Routledge Handbook of Corrections in the United States

The *Routledge Handbook of Corrections in the United States* brings together original contributions from leading scholars in criminology and criminal justice that provide an in-depth, state-of-the-art look at the most important topics in corrections. The book discusses the foundations of corrections in the United States, philosophical issues that have guided historical movements in corrections, different types of punishment and supervision, trends in incarceration, issues affecting race, ethnicity, and special populations in corrections, and a variety of other emerging issues.

This book scrutinizes innovative community programs as well as more traditional sanctions, and exposes the key issues and debates surrounding the correctional process in the United States. Among other important topics, selections address the inherent discrimination within the system, special issues surrounding certain populations, and the utilization of the death penalty as the ultimate punishment. This book serves as an essential reference for academicians and practitioners working in corrections and related agencies, as well as for students taking courses in criminal justice, criminology, and related subjects.

O. Hayden Griffin III, Ph.D., J.D. is an Associate Professor in the Department of Criminal Justice at the University of Alabama at Birmingham.

Vanessa H. Woodward, Ph.D. is an Associate Professor in the Department of Criminology at the University of West Georgia.

Routledge Handbook of Corrections in the United States

Edited by
O. Hayden Griffin III and
Vanessa H. Woodward

Routledge
Taylor & Francis Group
NEW YORK AND LONDON

First published 2018
by Routledge
711 Third Avenue, New York, NY 10017

and by Routledge
2 Park Square, Milton Park, Abingdon, Oxon, OX14 4RN

Routledge is an imprint of the Taylor & Francis Group, an informa business

Library of Congress Cataloging-in-Publication Data
Names: Griffin, O. Hayden, III, editor. | Woodward, Vanessa H., editor.
Title: Routledge handbook of corrections in the United States / edited by O. Hayden Griffin, III, and Vanessa H. Woodward.
Description: New York, NY : Routledge, 2018. | Includes index.
Identifiers: LCCN 2017013022 | ISBN 9781138183353 (hardback)
Subjects: LCSH: Corrections—United States. | Criminal justice, Administration of—United States.
Classification: LCC HV9466 .R68 2018 | DDC 364.60973—dc23
LC record available at https://lccn.loc.gov/2017013022

ISBN: 978-1-138-18335-3 (hbk)
ISBN: 978-1-315-64517-9 (ebk)

Typeset in Bembo
by Florence Production Ltd, Stoodleigh, Devon, UK

Contents

Preface

At the time of the founding of the English colonies, there was nothing particularly complex about corrections and punishment. Those who were in need of criminal justice sanction received it—through either corporal punishment or the death penalty. Additionally, many of the colonists who arrived in this new land were in fact offenders themselves—their sanction was banishment from England to the Americas. In fact, the irony of the United States is that its very independence was ostensibly criminal: rebelling against the King by declaring independence, by England's standards, treason.

After the 13 colonies became an independent nation and then eventually, a nation of 50 states with a population of nearly 320 million people, corrections has become exceedingly complex in its role, actions, and purposes. While original sanctions such as the death penalty and corporal punishment have become less common, incarceration and forms of community corrections became the predominant forms of punishment. For those who committed more violent and/or serious offenses, incarceration became the predominant punishment. For those offenders who committed petty or minor offenses, probation, community service, and monetary fines became the most common sanctions within the system. While these sanctions remain most common, a host of alternative sanctions have arisen.

On its face, corrections should primarily focus on correcting behavior, which may or may not be accomplished through mere punishment. This reflects the sheer complexity of the system: correcting an offender's behavior may require punishment, family support, community support, treatment, rehabilitation, and/or therapy. Moreover, even when these are provided, behavior may not be corrected within the offender. Further, even if it does correct behavior and prevent recidivism, it is still predominantly a reactive, rather than proactive approach, which makes it inevitable that another individual will transform into an offender in need of corrections. Thus, in addition to punishment, it is necessary to discuss the various philosophies that affect the imposition of punishment: whether it is treatment, revenge, retribution, general and/or specific deterrence, or some amalgamation of these philosophies. Along with these philosophies is a need to understand the differential treatment (both purposeful and unintended) of correctional populations; most notably, women and juveniles. Some of these differences in treatment are due to how they respond to different correctional interventions. Regarding women, they commit far fewer crimes (especially less violent crime) than men, lack the same frequent behavioral problems that men exhibit while incarcerated, and frequently require and/or are motivated to desist from crime by a host of different factors than men. Regarding juveniles, an entirely separate system has been created for their correctional treatment, as there is more of a rehabilitative framework surrounding the juvenile system. Furthermore, specific populations in the United States, particularly ethnic minorities and people who suffer from mental illness, are overrepresented in the correctional population. Additionally, constitutional safeguards have affected how people can be punished and different societal concerns (most notably the war on drugs and mass incarceration) have dramatically changed or altered the scope of who is punished in the criminal justice system.

This handbook is an edited volume comprising 45 chapters that are collectively written by 73 different authors and divided into six sections. Section 1, Correctional Philosophies, discusses many of the different philosophical beliefs that shape the way we view corrections. Section 2, Punishment and Correctional Sanctions in the United States, discusses the most common forms of punishment in the United States. Section 3, Community Corrections and Alternative Sanctions, discusses many of the different sanctions that have evolved over the years to divert people from incarceration. Section 4: Issues Affecting Corrections and Punishment, discusses many of the events and concerns that affect corrections and punishment beyond just philosophical concerns. Section 5: Issues Affecting Incarceration, discusses the myriad of issues that occur within or because of the presence of correctional facilities. Section 6: Effects of Corrections and Post-Sanction Issues, discusses many issues that are byproducts of corrections.

The corrections system in the United States is continually changing. Most often, these changes are based upon political movements that affect motives. The ebb and flow of philosophical ideals that we have observed throughout history will likely continue, with little understanding of the origin of each present movement. In addition to the constant change within the correctional system, so too is its complex nature—that will likely never cease. Thus, our goal within this handbook was to provide an in-depth analysis of the system throughout history and presently, in hopes of providing a better understanding of what is to come.

Author Biographies

Eileen M. Ahlin, Ph.D. is an assistant professor of Criminal Justice in the School of Public Affairs at Penn State Harrisburg. Her research focuses on corrections, neighborhoods, and violence.

Daniela Barberi is a Master's degree candidate in Criminal Justice in the School of Public Affairs at Penn State Harrisburg. Her research interests include corrections, recidivism, and minority populations.

Maude Beaudry-Cyr is a doctoral student in Criminology at the University of South Florida. She currently serves as the assistant managing editor of the *Journal of Crime & Justice*. Her research has been accepted for publication in *Justice Quarterly* and *Race & Justice*. Her research interests include racial/ethnic disparities in the juvenile justice system, the intersection of race/ethnicity, drug use, and mental illness, and criminological theory.

Robert M. Bohm is Professor Emeritus of Criminal Justice, University of Central Florida. He has published numerous books, book chapters, and journal articles in the areas of criminal justice and criminology. He is the author of *DeathQuest: An Introduction to the Theory and Practice of Capital Punishment in the United States*, 5th ed. (2017), *Capital Punishment's Collateral Damage* (2013), *The Past as Prologue: The Supreme Court's Pre-Modern Jurisprudence and Its Influence on the Supreme Court's Modern Death Penalty Decisions* (2012), *Ultimate Sanction: Understanding the Death Penalty Through Its Many Voices and Many Sides* (2010), and *A Concise Introduction to Criminal Justice* (2008). He is coauthor (with Keith N. Haley) of *Introduction to Criminal Justice*, 9th ed. (2017), and (with Brenda L. Vogel) *A Primer on Crime and Delinquency Theory*, 4th ed. (2015). He is also the editor of *The Death Penalty Today* (2008) and *The Death Penalty in America: Current Research* (1991), and coeditor (with James R. Acker and Charles S. Lanier) of *America's Experiment with Capital Punishment: Reflections on the Past, Present, and Future of the Ultimate Sanction*, 3rd ed. (2014), and (with Jeffery T. Walker) *Demystifying Crime and Criminal Justice*, 2nd ed. (2013).

Pauline K. Brennan received her Ph.D. in Criminal Justice from the University at Albany, SUNY, and is an Associate Professor and the Doctoral Program Chair for the School of Criminology and Criminal Justice at the University of Nebraska Omaha (UNO). She also serves as the Director of the London Program for UNO and is the Immediate Past-President for the Association of Doctoral Programs in Criminology and Criminal Justice. Her areas of research include inequity in court processing, correctional policy, and issues related to female offenders and victims.

Bridget Brew studies Race and Social Stratification as a Ph.D. student at Cornell University. She is particularly interested in inequality in secondary schools and criminal justice institutions. She has a minor in Demography and is an affiliate of the Cornell Population

Center, the Center for the Study of Inequality, and the Bronfenbrenner Center for Translational Research. She is also a mathematics instructor at Auburn Correctional Facility through the Cornell Prison Education Program.

Marilyn M. Brown, Ph.D. is Associate Professor of Sociology at the University of Hawai'i Hilo, where she serves as Chair of the Sociology Department. Her research specializations include corrections, reintegration of former prisoners, gender and punishment, corrections and families, and criminal justice policy. She is the author of articles on women, crime, and justice as well as chapters in edited volumes. Dr. Brown has also served as consultant on criminal justice programming for a number of Hawai'i State agencies.

Kyle A. Burgason is an Assistant Professor in the Department of Sociology at Iowa State University. His research interests include policing, ethics in criminal justice, criminological theory, structural and cultural context of violent crime and victimization, capital punishment, and optimal foraging theory's applications to crime. His recent work appears in *Deviant Behavior*, *Journal of Interpersonal Violence*, *the American Journal of Criminal Justice*, *Homicide Studies*, *Western Criminology Review*, and *Journal of Forensic Investigation*.

Meda Chesney-Lind, Ph.D. teaches Women's Studies at the University of Hawai'i. Nationally recognized for her work on women and crime, her testimony before Congress resulted in national support of gender responsive programming for girls in the juvenile justice system. Her most recent book on girls' use of violence, *Fighting for Girls* (co-edited with Nikki Jones), won an award from the National Council on Crime and Delinquency for "focusing America's attention on the complex problems of the criminal and juvenile justice systems." In 2013, the Western Society of Criminology named an award honoring "significant contributions to the field of gender, crime and justice" for Chesney-Lind and gave her the "inaugural" award.

Valerie A. Clark is the Director of Training, Research, and Communications at the Minnesota Department of Public Safety, Office of Justice Programs. In addition to corrections, her research has focused on sentencing, victimization, and intimate partner violence. Her recent research has been published in *Criminology & Public Policy*, *Journal of Experimental Criminology*, and *Crime & Delinquency*. She holds a Ph.D. from the Pennsylvania State University.

Danilo Freire is a Ph.D. Candidate in the Department of Political Economy at King's College London. He gratefully acknowledges the support of the Brazilian National Council for Scientific and Technological Development and the Faculty of Social Science and Public Policy at King's College London.

Brett Garland is a Professor in the Department of Criminology and Criminal Justice at Missouri State University. He received a Ph.D. in 2007 from the School of Criminology and Criminal Justice at the University of Nebraska, Omaha. Dr. Garland's research interests focus on criminal justice management and staff, prisoner reentry, and public opinion on justice related topics. He formerly worked as a pre-release coordinator for the Indiana Department of Corrections and as a caseworker in a juvenile group home.

Julie Garman received her M.S. from the School of Criminology and Criminal Justice at the University of Nebraska Omaha (UNO) in 2015, and is currently a second-year doctoral student in the same program. Her research interests lie in examining issues faced by those under correctional supervision, including the difficulties such individuals face in accessing mental-health treatment.

Lior Gideon, Ph.D. is a Professor of Criminal Justice at John Jay College of Criminal Justice in New York, New York. He specializes in corrections-based program evaluation and focuses his research on rehabilitation, reentry, and reintegration issues and in particular by examining offenders' perceptions of their needs. Dr. Gideon developed measurements to examine level of punitiveness, attitudes supportive of rehabilitation, and recently measures of social support. His research interests also involve international and comparative corrections-related public opinion surveys and their effect on rehabilitation and reintegration policy. Dr. Gideon published numerous manuscripts, including three previously published books on offenders' needs in the reintegration process: *Substance Abusing Inmates: Experiences of Recovering Drug Addicts on Their Way Back Home* (2010, Springer), *Rethinking Corrections: Rehabilitation, Reentry, and Reintegration* (with Hung-En Sung, 2011, Sage), and *Special Needs Offenders in Correctional Institutions* (2013, Sage). Aside from the above, Dr. Gideon has published three methodology books and textbooks. His works also appear in *The Prison Journal, International Journal of Offender Therapy and Comparative Criminology, Asian Journal of Criminology, International Journal of Criminal Justice Review*, and *Social Science Quarterly*.

Alyssa Goldman is a Ph.D. candidate in the Department of Sociology at Cornell University. Her research interests include incarceration and other contact with the criminal justice system, and their effects on health and wellbeing. Prior to pursuing her doctoral studies, she earned a Master's degree in Social Science from the University of Chicago.

Angela R. Gover, Ph.D. is a Professor in the School of Public Affairs at the University of Colorado Denver. She conducts research in the areas of crime victimization and intimate partner violence.

Edward L.W. Green is Assistant Professor in the Criminal Justice Department at Roosevelt University in Chicago, Illinois, specializing in critical criminology and corrections. He is actively engaged in qualitative prison research and the study of prisonization in order to better understand the consequences of mass incarceration. Dr. Green's dissertation, *Weight of the Gavel: Prison as a Rite of Passage*, has been nominated for the CGS/ProQuest Distinguished Dissertation Award; it focuses on identity transitions of long-term inmates in five Midwest prisons. More generally, he is interested in the relationship between citizen, culture, and state.

O. Hayden Griffin III, Ph.D., J.D. is a Professor in the Department of Associate Criminal Justice at the University of Alabama at Birmingham. His research interests are drug policy, corrections, and law and society. He is the author (along with Vanessa Woodward and John J. Sloan, III) of *The Money and Politics of Criminal Justice Policy* (Carolina Academic Press).

Jada N. Hector is a licensed mental health professional in the State of Louisiana with experience in addressing severe mental illness, substance use disorder, juvenile violence and delinquency, persistent trauma, and vicarious trauma, among other non-justice related topics such as relationships and sexual health. Ms. Hector specializes in forging systemic change for lasting success of mental health and substance abuse programming through education and consultation.

Brittany Hood is pursuing a Ph.D. in Criminal Justice at Indiana University. Her research focuses on examining treatments and interventions for offenders with a mental illness. She is currently involved in research assessing participant perceptions of procedural justice in specialty courts and evaluating a reentry program for the Indiana Department of Corrections.

Don Hummer, Ph.D. is an Associate Professor of Criminal Justice in the School of Public Affairs at Penn State Harrisburg. His research interests include institutional and community violence, and offender reintegration.

Elizabeth L. Jeglic, Ph.D. is a Professor of Psychology at the John Jay College of Criminal Justice in New York. Her research focuses on issues pertaining to the treatment and assessment of sex offenders and evidence-based public policy.

Lee "Mike" Johnson is Associate Professor of Criminology and Criminal Justice in the Department of Sociology at William Patterson University. He received his Ph.D. in Sociology from Iowa State University in 2001. Professor Johnson has published articles on juvenile justice, victimization, corrections, and policing in journals such as *Criminal Justice Policy Review*, *Journal of Interpersonal Violence*, *Drug and Alcohol Review*, *Policing: An International Journal of Police Strategies and Management*, *Southwest Journal of Criminal Justice*, *Victims & Offenders*, and *Youth and Society*. He is also author of *Professional Misconduct against Juveniles in Correctional Treatment Settings* (Anderson) and editor of *Experiencing Corrections: From Practitioner to Professor* (Sage).

W. Wesley Johnson earned his Ph.D. in Criminology from Florida State University. Dr. Johnson is currently the Criminal Justice Doctoral Program Director at the University of Southern Mississippi; he previously taught at South Carolina State College and Sam Houston State University. He is also a co-author of *Criminalization of Mental Illness: Crisis and Opportunity for the Justice System*, and has worked in the criminal justice system in the areas of juvenile corrections and substance abuse treatment. Dr. Johnson is editor of the journal *Corrections: Policy, Practice and Research*, is actively involved in the National Alliance on Mental Illness, and is a former President of the Academy of Criminal Justice Sciences.

Susan Jones, Ph.D. University of Colorado, Colorado Springs. Dr. Jones retired after working for 31 years in Colorado corrections in positions ranging from correctional officer through warden. Dr. Jones earned her doctorate from the University of Colorado, Colorado Springs. Dr. Jones' research interests revolve around issues that correctional employees face as well as the training and educational preparation provided to employees at all levels of the corrections systems. Dr. Jones believes that the challenges faced in the criminal justice system can be met by prepared employees that are given the tools and encouragement to provide the leadership necessary to change the systems.

Kent R. Kerley, Ph.D. is Professor and Chair in the Department of Criminology and Criminal Justice at The University of Texas at Arlington. His primary research interests include corrections, religiosity, and drug careers. He is author of the research monograph, *Religious Faith in Correctional Contexts* (2014, First Forum Press/Lynne Rienner Publishers). His research has appeared in many top journals, including *Aggression and Violent Behavior*, *Journal for the Scientific Study of Religion*, *Justice Quarterly*, *Social Forces*, and *Social Problems*. He has received research funding from the National Science Foundation, Google, and the Religious Research Association.

Natasha Khade, M.S. is a graduate student in the School of Criminology and Criminal Justice at Arizona State University. Her interests lie in the areas of criminological theory, cross-cultural criminology, and offender reentry. She is particularly interested in how culture, theory, and laws can be intertwined to improve offender reentry outcomes.

David N. Khey is the department head and assistant professor of Criminal Justice at the University of Louisiana at Lafayette. Since moving to Louisiana, Dr. Khey has specialized in reentry, crime and mental illness, and drug policy and has lent his expertise to expanding evidence-based programming in these areas in the state.

Ryan M. Labrecque, Ph.D. is an Assistant Professor in the Criminology and Criminal Justice Department at Portland State University. Dr. Labrecque's research interests focus on the evaluation of correctional interventions, the effects of prison life, the development of risk and needs assessments for community and institutional corrections settings, offender rehabilitation, and the transfer of knowledge to practitioners and policy makers. He has a number of published articles, book chapters, and conference presentations on these topics. Dr. Labrecque has also worked on several federal- and state-funded research projects in these areas and he is a former probation and parole officer.

Jenny L. Lau, B.A., is a graduate student at Washington State University in the Department of Criminal Justice and Criminology. Jenny discovered her passion for criminal justice reform after serving time in the Washington Corrections Center for Women. Since her release she received her undergraduate degree from Central Washington University in 2013 with *cum laude* honors, interned for the Washington State Senate, and has presented on various panels about chemical dependency and education after incarceration. Her current research interests include corrections, reentry, women and crime, racial disparity in the criminal justice system, labeling theory, and drug and alcohol addiction. Jenny has used her personal experience with the criminal justice system to fuel her research and academic goals.

Gavin Lee is an Assistant Professor at the University of West Georgia. His research interests include capital punishment and serial murder. His work has been published in the *American Journal of Criminal Justice*, the *International Journal of Crime, Criminal Justice and Law, International Criminal Justice Review*, and the *Southwestern Journal of Criminal Justice*.

Michael J. Leiber is the Chair and a Professor in Criminology at the University of South Florida. He earned his doctorate in Criminal Justice from the State University of New York at Albany. His main research interests and publications lie in juvenile delinquency, juvenile justice, and race/ethnicity. Currently, he serves as the editor of the Midwestern Criminal Justice Association journal, the *Journal of Crime & Justice*.

C. Cory Lowe is currently pursuing a Ph.D. in the Department of Sociology and Criminology & Law at the University of Florida. He received his M.A. in the Social Sciences at Georgia Southern University with a concentration in Sociology and Criminology, and his undergraduate degree in History and Political Science at Shorter University. His current interests include law and society, historical sociology, life-course criminology, gender and crime, and criminological theory. His work has appeared in *Public Understanding of Science*, and his M.A. thesis examined gender depictions in country music from 1944 through 2012.

Arthur J. Lurigio, a psychologist, is Senior Associate Dean for Faculty in the College of Arts and Sciences, and a Professor of Criminal Justice and Criminology and of Psychology at Loyola University Chicago. He is also a member of the Graduate Faculty and Director of the Center for the Advancement of Research, Training, and Education (CARTE) at Loyola University Chicago. In 2003, Dr. Lurigio was named a Faculty Scholar, the highest honor bestowed on senior faculty at Loyola. In 2013, he was named a Master Researcher by the College of Arts and Sciences at Loyola in recognition of his continued scholarly productivity.

Faith E. Lutze, Ph.D. is a Professor in the Department of Criminal Justice and Criminology at Washington State University. Her current research interests include community corrections, homelessness and reentry, correctional industries and offender employment, incarcerated veterans with traumatic brain injury, drug courts, and gender and justice with an emphasis on masculinity. Dr. Lutze is the author of the book *The Professional Lives of Community Corrections Officers: The Invisible Side of Reentry* (2014) and has published the results of her research in various journals including *Criminal Justice and Behavior*, *Justice Quarterly*, *Crime & Delinquency*, *Criminology and Public Policy*, *Journal of Offender Rehabilitation*, and the *Journal of Criminal Justice*. She teaches courses on gender and justice, violence toward women, and corrections. She is active in the community supporting violence prevention programs, promoting equality, and serving her rural community as an emergency medical technician.

Sean Maddan is Associate Professor in the Department of Criminology at the University of West Georgia. His research areas include criminological theory, statistics, research methods, and the efficacy of current sex offender policies. Dr. Maddan has authored over a dozen articles that have appeared in many outlets including *Justice Quarterly*, *Crime and Justice*, and the *Journal of Criminal Justice*. Dr. Maddan has also authored/co-authored several books. His most recent book is *Sex Offenders: Crimes and Processing in the Criminal Justice System* (2017).

Bryan Lee Miller, Ph.D. is an Associate Professor of Criminal Justice and Criminology at Georgia Southern University. His research focuses on drugs and society, offender reentry, and criminal justice policy. His research has evaluated novel psychoactive drugs, prescription drug abuse, drug panics, and restrictions on ex-offenders reintegrating into the community. He is an author or co-author of over 40 peer-reviewed publications and book chapters as well as the book *Emerging Trends in Drug Use and Distribution* (2014, Springer). Recent publications have appeared in scholarly journals such as *Pediatrics*, *Criminal Justice Review*, and *Journal of Research on Crime and Delinquency*.

Holly Ventura Miller is an Associate Professor of Criminology at the University of North Florida, a former National Institute of Justice W.E.B. DuBois Fellow, and a Past President of the Southern Criminal Justice Association. Her research interests include correctional policy, immigration and crime, and program evaluation. Recent research has appeared in *Journal of Criminal Justice*, *Prison Journal*, and *Criminology & Public Policy*. She is Editor, along with Anthony Peguero, of the forthcoming Routledge *Handbook of Immigration and Crime*.

Ojmarrh Mitchell is an Associate Professor in the Department of Criminology at the University of South Florida. Professor Mitchell earned his Ph.D. in Criminal Justice and Criminology from the University of Maryland with a doctoral minor in Measurement, Statistics, and Evaluation. His research interests include drugs and crime, race and crime, corrections and sentencing, and meta-analysis.

Kathryn (Kay) Morgan, Ph.D. is Professor of Criminal Justice and Director of the African American Studies Program at the University of Alabama at Birmingham. She was awarded degrees in Sociology and Criminology from Texas and Florida State University. Dr. Morgan's research and teaching areas include race, crime and social policy, gender issues in criminal justice, and correctional practices and policies. Her research has been published in *Journal of Criminal Justice*, *Justice Quarterly*, *Criminology and Public Policy*, *Criminal Justice Policy Review*, and *Criminal Justice Review*. Her book *Probation, Parole and Community Corrections in Theory and Practice* was published in 2015.

Elias Nader is a doctoral student in the School of Criminology and Justice Studies at the University of Massachusetts Lowell. He received his M.A. in 2016 from the School of Criminology and Justice Studies at the University of Massachusetts Lowell. His research interests include gender and crime, institutional misconduct, and social network analysis.

John C. Navarro is a graduate student at the University of Louisville working towards his doctorate degree in Criminal Justice. Navarro graduated with a Bachelor of Arts in Psychology with a minor in Criminal Justice Sciences in 2011 and Master's of Science in Criminal Justice Sciences in 2014 from Illinois State University. Current research interests include victimization, sex offenders, sexually variant behaviors, and crime mapping.

Graeme R. Newman is distinguished teaching professor at the School of Criminal Justice, University at Albany and Associate Director of the Center for Problem-Oriented Policing. Throughout his 40-year career in academia, he has written many books and major articles on the history, philosophy, and practices of punishment, international criminal justice, cybercrime, terrorism, migration and crime, community policing, and crime prevention. His recent books include: a new translation of Cesare Beccaria's *On Crimes and Punishments* with Pietro Marongiu (Transaction Press, 2009), *Crime and Punishment around the World* in four volumes (ABC-CLIO, 2010) and *Community Policing in Indigenous Communities* with Mahesh Nalla (CRC Press, 2013). Professor Newman has also written books for the trade market, including *Just and Painful: A Case for the Corporal Punishment of Criminals* (Macmillan, 1983, 1995).

Maria J. Patterson is pursuing her BA in Gender Studies and a minor in English at Mount Holyoke College. She plans to obtain a Ph.D. in Gender Studies and teach at the university level.

Lynn Pazzani is an Assistant Professor in the Department of Criminology at the University of West Georgia. Her research interests include gender and criminal justice, sexual assault and sex offenders, and research methods and statistics. Dr. Pazzani co-authored, with Dr. Maddan, *Sex Offenders: Crimes and Processing in the Criminal Justice System* (2017).

Dylan Pelletier is a doctoral student at Washington State University. He earned his Bachelor's degree from Missouri State University. His research interests include campus crime and policing. His work has appeared in *Criminal Justice Review* and *American Journal of Criminal Justice*.

Chad Posick is an Assistant Professor of Criminal Justice and Criminology at Georgia Southern University. He received his doctorate in Criminal Justice and Criminology from Northeastern University in 2012 and his Master's degree in Public Policy from the Rochester Institute of Technology in 2009. His major research interests include violence prevention, restorative justice, and police–community relations. He teaches in the areas of victimology, criminal behavior, and statistics. He is a board member of the Ogeechee Court-Appointed Special Advocates (CASA) program for abused and neglected children.

Roberto Hugh Potter had the opportunity to be among the few sociologist/criminologists employed at the Center for Disease Control and Prevention during the turn of the last century (1998–2008). This allowed him to employ his experiences working with correctional systems to problems such as violence prevention and correctional health issues. He was part of the team that developed the censored and never-published "Surgeon General's Call to Action on Corrections and Community Health." That document provides the core of ideas presented in his entry here. He received his doctorate in Sociology at the University of Florida in 1982. After that, he worked in state and federal government in the United States, state universities in the U.S. and Australia, and justice and family welfare non-profits in Florida and Georgia. He is currently a professor in the Department of Criminal Justice at the University of Central Florida. He continues his work in the areas of correctional health issues and the organization of criminal justice and allied fields.

Travis C. Pratt is a Fellow with the University of Cincinnati Corrections Institute. He received his Ph.D. in Criminal Justice from the University of Cincinnati. His work focuses primarily on criminological theory and correctional policy, with most of his research examining the nature and consequences of violent victimization. He is the author of *Addicted to Incarceration: Corrections Policy and the Politics of Misinformation in the United States* (2009, Sage), and his peer-reviewed work has been published *Criminology*, *Journal of Research in Crime and Delinquency*, *Journal of Quantitative Criminology*, *Justice Quarterly*, and the *Journal of Pediatrics*. He was the recipient of the Ruth Shonle Cavan Young Scholar Award from the American Society of Criminology.

Bradley Ray, Ph.D. is an Assistant Professor in the School of Public and Environmental Affairs at Indiana University–Purdue University Indianapolis. His research focuses on policy responses to mental illness and substance abuse. He has conducted research on drug courts and mental health courts using observational, survey, and administrative data.

Keramet Reiter is an Assistant Professor in the Department of Criminology, Law & Society and at the School of Law at the University of California, Irvine. Her research focuses on the law and theory of punishment. She is the author of *23/7: Pelican Bay Prison and the Rise of Long-Term Solitary Confinement* (2016, Yale University Press) on the history and uses of U.S. supermax prisons.

R. Barry Ruback is a Professor of Criminology and Sociology at Penn State University. His work on economic sanctions has been supported by the National Institute of Justice, the National Science Foundation, the Pennsylvania Commission on Crime and Delinquency, and the Pennsylvania Commission on Sentencing.

Jason Rydberg is an Assistant Professor in the School of Criminology and Justice Studies at the University of Massachusetts Lowell. He received his Ph.D. in 2014 from the School of Criminal Justice at Michigan State University. His research interests include prisoner reentry, recidivism, sex offender policy, and the evaluation of criminal justice programs. His research has recently been featured in *Corrections: Policy, Practice, and Research*, *Criminology and Public Policy*, and the *Journal of Criminal Justice*.

Llynea Sherwin, B.A., is a graduate student in the Department of Criminology and Criminal Justice at The University of Texas at Arlington.

David Skarbek is Senior Lecturer in Political Economy at King's College London.

Risdon N. Slate received his Ph.D. from the Claremont Graduate School in Claremont, California. He is Professor and Chair of the Criminology Department at Florida Southern College. He is lead author of the book entitled *Criminalization of Mental Illness: Crisis and Opportunity for the Justice System*, and his research interests include the interface of the mental health and justice systems and criminal justice practitioner stress. Dr. Slate is a former member of the Board of Directors of the National Alliance on Mental Illness, and he has prior work experience as a United States Probation Officer and as assistant to the warden at a medium/maximum, death row prison in Columbia, South Carolina.

Christopher E. Smith is Professor of Criminal Justice at Michigan State University. He is the author of *Law and Contemporary Corrections* and his research on corrections law has appeared in such journals as *Prison Journal*, *Criminal Justice Studies*, *Justice System Journal*, *Indiana Law Review*, and *Journal of Black Studies*.

Mark C. Stafford is a Professor in the School of Criminal Justice at Texas State University, where he is currently Doctoral Program Director. He also has been a faculty member at

Washington State University and The University of Texas at Austin, where he was one of the founders of the Center for Criminology and Criminal Justice Research. He has been a Postdoctoral Fellow at the Center for Advanced Study in the Behavioral Sciences at Stanford University and a Visiting Scholar at the University of Colorado, Boulder. He was an IEAT-FORD Chair of Criminality, Violence, and Public Policy in the Institute of Interdisciplinary Advanced Studies at Federal University of Minas Gerais, Belo Horizonte, Brazil. He has published extensively on deterrence and rational-choice behavior, victimization and fear of crime, and causes of crime and juvenile delinquency. He is a co-author of a forthcoming book on sex crimes and sex offenders.

Benjamin Steiner is an Associate Professor in the School of Criminology and Criminal Justice at the University of Nebraska, Omaha. He holds a Ph.D. from the University of Cincinnati. His research interests focus on issues related to juvenile justice and corrections. He has published over 80 journal articles and book entries related to these topics. Professor Steiner has received the Distinguished New Scholar award from the American Society of Criminology's Division on Corrections and Sentencing and the Outstanding Young Scholar award from the Academy of Criminal Justice Sciences' Juvenile Justice Section.

Melinda Tasca is an Assistant Professor in the Department of Criminal Justice and Criminology at Sam Houston State University. Her research interests include correctional policy, consequences of incarceration, and disparities in the criminal justice system. Her work has been published in outlets such as Criminal Justice and Behavior, Journal of Interpersonal Violence, and Punishment and Society.

Faye S. Taxman, Ph.D. is a University Professor in the Criminology, Law and Society Department and Director of the Center for Advancing Correctional Excellence at George Mason University. She developed the RNR Simulation Tool (www.gmuace.org/tools). Dr. Taxman has published more than 155 articles, including "Tools of the Trade: A Guide to Incorporating Science into Practice," and *Implementing Evidence-Based Community Corrections and Addiction Treatment* (Springer, 2012 with Steven Belenko). She is co-Editor of *Health & Justice*. The American Society of Criminology's Division of Sentencing and Corrections has recognized her as Distinguished Scholar twice as well as the Rita Warren and Ted Palmer Differential Intervention Treatment award. She has a Ph.D. from Rutgers University's School of Criminal Justice.

Richard Tewksbury is Professor of Criminal Justice at the University of Louisville. His work focuses on issues of sex offender registration, criminal victimization risks, and perceptions of sexual offenses and deviance.

Amanda L. Thomas, M.A. is a retired Sergeant from the New York City Police Department (NYPD). As a sergeant, Amanda authored and co-authored innovative crime control policies through the NYPD's Best Practice Forums that specifically pertained to decreasing crime in public housing developments. She holds a B.A. from Manhattan College in Sociology and Psychology and an M.A. from John Jay College of Criminal Justice in Criminal Justice with a concentration in Criminology and Deviance. Since her retirement, she has been an adjunct lecturer at John Jay College of Criminal Justice, in the Department of Law, Police Science and Criminal Justice Administration.

Sara Toto is a doctoral student in the School of Criminology and Criminal Justice at the University of Nebraska, Omaha. She holds an M.A. in Criminal Justice from the University of Nevada, Reno. Her primary research interests include institutional and community-based corrections.

Maren Trochmann is a Ph.D. student at the School of Public Affairs at the University of Colorado Denver. Her research interests include examining federal and local government and the intersections of race, class, gender, and public policy.

Christopher Wildeman is an Associate Professor of Policy Analysis and Management at Cornell University (in Ithaca, New York), a Senior Researcher at the Rockwool Foundation (in Copenhagen, Denmark), and a Visiting Fellow at the Bureau of Justice Statistics (in Washington, DC). His first book, *Children of the Prison Boom: Mass Incarceration and the Future of American Inequality* (with Sara Wakefield), was published by Oxford University Press in 2013.

L. Susan Williams is Associate Professor of Sociology and Criminology at Kansas State University, specializing in gender, prisons, and place. Dr. Williams has received several local and national grants involving gender, youth, and inequalities; she is currently engaged in prison ethnography, as well as survey-type research on social cohesion in five prison facilities. Dr. Williams has worked with state prisons for more than 20 years, involving thousands of students in *Beyond Walls*, a project that incorporates letter and face-to-face exchanges with prisoners. Dr. Williams resides part time in California and is involved in innocence and domestic violence organizations.

Georgia M. Winters, M.A. is a third-year clinical psychology Ph.D. student at John Jay College and the Graduate Center, City University of New York. Her research focuses on how sexual offenders are viewed by jurors in the criminal court system and the sexual grooming behaviors of child molesters.

Eric J. Wodahl is an Associate Professor of Criminal Justice at the University of Wyoming. Dr. Wodahl's research interests focus on the areas of prisoner reentry, alternatives to revocation in the supervision of offenders in the community, and correctional policy issues. Before entering academia, he worked in the correctional system for almost a decade, working with both juvenile and adult offenders in community and institutional settings. Dr. Wodahl's correctional experience includes over seven years as a probation and parole officer, during which time he supervised both traditional and intensive supervision caseloads.

Vanessa H. Woodward is an Associate Professor in the Department of Criminology at the University of West Georgia. Her research interests include sexual violence, campus crime, and corrections. Her work has been published in *Criminal Justice Review*, *Deviant Behavior*, and *Journal of Criminal Justice Education*.

Robert M. Worley is an Associate Professor of Criminal Justice at Lamar University. He received his Ph.D. in Criminal Justice from Sam Houston State University. Prior to entering academia, Dr. Worley worked as a correctional officer for seven years with the Texas Department of Criminal Justice. He has published articles in journals such as *Deviant Behavior, Criminal Law Bulletin, Criminal Justice Review, Journal of Criminal Justice Education*, and the *American Journal of Criminal Justice*, among others. Robert is currently the Editor of *ACJS Today* and an Associate Editor of *Deviant Behavior*.

Vidisha B. Worley is an Associate Professor of Criminal Justice at Lamar University, Beaumont, Texas; former Contributing Editor and Columnist with the *Criminal Law Bulletin* (January 2010 to December 2013); Founding Member of the Institute for Legal Studies in Criminal Justice, Sam Houston State University; and a Licensed Attorney in India and New York. She was a journalist in India for six years and worked at three national dailies, *The Asian Age*, *Business Standard*, and *The Financial Express*, respectively.

She presented a paper on intellectual disability and the death penalty at the Oxford Round Table, Oxford University, U.K. in March 2010. Professor Worley's research areas include police and prison officers' liabilities for the use of Tasers and stun guns, the death penalty, prison rape, correctional officer deviance, inappropriate relationships between inmates and correctional officers, cyberbullying and sexting, ethical issues in criminal justice, and terrorism. Her published books include *Press and Media Law Manual* (2002) and *Terrorism in India* (2006).

Kevin A. Wright, Ph.D. is an Associate Professor in the School of Criminology and Criminal Justice at Arizona State University. His research interests include criminological theory and correctional policy, with a particular interest in how the correction of crime may be tied to the causes of crime. His work has been published in *Criminology*, *Journal of Youth and Adolescence*, and *Justice Quarterly*.

Section 1

Correctional Philosophies

1 Deterrence and Imprisonment

Mark C. Stafford

A policy of mass incarceration in the U.S., beginning in the late 1970s and early 1980s, caused huge increases in the number of people in prisons and jails. Both the likelihood of incarceration and average sentence length increased substantially (Mauer 2006; Western 2006). While there were two million adults in the correctional system in 1980 (on probation or parole or in prisons and jails), the number ballooned to 6.5 million in 2000 and has remained fairly stable since then (Glaze and Herberman 2014; Mears, Cochran, and Cullen 2015). There were about seven million adults in the correctional system in 2014—4.7 million on probation or parole and 2.2 million in prisons or jails. One out of 36 adults (or about 3 percent of all adults) at the time was under some form of correctional supervision (Kaeble, Glaze, Tsoutis, and Minton 2015). The picture is worse for some populations, such as African Americans. Among men born in the late 1960s, "3 percent of whites and 20 percent of blacks had served time in prison by their early thirties" (Petit and Western 2004: 151).

Legal punishment, such as imprisonment, has diverse goals, including retribution, rehabilitation, incapacitation, and deterrence. Except for retribution which has ancient roots, deterrence is the oldest of the goals, with its foundations in the writings of eighteenth-century Enlightenment philosophers, such as Cesare Beccaria and Jeremy Bentham (Johnson and Wolfe 2003). Deterrence is also the most complex, which is one reason why, many years after Beccaria and Bentham, researchers still know very little about it. Part of the complexity is that the concept of deterrence is multidimensional; there are different types of deterrence, and the effects may vary from one type to the next. The causal logic of deterrence is also complex, and there are challenges in distinguishing deterrent effects from other effects of legal punishment, such as incapacitation.

This chapter focuses on the deterrent effects of imprisonment. Along with incapacitation, deterrence has been one of the principal justifications for mass incarceration in the U.S. (Mears and Cochran 2015; Mears et al. 2015). Increased imprisonment should incapacitate more people from committing crimes (i.e., prevent them from committing crimes while in prison) and/or deter more people from committing crimes because of fear of being imprisoned or re-imprisoned. The chapter also considers what constitutes relevant evidence of the deterrent effects of imprisonment and the quality of the evidence in existing research. A good place to begin is examination of crime trends.

In the U.S. from the early 1960s to the early 1980s, there were increases in both property and violent crime rates (Paternoster 2010). The increases were followed by decreases in both rates until the mid 1980s when they increased again. Both rates peaked in the early 1990s; but after that, there were substantial decreases that have been labeled "the great American crime decline" or simply "the crime drop" (Blumstein and Wallman 2000; Zimring 2006). The drop occurred at the time when mass incarceration in the U.S. was causing the imprisonment rate to double, raising the question whether increased imprisonment was responsible (Paternoster 2010). As Paternoster (2010: 801) indicated, "there is a general consensus that the decline in crime [was], at least in part, due to more and longer prison sentences," but there is disagreement about "how much of an effect imprisonment had" (also see Rosenfeld and Messner 2009). Spelman (2000) estimated that between 4 percent and 21 percent of the drop was due to increased imprisonment, while Levitt (2004) estimated it to be 33 percent. Whatever the magnitude of the effect, it has been difficult to estimate how much of it was due to deterrence and how much to incapacitation. It was probably both. Moreover, researchers have found the crime drop to be better explained by factors other than imprisonment, such as decreasing demand for crack and other hard drugs, an expanding national economy and increasing consumer confidence, changes in crime reporting, an aging population, and improvements in domestic security (e.g., Blumstein and Wallman 2000; Farrell, Tseloni, Mailley and Tilley 2011; Rosenfeld and Messner 2009; Steffensmeier and Harer 1999).

One of the goals of this chapter is to explain why caution is needed in considering all evidence about the deterrent effects of imprisonment. The evidence is mixed, with some studies suggesting that imprisonment deters, while other studies suggesting it does not. More importantly, many of the studies have serious shortcomings that limit their usefulness in assessing the deterrent effects of imprisonment and constructing effective crime-control policy.

Background

Briefly defined, deterrence is the omission or curtailment of crime out of fear of legal punishment, including imprisonment (Gibbs 1975). The terms *omission* and *curtailment* in the definition are important because they suggest two possibilities. People may refrain entirely from committing a crime out of fear of legal punishment, which is termed *absolute deterrence.* Or they may only curtail or restrict their crimes out of fear of legal punishment as when a burglar takes a temporary break, believing that additional burglaries will result in a substantial increase in the likelihood of being caught. This second possibility is termed *restrictive deterrence.*

Three properties of legal punishment are relevant for deterrence: certainty, severity, and celerity. Any type of legal punishment (e.g., community service, restitution, or probation) can be considered in terms of these properties, but for imprisonment, certainty has to do with the probability of being imprisoned for crime. Severity has to do with the amount of punishment from imprisonment, including sentence length. Celerity has to do with the speed or swiftness at which people are imprisoned after committing a crime (or, alternatively, the speed at which they are sentenced to prison).

Since Beccaria and Bentham's writings, the certainty of legal punishment has been considered a more effective deterrent than either severity or celerity and, consequently, has been the focus of most deterrence research (Paternoster 2010). Moreover, while traditional accounts of deterrence consider speedier punishments to be greater deterrents, some people may perceive delayed punishment as more severe because it gives them time to dread what is ahead for them. If so, speedy punishment should be less of a deterrent. Because the possibility of dread creates ambiguity about how the celerity of punishment works as a deterrent (if at all), there has been little research on it (for exceptions, see Clark 1988; Nagin and Pogarsky 2001). Consequently, the focus here is on the certainty and severity of imprisonment.

There are two ways to consider certainty and severity. The first is to consider them objectively. Objective legal punishments involve what legal officials actually do in the way of punishing offenders. For example, for a particular place and time, such as a U.S. state in a given year, the objective certainty of imprisonment for a type of crime could be estimated by dividing the number of persons imprisoned for the crime divided by the number of crimes. There are two predictions about the objective certainty and severity of imprisonment and the likelihood of crime:

1. The greater the objective certainty of imprisonment for a type of crime, the less the likelihood of the crime.
2. The greater the objective severity of imprisonment for a type of crime, the less the likelihood of the crime.

The second way to consider legal punishments is perceptually. People can be asked about their perceptions of the certainty and severity of imprisonment in a survey or in interviews. The distinction between objective and perceived punishments is important because, according to the causal logic of deterrence, objective punishments deter only indirectly through their effects on perceived punishments (Gibbs 1975). People's perceived punishments are believed to result from objective punishments (what legal officials actually do), and deterrence is believed to occur when people perceive legal punishments as certain and severe. There are two predictions about the perceived certainty and severity of imprisonment and the likelihood of crime:

1. The greater the perceived certainty of imprisonment for a type of crime, the less the likelihood of the crime.
2. The greater the perceived severity of imprisonment for a type of crime, the less the likelihood of the crime.

A complication is that there are two types of deterrence: *specific* and *general* (Gibbs 1975; Stafford and Warr 1993). Whereas specific deterrence has to do with the deterrent effects of people's direct experience with legal punishment (including avoidance of punishment), general deterrence has to do with the deterrent effects of people's indirect experience with legal punishment through observing or somehow learning about the punishment experiences of others (also including avoidance of punishment). To illustrate, if a judge sentences a burglar to prison to send him a message to refrain from burglary after release, the judge's goal is specific deterrence. If the judge sentences the burglar to prison to send a message to others to refrain from burglary, the judge's goal is general deterrence. While probably all judges sentence burglars to prison to achieve both types of deterrence, imprisonment may deter only specifically and not generally, or only generally and not specifically. The point is there is no reason to expect that imprisonment, or any type of legal punishment, will necessarily result in both specific and general deterrence.

Research on General Deterrence and Imprisonment

Despite its eighteenth-century foundations, discussions of deterrence were largely argumentative and ideological until the late 1960s when Gibbs (1968) and Tittle (1969) first tested two key deterrence predictions. Gibbs (1968) examined the relationship among U.S. states between the objective certainty and severity of imprisonment and the homicide rate (Predictions 1 and 2 above). Objective certainty was estimated for each state by dividing the number of persons admitted to prison for homicide during 1959–1960 by the average annual number of homicides during the same period. The objective severity of imprisonment for each state was estimated by the median number of months served in prison for homicide as of December, 1960. Consistent with Prediction 1 above, states with greater objective certainty of imprisonment had lower homicide rates. Consistent with Prediction 2 above, states with greater objective severity of imprisonment also had lower homicide rates, but the association was small and not statistically significant.

Tittle (1969) expanded on Gibbs' (1968) study by examining 1960s state-level imprisonment data for more types of crime—rape, robbery, assault, burglary, theft, and auto theft in addition to homicide. Across all crime types, states with greater objective certainty of imprisonment had lower crime rates. The magnitude of the association, however, varied from a large association in the case of rape to no association in the case of auto theft (Tittle 1969). Moreover, contrary to Prediction 2 above, states with greater objective severity of imprisonment had higher crime rates. Homicide was the only exception. Consistent with Prediction 2 above, the greater the objective severity of imprisonment for homicide in a state, the less the state's homicide rate. The objective certainty of imprisonment was, on average, greater for homicide than for other types of crime, which led to Tittle (1969) suggesting that greater objective severity may deter only when objective certainty is high. "It would seem that severity alone is simply irrelevant to the control of crime" (Tittle 1969: 416).

Alternative Interpretations

The importance of Gibbs' (1968) and Tittle's (1969) groundbreaking studies should not be underestimated, but the findings were subject to alternative interpretations. Gibbs (1968) observed that social condemnation of homicide could produce a lower homicide rate, and it also could produce greater objective certainty and severity of imprisonment for homicide. The observed association between the objective certainty/severity of imprisonment and the homicide rate could, therefore, be spurious. Erickson, Gibbs, and Jensen (1977: 316–317) later elaborated:

> A criminal law is seldom violated if the type of act is socially condemned to a marked degree, and that very condemnation prompts legal officials to pursue arrests and press for convictions. Those official activities could result in greater objective certainty of punishment than would otherwise be the case . . ., and the greater objective certainty may be perceived by the public . . . in terms of "what ought to be" . . . The combination of a low crime rate . . . and high objective or perceived certainty of legal punishment would reflect the social (extralegal) evaluations of particular types of crimes, *not deterrence*. That possibility is . . . important since there is no basis to assume that the social condemnation of particular types of crime (e.g., homicide) is even approximately constant from one state to the next.

Tittle (1969) likewise considered an alternative interpretation of his findings. Because his data were cross-sectional—the imprisonment and homicide data covered roughly the same period in the early 1960s—it was impossible to distinguish cause from effect. A low crime rate could have caused greater objective certainty of imprisonment rather than the other way around. "This may come about because fewer crimes permit police departments to assign more manpower to known crimes" (Tittle 1969: 420). Conversely, a high crime rate could have led to a low objective certainty of imprisonment. "High crime rates could result in overcrowded prison facilities, thus inducing judicial personnel to make greater use of probation and suspended sentences" (Tittle 1969: 420).

There is still another alternative interpretation of the Gibbs–Tittle findings. Imprisonment can eliminate opportunities to commit crime. It is difficult, if not impossible, to commit some types of crime, such as auto theft, in prison. Thus, imprisonment can incapacitate offenders from committing crimes. In such a case, "the greater the [objective] certainty [and severity] of imprisonment, the greater the incapacitation, and the less the crime rate" (Gibbs 1975: 60). The same association between the objective certainty and severity of imprisonment and the crime rate could reflect deterrence or incapacitation, or both.

Deterrence versus Incapacitation

Why is it important to distinguish the effects of deterrence from incapacitation? If imprisonment produces less crime, why ask the reason? Gibbs (1975: 59) answered this way:

> Consider two jurisdictions, A and B, with approximately the same population size. Suppose that in A during a particular year there were 100 cases of robbery, with 20 individuals accounting for 40 cases before being imprisoned. Now suppose that another 20 individuals committed robbery at least once without ever being imprisoned so that they accounted for the remaining 60 cases, or 3 per individual. Turning to jurisdiction B suppose that there were also 40 individuals who committed robbery at least once during a year, but that only 5 were imprisoned, having committed 10 robberies prior to arrest. So the remaining 35 committed 105 robberies (3 on the average) without being imprisoned . . . B's robbery rate (115 cases) would be greater than A's (the two having the same population size), and the [objective] certainty of imprisonment would be greater in A. Those differences would be consistent with the deterrence doctrine, but the contrasts in the robbery rates could be attributed entirely to incapacitation. Had 15 more B individuals been imprisoned before repeating the offense, the robbery rates of A and B would have been equal, and the [objective] certainty of imprisonment would have been equal.

It is important to emphasize that if imprisonment only incapacitates without deterring, it can only prevent crimes that offenders would commit if they were not in prison (in the Gibbs example above, 40 robberies in jurisdiction A and ten robberies in jurisdiction B). More crimes could be prevented if imprisonment deterred people outside of prison from committing crimes (general deterrence). Deterrence would have broader application as a crime-control policy. Imprisonment of fewer offenders could prevent more crime through deterrence than imprisonment of more offenders through incapacitation.

More Research on General Deterrence and Imprisonment

There was a second generation of studies of the deterrent effects of imprisonment in the 1990s. In contrast to the first-generation studies by Gibbs (1968) and Tittle (1969), the second-generation studies used longitudinal data that were analyzed not only across states but over time (Nagin 2013a, 2013b). The new studies did not attempt to separate the deterrent effects of objective certainty and objective severity. Instead, "they examined the relationship between the crime rate and rate of imprisonment (prisoners per capita)" (Nagin 2013b: 86).

In recent reviews, Nagin (2013a, 2013b; Durlauf and Nagin 2011) reported that, like the first-generation studies, many of the second-generation studies found a negative association between imprisonment rates and crime rates (the greater the imprisonment rate, the less the crime rate). The findings, however, were subject to the same alternative interpretations as before. Most could not distinguish deterrence from incapacitation, nor could they distinguish cause from effect. An exception was a study by Levitt (1996) who used court-ordered prison releases in an instrumental variable analysis to untangle cause and effect and found that for every one-prisoner increase, there were 15 fewer serious crimes each year. It was unclear, however, how much of the decrease in serious crimes was due to deterrence and how much to incapacitation.

Another exception was a study by Raphael and Ludwig (2003; Raphael 2006) who examined the deterrent effects of a sentence enhancement for gun laws in a Richmond, Virginia intervention called *Project Exile*. Offenders who committed violent or drug crimes involving firearms were targeted for federal prosecution with longer prison sentences than allowed by Virginia law. From a comparison of (1) adult arrest rates for homicide with juvenile arrest rates for homicide in Richmond and (2) Richmond's gun homicide rate with the gun homicide rate in comparable cities, Raphael and Ludwig (2003; Raphael 2006) concluded the sentence enhancement did not deter. The problem of distinguishing cause from effect was avoided because the intervention occurred before the arrests and the gun homicides the intervention was intended to prevent. It was unclear, however, whether *Project Exile*'s primary objective was deterrence or incapacitation (Rosenfeld, Fornango, and Baumer 2005). Moreover, other than to report an increase in convictions for gun crimes, there was no evidence the intervention increased the objective certainty and severity of imprisonment. The emphasis in *Project Exile* was on extensive advertising in print and electronic media that gun crimes would result in longer sentences. Even if there was an increase in the objective certainty and severity of imprisonment, there was no evidence the intervention increased the *perceived* certainty and severity of imprisonment.

Failure to consider perceived properties of imprisonment is a problem with other studies of sentence enhancements. For example, Kessler and Levitt (1999) examined the effects of Proposition 8, which was a California sentence-enhancement law passed in 1982. Proposition 8 predated the "three-strike" laws passed by many states in the 1990s. The criminal law usually provides sentence enhancements for repeat offenders, but Proposition 8 extended their scope. Before Proposition 8, sentence enhancements applied only to prior incarcerations. After, they included prior convictions. Kessler and Levitt (1999) estimated a 4 percent decrease in crime after Proposition 8 attributable to deterrence. There was a 20 percent decrease in crime within five to seven years, but this longer-term decrease included incapacitation. While there were methodological criticisms of Kessler and Levitt's (1999) estimates (e.g., Webster, Doob, and Zimring 2006), a serious shortcoming was the failure to consider perceived properties of imprisonment. There was no evidence that Proposition 8 increased the perceived certainty and severity of imprisonment for crime in California.

There is a plethora of deterrence studies of the perceived certainty and severity of legal punishments *other than imprisonment*, such as arrest, but few studies of the perceived certainty and severity of imprisonment (for reviews, see Nagin 1998, 2013a, 2013b; Paternoster 2010). Studies of perceived properties of imprisonment are important because they help to distinguish deterrence from incapacitation. To conclude that objective properties of imprisonment deter rather than incapacitate, it is necessary to show (1) an association between the objective certainty and severity of imprisonment and people's perceptions of the certainty and severity of imprisonment and (2) an association between the perceived certainty and severity of imprisonment and crime.

Evidence for the first association was provided by Hjalmarsson (2009) who examined the effects of moving from the jurisdiction of juvenile court to adult court when reaching the age of majority. There should be harsher sentences in adult court; thus, the move should lead to greater perceived certainty and severity of punishment as well. Consistent with expectations, Hjalmarsson (2009) reported that, compared to the percentage of referrals to juvenile court that resulted in placement in a residential facility, there was a greater percentage of arrests of adults that resulted in a sentence to jail or prison. Also consistent with expectations, she found "the perceived chance of jail increases by 5.2%, on average, when the individual becomes an adult in the eyes of the court. This effect is over and above the underlying trends in age" (Hjalmarrson 2009: 213).

Evidence for the second association (and Prediction 3 above) was provided by Erickson et al. (1977). In a study of Arizona high school students, they found that, among types of crime, the greater the perceived certainty of incarceration in a reformatory, the less the rate of self-reported crimes.

Summary of Research on General Deterrence and Imprisonment

After six decades of research on the general deterrent effects of imprisonment, there are more questions than answers. Consistent with the causal logic of deterrence, many studies have found a negative association between objective properties of imprisonment and crime. However, which is the cause, and which is the effect? Is the association due to deterrence or incapacitation? Are the objective certainty and severity of imprisonment associated with people's perceptions of the certainty and severity of imprisonment, and are these perceptions associated with crime?

Research on Specific Deterrence and Imprisonment

Recall that specific deterrence involves direct experience with legal punishment (including avoidance of punishment). The causal logic of specific deterrence is a variation of Predictions 1–4 above. The experience of certain and severe legal punishments for committing crime should cause offenders to perceive legal punishments as certain and severe, which should deter them from repeating their crime and possibly other crimes. Virtually all studies of specific deterrence and imprisonment, however, truncate the logic and ask whether imprisonment decreases the likelihood of recidivism for the instant offense (the crime for which the offender was imprisoned) and other crimes. The idea is that the pain of imprisonment (Sykes 1958) should deter any self-interested person from repeating the experience. Nagin, Cullen, and Jonson (2009: 124) further suggest that the "structure of the law itself may cause previously convicted individuals to revise upward their estimates of the likelihood or severity of punishment for future lawbreaking." Imprisonment may cause people to believe, now that they have a record, there is a greater chance they will be arrested, convicted, and given a longer prison sentence if they commit another crime. They may update or adjust their perceptions of punishment. Although pertaining to arrest rather than imprisonment, Matsueda, Kreager, and Huizinga (2006) found evidence of updating in a study of juveniles in high-risk neighborhoods in Denver. Net of prior perceptions of the certainty of arrest, the greater the experienced certainty of arrest (i.e., the ratio of the number of times ever arrested or questioned by the police to the number of self-reported crimes), the greater the perceived certainty of arrest. Hjalmarrson (2009) also found that, compared to "ever arrested males," "ever incarcerated males" perceived a greater chance of jail if arrested.

At first glance, there is reason to doubt that prisons are a strong specific deterrent. A recent report by the U.S. Department of Justice estimated that within three years of release, 49.7 percent of state prisoners returned to prison (Durose, Cooper, and Snyder 2014). Similar estimates have been reported by Langen and Levin (2002) and the Pew Center on the States (2011). Because most crimes do not result in arrest, let alone imprisonment, the true recidivism (reoffending) rate is considerably greater (Mears and Cochran 2015).

These estimates, however, may paint too bleak a picture. They are based on a narrow conception that people either recidivate or they do not, and this ignores the possibility that recidivism can be a matter of degree. Instead of refraining entirely from committing crime, released prisoners may commit fewer crimes than they would if they had not been imprisoned. This is akin to the distinction between absolute and restrictive deterrence mentioned at the beginning of this chapter. Imprisonment may cause released prisoners to curtail or restrict their crimes rather than refrain from crime entirely. As Mears and Cochran (2015: 149) illustrate, "if prior to incarceration, an individual committed 10 crimes per year and then, after prison, committed only five crimes per year, a significant improvement has occurred." The result would be less crime. Imprisonment may also extend the time it takes offenders to reoffend (e.g., from one year to two), which also would result in less crime.

In a recent review of the literature, Nagin et al. (2009:115) conclude that "compared with noncustodial sanctions, incarceration appears to have a null [deterrent effect] or a mildly criminogenic [i.e., crime-inducing] effect on future criminal behavior" (for a similar conclusion, see Gendreau, Goggin, Cullen, and Andrews 2000; Villettaz, Killias, and Zoder 2006). They are quick to add, however, that there are few rigorous studies that have produced a reasonably high quality of evidence. The "litmus test for assessing the [specific deterrent] impact of imprisonment on reoffending is to compare the experiences of offenders in prison with those of *similar* offenders given a noncustodial sanction" (emphasis added—Nagin et al. 2009: 120). The key word in the quote is *similar*, but this can be difficult to achieve.

In a study of serious juvenile offenders, Loughran, Mulvey, Schubert, Fagan, Piquero, and Losoya (2009) initially observed that institutionalized offenders had a greater recidivism rate than those on probation—1.2 arrests per year versus 0.63 arrests per year. The two groups, however, were not similar. Institutionalized offenders had characteristics that made them a greater recidivism risk. For example, they were older, had longer prior records, and committed more serious crimes. The problem was a "selection effect" where the "highest risk offenders are selected for the most . . . severe sanctions" (Loughran et al. 2015: 5). To rule out selection effects, Loughran et al. (2009) matched offenders on a large number of background characteristics. After matching, the difference in recidivism disappeared; the two groups had virtually the same recidivism rate.

The best way to achieve similar groups is through randomization in an experimental design. Nagin et al. (2009), however, identified only five studies that randomly assigned offenders to prison or a non-prison alternative. Taken as a whole, they showed little evidence of specific deterrence. In one study of three in-home intensive supervision programs in Wayne County (Detroit) Michigan, every youth recommended by the juvenile court for incarceration was randomly assigned to one of the in-home programs (the experimental or treatment group) or incarceration (the control group). The in-home programs were just as effective as incarceration in decreasing the likelihood of recidivism. "Two years after random assignment, the experimental and control group cases showed few differences in recidivism, either in official charges or by self-report" (Barton and Butts 1990: 238).

Randomization in an experimental design is used infrequently in studies of specific deterrence and imprisonment because of ethical concerns. The next best way to achieve similar groups is in a quasi-experimental study where imprisoned offenders are systematically matched with offenders sentenced to a non-custodial punishment. The control and treatment groups need to be as similar as possible so any difference in recidivism can be attributed to the type of punishment.

Nagin et al. (2009) identified 11 studies that matched to obtain similar groups (also see Cullen, Jonson, and Nagin 2011). Most studies found a slight criminogenic effect of imprisonment rather than deterrence. Using data from the Netherlands, Nieuwbeerta, Nagin, and Blokland (2009) studied 1,475 men, ages 28–38, who were imprisoned for the first time. The focus on first-time prisoners avoided problems of separating the effects of current as compared to prior imprisonment. The control group was comprised of 1,315 men who were convicted but not imprisoned, and the two groups were matched to minimize selection bias. Over a three-year follow-up, imprisonment was associated with slightly higher recidivism rates, suggesting a criminogenic effect of imprisonment. Similar findings were reported in the other ten matching studies.

An additional study warrants attention because its methods and findings differ from other studies. Instead of comparing similar groups from randomization or matching, Bhati and Piquero (2008) used a life-course approach. From arrest histories of a sample of U.S. state prisoners who were released in 1994 and followed for three years, they estimated the effects of imprisonment on subsequent offending trajectories. Their "goal was to estimate and compare a releasee's actual post-prison offending trajectory for the purpose of answering the question: 'How, if at all, has this incarceration experience deflected the trajectory the offender was on'" (Bhati and Piquero 2008: 218). Because imprisonment interrupts offenders' criminal careers, their pre-prison trajectories were used as controls for their post-prison trajectories. Downward reflection of criminal careers after imprisonment would suggest deterrence, while upward reflection would suggest a criminogenic effect. Incapacitation would be suggested if there were no changes in offending trajectories before and after imprisonment. In contrast to other studies, Bhati and Piquero (2008) found stronger deterrent and incapacitative than criminogenic effects. "Most releasees were either deterred from future offending (40%) or . . . incapacitated by their incarceration (56%). Only about 4% had a criminogenic effect" (Bhati and Piquero 2008: 207).

Summary of Research on Specific Deterrence and Imprisonment

The bulk of the evidence is inconsistent with prisons as a strong specific deterrent. There is a paucity of experimental or quasi-experimental studies that allow for meaningful comparisons of imprisoned offenders with similar offenders given non-custodial punishments. With few exceptions, most studies suggest imprisonment has either no specific deterrent effect or a criminogenic effect.

Discussion and Conclusions

There is no simple answer to whether imprisonment deters, and this holds for general deterrence and specific deterrence. Despite decades of research, remarkably little is known about it except that the deterrent effects of imprisonment are probably small. The magnitude of the effect is clearly too small to justify a prison-based crime-control policy, such as the mass incarceration in the U.S. in the late 1970s and early 1980s.

The ultimate question about deterrence and imprisonment is: What would the crime rate be if some legal punishment other than imprisonment were imposed (Mears et al. 2015)? In the case of general deterrence, this might involve large-scale substitution of an intermediate punishment (or some combination of different intermediate punishments) for imprisonment and comparison of crime rates before and after the substitution. Any difference in the crime rates, however, cannot be attributed to deterrence unless the substitution is associated with change in the objective certainty and severity of punishment and corresponding change in the perceived certainty and severity of punishment.

In the case of specific deterrence, it would be necessary to compare the experiences of released prisoners with those of similar offenders who completed intermediate punishments. The most common intermediate punishment is intensive supervision programming (ISP) (Gendreau et al. 2000). The specific deterrent effects of ISP, however, will probably be no better than imprisonment. Gendreau et al. (2000: 11) summarized results from

"47 comparisons of the recidivism rates of offenders in an ISP with those receiving regular probation" and, on average, found no difference in recidivism rates. Combining the ISP results with those of seven other intermediate punishments, including fines, restitution, and electronic monitoring, they found, on average, no effect on recidivism. Although these results do not come from a comparison of intermediate punishments with imprisonment, they are suggestive that intermediate punishments are no panacea.

Substantial investment in imprisonment in the U.S. suggests that policy makers believe it effectively deters crime. Most deterrence studies suggest otherwise. It needs to be emphasized, however, that many of the existing deterrence studies have serious shortcomings, and there may be different results from more rigorous studies. What is needed is a theory that combines deterrence with what we know about the causes of crime. This may be useful for identifying the conditions under which imprisonment deters. For example, it may be the threat of imprisonment is a more effective deterrent during periods of economic prosperity when there is more to lose for legal punishment for committing crime. Or it may be that imprisonment is a better specific deterrent when released prisoners stay away from friends who influenced them to commit crimes in the first place. The suggestion likely increases the complexity of deterrence, but that may be the requirement for a better understanding of it.

References

Barton, W.H., and J.A. Butts. 1990. "Viable Options: Intensive Supervision Programs for Juvenile Delinquents." *Crime and Delinquency* 36(2): 238–256.

Bhati, A., and A.R. Piquero. 2008. "Estimating the Impact of Incarceration on Subsequent Offending Trajectories: Deterrent, Criminogenic, or Null Effect?" *Journal of Criminal Law and Criminology* 98(1): 207–253.

Blumstein, A., and J. Wallman. 2000. *The Crime Drop in America.* Cambridge: Cambridge University Press.

Clark, R.D. 1988. "Celerity and Specific Deterrence: A Look at the Evidence." *Canadian Journal of Criminology* 30: 109–120.

Cullen, F.T., C.L. Jonson, and D.S. Nagin. 2011. "Prisons Do Not Reduce Recidivism: The High Cost of Ignoring Science." *The Prison Journal* 91(3): 48S–65S.

Durlauf, S.N., and D.S. Nagin. 2011. "Imprisonment and Crime: Can Both Be Reduced?" *Criminology and Public Policy* 10(1): 13–54.

Durose, M.R., A.D. Cooper, and H.D. Snyder. 2014. *Recidivism of Prisoners Released in 30 States in 2005: Patterns from 2005 to 2010.* Washington, DC: Bureau of Justice Statistics.

Erickson, M.L., J.P. Gibbs, and G.F. Jensen. 1977. "The Deterrence Doctrine and the Perceived Certainty of Legal Punishments." *American Sociological Review* 42(2): 305–317.

Farrell, G., A. Tseloni, J. Mailley, and N. Tillery. 2011. "The Crime Drop and the Security Hypothesis." *Journal of Research in Crime and Delinquency* 48(2): 147–175.

Gendreau, P., C. Goggin, F.T. Cullen, and D. Andrews. 2000. "The Effects of Community Sanctions and Incarceration on Recidivism." *Forum on Corrections Research* 12(2): 10–13.

Gibbs, J. P. 1968. "Crime, punishment, and deterrence." *The Southwestern Social Science Quarterly* 48(4): 515–530.

Gibbs, J.P. 1975. *Crime, Punishment, and Deterrence.* New York: Elsevier.

Glaze, L.E., and Herberman, E.J. 2014. *Correctional Populations in the United States, 2013.* Washington, DC: U.S. Department of Justice, Bureau of Justice Statistics.

Hjalmarrson, R. 2009. "Crime and Expected Punishment: Changes in Perceptions at the Age of Criminal Majority." *American Law and Economics Review* 11(1): 209–248.

Johnson H.A., and N.T. Wolfe. 2003. *History of Criminal Justice.* Cincinnati, OH: Anderson.

Kaeble, D., L. Glaze, A. Tsoutis, and T. Minton. 2015. *Correctional Populations in the United States, 2014.* Washington, DC: Bureau of Justice Statistics.

Kessler, D.P., and S.D. Levitt. 1999. "Using Sentence Enhancements to Distinguish between Deterrence and Incapacitation." *Journal of Law and Economics* 42: 343–363.

Langen, P.A., and Levin, D.J. (2002). *Recidivism of Prisoners Released in 1994*. Washington, DC: Bureau of Justice Statistics.

Levitt, S.D. 1996. "The Effect of Prison Population Size on Crime Rates: Evidence from Prison Overcrowding Litigation." *Quarterly Journal of Economics* 111(2): 319–352.

Levitt, S.D. 2004. "Understanding Why Crime Fell in the 1990s: Four Factors that Explain the Decline and Six that Do Not." *Journal of Economic Perspectives* 18(1): 163–190.

Loughran, T.A., E.P. Mulvey, C.A. Schubert, J. Fagan, A.R. Piquero, and S.H. Losoya. 2009. "Estimating a Dose-response Relationship between Length of Stay and Future Recidivism in Serious Juvenile Offenders." *Criminology* 47(3): 699–740.

Matsueda, R.L., D.A. Kreager, and D. Huizinga. 2006. "Deterring Delinquents: A Rational Choice Model of Theft and Violence." *American Sociological Review* 71(1): 95–122.

Mauer, M. 2006. *Race to Incarcerate*. New York: The Free Press.

Mears, D.P., and J.C. Cochran. 2015. *Prisoner Reentry in the Era of Mass Incarceration*. Los Angeles, CA: Sage.

Mears, D.P., J.C. Cochran, and F.T. Cullen. 2015. "Incarceration Heterogeneity and Its Implications for Assessing the Effectiveness of Imprisonment on Recidivism." *Criminal Justice Policy Review* 26(7): 691–712.

Nagin, D. S. 1998. "Criminal Deterrence Research at the Outset of the Twenty-first Century." *Crime and Justice* 23: 1–42.

Nagin, D.S. 2013a. "Deterrence in the Twenty-first Century." *Crime and Justice* 42(1): 199–263.

Nagin, D.S. 2013b. "Deterrence: A Review of the Evidence by a Criminologist for Economists." *Annual Review of Economics* 5(1): 83–105.

Nagin, D.S., and G. Pogarsky. 2001. "Integrating Celerity, Impulsivity, and Extralegal Sanction Threats into a Model of General Deterrence: Theory and Evidence." *Criminology* 39(4): 865–891.

Nagin, D.S., F.T. Cullen, and C.L. Jonson. 2009. "Imprisonment and Reoffending." *Crime and Justice* 38(1): 115–200.

Nieuwbeerta, P., D.S. Nagin, and A. Blokland. 2009. "The Relationship between First Imprisonment and Criminal Career Development: A Matched Samples Comparison." *Journal of Quantitative Criminology* 25(3): 227–257.

Paternoster, R. 2010. "How Much Do We Really Know about Criminal Deterrence?" *Journal of Criminal Law and Criminology* 100(3): 765–823.

Petit, B., and B. Western. 2004. "Mass Incarceration and the Life Course: Race and Class Inequality in U.S. Incarceration." *American Sociological Review* 69(2): 151–169.

Pew Center on the States. 2011. *State of Recidivism: The Revolving Door of America's Prisons*. Washington, DC: The Pew Charitable Trusts.

Raphael, S. 2006. "The Deterrent Effects of California's Proposition 8: Weighing the Evidence." *Criminology and Public Policy* 5(3): 471–478.

Raphael, S., and J. Ludwig. 2003. "Prison Sentence Enhancements: The Case of Project Exile." Pp. 251–286 in *Evaluating Gun Policy: Effects on Crime and Violence*, edited by Jens Ludwig and Philip J. Cook. Washington, DC: Brookings Institution Press.

Rosenfeld R., and S.F. Messner. 2009. "The Crime Drop in Comparative Perspective: The Impact of the Economy and Imprisonment on American and European Burglary Rates." *The British Journal of Sociology* 60(3): 445–470.

Rosenfeld, R., R. Fornango, and E. Baumer. 2005. "Did *Casefire*, *Compstat*, and *Exile* Reduce Homicide?" *Criminology and Public Policy* 4(3): 419–449.

Spelman, W. (2000). "What Recent Studies Do (and Don't) Tell Us about Imprisonment and Crime." *Crime and Justice* 27: 419–494.

Stafford, M.C., and M. Warr. 1993. "A Reconceptualization of General and Specific Deterrence." *Journal of Research in Crime and Delinquency* 30(2): 123–135.

Steffensmeier, D., and M.D. Harer. 1999. "Making Sense of Recent U.S. Crime Trends, 1980 to 1996/1998: Age Composition Effects and Other Explanations." *Journal of Research in Crime and Delinquency*, 36(3): 235–274.

Sykes, G.M. 1958. *Society of Captives: A Study of a Maximum Security Prison*. Princeton, NJ: Princeton University Press.
Tittle, C.R. 1969. "Crime rates and legal sanctions." *Social Problems* 16(4): 409–423.
Villettaz, P., M. Killias, and I. Zoder. 2006. *The Effects of Custodial vs. Non-custodial Sentences on Re-offending: A Systematic Review of the State of Knowledge*. Oslo: Campbell Collaboration Crime and Justice Group.
Webster, C., A. Doob, and F.E. Zimring. 2006. "Proposition 8 and Crime Rates in California: The Case of the Vanishing Deterrent." *Criminology and Public Policy* 5(3): 417–448.
Western, B. 2006. *Punishment and Inequality in America*. New York: Russell Sage Foundation.
Zimring, F.E. 2006. *The Great American Crime Decline*. New York: Oxford University Press.

2 Victim Rights and Retribution

Maria J. Patterson, Angela R. Gover, and Maren Trochmann

Crime Victims' Rights Movement

The American criminal justice system has historically focused largely on deterring, capturing, convicting, punishing, and rehabilitating the offender. More recently, however, government agencies and the public at large have become further aware of and involved in meeting the needs of the innocent human beings at the other end of the crimes: the victims. Practitioners in the fields of law, media, politics, and social justice have shone new light on the hardships victims face within the criminal justice system, and as a result, today's public as well as government agencies have become more aware of victims' needs and experiences than they were in the past.

Crime victims come from all walks of life in terms of race/ethnicity, socioeconomic status, religion, politics, gender, and age; these differences have complicated efforts to unite as a group in order to foster social change. However, it is widely acknowledged that despite such diversity, victims as a whole have reaped tremendous benefits through mutual support, systematic acknowledgement, and the opportunity to participate in the criminal justice process. As both practitioners and the general public gained more awareness of these needs, a crime victims' movement arose starting in the 1970s. This movement was largely influenced by previous social crusades such as the civil rights movement, the feminist movement, and the law-and-order movement.

Influences on the Crime Victims' Rights Movement

Law-and-Order Groups

Emerging in the 1960s, the law-and-order movement resulted from increasing public dissatisfaction with higher crime rates and a perceived systemic bias towards offenders. Conservatives responded by advocating for harsher penalties and other hardline crime policies. Casting the criminal justice system in the role of savior from certain societal bedlam and annihilation, they determined to protect the public at large by strengthening the "thin blue line" of law enforcement. Citing a previously lax response on the part of the criminal justice system, law-and-order advocates called for a crackdown on the wrongdoers who would ignore society's social and political rules. Hardliners promoted widespread fear among the public about becoming victims of crime in order to increase support for enhanced powers within criminal justice agencies including police forces, court systems, and the prison system, despite potential for false convictions and excessive punishments (Hook 1972). Hardcore advocates further asserted that the scales of justice were unfairly weighted in favor of criminals at the expense of honest, law-abiding citizens and their partners in law enforcement and the courts.

Championing a rehabilitated justice system characterized by swift and sure punishment, advocates worked to strike down legal procedures benefitting defendants, dismissing them as technicalities and loopholes that allowed hardened criminals to go free and undermined government efforts to protect the public. As a result, sentences were lengthened, fewer accused were granted bail, and fewer offenders were granted probation or parole. Dissenting voices against these new policies as too extreme were accused of being "pro-criminal" and "anti-victim" (Carrington 1975; Miller 1973).

Women's Movement

In the late 1960s, the women's rights movement began to direct more attention towards women crime victims, particularly in terms of female victims of male perpetrators. Adding insult to injury, these victims were often treated dismissively by a male-dominated criminal justice system. Highlighting the need for support and resources for rape and domestic violence victims, feminists responded by founding the first rape crisis centers in 1972 (Berkeley, CA, and Washington, DC) and the first battered women's shelter in 1974 (St. Paul, MN). These resources offered victims much-needed support and consolation, providing a safe place for many who would have otherwise suffered in silence and isolation. In addition, these locations often became community centers for feminist political outreach and organization.

Anti-battering and anti-rape campaigns shared many commonalities, including often being spearheaded by former victims' intent on combatting the societal and institutionalized misogyny leading to violence against women. Both campaigns focused on female empowerment by exposing and confronting systemic patriarchal bias, establishing support communities, and providing safe spaces.

A centralized theme driving these feminist campaigns was the belief that crimes typically characterized by male offenders against female victims such as domestic violence, rape, sexual abuse, and sexual harassment imperil the security of *all* women and impede progress towards an equal and just society for all. Victims who were also women of color and/or economically disadvantaged were recognized as among the most vulnerable in society, first victimized by males and then forced to depend on a criminal justice system dominated by privileged males who were unmotivated to empower women. As a result, women turned to one another for their own empowerment.

Other Social Movements

Activists from other social movements including the civil liberties, children's rights, seniors' rights and LGBTQ rights movements have had a strong influence on improving crime victims' rights. The civil liberties movement emphasizes constitutional protections and the guarantee of due process for suspects, defendants, and convicted offenders in the criminal justice system. Civil liberties advocates have prevailed in court battles that served to benefit crime victims as well by promoting law enforcement professionalism and by reinforcing equal protection under the law. The children's rights movement also protects crime victims through combatting sexual abuse, child battering, child neglect, and other types of child maltreatment. Advocacy efforts have resulted in more exacting guidelines for reporting suspected maltreatment, increased focus on the expedient arrest and prosecution of perpetrators, improved procedures for vulnerable child victims testifying in court, and improved efforts in terms of child protection and abuse prevention services.

History of Victim Rights Movement

Following the Industrial Revolution, criminal legislation has evolved to place more concern regarding the effects of crime on the state rather than on the victim. This was beneficial for the state, as it allowed the state to collect fines from these crimes; however, this shift isolated victims from the workings of the justice system. In 1972, the first National Crime Survey (now called the National Crime Victimization Survey) found large discrepancies between the number of crimes reported to law enforcement and the number of crimes that survey respondents were willing to report (Boland and Butler 2009). These discrepancies led to a focus, consideration, and treatment of crime victims within the criminal justice system. As a result, over the last two decades, both state and federal governments have expanded victims' rights through a number of acts designed to increase victim participation through providing information, support, and restitution to crime victims.

The first federal victim legislation was passed in 1982. The Victim and Witness Protection Act of 1982 advocated for the fair treatment of federal crime victims and witnesses by offering victims certain rights, namely allowing for victim impact statements and restitution, and calling for the attorney general to issue guidelines for further crime victim policy development (Goldstein 1984). In the same year, President Ronald Reagan assembled a Presidential Task Force on Victims of Crime in order to inquire into the needs of crime victims and the manner in which the criminal justice system attempted to meet victims' needs. The Task Force's 1982 report recommended extending such procedural rights as requiring pre-sentencing reports to include information about victim loss and suffering as well as expanded compensation for victims of crimes. The 1984 Victims of Crime Act (VOCA) reflected the Task Force's report by establishing a process through which the funds collected from federal offenders would be distributed to states in order to support crime victims.

The 1990 Victim Rights and Retribution Act further improved procedural rights for crime victims by extending their right to be notified of significant changes in the federal cases in which they are involved. Namely, the act afforded the victims the right to be made aware of dates and times of court proceedings and their right to attend them; the right to communicate with the prosecutor, the right to protection from the offender, and the right to be notified when the defendant's detention status changes. These rights were increased further four years later when, under President Clinton's presidency, the 1994 omnibus Violent Crime Control and Law Enforcement Act granted federal crime victims the right to speak at sentencing hearings. The 1994 Act also significantly increased the funding reserved for local victim services and made restitution mandatory for all sexual assault cases through the Violence Against Women Act (VAWA), which also provided additional protections for women. As a result of the passage of these acts and other statutes, victims are now afforded several rights at the federal level.

Crime Victims' Rights at the Federal Level

Some of the basic rights afforded to crime victims include notification of various situations, the right to participate in the criminal justice system and consult with prosecutors, the right to compensation and protection, the right to protection, and the right to a speedy trial. A victim's right to notification is one of the most essential rights afforded to a victim because victims cannot exercise the rights they have if they are not made aware of the fact that they have these rights and protections. Victims find the right to be notified highly important, especially notification of events such as the arrest of a suspect (Davis and Mulford 2008). Unfortunately, not all states consistently ensure that victims are given the required information, even when the state has strong, specific, and comprehensive legislation about victim rights to notification (Kilpatrick, Beatty, and Smith Howley 1998).

Restitution

Another important right afforded to crime victims is restitution. Victims of crimes can incur numerous types of loss or damages, many of which are financial in form or have financial repercussions. For example, victims can face costs to repair property damage, medical costs as a result of emotional or physical trauma, and loss of productive time that correlates to a loss of income. In spite of the financial damages most crime victims endure, however, not all victims receive restitution. Rather, oftentimes states may base the payment of restitution on the offender's ability to pay, and victims may wait years for restitution or never receive the full amount of restitution ordered (Office for Victims of Crime 2013).

Restitution statutes state that these financial losses are to be compensated in one of two ways. The first way in which victims can receive monetary compensation is by receiving restitution paid by the offender. Restitution can be required as a condition of parole in many states or offered as a required condition of a suspended sentence. On the other hand, victim compensation can come from victim compensation programs rather than offender-paid restitution. As a result of the 1984 Victims of Crime Act, states have established a public victim compensation program that aids victims in receiving financial compensation, including victims of drunk driving and domestic violence (per the 1988 amendment of the Act). As long as state compensation programs satisfy VOCA's guidelines, the programs can receive subsidies from the federal Crime Victims' Fund. Made up primarily of money from fines paid by persons convicted of federal crimes, the Fund's assets are distributed by state governments through state compensation programs, and up to 40 percent of a state program's payments to victims can be covered by this federal subsidy. It should be noted, however, that restitution is used as a means to encourage victim participation; in all states, only victims who report crimes and assist in the prosecution of offenders are considered eligible for restitution.

Right to Participation

Another key right that crime victims have is the right to be present and participate in the criminal justice system process, from the time the case is being investigated by law enforcement through the time of prosecution. Victims of all crime have the right to attend court proceedings and submit a victim impact statement (VIS) at the time of sentencing. A VIS may be read by the victim in court or submitted directly to the judge. A VIS describes how the victimization impacted the victim physically, emotionally/psychologically, financially, etc., and how it impacted others the victim may live with such as children or spouse/partner.

The expansion of victims' rights has been met with some resistance. Those opposed to expanding victims' rights have been concerned for defendants' due process. It is suggested that, as a result of such expansion of victims' rights, convicted offenders would be more likely to be treated unfairly and receive harsher sentences (Davis and Mulford 2008). However, it is also possible that judges and prosecutors may not be applying victim impact statements to their cases with regularity. This suggests that it may be judges' lack of integrating victim impact statements into their sentencing decisions, rather than using them as aggravating factors in their sentencing considerations, thus causing the lack of uniformity in sentencing.

Right to a Speedy Trial

Just as defendants attain due process through a right to a speedy trial, many states afford this right to victims as well. According to Howley and Dorris (2007), this right is explicitly clear through statutory language in about half the states. This right is often seen in relation to rulings for motions of continuance of a case, as several states have implemented a limitation on the number of continuances possible for each case. In addition, some states will allow for accelerated dispositions in cases involving certain victims—such as minors, people with disabilities, or seniors—who would be more likely to suffer harm if court proceedings were delayed. As such, when a party requests a continuance, many states require a consideration of the impact such a continuance would have on the victim prior to ruling.

Right to Protection

Finally, victims have a right to protection. Introduced in the Victim and Witness Protection Act of 1982, it was decided that victims and witnesses of federal crimes are to be protected from harm and intimidation during their involvement in the criminal justice process. Most states have also implemented measures to provide victims and witnesses of crimes—especially victims who are involved in cases of gang crimes, interpersonal violence, or other violent crimes—with some right to protection. In the majority of states, protections given to victims include a secure waiting area separate from that of the defendant in court buildings, information regarding protocol for reacting to a defendant's intimidation or threat of intimidation, as well as the issuing of non-contact or restraining orders. Further, an increasing trend across states continues to be to further protect victims from intimidation by refraining from disclosing identifying details about victims, such as address or place of employment, in court testimonies (Howley and Dorris 2007). In these states, nonessential information can also be limited in disclosures to law enforcement and kept out of court records for purposes of protection.

There have been a variety of challenges in implementing victim rights legislation, and victim rights research frequently finds that victims often fail to receive due notification, restitution, and opportunities to be heard (Davis and Mulford 2008). Despite state and federal legislation, criminal justice systems do not consistently comply and implement victim rights legislation. As a result, a number of states have developed offices that serve to help victims by providing referrals to state and community-based organizations that provide direct services. These state-level offices also act as a form of oversight and monitor compliance with victim rights legislation.

Do Sentencing Philosophies Serve the Interests of the Victim?

Crime victims' rights and needs are secondary in importance to the rights of those who are accused of committing criminal offenses because of the due process rights the U.S. Constitution affords to those accused of committing such acts. The Sixth Amendment guarantees the rights of criminal defendants, but no such constitutional rights and protections are afforded to victims despite the various state and federal laws discussed previously. In the American criminal justice system, the commission of a crime is viewed as a crime committed against the state and the laws of the state, rather than a crime committed against a victim. In fact, if a case makes it from the law enforcement stage to the prosecution stage, which can normally only be done with the victim's cooperation, the case is still prosecuted on the state's behalf rather than on behalf of the victim. Despite the various rights victims have under state and federal law, this philosophy underlies the criminal justice process.

Retribution as a Sentencing Philosophy

Retribution was the first philosophy of justice that prioritized the victim, as evidenced by early criminal codes such as the Babylonian Code of Hammurabi in the seventeenth century BCE. However, today retribution as a sentencing philosophy is sometimes thought to be too moralistic and has been replaced by more utilitarian sentencing methods such as rehabilitation and incarceration. It can be argued, though, that in placing so much emphasis on the offender and the offender's effect on society, current sentencing philosophies fail to address the needs of those who are most impacted by an offense—the victim. In order to understand why retribution as a punishment philosophy has fallen out of favor, it is important to consider retribution in its historical context, both its philosophical origins and its relevance in currently existing crime victim legislation. In doing so, it is clear that the era of retribution may not be over; rather, retribution may be an essential component to prioritizing victims in an era that is so focused on how crimes harm the state.

In the seventeenth century BCE the king of Mesopotamia, Hammurabi, produced the Code of Hammurabi, a code of 282 laws. The 196th law of the Code stated, "If a man put out the eye of another man, his eye shall be put out" (Ascaso, Singh, and Dua 2011). This idea was later simplified to "an eye for an eye" in the biblical *lex talionis* doctrine, but the meaning remained largely unchanged: a criminal's punishment should be equal to the harm suffered by the victim. This victim-focused philosophy remained prevalent throughout the Middle Ages, though this was not necessarily by design as early criminal justice systems were far less formal and structured than they are today. It was, therefore, up to the victim to seek justice, and he often did so through demanding of the offender what he as the victim lost—often, an eye for an eye or a death for a death. Additionally, an offender was expected to pay restitution to the victim. This method of punishment may have more closely resembled revenge than retribution, but two ideas in this philosophy of punishment remain true in the spirit of retribution: first, the punishment was proportional to the harm the victim suffered; and second, the crime was considered to be harmful primarily to the victim, rather than to the state or governing body.

During the Industrial Revolution, however, criminal law started to focus on the effects of crimes on the state. This was a financially advantageous move for the state; if crimes negatively impacted the state, rather than the victim, fines could be collected from offenders. When the focus of the impact of crime shifted from the victim to the state, victims were neglected and no longer seen as a valued participant in the criminal justice process. This disregard for victims remained until the 1940s, when activists and researchers attempted to bring more focus back to the victims. On the other hand, researchers at the time no longer thought of victims the same way. Instead, research started to see victims as potentially culpable in their own victimization, and aimed to identify the extent to which victims could reasonably be held responsible for their victimization. Though victims were no longer invisible, the harm victims suffered still failed to be the primary focus.

Today the meaning and role of retribution has remained a topic of debate, especially in relation to victim participation in criminal justice proceedings. Some worry that victims' primary motivations for participation are rooted in revenge and that above all victims hope to see the offender suffer as they have (Starkweather 1992). For many, retributive justice has been difficult to separate from its revenge-based origins. For this reason, some regard retributive justice as uncivilized, especially when compared to more utilitarian sentencing philosophies that aim to prevent future crimes. In considering the effects of a crime on a victim, however, the desire for retributive justice is clear. It can be difficult to determine who the victim of a crime is, especially if a crime affects many people. However, retributive justice focuses on the true victims, those most afflicted by the crime, rather than on theoretical victims of potential future crimes. Retribution, for this reason, may serve as a theory that would help prioritize the rights of crime victims.

Though there is not one universally accepted definition of retribution, the theory of retribution approaches crimes as violations of order, morality, or society and asserts that a criminal must be deservedly punished for violating this order (Fletcher 1999). This is the "just deserts" justification of punishment: an offender is punished because he is a rational human being able to decide whether to commit a crime, so if he chooses to commit the crime he deserves to be punished (Starkweather 1992). A related goal of retribution is to bring the parties back to the equilibrium that has been violated by the crime. The offender must reestablish the equilibrium by compensating for the damage he caused the relationship by committing the crime (Henderson 1985). He thus must not only be punished, but his punishment must be proportionate to the damage he caused by committing the crime. The just deserts model of punishment factors harm to a victim into an offender's sentence because this harm directly effects what he deserves (his deserts). Retribution is not about what the beneficial outcomes may be of a punishment; in fact, if a punishment has significant benefits to society, but the offender does not deserve that punishment, then that punishment cannot be justified.

Retribution Compared to Deterrence, Rehabilitation, and Incapacitation

There are many philosophies regarding the purposes of punishment, though these purposes are typically grouped into utilitarian and nonutilitarian purposes (Frase 2005). While utilitarian purposes seek net benefits as a result of the punishment, such as a decrease in offenses of that crime committed in the future, nonutilitarian purposes of punishment understand punishment to be necessary for justice. According to the nonutilitarian theory, punishment is the goal itself because it is the fair response to the harm caused by the crime. Incapacitation, rehabilitation, and deterrence as forms of punishment all serve a utilitarian purpose, while retribution is categorized as a nonutilitarian form of punishment (Weiner, Graham, and Reyna 1997).

As methods intended to inhibit an offender's ability to commit future crimes, incapacitation, rehabilitation, and deterrence all serve both a practical and utilitarian goal. Incapacitation prevents future crimes by literally making offenders incapable of committing further crimes, often through incarceration. Rehabilitation, on the other hand, is rooted in the belief that identifying and addressing the problems that prompted an offender's past crimes can prevent the offender from committing future crimes. In the 1970s, rehabilitation was the dominant philosophy of punishment; however, rehabilitation's popularity was brought to an end by the "nothing works" debate. This debate was sparked by Robert Martinson's conclusion in his 1974 article "What Works?—Questions and Answers About Prison Reform" that rehabilitation has no positive effect on offender recidivism (Sarre 2001). The article garnered the nickname, "Nothing Works!" and encouraged the movement towards other sentencing philosophies, especially deterrence. Similarly, the juvenile justice system long viewed rehabilitation to be the purpose of juvenile punishment. However, the increasing severity of juvenile punishments over the last few decades suggests that incapacitation has replaced rehabilitation as the goal (Weiner et al. 1997).

Deterrence, meanwhile, uses the philosophy that punishment must be "swift, certain, and severe" in order to discourage future crimes of that kind (Frase 2005). Deterrence was borne of rational choice theory, which operates on the assumption that people are rational and able to be deterred. There are two types of deterrence: specific and general. While specific deterrence (also called individual deterrence) functions on the level of an individual offender, general deterrence seeks to deter a larger subgroup of the public from offending. Specific deterrence operates on the belief that severe punishment will make an offender fearful of committing more crimes because he or she does not want to receive the same or harsher punishment in the future. Similarly, general deterrence aims to prevent members of society, either a subgroup or the public in general, from committing the crime as a result of their fear of getting a harsh penalty that an offender would receive.

Unlike deterrence, rehabilitation, and incapacitation, retribution is a nonutilitarian principle. There is a negative and a positive version of retributive theory (Frase 2005). The negative version suggests that retributive theory is best used for setting limits on punishment severity according to each case. The positive version, however, follows the purpose theory, which sees retribution as the purpose of punishment. In this view, offenders deserve punishment because they committed a crime, and the severity of their punishment should be defined by what they deserve based on the crime they committed.

Proportional and uniform sentencing is thus an essential aspect of retributive theory: that punishment should be proportional in scale to the blameworthiness (also called desert) of the offender (Henderson 1985). Further, sentencing should be uniform, meaning that offenders with the same level of blameworthiness should receive sanctions of the same magnitude. Blameworthiness is directly tied to moral arguments of fairness: what sentence is fair to the offender, given his crime? What is fair to society and those within society who have abided by the law? And, significantly, what is fair to the victim of this crime? In this way, retribution, in considering what is fair to the victim, takes into account the harm done to victims in ways that deterrence, rehabilitation, and incapacitation do not.

Conclusion: What Does the Future Look Like for Victims' Rights and Retribution?

The criminal justice landscape in the U.S. was founded upon a belief that crimes are committed primarily against the state. Moreover, the state has a constitutional duty to protect the due process and presumed innocence of any accused offender. Not until recent social movements drawing attention to victims of crime, such as the law-and-order and women's rights movements, did the scales of justice begin to tip in a way that acknowledged the other side of a crime—the victim. These movements brought attention and awareness to the oft-neglected rights of the victim, and states and the federal government began to take note and follow suit through legislative reforms and changes.

In the past decades, federal and state legislation has been implemented to protect and honor key rights of victims in the criminal justice system. These rights include the right to restitution or compensation for any losses due to the crime, the right to participation in the prosecution and criminal justice process, and the right to a speedy trial. These rights also now afford the victim the right to protection from intimidation and threat from the offender. Yet, despite these widely recognized rights and increased recognition and services granted to victims, the sentencing philosophy within the U.S. criminal justice system may not fully serve the victim.

The American Constitution protects and enshrines the rights of offenders to due process, encapsulating the core ideal that any accused is innocent until proven guilty. Despite the various laws and increasing rights of victims, those rights are protected with less strength, permanence, and are secondary to those rights protected by a constitutional amendment. The state has taken on the onus of prosecuting, sentencing, and punishing offenders, an onus that in previous times was borne by the victims themselves who may have sought retribution from the time of Hammurabi to the Middle Ages.

In the current system, crimes are viewed and prosecuted as violent or unlawful acts committed against the state, against order, and against society rather than as acts committed against an actual victim or multiple victims. The justice system has, thus, taken a utilitarian approach promoting general and specific deterrence as its primary objective. Along with deterrence, incarceration and rehabilitation of offenders have been emphasized and embraced historically. Any form of retribution is no longer a personal matter in the hands of the victim, but rather the state and criminal justice system undertakes sentencing. Such retribution may be viewed as morally uncivilized and revenge-based at the worst, and a non-utilitarian form of punishment at the very least.

While legislative and advocacy efforts may continue to strengthen and assert victims' rights, it seems unlikely that the core sentencing philosophy of the American criminal justice system will drastically change. Victims may continue to seek more rights and recognition of the pain suffered through a sentencing philosophy of retributive justice, yet even such non-utilitarian retribution does not make a crime victim truly whole. While retribution or the *lex talionis* doctrine of "an eye for an eye" may impart equal harm to an offender, it cannot take away the harm and pain brought to the victim of the crime. Thus, it is likely the state will continue to prosecute crime through utilitarian means, perhaps enhancing victims' rights over time, but continuing a sentencing philosophy that places primacy on the rights of the offender and provides a utilitarian form of justice.

References

Ascaso, Francisco J., Arun D. Singh, and Harminder S. Dua. 2011. "Decoding Eyes in the Code of Hammurabi." *British Journal of Ophthalmology* 95(6): 760.

Boland, Mary L., and Richard Butler. 2009. "Crime Victims' Rights: From Illusion to Reality." *Criminal Justice* 24(4): 1–7.

Carrington, Frank. 1975. *The Victims*. New Rochelle, NY: Arlington House.

Davis, Robert C., and Carrie Mulford. 2008. "Victim Rights and New Remedies: Finally Getting Victims their Due." *Journal of Contemporary Criminal Justice* 24(2): 198–208.

Fletcher, George. 1999. "The Place of Victims in the Theory of Retribution." *Buffalo Criminal Law Review* 3(1): 51–63.

Frase, Richard. 2005. "A More Perfect System: Twenty-five Years of Guidelines Sentencing Reform." *Stanford Law Review* 58(1): 67–83.

Goldstein, Abraham S. 1984. "The Victim and Prosecutorial Discretion: The Federal Victim and Witness Protection Act of 1982." *Law and Contemporary Problems* 47(4): 225–248.

Henderson, Lynne N. 1985. "The Wrongs of Victim's Rights." *Stanford Law Review* 37: 937–1021.

Hook, S. 1972. "Victims of Crime." *Student Law* 1, 48.

Howley, Susan, and Carol Dorris. 2007. "Legal Rights for Crime Victims in the Criminal Justice System." Pp. 299–317 in *Victims of Crime*, edited by R.C. Davis, A.J. Lurigio and Susan Herman. Thousand Oaks, CA: Sage.

Kilpatrick, Dean G., David Beatty, and Susan Smith Howley. 1998. *The Rights of Crime Victims: Does Legal Protection Make a Difference?*. Washington, DC: U.S. Department of Justice, Office of Justice Programs, National Institute of Justice.

Miller, Walter B. 1973. "Ideology and Criminal Justice Policy: Some Current Issues." *Journal of Criminal Law and Criminology* 64(2): 141–162.

Office for Victims of Crime. 2013. *Crime Victims Fund*. Retrieved June 9, 2016, from www.ovc.gov/pubs/crimevictimsfundfs/index.html

Sarre, Rick. 2001. "Beyond 'What Works?' A 25-year Jubilee Retrospective of Robert Martinson's Famous Article." *Australian & New Zealand Journal of Criminology* 34(1): 38–46.

Starkweather, David A. 1992. "Retributive Theory of 'Just Deserts' and Victim Participation in Plea Bargaining." *The Indiana Law Journal* 67: 853–878.

Weiner, Bernard, Sandra Graham, and Christine Reyna. 1997. "An Attributional Examination of Retributive versus Utilitarian Philosophies of Punishment." *Social Justice Research* 10(4): 431–452.

3 Incapacitation and Sentencing

Pauline K. Brennan and Julie Garman

Punishments may serve multiple purposes, and these may include rehabilitation, retribution, deterrence, and incapacitation. This chapter focuses on the punishment goal of incapacitation, which is accomplished when a judge imposes a sentence that limits or completely does away with an offender's physical ability to commit a crime. The ultimate form of incapacitation, because it completely neutralizes an offender, is death. A less drastic example is the surgical or chemical castration of a sex offender, because such an action alters the individual's physiological state and, thereby, minimizes his likelihood of reoffending. But, the death penalty is not often imposed and sentences that require an offender to undergo a process of castration are far from common. In comparison, jail and prison sentences are imposed far more frequently; the primary method of offender incapacitation in the United States is incarceration. Prison and jail inmates are incapacitated due to their secure isolation from the general public; individuals who are physically removed from society cannot harm law-abiding citizens.

More than two million Americans are currently incarcerated in the United States, and rates of incarceration have increased markedly over time (Kaeble, Glaze, Tsoutis, and Minton 2015). Changes in sentencing policy largely explain the current extent of American incarceration. To put it another way, sentences to incarceration are far more likely today than they once were because punishment laws were modified over time to reflect the goal of crime prevention through incapacitation.

This chapter begins with an overview of the use of incarceration in the United States, and highlights increases over time. The section that follows explains how a sizeable amount of the spike in incarceration resulted from the passage of laws that mandated determinate sentences, guidelines-based sentences, mandatory-minimum prison sentences for first-time offenders convicted of specified crimes, lengthy prison terms for repeat offenders (sometimes with no opportunity for release), and fewer days of credit that could be earned by prison inmates to reduce their time behind bars. The chapter then turns to an examination of research findings from studies of the effects of such laws. The conclusion provides a discussion of some recently implemented sentencing reforms.

American Lockup

The rate of incarceration in the U.S. more than tripled from 1980 to 2014. In 1980, slightly more than 500,000 individuals were incarcerated in jails and prisons across the United States and the rate of incarceration was 221 inmates per 100,000 U.S. residents (Beck and Gillard 1995: 2). By 1994, the rate of incarceration increased to 562 inmates per 100,000 people and over 1.4 million individuals were in custody (Gillard and Beck 1996: 2). At year-end 2014, over two million people were housed in U.S. jails and prisons and the estimated rate of incarceration was 690 inmates per 100,000 Americans (Kaeble et al. 2015: 2–3).

To provide a bit more context to these figures, the current U.S. rate of incarceration is more than five times higher than the rate found for almost every other country (Wagner and Walsh 2016). In fact, "38 states lock up greater portions of their populations than El Salvador, a country that recently endured a civil war and now has one of the highest homicide rates in the world" (Wagner and Walsh 2016: n.p.).

The size of prison populations and the rate of incarceration are, of course, determined by the number of admissions to prison and by inmate length of stay. The number of inmates in federal and state prisons for violent, property, drug, and public-order (e.g., drunk driving, obstruction of justice, gambling) offenses has increased dramatically over time. Increases have been especially notable for inmates serving time for drug offenses; the likelihood of being sent to prison for a drug-related crime increased by 350 percent from 1980 to 2010 (Mitchell and Leachman, 2014: 5). At the federal level, 25 percent of the U.S. prison population (4,900 inmates in total) consisted of drug offenders in 1980 (Brown, Gilliard, Snell, Stephan, and Wilson 1996: 12). In 2014, nearly half of all federal inmates (96,500 inmates) were serving time for drug offenses (Carson 2015). Across state prisons, only 6.4 percent of inmates (19,000 in total) were incarcerated for drug offenses in 1980 (Brown et al. 1996: 10). By yearend 2013, about 16 percent of state prison inmates (208,000 in total) were drug offenders (Carson 2015). In short, the number of people incarcerated in state prisons for a drug offense has increased more than ten-fold since 1980. It is also interesting to point out that "most of these people [were] not high-level actors in the drug trade, and most [had] no prior criminal record for a violent offense" (Sentencing Project 2015: 3).

Furthermore, inmates are serving longer prison sentences today than they did decades ago. Researchers from the Pew Center on the States (2012: 13) reported that inmates released from state prisons in 2009 spent an average of nine months longer behind bars than inmates released in 1990. From 1990 to 2009, the average length of time served in state prisons increased by 37 percent for violent offenders, 36 percent for drug offenders, and 24 percent for property offenders (Pew Center on the States 2012: 3). And, among specific categories of violent crime, time served in state prisons for aggravated assault, burglary, and robbery increased by 83 percent, 41 percent, and 79 percent, respectively, from 1980 to 2010 (National Research Council 2014: 53).

Similar trends have also been observed among federal inmates. The average amount of time served by federal inmates was more than two and a half times longer in 2012 (Motivans 2015: 39) than in 1986 (Bureau of Justice Statistics 1996: 18). With regard to increases among specific categories of federal inmates, from 1986 to 2012, the average amount of time served increased by more than two years (from 46.4 months to 71.6 months) for those convicted of violent crimes and by more than three years (from 20.6 months to 58.6 months) for those convicted of drug offenses (Bureau of Justice Statistics 1996: 18; Motivans 2015: 39). Lengthier average prison sentences, particularly among drug offenders, have significantly increased the federal inmate population. In fact, researchers from the Urban Institute concluded "the increase in expected time served by drug offenders was the single greatest contributor to growth in the federal prison population between 1998 and 2010" (Mallik-Kane, Parthasarathy, and Adams 2012: 3).

It is also worth noting that more inmates are serving life sentences today than during the 1980s. Since 1984, the number of people serving life sentences has more than quadrupled (Sentencing Project 2015: 8); an estimated one in nine prison inmates is currently serving a life sentence (Sentencing Project 2015: 8) and one third of these inmates is serving a sentence without the possibility of parole (Nellis 2013: 1). Before 1970, only seven states authorized judges to impose life sentences without the opportunity for parole (LWOP), but even though allowed, LWOP was infrequently given and was generally used only as an alternative to the death penalty for those convicted of homicide (Nellis 2013: 3–7). However, beginning in the 1980s when incapacitation gained prominence as a punishment goal, and as support for the goal of rehabilitation diminished, policymakers and the public got behind the idea of putting many different sorts of offenders away for the rest of their lives. Today, the federal government and every state (with the exception of Alaska) allow judges to impose LWOP sentences, and life sentences are authorized for individuals convicted of homicide, assault, robbery, sex-related crimes, drug offenses, and some property offenses (Nellis 2013: 5–7). While most lifers are serving time for violent offenses, "more than 10,000 people serving life sentences have been convicted of a nonviolent crime, including more than 2,500 for a drug offense and 5,400 for a property crime" (Nellis 2013: 7).

Changes in Sentencing Policy

A review of sentencing policy is necessary in order for one to better grasp how an offender may end up serving time behind bars, as well as how changes in sentencing policy have resulted in increases in imprisonment likelihood and length. During the 1970s and earlier, judges exercised considerable discretion when deciding which punishments to impose on convicted offenders. Judges were free to impose punishments that were generally not limited by legislators, and sentences were intended to be tailored to an individual offender's needs and unique circumstances; most offenders could be given community-based punishments (e.g., such as probation) and prison or jail sentences were (for the most part) not mandatory (Ellison and Brennan 2016; Spohn 2009; Tonry 2013). Moreover, in 1970, every state and the federal government allowed judges to impose indeterminate prison sentences, which meant that a sentencing judge set the minimum and maximum amount of time that a convicted offender could serve in prison but the exact amount of time would ultimately rest with a discretionary parole board (Tonry 2013). For example, a judge could sentence an offender to serve one to five years in prison. Such an inmate, if deemed by a parole board to be sufficiently rehabilitated and no longer a risk to society, could be released before the five-year mark. But, a parole board could also deny early release, which meant that an inmate could end up serving the maximum set prison term. In short, under indeterminate sentencing systems, some inmates served mere fractions of their possible prison sentences while other inmates ended up serving considerably longer periods of time behind bars.

Because a wide-range of punishment options were possible prior to the 1980s and because there did not seem to be consistency in the likelihood of imprisonment or in the imposed length of prison sentences for similar offenders, critics argued that punishments were often wildly disproportionate to the types of offenses committed, highly disparate across offenders, not sufficiently punitive, and did not work to reduce the likelihood of reoffending (Frankle 1972; Martinson 1974; Von Hirsch 1976). Due process advocates (i.e., liberals) stressed that courts should impose equitable punishments across similar offenders, and that evidence of possible discriminatory treatment undermined notions of fair treatment and threatened the legitimacy of the criminal justice system (Ellison and Brennan 2016; Packer 1968). Conservatives, on the other hand, advocated for the adoption of a crime control model and argued that inconsistent punishments undermined the crime prevention goals of retribution (because punishments were often too lenient), deterrence (because prison sentences ended up being shorter than expected), and incapacitation (because inmates who were released from prison on parole ended up reoffending) (Packer 1968). As concern over the criminal justice system grew, sentencing policies changed across the nation. Changes to sentencing policy came in the form of determinant sentencing, sentencing guidelines, mandatory imprisonment, habitual offender laws, and truth-in-sentencing legislation.

Critics of indeterminate sentencing structures argued that determinate, or fixed, prison sentences were necessary. With determinate sentencing, a judge is required to impose a specified amount of prison time at the time of the sentencing hearing, which eliminates the need for a later decision about possible early release from prison by a discretionary parole board. In other words, under determinate sentencing, early release from prison via parole is not possible. The California legislature was the first to enact a determinate sentencing law in 1976, and shortly thereafter "the number of adults incarcerated by the state rose substantially" and prisons became overcrowded (California Budget and Policy Center 2015: 4). Determinate sentencing laws were also passed in Illinois, Indiana, and Arizona (Tonry 2013). Like California, prison populations increased in each of these states after indeterminate sentencing ceased to exist. In Illinois, for example, roughly 11,000 prison inmates were incarcerated in 1977, the year when its legislature passed a determinate sentencing law (Peters and Norris 1991: 829). By 1991, close to 29,000 inmates were housed in prisons across the State (Peters and Norris 1991: 829).

Sentencing guidelines were another type of sentencing reform intended to assure that similar offenders received equally punitive sanctions, and Minnesota was the first jurisdiction to initiate the use of guidelines-based sentencing in 1980 (Tonry 2013). The federal government and 19 states currently require judges to use some form of sentencing guidelines when imposing punishments (Harmon 2014). In 1984, for example, Congress passed the Sentencing Reform Act (SRA), which did away with parole and mandated that federal judges impose stipulated punishments for convicted offenders (Nagel and Schulhofer 1992; Spohn 2009). To be more specific, the SRA required judges to use a predetermined grid of presumptive punishments at the sentencing hearing—the point at which an offender's criminal history and offense seriousness intersected on the grid specified the intended punishment. If incarceration ended up being the designated punishment (which is the result in 89 percent of the cells in the guidelines grid), a judge was required to impose the denoted length of prison time (USSC 2015a: 403). A judge who decided to impose a different punishment (i.e., meaning a departure from the guidelines occurred) had to specify his or her reasons in writing and the decision was subject to review (Spohn 2009).

A United States Sentencing Commission (USSC) report on the consequences of the SRA for the first 15 years after implementation indicated that sentence severity in the federal courts increased after 1990 and the use of probation as a sanction declined (USSC 2004: 42–43). The 2004 USSC report also found that the average length of federal prison sentences more than doubled from 1986 to 1992, immediately following the implementation of sentencing guidelines. To put it another way, the average sentence received by a federal inmate in 2002 was more than twice the going rate for 1986 (USSC 2004: 46). In short, the mandated use of federal sentencing guidelines increased imprisonment likelihood and length for many federal offenders. Similar outcomes were observed in Washington State after it enacted sentencing guidelines in 1981 (Boerner 1993; Engen and Steen 2000).

An array of new mandatory minimum sentencing laws that greatly expanded the use of prison time also emerged during the 1980s and 1990s. In fact, "between 1975 and 1996, mandatory minimums were the most frequently enacted change in sentencing law in the United States" (National Research Council 2014: 83). With mandatory minimum laws, those found guilty of stipulated crimes, regardless of their criminal histories, must be sent to prison. Thus, judges cannot use their discretion to impose other punishments, even when mitigating circumstances may warrant alternatives to incarceration. By 1994, every state required mandatory prison terms for certain first-time offenders (Austin, Jones, Kramer, and Renninger 1996). At the federal level, "between mid-1985 and mid-1991, the U.S. Congress enacted at least 20 new mandatory penalty provisions; by 1991, more than 60 federal statutes subjected more than 100 crimes to mandatory penalties" (Tonry 2013: 165).

Most mandatory minimum laws apply to those convicted of drug offenses, murder, sex crimes, and felonies involving firearms (National Research Council 2014; Tonry 2013).

Some offenders convicted of property crimes must also be given mandated prison sentences. Prior to the enactment of mandatory minimum laws, judges could impose community-based punishments, such as probation and community service, on almost all offenders.

Oregon's Measure 11 provides an example of a mandatory sentencing law that went into effect in 1995 (Merritt, Fain, and Turner 2006). The law required the imposition of lengthy mandatory minimum prison sentences for individuals convicted of 16 designated crimes (Merritt et al. 2006). Five more offenses were added to the list via an amendment to the law in 1997. For the 21 offenses ultimately included in Measure 11, the stipulated mandatory terms of imprisonment ranged from a minimum of 70 months for second-degree assault, kidnapping, robbery, and certain sex offenses to a minimum of 300 months for murder (Merritt et al. 2006: 16). Penalties could not be reduced for first-time offenders or for juveniles.

Researchers found that Oregon's law increased both the likelihood of incarceration and the length of incarceration for individuals convicted of the 21 offenses included in Measure 11. Before implementation of the law, 66 percent of those convicted of the eligible offenses received prison terms, but more than 90 percent of eligible offenders were sentenced to prison by 1998 (Merritt et al. 2006: 23). Moreover, within one year of implementation, "the average sentence length for M11-eligible cases increased from 77 to 105 months. Average prison sentence lengths continued to rise through the end of the decade, peaking at 118 months in 1999" (Merritt et al. 2006: 29).

Connecticut, like Oregon and all other states, also requires the imposition of mandatory minimum prison sentences on some of its convicted offenders. In fact, there are now 74 crimes in Connecticut that require minimum prison sentences of varying durations (Office of Legislative Research 2015: 1). For example, a minimum of 25 years in prison must be given to a first-time offender convicted of murder or aggravated sexual assault of a minor (Office of Legislative Research 2015: 4). An individual convicted for a second time of sexual assaulting a minor in an aggravated manner must serve at least 50 years in prison. With regard to other crimes, at least ten years must be given to those found guilty of home invasion or first-degree kidnapping with a firearm. At least two years must be spent in prison by anyone convicted of second-degree larceny involving property taken from an elderly, blind, physically disabled, pregnant, or intellectually disabled person. And, with regard to certain drug offenses, those found guilty of selling drugs to minors must be sentenced to serve at least two years in prison and, with some exceptions, at least one year of incarceration must be imposed on non-students found guilty of using, possessing, or delivering drug paraphernalia near a school (Office of Legislative Research 2015: 8–9). It is worth nothing that prior to the 2014 legislative session, Connecticut's law mandated a minimum three-year prison sentence for anyone who committed a drug offense within 1,500 feet of a school, public housing complex, or day care center (Porter and Clemons 2013: 3).

All 50 states have drug-free-zone laws that mandate prison time for individuals convicted of certain drug crimes near places where children are most likely to be present (Porter and Clemons 2013: 1). While most of these laws pertain to those convicted of selling or distributing drugs within protected areas, "in nine states—Alaska, Arkansas, Arizona, Connecticut, Indiana, Minnesota, New Mexico, Michigan, and Oklahoma—defendants in drug-free zones can also face enhanced penalties even for simple drug possession that does not involve sale to school children" (Porter and Clemons 2013: 1). In Arkansas, for example, simple possession of two grams of methamphetamine in a drug-free zone—which may include a public park, school, university, school bus stop, skating rink, community center, public housing complex, or church—is sufficient to trigger a ten-year prison sentence (Porter and Clemons 2013: 1–7).

At the federal level, Congress passed a series of laws mandating prison sentences for many first-time drug offenders. One of these laws, the Anti-Drug Abuse Act of 1986, required a minimum of five or ten years in prison for those convicted of selling certain quantities of specific drugs (USSC 1991: 10). To elaborate, the federal law mandated at least a five-year prison sentence for the sale of 1 gram of LSD, which is roughly the equivalent of a single packet of sweetener, and a ten-year sentence for the sale of 10 grams of LSD (Families Against Mandatory Minimums (FAMM) 2011: 4). Sale of 5 grams of crack cocaine triggered a five-year prison sentence, while 50 grams resulted in at least a ten-year term. For powder cocaine, sale of 500 grams netted a five-year minimum prison sentence and 5 kilos (or 11 pounds) triggered a mandatory ten years. "Congress established [these] mandatory sentences with the intention of locking up high-level drug traffickers. But only 11% of those incarcerated in federal prisons on drug charges fit that definition . . . The rest are low-level offenders" (FAMM 2011: 8).

Congress then passed the Omnibus Anti-Drug Abuse Act of 1988, which required a mandatory minimum sentence of five years for individuals convicted of possessing more than 5 grams of crack cocaine (USSC 1991: 10). One hundred times that amount of powder cocaine (500 grams) also triggered a minimum sentence of five years in prison (Spohn 2009: 242). The Act also doubled the amount of required prison time for those who "engaged in a continuing drug enterprise" from a minimum of 10 years to a minimum of 20 years (USSC 1991: 10). Moreover, mandatory minimum penalties increased substantially for those convicted of conspiring to sell or distribute drugs (USSC 1991:10).

A recent report by the USSC found steady increases over a 20 year period in the number of offenders in federal custody who were subject to a mandatory minimum penalty at sentencing (USSC 2011: xxix). Almost 25 percent of all offenders sentenced in the federal courts in fiscal year 2014 were convicted of an offense that carried a mandatory minimum amount of prison time (USSC 2014: 1). More than two-thirds of offenders convicted of an offense carrying a mandatory minimum penalty in 2014 were drug offenders, with crack cocaine offenders subject to such penalties most often (USSC 2014: 1–2). These figures serve to demonstrate the extent to which federal offenders are affected by mandatory minimum sentencing laws.

Similar to mandatory-minimum sentencing laws, habitual offender laws restrict judicial discretion at sentencing by requiring judges to impose lengthy prison terms. Habitual offender laws are known by a variety of names, including three-strike laws, repeat offender laws, persistent offender laws, and prior and persistent offender laws. The purpose of these laws is to assure that individuals who have shown a propensity to reoffend will be locked away in prison for long periods of time, in order to protect the general public from further harm (Auerhahn 1999; Russell 2010; Shichor 1997).

All states had some form of enhanced sentencing for repeat offenders prior to 1970, but a variety of new laws for repeat offenders were enacted across the U.S. during the early 1990s that were less flexible, applied to a longer list of felonies, and significantly increased the duration of required time behind bars (Russell 2010: 1149; Spohn 2009: 265). Between 1993 and 1995, 24 states and the federal government passed laws that mandated very lengthy prison terms, often life sentences, for repeat felony offenders (Clark, Austin, and Henry 1997: 1). Three prior convictions or "strikes" were required in most states for an offender to be taken "out" of society for a prolonged period of time, but "two-strikes" were enough to trigger recidivist enhancements in nine states (Clark et al. 1997).

For example, a second felony conviction in Georgia for kidnapping, armed robbery, rape, aggravated sodomy, aggravated sexual battery, or aggravated child molestation requires a life sentence without the option of parole (Nellis 2013: 15). LWOP is also mandatory for anyone convicted of homicide (Nellis 2013: 15). More than 700 prison inmates in Georgia were serving LWOP by the end of 2012, and more than 40 percent were convicted of something other than homicide (Nellis 2013: 15).

In California, an offender may end up serving a minimum of 25 years in prison if convicted of a second qualifying felony (Clark et al. 1997: 7). A sentence of 25 years to life is mandated for a person found guilty of a third felony, no matter how minor, if the offender has two prior serious or violent felony convictions (Nellis 2013: 15). Under California's law, people have been sentenced to 25 years to life for stealing golf clubs from a country club, stealing meat from a grocery store, and stealing cookies from a restaurant (Spohn 2009: 264). While California's three-strike law was intended to take persistent offenders off the street, by 2008 fewer than half the individuals sentenced under the law were convicted of a violent offense as their third strike; "55% were convicted of a nonviolent offense, including 16% for a drug offense and 30% for a property crime" (Nellis and King 2009: 28). An estimated 22 percent of inmates currently serving life terms in California received their sentences under the State's three-strike law (Nellis 2013: 15). An even higher percentage of lifers in the State of Washington (68 percent) is estimated to be serving LWOP sentences due to a three-strike law that went into effect in 1994 (Nellis 2013: 16).

Truth-in-sentencing (TIS) laws, which generally limit the amount of good-time credit inmates may earn in order to gain early release from prison, have also lengthened prison sentences. These laws were enacted throughout the United States due to the Violent Crime Control and Law Enforcement Act of 1994, which awarded federal funds for prison construction to states that (a) increased the percentage of violent offenders sent to prison, (b) lengthened prison sentences for violent offenders, and (c) required violent offenders to serve at least 85 percent of their imposed sentences (Tonry 2013: 162). Many reasoned that the 85 percent rule would make prison sentences more "truthful," because inmates would be required to serve the vast majority of their imposed sentences. By 1999, 42 states and the District of Columbia had enacted some form of a TIS policy (Sabol, Rosich, Mallik-Kane, Kirk, and Dubin 2002: 7). Shortly after these laws were enacted, researchers from the Urban Institute concluded that "when implemented as part of a larger sentencing reform process, TIS reforms are associated with large changes in prison population outcomes" (Sabol et al. 2002: vi). Evaluators from the RAND Corporation also found that TIS laws contributed to increases in prison populations (Turner, Fain, Greenwood, Chen, and Chiesa 2001: 134).

Research on the Effectiveness of Sentencing and Incapacitation

Numerous issues have been raised regarding America's use of imprisonment as a crime-prevention strategy. To begin, mass incarceration has little or no clear influence on crime rates (National Research Council 2014: 337; Mauer 2010: 6; Tonry 2013: 147). While some may disagree and point to the widely noted inverse relationship between violent crime rates and rates of incarceration in the U.S. during the 1990s as "proof" that incarceration reduces crime, scholars stress that the predictors of crime are complex, so the extent of crime in any society cannot simply be due to the number of people incarcerated (Austin and Irwin 2001; Gainsborough and Mauer 2000; King, Mauer, and Young 2005). For example, the relationship between age and crime is well-known; crime is disproportionately committed by individuals in their late teens and early twenties, and the likelihood of engaging in crime diminishes notably with age (Hirschi and Gottfredson 1983). Therefore, crimes rates will be higher in places with large percentages of young people.

Those who believe incarceration offers a simple panacea to the crime problem also fail to consider the phenomenon of replacement for certain types of offenders. To elaborate, researchers find that incarcerated drug dealers are quickly replaced by individuals with limited options who overestimate the benefits that may materialize through illegal pursuits (National

Research Council 2014: 345–346). Further flaws in the argument that "prison works" become apparent after one considers trends in different places. For example, as was the case in the United States, the crime rate in Canada decreased during the 1990s, yet this occurred as the Canadian prison population declined (Mauer 2010: 7). New York also experienced a crime drop during the 1990s, when "New York State had the second slowest growing prison system in the country" and at a time when its largest city jail system downsized (Justice Policy Institute 2000: 4). This finding is all the more poignant when one also takes into account rates of imprisonment and crime in California during the same time period:

> California's prison population grew by 30%, or about 270 inmates per week, compared to New York State's more modest 30 inmates a week. Between 1992 and 1997, New York State's violent crime rate fell by 38.6%, and its murder rate by 54.5%. By contrast, California's violent crime rate fell by a more modest 23%, and its murder rate fell by 28%. Put another way, New York experienced a percentage drop in homicides which was half again as great as the percentage drop in California's homicide rate, despite the fact that California added 9 times as many inmates to its prisons as New York.
>
> (Justice Policy Institute 2000: 4)

In other words, changes in the use of incarceration do not necessarily result in the same changes in crime rates in all places.

Furthermore, lengthy terms of imprisonment are not necessary to secure the goal of community protection, although many people believe that select offenders are certain to reoffend if released from prison and must, therefore, be locked up for the rest of their lives. In a recent study, researchers from Stanford University examined recidivism outcomes for a cohort of 860 California inmates who were convicted of homicide, sentenced to life, and then released on parole (Weisberg, Mukamal, and Segall 2011). Among the group of 860 inmates released from prison beginning in 1995, only five individuals (less than 1 percent) were returned to jail or prison for new felonies by 2010 (Weisberg et al. 2011: 17). Marquart and Sorensen (1988) reported similar outcomes for a group of inmates who once sat on Texas' death row. All the inmates became eligible for parole after their death sentences were commuted to life terms as a result of the U.S. Supreme Court's 1972 ruling in *Furman v Georgia*, and 31 were released from prison between 1973 and 1986 (Marquart and Sorensen 1988). Of the entire group, only two committed subsequent felonies—one was returned to prison for burglary and one murdered his girlfriend and then committed suicide. While two crimes would have been prevented if these inmates had remained incarcerated, the execution or the permanent detention of all 31 inmates would not have greatly protected society. In fact, the vast majority of inmates remained crime-free while in the community. "These so-called 'successes' or 'false positives' demonstrate the futility of trying to predict future dangerousness" (Marquart and Sorensen 1988: 690). In fact, findings from multiple other studies stress that it is not possible to identify high-rate future offenders with sufficient accuracy (Auerhahn 1999; Blumstein, Cohen, Roth, and Visher 1986; Tonry 2013).

The problem with false prediction is that it leads to unnecessary detention, which is both unfair to affected individuals and a waste of money for taxpayers. The estimated cost to house an offender is high, at approximately $28,000 per year for a federal inmate (National Association of State Budget Officers [NASBO] 2013: 2) and about $31,000 per year for a state inmate (Henrichson and Delaney 2012: 10). It is even more expensive to house an elderly inmate due to added costs related to health care (e.g., required medications, hearing aids, walkers, breathing machines), dental care (e.g., root canals and dentures), and required modifications to prisons (e.g., installation of ramps for wheel chairs) and prison cells (e.g., widening doorways and adding hand rails near toilets) in order to accommodate physical issues that come with age. Indeed, prisons spend "two to three times more to incarcerate geriatric individuals than younger inmates" (Chiu 2010: 5). These costs can be quite high when one considers that 10 percent of all state prisoners (131,500 inmates in total) are 55 years old or older, and the number of such inmates more than quadrupled between 1993 to 2013 (Carson 2016: 1). Habitual offender laws and mandatory minimums account for the increase in the elderly inmate population.

Increases in prison populations have been matched with surges in correctional spending. Between 1980 and 2013, annual spending for the federal prison system rose 595 percent, from $970 million to more than $6.7 billion (The Pew Charitable Trusts 2015: 2). From 1986 to 2012, state-level spending on corrections increased by more than 400 percent, from approximately $10 billion to over $50 billion (NASBO 2013: 4). In 2002, America spent more money incarcerating non-violent offenders than the federal government spent on welfare programs that served over eight million people (Justice Policy Institute 2000: 6). And, in 2013, 11 states spent more money on corrections than on higher education (Mitchell and Leachman 2014: 8). The high cost of corrections to taxpayers is clear.

There are also hidden costs of incarceration for offenders and their families. Incarceration is a stressful experience for inmates, due to separation from loved ones, concerns over safety, limited autonomy, and shame. Moreover, the stigma of being an ex-prisoner may make it difficult for released inmates to find employment and housing (Pew Center on the States 2010a: 22). With regard to the collateral consequences of incarceration for families, "it strains them financially, disrupts parental bonds, separates spouses, places severe stress on the remaining caregivers, leads to a loss of discipline in the household, and to feelings of shame, stigma, and anger among the children left behind" (Barreras, Drucker, and Rosenthal 2005: 168; see also Turanovic, Rodriguez, and Pratt 2012: 916–919).

These hidden costs of incarceration have been disproportionately felt by racial and ethnic minorities. Approximately 60 percent of people in prison today are black or Hispanic (Carson 2015). In 2014, black men were almost six times more likely to end up behind bars than white men (Carson 2015: 15). The rate of incarceration for Hispanic men was 2.3 times higher than the rate for white men. When compared to white women, incarceration was twice as likely for black women and 1.2 times as likely for Hispanic women (Carson 2015: 15). Differential treatment by the criminal justice system provides a reason for the racial and ethnic disparities in imprisonment. For example,

> the War on Drugs has been waged in racially disparate ways. From 1999–2005, African Americans constituted roughly 13% of drug users on average but 36% of those arrested for drug offenses and 46% of those convicted for drug offenses. While the War on Drugs creates racial disparity at every phase of the criminal justice process, disparities in sentencing laws for various types of drugs and harsh mandatory minimum sentences disproportionately contribute to disparity.
>
> (Sentencing Project 2013: 14–15)

In particular, upon assessing the federal sentencing guidelines for 15 years, the USSC concluded that mandatory penalties for crack cocaine contributed significantly to differences in average sentences for blacks and whites (USSC 2004: 132). Until recently, 100 times more powder cocaine than crack cocaine was required for the same mandatory prison sentence; the ratio is now 18:1, which still means that notably higher amounts of powder cocaine are necessary to elicit the same penalties (FAMM 2011: 4; Sentencing Project 2013: 15). When one considers that 83 percent of those sentenced under federal crack cocaine laws are black (USSC 2015b), harsher penalties for black offenders are the result.

It is also worth mentioning that close to half of those convicted of offenses that require mandatory amounts of prison time will end up with more lenient punishments, due to "safety valve" provisions linked to offender acceptance of responsibility or prosecutorial requests for departures for defendants who provide assistance with criminal investigations (USSC 2011: xxix). A recent report from the United States Sentencing Commission indicated that black offenders were the least likely to escape the imposition of a mandatory penalty (USSC 2011: xxix). With regard to the effect of prosecutorial discretion on sentencing disparity, Hartley and colleagues (2007: 404) found that federal prosecutors filed motions for substantial assistance to mitigate the sentences of offenders perceived to be sympathetic and non-dangerous, and found that such departures were likely for females, whites, and more educated offenders. In another study, Spohn and Brennan (2011: 59) reported that close to 40 percent of drug defendants in Iowa, Minnesota, and Nebraska received substantial assistance departures, which (on average) cut their sentences in half. An offender's ethnicity mattered; Hispanics were less likely than whites to be given substantial assistance departures (Spohn and Brennan 2011: 62). Overall, these findings suggest that prosecutors' discretionary decisions regarding departures for substantial assistance result in unwarranted disparity in the federal sentencing process.

State-specific sentencing laws have also resulted in racial and ethnic disparities in imprisonment. "In California, for example, the state with the most far-reaching [three-strike] law, African Americans constitute 29% of persons serving a felony sentence in prison, but 45% of persons sentenced under California's three-strike law" (Mauer 2010:8). In Florida, Crawford, Chiricos, and Kleck (1998: 498) examined outcomes for 9,690 males who met the requirements to be sentenced as habitual offenders and found that the race of the defendant mattered. Among eligible property offenders, blacks were sentenced as habitual offenders 2.3 times as often as nonblacks. And, among drug offenders, blacks were 3.6 times more likely to be incarcerated as habitual offenders (Crawford et al. 1998: 498). These findings shed light on the issue of inequality under the law and, therefore, the need for one to reconsider many current sentencing policies.

Summary and Concluding Thoughts

Prison and jail populations have increased significantly over time due to sentencing policies that stressed incapacitation as the primary purpose of punishment, despite evidence that imprisonment offers few (if any) long-term benefits for community protection. Soaring prison populations have resulted in concomitant increases in correctional costs, often at the expense of education and other socially beneficial programs. Offenders and their families have also fallen victim to immense collateral consequences of incarceration, and these adverse effects have been disproportionately felt by racial and ethnic minorities.

Given the costs of imprisonment, research findings that question the necessity of mass incarceration, and obvious disproportionate minority confinement, one must wonder whether alternative punishments would provide a better option. A 2013 online report by the Administrative Office of the U.S. Courts (AOC) indicated that the annual cost of supervision by a federal probation officer (about $3,000 per probationer) was about eight times lower than the cost of incarceration in a federal prison (about $28,000 per inmate) (AOC 2013). In addition, some researchers find that rates of reoffending are lower among probationers than among inmates released from prison. In a study of 1,077 offenders convicted of felonies in Kansas City, Spohn and Holleran (2002: 350) found that offenders who had been incarcerated were more likely to be charged with a new offense, convicted of a new offense, and incarcerated for a new offense than those who were put on probation. Moreover, released prisoners reoffended more quickly than probationers. Differences were especially pronounced among drug offenders; incarcerated drug offenders were five to six times more likely to reoffend upon release than drug offenders who remained in the community on probation (Spohn and Holleran 2002: 350). Gendreau, Goggin, Cullen, and Andrews (2000) also reported that recidivism was more likely for individuals who had been incarcerated than for those given community sanctions. In short, alternatives to incarceration, such as probation, may provide more cost-effective methods for crime prevention. Such alternatives may also alleviate the collateral consequences of incarceration that are felt by so many individuals.

In line with such a suggestion, steps have been taken across jurisdictions in recent years to reduce inmate populations and direct resources to incarceration alternatives. For example, California voters approved Proposition 47 in 2014, which reclassified some drug and property offenses from felonies to misdemeanors (Sentencing Project 2016). The measure also mandated redirection of resources to mental health services, drug treatment, and diversion programs to enable offenders to reduce their likelihoods of reoffending (Mitchell and Leachman 2014: 17). A year after the law went into effect, a study conducted by the Justice Advocacy Project at Stanford University reported that Proposition 47 reduced California's prison population by 13,000 inmates and saved taxpayers an estimated $150 million (Romano 2015: 1). South Carolina changed its sentencing practices in 2010 to allow for certain nonviolent offenders to be given community-supervision options in lieu of imprisonment (Henrichson and Delaney 2012: 11), and analysts estimated that South Carolina would reduce correctional costs by $241 million as a result (McLeod 2011: 1).

Other states have taken steps to reduce time spent in prison by allowing inmates to earn more good-time credits towards their release. For example, in 2008, Mississippi reduced the percentage of sentences that nonviolent offenders were required to serve prior to parole eligibility from 85 percent to 25 percent (Henrichson and Delaney 2012: 11). After just one year, the State's prison population decreased by over 1,000 inmates (Pew Center on the States 2010b: 2). In Nevada, State legislators feared that prison populations would increase by 60 percent and would cost taxpayers $2 billion (Pew Center on the States 2010b: 4). Therefore, the 2007 Nevada legislature "voted nearly unanimously" to increase the number of good-time credits that inmates could earn for in-prison participation in educational programs, vocational training, and substance abuse treatment. This change in policy helped Nevada save $38 million in operating expenditures (McLeod 2011: 1; Pew Center on the States 2010b: 4). As evidence of cost-effective solutions to incarceration will continue to amass, it is likely that even more energy will be directed at strategies designed to reduce the number of people in U.S. prisons in the years to come.

References

Administrative Office of the U.S. Courts (AOC). 2013. *Supervision Costs Significantly Less than Incarceration in the Federal System*. Washington, DC: AOC. Retrieved May 15, 2017 from www.uscourts.gov/news/2013/07/18/supervision-costs-significantly-less-incarceration-federal-system

Auerhahn, Kathleen. 1999. "Selective Incapacitation and the Problem of Prediction." *Criminology* 37(4): 703–734.

Austin, James, and John Irwin. 2001. *It's About Time: America's Imprisonment Binge*. 3rd ed. Belmont, CA: Wadsworth.

Austin, James, Charles Jones, John Kramer, and Phil Renninger. 1996. *National Assessment of Structured Sentencing*. Washington, DC: U.S. Department of Justice, Office of Justice Programs.

Barreras, Ricardo E., Ernest M. Drucker, and David Rosenthal. 2005. "The Concentration of Substance Use, Criminal Justice Involvement, and HIV/AIDS in the Families of Drug Offenders." *Journal of Urban Health* 82(1): 162–170.

Beck, Allen J., and Darrell K. Gilliard. 1995. *Prisoners in 1994*. Washington, DC: U.S. Department of Justice, Bureau of Justice Statistics.
Blumstein, Alfred, Jacqueline Cohen, Jeffrey A. Roth, and Christy Visher (Eds.). 1986. *Criminal Careers and "Career Criminals."* Washington, DC: National Academies Press.
Boerner, David. 1993. "The Role of the Legislature in Guidelines Sentencing in 'The Other Washington.'" *Wake Forest Law Review* 28: 381–420.
Brown, Jodi M., Darrell K. Gilliard, Tracy L. Snell, James J. Stephan, and Doris James Wilson 1996. *Correctional Populations in the United States, 1994*. Washington, DC: U.S. Department of Justice, Bureau of Justice Statistics.
Bureau of Justice Statistics. 1996. *Federal Criminal Case processing, 1982–93*. Washington, DC: U.S. Department of Justice.
California Budget and Policy Center. 2015. *Sentencing in California: Moving toward a Smarter, More Cost-Effective Approach*. Sacramento, CA: California Budget and Policy Center.
Carson, E. Ann. 2015. *Prisoners in 2014*. Washington, DC: U.S. Department of Justice, Bureau of Justice Statistics.
Carson, E. Ann. 2016. *Aging of the State Prison Population, 1993–2013*. Washington, DC: U.S. Department of Justice, Bureau of Justice Statistics.
Chiu, Tina. 2010. *It's About Time: Aging Prisoners, Increasing Costs, and Geriatric Release*. New York: Vera Institute of Justice, Center on Sentencing and Corrections.
Clark, John, James Austin, and D. Alan Henry. 1997. *"Three Strikes and You're Out": A Review of State Legislation*. Washington, DC: U.S. Department of Justice, National Institute of Justice.
Crawford, Charles, Ted Chiricos, and Gary Kleck. 1998. "Race, Racial Threat, and Sentencing of Habitual Offenders." *Criminology* 36(3): 481–511.
Ellison, Jared M., and Pauline K. Brennan. 2016. "Sentencing Outcomes and Disparity." Pp. 328–350 in *The Handbook of Measurement Issues in Criminology and Criminal Justice*, edited by B. M. Huebner and T. S. Bynum. Hoboken, NJ: John Wiley & Sons.
Engen, Rodney L., and Sara Steen. 2000. "The Power to Punish: Discretion and Sentencing Reform in the War on Drugs." *American Journal of Sociology* 105(5): 1357–1395.
Families Against Mandatory Minimums (FAMM). 2011. *Mandatory Sentencing Was Once America's Law-and-Order Panacea: Here's Why It's Not Working*. Washington, DC: FAMM.
Frankel, Marvin E. 1972. "Lawlessness in Sentencing." *University of Cincinnati Law Review* 41(1): 1–54.
Gainsborough, Jenni, and Marc Mauer. 2000. *Diminishing Returns: Crime and Incarceration in the 1990s*. Washington, DC: The Sentencing Project.
Gendreau, Paul, Claire Goggin, Francis T. Cullen, and Don A. Andrews. 2000. "The Effects of Community Sanctions and Incarceration on Recidivism." *Forum on Corrections Research* 12(2): 10–13.
Gilliard, Darrell K., and Allen J. Beck. 1996. *Prison and Jail Inmates, 1995*. Washington, DC: U.S. Department of Justice, Bureau of Justice Statistics.
Harmon, Mark G. 2014. "Sentencing Guidelines." Pp. 1–5 in *The Encyclopedia of Criminology and Criminal Justice*, edited by J.S. Albanese. New York: Wiley Blackwell.
Hartley, Richard D., Sean Maddan, and Cassia C. Spohn. 2007. "Prosecutorial Discretion: An Examination of Substantial Assistance Departures in Federal Crack-Cocaine and Powder-Cocaine Cases." *Justice Quarterly* 24(3): 382–307.
Henrichson, Christian, and Ruth Delaney. 2012. *The Price of Prisons: What Incarceration Costs Taxpayers*. New York: Vera Institute of Justice, Center on Sentencing and Corrections.
Hirschi, Travis, and Michael Gottfredson. 1983. "Age and the Explanation of Crime." *The American Journal of Sociology* 89(3): 552–584.
Justice Policy Institute. 2000. *The Punishing Decade: Prison and Jail Estimates at the Millennium*. Washington, DC: Justice Policy Institute.
Kaeble, Lauren, Lauren Glaze, Anastasios Tsoutis, and Todd Minton. 2015. *Correctional Populations in the United States, 2014*. Washington, DC: U.S. Department of Justice, Bureau of Justice Statistics. Retrieved May 15, 2017 from www.bjs.gov/content/pub/pdf/cpus14.pdf
King, Ryan S., Marc Mauer, and Malcolm C. Young. 2005. *Incarceration and Crime: A Complex Relationship*. Washington, DC: The Sentencing Project.

Mallik-Kane, Kamala, Barbara Parthasarathy, and William Adams. 2012. *Examining Growth in the Federal Prison Population, 1998 to 2012*. Washington, DC: Urban Institute, Justice Policy Center.

Marquart, James W. and Jonathan R. Sorensen. 1988. "Institutional and Postrelease Behavior of Furman-commuted Inmates in Texas." *Criminology* 26(4): 677–694.

Martinson, Robert. 1974. "What Works? Questions and Answers about Prison Reform." *Public Interest* 35(1): 22–54.

Mauer, Marc. 2010. "The Impact of Mandatory Minimum Penalties in Federal Sentencing." *Judicature* 94(1): 6–8, 40.

McLeod, Jeffrey S. 2011. *State Efforts in Sentencing and Corrections Reform*. Washington, DC: National Governors Association for Best Practices.

Merritt, Nancy, Terry Fain, and Susan Turner. 2006. "Oregon's Get Tough Sentencing Reform: A Lesson in Justice System Adaptation." *Criminology and Public Policy* 5(1): 5–36.

Mitchell, Michael, and Michael Leachman. 2014. *Changing Priorities: State Criminal Justice Reforms and Investments in Education*. Washington, DC: Center on Budget and Policy Priorities.

Motivans, Mark. 2015. *Federal Justice Statistics, 2012—Statistical Tables*. Washington, DC: U.S. Department of Justice, Bureau of Justice Statistics.

Nagel, Ilene H., and Stephen J. Schulhofer. 1992. "A Tale of Three Cities: An Empirical Study of Charging and Bargaining Practices under Federal Sentencing Guidelines." *California Law Review*: 66 (November): 501–561.

National Association of State Budget Officers (NASBO). 2013. *State Spending for Corrections: Long-term Trends and Recent Criminal Justice Policy Reforms*. Washington, DC: NASBO.

National Research Council. 2014. *The Growth of Incarceration in the United States: Exploring Causes and Consequences. Committee on Causes and Consequences of High Rates of Incarceration*. J. Travis, B. Western, & S. Redburn (Eds.). Committee on Law and Justice, Division of Behavioral and Social Science Education. Washington, DC: The National Academies Press.

Nellis, Ashley. 2013. *Life Goes On: The Historic Rise in Life Sentences in America*. Washington, DC: The Sentencing Project.

Nellis, Ashley, and Ryan S. King. 2009. *No Exit: The Expanding Use of Life Sentences in America*. Washington, DC: The Sentencing Project.

Office of Legislative Research. 2015. *Crimes with Mandatory Minimum Prison Sentences—Updated and Revised*. Hartford, CT: Connecticut General Assembly, author.

Packer, Herbert L. 1968. *The Limits of the Criminal Sanction*. Stanford, CA: Stanford University Press.

Peters, Thomas, and David Norris. 1991. "Reconsidering Parole Release Decisions in Illinois: Facts, Myths and the Need for Policy Changes." *The John Marshall Law Review* 24(4): 815–841.

Pew Center on the States. 2012. *Time Served: The High Cost, Low Return of Longer Prison Terms*. Washington, DC: The Pew Charitable Trusts.

Pew Center on the States. 2010a. *Collateral Costs: Incarceration's Effect on Economic Mobility*. Washington, DC: The Pew Charitable Trusts.

Pew Center on the States. 2010b. *Prison Count 2010: State Population Declines for the First Time in 38 Years*. Washington, DC: The Pew Charitable Trusts.

Pew Charitable Trusts. 2015. *Prison Time Surges for Federal Inmates: Average Period of Confinement Doubles, Costing Taxpayers $2.7 Billion a Year*. Washington, DC: The Pew Charitable Trusts.

Porter, Nicole D., and Tyler Clemons. 2013. *Drug-free Zone Laws: An Overview of State Policies*. Washington, DC: The Sentencing Project.

Romano, Michael. 2015. *Proposition 47 Progress Report: One Year Implementation*. Stanford, CA: Stanford Law School, Stanford Justice Advocacy Project.

Russell, Sarah F. 2010. "Rethinking Recidivist Enhancements: The Role of Prior Drug Convictions in Federal Sentencing." *UC Davis Law Review* 43(4): 1135–1233.

Sabol, William J., Katherine Rosich, Kamala Mallik-Kane, David Kirk, and Glenn Dubin. 2002. *The Influences of Truth-in-sentencing Reforms on Changes in States' Sentencing Practices and Prison Populations*. Washington, DC: The Urban Institute.

Shichor, David. 1997. "Three Strikes as Public Policy: The Convergence of the New Penology and the McDonaldization of Punishment." *Crime and Delinquency* 43(4): 470–492.

Sentencing Project. 2013. *Report of the Sentencing Project to the United Nations Human Rights Committee: Regarding racial disparities in the United States criminal justice system*. Washington, DC: The Sentencing Project.

Sentencing Project. 2015. *Fact Sheet: Trends in U.S. corrections*. Washington, DC: The Sentencing Project.

Sentencing Project. 2016. *Criminal Justice Facts: Our Criminal Justice system is like a Bicycle Stuck in One Gear—The Prison Gear*. Washington, DC: The Sentencing Project. Retrieved May 15, 2017 from www.sentencingproject.org/criminal-justice-facts/

Spohn, Cassia. 2009. *How Do Judges Decide? The Search for Fairness and Justice in Punishment*. Thousand Oaks, CA: SAGE.

Spohn, Cassia, and Pauline K. Brennan. 2011. "The Joint Effects of Offender Race/Ethnicity and Gender on Substantial Assistance Departures in Federal Courts." *Race and Justice* 1(1): 49–78.

Spohn, Cassia, and David Holleran. 2002. "The Effect of Imprisonment on Recidivism Rates of Felony Offenders: A Focus on Drug Offenders." *Criminology* 40(2): 329–258.

Tonry, Michael. 2013. "Sentencing in America, 1975–2025." *Crime and Justice* 42(1): 141–198.

Turanovic, Jillian J., Nancy Rodriguez, and Travis C. Pratt. 2012. "The Collateral Consequences of Incarceration Revisited: A Qualitative Analysis of the Effects of Caregivers of Children of Incarcerated Parents." *Criminology* 50(4): 913–959.

Turner, Susan, Terry Fain, Peter W. Greenwood, Elsa Y. Chen, and James R. Chiesa. 2001. *National Evaluation of the Violent Offender Incarceration/truth-in-sentencing Incentive Grant Program*. Final Report to the U.S. National Institute of Justice. Santa Monica, CA: RAND Corporation.

United States Sentencing Commission (USSC). 1991. *Special Report to the Congress: Mandatory Minimum Penalties in the Federal Criminal Justice System*. Washington, DC: USSC.

USSC. 2004. *Fifteen years of Guidelines Sentencing: An Assessment of How Well the Federal Criminal Justice System is Achieving the Goals of Sentencing Reform*. Washington, DC: USSC.

USSC. 2011. *2011 Report to the Congress: Mandatory Minimum Penalties in the Federal Criminal Justice System*. Washington, DC: USSC.

USSC. 2014. *Quick facts: Mandatory Minimum Penalties*. Washington, DC: USSC.

USSC. 2015a. *Guidelines Manual*. Washington, DC: USSC.

USSC. 2015b. *U.S. Sentencing Commission's 2014 Sourcebook of Federal Sentencing Statistics*. Washington, DC: USSC. Retrieved May 15, 2017 from www.ussc.gov/research/2015-sourcebook/archive/sourcebook-2014

Von Hirsch, Andrew. 1976. *Doing Justice: The Choice of Punishments*. New York: Hill & Wang.

Wagner, Peter, and Allison Walsh. 2016. *States of Incarceration: The Global Context 2016*. Northampton, MA: The Prison Policy Initiative. Retrieved May 15, 2017 from www.prisonpolicy.org/global/2016.html

Weisberg, Robert, Debbie A. Mukamal, and Jordan D. Segall. 2011. *Life in Limbo: An Examination of Parole Releases for Prisoners Serving Life Sentences with the Possibility of Parole in California*. Stanford, CA: Stanford Law School, Stanford Criminal Justice Center.

4 Rehabilitation and the Rehabilitative Ideal

Lior Gideon and Amanda L. Thomas

Introduction

Since the 1980s, the incarceration rate has quadrupled in the United States, thus, positioning the nation as the frontrunner in incarceration among all other industrialized nations. This precipitous increase can be credited to the "get tough on crime polices" along with the "war on drugs" that marked the beginning of a new era in correctional practices; an era characterized by longer mandatory sentences. While the numbers of individuals sentenced to prison, both state and federal, and to jail reached its highest number of over 2.4 million during 2007–2009, recent years have been characterized by some slight decrease. In fact, the United States' Bureau of Justice Statistics (2015) reported that there were approximately 1,561,500 prisoners in state and federal custody at the end of 2014, which amounts to the smallest total prison population since 2005, and the second largest decline in more than 35 years. However, such numbers exclude the local jail population, which was estimated at about 744,600 during midyear of 2014 (Minton and Zeng 2015); thus causing the number of individuals admitted into correctional institutions to roughly total 2.3 million. The number appears to be more catastrophic when one looks at the total correctional population—not just those held in prisons and jails, but also those under correctional supervision—of over 7 million individuals (the Bureau of Justice Statistics estimates that about 4,708,100 were under probation and parole supervision at yearend of 2014). These numbers suggest that with the amount of individuals who are under some form of correctional supervision, correctional scholars are faced with addressing three major social challenges—successful rehabilitation, reentry and reintegration. Specifically, recent data suggest that anywhere between 600,000 and 700,000 (Latessa and Holsinger 2016) incarcerated individuals are released every year in the United States, which roughly translates into approximately 1,900 individuals that are reentering society and our communities every day (Walker 2015). Such alarming data mandate a shift in penological perspective and ideology that will address the need of many individuals returning home after longer periods of incarceration. Indeed, the increase in individuals placed in correctional institutions had a direct effect on the volume of individuals being supervised in the community (Travis and Petersilia 2001). The exorbitant growth of the parole population has strained parole departments and their ability to function effectively. Prisoner reentry and reintegration has now become, according to Petersilia (2003: 3), "one of the most profound challenges facing American society" today.

Not surprisingly, penologists can agree that while correctional facilities are intended to incapacitate, deter, impose retribution on convicted offenders, such environments are not conducive to the idea of rehabilitation. While these four correctional perspectives are interrelated, rehabilitation is markedly different. For example, Halleck (2001: 275) explains that rehabilitation may not be achieved if a program places "too much emphasis on retribution." That being said, incapacitation and deterrence are similar to rehabilitation in the sense that both philosophies share a similar *utilitarian goal* (Cullen and Jonson 2012: 26).

Rehabilitation Ideal in Philosophical Context

The utilitarian approach to punishment requires that a punishment will have a clear effect to it. In particular, a utilitarian approach to punishment tends to focus on the future of the offender, rather than on what she or he did. According to such approach, a punishment will be effective if it prevents future crimes. It is within this context that the idea of rehabilitation draws penologists' attention. More specifically, those who support the rehabilitative ideal call for correctional institutions to address the needs and risks of the offender in order to prevent her/him from committing future crimes. Von Hirsh (1976: 11) defines rehabilitation as "any measure taken to change offender's character, habits, or behavior patterns so as to diminish his criminal propensities." As such, rehabilitation can actually be viewed as crime prevention strategy, while at the same time a method by which we treat offenders and improve their lives (Cullen and Jonson 2011). Another definition of rehabilitation also considers the greater good of the community who would essentially benefit from the successful rehabilitation of individual offenders. Allen (1981), for example, suggests that rehabilitation should have an effect on the character, attitudes, and behavior of the individual in such a way that it will strengthen the community's social defense. Both of the aforementioned definitions suggest that rehabilitation is not limited to one single dimension, and as such must address the multiple needs and risks of individual offenders if a positive outcome is desired.

Considering that thousands of inmates are being released per month, it is no wonder that rehabilitation is once again in the spotlight. Rehabilitation is thus an important goal of corrections, and as such receives a great deal of attention by correctional scholars. In fact, rehabilitation as a correctional practice has gained massive momentum in the past decades by becoming the focus of many debates on its effectiveness in reducing recidivism, and changing offenders' behavior, habits, and character. Yet, correctional practices of recent years suggest that the rehabilitation ideal has more to offer than the "get tough" correctional policies of incarcerating and incapacitating offenders for the sole sake of removing them from society. Therefore, deductively speaking, correctional scholars support the notion that correctional intervention programs that aim to rehabilitate offenders should focus on teaching offenders the attitudes and skills needed to avoid crime while embracing a productive and normative lifestyle (Cullen and Jonson 2012).

Successful correctional interventions aimed at rehabilitation are the result of criminal justice professionals vetting the intersection of a multitude of dynamic factors (societal, political, psychological and theoretical ideologies). Additionally, Sung and Gideon (2011: 71) argued, "successful correctional interventions are clinically effective, politically relevant, and theoretically meaningful." Further, Applegate, Cullen, and Fisher (1997) conducted a national survey that aimed to measure whether or not the general public were supportive of rehabilitation and treatment for convicted offenders. Their research affirmed that the public is highly responsive to the ideas and goals of rehabilitation. Similar findings, from an international comparative study, further validated the public's support of rehabilitation (see Gideon and Hsiao 2012; Gideon and Loveland 2011; Gideon and Sherman-Oren 2014).

Cullen and Jonson (2012: 32) explained "the rehabilitative ideal would hold sway over corrections in the United States into the early 1970s." However, a shift in theoretical and ideological paradigms within the field of corrections began to emerge as early as the 1960s, when the social and political climate in the United States started to change. As crime rates skyrocketed nationally (up until the 1990s), the "get tough on crime" approach also gained momentum and public support. As such, legislation became more punitive (i.e., Rockefeller drug laws, mandatory sentences, "Truth-in-Sentencing" laws, and the "Three-Strikes" laws), and less rehabilitative. Yet, the pendulum swung again in the direction of the rehabilitative ideal toward the middle of the 1990s.

In the mid 1990s the idea of rehabilitation gained a renewed interest when Janet Reno, who was the United States Attorney General under the President Clinton administration, presented the inevitable question seeking to learn what happens with all those individuals that are being released from incarceration. Her question, simple as it may have sounded, ignited a vibrant research agenda into the reentry and reintegration process of convicted offenders (Travis 2005). Yet, these terms were not to be mixed or mistaken with the actual rehabilitative idea, which begins much earlier in the correctional process, from the pre-sentencing report, through the sentencing process, and its correctional intervention(s), and, lastly, through the services administered by parole agencies. Nonetheless, Janet Reno's question helped push the rehabilitative idea and its related practices to the top of the correctional agenda, by focusing more attention on practices that are empirically proven to help alleviate the harsh transition that many incarcerated individuals face when released back into their home and communities.

Successful rehabilitation thus leads to successful reentry and reintegration of convicted offenders. It is because of its potential positive outcome to the individual offender, his/her family, their community, and society as a whole, that we must rethink our correctional practices. In particular, we must rethink how we rehabilitate those convicted of a crime so that they can return back to society as productive and normative functioning individuals. Therefore, for rehabilitation to achieve this goal one must first identify the needs and risks of individual offenders and tailor a custom rehabilitation suite that will fit their needs. This can be done only when we are willing to acknowledge that not all convicted offenders are alike (Gideon 2013), and that individual differences shape the way in which people behave (Cullen and Jonson 2012). Indeed, different scholars, such as Hawkins and Alpert (1989) and May and Wood (2010), acknowledge that even though individuals may be exposed to similar forms of punishment they may, in fact, report different impacts and results than one another; such is the case with intervention and rehabilitation strategies.

Consequently, the current chapter will identify specific intervention approaches and how they address the needs of rehabilitation among convicted offenders. While there are many different programs aimed at rehabilitation, they are too broad in scope for this chapter to cover, and thus we focus on a few of those approaches and theories believed to yield the best rehabilitative results. We begin by a short discussion on the rehabilitation theory.

Rehabilitation Theory

At the core of each and every rehabilitative initiative lies a well-thought-out treatment modality or intervention strategy. Each treatment modality or intervention strategy that is developed must logically address the criminogenic needs of the offenders they are targeting, with the aim to minimize, as much as possible, the effects of such causes. Accordingly, the various factors that are being considered by each modality must be carefully examined and evaluated to provide evidence-based knowledge about their effects. Thus, theories of rehabilitation develop from careful systematic observations of the various treatment and intervention modalities available to criminal justice clients. Such systematic observations seek to evaluate the effectiveness of each specific modality by looking at the different measures and definitions of recidivism (e.g., substance relapse, further criminality, further arrests and convictions, and in the case of the mentally ill, further hospitalization due to mentally ill episodes). Once evaluation research provides systematic support for the effectiveness of an intervention, the corresponding intervention strategy may then be elevated within the hierarchy to a theory. Once an intervention or treatment modality becomes an official theory, it may then be utilized as a guide for practitioners so that they can determine who is suitable for such intervention, what to do, how to do it, and what may be the potential outcomes of such intervention. The theory then needs to be confronted with the harsh reality of practice and real-world implementation. Yet policymakers, practitioners and clients should understand that even the strongest theory is not a panacea to all criminal aliments, and as such does not provide a fool-proof blanket of success. Hence, controlled examination of the theory is essential to examine its predictive and external validity. These are essential for practitioners to gain confidence in the potential outcome of their intervention.

Rehabilitation and correctional intervention modalities were subjected to immense scrutiny after the publication of the Martinson report (1974). The Martinson report was a meta-analysis that reviewed approximately 230 studies that analyzed the effectiveness of correctional intervention and rehabilitation programs for inmates. These studies were reviewed to determine whether certain treatment programs were empirically proven to lower recidivism rates in released offenders. Martinson (1974) concluded that the majority of treatment programs, with limited exception, had little effect on the recidivism rates of released inmates. As a result of this publication, the political arena began to push the "nothing works" doctrine as it related specifically to the goals of rehabilitation programs administered within correctional facilities. Politicians and other interest groups used Martinson's conclusion to further push the combatant agenda of "get tough on crime" proposals, thus inviting more support for policies to be more control oriented than rehabilitation oriented. Cullen and Jonson (2012: 36) argue that this report fueled the "*theoretical crisis in corrections*" (emphasis in original). However, as Walker (2015: 284) correctly points out, Martinson actually "found positive outcomes in 48 percent of the program evaluations he reviewed." Although this is not the focus of this chapter, a few cautionary words are needed. Martinson's study suffered from some major methodological limitations that impede it from generalization and prediction. Further, it is very difficult for one study to evaluate various studies that implement different intervention programs operating under various conditions and in various locations (Latessa and Holsinger 2016).

One positive aspect of the Martinson report, however, is that it proposed a new paradigm for corrections. This paradigm shift caused correctional programs to become more evidence-based and insisted that guidelines should be implemented to evaluate the performance of the programs that are being offered to inmates. Consequently, progressive correctional researchers shifted their focus by carefully evaluating correctional-based interventions that were associated with fortuitous results (Schaefer, Cullen, and Eck 2016). As a result, multiple studies, implementing the practice of meta-analyses, began to emerge questioning the "nothing works" doctrine. At the same time, even more evidence-based research and practice began to emerge and provide evidence that some correctional intervention and rehabilitative initiatives do work. The following sections briefly discuss a few rehabilitative intervention techniques currently used in correctional settings. However, before turning the discussion to such techniques, it is essential to present a clear definition of rehabilitation. As noted earlier, Allen (1981: 2) defines rehabilitation as:

> the notion that the primary purpose of penal treatment is to effect changes in the character, attitudes, and behavior of convicted offenders, so as to strengthen the social defense against unwanted behavior, but also to contribute to the welfare and satisfaction of others.

Cullen and Jonson (2012) supplement the aforementioned definition by also placing emphasis on correctional-based interventions that target social criminogenic factors with the goal of reducing recidivism while improving other aspects of an offender's life. Such definitions are important to our brief discussion of the various intervention programs discussed below.

Cognitive-Behavioral Therapy (CBT)

According to Sung and Gideon (2011), cognitive-behavioral therapy/treatment (CBT) is a diverse family of treatment interventions rooted in the merging of behavioral modification, cognitive therapy and social learning theory. Their techniques are part of a larger approach that leans on learning theories and the use of positive reinforcement and negative sanctions. Specifically, the approach assumes that just as behavioral patterns are conditioned by rewards or punishments during the course of one's life, they are also susceptible to planned change through careful administration of rewards and punishments. Yet, self-defeating experiences are also an important factor in the individual's past that needs to be addressed. Thus, the application of merging these theories is set to address an offender's "dysfunctional patterns of thinking" (Milkman and Wanberg, 2007: 5). As such, "Cognitive-behavioral techniques are part of a larger approach known as functional contextualism" (Schaefer et al. 2016: 114), which emphasizes beliefs, expectations, ideas, and attitude in the context of previous and future social situations. This axiom purports that in order "to influence maladaptive *thoughts*, the practitioner should first aim to manipulate *behavior*" (as cited by Schaefer et al. 2016: 114). Furthermore, in order to be successful, Milkman and Wanberg (2007: xiii) suggest, "[t]herapy must also include a sociocentric approach to treatment that focuses on responsibility toward others and the community."

Currently, there are six prominent CBT programs used in the criminal justice system for offenders. These include: Aggression Replacement Training (ART), Criminal Conduct and Substance Abuse Treatment: Strategies for Self-Improvement and Change (SSC), Moral Reconation Therapy (MRT), Reasoning and Rehabilitation (R&R and R&R2), Relapse Prevention Therapy (RPT), and Thinking for a Change (T4C) (Milkman and Wanberg 2007). "Generally, cognitive behavioral therapies in correctional settings consist of highly structured treatments that are detailed in manuals (Dobson and Khatri 2000) and typically delivered to groups of 8 to 12 individuals in a classroom-like setting" (Milkman and Wanberg 2007: 15).

Milkman and Wanberg (2007) further conclude that there have been significant successful outcomes reported in each of the six CBT programs mentioned above. Landenberger and Lipsey's (2005) meta-analysis also yielded positive results. Their research "confirmed the findings of positive CBT effects on the recidivism of offenders that have been reported in other recent meta-analyses" (as cited by Landenberger and Lipsey 2005: 470). MacKenzie (2000) who also assessed two CBT methods—Reasoning and Rehabilitation (R&R) and Moral Reconation Therapy (MRT)—found that both programs were found to be effective in reducing recidivism. In essence, these programs accomplished this by "focus[ing] on changing participants' thoughts and attitudes, either through moral development (moral recognition) or problem solving (reasoning and rehabilitation)" (MacKenzie 2000: 465).

Substance Abuse Treatment (SAT)

With the declaration of the "war on drugs and crime" by President Nixon in the early 1970s, and later in the renewed emphasis and declaration of the "war on drugs" by President Reagan, the United States saw a precipitous increase in both federal and state inmates convicted of a drug-related offense. However, once they were incarcerated there was minimal attention focused on their actual treatment (Pager 2003; Petersilia 2003). It was not until the early 1990s that the federal Bureau of Prisons (BOP) was legislatively commissioned to provide substance abuse treatment or drug education to every eligible inmate through the passage of the Violent Crime Control and Law Enforcement Act of 1994. Even still, by 2000 a Health and Human Services (HHS) survey concluded that "45 percent of state prisons and 68 percent of jails had *no* substance abuse treatment of any kind" (Petersilia 2003: 97).

This issue is immensely important, taking into consideration the grim fact that more than three-quarters of offenders sentenced to jails and prisons suffer from some form of substance dependency, further supporting the notion that substance abuse intervention has become a much needed and essential intervention priority. Yet only 11 percent of those in need of substance abuse treatment receive such treatment that will address their addiction (Sung, Richter, Vaughan and Foster 2013). Such approach is proving to be counter-productive to the rehabilitation of substance-abusing offenders, who as a sub-set category are plagued by high recidivism rates, further substance abuse, and high reincarceration rates (Wexler, Lipton and Johnson 1988; Welsh 2011), thereby perpetuating a never-ending cycle of the revolving door of the criminal justice system.

It is important to note that substance abuse treatment for convicted offenders may occur either within a correctional facility or outside in the community. This section of the chapter will provide a brief glance of some prison-based substance abuse programs, while also reviewing some results from programs aimed at diverting individuals from penal institutions.

"Correctional approaches to Alcohol or Other Drug (AOD) treatment are often informed by a holistic health model that treats substance abuse as a complex and multifaceted problem" (Sung and Gideon 2011:159). Accordingly, effective rehabilitation of substance-abusing offenders is thought to be achieved by treatment programs that are tasked with the overall goal of not only reducing future drug use and recidivism rates, but also changing and modifying the offender (both psychologically and socially) so that successful reintegration can be achieved. As suggested by Seiter and Kadela's (2003) research, such drug rehabilitation programs ease the transition, for the released substance-abusing offender, back into the community. In fact, many studies that aimed to evaluate prison-based drug treatment programs provide solid proof to the fact that drug treatment intervention is one of the most viable rehabilitation techniques (see Chandler, Fletcher, and Volkow 2009; De Leon 2000; Gideon, Shoam, and Weisburd 2010; Inciardi, Martin, and Butzin 2004; Welsh 2011; Weisburd et al. 2010). In sum, Sung and Gideon (2011: 159) argued, "There is strong evidence that drug treatment, when well implemented, can significantly reduce recidivism, relapse, and costs of incarceration."

Furthermore, with the ever-burgeoning stresses placed on correctional institutions, other avenues have been explored to deal with convicted drug offenders. These include developing specialized problem-solving courts (i.e., drug courts, juvenile courts, family courts). Drug courts were developed as means of diverting low-risk substance-abusing individuals from correctional institutions. Established in the late 1980s and early 1990s, these courts took an individualized approach in dealing with substance-abusing offenders. These courts did so by targeting the individuals' needs and risks, focusing on changing their behavior, all while also targeting social criminogenic factors that are present in the life of the offender. Accordingly, Walker (2015: 306) defines a drug court as, "a specialized criminal court that handles substance abuse cases through a comprehensive program of treatment, supervision, and alternative sanctions." This specialized problem-solving court gained tremendous support as prison overcrowding surfaced and reached national attention and concern.

MacKenzie (2000) conducted a thorough meta-analysis to determine the effectiveness of drug-courts. Examining ten years of drug-court research, MacKenzie (2000) found that drug courts that focus on both control and rehabilitation show considerable promise. Similar results were found by Rossman and colleagues who evaluated 23 different drug courts in a Multi-Site Adult Drug Court Evaluation (MADCE) project (Rossman, Roman, Zweig, Rempel, and Lindquist, 2011). Specifically, findings showed positive support for the effectiveness of drug courts not only in the categories of substance abuse and crime, but also in other psychological aspects. Furthermore, the study inexorably links the role of the judges to the participants' success through a positive correlation (Rossman et al. 2011). Lastly, the MADCE also concluded "the net benefit for drug courts is an average of $5,680 to $6,208 per participant, returning $2 for every $1 of cost" (Rossman et al. 2011:8).

Vocational and Educational Programs (VEP)

As the U.S. became more punitive, the options for inmates to participate in "in-house" programming (i.e., educational, vocational/job-training, substance abuse programs, and therapy) began to decrease dramatically; thus further eroding the rehabilitative ideal. The decreased opportunity for inmates to engage in, and develop, pro-social behaviors while still in prison have also been shown to increase their likelihood of recidivating on the outside. It wasn't until prison populations began to swell by the early twentieth century that elected officials began to question the effectiveness of our nation's correctional institutions. As such, a new correctional ideology emerged. This new, yet simplistic, philosophy "emphasized the idea that inmates needed to work so they would be prepared with a trade and good work habits that would help them find employment upon their release" (Regoli, Hewitt, and Maras 2013: 284). Such philosophy paved the way to develop what is now known as vocational and educational programs for rehabilitation.

Petersilia (2003: 4) notes that, "just 60 percent of inmates have a GED or high school diploma (compared to 85 percent of the U.S. adult population" thereby decreasing the likelihood that they could be gainfully employed. Additionally, Regoli et al. (2013: 310) report, "about one-third of all men and more than half of all women in prison were not employed at the time of their arrest." While these two conditions may or may not have directly impacted the fact that an individual was in fact arrested, all three of them combined will, more than likely, affect them once they are released (Regoli et al. 2013). Therefore, in order to better prepare inmates for release and make them more likely to successfully reintegrate into their community, correctional facilities must address these issues.

Today, prisons typically provide the following types of educational programs: adult basic education, study release, adult secondary education, vocational education, special education, and college coursework (Guerrero 2011). However, over the last 15 years government financial endorsement for these types of programs has wavered and enrollment in these programs has been significantly cut (Guerrero 2011; Petersilia 2003). Due to decreased funding, society's changed ideology of prisons, and the high volume of people behind bars, there are fewer opportunities for incarcerated individuals to take advantage of educational and vocational training programs. Even when such programs are offered, far fewer prisoners have the opportunity to take advantage of them because of limited space and steep eligibility criteria (Frazier 2011). Petersilia (2003: 94–95) reports:

> In 1997, fewer than half of the inmates in either prison system (federal, 45 percent, and state, 38 percent) had been involved in an education program since being admitted. And less than one-third of the inmates received any vocational training.

With that being said, ironically, research continues to support the idea that such educational, vocational training, and/or work release programs are effective in reducing recidivism rates as well as improving job readiness skills for ex-offenders (Seiter and Kadela 2003), as these types of programs not only provide individuals with the skills they need, but further improve their self image, and target internal change in attitudes. Similar findings were also noted by MacKenzie (2000: 465), who argued that "the research on vocational education programs demonstrates that these programs are effective in reducing the recidivism of offenders." Shuler (2004) further adds that such programs are cost effective and that for every dollar spent, two dollars are saved (also see Guerrero 2011).

Faith-Based Programs

Faith-based programs have historically played a critical role in the rehabilitation of offenders (Frazier 2011). As evidenced by their presence as early as the eighteenth century, Quakers attempted to reform American correctional facilities by implementing the idea of repentance and rehabilitation through religion. Nowadays, religion is an integral part of federal, state, and private prisons, and inmates enjoy instruction and services in all main streams of religion. The emphasis on religion in prison has recently grown due to the creation of a White House Office of Faith-Based and Community Initiatives by President George W. Bush, in January of 2001. Such initiative resulted in the immersion of a variety of worship services inside prisons that provide counseling and services to individual inmates in a professional manner. To date, this program continues with bi-partisan support under the direction of President Obama (Walker, 2015).

According to Siegel and Bartollas (2016: 265), such professional religious services deliver a continuum of care that approaches and treats an inmate as a total person while addressing social problems such as addiction, education, and faith. As Petersilia (2003) notes, individuals who are blocked from engaging in and developing pro-social behaviors while still in prison have also been shown to increase their likelihood of recidivating on the outside. Hence, there is no surprise when participants in prison-based faith-based programs tend to have fewer behavioral infractions, and tend to have better rehabilitative prospects, as they become part of a bigger social support group.

Another important aspect that should not be downplayed is inmates' assimilation into prison life. Whether it is for short term or long term, inmate assimilation into prison life is not always an easy task, and is often guided by the combination of various dynamic and static factors. Additionally, social interactions within prisons, similar to those on the outside, are subject to social and structural hierarchies that follow certain formal and informal rules. Zaitzow and Jones (2013: 328), citing Sykes' (1958) famous work on the culture of prison, note that "[T]he inmate subculture helps inmates cope with the challenges, frustrations, deprivations, and pains of imprisonment that are part of the prison experience." This subculture, which is dominated by control, is often expressed through acts of violence and aggression, and it is within this context that faith-based programs mitigate such acts and serve as buffers of strain and aggression. Consequently, it is not surprising that religion-based correctional programs aimed at rehabilitation are very common in correctional practice, as pointed out by Zaitzow and Jones (2013: 331), who state that such programs "are not only among the oldest but also among the most common forms of rehabilitative programs found in correctional facilities today."

Currently there are several different kinds of faith-based treatment programs that are offered in correctional facilities. Generally speaking, however, most of these programs are either based in organic religion or intentional religion. Johnson, Tompkins, and Webb (2002: 8) define organic religion as "the influence of religion practiced over time," as an imbedded part of one's upbringing and experiences. Whereas, "Intentional religion is the exposure to religion one receives at a particular time in life for a particular purpose" (Johnson et al. 2002: 8) or as a result of experiencing a particular crisis.

Aligned with the rehabilitative ideal, as presented earlier in this chapter, Johnson and colleagues (2002) conducted a thorough analysis of 800 studies, in which 669 studies focused on organic religion. Results from the study show promise. Specifically, Johnson and colleagues (2002: 9) were attempting to determine "the role of organic religion in not only protecting people from harmful outcomes, but promoting pro-social outcomes as well", which it did on all accounts. Further, Johnson and colleagues (2002: 21) state that a more thorough examination of intentional religion as a correctional-based rehabilitative intervention is needed, as few of the studies that did focus on such intervention were "plagued with methodological shortcomings."

Another study, by Zaitzow and Jones (2013), further examines the role of religion and spirituality in the rehabilitation process. Zaitzow and Jones outline four examples of faith-based programs that are offered through a multitude of correctional facilities. These include the Aleph Institute, the Kairos Prison Ministry International, the Prison Fellowship, and the Prisoner & Family Ministry. While each of these programs is different, they all share similar attributes, such as: (a) the belief that people can change; (b) they address the special needs of the inmates, both inside prison and once released; and in the Aleph Institute (c) the program seeks to accomplish behavior modification through the integration of Jewish law and tradition with psychological principles (Zaitzow and Jones, 2013: 325). Not surprisingly, many officials across the nation now realize the important potential of faith-based programs in promoting rehabilitation among incarcerated individuals, as well as their potential in managing and controlling inmates' behavior.

Throughout this chapter we have surmised that in order to effectively rehabilitate inmates we need to mandate that inmates: (1) attend (individual, group, and/or family) counseling sessions, (2) participate in educational and/or vocational training, and, for those that require it, (3) participate in a substance abuse program. However, as Zaitzow and Jones (2013) points out, efforts at rehabilitating inmates must also target core values and basic morals, which many offenders are lacking. Therefore, to ignore the possible positive effect that faith-based programs could provide to inmates, their families, and to society would be terribly irresponsible of us.

Conclusion

The rehabilitative ideal aims to intervene so as to change those factors that are causing the offender to break the law (Cullen and Jonson 2012). In order for rehabilitation to prevail, antisocial attitudes, dysfunctional family life, and the presence of bad companions must be addressed and alternatives must be presented and taught. Such criminogenic factors are at the heart of any rehabilitative initiative as was discussed briefly above. The ultimate goal for rehabilitation is a utilitarian one—to diminish criminal propensities. In this regard, the rehabilitative ideal also aims at crime prevention by altering maladaptive behaviors and attitudes, and by providing personal and social tools that can be utilized in the long process of reintegration back into the normative society.

Prisoner rehabilitation is an incredibly complex and multifaceted problem. And as such, rehabilitation cannot be viewed as a one-dimensional issue, for it encompasses multiple layers of social, behavioral, and cognitive aspects. Rehabilitation will not be the same for all offenders, and cannot be thought of in similar terms for all offenders. Each offender has their own individual characteristics that dictate their specific needs and risks, and accordingly must also have a specific rehabilitation program that is tailored to such individual needs and risks.

Although, a majority of incarcerated individuals suffer from some form of substance dependency, their dependency may not be the sole cause of their criminality. Thus, their rehabilitation may require a multisystemic approach that takes into consideration human ecology and pragmatic family systems (Sung and Gideon 2011), but also the needs of offenders to be able to find a job upon release and to maintain healthy self-esteem. It is in this context that cognitive-behavioral therapy (CBT), substance abuse treatment (SAT), vocational and educational programs (VEP), and faith-based programs were discussed. While each addresses different needs, they all share a common goal—to provide emotional and social support that will reduce the effect of criminogenic factors and increase the offender's ability to successfully reintegrate and desist from engaging in any form of criminal behavior. By achieving these goals, the complete spectrum of the rehabilitative ideal will be accomplished.

References

Allen, Francis A. 1981. *The Decline of the Rehabilitative Ideal: Penal Policy and Social Purpose*. New Haven, CT: Yale University Press.

Applegate, Brandon K., Francis T. Cullen, and Bonnie S. Fisher. 1997. "Public Support for Correctional Treatment: The Continuing Appeal of the Rehabilitative Ideal." *The Prison Journal* 77(3): 237–258.

Bureau of Justice Statistics. 2015. *Prisons in 2014: Summary*. Washington, DC: Bureau of Justice Statistics.

Chandler, Redonna K., Bennett W. Fletcher, and Nora D. Volkow. 2009. "Treating Drug Abuse and Addiction in the Criminal Justice System: Improving Public Health and Safety." *Journal of the American Medical Association* 301(2): 183–190.

Cullen, Francis T., and Cheryl L. Jonson. 2011. "Rehabilitation and Treatment." Pp. 293–344 in *Crime and Public Policy*, edited by J.Q. Wilson and J. Petersilia. New York: Oxford University.

Cullen, Francis T., and Cheryl L. Jonson. 2012. *Correctional Theory: Context and Consequences*. Thousand Oaks, CA: SAGE.

De Leon, George. 2000. *The Therapeutic Community: Theory, Model and Method*. New York, NY: Springer-Verlag.

Frazier, Beverly D. (2011). "Faith-based Prisoner Reentry." Pp. 279–306 in *Rethinking Corrections: Rehabilitation, Reentry and Reintegration*, L. Gideon and H.E. Sung Thousand Oaks, CA: Sage.

Gideon, Lior. 2013. "Introduction: Special Needs Offenders. Pp. 1–20 in *Special Needs Offenders in Correctional Institutions*, edited by L. Gideon. Thousand Oaks, CA: Sage.

Gideon, Lior, and Yuhsu G. Hsiao. 2012." Stereotype and Age in the Prediction Taiwanese Public Support of Rehabilitation." *Asian Journal of Criminology* 7(4): 309–326.

Gideon, Lior, and Natalie Loveland. 2011. "Public Attitudes toward Rehabilitation and Reintegration—How Supportive are People of the Getting-Tough-on-Crime Policies?" Pp. 19–36 in *Rethinking Corrections: Rehabilitation, Reentry and Reintegration*, edited by L. Gideon and H.E. Sung. Thousand Oaks, CA: Sage.

Gideon, Lior, and Ayala Sherman-Oren. 2014. "The Role of Social Distress, Political Affiliation and Education in Measuring Punitive Attitudes: Israel as a Case Study." *International Journal of Criminal Justice Review* 24(2): 151–171.

Gideon, Lior, Efrat Shoam, and David L. Weisburd. 2010. "Changing Prison to Therapeutic Milieu: Evidence from the Sharon Prison." *The Prison Journal* 90(2): 179–202.

Guerrero, Georgen. 2011. "Prison-based Educational and Vocational Training Programs." Pp. 193–218 in *Rethinking Corrections: Rehabilitation, Reentry and Reintegration*, edited by L. Gideon and H.E. Sung. Thousand Oaks, CA: Sage.

Halleck, S. 2001. "Violence: Treatment versus Correction." Pp. 273–279 in *Understanding Violence*, edited by D.P. Barash. Needham Heights, MA: Pearson Education.

Hawkins, Richard, and Geoffrey P. Alpert. 1989. *American Prison Systems: Punishment and Justice*. Englewood Cliffs, NJ: Prentice Hall.

Inciardi, James A., Steven S. Martin, and Clifford A. Butzin. 2004. "Five-year Outcome of Therapeutic Community Treatment of Drug Involved Offenders after Release from Prison." *Crime and Delinquency* 50(1): 88–107.

Johnson, Byron R., Ralph Brett Tompkins, and Derek Webb. 2002. *Objective Hope: Assessing the Effectiveness of Faith-Based Organizations: A Review of the Literature*. Philadelphia, PA: Center for Research on Religion and Urban Civil Society.

Landenberger, Nana A., and Mark W. Lipsey. 2005. "The Positive Effects of Cognitive-behavioral Programs for Offenders: A Meta-analysis of Factors Associated with Effective Treatment." *Journal of Experimental Criminology* 1: 451–476.

Latessa, Edward J., and Alexander M. Holsinger. 2016. "Offender Programming and Treatment." Pp. 189–192 in *Correctional Context: Contemporary and Classical Readings*, 5th ed., edited by E.J. and A.M. Holsinger. New York: Oxford University Press.

MacKenzie, Doris L. 2000. "Evidence-based Corrections: Identifying What Works." *Crime & Delinquency* 46(4): 457–471.

Martinson, Robert. 1974. "What Works? Questions and Answers about Prison Reform." *The Public Interest* 35: 22–54.

May, David C., and Peter B. Wood. 2010. *Ranking Correctional Punishments: Views from Offenders, Practitioners, and the Public*. Durham, NC: Carolina Academic Press.

Milkman, Harvey B., and Kenneth W. Wanberg. 2007. *Cognitive-Behavioral Treatment: A Review and Discussion for Corrections Professionals*. Washington, DC: U.S. Department of Justice, National Institute of Corrections.

Minton, Todd D., and Zhen Zeng. 2015. *Jail Inmates at Midyear 2014*. Washington, DC: Bureau of Justice Statistics.

Pager, Devah. 2003. "The Mark of a Criminal Record." *American Journal of Sociology* 108(5): 937–975.

Petersilia, Joan. 2003. *When Prisoners Come Home*. New York: Oxford University Press.

Regoli, R.M., Hewitt, J.D., and Maras, M.H. (2013). *Exploring Criminal Justice: The Essentials*. 2nd ed. Burlington, MA: Jones & Bartlett.

Rossman, Shelli B., John K. Roman, Janine M. Zweig, Michael Rempel, and Christine H. Lindquist. (2011, November). *The Multi-site Adult Drug Court Evaluation: Executive Summary* (Document No. 237108). Washington, DC: U.S. Department of Justice.

Schaefer, Lacey, Francis T. Cullen, and John E. Eck. 2016. *Environmental Corrections: A New Paradigm for Supervising Offenders in the Community*. Thousand Oaks, CA: SAGE.

Seiter, Richard P., and Karen R. Kadela. 2003. "Prisoner Reentry: What Works, What does not, and What is Promising." *Crime & Delinquency* 49(3): 360–388.

Shuler, P. 2004. "Educating Prisoners is Cheaper than Locking them up Again." *City Beat,* retrieved December 21, 2015 from: http://citybeat.com/cincinnati/article-6662-educating_prisoners_is_cheaper_than_locking_them_up_again.html

Siegel, L., and Bartollas, C. (2016). *Corrections Today*, 3rd ed. Boston, MA: Cengage Learning.

Sung, Hung-En, and Lior Gideon. 2011. "Major Rehabilitative Approaches." Pp. 71–96 in *Rethinking Corrections: Rehabilitation, Reentry and Reintegration*, edited by L. Gideon and H.E. Sung. Thousand Oaks, CA: Sage.

Sung, Hung-En., Linda Richter, Roger Vaughan, R., and Susan E. Foster. 2013. "Substance Use and Addiction and American Prison and Jail Inmates." Pp. 459–494 in *Special Needs Offenders in Correctional Institutions*, edited by L. Gideon. Thousand Oaks, CA: Sage.

Travis, Jeremy. 2005. *But They All Come Back: Facing the Challenges of Prisoner Reentry*. Washington, DC: Urban Institute Press.

Travis, Jeremy, and Joan Petersilia. 2001. "Reentry Reconsidered: A New Look at an Old Question." *Crime & Delinquency* 47(3): 291–313.

Von Hirsh, Andrew. 1976. *Doing Justice: The Choice of Punishment*. New York: Hill & Wang.

Walker, Samuel. 2015. *Sense and Nonsense about Crime, Drugs, and Communities*, 8th ed. Stamford, CT: Cengage Learning.

Weisburd, David, E. Shoam, B. Ariel, M. Manspeizer, and Lior Gideon. 2010. "Follow-up Study among Released Substance Abusing Inmates Who Graduated from the Sharon Prison-based Therapeutic Community." *Megamot* 47(2): 236–253.

Welsh, W.N. 2011. Prison-Based Substance Abuse Programs. Pp. 157–192 in *Rethinking Corrections: Rehabilitation, Reentry and Reintegration*, edited by L. Gideon and S.H.E. Sung. Thousand Oaks, CA: Sage Publishing.

Wexler, H. K., D.S. Lipton, D. S., and B.D. Johnson. 1988. *A Criminal Justice System Strategy for Treating Cocaine-heroin Abusing Offenders in Custody* (Vol. 90, No. 10). Washington, DC: U.S. Department of Justice, National Institute of Justice, Office of Communication and Research Utilization.

Zaitzow, B.H., and R.S. Jones. 2013. "Redemption from the Inside-out: The Power of Faith Based Programming." Pp. 319–344 in *Special Needs Offenders in Correctional Institutions*, edited by L. Gideon. Thousand Oaks, CA: Sage.

5 Restorative Justice

Chad Posick

What is Restorative Justice?

When someone commits a crime in the United States, the process to determine guilt and hold the offender accountable is generally taken over by the formal criminal justice system. Here we see a prosecutor take the place of the victim and a defense attorney represent the accused. A judge sits in the place of society or the community that was harmed. The victim and the offender have almost no place in this process. The default response to violent crime is to place the offender in prison. This has led to an incredible increase in incarceration within the United States and a high rate of recidivism (Clear and Frost 2015).

Restorative justice (RJ), on the other hand, seeks to include all parties affected by a crime in decisions on how to address the harm done by the act. RJ aims to: (1) provide a space for active participation in victim support; (2) hold offenders directly accountable for their actions; (3) restore the emotional health of victims; (4) restore victim's material loss; (5) provide a range of opportunities for dialogue and problem-solving; (6) offer opportunities for the offender to be reintegrated back into the community; and (7) increase public safety through community building (Umbreit 2000a). This process puts the victim in the center of the justice process and focuses on how to help assist them in recovering from the crime. Additionally, the process is concerned with the offender and meeting their needs in successfully making things right and being reintegrated into the community. Many proponents and advocates of this approach to addressing harm are much broader in their conceptualization of the philosophy of RJ, arguing that restorative justice is "a holistic change in the way we do justice in the world" (Braithwaite 2003: 1). In this sense, RJ is a broad philosophy on how we are to treat each other and achieve justice when harm occurs.

There is never a one-size-fits-all solution to accomplishing what RJ sets out to do, but the process allows for a wide range of avenues to do so—unlike traditional approaches to criminal justice. RJ techniques range from sentencing offenders (sentencing circles), monitoring offenders in the community (community reparation boards), and bringing together victims and offenders for dialogue. It would be difficult to cover in any detail all of the approaches to restorative justice, so three of the most popular approaches will be covered here: (1) family group conferencing (FGC); (2) victim–offender mediation (VOM); and (3) peacemaking circles. These three approaches have wide application and are appropriate in various types of situations and cases. They also have been the focus of rigorous empirical evaluation.

Family group conferencing includes the involvement of the victim, offender, community, and support individuals of each party who come together to speak, one at a time, to each other, facilitated by a trained outside observer. Many times the facilitator is a criminal justice official such as a probation or police officer but other times it can be a civilian community member. Each FGC is different and, particularly, the individuals there for support differ depending on the dynamics of the situation. Sometimes law enforcement officials attend (e.g., police, probation officers, judges) especially when sentencing an offender within the criminal justice system is an option. If the FGC addresses issues within a school, school officials (e.g., principals, teachers, counselors) might join the group. If the crime was particularly damaging to the victim, broader victims support advocates may attend. There may also be more than one offender present at the FGC, depending on the particular offense and situation.

Generally, an FGC proceeds in a structured way: (1) the facilitator of the FGC contacts the victim first and the offender second to explain the process and invite the parties to attend—both must agree voluntarily and the offender must admit—in some part—to the offense; (2) the participants are asked to invite supporters such as family, friends, and advocates; (3) a pre-conference meeting is set up to reiterate the process and confirm participation of each individual—this is also a time where the facilitator and participants can meet face-to-face; (4) the conference is initiated with the offender discussing their involvement in the offense, followed by the others, primarily the direct victim, describing the impact of the offense on them personally; (5) a decision is made, jointly, on how to address the harm caused by the offense. Many times the ultimate goal of an FGC is to make a decision on how to repair the harm caused by the offense. Alternative goals may be restitution to the victim or an offender apology, but RJ cautions against the expectation of specific outcomes of the process. FGCs have gained appeal in New Zealand, Australia, Canada, and the United States, among other countries, and have seen growth in each of these areas which likely will continue in the future.

Victim–offender mediation includes only the victim and offender (along with a facilitator) who engage in a dialogue to better understand the criminal incident. Again, this is led by a facilitator and the goal is to achieve greater understanding of the damaging event. The primary driver of VOM is open-dialogue between the victim and offender with little interference by the facilitator. Commonly, but secondarily, some form of restitution is agreed upon by the parties. Both family group conferences and victim–offender mediation take place on neutral ground (as defined by the victim) and only proceed if the victim wants to entertain the process and the offender accepts responsibility for the act. If the facilitator envisions any problems, they may call off the meeting (Umbreit 2000b). One special case is when the offender is incarcerated, in which case the only option for a meeting is inside the prison under the specific regulations of the institution.

Finally, peacemaking circles are broader than both FGCs and VOMs and have several diverse applications. The main purpose of peacemaking circles is to either prevent crime or intervene when conflict arises to thwart escalation. Peacemaking circles are gaining traction in schools as a way to intervene in bullying and other conflicts. Some schools regularly participate in circles as a way to give students a space to voice concerns and address classroom issues that present a particular challenge (Pranis, Stuart, and Wedge 2003). Peacemaking circles have even been used to address longstanding violence, such as between rival gangs and ethnic conflicts (e.g., Hutus and Tutsis/Israelis and Palestinians) with success (Boyes-Watson 2013). Peacemaking circles are a common RJ approach when there is no clear offender and victim, and in cases when there has been a history of conflict and harm on both (or all) sides.

The Empirical Evidence

Evaluations of RJ programs picked up in the 1990s and early 2000s to assess the outcomes of the first set of formal efforts in the United States and abroad. A meta-analysis of this body of research was carried out in 2005 and found that RJ is a profitable practice for intervention and prevention. Victims who participated in RJ were more likely to be satisfied with the process than those who went through traditional criminal justice practices, offenders were more likely to pay back restitution to victims than those who were punished by the criminal justice system, and offenders were less likely to recidivate than their counterparts punished by the criminal justice system (Latimer, Dowden and Muise 2005). A recent study on the effectiveness of the reintegrative shaming experiments (RISE) in Canberra, Australia from 1995–2000 highlighted the positive outcomes of an RJ diversionary program that produced higher levels of offender engagement and higher levels of ethical treatment of offenders and victims when compared to the normal court process (Barnes et al. 2015).

The results of recent rigorous research on the effectiveness of restorative justice echoes what was revealed in the 1990s and 2000s—that, in most cases, restorative justice is *at least* on par with outcomes from the traditional criminal justice system and often *better* than traditional court processes (Sherman et al. 2015a; Sherman et al. 2015b). A randomized-control study of the effectiveness of restorative justice to reduce post-traumatic stress symptoms (PTSS) among a sample of robbery and burglary victims revealed that there were 49 percent fewer victims who showed PTSS in those randomly assigned to an FGC style process than those who went through the formal criminal justice system alone without an FGC (Angel et al. 2014). A meta-analysis of ten RJ programs in the UK and Australia (seven programs from 2001–2005 and three from the mid 1990s) found support for RJ in reducing 2-year recidivism rates among offenders who participated in RJ compared to regular criminal justice processes (Sherman et al. 2015b).

Restorative Justice in Prisons

While RJ is often used as a diversionary strategy to avoid incarceration, it does not have to be so. Sometimes an RJ intervention ends with the offender being incarcerated. In fact, RJ has found a prominent place within the prison setting. Prison separates an offender from his or her community and, essentially, from their victim. Often it is the case that an offender is *legally restricted* from having any contact with their victim(s) and would be punished for trying to make any contact. Likewise, victims often do not have any avenue for reaching out to contact those who have wronged them. This separation prohibits the victim from reaching further understanding of their victimization and it prevents the offender from taking steps to make things right. Restorative justice inside prison attempts to break this barrier and reconnect the web between offenders and victims and their communities.

Programs have been set up so that offenders who are incarcerated can meet with their victims if both parties agree to meet inside the prison. Often these meetings are attended by prison guards (per prison rules) as well as a facilitator to lead the face-to-face meeting. However, understandably, sometimes one party does not want to meet face-to-face with the other party. In this case, there are alternative initiatives to achieve restoration. If the direct victim does not want to meet, victims of similar crimes are often willing to "stand in" for the victim and meet with offenders on the inside—generally in small groups. Similar processes are available when the victim wants to meet, but the offender does not. Groups of prisoners, convicted of similar crimes, meet with victims who have suffered from harms. Even though these processes do not link the direct offender with the direct victim, participants report that they have a better understanding of why they were victimized, offenders have a chance to apologize and explain why they did what they did, and each party leaves with a better sense of finality that would not have been possible without dialogue. Prison participants of RJ have been found to have lower recidivism rates than those in the general prison population by increasing empathy for victims and holding offenders directly accountable for the harm they caused (Armour et al. 2005).

Just as schools are moving toward using RJ to address harm, so too are prisons. Barb Toews (2006) outlines four major uses of RJ inside prison, including: (1) dealing with conflicts between prisoners and staff; (2) addressing harm from crimes that happen inside prison; (3) restoring relationships between family and prisoners; and (4) dealing with disciplinary infractions. The prison community is a community in and of itself and the health of those in the system depend on effectively dealing with harm when it arises. While there have not been many empirical evaluations of these types of prison programs, there is potential to achieve the same positive effects on the inside as are seen on the outside. Given the heightened level of conflict and crime in prison when compared with the general population, RJ might offer a viable solution that increases safety and reduces institutional costs.

Toews (2006: 86) also suggests using an RJ framework more broadly while inside prison. This takes advantage of the benefits of a restorative justice philosophy regardless of the level of institutional support for the approach. She recommends: (1) getting on a healing path; (2) embracing restorative values; (3) creating a sanctuary; (4) walking with those who offend; (5) walking with victims; and (6) walking with families in an effort to "restore living for the common good." Wider efforts to promote positive living on the inside, by connecting with others, sharing stories, and creating a space to address harm, might go far in reducing disciplinary infractions and crime in prison—however, this has yet to be empirically tested.

The Future of Restorative Justice

Given the empirical status of restorative justice in producing positive results in the general population and inside prison, it is anticipated that the United States and other countries will see more of its use in place of, or parallel with, the traditional school and prison systems. Given continuing state budget cuts and deficits in the states (the major funder of prisons and correctional programming), alternatives to incarceration may become more attractive and policymakers may take cost-effective prevention more seriously.

Restorative justice is theoretically attractive given its connection with contemporary understanding of antisocial behavior. First, it reduces the chance of stigmatization of offenders by dealing with issues informally, outside of the criminal justice system where labels such as "felon" and "convict" follow individuals around for life. Second, RJ provides an avenue for reintegration back into the community by providing supportive connections and bonds with the community. Together, these factors increase perception of legitimacy of the law—and these perceptions of legitimacy relate to obeying and cooperating with the law. Third, RJ has implications across the life-course in providing "turning points" for offenders in shaping their life for better increasing the chances of desistance from crime. Finally, RJ coincides with recent neuro-scientific, biological, and psychosocial theories of behavior. All people are biological beings with innate sensory systems and behavioral responses to environmental stimuli. RJ confers benefits on appropriate cognitive and affective systems (that are hardwired into our central nervous system) by engaging in dialogue to understand their social situations and connect people on a biological level which likely contributes to the positive outcomes that evaluation studies have uncovered.

Despite evidence that RJ produces positive outcomes for participants, there is reason for caution in wholesale acceptance of RJ practices. In other words, not all restorative justice practices are created equal. Leading researchers and assessors of RJ practices have found that there are three major implications of current RJ practices: (1) Many RJ practices are untested and claims that *some* RJ practices are effective does not mean that *all* RJ practices are effective—in fact, some untested practices may be *causing* harm; (2) Practices that have been rigorously tested and found to be effective are not widely used, while untested RJ practices have arguably *caused* harm by diverting essential, and limited, resources to ineffective programs; and (3) Victims of violent crime are indirectly harmed by the diversion of resources to property crime where RJ is found to be less effective (Strang and Sherman 2015). Practitioners should heed the advice of Heather Strang and Lawrence Sherman (2015: 1) who state that there is:

> a moral obligation for RJ practitioners to assure that their work does no harm by promoting rigorous evaluations of what they are doing, and encouraging investment in tested strategies for the kinds of victims and offenders with whom RJ is known to have the strongest effects.

As always, theoretically strong and empirically validated approaches to crime prevention and intervention are the key to success and time will tell whether RJ lives up to the most promising of these practices.

References

Angel, Caroline M., Lawrence W. Sherman, Heather Strang, Barak Ariel, Sarah Bennett, Nova Inkpen, Anne Keane, and Therese S. Richmond. 2014. "Short-term Effects of Restorative Justice Conferences on Post-traumatic Stress Symptoms among Robbery and Burglary Victims: A Randomized Controlled Trial." *Journal of Experimental Criminology* 10(3): 291–307.

Armour, Marilyn Peterson, John Sage, Allen Rubin, and Liliane C. Windsor. 2005. "Bridges to Life: Evaluation of an In-prison Restorative Justice Intervention." *Medicine and Law* 24: 831–851.

Barnes, Geoffrey C., Jordan M. Hyatt, Caroline M. Angel, Heather Strang, and Lawrence W. Sherman. 2015. "Are Restorative Justice Conferences more Fair than Criminal Courts? Comparing Levels of Observed Procedural Justice in the Reintegrative Shaming Experiments (RISE)." *Criminal Justice Policy Review* 26(2): 103–130.

Boyes-Watson, Carolyn. 2013. *Peacemaking Circles and Urban Youth*. St. Paul, MN: Living Justice Press.

Braithwaite, John. 2003. "Principles of Restorative Justice." Pp. 1–20 in *Restorative Justice and Criminal Justice: Competing or Reconcilable Paradigms*, edited by A. Von Hirsch, J. Roberts, A. Bottoms, J. Roach, and M. Schiff. Oxford, UK: Hart.

Clear, Todd R., and Natasha A. Frost. 2015. *The Punishment Imperative: The Rise and Failure of Mass Incarceration in America*. New York: New York University Press.

Latimer, Jeff, Craig Dowden, and Danielle Muise. 2005. "The Effectiveness of Restorative Justice Practices: A Meta-analysis." *The Prison Journal* 85(2): 127–144.

Pranis, Kay, Barry Stuart, and Mark Wedge. 2003. *Peacemaking Circles: From Crime to Community*. St. Paul, MN: Living Justice Press.

Sherman, Lawrence W., Heather Strang, Geoffrey Barnes, Daniel J. Woods, Sarah Bennett, Nova Inkpen, Dorothy Newbury-Birch, Meredith Rossner, Caroline Angel, and Malcolm Mearns. 2015a. "Twelve Experiments in Restorative Justice: The Jerry Lee Program of Randomized Trials of Restorative Justice Conferences." *Journal of Experimental Criminology* 11(4): 501–540.

Sherman, Lawrence W., Heather Strang, Evan Mayo-Wilson, Daniel J. Woods, and Barak Ariel. 2015b. "Are Restorative Justice Conferences Effective in Reducing Repeat Offending? Findings from a Campbell Systematic Review." *Journal of Quantitative Criminology* 31(1): 1–24.

Strang, Heather, and Lawrence Sherman. 2015. "The Morality of Evidence: The Second Annual Lecture for Restorative Justice: An International Journal." *Restorative Justice* 3(1): 6–27.

Toews, Barb. 2006. *Little Book of Restorative Justice for People in Prison: Rebuilding the Web of Relationships*. Intercourse: Good Books.

Umbreit, Mark S. 2000a. *Family Group Conferencing: Implications for Crime Victims*. U.S. Department of Justice. Office of Justice Programs. Office for Victims of Crime.

Umbreit, Mark S. 2000b. *Guidelines for Victim-sensitive Victim-offender Mediation: Restorative Justice through Dialogue*. U.S. Department of Justice. Office of Justice Programs. Office for Victims of Crime.

Section 2

Punishment and Correctional Sanctions in the United States

6 Banishment and Residency Restrictions in the United States

O. Hayden Griffin III

Introduction

Banishment is one of the most ancient and basic punishments of people. While banishment has taken many forms, essentially, it is the forced removal of a person from society. In some instances, such a person is simply told to leave; while in others, a person is literally transported to another place or society. History is replete with examples of this form of punishment: the founding of the United States, Russian persons being sent to Siberia, and Napoleon Bonaparte being forced to live his final days on a remote island in the South Atlantic (St. Helena). However, as the United States has evolved into modernity, there are very few examples of the classical punishment of banishment being practiced. Yet, while the practice of simply telling people to leave has largely vanished in the United States, a similar type of punishment has emerged—residency restrictions. This type of sanction is especially prevalent against sex offenders and dictates where some offenders may live and visit, with the threat of incarceration looming for those who fail to abide by these restrictions. This chapter discusses these two types of punishment.

Banishment

Banishment or as some people refer to it, exile, is an ancient form of punishment. As Beckett and Herbert (2010) noted, banishment has been used as a punishment in ancient societies such as Babylon, Greece, and Rome. Indeed, two of the most frequently cited examples of banishment come from the Old Testament, with the banishment of Adam and Eve from the Garden of Eden; and later, the banishment of their son Cain from God's presence after Cain killed his brother Abel (Kunesh 2007). While the complete permutations of banishment may vary, in general, there are two different practices of banishment. The first is that people who are convicted of crimes or in some similar manner adjudged guilty are told to leave the society that has made that determination. It does not matter so much where they go, just so long as they leave. This form of banishment can be either permanent or in effect for a specified number of years. The second practice of banishment is that after being convicted of a crime or in some similar manner adjudged guilty, a person is transported to a penal colony. In some instances, the transportation itself is the punishment. In more extreme cases, along with the transportation, the exiled person must perform hard labor and/or serve as a slave. While the motivations in different societies for utilizing banishment might vary, England's primary motivation for the imposition of banishment, which contributed to the settlement of the United States and Australia, was an alternative to the overreliance on capital punishment. From 1100 to 1700, so many people were executed in England that the legal code gained the moniker the "Bloody Code" (Hanser 2017).

In the age of exploration in which many European countries sought to claim colonies in the Americas and elsewhere, it became commonplace for these countries to send their offenders to these new colonies. Such a punishment was practical for two reasons: removal of offenders from the so-called mother country and for the settlement and protection of newly claimed land. Within England, this policy officially began with the passage of the Vagrancy Act of 1597. If an offender returned to England before they had completed the time or terms of their sentence, the punishment was execution. From approximately 1718 to 1776, approximately 50,000 convicts were transported from England to what would become the United States. After the Revolutionary War, England resumed transporting convicts to other colonies, most notably Australia (Clear, Cole, and Reisig 2013). While most people who were exiled from England never returned, the typical term of banishment was seven years (Yung 2007). Essentially, banishment serves two forms of punishment. It incapacitates offenders since they can no longer commit crimes against people within the society from which they were banished. Second, it can serve a deterrent effect, both specific and general, in that a person will no longer be able to commit a similar crime against a similar group of people (specific) and learning that a person could be banished from a place, might deter them from committing a future crime (general).

While banishment may have been effective in less modern societies, to some degree, this form of punishment was slated to become a historical relic. As transportation methods have evolved and nearly every corner of the Earth has become settled, there are simply no places left to send convicts that would mirror the British transportation of convicts to the United States and Australia (Alloy 2002). Beyond the practicalities of enforcing banishment and despite the United States essentially being founded on such a policy, since colonial times, banishment has rarely been used as a punishment in the United States. As Armstrong (1963) argued, the idea of banishment as a punishment was "repulsive" to the Founding Fathers of the United States. Beyond mere repulsion, a more legalistic reason that banishment has been used so infrequently in the United States is that many states have abolished banishment within their state constitutions (Borrelli 2002). Furthermore, although the federal courts have not really considered this issue, many legal scholars believe banishment is not constitutionally permissible. Perhaps the closest issue the federal courts have considered are deportation orders, but that involves people who are not citizens (Yung 2007). Despite a lack of applicable case law, many people have argued that banishment as a punishment violates the constitutional right to travel. The only recent documented case of a person being officially banished from a state was in 2000 when a Kentucky state court banned a man from the state for one year. This was a result of his punishment for domestic violence (Borrelli 2002).

Federal and state level banishment may be rare to non-existent, but different states have experimented with punishments that ban people from counties in which they have been convicted of crimes. As Borrelli (2002) has noted, different counties within Wisconsin, Georgia, and Mississippi have supported banishment. However, perhaps one of the most extreme (or clever depending upon perspective) instances of a state attempting to circumvent a state prohibition of banishment is in Georgia. In that state, judges, as part of the terms of a criminal sentence, have forbidden offenders from entering 158 out of the 159 counties within the state. When this occurs, a judge does not confine an offender to the county in which they reside, but to a county in another part of the state, typically far away. One example of this happened to a man named Paul Demetrius. He lived in Cobb County, Georgia, and had been convicted of possession of car theft tools. As part of his sentence, the judge banished Demetrius to Bulloch County, more than 200 miles away. Rather than move to the county, Demetrius moved to Maryland where he had family. Another offender, Armando Amador, was convicted of burglarizing a restaurant. He was sentenced to six years in prison and 14 years of probation. As part of Amador's probation, the judge in the case banished Amador to Rabun County, the farthest county away from his home in Tifton, Georgia. Much like Demetrius, Amador moved from the state. Thus, while the state constitution of Georgia officially prohibits the punishment of banishment, judges have found ways around such restrictions (Alloy 2002).

Residency Restrictions

While there may be a shortage of legal punishments that mirror the traditional punishment of banishment, many punishments in the United States certainly resemble this ancient practice. As Beckett and Herbert (2010) argued, states have begun to increasingly use policies of spatial exclusion to control the actions of offenders. They noted that spatial regulation has long been a method of social control. These types of tactics can essentially be placed into two categories: the aforementioned punishment of banishment and policies of containment. According to Beckett and Herbert, as societies have approached modernity, strict policies of exclusion have gradually developed into policies of containment. Much of the work of Michel Foucault (1975), especially his work *Discipline and Punish*, documents the different efforts societies have engaged in to control certain groups of citizens. In particular, prisons and mental hospitals have been used as facilities to control societies' dangerous people. Within the United States, perhaps the key groups of people who have been targeted for containment were African Americans (Armstrong 1963) and the homeless. Many different vagrancy and loitering statutes were enacted for this purpose of containing these groups of people. During the 1960s and 1970s, many of these laws were struck down by federal courts because it was believed that the laws' enactment was done for discriminatory purposes (Beckett and Herbert 2010).

Beyond the traditional form/s of banishment, the first time that spatial exclusion began to be used as a tool of the criminal justice system was through the use of probation or parole. As either an alternative to incarceration or an early release from it, probationers and parolees have to agree to various restrictions or constraints upon their behavior. In some instances, these limits can be on where a person may work, the types of places they may visit, or the type of people with whom they are allowed to interact. A common restriction on probationers or parolees is that they cannot spend time with other people who have been convicted of crimes (Clear et al. 2013; Hanser 2017). Additionally, some jurisdictions have more intensive supervision programs for parolees or probationers who are deemed a greater risk to recidivate. It is believed that some of these offenders will fight such an urge if they are more carefully watched and restricted (Petersilia 1999). Failure to comply with these terms may result in incarceration. Due to this fear, many probationers or parolees are often reluctant to fight the terms of their restrictions. Thus, few challenges to these restrictions end up in court (Alloy 2002). Furthermore, civil commitment statutes have been used to target specific populations, especially sex offenders (Levenson 2004) and gang members (Smith 2000). Additionally, some laws have been designed to specifically punish the actions of certain people. As Beckett and Herbert (2010) noted, rather than merely punish homelessness, many localities in the United States have enacted regulations against panhandling, sitting or lying on sidewalks, and camping in placing not designated for that purpose to combat homelessness.

In the United States, perhaps the most widespread form of residency restrictions are laws meant to control the behavior of sexual offenders. While sex offenders have often been viewed as the most loathsome criminals, beginning in the mid 1990s, especially with the passage of the Jacob Wetterling Act and Megan's Law, sex offenders began to experience a wide range of regulations beyond incarceration or other more traditional punishments from the American criminal justice system. The Jacob Wetterling Crimes against Children and

Sexually Violent Offender Registration Act, passed in 1994, implemented the process of registering sex offenders in centralized databases. Two years later, with the passage of Megan's Law, law enforcement agencies were required to make the contents of these databases publicly available. To comply with probation, parole, or a separate crime, many different types of sex offenders have been forced to comply with these laws or risk being sent to prison (Tewksbury and Lees 2006). Sex offender registration laws essentially serve the function of allowing people to know where the "dangerous" people may reside. Yet, many researchers have pondered whether these policies are effective to prevent future recidivism (Tewksbury and Jennings 2010). As Sandler, Freedman and Socia (2008) documented after a study of registered sex offenders in New York, more than 95 percent of all sexual offense arrests were perpetrated by first-time offenders. Thus, it seemed to them that there was little value in trying to catch repeat offenders, especially since many of the worst sexual offenders will never be released from prison. Furthermore, many scholars have questioned whether the registry actually inhibits the ability of sex offenders to reintegrate into their communities upon their release from incarceration (Tewksbury and Lees 2006). It has been documented that sex offenders listed on such registries have experienced threats or harassment from neighbors as well as property damage (Levenson and Cotter 2005b).

It is doubtful that any sex offender would be willing to sign up to be on a registry without any tangible benefit. Beyond the shaming aspect, there is no official constraint on a sex offender's life. However, many states have gone beyond merely placing sex offenders on a website or list and restrict where they are allowed to live. In 2005, Levenson and Cotter (2005a) found 14 states that placed restrictions on where sex offenders were allowed to live. Seven years later, Nobles, Levenson, and Youstin (2012) found that more than 30 states had such laws. Furthermore, thousands of municipalities have such restrictions. The purpose of these laws seem to be to create "buffer zones" between sex offenders and the people upon which they might victimize. Among the different places that sex offenders must avoid when deciding where to live are schools, parks, day care centers, or school bus stops; essentially, any place that children are likely to congregate. Levenson and Cotter (2005a) found the shortest such buffer to be in Illinois (500 feet), while the most common buffer zone was 1,000 to 2,000 feet. In California, sex offenders on parole are forbidden from living within one quarter mile of an elementary school and not within 35 miles of a victim or witness.

Needless to say, sex offenders with residency restrictions may have difficulty finding a place to live after their release from incarceration. Reintegrating into society is challenging for any offender, never mind the addition of residency restrictions. Indeed, there are many collateral consequences of these policies. Many sex offenders have been forced to move from their original homes to comply with residency restrictions and, in many instances, the places they end up are not conducive to reform. Such policies may place many sex offenders into socially disorganized neighborhoods, the type of neighborhoods that foster crime regardless of whether someone who is prone to offend arrives. According to Mustaine (2014), this will cause most sex offenders to move to worse places than they lived before they were convicted. Many of these neighborhoods lack collective efficacy, educational resources, and employment opportunities. While residency restrictions may seem well-intentioned, the collateral consequences actually seem to cause the behavior these policies were intended to stop.

Four major critiques of residency restrictions have been asserted. The first critique of these restrictions is a common one among many crime policies – residency restrictions ignore the fact that most sexual assaults are committed by people whom the victims already know. Thus, protections against sex offender strangers interacting with victims are unlikely to prevent many instances of future offending (Meloy, Miller, and Curtis 2008). The second critique is that there is little-to-no evidence that sex offenders recidivate at higher levels than other criminals (Tewksbury and Jennings 2010). The third critique is that there is no consensus on whether sex offenders actually attempt to live in places near where children congregate. As Levenson and Cotter (2005a) found, the results are "mixed" and several studies have found that sex offenders actually travel to other places to commit sex crimes. To these offenders, there is a decreased likelihood of being caught. The fourth critique and perhaps most important, is that residency restrictions have shown no evidence of being effective (Huebner et al. 2014; Nobles et al. 2012).

Some people might be willing to disregard such critiques and merely believe that it is better to be safe than sorry, even in the face of considerable evidence that these policies seem to make offenders' lives worse and have limited utility in preventing future crime. Yet, some of these policies go beyond these critiques. While some offenders will merely have these restrictions as a condition of probation or parole, many of these laws make a failure to comply with these restrictions a separate crime. For instance, in the state of Georgia, if a sex offender resides, is employed, or loiters within 1000 feet of a school, childcare facility, church, public or private park, recreation facility or playground, skating rink, neighborhood center, gymnasium, community swimming pool, or school bus stop, that person can be convicted of a felony that is punishable from ten to 30 years in prison (Tewksbury 2007). As Geraghty (2007:513) argued, this law is tantamount to banishment. Much like the 158 out of 159 county restrictions, Geraghty stated that Georgia's law is essentially a legislative mechanism to "rid itself of its 12,000 registered sex offenders." Thus, through a design of residency restrictions, many states may actually be employing a de facto policy of banishment.

Conclusion

Banishment is an ancient punishment that was widely employed as an alternative to the death penalty. While such a punishment does not seem to have a place in the modern world, other policies, such as spatial exclusion and residency restrictions seem to have a similar purpose. Furthermore, while these types of punishments might not literally resemble banishment, the practical effect of these punishments may essentially encourage people to leave certain jurisdictions. Thus, while these punishments are not explicitly banishment, the application of these policies may work in a similar manner and have the same practical goal—to either remove certain groups of people or encourage them to leave.

References

Alloy, Jason S. 2002. "158-County Banishment in Georgia: Constitutional Implications under the State Constitution and the Federal Right to Travel." *Georgia Law Review* 36: 1083–1108.

Armstrong, Michael F. 1963. "Banishment: Cruel and Unusual Punishment." *University of Pennsylvania Law Review* 111: 758–786.

Beckett, Katherine, and Steve Herbert. 2010. "Penal Boundaries: Banishment and the Expansion of Punishment." *Law & Social Inquiry* 35(1): 1–38.

Borrelli, Matthew. 2002. "Banishment: The Constitutional and Public Policy Arguments against this Revived Ancient Punishment." *Suffolk University Law Review* 36: 469–486.

Clear, Todd R., George F. Cole, and Michael D. Reisig. 2013. *American Corrections*, 10th ed. Belmont, CA: Cengage.

Foucault, Michel. 1975. *Discipline and Punish: The Birth of the Prison*. New York: Vintage Books.

Geraghty, Sarah. 2007. "Challenging the Banishment of Registered Sex Offenders from the State of Georgia: A Practitioner's Perspective." *Harvard Civil Rights-Civil Liberties Law Review* 42: 513–529.

Hanser, Robert D. 2017. *Introduction to Corrections*, 2nd ed. Thousand Oaks, CA: Sage.

Huebner, Beth M., Kimberly R. Kras, Jason Rydberg, Timothy S. Bynum, Eric Grommon, and Breanne Pleggenkuhle. 2014. "The Effect and Implications of Sex Offender Residence Restrictions." *Criminology & Public Policy* 13(1): 139–168.

Kunesh, Patrice H. 2007. "Banishment as Cultural Justice in Contemporary Tribal Legal Systems." *New Mexico Law Review* 37: 85–145.

Levenson, Jill. 2004. "Sexual Predator Civil Commitment: A Comparison of Selected Released Offenders." *International Journal of Offender Therapy and Comparative Criminology* 48(6): 638–648.

Levenson, Jill, and Leo P. Cotter. 2005a. "The Impact of Sex Offender Residence Restrictions: 1,000 Feet from Danger or One Step from Absurd?" *International Journal of Offender Therapy and Comparative Criminology* 49(2): 168–178.

Levenson, Jill and Leo P. Cotter. 2005b. "The Effect of Megan's Law on Sex Offender Reintegration." *Journal of Contemporary Criminal Justice* 21(1): 49–66.

Meloy, Michelle L., Susan L. Miller, and Kristin M. Curtis. 2008. "Making Sense out of Nonsense: The Deconstruction of State-Level Sex Offender Residence Restrictions." *American Journal of Criminal Justice* 33(2): 209–222.

Mustaine, Elizabeth Ehrhardt. 2014. "Sex Offender Residency Restrictions: Successful Integration or Exclusion? *Criminology & Public Policy* 13(1): 169–177.

Nobles, Matt R., Jill S. Levenson, and Tasha J. Youstin. 2012. "Effectiveness of Residence Restrictions in Preventing Sex Offense Recidivism." *Crime & Delinquency* 58(4): 491–513.

Petersilia, Joan. 1999. "Parole and Prisoner Reentry in the United States." *Crime and Justice* 26: 479–529.

Sandler, Jeffrey C., Naomi J. Freeman, and Kelly M. Socia. 2008. "Does a Watched Pot Boil? A Time-Series Analysis of New York State's Sex Offender Registration and Notification Law." *Psychology, Public Policy, and Law* 14(4): 284–302.

Smith, Stephanie. 2000. "Civil Banishment of Gang Members: Circumventing Criminal Due Process Requirements?" *The University of Chicago Law Review* 67(4): 1461–1487.

Tewksbury, Richard. 2007. "Exile at Home: The Unintended Collateral Consequences of Sex Offender Residency Restrictions." *Harvard Civil Rights-Civil Liberties Law Review* 42: 531–540.

Tewksbury, Richard, and Wesley G. Jennings. 2010. "Assessing the Impact of Sex Offender Registration and Community Notification on Sex-Offending Trajectories." *Criminal Justice and Behavior* 37(5): 570–582.

Tewksbury, Richard, and Matthew Lees. 2006. "Perceptions of Sex Offender Registration: Collateral Consequences and Community Experiences." *Sociological Spectrum* 26(3): 309–334.

Yung, Corey Rayburn. 2007. "Banishment by a Thousand Laws: Residency Restrictions on Sex Offenders. *Washington University Law Review* 85(1): 101–160.

7 Economic Sanctions

R. Barry Ruback

Economic Sanctions

Economic sanctions are court-imposed financial obligations following a criminal conviction. In the criminal justice system these economic sanctions are of four primary types: restitution, fees/costs, fines, and criminal forfeiture. In this chapter I define each of these sanctions, describe how they are imposed, and examine their effects. Then I discuss the issues regarding economic sanctions that will be faced in coming years. I conclude by discussing the economic sanctions in terms of their impact on victims, offenders, and society.

Restitution

Restitution is a court-ordered payment to victims as compensation for the financial losses that they suffered as a result of the crime. As such, its goal is concern for the victim (Moen 2013), but the payment also addresses issues of just deserts and justice for both the victim and society (Harland 1981). The amount of restitution must be for "easily ascertainable" economic losses (McGillis 1986: 36). In some states, the statutory language refers to "losses and damages," whereas in other states, specific types of losses (e.g., stolen property, medical expenses) are listed. Typically, general damages, including pain and suffering, are not permitted as restitution, in the belief that compensation for these harms should be handled in civil courts. Restitution has been handled in one of four different ways (McGillis 1986): (1) through victim/witness assistance programs, (2) through victim/offender reconciliation programs, (3) through probation supervision, and (4) through court-based employment programs. Although restitution is recognized as a victim right in all 50 states, it is a constitutional right in only 20 and its imposition is mandated by law in only 33 (Haynes, Cares, and Ruback 2015).

Nationally, offenders in state courts are ordered to pay restitution in 18 percent of all conviction offenses: 18 percent of violent offenses, 27 percent of property offenses, 14 percent of drug offenses, 8 percent of weapons offenses, and 13 percent of other offenses (Rosenmerkel, Durose, and Farole 2009: Table 1.5). Despite the fact that restitution is imposed more often than it was earlier (Durose and Langan 2003), for three reasons restitution programs have not been as successful as they might be (Office for Victims of Crime 1998). First, judges may consider offenders' ability to pay, and often do not impose restitution on those who they believe are unable to pay it. Second, the payment of restitution typically follows the payment of costs and fines, which may mean that the offender does not have the money to pay the restitution. Third, the responsibility for monitoring, collecting, and enforcing restitution payments can be ambiguous, and with no clear lines of responsibility, offenders may escape having to pay.

There have been three experimental studies of restitution. Lurigio and Davis (1990) found that adult probationers who were delinquent in paying restitution were significantly more likely to pay their restitution if they had received a letter telling them what they owed, how to make payment, and threatening them with serious consequences if they did not. The effect of this letter was especially strong for those who had jobs and who had shorter criminal records, suggesting that they had the ability to pay and that they were more concerned about the effects of probation revocation. Weisburd, Einat, and Kowalski (2008) investigated the payment of financial obligations, including restitution, by testing what they called "the miracle of the cells." That is, if offenders are threatened with incarceration they will find the money. Ruback, Gladfelter, and Lantz (2014) suggested that this sort of compliance can be expensive, because it can be obtained only as long as the rules will be enforced.

In their experiment, Ruback et al. (2014) assigned offenders who were delinquent in paying restitution to one of four experimental conditions. Over a six-month period, three-quarters of the offenders received a letter once a month that contained (a) information about the economic sanctions they had paid and what they still owed (Information manipulation), (b) a statement about reasons for paying restitution (Rationale manipulation), or (c) both the Information manipulation and the Rationale manipulation. The remaining quarter of the offenders did not receive any letters. Over a one-year period (the six months of letters and a six-month follow-up period), offenders who had received letters containing Information paid significantly more money and made significantly more monthly payments than did offenders in the other three experimental conditions. A cost-effectiveness analysis indicated that for every dollar spent on the experimental manipulation about $6.44 in restitution was received. Because the offenders in the Information condition continued to pay restitution even after the letters were no longer being sent, Ruback et al. concluded that the offenders had internalized the need to pay restitution, consistent with the rationale for restorative justice.

Fees/Costs

Fees and costs refer to required payments to reimburse the government (local and state) for the costs associated with administering the criminal justice system. These costs can include backward-looking charges for the costs of prosecution (e.g., witness costs), as well as forward-looking charges for future expenses (e.g., probation supervision). In other places, costs refer to blanket charges for program participation (e.g., a diversion program), whereas fees refer to specific charges in an individual case (e.g., a fee for DNA analysis). However, the distinction between costs and fees is not consistent across jurisdictions, and most discussions, as here, combine the two.

Because of high probation caseloads, the most common type of fees relate to supervision (Bonczar 1997), including supervision through electronic monitoring. About two-thirds of convicted offenders are placed on community supervision, but only one-tenth of corrections budgets go toward supervision (Petersilia 1997). Thus, there is pressure on probation departments to become self-supporting (Olson and Ramker 2001).

Not much research has been conducted on the imposition and payment of fees/costs. There is some evidence that fees are more likely to be imposed in rural than urban counties, and, in terms of individual characteristics, more likely for white offenders, offenders with higher incomes, and offenders convicted of misdemeanors rather than felonies (Olson and Ramker 2001). Judges in rural areas may be more responsive to their communities and therefore more concerned with imposing justice in individual cases, whereas judges in urban areas may be more concerned with processing large numbers of cases (Olson and Ramker 2001). Rural areas also tend to have smaller budgets and therefore might have a greater need for the fees (Olson, Weisheit, and Ellsworth 2001). Most of the objections to economic sanctions are to fees/costs, especially economic surcharges (interest, plan fees, late fees), as these surcharges are particularly likely to impact the poor.

Fines

Fines are monetary penalties for crimes. Most of the research on fines was conducted 30 years ago, in connection with proposals to make fines more attractive as alternatives to incarceration. Hillsman (1990), a leader in this research, suggested that fines have several advantages over other types of sentencing options: (1) their level of punitiveness can be adjusted to the seriousness of the particular crime and the individual offender's criminal history and resources; (2) they are flexible in that they can be used as sole penalties or in combination with other sanctions; and (3) the funds generated through fines can be used to support the collections office and victim compensation.

Judges in the United States are often opposed to fines because they believe that fines cannot be enforced against the poor and have little effect on the wealthy (Hillsman 1990). Judges also generally do not believe that fines can be used as an alternative to probation or to incarceration (Cole, Mahoney, Thornton, and Hanson 1987).

As a result of these beliefs, in the United States fines are used primarily in courts of limited jurisdiction, particularly traffic courts (Hillsman, Sichel, and Mahoney 1984). Fines are also used for minor offenses, such as shoplifting, especially when the offender has no prior offenses and can pay the fine (Hillsman, Mahoney, Cole, and Auchter 1987). Nationally, offenders in state courts are ordered to pay fines in 38 percent of all conviction offenses: 36 percent of violent offenses, 37 percent of property offenses, 41 percent of drug offenses, 27 percent of weapons offenses, and 40 percent of other offenses (Rosenmerkel et al. 2009: Table 1.5).

In contrast to the United States, in Europe fines are much more likely to be used as the primary criminal penalty. They are the legally presumptive penalty in 80 percent to 90 percent of all sentences in the Netherlands, Germany, and Sweden, primarily because incarceration is believed to have negative effects and fines are seen as effective in preventing recidivism (Tonry and Lynch 1996). Europe uses two types of fines, prosecution diversion systems and day fines. As a diversion device, the offender agrees to pay a fine (generally the amount that would have been imposed had the offender been convicted), and the prosecutor dismisses the charges. Day fines are based on the degree of punishment needed (relating to the severity of the crime) and a specific monetary amount based on the offender's ability to pay (Hillsman 1990).

In the U.S. typically judges apply the "going rate" for fines, so that for a particular offense, all offenders are ordered to pay the same amount. However, their use of the going rate undermines one of the advantages of fines, that the amount can be adjusted to the individual offender. And, because this going rate tends to be at the lower end of the range of possible penalties, so as to accommodate the majority of offenders who are poor, the fine amount has little penalty value for wealthy offenders.

Forfeitures

Forfeitures refer to the government's seizing of property for one of four reasons: the property is illegal contraband, the property was obtained illegally, the property was gained through resources that were illegally obtained, or the property was used in connection with illegal activity. Forfeitures prevent offenders from enjoying the benefits of illegal activity, and serve a secondary purpose of providing resources to the government, which can be used or sold.

Forfeitures can be either criminal or civil (Campbell 1991). Civil forfeitures are the most common type of forfeitures (about 80 percent of all forfeitures; Blumenson and Nilsen 1998), because the standard of proof is "preponderance of the evidence." In civil forfeitures, the lawsuit is against the property that was used in the criminal activity (Williams 2002), not the owner of the property. Thus, a criminal conviction of the owner is not necessary and, according to the law, the forfeiture is not punitive. In contrast to civil forfeiture, criminal forfeiture requires that the owner be convicted of a crime "beyond a reasonable doubt." Criminal forfeiture involves the taking of assets involved in crime, and this taking is intended to be punitive.

Forfeiture laws were developed in the early years of the United States from seventeenth century English maritime law, as a means for the federal government to seize ships and cargo when their owners did not pay duties (Carpenter, Knepper, Erickson, and McDonald 2015: 10). However, it was not until 1970, with the passage of the Racketeer Influence and Corrupt Organizations Act and the Continuing Enterprise Act, supplemented by laws in 1984 and 1986 (Spaulding 1989), that forfeitures became an important part of the federal government's efforts to remove the profit motive from drug crime. Forfeitures also provide a strong incentive to law enforcement agencies to pursue drug offenders, because law enforcement agencies can use or sell the forfeited assets. The Supreme Court in *United States v. Ursery* (1996) held that the primary goals of forfeiture are remedial and nonpunitive: making sure that criminals do not benefit from their illegal actions and encouraging property owners to prevent their property from being used in criminal activities.

Annually there are about 40,000 asset seizures in the United States, almost none of which are contested (Biewen 2002). Forfeitures have been criticized because of claims that they are disproportionately instituted against racial minorities. There are also criticisms that forfeitures skew law enforcement priorities, in that the police are likely to focus on low-level drug cases in order to seize money and property (especially cars) because the funds go directly to law enforcement agencies rather than to the general government coffers (Blumenson and Nilsen 1998).

In 2014, the Justice Department's Assets Forfeiture Fund took in $4.5 billion (Carpenter et al. 2015: 5). Almost all of these forfeitures (87 percent) were civil forfeitures, which means that the burden of proof is on "property owners to prove their innocence in order to recover property" (Carpenter et al. 2015: 43). Under the equitable sharing provision of the federal civil forfeiture law, state and local law enforcement can receive up to 80 percent of proceeds. Thus, police have an incentive to cooperate with federal authorities, since state laws may be more restrictive (Carpenter et al. 2015: 6).

Problem of Setting the Amount of Sanctions

In Europe, courts generally have a great deal of information about offenders' assets and income. In contrast, in state courts in the United States, judges generally do not have much information about the offender's ability to pay. In the federal court system, where judges probably have better information about an offender's income and assets, as would be expected, fines are strongly related to ability to pay (Waldfogel 1995).

Efforts are being made in the United States to obtain better information about offenders' assets and income. The best example is the detailed eight-page survey used in Maricopa County (Phoenix) Arizona. This survey asks about four types of information: (1) 11 types of assets for the offender and the offender's spouse, (2) 23 sources of income for the offender and the offender's spouse, (3) self-employed income, and (4) 64 different monthly expenses. Verification for all of the information is required. In Maricopa County, offenders must complete the survey only if they have been delinquent in making payments. Even with such a complete data collection, however, determining ability to pay can still be problematic because work may be irregular and other monetary obligations, such as child support and formal or informal loans, can change (Katzenstein and Nagrecha 2011).

Setting the amounts of economic sanctions is especially problematic when there are multiple crimes and multiple victims. There also appears to be some unfairness in the imposition of economic sanctions as a function of location (rural vs. urban areas; Olson and Ramker 2001; Ruback, Ruth, and Shaffer 2005), type of crime (Gordon and Glaser 1991), and offender characteristics (Ruback and Shaffer 2005).

Imposition and Enforcement of Payment

Most typically in the United States, economic sanctions are used as penalties in addition to other sanctions, such as probation and incarceration (Hillsman 1990). Under the Constitution, persons cannot be imprisoned for debt. In the criminal justice system, this standard means that a probationer who does not pay fees, fines, or restitution cannot be incarcerated for nonpayment, unless after a hearing, the judge determines that the offender has the ability to pay but willfully does not (*Bearden v. Georgia*, 1983).

The different types of economic sanctions are almost always imposed together. That is, convicted offenders are given fines, fees/costs, and, if appropriate, restitution. Obviously, for offenders with limited funds, the requirement to pay one type of economic sanction means that other economic sanctions will not be paid. Although there is research indicating that sometimes judges take this zero-sum situation into account in their sentencing, that is, that there is a negative relationship between the two types of sanctions (e.g., Ruback 2004), other research has found a positive relationship between economic sanctions, suggesting that when judges believe an offender will pay one type of economic sanction they also believe that the offender will pay other types of sanctions as well.

Studies suggest that judges are more likely to order restitution for offenders who will be able to pay, meaning that better-educated and employed offenders are more likely to be ordered to pay restitution (Lurigio and Davis 1990). On average, though, less than half of court-ordered restitution is paid (Lurigio 1984; Smith, Davis, and Hillenbrand 1989). Offenders are more likely to pay restitution if they are given employment opportunities, are closely supervised, and allowed to pay in installments (Van Voorhis 1985).

In many jurisdictions, the economic sanctions, particularly fees/costs are essentially automatically imposed in every case. There is some evidence that judges impose these sanctions fairly rather than by the letter of the law. For example, in Pennsylvania judges are required to impose a fine for each conviction offense, the monies of which would be directed toward victim/witness programs in the state. Rather than impose a fine for each conviction offense in proceedings in which there were more than one conviction offense, judges tended to impose one fine for the entire proceeding rather than one fine for each conviction (Ruback and Clark 2011).

Offenders are likely to have difficulty paying economic sanctions because they have little income and few assets (Wheeler, Hissong, Slusher, and Macan 1990). Payment is more likely if the offender has ties to the community (such as being employed, attending school) and less likely if the offender has a longer criminal record (Davis and Lurigio 1992). Fines are more likely to be paid if the amounts are reasonable in light of the offender's ability to pay, if the offender's payments are closely monitored, and if there are penalties for nonpayment (Hillsman 1990). In many cases, there is no penalty for nonpayment of court-ordered fines (Langan 1994; Petersilia and Turner 1993), and judges are reluctant to revoke probation for failing to pay (Wheeler et al. 1990).

There is limited research on the extent to which individual and contextual factors affect the imposition of economic sanctions. With regard to individual-level factors, the assumption is that factors related to ability to pay should be related to the imposition of economic sanctions. Thus, judges should be more likely to impose economic sanctions on wealthy rather than poor offenders, on older rather than younger offenders, on white rather than minority offenders, and perhaps on male rather than female offenders.

With regard to contextual factors, the assumption is that judges would take into account the overall poverty of the jurisdiction and would be less likely to impose economic sanctions in areas where rates of poverty were higher. Enforcement of economic sanctions varies across jurisdictions in part because there are variations in the extent to which jurisdictions use these monies to fund the operation of the criminal justice system. Ruback, Ruth, and Shaffer (2005) found that a change in Pennsylvania law mandating restitution imposition increased the rate of imposition of restitution for eligible cases from 38 percent before the law to 63 percent after the law. This increase was due to judges' agreement with the law, mechanisms in place to help victims, and the location of the victim/witness assistance office within the judiciary (Ruback and Shaffer 2005).

Unfairness of Costs and Fees

Most economic sanctions are costs and fees. At the individual level, offenders who committed traffic offenses had the highest amounts of economic sanctions imposed, followed by drug offenders, person offenders, and property offenders (Ruback and Clark 2011). These costs and fees are unfair to many offenders who may have little or no money but who face charges of hundreds or thousands of dollars, which they are unlikely to ever be able to pay. In addition, aside from affecting their time under criminal justice supervision, these economic sanctions may adversely affect their ability to obtain employment, credit, and housing (Harris, Evans, and Beckett 2011). Other collateral effects include interference with paying living expenses and child support, and with employment, especially if a car is needed to get to employment.

Costs and fees are unfair, especially to the poor. As argued in the American Law Institute's Model Penal Code, "criminal offenders should not be treated as a special class of taxpayers who may be called upon to pay for criminal justice programs and operations that are otherwise underfunded by state legislatures" (Reitz 2015). Because these added costs are borne by offenders, they amount to an additional punishment beyond what has traditionally been imposed on convicted offenders.

These user fees are explicitly intended to raise revenue (Bannon, Nagrecha, and Diller 2010). In recent years, private corporations have begun operating criminal justice services that had previously been performed by the government. Because they have a pecuniary interest in the behavior of the offenders they deal with, specifically wanting the offenders to continue making payments on the original owed amounts and on any additional fees, penalties, and surcharges that may have accrued, the field has become known as "poverty capitalism" (Edsall 2014) and an "offender-funded probation industry" (Albin-Lackey 2014). One of the primary criticisms of private companies being involved in the criminal justice system is that they are profiting from the misfortunes of victims and offenders. Furthermore, the private companies' focus on profit may cause them to want offenders not to succeed, so that they can make more money.

Particularly in the South, costs and fees are used to transfer governmental responsibilities to private agencies, which is one reason why the Southern Poverty Law Center successfully sued the City of Montgomery, Alabama for what is termed "pay-only probation." Not surprisingly then, studies have recommended that fees be discontinued, particularly fees that impose additional costs on the indigent, such as payment plan fees, late fees, collection fees, and interest (Bannon et al. 2010).

Aside from being unfair, in general, fees are likely counterproductive—what O'Malley (2011) calls "economically irrational"—because they cost more to implement than the money that is brought in. Additionally, the use of fees can interfere with other economic sanctions (Ruback 2015), specifically restitution to victims and fines to the state, which could be used as alternatives to incarceration.

In Pennsylvania, there is significant variation between counties both in the number of different types of economic sanctions imposed (and the resulting complexity of the system of economic sanctions), and in the average and median amounts of economic sanctions imposed per case (Ruback and Clark 2011). Costs/fees that are unique to a county raise a troubling question. How fair is it to an offender if the burden of paying for the costs of criminal justice is shifted to offenders only if the county is poor and therefore cannot afford to pay?

The poor, relative to the non-poor, have to pay a larger percentage of their net worth for fees and costs, and, when economic surcharges (interest, late fees) are included, the poor may have to pay larger absolute amounts, because wealthier offenders can pay the entire amount owed and will not have to pay interest. Given low skills, low education, and unemployment, offenders' payment of these sanctions may interfere with their ability to live without committing crime.

Although there is little research on the topic, payment and recidivism are likely affected by four factors: (1) the type of economic sanction—costs and fees leading to higher recidivism, (2) the type of offender—those who are more tied to the community should be more likely to pay and less likely to recidivate, (3) the type of county—counties differ in their level of imposition, their level of monitoring, and their level of enforcement of punishment, and (4) the type of offense—poor offenders are probably more likely to commit crimes aimed at obtaining money. The early research on restitution was conducted with juveniles (Galaway and Hudson 1975) and generally found support for the effectiveness of restitution payment in lowering recidivism. Other research also suggests that the payment of restitution can reduce recidivism for both juveniles (e.g., Farrington and Welsh 2005; Haynes, Cares, and Ruback 2014) and adults (Heinz, Galaway, and Hudson 1976; Outlaw and Ruback 1999), consistent with theoretical work on restorative justice (Sherman, Schmidt and Rogan 1992) and reintegrative shaming (Braithwaite 1989). Research is needed regarding the effect of costs/fees on recidivism.

For the wealthy, economic sanctions have little impact, because the amounts are set for the average offender, not the wealthy, and thus are less of a burden for the wealthy. Moreover, amounts are generally not adjusted for inflation, meaning that the actual economic impact has eroded over the years. For the poor, economic sanctions have little impact because the amounts are simply one more debt that they will not pay. However, it can be onerous, because courts often rely on family members to make payments, putting an additional burden on them. Whoever makes the payment, for the poor the amounts that are paid could be going to living expenses (rent, transportation) and child support.

The Future of Economic Sanctions

What is likely to happen to economic sanctions in the next 25 years? First, it is important to recognize the continuing pressures that economic sanctions continue, particularly by having offenders pay for more of their interactions with the criminal justice system. There is also increasing concern that crime victims receive restitution (Ruback and Bergstrom 2006).

Despite these pressures for more economic sanctions, however, dissatisfaction with economic sanctions may bring about change. The most important of these criticisms concern costs/fees. These criticisms include philosophical issues, one being that the imposition of punishment is a governmental function that should not be borne by defendants, particularly when, as with the costs of a defense attorney for the poor, the issue involves a constitutional right (Ruback 2015). Other criticisms include the heavy burden these costs/fees impose on the poor and the fact that the payments of these costs/fees interfere with the payment of restitution to victims and of fines to the state (Ruback 2015). In 2016, the Department of Justice criticized the policies targeting the poor that courts used to maximize fee collection (Apuzzo 2016), and the Model Penal Code has called for an end to costs/fees.

Regarding fines, the primary criticism comes from the Model Penal Code: judges imposing fines should take into account the offender's ability to pay. One way to address this and other problems associated with fines is to follow the European concept of day fines, by which offenders are punished in units (based on the severity of the conviction offense) that are translated into fine amounts depending on the income of the defendant, the idea being that, even though the amounts of the fine might differ because of different income levels, the punitive component would be the same because the fine amount would be relative to income. This income-driven standard has been used in other governmental functions, such as income-based student loan repayment in Australia (Supiano 2016).

Conclusion

All economic sanctions are not alike, and how they should be thought of depends on the function they serve (Ruback 2015). Restitution to victims is important because it can provide an institutional mechanism for compensating victims for their losses. It may help offenders take responsibility for their crime, and payment may result in lower recidivism. Thus, restitution promotes the notion of restorative justice, whereby victims receive compensation for their losses and offenders can be reintegrated into their communities. Fines may serve the goals of punishment and deterrence and may be used as intermediate sanctions instead of incarceration, although they are generally not used that way in the United States today. The money from fines can be used for general governmental purposes or for specific goals, such as a victim compensation fund). Costs/fees can cover some of the costs of criminal justice, but those costs are governmental duties that should be borne by government and that may cause a conflict of interest in the courts and agencies that impose and collect these sanctions (Reitz 2015). Moreover, the payment of costs/fees interferes with the payment of restitution and fines. In recent years, scholars have generally been opposed to costs/fees (Bannon et al. 2010; Harris et al. 2011; Reitz 2015; Ruback 2015).

Overall, unless the amounts are set in light of offenders' salary and assets, economic sanctions are likely to be unjust to the poor and to generally have little impact on the wealthy. The issues created by economic sanctions concerning fairness, effectiveness, and recidivism have been the focus of the Model Penal Code (Reitz 2015) and will be the subject of much debate in coming years.

References

Albin-Lackey, Chris. Human Rights Watch, *Profiting from Probation*. February 5, 2014. Retrieved May 10, 2017 from www.hrw.org/print/reports/2014/02/05/profiting-probation

Apuzzo, Matt. 2016. "Justice Dept. Condemns Profit-minded Court Policies Targeting the Poor." The *New York Times*, March 14. Retrieved May 10, 2017 from www.nytimes.com/2016/03/15/us/politics/justice-dept-condemns-profit-minded-court-policies-targeting-the-poor.html?emc=eta1

Bannon, Alicia, Mitali Nagrecha, and Rebekah Diller. 2010. *Criminal Justice Debt: A Barrier to Re-entry*. New York: Brennan Center for Justice.
Bearden v. Georgia, 461 U.S. 660 (1983).
Biewen, J. 2002, April 27. "Weekend Edition: Asset Forfeiture from Drug-related Arrests and How Some Law Enforcement Agencies Use the Funds." [Radio broadcast]. Washington, DC: National Public Radio.
Blumenson, Eric, and Eva Nilsen. 1998. "Policing for Profit: The Drug War's Hidden Economic Agenda." *University of Chicago Law Review* 65: 35–114.
Bonczar, Thomas P. 1997. "Characteristics of Adults on Probation, 1995." *Traffic* 4(9): 10–12.
Braithwaite, John. 1989. *Crime, Shame and Reintegration*. Cambridge: Cambridge University Press.
Campbell, A.W. 1991. *Law of Sentencing*, 2nd ed. Deerfield, IL: Clark Boardman.
Carpenter, Dick M., Lisa Knepper, Angela C. Erickson, and Jennifer McDonald. 2015. *Policing for Profit: The Abuse of Civil Asset Forfeiture*, 2nd ed. Washington, DC: Institute for Justice.
Cole, George F., Barry Mahoney, Marlene Thornton, and Roger A. Hanson. 1987. *The Practices and Attitudes of Trial Court Judges Regarding Fines as a Criminal Sanction*. Washington, DC: National Institute of Justice.
Davis, Robert C., and Arthur J. Lurigio. 1992. "Compliance with Court-ordered Restitution: Who Pays?" *Perspectives* 16: 25–31.
Durose, Matthew R., and Patrick A. Langan. 2003. *Felony Sentences in State Courts, 2003*. (BJS Bulletin NCJ 198821). Washington, DC: U.S. Department of Justice.
Edsall, Thomas B. 2014. "The Expanding World of Poverty Capitalism." *The New York Times*, August 26. Retrieved May 10, 2017 from www.nytimes.com/2014/08/27/opinion/thomas-edsall-the-expanding-world-of-poverty-capitalism.html
Farrington, David P., and Brandon C. Welsh. 2005. "Randomized Experiments in Criminology: What Have We Learned in the Last Two Decades?" *Journal of Experimental Criminology* 1: 9–38.
Galaway, Burt, and Joe Hudson. 1975. "Restitution and Rehabilitation: Some Central Issues." Pp. 255–264 in *Considering the Victim: Readings in Restitution and Victim Compensation*, edited by J. Hudson and B. Galaway. Springfield, IL: Thomas.
Gordon, Margaret A., and Daniel Glaser. 1991. "The Use and Effects of Financial Penalties in Municipal Courts." *Criminology* 29: 651–676.
Harland, Alan T. 1981. *Restitution to Victims of Personal and Household Crimes*. Washington, DC: Bureau of Justice Statistics.
Harris, Alexes, Heather Evans, and Katherine Beckett. 2011. "Courtesy Stigma and Monetary Sanctions: Toward a Socio-cultural Theory of Punishment." *American Sociological Review* 76: 234–264.
Haynes, Stacy Hoskins, Allison C. Cares, and R. Barry Ruback. 2014. "Juvenile Economic Sanctions: An Analysis of their Imposition, Payment, and Effect on Recidivism." *Criminology & Public Policy* 13: 31–60.
Haynes, Stacy Hoskins, Allison C. Cares, and R. Barry Ruback. 2015. "Reducing the Harm of Criminal Victimization: The Role of Restitution." *Violence and Victims* 30: 450–469.
Heinz, Joe, Burt Galaway, and Joe Hudson. 1976. "Restitution or Parole: A Follow-up Study of Adult Offenders." *Social Service Review* 50: 148–156.
Hillsman, Sally. 1990. "Fines and Day Fines." Pp. 49–98 in *Crime and Justice: A Review of Research*, edited by M. Tonry and N. Morris. Chicago, IL: University of Chicago Press.
Hillsman, Sally, Barry Mahoney, George F. Cole, and B. Auchter. 1987. *Fines as Criminal Sanctions*. National Institute of Justice.
Hillsman, Sally, Joyce L. Sichel, and Barry Mahoney. 1984. *Fines in Sentencing: A Study of the Use of the Fine as a Criminal Sanction*. Washington, DC: National Institute of Justice.
Katzenstein, Mary F., and Mitali Nagrecha. 2011. "A New Punishment Regime." *Criminology & Public Policy* 10: 555–568.
Langan, Patrick A. 1994. "Between Prison and Probation: Intermediate Sanctions." *Science* 264: 791–793.
Lurigio, A. 1984. *The Relationship between Offender Characteristics and Fulfillment of Financial Restitution*. Chicago, IL: Cook County Adult Probation Department.

Lurigio, Arthur J., and Davis, R. C. 1990. "Does a Threatening Letter Increase Compliance with Restitution Orders? A Field Experiment." *Crime and Delinquency* 36: 537–548.

McGillis, Daniel. 1986. *Crime Victim Restitution: An Analysis of Approaches*. Washington, DC: NIJ.

Moen, Kelse. 2013. "Choice in Criminal Law: Victims, Defendants, and the Option of Restitution." *Cornell Journal of Law and Public Policy* 22: 733–767.

Office for Victims of Crime. 1998. *New Directions from the Field: Victims' Rights and Services for the 21st Century*. Washington, DC: U.S. Department of Justice.

Olson, David E., and Gerard F. Ramker. 2001. "Crime Does Not Pay, but Criminals May: Factors Influencing the Imposition and Collection of Probation Fees." *Justice System Journal* 22: 29–46.

Olson, David E., Ralph A. Weisheit, and Thomas Ellsworth, T. 2001. "Getting Down to Business: A Comparison of Rural and Urban Probationers, Probation Sentences, and Probation Outcomes." *Journal of Contemporary Criminal Justice* 17: 4–18.

O'Malley, Pat. 2011. "Politicizing the Case for Fines." *Criminology and Public Policy* 10: 547–553.

Outlaw, Maureen C., and R. Barry Ruback. 1999. "Predictors and Outcomes of Victim Restitution Orders." *Justice Quarterly* 16: 847–869.

Petersilia, Joan. 1997. "Probation in the United States." Pp. 149–200 in *Crime and Justice: A Review of Research*, edited by M. Tonry. Chicago, IL: University of Chicago Press.

Petersilia, Joan, and Susan Turner. 1993. "Intensive Probation and Parole." Pp. 281–335 in *Crime and Justice: A Review of Research*, edited by M. Tonry. Chicago, IL: University of Chicago Press.

Reitz, C.E. 2015. "The Fees Collected by All Governmental Agencies in a Representative Kansas County in 1938." Master's Thesis, Kansas State University, Department of Economics and Sociology.

Rosenmerkel, Sean, Matthew Durose, and Donald Farole. 2009. "Felony Sentences in State Courts, 2006—Statistical Tables." *NCJ 226846*. Washington, DC: Bureau of Justice Statistics.

Ruback, R. Barry. 2004. "The Imposition of Economic Sanctions in Philadelphia." *Federal Probation* 68: 21–26.

Ruback, R. Barry. 2015. "The Benefits and Costs of Economic Sanctions: Considering the Victim, the Offender, and Society." *Minnesota Law Review* 99: 1779–1836.

Ruback, R. Barry, and Mark H. Bergstrom. 2006. "Economic Sanctions in Criminal Justice: Purposes, Effects, and Implications." *Criminal Justice and Behavior* 33: 242–273.

Ruback, R. Barry, and Valerie A. Clark. 2011. "Economic Sanctions in Pennsylvania: Complex and Inconsistent." *Duquesne Law Review* 49: 751–772.

Ruback, R. Barry, Andrew S. Gladfelter, and Brendan Lantz. 2014. "Paying Restitution: An Experimental Analysis of the Effects of Information and Rationale." *Criminology & Public Policy* 13: 405–436.

Ruback, R. Barry, Gretchen R. Ruth, and Jennifer N. Shaffer. 2005. "Assessing the Impact of Statutory Change: A Statewide Multilevel Analysis of Restitution Orders in Pennsylvania." *Crime & Delinquency* 51: 318–342.

Ruback, R. Barry, and Jennifer N. Shaffer. 2005. "The Role of Victim-related Factors in Victim Restitution: A Multi-method Analysis of Restitution in Pennsylvania." *Law and Human Behavior* 29: 657–681.

Sherman, Lawrence W., Janell Schmidt, and Dennis P. Rogan. 1992. *Policing Domestic Violence: Experiments and Dilemmas*. New York: Free Press.

Smith, Barbara, Robert Carl Davis, and Susan W. Hillenbrand. 1989. *Improving Enforcement of Court-ordered Restitution*. Chicago, IL: American Bar Association.

Spaulding, Karla R. 1989. "'Hit them Where it Hurts': RICO Criminal Forfeitures and White-collar Crime." *Journal of Criminal Law and Criminology* 80: 197–292.

Supiano, B. 2016. "What America Can Learn from Australia's Student-loan System." *The Chronicle of Higher Education*, January 5. Retrieved May 16, 2017 from http://chronicle.com/article/What-America-Can-Learn-From/234796?cid=at&utm_source=at&utm_medium=en&elq=579c4036542 4411f8c2f0f1e7ecc532f&elqCampaignId=2154&elqaid=7398&elqat=1&elqTrackId=92adbbe4dc0d 4ed49ebc5cfcc9d8119f

Tonry, Michael, and Mary Lynch. 1996. "Intermediate Sanctions." Pp. 99–144 in *Crime and Justice: A Review of Research*, edited by M. Tonry. Chicago, IL: University of Chicago Press.

United States v. Ursery 518 U.S. 216 (1996).

Van Voorhis, Patricia. 1985. "Restitution Outcome and Probationers' Assessments of Restitution: The Effects of Moral Development." *Criminal Justice and Behavior* 12: 259–287.

Waldfogel, Joel. 1995. "Are Fines and Prison Terms Used Efficiently? Evidence on Federal Fraud Offenders." *The Journal of Law and Economics* 38: 107–139.

Weisburd, David, Tomer Einat, and Matt Kowalski. 2008. "The Miracle of the Cells: An Experimental Study of Interventions to Increase Payment of Court-ordered Financial Obligations." *Criminology & Public Policy* 7: 9–36.

Wheeler, Gerald R., Rodney V. Hissong, Morgan P. Slusher, and Therese M. Macan. 1990. "Economic Sanctions in Criminal Justice: Dilemma for Human Service?" *Justice System Journal* 14: 63–77.

Williams, Marian R. 2002. "Civil Asset Forfeiture: Where Does the Money Go?" *Criminal Justice Review* 27: 321–329.

8 Corporal Punishment

Graeme R. Newman

There are two major misconceptions about corporal punishment in criminal justice: (1) that it is never used in the USA and other Western countries, and (2) if used it would violate the Eighth Amendment of the U.S. Constitution. While judicial corporal punishment was last administered in Delaware in 1952, corporal punishment continues to be used inside prisons as a means of prison discipline, though its extent is unknown. It is probably also used in juvenile institutions, considering that currently at least 20 states of the U.S. still allow corporal punishment in schools. The U.S. Supreme Court has never ruled judicial corporal punishment as cruel and unusual, though in the recent case *Brown v. Plata* (2011), it has ruled that excessive punishment in the form of prison is. Moreover, some argue that prison is a form of corporal punishment.

Definition of Corporal Punishment

There are two ways of defining corporal punishment: narrow or broad. The narrow definition is the intentional infliction of acute temporary pain on the body for an infraction against a rule. Examples of this kind of punishment are the whip, lash, electric shock, paddle (as in the Michael Fay case in 1994), the strap, switch, cane and so on. The broad definition is the intentional infliction of pain on a person for an infraction against a rule. Examples of this type of punishment include denial of sleep, harsh diet, solitary confinement, mutilation including castration, branding and the various pains of imprisonment including rape in prison and prison violence. Some of the pains of imprisonment are not "intentional" but simply come with the punishment of prison. That is to say, a judge does not sentence an offender to be raped in prison. The sentence is simply for a certain number of months or years in prison.

Corporal Punishment and Torture

Corporal punishment is widely assumed to be the equivalent of torture since many techniques of torture do inflict pain on the body. However, torture is vastly different from corporal punishment because it aims not so much to inflict pain on the body as to completely overwhelm the individual, to take over both body and mind. Its technique is to establish four conditions in the accused: debility, dependency, dread, and disorientation (Suedfeld 1990: 3) by intimidating, isolating, and indoctrinating the accused. Torture is a process essentially used to extract information, usually in the form of confessions or names of accomplices. Judicial corporal punishment is not used to those ends, or if it is, it is torture. A paradox of torture is that the torturer depends totally on the accused to give up information, confess. Thus, there is always the tendency for the torturer to use pain in excess, the paradox being of course, that the accused may say anything to stop the pain, which means that confessions under torture can never really be trusted. The torturer is therefore doomed to failure. However, it is the excess of punishment, infliction of extreme pain, in the process of torture that is often mistakenly equated with corporal punishment. Historically, this is probably why corporal punishment as a sentence was abolished.

Corporal Punishment and Capital Punishment

There is some confusion between corporal punishment and capital punishment because some methods of putting to death may include the infliction of pain on the offender. Beheading, presumably the forerunner of the guillotine, has traditionally been thought of as offering the most "painless" death if administered expertly. The invention of the "trap" for hanging was also designed to avoid the long and dreadful jiggling of the hanged offender as he convulsed his way to death on the gallows. The firing squad used in the state of Utah is also "painless" so long as the squad is well trained. The method of lethal injection accompanied by various muscle relaxing drugs in the USA is an extension of the idea of painless killing. It is an effort to avoid the accusation that killing someone is inhumane, as though doing it painlessly removes this blemish. It also has the advantage of being bloodless. However, other forms of the death penalty also incorporate corporal punishment by intentionally inflicting pain on the accused, sometimes even leaving it open as to whether the offender will die or not, such as stoning to death or crucifixion under Shari'a law. In any case, the recent history of corporal punishment in Western countries is closely bound to the history of the death penalty and its eventual abolition in the U.K. and elsewhere in Europe. In the nineteenth century various campaigns were conducted to abolish corporal punishment from criminal justice throughout Europe, Russia, the U.K. and the Americas, these coming to fruition early in the twentieth century.

History of Corporal Punishment

The Romans and the Greeks used corporal punishments extensively. The Romans used torture as a matter of course in conducting interrogations, especially of slaves whose testimony as witnesses was never allowed unless obtained under torture. The paddling of children by their tutors was routine and the whipping of slaves common. However, well before the Romans whipping was a recommended punishment in the Bible, in particular, "If the guilty man deserves to be beaten, the judge shall make him lie down and have him flogged in his presence with the number of lashes his crime deserves, but he must not give him more than forty lashes" (Deuteronomy 25: 2–3). Note here that the insistence on proportionality (matching the punishment to the crime) and the placing of limits to avoid excess, both principles that were largely lost in the eighteenth and nineteenth centuries AD. Of particular significance was the excessive use of the lash in the various navies of the world as the countries of Europe and U.K. sailed the oceans to further their colonial interests. Five hundred lashes and more were not uncommon for offences such as disobeying an officer. In 1776, General George Washington petitioned the Continental Congress for authority to impose 100 lashes in lieu of the former limit of 39 (Gleissner 2013). However, by the turn of the nineteenth century, the use of the lash in the navy and military was abolished in all these countries, possibly brought to a head by the Revolt of the Whip in Rio De Janeiro by Afro-American seamen that lasted for two weeks in 1910 (Morgan 2014).

There is a long history of the use of corporal punishment on slaves, dating from at least Roman times as noted above. However, there was an inbuilt limit to avoid excessive use of corporal punishment on slaves because they were valuable property and their resale value was affected if they had signs of stripes from whipping. In the U.S. disciplinary corporal punishment of slaves was legal but "prohibited or discouraged" from being cruel, unusual or excessive (Gleissner 2013: 727). Florida established a punishment of up to 39 stripes of corporal punishment or the pillory for wandering ex-slaves after the civil war. However, the Civil Rights Act of 1866 made it a crime to subject former slaves to "different punishment, pains or penalties" (Gleissner 2013: 727).

Abolition of Corporal Punishment

Michel Foucault, in his book *Discipline and Punish* argued that prison arose as a unique punishment to replace the punishments of the body. Though he did not explicitly show that corporal punishments were replaced by prison, he did show that the abolition of capital punishment, especially the gory and public methods of administering the death penalty such as drawing and quartering in Europe and England did signify the rise of punishment of the "soul" by the use of prison as a substitute for the death penalty. The idea that prison punished the mind rather than the body introduced a serious misconception about prison as a punishment among liberal reformers and criminologists who frequently cited the "father" of modern criminal justice, Cesare Beccaria, in support of this notion. Beccaria did oppose the death penalty with his famous critique that life in prison was far worse a punishment, but he still favored corporal punishment for violent crimes. Some have argued in fact that corporal punishment increased in use in the U.K. as a substitute for the abolition of the death penalty, or at least its partial abolition when moved behind prison walls out of public view (Gleissner 2013). It is likely that in fact it was the abolition of corporal punishment as well as capital punishment that began the rise of prison as a substitute. In the early nineteenth century we also saw the use of transportation as a punishment for those crimes not receiving the death penalty, which also brought with it (like prison) various corporal punishments of whipping on the ship on the way to the colony, and corporal punishment of the lash within the prison colony. By the 1950s, judicial corporal punishment had been abolished or fallen out of use in most countries of the Western world, replaced mainly by prisons that would become mass incarceration in the USA and the Gulag Archipelago in Russia.

Varieties of Corporal Punishment

There have been many kinds of corporal punishments used throughout history, though few of them remain today. The common element of all such punishments has been their administration in public view, though more recently judicial corporal punishment has been administered within prison walls, as was the well-known case of the paddle applied to Michael Fay in Singapore in 1994. A short, though incomplete list of corporal punishments is as follows (Newman 2008):

- the pillory and stocks: in which the offender was constrained by wooden devices, head and hands locked in place, erected in the town square. Onlookers were usually free to post notes on the device either of encouragement or derision. Similarly, they could pelt them with rotten eggs or vegetables or even stones if they so wished;
- stoning to death: this is possibly the oldest corporal punishment—though technically speaking it is an aggravated form of the death penalty—mentioned very early in the Bible, still used in Islamic countries that have retained Shari'a law;
- the ducking stool: the offender (usually a nuisance or disobedient wife) was affixed to a chair that was then dipped into a pool or stream and out again;
- scold's bridle: usually for a wife who talked too much. A metal contraption that fitted over the head and constrained the mouth. More severe forms clamped or pierced the tongue.

- castration, mutilation, severing of limbs, branding on face and elsewhere: the modern use of castration is of course not done in public, but mutilations are public in Shari'a law;
- prison-related corporal punishments: solitary confinement, restricted diet, deprivation of sleep, whip or lash, confinement in small space, are just a few of the bodily pains of imprisonment;
- the whip, lash, strap, paddle, "cat-o'-nine-tails", the knout, the birch, and many instruments used to apply acute pain to the offender: this is by far the most common corporal punishment to this day. Its advantages are many: it can be varied in intensity, given the type of instrument used and part of the body to which it is applied. It can be varied in amount by counting the number of stripes applied. It can be applied over a period of time in different schedules, all at once, or in small numbers of stripes in batches over a longer period of time. It is portable and requires no special equipment, although there are many such instruments available. Compared to prison, it is cheap. The negative is that, probably, the punisher needs some training in how to wield the whip, consistently strike the desired part of the body, consistently administer each stripe with the same intensity, have the stamina to endure administration of the required number of lashes. It is also, obviously, a blatantly violent punishment that may be, to some, unpleasant to administer, though to onlookers it may inflame the senses, or "teach violence" which may be the very type of act for which the offender is being punished.
- the Scarlet Letter, not strictly speaking a corporal punishment, requiring the offender to wear a letter or carry a sign depicting the crime: this punishment is the pure form of public humiliation that accompanies most if not all corporal punishments administered in public view.

Corporal Punishments of Shari'a Law

Because of the growing population of Muslims in the United States and other Western nations, the role of Shari'a law and its punishment has come considerably more into public view. There is even the call for Shari'a law to be available to Muslim communities in the USA. Various opinion polls have reported that a slight majority of U.S. resident Muslims would support Shari'a law in their communities (Arafa and Burns 2015; Ghassemi 2009). The majority of punishments laid down by Shari'a are corporal punishments. In contrast to Western law, Shari'a has few actual crimes (though many religious infractions derived from the Koran and related scholarly treatises), and probably a greater variety of punishments. The list below compiled from Peters (2005) and Abdel-Haleem, Sherif, and Daniels (2003) summarizes the corporal and capital punishments generally available in Islamic countries. To the Western eye some of the punishments may seem barbaric. However, there is considerable debate as to how often such punishments are used for particular crimes. Defenders of Shari'a law argue that, just as the death penalty in the United States is administered only for a tiny portion of murderers, the same applies in Shari'a law for cases that might receive mutilating or capital punishments and even flogging. The claim is that the harsh-looking punishments are maximum punishments that are rarely applied. Unfortunately, there are no statistics to back up this claim.

- reprimand—the least severe, usually reserved for the elite classes;
- fines—compensation to victims; there is much controversy as to whether money can be paid to the State;
- some property confiscated until offender "goes straight";
- exposure to public scorn—all serious punishments public (except prison);

- banishment—for banditry, unlawful sexual intercourse. Not allowed for women;
- imprisonment—supposedly only for debtors, not a penal punishment. However, it is now used for *ta'zir* crimes;
- flogging—probably the most common punishment. Must be with a leather whip, stripes deposited all over the body excluding the head and genital area. Exceptions or adjustments may be made for health of sickness of the offender;
- amputation of the right hand—cut off and cauterized in boiling oil. If the hand has been previously cut off, the left foot is amputated;
- cross amputation—four fingers of the hand and four toes cut off (Shiite law);
- retaliation for injuries—amputation or blinding may be done to one who has inflicted such injuries on others;
- death penalty—mostly beheading by sword. For a pregnant woman, postponed until she has given birth;
- stoning to death—with medium sized stones; first stones (according to some sects) must be thrown by significant witnesses who testified to the crime;
- crucifixion—sometimes crucified after death, others first crucified then stabbed in chest, others (Shiite) crucified for three days and if still alive, the life is spared.

Cruel and Unusual?

It is widely believed that the infliction of corporal punishment is cruel because it intentionally causes pain or suffering of the offender and, depending on the method of inflicting it, may result in blood being shed, screaming, or other behavior of the offender denoting pain. However, on further inspection, it is likely that the most abhorrent aspect of corporal punishment is that it displays in full view the subjection of an individual by one who represents the heavy weight of government authority. This nexus between individual and authority is depicted most clearly by a violent stroke of the lash. Not only is it a shocking thing to suffer, but it also is a shocking thing to witness. It is the raw view of government that has the monopoly on force. The same nexus occurs when a police officer arrests a suspect. It is a physical confrontation between the State and a citizen. Offenders may deserve to be punished for their crimes, but for the last couple of centuries we have pushed criminal punishment into the bureaucracies of court processing and especially into the secrecy of prisons. The enlightenment thinkers viewed punishment as a necessary evil, that we grudgingly gave up part of our liberty to the State in order to enjoy an ordered society (Newman and Marongiu 2009). In sum, intentionally inflicting pain is not in and of itself cruel, otherwise we would call dentists cruel, not to mention violent sports. What makes it cruel is its excess, not the physical infliction of pain itself. But is corporal punishment "cruel and unusual," echoing the Eighth Amendment of the U.S. Constitution?

The classic case of judicial corporal punishment decided by the Supreme Court is that of *Weems v. U.S.* on May 2, 1910; the United States Supreme Court considered the case of Mr. Weems who had been convicted of falsifying official records of the United States Coastguard, which resulted in the government being defrauded of 612 pesos (the crime occurred in the Philippines). The Philippine Criminal Code mandated 15 years in prison with hard labor for this offense, plus the added punishment of *cadena temporal*, which required him to be constantly in chains. In addition, he lost all political rights during imprisonment, was subject to permanent surveillance after his release, and was fined 4,000 pesetas.

The Philippine Constitution contains the same clause about cruel and unusual punishment as does the Eighth Amendment to the U. S. Constitution that was adopted in 1791: "That excessive bail ought not be required, nor excessive fines imposed, nor cruel and unusual punishments inflicted."

The Supreme Court struck down the sentence as cruel and unusual. However, the reasons it gave for this decision have been the subject of debate until this day. A number of legal scholars and historians argue that it is a fallacy to believe that the phrase "cruel and unusual," lifted from the English Bill of Rights of 1689, was included in that Bill of Rights specifically to exclude barbarous bodily punishments (Granucci 1969: 839–865, Hall 1995). This could not have been the intent of the framers of the English Bill of Rights, since barbarous punishments were used for at least another hundred years after 1689. What is clear is that their intent was to forbid the abuse of governmental power. This was the preoccupation of the English in the seventeenth century. As such, the phrase could apply to any kind of punishment at all.

It is true that the court in *Weems* did consider the interpretation of abuse of governmental power as a factor in the intent of the framers of the English Bill of Rights. But the Court seemed to find it necessary to go further in justifying its decision, especially that part of it that focused on proportionality: that is, the idea that 15 years of prison was too much compared to the seriousness of the offense. This opened the way for subsequent appeals against excessive prison terms for seemingly minor crimes. It also established a precedent for the arguments in the 2011 case of *Brown v. Plata* that prison was an excessive punishment both in amount and quality (deplorable prison conditions). This decision came after many cases in which the Supreme Court refused to rule any prison term as excessive. In fact, in 1991, the court even refused to overturn a sentence of life in prison without parole for possession of 672 grams of cocaine (*Harmelin v. Michigan* 1991). So it would appear that while the Supreme Court had introduced the notion of proportionality in *Weems*, it had never taken the rule very seriously and therefore the only way to explain its decision was to conclude that it was the "extras" of *cadena* (the corporal punishment) that were enough to make the Philippine case cruel and unusual.

Why did the Court make trouble for itself by addressing the proportionality question in *Weems*? One can only speculate on this, but it is likely that the reason was the wholly "quantitative" conception of prison as a punishment so that it is the *amount* of punishment that is linked to proportionality, not the *type* of punishment (with the minor exception that it found the death penalty disproportionate for rape in *Coker v. Georgia*). But the framers of the English Bill of Rights could not have had proportionality in mind, because there was no conception of the numerical base of punishment until the utilitarians such as Beccaria and Bentham introduced it in the eighteenth century (Newman and Marongiu 2009). Before that time, an offender was not sentenced to a certain number of lashes, but merely to be whipped. By the time the Americans came to frame their Constitution, the utilitarians had reached the height of their ideological power and there is good reason to believe that Beccaria's ideas had penetrated the minds of the framers of the American Constitution (Bessler 2014; Newman and Marongiu 2009; Schwartz and Wishingrad 1975). So the chances are that the framers of the Constitution believed "cruel and unusual" included the quantitative notion of proportionality.

Notwithstanding the different interpretations of the framers of the Constitution, most decisions on cruel and unusual punishment have assumed that the Eighth Amendment "expresses the revulsion of civilized man against barbarous acts—the 'cry of horror' against man's inhumanity to his fellow man" (*Robinson v. California* 1962, Mr. Justice Douglas concurring). Other interpretations have made similar pronouncements referring to the "traditional humanity of modern Anglo-American law." Clearly, this "humanity" was assumed, or defined, merely in terms of the absence of corporal punishment, since the court had consistently failed to rule as cruel and unusual a number of prison terms that were clearly out of proportion and excessive by anyone's standards.

Until *Brown v. Plata*, not only did the Supreme Court consistently refuse to overturn excessive prison sentences, it also refused to rule on the question of whether particular conditions in prisons violated the cruel and unusual clause. For example, in 1979 the Court overturned a lower federal court decision that found that numerous practices and conditions in a New York City detention center were cruel and unusual. These conditions included: the inmates were defendants awaiting trial, they were subject to unannounced searches, strip searches were conducted of friends and family, and Christmas packages were refused (*Bell v. Wolfish* 1979).

The court made a similar decision in June, 1981, when it rejected the opinion of a federal district court that double-celling in an Ohio state prison in cells designed for one constituted cruel and unusual punishment. The majority of the Supreme Court Justices concluded that "the constitution does not mandate comfortable prisons, and prisons of (this) type which house persons convicted of serious crimes, cannot be free of discomfort" (*Rhodes v. Chapman* 1981).

The Court also refused to rule that brutality and violence in prisons constitute cruel and unusual punishment. In *Ingraham v. Wright* (1977) the Court noted that although prison brutality is part of the total punishment that an individual is subjected to for his crime and, as such, is a proper subject for Eighth Amendment scrutiny, nevertheless, the protection afforded by the Eighth Amendment is limited after incarceration; only the unnecessary and wanton infliction of pain constitutes cruel and unusual punishment.

One can agree with the Court, that there is no compelling reason to make prisons comfortable. But the clear irony of the Court's position was that it seemed to affirm the infliction of harsh conditions, especially violence, upon the inmates largely because they are by-products of prison itself, whereas if we specifically chose to apply a violent or harsh punishment on a criminal, then this would be unconstitutional, because it would be an act of "barbarous punishment." In fact, in the case of *Jackson v. Bishop* (1968), the use of a leather strap for prison discipline was found to be cruel and unusual. The case concerned an injunction brought against the superintendent of the Arkansas State Penitentiary, to cease using the strap against prisoners for disciplinary purposes. The Court of Appeals held, among other things, that any use of the strap (even when due process of the Fourteenth Amendment was demonstrated) violated the Eighth Amendment of the Constitution which prohibits cruel and unusual punishment, simply because it was cruel. However, after a thorough review of Supreme Court cases through the 1990s, Maddan and Hallahan (2002: 116) concluded that there was a clear sign that the Supreme Court would allow corporal punishment, properly administered according to established guidelines, to be used within prison for disciplinary purposes. After a similar review, Edwards also concluded: "today, in a different setting, one in which corporal punishment was authorized and implemented in accordance and compliance with these guidelines, that a court would find the practice constitutional, in that it did meet the contemporary standards of decency" (Edwards 1999: 227).

Is There a Place for Corporal Punishment in American Corrections?

Depending on how one defines it, corporal punishment is probably already in use in correctional institutions throughout America, especially the use of solitary confinement and various forms of paddling in juvenile institutions. These practices are only to be decried because of the isolated secret settings in which they occur. Without machinery to guarantee limits, not to mention due process, the use of corporal punishment runs the risk of a slippery slope to torture or, its sibling, wanton violence, and in many cases with explicit sexual overtones, as was the case with the Abhu Graib scandal. The use of corporal punishment in isolated settings such as prisons and other closed institutions occurs because of the lack of accountability or transparency that the secrecy of closed institutions offers.

As a judicial punishment, Newman (1983, 1995) argued for the introduction of corporal punishment, specifically short sharp shocks of electricity as an intermediate punishment to fill the gap between probation or other non-punishments and prison. At the time, Newman's argument was set against the then huge number of individuals behind bars, pointing out that an intermediate, credible punishment was needed to take the place of prison for mildly serious crimes. Recent scholars have taken up this argument again, pointing to the continued increase in the use of prison as a punishment, calling it "mass incarceration" (Murtagh 2012; Scarre 2003). The argument has also gained considerable ground with the *Brown v. Plata* case that essentially acknowledges that any punishment used in excess is cruel and unusual. Briefly, Newman puts the case for judicial corporal punishment as follows.

Liberal penologists have tried to reduce the prison population by introducing alternatives to prison that were not true alternatives because they lacked the credibility of punishments. That is, they were not painful enough. Examples of such punishments are probation, community service, and work release. Further, they destroyed the credibility of prisons by trying to minimize the pains of imprisonment by introducing prison farms and minimum security prisons for white-collar type offenders. This resulted in the inconvenient fact that the public is of the opinion that prisons are not tough enough, even though penologists know that the mildest of them are horrible places. The public's demand for more punishment and the conservative reformers' swing to "just deserts" in the late 1970s resulted in more people being put in prison, yet at the same time, researchers found that prisons generally do not rehabilitate, nor do they deter (above a minimum level). This has resulted in mass incarceration of huge numbers of offenders, America having the highest prison rate in the world and, worse, with an embarrassing disproportionate representation of minorities in the prison population. Both the conservative and liberal approaches to corrections are doomed to repeat the failures of the past because they do not face up to the reality that prisons are the most expensive and least morally defensible form of severe punishment. In their present form they are an aberration of the twentieth and twenty-first centuries that historians of the future will look back on and view as barbaric.

While recent scholars have argued for the reintroduction of flogging as a substitute for prison, Newman argued for the introduction of what might be called "electronic" flogging. That is, the administration of electric shocks by carefully controlled and calibrated machine, a robot. Such a machine was envisaged by Jeremy Bentham, one of the founders of modern corrections (but that is another story). It is superior to flogging because it removes the possibility of human error from the administration of pain (floggers get tired, may be sadistic, or motivated by hate or whatever), and its application is more easily directed to specific parts of the body. Electric shock properly administered does not leave lasting damage or scars on the body, it is not a violent punishment as is flogging, and it can be calibrated in terms of intensity, duration, and intervals more easily than traditional flogging. In other words, it is obviously a far more humane punishment than both prison and traditional flogging.

Conclusions

In an attempt to find the "place" for corporal punishment in American corrections, Newman argues that the measure of "what works" for comparing judicial punishments should be tied to the specific outcomes and effects of the punishments. The criteria for comparison he identifies as:

Control. Can the specific effects of the punishment be confined to particular outcomes? For example, temporary acute corporal punishment such as electric shock can confine the pain to specific parts of the body, and at specific intervals and intensities. If administered carefully, any long-term effects will also be minimized.

Credibility. Are the punishments demonstrably painful so as to ensure the public's acceptance of them as true punishments?

Visibility. How visible are the punishments to the public? It is especially difficult to make prisons visible to the public, because by definition they keep those punished out of sight.

Calibration. Can the punishments be calibrated easily? Prison does it in terms of time, but only that. The temporary corporal punishment of electric shock can be calibrated according to the intensity of pain inflicted, length of time of the application of pain, the number of times the pain is applied, the time between application of each shock, and even length of punishment sessions, and time between such sessions. Conventional flogging can be calibrated, though not with the precision of electric shock, since the variation of each stroke of the lash depends on the skill and training of the punisher, thus subject to human error.

Side effects on the offender. All punishments have side effects. The question is which ones have the least? Prison for example has far-reaching side effects on an offender. And the longer the term of course, the side effects are greater and many continue well after the offender has been released. Those corporal punishments that mutilate also carry long-term side effects. But temporary corporal punishment such as electric shock has minimal long-term effects, if administered correctly. The irony of prison as a punishment is that an entire industry of doing good has arisen to help the prisoner on re-entry. By comparison, after temporary corporal punishment has been administered, the recipient can be given a pain killer and sent home.

Overflow effects. One need hardly point to the obvious uncontrollable overflow effects of prison as a punishment. Family members of the offender are directly affected and this effect can be for a lifetime. Does an offender's family deserve to be punished for his or her crime?

Cost. The cost of initial set-up of infrastructure to administer temporary corporal punishment would be minimal compared to prison, which requires an enormous infrastructure that, once built, is difficult to dismantle. The cost to maintain one inmate runs to close to $100,000 a year.

Portability. Prisons, once built, cannot be moved or in most cases closed. The apparatus of corporal punishment, especially electric shock, is relatively simple and small, can be moved easily from place to place. In fact, it facilitates one of the most important principles of criminal punishment: it can be administered as close as possible to the pronouncement of the sentence by the judge, administered in much the same way that fines are collected, often in an office adjacent to the local courthouse. In contrast, the offender has to be sent away to prison, often hundreds of miles away.

References

Abdel-Haleem, Muhammad, Adel Omar Sherif, and Kate Daniels. 2003. *Criminal Justice in Islam*. London: I.B.Tauris.

Arafa, Mohamed A., and Jonathan G. Burns. 2015. "Judicial corporal punishment in the United States? Lessons from Islamic criminal law for curing the ills of mass incarceration." *Indiana International & Comparative Law* Review 25(3): 385–420.

Bell v. Wolfish 411 U. S. 520 99 S. Ct. 1861 (1979).

Bessler, John. 2014. *The Birth of American Law: An Italian Philosopher and the American Revolution*. Durham, NC: Carolina Academic Press.

Brown v. Plata, 131 S. Ct. 1910 (2011).

Coker v. Georgia 433 U.S. 584; 53 LEd., 2d. 982 (1977).

Edwards, T.D. 1999. "Can (or Should) We Return to Corporal Punishment?—Yes." Pp. 219–239 in *Controversial Issues in Corrections*, edited by C.B. Fields. Boston, MA: Allyn & Bacon.

Ghassemi, Ghassem. 2009. "Criminal Punishment in Islamic Societies: Empirical Study of Attitudes to Criminal Sentencing in Iran." *European Journal Criminal Policy Research* 15: 159–180.

Gleissner, John Dewar. 2013. "Prison Overcrowding Cure: Judicial Corporal Punishment of Adults. *Criminal Law Bulletin* 49(4): ART 2.

Granucci, Anthony F. 1969. "Nor Cruel and Unusual Punishments Inflicted: The Original Meaning," *California Law Review* 57(4): 839–865.

Hall, Daniel E. 1995. "When Caning meets the Eighth Amendments: Whipping Offenders in the United States." *Widener Journal of Public Law* 4(2): 403–459.

Harmelin v. Michigan, 502.U.S. 957 (1991).

Ingraham v. Wright 97 S. Ct. 1401 (1977).

Jackson v. Bishop 404 F. 2d 571 (1968)

Maddan, Sean, and William Hallahan. 2002. "Corporal Punishment in the 21st Century: An Examination of Supreme Court Decisions in the 1990s to Predict the Reemergence of Flagellance." *Journal of Criminal Justice* 25(2): 97–120.

Morgan, Zachary. 2014. *Legacy of the Lash: Race and Corporal Punishment in the Brazilian Navy and Atlantic World*. Bloomington and Indianapolis, IN: Indiana University Press.

Murtagh, Kevin J. 2012. "Is Corporally Punishing Criminals Degrading? *Journal of Political Philosophy* 20(4): 481–498.

Newman, Graeme R. 1983. *Just and Painful: A Case for the Corporal Punishment of Criminals*,1st ed. New York: Macmillan The Free Press.

Newman, Graeme R. 1995. *Just and Painful: A Case for the Corporal Punishment of Criminals*, 2nd ed. New York: Harrow & Heston.

Newman, Graeme R. 2008. *The Punishment Response*, 3rd. ed. Rutgers University, NJ: Transaction.

Newman, Graeme R., and Pietro Marongiu. 2009. "Introduction" to their *Translation: Beccaria: On Crimes and Punishments*. Rutgers University, NJ: Transaction Press.

Peters, Rudolph. 2005. *Crime and Punishment in Islamic Law: Theory and Practice from the Sixteenth to the Twenty-first Century*. Cambridge: Cambridge University Press.

Rhodes v. Chapman 101 S. Ct. 1401 (1981).

Robinson v. California 82 S. Ct. 1417 (1962).

Scarre, Geoffrey. 2003. "Corporal Punishment." *Ethical Theory and Moral Practice* 6: 295–316.

Schwartz, Deborah A., and Jay Wishingrad. 1975 "The Eighth Amendment, Beccaria, and the Enlightenment: An Historical Justification for the *Weems v. U. S.* Excessive Punishment Doctrine," *Buffalo Law Review* 24: 783–838.

Suedfeld, Peter. 1990. (Ed.) *Psychology and Torture*. New York: Taylor & Francis.

Weems v. United States 30 S. Ct. 544 (1910).

9 Capital Punishment in America

Gavin Lee and Robert M. Bohm

Introduction

The death penalty, or capital punishment, is an area of American criminal justice policy that has caused heated debates, even though most people in the United States know little about it (Bohm 2017). Bohm (2017: xix) has described the practice as representing "two profound concerns to nearly everyone: the value of human life and how best to protect it." This chapter examines various aspects of capital punishment in the United States, starting from colonial times to the present. The chapter is divided into seven sections: (1) a brief history of the death penalty in the United States, (2) the United States Supreme Court and the death penalty, (3) methods of execution, (4) deterrence, (5) incapacitation and economic costs, (6) miscarriages of justice, and (7) arbitrariness and discrimination.

A Brief History of the Death Penalty in the United States

Laws in the American colonies were based on the laws of England, with slight variations among colonies. Differences notwithstanding, all 13 colonies allowed public hangings as punishment for certain "crimes against the state, the person, and property" (Bedau 1998: 4). The first person executed in America was Captain George Kendall in 1608. He was executed by firing squad for espionage in the Virginia colony's Jamestown settlement (Bohm 2017: 1). Kendall's execution was unusual for two reasons: he was executed for a rarely committed crime, and he was shot instead of hanged (Bohm 2017: 5). Forty percent of the executions in the English colonies during the seventeenth century were for murder, 25 percent were for witchcraft, and 15 percent for piracy (Bohm 2017: 5). Hanging was the method used in the vast majority (88 percent) of those executions (Bohm 2017: 5).

Several prominent abolitionists voiced their objections to capital punishment during the colonial era (Banner 2002). The leading abolitionist during this period was Dr. Benjamin Rush, a physician and prison reformer from Philadelphia. Rush opposed capital punishment on the grounds that it did not deter capital crimes or comport with Christian beliefs (Bohm 2017: 6–7).

Public disquiet about the death penalty caused executions to be hidden from the general public behind the walls of prisons or jails, starting with Connecticut in 1830 (Banner 2002). The last public execution in the United States was carried out in Mississippi during the late 1940s (Bohm 2017: 10).

The abolitionist movement won a huge victory in 1846, when the state of Michigan abolished the death penalty for all crimes except treason. This made Michigan the first English-speaking jurisdiction in the world to abolish the death penalty (Bohm 2017: 11–12). In 1852, the state of Rhode Island abolished the death penalty for *all* crimes including treason (Bedau 1982). Over the next 100 years several states abolished, and in some cases, reinstated the death penalty. Most of these states were in the northeastern or western United States, and to this day, the death penalty remains a largely southern phenomenon (Bohm 2017). Currently, 32 jurisdictions in the United States have the death penalty (30 states, the U.S. government, and the U.S. military), and 21 jurisdictions do not (20 states and the District of Columbia). Since 2007, eight states have abolished the death penalty (New Jersey and New York in 2007, New Mexico in 2009, Illinois in 2011, Connecticut in 2012, Maryland in 2013, Nebraska in 2015, and Delaware in 2016) (DPIC 2016h).

The United States Supreme Court and the Death Penalty

From the late eighteenth century to the early 1960s, the United States Supreme Court ("the Court") largely left matters relating to the death penalty and the criminal justice system to the various states (Bohm 2017). This position began to change when the Court started to apply the Bill of Rights to the states using the doctrine of "selective incorporation" (Foley 2003: 3).

Some of the earliest death penalty cases the Court addressed dealt with methods of execution. For example, in the case of *Wilkerson v. Utah* (1878), Wallace Wilkerson claimed that Utah's method of execution at the time—the firing squad—was unconstitutional because it violated the Eighth Amendment's prohibition against cruel and unusual punishment. The alleged problem was that Utah's death penalty statute did not specify how the condemned were to be put to death (Bohm 2017: 49). The Court held that there was nothing unconstitutional about Utah's method. According to the Court, for a punishment to be considered cruel and unusual in violation of the Eighth Amendment, it had to involve torture or unnecessary cruelty, something that the Court opined shooting did not (Bohm 2017: 49). Ironically, Wilkerson's execution was botched. It took Wilkerson 27 minutes to die because the firing squad missed his heart (Bohm 2017: 49).

In *In Re Kemmler* (1890), the Court ruled on the constitutionality of electrocution as a method of execution. Because William Kemmler's upcoming execution was to be the first using the electric chair, the Court conceded the method was indeed unusual; however, it did not accept the argument that the punishment was cruel. The Court wrote: "punishments are cruel when they involve torture or lingering death . . . something more than the mere extinguishment of life . . . [such as] burning at the stake, crucifixion, breaking on the wheel, or the like" (*In Re Kemmler* 1890). Kemmler's execution, incidentally, like Wilkerson's, was botched. Kemmler did not die "instantaneously"—a second jolt of electricity had to be administered 4.5 minutes after the first one (Bohm 2017: 201). During the second jolt, witnesses observed Kemmler's hair and flesh burning and blood on his face. His body emitted a horrible stench. Whether his death was a "painless" one is uncertain. Electricians blamed faulty equipment for the botched execution.

The Court revisited the method of electrocution in 1947, in the case of *Louisiana ex rel. Francis v. Resweber.* Willie Francis, a sixteen-year-old black male, had been convicted and sentenced to death for the killing of a popular white druggist (Bohm 2017: 50). On the day of his execution he was secured in the electric chair, and the executioner (who was drunk) threw the switch; however, the current did not kill Francis. After it became clear that the execution attempt had failed, Sheriff Resweber, who was overseeing the proceedings, ordered Francis to be taken back to his cell. The state of Louisiana immediately began to plan a second attempt at the execution but was challenged by Francis on the grounds that a second attempt would constitute torture. The Court, however, disagreed with Francis, holding that the state had carried out its duties in "a humane manner," and that the event represented "an unforeseeable accident," Francis was executed on May 9, 1947 (Miller and Bowman 1982).

In 1972, the Court decided three cases that challenged the constitutionality of death penalty statutes: *Branch v. Texas, Furman v. Georgia*, and *Jackson v. Georgia* (Bohm 2017). In the three cases, which were consolidated for trial under *Furman v. Georgia*, the Court held that the capital punishment statutes in the challenged states were unconstitutional because they gave the jury unfettered discretion to impose a death sentence or a sentence of imprisonment. In a 5–4 decision, the majority wrote that the death penalty had been imposed arbitrarily, infrequently, and often selectively against minorities and that, as such, was unconstitutional in violation of the Eighth and Fourteenth Amendments (*Furman v Georgia* 1972). The decision resulted in the Court rendering 41 jurisdictions' death penalty statutes unconstitutional, and almost 600 inmates on death rows in 32 states and the District of Columbia at the time had their sentences commuted to either life imprisonment or a term of years (Bohm 2017: 85).

Four years later, in *Gregg v. Georgia* (the lead case), *Jurek v. Texas*, and *Proffitt v. Florida* (1976), the Court accepted the revised death penalty statutes in the three states because the Court believed they would overcome the objections it had raised in *Furman*. The new Georgia death penalty statute, for example, contained four reforms approved by the Court. First, Georgia's capital trials were to be bifurcated (in other words, a death-penalty trial would have a separate guilt phase, in which the sole issue would be guilt or innocence, and a separate penalty phase, in which the only issue would be the appropriate penalty to be imposed). Second, after finding a defendant guilty, the jury would determine the sentence by weighing aggravating circumstances against mitigating circumstances. Aggravating circumstances (or factors) or "special circumstances," as they are called in some jurisdictions, refer to the particularly serious features of a case, for example, evidence of extensive premeditation and planning by the defendant, or torture of the victim by the defendant (Bohm 2017: 92). Mitigating circumstances (or factors), or "extenuating circumstances," on the other hand, refer to features of a case that explain or particularly justify the defendant's behavior, even though they do not provide a defense to the crime of murder, for example, youth, immaturity, or being under the influence of another person (Bohm 2017: 92). Third, the prosecution had to prove any aggravating circumstance beyond a reasonable doubt. No standard of proof was required of mitigating circumstances. Finally, all death sentences had to be reviewed by the Georgia Supreme Court to decide whether, in each case, the death sentence was appropriate. In *Gregg*, in short, the Court found that the death penalty was not *per se* in violation of the Eighth and Fourteenth Amendments. With the *Gregg* ruling, the so-called modern era of capital punishment began (Foley 2003). The following year, 1977, Gary Gilmore was executed by firing squad in Utah. He was the first person executed in the United States in a decade (Bohm 2017: 77).

Since the Court's reinstatement of the death penalty with its *Gregg* decision, several landmark cases have greatly changed the way capital punishment is applied. Arguably the most important of these cases have dealt with limitations to the crimes eligible for the death penalty and on whom the death penalty can be imposed. A series of cases have effectively limited the death penalty to the crime of capital or "aggravated" murder. Indeed, all persons executed during the modern era were sentenced to death for capital or "aggravated" murder (Bohm 2017: 113). The first case in this series was *Coker v. Georgia* (1977). In *Coker*, the Court ruled that the death penalty is not warranted for the crime of rape of an adult woman in cases in which the victim is not killed. The Court held that the death penalty for such a rape was "grossly disproportionate and excessive punishment" (Bohm 2017: 113). In 2008, the Court expanded its *Coker* decision in the case of *Kennedy v. Louisiana*, ruling that the rape of a child is unconstitutional under the Eighth and Fourteenth Amendments because it is disproportionate to the crime where the crime did not result, and was not intended to result, in the death of the child (Bohm 2017: 113). Also in 1977, in *Eberheart v. Georgia* and

Hooks v. Georgia, the Court, on proportionality grounds, held that the death penalty is not warranted for the crimes of kidnapping in cases in which the victim is not killed and armed robbery, respectively (Bohm 2017: 113). Traditionally, kidnapping and armed robbery, like rape, had been capital crimes, regardless of whether the victim died. These four cases, then, for all intents and purposes, have limited the death penalty to only capital or "aggravated" murder.

A second series of important cases addressed the issue of on whom the death penalty can be imposed. In the first case, *Enmund v. Florida* (1982), the Court ruled that to impose the death penalty on someone who did not kill or intend to kill violated the Eighth Amendment. Enmund was the driver of the getaway car in a robbery in which the victims were murdered (Bohm 2017: 134–135). In 1987, the Court revisited its *Enmund* decision in the case of *Tison v. Arizona*. As in *Enmund*, Raymond and Ricky Tison were participants in felony murders—in this case, involving robbery and kidnapping. Also like Enmund, the Tison brothers did not do the killing or intend to kill. However, unlike Enmund, the Tisons were major participants in the crimes and showed a "reckless indifference to human life." The Court held that even though the killing and intent to kill were absent, the other circumstances were sufficient to support a judgment of death (Bohm 2017: 136).

In 1986, in *Ford v. Wainwright*, the Court considered the issue of whether states may execute people who have literally gone crazy on death row, which is not uncommon because death row inmates currently average more than 15 years on death row before they are executed (Bohm 2017: 192). Some inmates have been on death rows for more than 30 years (Bohm 2017: 192–193). The Court ruled that states could not execute "crazy" death row inmates. The implication is that death row inmates must first be cured of their insanity before they are executed (Bohm 2017: 136). Apparently, the Court does not object to states forcibly medicating death row inmates who have become insane on death row for the sole purpose of rendering them competent for execution (Bohm 2017: 136).

In 2002, in the case of *Atkins v. Virginia*, the Court ruled that it is cruel and unusual punishment to execute the mentally retarded; thus, reversing its decision in the 1989 case of *Penry v. Lynaugh*. A problem with the *Atkins* decision is that the Court did not set a standard for what constitutes mental retardation (now called "intellectual disability"). That issue was left to the states to decide.

Finally, in 2005, in *Roper v. Simmons*, the Court held the Eighth and Fourteenth Amendments forbid the imposition of the death penalty on offenders who were under the age of 18 at the time their crimes were committed. The Court's *Roper* decision overturned its previous positions in the 1988 and 1989 cases of *Thompson v. Oklahoma*, *Stanford v. Kentucky*, and *Wilkins v. Missouri* that permitted the execution of 16- and 17-year-olds (Bohm 2017: 139–140).

In sum, in this second series of cases, the Court forbade imposition of the death penalty on (1) participants in felony-murders who did not kill or intend to kill (but not for participants who show "a reckless indifference to human life"), (2) death row inmates who have become insane while on death row (until they become sane again), (3) defendants who are mentally retarded or have an intellectual disability, and (4) offenders who were under the age of 18 at the time their crimes were committed.

Methods of Execution

Various means of execution have been used in the history of the American colonies and the United States, including beheading, pressing to death, drawing and quartering, breaking on the wheel, drowning, and, in rare instances, burning at the stake (Bohm 2017: 189). However, none of these methods has been used in the modern era of the death penalty

(Banner 2002). Currently, there are five methods by which people may be put to death in the United States: hanging, firing squad, electrocution, lethal gas, and lethal injection (Bohm 2017: 197). Each method of execution was promoted by its proponents as being more humane than the method it was replacing.

Hanging was one of the first execution methods used in colonial America and was last used in the United States to execute double murderer Billy Bailey in Delaware in 1996 (DPIC 2016e). Since 1608, more than 70 percent of all American executions have been carried out using this method, and it still remains an option in New Hampshire and Washington (DPIC 2016e).

The firing squad was also used in colonial America. As noted previously, it was the method used to execute Captain George Kendall in 1608. The firing squad was also the method used in the first post-*Furman* execution (that of Gary Gilmore in Utah in 1977, as noted previously). It still is an option in two states: Oklahoma and Utah, although both states have lethal injection as their primary method of execution (DPIC 2016e). The last person executed by firing squad in the United States was Ronnie Lee Gardner in Utah in 2010 (DPIC 2016e).

Electrocution, as a method of execution, was first used in 1890, to execute William Kemmler in the state of New York (Bohm 2017: 201). It has been used as a method of execution in 11 percent of the 1,435 post-*Furman* executions (as of April 2016), and was last used in Virginia in 2013, to execute Robert Gleason Jr. (DPIC 2016e). It currently is a potential method of execution in eight states: Alabama, Arkansas, Florida, Kentucky, Oklahoma, South Carolina, Tennessee, and Virginia (DPIC 2016e). Electrocution has been declared unconstitutional in two states: Georgia in 2001, and Nebraska in 2008 (DPIC 2016e).

Another method of execution currently available in the United States is asphyxiation by lethal gas, which has been used only 11 times in the post-*Furman* era (DPIC 2016e). The first person executed by lethal gas was Gee Jon in Nevada in 1924. It currently is available as a method of execution in five states: Arizona, California, Missouri, Wyoming and Oklahoma (DPIC 2016e). It was last used to execute Walter B. LeGrand in Arizona in 1999 (DPIC 2016e).

The primary method of execution in the United States is lethal injection, which has been used in nearly 90 percent of all post-*Furman* executions (DPIC 2016e). The method was developed in 1977, in the state of Oklahoma by the state's Chief Medical Examiner, Dr. Jay Chapman. Chapman's protocol consisted of a drug combination that he described as "a lethal quantity of an ultra-short acting barbiturate or other similar drug in combination with a chemical paralytic to cause death" (Bohm 2017: 204). Chapman stated that he didn't carry out any research before deciding on the protocol, and that he "didn't care which drug killed the prisoner, as long as one of them did" (Bohm 2017: 205). Later, Chapman decided to add a third drug, potassium chloride, which stops the heart. When asked why he added the third drug, he responded, "Why not . . . You wanted to make sure the prisoner was dead at the end, so why not just add a third drug. I didn't do any research . . . it's just common knowledge" (Bohm 2017: 206). The first person executed by lethal injection was Charles Brooks Jr. in Texas in 1982 (Bohm 2017: 207).

Since the first use of lethal injection, at least 35 lethal injection executions have been botched, resulting in several legal challenges to the lethal injection procedure (DPIC 2016a). One of the most important of these cases was *Baze et al. v. Rees*, which was decided by the U.S. Supreme Court in 2008. In *Baze*, the plaintiffs challenged Kentucky's lethal injection procedure, which was similar to the three-drug protocol used in most other death penalty states. The plaintiffs claimed that there was substantial risk that the state's execution protocol would not be followed correctly, resulting in significant pain in violation of the Eighth

Amendment. In a 7–2 decision, the Court ruled that the plaintiffs had failed to show that there was a substantial risk of serious harm (Denno 2013). Ironically, today, no state uses the protocol the Court tacitly approved in *Baze*, and botched lethal-injection executions continue (Denno 2013).

One of the problems with lethal-injection executions, besides some of them being botched, is the recent difficulty in obtaining lethal-injection drugs. Under international pressure, drug companies have refused to sell their drugs if they are to be used in executions (Bohm 2017: 213–216). This has resulted in an unseemly scramble by various corrections departments to obtain the drugs. Many states have been forced to switch the drugs they use, and many of them have departed from a three-drug protocol altogether, instead opting for a one- or two-drug protocol (Bohm 2017: 212–220). Some states have turned to compounding pharmacies for the drugs they need (Bohm 2017: 220–221).

Denno (2013) reported that she analyzed more than 300 cases citing *Baze* between 2008 and 2013, and, based on that analysis, concluded that "states can—and do—modify virtually any aspect of their lethal injection procedures with a careless frequency that is unprecedented among execution methods in this country's history." She added that "lethal injection challenges 'have already held up more executions, and for a longer time than appeals involving such . . . issues as race, innocence, and mental competency'" (Denno 2013). If the current trend continues, one wonders what the next execution method will be? No doubt it will be promoted as more humane than lethal injection.

Deterrence

Historically, the idea that the death penalty deters or prevents people-in-general or would-be capital offenders from committing capital crimes has been a mainstay argument used by many death penalty proponents. The argument is based on the simple logic that a more severe penalty has a greater deterrent effect than a less severe penalty; thus, the most severe penalty —the death penalty—must have a greater deterrent effect than any other punishment (see Van den Haag 1982). This logical assumption is questionable for at least two reasons. First, the belief that a more severe penalty has a greater deterrent effect than a less severe penalty generally is true; however, beyond a point added severity is likely to reduce deterrence. For example, in England during the eighteenth century, about 150 crimes (some put the number at more than 200) were death-eligible. Because many of the crimes were so petty, juries chose not to convict clearly guilty defendants rather than having to condemn them to die. The practice is called jury nullification, and such a practice likely reduces any general deterrent effect. Second, the assumption that the death penalty is the most severe penalty is not true for some people: the prospect of spending the rest of one's life in prison may be more terrifying than death, as it apparently was for Gary Gilmore, who waived his appeals and actively sought his execution.

Even if there was a general consensus that the death penalty is the severest penalty (and that at least some capital crimes are deterred), the problem remains that there is no scientific evidence showing conclusively that the death penalty has any marginal effect. That is, there is no scientific evidence that proves capital punishment deters more than an alternative noncapital punishment, such as life imprisonment without opportunity of parole (LWOP). Instead, most statistical analyses have indicated that capital punishment makes no discernible difference on homicide or murder rates (Bohm 2017: 239).

An exception to decades of previous research that failed to find a unique deterrent effect for capital punishment was the iconic 1975 study by economics professor Isaac Ehrlich. Ehrlich was the first to use a relatively new and sophisticated statistical analytic technique—multiple regression—to examine the impact of capital punishment on murder rates between 1933 and

1969 (Ehrlich 1975). Results of his study suggested that each execution per year during the study period might have resulted in about seven or eight fewer murders (Ehrlich 1975).

Ehrlich's findings have been influential. For example, the solicitor general of the United States Robert Bork introduced Ehrlich's prepublished results in *Fowler v. North Carolina* (1976) as evidence in support of the death penalty (Zimring and Hawkins 1986: 175). The study was also cited in the majority's opinion in *Gregg v. Georgia* (1976) to support the more modest contention that scientific evidence concerning the death penalty's general deterrent effect was "inconclusive" (Bowers, 1984: 281, n.13). Finally, Ehrlich's research continues to inform the opinions of some Supreme Court justices, who believe that capital punishment deters many types of murder (Haney and Logan 1994: 87–90; Peterson and Bailey 2003).

However, most of the attention devoted to Ehrlich's study was critical, and numerous methodological flaws with his research were cited (see Bohm 2017: 258, n.41 for a list of critical studies). Among the problems were (1) the failure to compare the effectiveness of capital punishment with that of particular prison terms (the marginal effect issue), (2) his finding of a deterrent effect does not hold if the years between 1965 and 1969 are omitted from his statistical model, (3) his use of aggregate U.S. data ignores important regional differences, and (4) he fails to consider the possible influences of racial discord, the Vietnam conflict, the sexual revolution, and increased handgun ownership—to name only a few possible factors—on the homicide or murder rate during the study period (Bohm 2017: 242).

One of the first and most forceful critiques of Ehrlich's research came from a panel established in 1975 by the National Academy of Sciences (see Zimring and Hawkins 1986: 179–181). The panel's final report, published in 1978, was based in part on several commissioned papers. One of the more influential papers was by Lawrence R. Klein, a past president of the American Economic Association, and his colleagues (Klein, Forst, and Filatov 1982). Most of the aforementioned problems, as well as several others, were first described in this paper. Klein and his colleagues were more generous than the full panel would be in their assessment of Ehrlich's research. They wrote, "The deterrent effect of capital punishment is definitely not a settled matter, and this is the strongest social scientific conclusion that can be reached at the present time" (Klein et al. 1982: 158). The panel's report emphasized that Ehrlich's research provides "no useful evidence on the deterrent effect of capital punishment" and that "the current evidence on the deterrent effect of capital punishment is inadequate for drawing any substantive conclusions" (cited in Zimring and Hawkins 1986: 180). Although not all members agreed, the report concluded on a pessimistic note: "research on this topic is not likely to produce findings that will or should have much influence on policy makers" (cited in Zimring and Hawkins 1986: 180).

Critiques of Ehrlich's research prompted a new wave of deterrence studies, many of them conducted by economists such as Ehrlich (including Ehrlich himself) (for a list of these studies, see Bohm 2017: 258, n.47). All of these econometric studies found a deterrent effect for capital punishment. Testifying before Congress in 2003, one of these economists, Joanna Shepherd, remarked that there is a "strong consensus among economists that capital punishment deters crime" and that "the studies are unanimous" (cited in Donohue and Wolfers 2005: 793, n.11). When asked by the committee chairman about "the findings of anti-death penalty advocates that are 180 degrees from your conclusion," she stated:

> There may be people on the other side that rely on older papers and studies that use outdated statistical techniques or older data, but all of the modern economic studies in the past decade have found a deterrent effect. So I am not sure what the other people are relying on.
>
> (cited in Donohue and Wolfers 2005: 793, n.11)

As recently as June 29, 2015, in his concurring opinion in *Glossip v. Gross*, former U.S. Supreme Court Justice Scalia cited the studies by Zimmerman (2004) and Dezhbakhsh, Rubin, and Shepherd (2003) to support his belief that the death penalty has a significant deterrent effect.

In 2008, Yang and Lester conducted a meta-analysis of studies on the deterrent effect of capital punishment published in peer-reviewed journals after 1975 (Yang and Lester 2008). (A meta-analysis is the statistical examination of a large collection of study results for the purpose of integrating the findings.) They found 104 studies, of which 95 contained enough data to show an adequate effect size. They reported that 60 of the studies found a deterrent effect, while 35 of the studies discovered a counterdeterrent or brutalization effect (that is, executions may cause murders rather than deter them).

The new econometric death penalty deterrence studies prompted a fresh look by the National Academy of Sciences, which published its findings in 2012—nearly 35 years after its previous review. This time the review focused on studies conducted between 2003 and 2010 (National Research Council 2012). The researchers reported the now familiar criticisms with the econometric studies and concluded with a statement remarkably similar to the one issued more than three decades ago:

> [R]esearch to date on the effect of capital punishment on homicide is not informative about whether capital punishment decreases, increases, or has no effect on homicide rates. Therefore, the committee recommends that these studies not be used to inform deliberations requiring judgments about the effect of the death penalty on homicide. Consequently, claims that research demonstrates that capital punishment decreases or increases the homicide rate by a specified amount or has no effect on the homicide rate should not influence policy judgments about capital punishment.
>
> (National Research Council 2012: 2)

In sum, there is absolutely no evidence showing that capital punishment deters more than an alternative noncapital punishment such as LWOP, and, in fact, to carry out such a study is fraught with methodological complexities. Yet, policymakers continue to rely on flawed studies that do show a deterrent effect, however small that effect may be, to support the continued use of the death penalty in the United States.

Incapacitation and Economic Costs

There is no doubt that executing a prisoner removes his ability to harm society. The death penalty is the only sentence that guarantees an offender's permanent incapacitation. Despite this fact, many death penalty opponents believe that such a drastic measure is unnecessary. They argue that if an alternative penalty, such as LWOP, accomplishes the same purpose, it would be preferable because of the other costs associated with the death penalty (e.g., a possible brutalizing effect and execution of innocent people) (Bohm 2017: 263).

Death penalty proponents, on the other hand, argue that some capital offenders are incorrigibly anti-social and will pose a threat to society as long as they remain alive (Bohm 2017: 263). Many death penalty proponents, including some prison officials, believe that the prospect of the death penalty is the only sanction that might deter inmates who already are serving life sentences from committing murders while they are in prison. Death penalty proponents also argue that unless an inmate is executed, there remains a risk that the inmate may escape from prison or be paroled, pardoned, or have his sentence commuted, either mistakenly or legitimately, to prey upon society once again. Further, proponents maintain that inmates can remain a risk to society, even while they remain incarcerated, by contacting victims or witnesses, threatening their lives, or coercing them to alter their testimony.

Despite these concerns, and they are legitimate concerns, to ensure that no convicted capital offender killed again, all convicted capital offenders would have to be executed. Such a policy has two major problems. First, as described in the next section, innocent people, wrongfully convicted of capital crimes, would be executed. If all convicted capital offenders were executed to prevent any one of them from killing again, it would be impossible to rectify the injustices done to the innocent people executed, their families and friends, and to a society that considered such acts immoral (Bohm 2017: 266). To prevent such miscarriages of justice and still retain the death penalty, identifying convicted capital offenders who are innocent and sparing them from death would be necessary. However, that is no easy task because nearly all convicted capital offenders claim they are innocent, even though only a small percentage of them really are. Generally, it is only after considerable effort that proof of innocence is ever discovered, and rarely is such effort expended on death row inmates. For those family members and friends who would like to try, the financial and psychological resources necessary for such an endeavor are often not available (Bohm 2017: 266).

Second, the threat posed by either released death row inmates or inmates serving life sentences is more imagined than real. A large body of evidence shows that murderers, including capital murderers, do sometimes kill again even after having been imprisoned for many years, but the data also reveal that the number of such repeat killers is very small. A somewhat larger percentage of paroled death row inmates commit other offenses. However, most paroled death row inmates are returned to prison for parole violations rather than for committing new crimes. Most convicted capital offenders will not kill again, even if they are released from prison, and a large majority of them will not be arrested for any new crimes (see Bohm 2017: 268–273). Unfortunately, it is impossible to predict reliably which released death row inmates or inmates serving life sentences will kill again, and which ones will not.

An alternative to capital punishment, and one that eliminates entirely the possibility of executing an innocent person, is true LWOP. LWOP also eliminates entirely the possibility of an LWOP inmate killing outside of prison. However, some people oppose LWOP because they believe it would be too costly; they assume that the death penalty is cheaper than LWOP. If they have in mind only the costs of the eventual execution, they are right, but if they consider the entire process of capital punishment, including trials, appeals, and executions, then they are wrong. The financial costs of capital punishment are addressed next.

Although the actual death-causing procedure may be relatively inexpensive, the process of getting to that point is quite costly under post-*Furman* statutes. The Supreme Court requires that defendants charged with capital crimes be provided with "super due process" (Radin 1980), and super due process is expensive. Super due process refers to the unique procedural safeguards afforded to people charged with capital crimes, such as bifurcated trials, consideration of aggravating and mitigating circumstances, and automatic appellate review. Below are some estimates of the economic costs of capital punishment.

- A 2016 study of Nebraska's death penalty found that each death penalty prosecution cost the state about $1.5 million more than an LWOP prosecution, and that Nebraska spent approximately $14.6 million a year to maintain its capital punishment system (DPIC 2016b). Nebraska abolished its death penalty in 2015.
- A 2015 study of the state of Washington's death penalty discovered that a death penalty case cost, on average, $1 million dollars more than a similar case where the state did not seek the death penalty ($3.07 million vs. $2.01 million). Since it reinstated the death penalty in 1981, Washington has executed five people at a cost of about $120 million, or $24 million per execution. In three of the five cases, the inmate waived parts of his appeals; thus, reducing costs (DPIC 2016b).

- A 2014 study of Nevada's death penalty showed that the average death penalty case costs a half million dollars more than a case in which the death penalty is not sought ($1.03 to $1.3 million vs. $775,000) (DPIC 2016b).
- A 2014 study of Kansas' death penalty examined 34 potential death penalty cases from 2004–2011. The study found that (1) defense costs for death penalty trials averaged nearly $400,000 per case, compared to about $100,000 per case when the death penalty was not sought; (2) trial court costs averaged about $72,500 in death penalty cases and approximately $21,500 in cases not involving the death penalty; and (3) housing an inmate on death row cost approximately $49,000 per year compared to about $25,000 per year for housing an inmate in the general prison population (DPC 2016b). Kansas has not conducted any executions under its post-*Furman* death penalty statute.
- A 2011 study of California's death penalty (which was updated in 2012) revealed that the state has spent more than $4 billion dollars on its death penalty system since 1978, or about $137 million a year, despite having executed only 13 people during that time period. That equates to about $300 million dollars per execution. By contrast, a comparable system that sentenced the same inmates to LWOP was estimated to cost about $11.5 million a year (DPIC 2016b).
- New York reinstated the death penalty in 1995 only to repeal it in 2004. During the nine-year period, the state spent $170 million on its death penalty system but did not execute a single person (DPIC 2016b).
- Similarly, since 1983, New Jersey spent $253 million dollars on its death penalty without conducting a single execution (DPIC 2016b). New Jersey abolished its death penalty in 2007.

Several points are worth noting about these data. First, the states discussed previously either have abolished their death penalties, executed very few capital offenders under their post-*Furman* death penalty statutes, and/or, with the exception of California, had very few inmates on their death rows. Still, with the exception of California, they are typical of most death penalty states. None of these states has been able to take advantage of economies of scale like Texas has. Because Texas conducts so many more capital trials and executes so many more inmates than any other state, it has become more economically efficient than any other death penalty states, probably resulting in a lower cost per execution (no data are available on this conjecture).

Second, as Richard Dieter, former executive director of the Death Penalty Information Center, pointed out, "Death penalty costs are accrued upfront, especially at trial and for the early appeals, while life-in-prison costs are spread out over many decades." "A million dollars spent today," Dieter notes, "is a lot more costly to the state than a million dollars that can be paid gradually over 40 years" (Dieter 2005).

Third, whenever a capital trial does not result in a death sentence and execution, as is often the case, the added costs associated with the death penalty process are incurred without any "return" on the state's investment of resources. In other words, the enormous costs of capital punishment are not a product of the number of executions but rather the number of people death penalty jurisdictions attempt to execute (Haines 1996: 170).

The average cost per execution in the United States (that is, the entire process) is estimated to range from about $1.4 million to $7 million (in 2015 dollars) (Bohm 2017: 277). Extraordinary cases can cost much more. The state of Florida, for example, reportedly spent $10 million to execute serial murderer Ted Bundy in 1989 (19 million in 2015 dollars). Orange County, California, spent more than $10 million just to convict serial killer Randy Kraft the same year (19 million in 2015 dollars). (At this writing, Kraft remains on California's death row.) Finally, the federal government spent more than $100 million to execute mass murderer Timothy McVeigh in 2001 (more than $135 million in 2015 dollars) (Bohm 2017: 277).

Because of the conditions of prison life, such as violence, HIV and other diseases, poor diets, and poor health conditions, an inmate sentenced to LWOP is estimated to live an average of 31 years in prison (Bohm 2017: 297, n.96). If an inmate sentenced to LWOP lives 31 years, and the average annual cost of imprisonment for the first 21 years is about $34,140 per inmate (in 2015 dollars), and the average annual cost of imprisonment for the last 10 years is around $70,442 per inmate (in 2015 dollars), then the cost of that LWOP sentence is roughly $1.4 million (in 2015 dollars, assuming the LWOP sentence was the result of a successful plea bargain), making capital punishment, on average, as much as five times more expensive than LWOP imposed as a result of plea bargaining (Bohm 2017: 277). If the LWOP sentence is imposed after a trial and includes other post-conviction proceedings (which is unlikely), then the difference will be much smaller. Nevertheless, the costs of a death sentence probably will always be more expensive than the costs of an LWOP sentence because super due process is required only in capital cases (Bohm 2017: 277).

Miscarriages of Justice

Miscarriages of justice, that is, wrongful convictions and executions, are a concern of nearly everyone in the death penalty debate, regardless of position. Although super due process is supposed to minimize the risk of miscarriages happening, the administration of the death penalty is a human endeavor and, as such, mistakes are bound to occur. Recently, law professor Samuel Gross and his colleagues (2014) conservatively estimated that 4.1 percent, or 307, of the 7,482 defendants sentenced to death in the United States from 1973 through 2004, were innocent (or at least falsely convicted). As of August 2016, 156 people have been exonerated and freed from death rows during the post-*Furman* era (DPIC 2016d).

Death penalty proponents have pointed to exonerations as confirmation that the system works. They also maintain—correctly—that no incontrovertible proof exists that shows an innocent person has been executed. Unsurprisingly, no state or jurisdiction has ever admitted to carrying out a wrongful execution (Bohm 2017: 305). Justice Scalia noted in 2006, that "there is no evidence showing any wrongful execution." "If there was," Scalia stated, "we would not have to hunt for it; the innocent's name would be shouted from the roof tops by the abolition lobby" (Carasik 2014).

Perhaps the highest profile case of a potentially innocent man being executed is that of Cameron Todd Willingham, who was executed in Texas in 2004, for setting fire to his house, killing his three daughters. Several expert arson investigators have stated that, after examining the evidence presented at trial, they found the original findings to be incorrect and that, in fact, the fire was not deliberately set; rather, it was caused by a faulty electrical wire in the attic (Grann 2009). Despite this revelation, in April 2011, the Texas Forensic Science Commission, which was tasked with re-examining the evidence on behalf of the state, simply suggested that more education and training for fire investigators was required (Innocence Project 2010).

The causes of wrongful convictions are many and varied. They include police and prosecutorial misconduct, eyewitness misidentification, perjury by prosecution witnesses, false confessions, judicial misconduct or error, bad defense lawyers, and several problems with the jury (see Bohm 2017: 314–335).

The often-overlooked tragedy of wrongful convictions is that many innocent individuals serve lengthy stretches on death row before they are exonerated. For example, seven of the eight individuals exonerated in 2013 and 2014 served at least 30 years on death row before they were released (DPIC 2015). Three of them—Ricky Jackson, Wiley Bridgeman, and

Kwame Ajamu—served 39 years each on Ohio's death row before their charges were dismissed in 2014 (DPIC 2015). The average number of years between death sentencing and exoneration for those death row inmates exonerated from 1973 into 2015 was 11.3 years (DPIC 2015). The tragedy likely would be compounded if the appellate process were streamlined further, as critics of the process advocate, because the death row inmates freed because of evidence of their innocence surely would have been executed before they were exonerated or, in some cases, exonerated posthumously.

Some death penalty proponents argue that even if some innocent persons are executed, the mistakes, though regrettable, are justified nonetheless by the protection executions provide society (see, for example, Markman and Cassell 1988). Those who make the argument clearly believe that executions (whether of the guilty or the innocent) have a general deterrent effect. As shown in a previous section of this chapter, however, no credible evidence exists to support such a belief. The view also is misguided for another reason. Most miscarriages of justice in capital cases, especially wrongful convictions, mean that the actual killer has gone free and remains able to prey upon an unsuspecting public (Bohm 2017: 358).

Arbitrariness and Discrimination

Two major goals of the Court's decision in *Gregg v. Georgia* (1976) were to remove unconstitutional forms of arbitrariness and discrimination from the capital punishment process. A large body of evidence indicates that this has not happened. Arbitrariness refers to random, capricious, irregular, or disproportionate application; discrimination involves deliberate application based on extra-legal factors such as race, sex, or wealth (see Nakell and Hardy 1987: 16). As evidence of arbitrary application of the death penalty under post-*Furman* statutes, critics point to the small percentage of all death-eligible offenders who are executed and to the patterns in which the death penalty has been applied across jurisdictions and over time.

Only 1–2 percent of all death-eligible offenders have been executed from 1930 to the present (Bohm 2017: 369). Thus, not only are the vast majority of capital offenders able to escape execution, but no meaningful way exists to distinguish between the eligible offenders who were executed and those who were not. One might assume that the few death-eligible offenders that are executed represent the "worst of the worst," but the "worst of the worst" sometimes escape execution, while murderers who clearly are not among the "worst of the worst" do not. Regarding the first category, in 2003, Gary Ridgeway, the so-called "Green River Killer," admitted to killing 48 women during a span of two decades. He was allowed to escape the death penalty by pleading guilty to the murders and, in doing so, gained the distinction of pleading guilty to more murders than any other serial killer in American history. He was sentenced to consecutive LWOP sentences for each murder. The prosecutor reluctantly agreed to the plea deal because investigators and victims' relatives wanted the murders resolved and cases closed. Had the victims not been prostitutes, drug addicts, and/or runaways, perhaps the prosecutor's decision might have been different (Tizon 2003).

Arbitrariness also is evident in the way the death penalty has been applied across jurisdictions and over time. As Anthony Amsterdam, who has defended dozens of capital offenders, described:

> [T]here is a haphazard, crazy-quilt character about the administration of capital punishment that every knowledgeable lawyer or observer can describe but none can rationally explain. Some juries are hanging juries, some counties are hanging counties, some years

> are hanging years; and men live or die depending on these flukes. However atrocious the crime may have been for which a particular defendant is sentenced to die, "experienced wardens know many prisoners serving life or less whose crimes were equally, or more atrocious."
>
> (Amsterdam 1982: 351)

Only five of the 32 death penalty jurisdictions in the United States (30 states, the U.S. government, and the U.S. military) account for about 65 percent of the 1,437 people executed under post-*Furman* statutes as of July 15, 2016 (the states are Texas, Oklahoma, Virginia, Florida, and Missouri); three states (Texas, Oklahoma, and Virginia) can lay claim to about 53 percent of the total; and one state (Texas) has executed more than 37 percent of the total (calculated from data at DPIC 2016f). Still, even Texas executes only a small percentage of its death-eligible offenders.

Regional variation in executions also suggests arbitrariness in application. More than 80 percent of post-*Furman* executions have been conducted in the South (calculated from data at DPIC 2016f), even though fewer than half of all murders occur in the South (see, for example, Federal Bureau of Investigation 2014). Note the "fewer than half of all murders" is for all murders and not just death-eligible murders, and data separating the two categories are not available. Thus, it is still possible, though improbable, that a much larger proportion of murders are death eligible in the South than in other regions of the country.

There is also regional variation within states, and such disparities are not limited to the South. Data of regional variation within states suggest that greater numbers of death-eligible homicides do not increase the overall probability of a death sentence, as one might expect. Rather, the data show that the odds of being sentenced to death are either greater in regions with fewer death-eligible homicides or not related to the number of death-eligible homicides at all. It may be that where capital murders are few, those that are committed receive harsher punishment (Bohm 2017: 372). Another explanation has to do with the costs of capital punishment. Counties that can afford it may seek the death penalty in all cases that warrant it, while "poor" counties may have to pick and choose among death-eligible cases, pursuing the death penalty in only some cases or not at all. "Poor" counties simply may not be able to afford the death penalty (Dieter 2005; Chammah 2014; Clancy and O'Brien 2013: 330–331).

Arbitrariness is most evident, and death sentences resulting in executions are most concentrated, at the county-level, where the usually locally elected prosecutor serves as the gatekeeper to the entire capital punishment process. A recent study found that (as of January 1, 2013) only 15 percent of all 3,143 U.S. counties or county-equivalents accounted for all of the executions in the United States since executions resumed in 1977, and only 2 percent of U.S. counties accounted for 52 percent of those executions (Dieter 2013). By contrast, 85 percent of U.S. counties have not conducted a single execution in more than 45 years. The executing counties represent only 15.9 percent of the U.S. population. Perhaps not surprisingly, nine of the 15 counties (60 percent) are in Texas. A previous study of death sentences by county discovered that the concentration of death sentences in those counties was not a function of the heinousness of the murders committed or the incorrigibility of the offenders. Rather, in some counties prosecutors sought the death penalty, and in other counties in the same state they did not, even for the same or more aggravated death-eligible murders (Smith 2010, 2012). In sum, these data show that the application of the death penalty under post-*Furman* statutes, in the words of the Court in its *Furman* decision, has been "rare," "uncommon," and "freakish."

As noted previously, only a select few of all death-eligible murderers are ever actually executed. Consideration of their unique characteristics, the laws under which they are prosecuted, and the behavior of defense attorneys, prosecutors, and jurors reveals unconstitutional forms of discrimination. Here we describe discrimination by social class, sex, age, and race.

The death penalty in the United States is reserved almost exclusively for the poor. As U.S. Supreme Court Justice William Douglas wrote in his *Furman* decision, "One searches our chronicles in vain for the execution of any member of the affluent strata of this society" (at 251–252). Chief Justice Earl Warren remarked in the *Maxwell v. Bishop* case conference in 1968: "Death seems to be reserved for the poor and the underprivileged. No person of any affluence is ever executed. Death falls unequally on the poor and the unpopular" (cited in Garland 2010: 371, n.60). Former San Quentin warden Clinton T. Duffy stated that he knew of no one of means who was ever executed (cited in Meltsner 1973: 70). Former Sing Sing (New York) warden Lewis Lawes elaborated:

> The defendant of wealth and position, of influence, seldom goes to the electric chair. Through good counsel, through legal technicalities and delay, through influence, he manages to escape death while the man who is friendless and destitute pays the extreme penalty. This statement is borne out by an examination of the data concerning the men who have been executed in this state during the past thirty years.
>
> (Lawes 1969: 10)

Finally, attorney Bryan Stevenson has pointed out that capital punishment really means "them without the capital gets the punishment" (Stevenson 2004: 95). A major reason wealth matters, as Warden Lawes observed, is that the wealthy are able to hire the best attorneys. In many capital cases, the outcome depends more on an attorney's skill than what actually happened (Dow 2005: 7).

The death penalty in the United States also is reserved almost exclusively for men. It is rarely inflicted on women, even though women commit roughly 10 percent of all criminal homicides (where the gender of the offender is known) (Federal Bureau of Investigation 2013). (The percentage of women who commit death-eligible homicides is unknown.) Approximately 20,000 people have been legally executed in the United States since 1608, and about 3 percent (approximately 574) of them have been women. Nearly 90 percent of the women were executed prior to 1866 (Schneider and Smykla 1991: 6, Table 1.1).

It has been estimated that under current death penalty laws, if women and men were treated equally, and no factor other than offense was considered, women would receive between 4 percent and 6 percent of all death sentences (Rapaport 1993: 147). Under post-*Furman* statutes, however, women have received about 2 percent of all death sentences (Streib 2013). The reason for the difference is that from arrest through execution, women are filtered from the process. Only 16 women have been executed under post-*Furman* statutes as of this writing (about 1 percent of the 1,437 executions) (DPIC 2016f; 2016i).

The ethical dilemma posed by sex discrimination in the administration of the death penalty is nicely expressed by law professor Victor Streib:

> One need not be a supporter of the death penalty to observe that if men are eligible for it then women should be also. Otherwise, women are lumped in with children and the mentally retarded as not fully responsible human beings.
>
> (Streib 2003: 322)

In short, if women are to be accorded full dignity as human beings, and illegal discrimination is to be avoided, then, as Streib contends, women either must be executed for their capital crimes, or no one should be executed for a capital crime.

The age of the offender is another source of discrimination in the administration of the death penalty. In 2005, in the case of *Roper v. Simmons*, the U.S. Supreme Court prohibited the death penalty for anyone less than 18 years of age at the time of the crime. However, while the practice existed, juveniles, like women, were filtered from the process. Although juveniles accounted for about 8 percent of murder arrests since the death penalty was reinstated in 1976 through the *Roper* decision in 2005, only about 2 percent of the death-eligible juveniles were executed (23 out of 949 executions) (Streib 2005). About 90 percent of the juveniles sentenced to death during this period had their death sentences reversed (Streib 2014: 324).

What makes the current practice of excluding juveniles from the death penalty discriminatory is that the designation of "juvenile" is arbitrary. Is there really a significant difference on any relevant social characteristic between a 17- and 18-year-old, other than what has been created by law? Is it really meaningful to consider a 17-year-old a juvenile and an 18-year-old an adult? Law professor Joseph Hoffmann pointed out that age is largely irrelevant. It is used because it serves as an imperfect proxy for more relevant social characteristics. Whether a murderer, regardless of age, deserves the death penalty depends, not on age, argues Hoffmann, but on maturity, judgment, responsibility, and the capability to assess the possible consequences of his or her actions (Hoffmann 1993: 118–119). Some juveniles possess these characteristics in greater quantity than some adults, or in sufficient quantities to be death eligible; some do not. The use of age as a basis for determining who is or is not death eligible is therefore discriminatory. Thus, the *Simmons* decision did nothing more than change the age at which death penalty states are allowed to discriminate.

Finally, post-*Furman* statutes have failed to end racial discrimination in the imposition of the death penalty. In the past, discussions of racial discrimination focused almost entirely on the race of those executed; however, more recent research has revealed a second, less obvious form of racial discrimination in the death penalty's administration: race-of-victim discrimination. We consider race-of-offender discrimination first.

From 1800 to 2002, half of all persons executed in the United States were black, even though they comprised only about 11 percent of the population (Baumgartner, DeBoef, and Boydstun 2008: 33). Put differently, from the early eighteenth century through the mid-twentieth century, black execution rates were, on average, about nine times higher than white execution rates (Allen and Clubb 2008: 21). In some states, however, the disparity was much greater. For example, in Mississippi, during the hundred years following the Civil War, 87 percent of the 433 people legally executed were black, and every execution for a nonlethal crime during that period—33 for rape and eight for armed robbery—involved a black defendant and white victim (Oshinsky 2010: 10; Garland 2010: 218–219).

The statistics for rape are particularly telling. Between 1930 and 1980, when rape was punishable by death, 455 men were executed for the crime. Of them, 11 percent (48) were white, and 89 percent (405) were black. Ninety-seven percent (443) were executed in the South (see Bedau 1982: 58–61). Apparently, no white man has ever been executed for the rape (only) of a black victim (Radelet 1989).

According to an "evaluation synthesis" of 28 post-*Furman* studies prepared by the U.S. General Accounting Office (GAO) and published in 1990:

> more than half of the studies found that race of defendant influenced the likelihood of being charged with a capital crime or receiving the death penalty . . . [and in] more than three-fourths of the studies that identified a race-of-defendant effect . . . black defendants were more likely to receive the death penalty.
>
> (U.S. General Accounting Office 1990: 6)

An update of the GAO study prepared for the American Bar Association (ABA) and published in 1997, showed that in nearly half of the death penalty states race of defendant was a significant predictor of who would receive a death sentence. In all but two of these states (Florida and Tennessee), black defendants were more likely to receive a death sentence (Baldus and Woodworth 1997). As of July 15, 2016, nearly 35 percent of the people executed under post-*Furman* statutes in the United States have been black males (DPIC 2016g), even though black males comprise only about 6 percent of the U.S. population (calculated from data at United States Census Bureau 2015).

As noted, available evidence indicates that post-*Furman* statutes have not eliminated a second, less obvious form of racial discrimination: race-of-victim discrimination. Whether the death penalty is imposed depends on the race of the victim. Research shows that the killers of whites, regardless of their race, are much more likely to be sentenced to death than are the killers of nonwhites. On the other hand, the killers of black male victims are the least likely to be sentenced to death (Williams, Demuth, and Holcomb 2007: 885). Consider these recent data on defendant–victim racial combinations for post-*Furman* executions, as of January 1, 2016 (Death Row USA 2016). Focusing only on whites and blacks, the data reveal that about 76 percent of the victims of those persons executed under post-*Furman* statutes have been white, and that only about 13 percent have been black. Yet, approximately 55 percent of defendants executed have been white, and nearly 35 percent have been black. Discrimination seems apparent because, historically, capital crimes generally have been intraracial (Baumgartner, Grigg, and Mastro 2015; Zahn 1989). For example, in 2014, white offenders murdered 82 percent of white victims, and black offenders murdered 90 percent of black victims (when race of victim and offender was known) (Federal Bureau of Investigation, 2014). Still, uncertainty remains about whether the data show discrimination because only about 20 percent of murders and nonnegligent manslaughters (the FBI category) are capital crimes. It seems likely that the percentage of interracial murders may be somewhat greater for capital murders than it is for noncapital murders.

In sum, the Supreme Court has not and likely cannot rid the imposition of the death penalty from repugnant forms of racial discrimination. Yet, in *Zant v. Stephens* (1983), *McCleskey v. Kemp* (1987), and other cases, it has clearly indicated that neither race-of-defendant nor race-of-victim racial discrimination in the administration of capital punishment is constitutionally permissible. Even under post-*Furman* statutes, Bowers and Pierce (1982: 220) observe that:

> race is truly a pervasive influence on the criminal justice processing of potentially capital cases, one that is evident at every stage of the process . . . it is an influence that persists despite separate sentencing hearings, explicitly articulated sentencing guidelines, and automatic appellate review of all death sentences.

The same also could be said about social class, sex, and age discrimination.

Conclusion

As of January 1, 2016, 2,943 people were on death rows in the United States (Death Row USA 2016), and, since executions resumed in 1977, 1,435 people have been put to death (DPIC 2016c). However, many observers have opined that the death penalty is in decline, potentially heading for extinction (see, for example, Bohm 2017). The discovery of innocent people being sentenced to death, awareness of the exorbitant costs of the penalty, the continuing controversy over lethal injection, evidence of arbitrary and discriminatory application, the reduction in public support for the practice, and the trend of states abolishing the death penalty have convinced many people of this conclusion. In fact, before his death, conservative Supreme Court Justice Antonin Scalia, a resolute death penalty proponent, suggested that the death penalty's days were numbered (Martelle 2015). Only time will tell if Scalia was right.

References

Allen, Howard W., and Jerome M. Clubb. 2008. *Race, Class, and the Death Penalty*. Albany, NY: State University of New York Press.

Amsterdam, Anthony G. 1982. "Capital Punishment." Pp. 346–358 in *The Death Penalty in America*, 3rd ed., edited by H.A. Bedau. New York: Oxford University Press.

Baldus, David C., and George Woodworth. 1997. Race Discrimination in America's Capital Punishment System since *Furman v. Georgia* (1972): The Evidence of Race Disparities and the Record of Our Courts and Legislatures in Addressing This Issue. Report prepared for the American Bar Association. Cited in Dieter, R. C. (1998) *The Death Penalty in Black & White: Who Lives, Who Dies, Who Decides*. Death Penalty Information Center. Retrieved May 15, 2017 from www.deathpenaltyinfo.org/racerpt.html

Banner, Stuart. 2002. *The Death Penalty: An American History*. Cambridge, MA: Harvard University Press.

Baumgartner, Frank R., Suzanna L. DeBoef, and Amber E. Boydstun. 2008. *The Decline of the Death Penalty and the Discovery of Innocence*. New York: Cambridge University Press.

Baumgartner, Frank R., Amanda J. Grigg, and Alisa Mastro. 2015. "#BlackLivesDon'tMatter: Race-of-Victim Effects in US Executions, 1976–2013." *Politics, Groups, and Identities* 3: 209–221.

Bedau, Hugo A. 1982. *The Death Penalty in America*, 3rd ed. New York: Oxford University Press.

Bedau, Hugo A. (Ed.) 1998. *The Death Penalty in America: Current Controversies*. New York: Oxford University Press.

Bohm, Robert M. 2017. *DeathQuest: An Introduction to the Theory and Practice of Capital Punishment in the United States*, 5th ed. New York: Routledge.

Bowers, William J., with Glenn L. Pierce, and John F. McDevitt. 1984. *Legal Homicide: Death as Punishment in America, 1864–1982*. Boston, MA: Northeastern University Press.

Carasik, Lauren. 2014. "Exoneration of Death Row Convict Supports Abolitionists" Aljazeera America (September 10). Retrieved May 15, 2017 from http://america.aljazeera.com/opinions/2014/9/henry-mccollum-deathpenaltynorthcarolinadnatest.html

Chammah, Maurice. 2014. "The Slow Death of the Death Penalty: The Public Supports It, But the Costs Are Lethal." The Marshall Project. Retrieved May 15, 2017 from www.themarshallproject.org/2014/12/17/the-slow-death-of-the-deathpenalty

Clancy, Martin, and Tim O'Brien. 2013. *Murder at the Supreme Court: Lethal Crimes and Landmark Cases*. Amherst, NY: Prometheus Books.

Death Penalty Information Center (DPIC). 2015. *Innocence List of Those Freed from Death Row*. Retrieved May 15, 2017 from www.deathpenaltyinfo.org/innocence-list-those-freed-death-row

Death Penalty Information Center (DPIC). 2016a. *Botched Executions*. Retrieved May 15, 2017 from www.deathpenaltyinfo.org/some-examples-post-furman-botched-executions.

Death Penalty Information Center (DPIC). 2016b. *Costs of the Death Penalty*. Retrieved May 15, 2017 from www.deathpenaltyinfo.org/costs-death-penalty

Death Penalty Information Center (DPIC). 2016c. *Facts about the Death Penalty*. Retrieved May 15, 2017 from www.deathpenaltyinfo.org/documents/FactSheet.pdf

Death Penalty Information Center (DPIC). 2016d. *Innocence and the Death Penalty*. Retrieved May 15, 2017 from www.deathpenaltyinfo.org/innocence-and-death-penalty

Death Penalty Information Center (DPIC). 2016e. *Methods of Execution*. Retrieved May 15, 2017 from www.deathpenaltyinfo.org/methods-execution?scid=8&did=245#state

Death Penalty Information Center (DPIC). 2016f. *Number of Executions by State and Region since 1976*. Retrieved May 15, 2017 from www.deathpenaltyinfo.org/number-executions-state-and-region-1976

Death Penalty Information Center (DPIC). 2016g. *Race of Death Row Inmates Executed Since 1976*. Retrieved May 15, 2017 from www.deathpenaltyinfo.org/race-death-row-inmates-executed-1976

Death Penalty Information Center (DPIC). 2016h. *States With and Without the Death Penalty*. Retrieved May 15, 2017 from www.deathpenaltyinfo.org/states-and-without-death-penalty

Death Penalty Information Center (DPIC). 2016i. *Women and the Death Penalty*. Retrieved May 15, 2017 from www.deathpenaltyinfo.org/women-and-death-penalty.

Death Penalty Information Center (DPIC). 2016j. States With and Without the Death Penalty. Retrieved from www.deathpenaltyinfo.org/states-and-without-death-penalty

Death Penalty Information Center (DPIC). 2016k. Women and the Death Penalty. Retrieved from www.deathpenaltyinfo.org/women-and-death-penalty

Death Row USA. 2016. *Criminal Justice Project (January 1). New York, NY: NAACP Legal Defense and Educational Fund, Inc.* Retrieved May 15, 2017 from www.deathpenaltyinfo.org/documents/DRUSAWinter2016.pdf

Denno, Deborah W. 2013. "Lethal injection Chaos Post-*Baze*." *Georgetown Law Journal* 102: 1331–1382.

Dezhbakhsh, Hasheem, Paul H. Rubin, and Joanna M. Shepherd. 2003. "Does Capital Punishment Have a Deterrent Effect? New Evidence from Post-Moratorium Panel Data." *American Law and Economic Review* 5: 344–376.

Dieter, Richard C. 2005. *Costs of the Death Penalty and Related Issues, Testimony before the New York State Assembly: Standing Committees on Codes, Judiciary, and Correction (January 25)*. Retrieved May 15, 2017 from www.deathpenaltyinfo.org ("Costs").

Dieter, Richard C. 2013. *The 2% Death Penalty: How a Minority of Counties Produce Most Death Cases at Enormous Costs to All (October)*. Retrieved May 15, 2017 from http://deathpenaltyinfo.org/documents/TwoPercentReport.pdf

Donohue III, John J., and Justin Wolfers. 2005. "Uses and Abuses of Empirical Evidence in the Death Penalty Debate." *Stanford Law Review* 58: 791–846.

Dow, David R. 2005. *Executed on a Technicality: Lethal Injustice on America's Death Row*. Boston, MA: Beacon Press.

Ehrlich, Isaac. 1975. "The Deterrent Effect of Capital Punishment: A Question of Life and Death." *The American Economic Review* 65: 397–417.

Federal Bureau of Investigation. 2013. *Crime in the United States 2013*. Washington, DC: U.S. Department of Justice.

Federal Bureau of Investigation. 2014. *Crime in the United States 2014*. Washington, DC: U.S. Department of Justice.

Foley, Michael A. 2003. *Arbitrary and Capricious: The Supreme Court, the Constitution, and the Death Penalty*. Westport, CT: Greenwood/Praeger.

Garland, David. 2010. *Peculiar Institution: America's Death Penalty in an Age of Abolition*. Cambridge, MA: The Belknap Press.

Grann, David. 2009. "Trial by Fire: Did Texas Execute an Innocent Man?" *The New Yorker*. Retrieved May 15, 2017 from www.newyorker.com/magazine/2009/09/07/trial-by-fire

Gross, Samuel R., Barbara O'Brien, Chen Hu, and Edward H. Kennedy. 2014. "Rate of False Conviction of Criminal Defendants Who Are Sentenced to Death." *Proceedings of the National Academy of Sciences* 111(20): 7230–7235.

Haines, Herbert H. 1996. *Against Capital Punishment: The Anti-Death Penalty Movement in America, 1972–1994*. New York: Oxford University Press.

Haney, Craig and Deana Dorman Logan. 1994. "Broken Promise: The Supreme Court's Response to Social Science Research on Capital Punishment." *Journal of Social Issues* 50: 75–100.

Hoffmann, Joseph L. 1993. "On the Perils of Line-Drawing: Juveniles and the Death Penalty." Pp. 117–132 in *A Capital Punishment Anthology*, edited by V.L. Streib. Cincinnati, OH: Anderson Publishing.

Innocence Project. 2010. *Cameron Todd Willingham: Wrongfully Convicted and Executed in Texas*. Retrieved May 15, 2017 from www.innocenceproject.org/cameron-todd-willingham-wrongfully-convicted-and-executed-in-texas/

Klein, L.R., Forst, B. and Filatov, V. 1982. "The Deterrent Effect of Capital Punishment: An Assessment of the Evidence." Pp. 138–159 in *The Death Penalty in America*, 3rd ed., edited by H. A. Bedau. New York: Oxford University Press.

Lawes, L.E. 1969, orig. 1924. *Man's Judgement of Death: An Analysis of the Operation and Effect of Capital Punishment Based on Facts, not on Sentiment.* Montclair, NJ: Patterson Smith.

Markman, Stephen J., and Paul G. Cassell. 1988. "Protecting the Innocent: A Response to the Bedau–Radelet Study." *Stanford Law Review* 41:121–160.

Martelle, Scott. 2015. "Justice Antonin Scalia "Wouldn't Be Surprised" If Supreme Court Ends the Death Penalty." *LA Times* (September 25). Retrieved May 15, 2017 from www.latimes.com/opinion/opinion-la/la-ol-scalia-death-penalty-pope-francis-xi-jinpeng-trump-boehner-20150925-story.html

Meltsner, Michael. 1973. *Cruel and Unusual: The Supreme Court and Capital Punishment.* New York: Random House.

Miller, Arthur S., and Jeffrey H. Bowman. 1982. "Slow Dance on the Killing Ground: The Willie Francis Case Revisited." *DePaul Law Review* 32: 1–75.

Nakell, Barry and Kenneth A. Hardy. 1987. *The Arbitrariness of the Death Penalty.* Philadelphia, PA: Temple University Press.

National Research Council. 2012. *Deterrence and the Death Penalty, Committee on Deterrence and the Death Penalty*, edited by D. S. Nagin and J. V. Pepper. Committee on Law and Justice, Division of Behavioral and Social Sciences and Education. Washington, DC: The National Academic Press.

Oshinsky, David M. 2010. *Capital Punishment on Trial: Furman v. Georgia and the Death Penalty in Modern America.* Lawrence, KS: Kansas University Press.

Peterson, Ruth D., and William C. Bailey. 2003. "Is Capital Punishment an Effective Deterrent for Murder? An Examination of Social Science Research." Pp. 251–282 in *America's Experiment with Capital Punishment: Reflections on the Past, Present and Future of the Ultimate Penal Sanction*, 2nd ed., edited by J.R. Acker, R.M. Bohm, and C.S. Lanier. Durham, NC: Carolina Academic Press.

Radelet, Michael L. 1989. "Executions of Whites for Crimes against Blacks: Exceptions to the Rule?" *The Sociological Quarterly* 30: 529–544.

Radin, Margaret J. 1980. "Cruel Punishment and Respect for Persons: Super Due Process for Death." *Southern California Law Review* 53: 1143–1185.

Rapaport, Elizabeth. 1993. "The Death Penalty and Gender Discrimination." Pp. 145–152 in *A Capital Punishment Anthology*, edited by V.L. Streib. Cincinnati, OH: Anderson Publishing.

Schneider, Victoria and John O. Smykla. 1991. "A Summary Analysis of Executions in the United States, 1608–1987: The Espy File." Pp. 1–19 in *The Death Penalty in America: Current Research*, edited by R.M. Bohm. Cincinnati, OH: Anderson Publishing.

Smith, R. 2010. *Arbitrariness as Ever: Only 10% of Counties in the Country Have Imposed a Death Sentence in the Last 6 Years. Second Class Justice.* Retrieved May 15, 2017 from www.secondclassjustice.com/?p=116

Smith, Robert J. 2012. "The Geography of the Death Penalty and Its Ramifications." *Boston University Law Review* 92: 227–289.

Stevenson, Bryan. 2004. "Close to Death: Reflections on Race and Capital Punishment in America." Pp. 76–116 in *Debating the Death Penalty: Should America Have Capital Punishment? The Experts on Both Sides Make Their Best Case*, edited by H.A. Bedau and P.G. Cassell. New York: Oxford University Press.

Streib, Victor L. 2003. "Executing Women, Juveniles, and the Mentally Retarded: Second Class Citizens in Capital Punishment." Pp. 301–323 in *America's Experiment with Capital Punishment: Reflections on the Past, Present and Future of the Ultimate Penal Sanction*, 2nd ed., edited by J.R. Acker, R.M. Bohm, and C.S. Lanier. Durham, NC: Carolina Academic Press.

Streib, Victor L. 2005. *Death Sentences and Executions for Juvenile Crimes, January 1, 1973–February 28, 2005.* Retrieved May 15, 2017 from www.deathpenaltyinfo.org/documents/StreibJuvDP2005.pdf

Streib, Victor. 2013. *Death Penalty for Female Offenders, January 1, 1973, Through October 31, 2010.* Retrieved May 15, 2017 from www.deathpenaltyinfo.org/documents/FemDeathDec2012.pdf

Streib, Victor L. 2014. "Women and Children First." Pp. 309–333 in *America's Experiment with Capital Punishment: Reflections on the Past, Present and Future of the Ultimate Penal Sanction*, 3rd ed, edited by J.R. Acker, R.M. Bohm, and C.S. Lanier. Durham, NC: Carolina Academic Press.

Tizon, T.A. 2003. "I Killed the 48 Women." *The Orlando Sentinel* (November 6), p. A1.

United States Census Bureau. 2015. *American FactFinder* (July 1). Retrieved May 15, 2017 from http://factfinder.census.gov/faces/tableservices/jsf/pages/productview.xhtml?src=bkmk

U.S. General Accounting Office. 1990. *Death Penalty Sentencing: Research Indicates Pattern of Racial Disparities*. Report to Senate and House Committees on the Judiciary. Washington, DC: GAO.

Van den Haag, Ernest. 1982. "The Criminal Law as a Threat System." *The Journal of Criminal Law and Criminology* 73: 769–785.

Williams, Marian R., Stephen Demuth, and Jefferson E. Holcomb. 2007. "Understanding the Influence of Victim Gender in Death Penalty Cases: The Importance of Victim Race, Sex-Related Victimization, and Jury Decision Making." *Criminology* 45: 865–891.

Yang, Bijou and David Lester. 2008. "The Deterrent Effect of Executions: A Meta-Analysis Thirty Years after Ehrlich." *Journal of Criminal Justice 36*: 453–460.

Zahn, Margaret A. 1989. "Homicide in the Twentieth Century: Trends, Types, and Causes." Pp. 216–234 in *Violence in America: The History of Crime*, Vol. 1, edited by T.R. Gurr. Newbury Park, CA: Sage.

Zimmerman, Paul R. 2004. "State Executions, Deterrence, and the Incidence of Murder." *Journal of Applied Economics* 7: 163–193.

Zimring, Franklin E. and Gordon Hawkins. 1986. *Capital Punishment and the American Agenda*. Cambridge: Cambridge University Press.

Cases Cited

Atkins v. Virginia 536 U.S. 304 (2002).
Branch v. Texas 408 U.S. 238 (1972).
Coker v. Georgia, 433 U.S. 584, (1977).
Furman v. Georgia 408 U.S. 238 (1972).
Gregg v. Georgia 428 U.S. 153 (1976).
In Re Kemmler 136 U.S. 436 (1890).
Jackson v. Georgia 408 U.S. 238 (1972).
Louisiana ex rel. Francis v. Resweber 329 U.S. 459 (1947).
McCleskey v. Kemp 481 U.S. 279 (1987).
Roper v. Simmons 543 U.S. 551 (2005).
Wilkerson v. Utah 99 U.S. 130 (1878).
Zant v. Stephens 462 U.S. 862 (1983).

10 Jails in America

Arthur J. Lurigio

The correctional population in the United States is prodigious. At the end of 2014, 6.8 million adults, nearly 3 percent of all residents of the country, were under correctional authority, either incarcerated in prisons or jails (institutional corrections) or mandated to parole or probation supervision (community corrections). The community corrections population (roughly 5 million adults) was more than double the institutional corrections population (roughly 2 million adults). In addition, the number of people in prisons (also known as penitentiaries) was significantly greater than the number of those in jails (also known as detention centers)—roughly 1.6 million versus roughly 750,000, respectively (Kaeble, Glaze, Tsoutis, and Minton 2015).

Brief History of Institutional Corrections

During the Colonial Era, the most common punishments were corporal: whipping, branding, and cutting off ears. Public shaming was another type of corporal punishment in which people were forced to stand in a pillory, which is a post with a wooden or metal framework with holes to secure an accused's head and hands. Being "pilloried" subjected rule-breakers to great discomfort and physical abuse as well as public torment and scorn. For the severest crimes, such as murder and rape, criminals were publicly executed, generally by hanging (Morris 1974).

The colonialists built the first jail in 1606 in Jamestown, Virginia (Zupan 1991). Philadelphia's Walnut Street Jail morphed into the first prison in 1790 with the addition of a new cell house to hold people convicted of crimes (post-disposition) for more sustained periods of confinement than those imposed on people held in the jail houses, who were largely detained before their cases were tried (pre-disposition) (Morris 1974). A forerunner to prisons, local jails or longer-term facilities, known as workhouses, grew in number and size throughout the nineteenth century with the increasing need to control the "dangerous classes," especially in the country's ever-increasing, more expansive, and densely populated urban centers where the "rabble" were considered to be more threatening and difficult to manage (Hirsh 1992; Irwin 1985; Mattick 1969).

Prisons and jails began to populate the landscape after the Revolutionary War Period. They were constructed in an effort to modernize and reform existing social control mechanisms by eschewing corporeal and capital punishments in favor of more humane options designed to achieve justice and to deter and control lawlessness (Rothman 2011). Post-revolutionary activists envisioned prisons as institutions in which incarcerees could develop character and be rehabilitated through hard physical labor and spiritual redemption (Hirsh 1992). By the 1820s, however, a prison sentence had become the most feared punishment in the country. Prisons were viewed as veritable dungeons of horrors in which incarcerees were beaten, starved, and worked to exhaustion (Morris and Rothman 1998).

Untrained and unprofessional detention officers ran jails, which frequently operated for profit. The term "catch-all" jail captures the historical role of the county jail, which became a repository for the mentally ill, the poor, and the homeless (Casey 1954). Witnesses to crimes and juvenile offenders were housed alongside adult criminals. As noted previously, similar to current detention facilities, the earliest jails confined mostly suspects accused of committing a crime and awaiting their appearance in court. Few were actually serving time after being sentenced for a criminal conviction or pleading guilty to a crime. Moreover, the poor or the destitute were forced to endure the pitiful conditions of jail confinement for lengthy terms due to their inability to pay even a modest bail or fine. Thus, similar to their contemporary counterparts, the first jails were intended as temporary housing facilities for people prior to case disposition (Casey 1954).

Reformers of the Antebellum Era thought that jails, like prisons, also could be transformed into places where misdemeanant or petty offenders would be rehabilitated (Morris 1974). A first major step in the reform process was to separate vulnerable children and adolescents from hardened career criminals who regularly shared the same cell. Social activists, namely, Dorothea Dix and Louis Dwight, raised public awareness regarding the unsuitability and inhumaneness of the jail as a holding facility for people with mental illness; detention centers provided neither the treatment nor the safe environment needed for detainees with psychiatric disorders (Gollaher 1995). Despite these genuine reform initiatives, at the turn of the century, jails remained dirty and repugnant places run by corrupt sheriffs whose political affiliations shaped the type of services and treatment that jail detainees received (Fishman and Perlman 1923). Indeed, many of the jail reforms that were eagerly anticipated never occurred in the aftermath of initiatives, and many still have not yet been realized (Morris and Rothman 1998).

Differences between Jails and Prisons

"Prisons" and "jails" are terms used synonymously but erroneously in common discourse and the media, even by major political office holders. Jails and prisons do share common characteristics. They are both secure facilities that are typically housed under the executive branch of government. People are physically confined in both settings and deprived of some of their Constitutional rights (e.g., freedom of liberty, movement, and speech). They also pursue common goals. As correctional institutions, they are intended to punish, incapacitate, deter, and rehabilitate people who are accused or convicted of crimes (Cornelius 2008). Along with these shared aims, periods of confinement in both prisons and jails ostracize, marginalize, and stigmatize former incarcerees, often causing them to lose their jobs, homes, and families, and barring them permanently from the community as full-fledged "respectable" citizens (Irwin 1985).

Size

Prisons and jails also differ in many of their fundamental features. The first difference between jails and prisons is size. Generally, jails are much smaller facilities than prisons in terms of their square footage and population capacities. For both jails and prisons, capacities are categorized as "design" (as estimated by architects and planners), "rated" (as deemed by a rating official in a jurisdiction), and "operational" (as determined by correctional administrators based on available staff, programming, and services) (Carson 2015). Exceeding a facility's capacity leads to overcrowding (more inmates and detainees arrive than depart), generating many adverse consequences. For example, jail overcrowding creates inhumane conditions and safety hazards for detainees and detention officers, such as, an increase in assaults, batteries, accidents, injuries, and fatalities as well as the heightened spreading of infectious diseases. Courts have ordered jails to reduce overcrowding by issuing consent decrees that specify a timetable of population reduction and a series of consequences for the failure to comply with such orders (e.g., daily fines for exceeding population limits) (Welsh 1995).

As expected, the largest states have the highest number of jails and the largest jail populations (in 2014): Texas (111; 153,000, respectively), California (33; 119,000, respectively), and Florida (143; 109,000, respectively) (Carson 2015). The average daily population of two-thirds of the country's jails is fewer than 100 people, whereas the average daily population of prisons is more than 400 people (Schlanger 2003). Despite this population differential, the number of jails in America (approximately 3,000) is double the number of prisons (approximately 1,500) (American Jail Association 2015; Schlanger 2003). The smallest venues for housing individuals who have entered the criminal justice system are lock-ups. Neither jails nor prisons, lock-ups are temporary holding facilities in police departments (headquarters or stationhouses) for arrestees who are awaiting transport to a bond court or a jail facility.

The most and largest jails are located in urban centers or conurbations; the least and the smallest are located in rural and other sparsely populated regions of the country. This difference is axiomatic. Large population centers have more people and contain more densely populated and more criminogenic environments compared with more isolated, smaller, and less urbanized environments. More residents commit crimes, leading to more arrests and a greater need for local correctional facilities to house them for further criminal justice system processing or punishment. For example, the three most populous jails in the United States in 2009 were located in Los Angeles County (20,000), New York City (13,000), and Harris County (Houston) (11,000); all of them had larger populations than many of the country's prisons and expectedly are located in some of the country's largest cities (correctionsone.com).

Many jails in large cities house people in more than one facility. For example, New York City has twelve jails; Los Angeles has seven. In contrast, Chicago has one jail, the Cook County Department of Corrections (CCDOC), which is located on 96 acres of land. Each year, the CCDOC admits 100,000 detainees and has an average daily population of more than 9,000 detainees (Olson 2012). The largest cities' jails, called "mega-jails" or "super jails," are defined as those with a bed capacity of 1,000 or more detainees. Large jails have a bed capacity of 250 to 999; medium jails have a bed capacity of 50 to 249; and small jails have a bed capacity of up to 49. The largest number of jails is classified as small, followed by medium, large, and mega-capacity jails (American Jail Association 2015). Super jails are now found in mostly mid-sized rather than large-sized counties (Subramanian, Henrichson, and Kang-Brown 2015).

Governance and Jurisdiction

The second difference between jails and prisons is their auspices or governing authority. An elected or appointed official, known as a sheriff, usually administers jails at the county level. By definition, jails are "municipality-run, confinement facilities" (Subramanian et al. 2015: 4). Sheriffs have been the chief administrators of jails since their inception (Irwin 1985). An appointed official, known as a director, administers prisons at the state level. Individual state and federal prisons are one of a collection of facilities under the aegis of a State Department of Corrections or the Federal Bureau of Prisons, respectively. Prisons are located in various areas throughout a state; typically, they are built in sparsely populated rural areas away from large population centers.

Prison facilities and jail divisions are also categorized with respect to levels of security, which segregate inmates in accordance with their needs for supervision and services. These levels usually range from minimum to super-maximum and are based on incarcerees' history of assaultive, violent, or disruptive behaviors; escape attempts; offense seriousness; medical status; and previous adjustment in a more or less restrictive security level. The higher the level of security, the more fortifications in terms of physical barriers to reduce escapes (e.g., higher walls and triple concertina wire) and the more rules to control and minimize incarcerees' interactions with other detainees (e.g., solitary confinement units) and to restrict communications with visitors and outsiders (e.g., limited visiting hours and partitions to prevent physical contact with visitors). Hence, within a larger jail complex or campus, there are minimum-, medium-, and maximum-security divisions, whereas usually an entire prison is constructed to provide a particular level of security (i.e., minimum, medium, or maximum).

State prisons comprise a system of facilities under the aegis of a statewide department of corrections. With the exception of those found in the country's largest cities, jails are generally individual facilities located in a single central area of a jurisdiction and are named the (County Name) Department of Corrections. For practical and logistical purposes, jails must be situated in proximity to police stations from which arrestees are transported to jail for further booking, processing, and detention. From jails, detainees are then escorted to the courthouse for arraignments, bond assessments, preliminary examinations, continuances, trials, and sentencing hearings.

Purpose and Length of Stay

Although jails and prisons share fundamental correctional goals, they adopt different orientations toward those goals due to basic differences in their sizes, resources, functionalities, and mandates, which is the third set of differences between these institutions. Jail populations are subject to high rates of turnover. People enter and leave jails continually and in large numbers in large jurisdictions. Called the "flow," detainee movements (i.e., admissions, transfers, and discharges) are continual, absent lockdowns for security purposes or cell confinements for headcounts. Detainees are admitted for highly variable stays and can exit the jail at any time, on any day. Unless bond is extremely high or denied, detainees can leave the jail as soon as their bond payment is collected. Detainees are denied bond or levied with a high bond amount due to the serious nature of their alleged criminal activity or offense history, their risk of flight, their tenuous attachment to the community, their membership in a criminal organization, and/or their imminent threat to public safety. They can also exit the jail as soon as their case is dismissed at a preliminary or sentencing hearing. Confinement in a jail is usually measured in hours or days. Hence, the jail population is generally short-term and highly transient (Subramanian et al. 2015). In contrast, prison sentences are always longer than one year and can be a lifetime or longer (e.g., 300 years for convictions on multiple counts, served consecutively).

Jail Operations

Booking Process

All arrestees are subjected to the booking process. The booking process collects information about detainees at the point of entry to the jail in a division generally referred to as the reception and classification or intake unit. Even arrestees who are able to post bail immediately or who receive citations in lieu of jail confinement are booked in order to create an official arrest record. The booking process can take several hours, particularly in large jails following active periods of arrests and staff shortages (e.g., weekends). The first step is to record suspect data for an intake sheet, for example: name, aliases, address, place of employment, physical characteristics (height, weight, eye color), tattoos, next of kin, and current charges. A photograph is taken to differentiate two arrestees with the same name and to establish the visible appearance of any injuries, bruises, wounds, fresh sutures, etc. The suspect's physical condition at arrest is germane to allegations of police use of unnecessary or unlawful force or to questions of the suspect's participation in a prearrest altercation.

At suspects' request, booking officers may allow them to retain small personal items (e.g., a wristwatch). Any articles removed from suspects are inventoried and must be returned to detainees upon their release from jail, unless those items constitute contraband or criminal evidence. Fingerprinting is a standard component of a booking record. Fingerprints are typically entered into a statewide database maintained by the State Police and a nationwide database maintained by the FBI. Fingerprint data are accessible to local, state, and federal police agencies. Police investigators can identify offenders by comparing the fingerprints left at a crime scene to those discovered in a state or federal database. Suspects also can be required to provide a DNA sample (e.g., from a cheek swab), which is submitted to a national DNA database.

A thorough physical search of a detainee is another routine aspect of the booking process. To prevent weapons and drugs from entering a jail, booking officers frequently require arrestees to remove all their clothing and submit to a full-body search. Strip searches are generally legal even when the arrestee has been detained for a relatively minor crime (e.g., unpaid traffic tickets) and even when no facts suggest that the arrestee is carrying a weapon or contraband. For example, the U.S. Supreme Court ruled in 2012 that such a search was legitimate even in the case of a person who was stopped for a traffic violation and arrested for the failure to pay an outstanding fine (the fine had, in fact, already been paid in this case) (*Florence v. Bd. of Chosen Freeholders of City of Burlington, 132 S. Ct. 1510 (2012)*).

The booking officer verifies whether an arrestee has any pending changes; suspects with outstanding warrants are usually denied bail. To protect the health and safety of detention officers and other detainees, the booking process can include, for example, X-rays to detect tuberculosis and blood tests to detect sexually transmitted diseases such as gonorrhea, hepatitis, and AIDS. To reduce the likelihood of violence and injuries, booking officers may ask arrestees about current and former gang affiliations, as well as other criminal relationships, which will determine the placement of a detainee in the proper level of housing (e.g., maximum security, protective custody, or solitary confinement).

Routine questioning during booking could constitute an interrogation that requires detention officers to give a Miranda warning to the suspect. Information that suspects disclose in response to a booking officer's questions may be admitted as evidence under the routine-booking question exception to Miranda. Incriminating information that an arrestee offers in response to a jailer's question about a gang affiliation is generally inadmissible if the defendant had not been accorded Miranda rights, according to *Pennsylvania v. Muniz, 496 U.S. 582* (1990) and *People v. Elizalde, 61 Cal. 4th 523* (2015).

Housing

Unlike early detention centers, modern jails (i.e., those constructed since the 1970s) were designed as safe and humane facilities that are equipped to respond to the medical and behavioral healthcare needs of incarcerees. For the sake of efficiency and safety, many newer jails are adjacent to the courts as well as other public and social service agencies. In the jail, the intake unit (booking and classification) is separated from the housing divisions. As they await booking, detainees are held in a large, open confinement space known as a "bullpen" or "cage." In large jails, the bullpen can be an odiferous, loud, chaotic, and violent environment. From those spaces, detainees are escorted for the booking and assessment process and then assigned to a division for housing, for example, in the general or maximum-security population or to a separate building or division of the jail for substance abuse, psychiatric, or other types of medical treatment. Each division is further divided into blocks or tiers of cells for the purpose of better controlling and serving the detainee population.

The confinement areas for detainees are typically organized in a pod-like or module configuration, which are self-contained and circumscribed living units that vary in size as a function of the overall number of people housed in the jail or in a jail division. Based on a direct supervision model of detainee management, pod designs create a more social environment; diminish the need for detainee movement; enhance security; reduce detainee tension, stress, and suicide attempts; and increase supportive contacts between detainees and detention officers (Farbstein, Liebert, and Sigurdson 1996; Wener 2006). Detention officers are assigned in shifts to oversee each pod and often sit in a protected area with a 360-degree view of the pod. Inside the officers' station, built-in monitors display the running visuals from camera feeds that blanket all of the space in the module.

Officers walk freely around the public and cell areas, interacting with detainees in order to monitor them and respond to their pressing needs for attention and service. Within a module, bi-level adjacent detainee cells, on upper and lower decks, encircle an open space ("public space") with secured round tables and attached seats, immovable chairs and couches, televisions, drink dispensers, bookcases, microwave ovens, and telephones. Special rooms are designated for visiting, programming, and recreation. Many pods also have exercise space.

Cells have one or two beds (a foam cushion on a hard flat surface), a desk and seat, a mirror, a sink with running water and connected toilet, and shelves for books and toiletries. Cells are typically six by six feet or six by ten feet and are dank, dark, and desolate places. Each numbered cell is secured with a steel door with hinges or sliding cell bars both with locks and a slot for food dispensing. Every piece of furniture in the cell and pod is anchored and constructed with industrial-grade durable materials to minimize vandalism and preclude the use of furniture as weapons. In minimum-security jail divisions, detainees are housed in dormitory fashion with cots neatly arrayed in open cubicles with personal storage space underneath. In maximum-security divisions, detainees are in individual cells with less or no time for recreation or contact with other detainees. Cells and personal storage containers are routinely subjected to unannounced, random searches for contraband or weapons.

Jail Population

Overview

The jail population consists of people sentenced to a period of incarceration of up to one year or less for an ordinance violation or misdemeanor conviction. As previously mentioned, the majority of detainees, particularly in large jails, are held pending the disposition of their cases at a preliminary hearing or trial. These incarcerees can include current prison inmates who must return to the local courts to face additional charges or further sentencing on subsequent convictions. In some jurisdictions, jails can incarcerate prison inmates from overcrowded state institutions. However, most detainees are confined to jail because they are unable to raise money for bail or comply with the conditions of pretrial release (Subramanian et al. 2015).

Jail admissions are the number of people who enter the jail in a particular year. The jail population consists of all the people confined on a given day or the average number of people confined daily in a given year, in a given facility, in a given jurisdiction. The per-capita jail incarceration rate is calculated by dividing the number of detainees by the total number of residents (aged 15–64) in the jail's jurisdiction (i.e., city or county) multiplied by the population size that is used to report the rate (i.e., per 1,000, per 10,000, per 100,000 residents). Jail admissions and discharges are the number of people entering and exiting the jail, respectively, in a given year. The numbers of admissions and discharges always exceed the number of individuals in each group, as detainees can enter and leave the jail two or more times throughout a given year.

Recent Population Growth

From 1970 to 2014, the number of detainees in the United States increased fourfold from 157,000 to 690,000. Similarly, the number of super jails increased sevenfold from 21 to 145, with the highest growth by far in small- and mid-sized counties, which encompassed 106, or 73 percent, of such facilities. Jail populations also grew at much faster rates in small- (less than 250,000 residents) (an increase of 6.8 percent) and mid-sized counties (greater than 250,000 but less than 1 million) (an increase of 4.1 percent) than they did in large-sized counties (greater than 1 million) (an increase of 2.8 percent). The growth in the jail population can be attributed to significant increases in the average length of stay, which more than doubled from nine days in 1978 to 23 days in 2014 (Subramanian et al. 2015).

From mid-year 2007 to mid-year 2014, the jail population rate decreased from 259 per 100,000 to 234 per 100,000. During the 2000s, the midyear jail population reached its peak in 2008 (785,500) and in 2014 fell to 744,600, when 11.4 million people were admitted to local jails in a 12-month period. The rated capacity of jails at the time was 890,500 beds. From 2000 to 2014, the jail population was at its lowest in 2000 (621,149). Nearly all (95 percent) of the growth in the jail population during the aughts was attributed to the rise in the numbers of unconvicted detainees. The racial distributions of detainees at mid-year 2014 was 47 percent White, 35 percent African American, and 15 percent Latino (Minton and Zeng 2015).

Special Subpopulations

The criminalization of the mentally ill has been a concern in the literature since the early 1970s. The growing number of people with serious mental illnesses housed in jails in the United States is attributable to several historical factors, including the closure of state psychiatric hospitals without the creation of community-based follow-up care as well as the war on drugs, which arrested and detained a steady flow of people with addictions who have a high rate of co-occurring other psychiatric disorders (Lurigio 2013). In a national survey, more than 40 percent of jail detainees (approximately 184,500 incarcerees) reported that they experienced symptoms of a psychiatric disorder (e.g., major depression, bipolar disorder, schizophrenia, and anxiety disorder) in the 30 days preceding the interview. Respondents indicated that these symptoms caused them serious psychological distress (Beck, Berzofsky, Caspar, and Krebs 2013).

Along with the rise in the representation of the mentally ill in detention centers, the proportion of female detainees has risen at a rapid pace since the 1970s and has necessitated the provision of gender-responsive services and housing. Specifically, the population of women in jail grew fourteen-fold, from fewer than 8,000 in 1970 to nearly 110,000 in 2014 (Subramanian et al. 2015). Jails have also encountered appreciable growth in the percentages of detainees with disabilities. For example, in 2011–2012, a study of the jail population indicated that one-third of detainees suffered from one or more medical problems related to ambulation, cognition (the most common disability), hearing, vision, self-care, and independent living. These problems were many times higher than the prevalence of such disabilities in the general U.S. population (Bronson, Maruschak, and Berzosky 2015).

In conclusion, jails in the early 2000s have vastly improved compared with the previous few decades. The direct supervision model has resulted in the better management of the detainee population as well as significant improvements in the quality of life and safety of detainees. More attention is being paid to the healthcare needs of detainees, and jails have become more gender-responsive. Despite these numerous inroads into improved care for incarcerees, jails today resemble their earliest incarnations in many respects. They remain disproportionately populated by people of color and persons with mental illness and communicable diseases, as well as the poor, the homeless, and the marginalized. A stint in jail, by itself, increases the likelihood of a conviction, infectious illness, a sentence to prison, and subsequent criminal activity, "making jail a gateway to deeper and more lasting involvement in the criminal justice system at considerable costs to the people involved and to society at large" (Subramanian 2015: 5).

References

American Jail Association. 2015. *Statistics of Note*. Hagerstown, MD: Author.

Beck, Allen J., Marcus Berzofsky, Rachel Caspar, and Christopher Krebs. 2013. *Sexual Victimization in Prisons and Jails Reported by Inmates, 2011–12*. Washington, DC: U.S. Department of Justice, Office of Justice Programs, Bureau of Justice Statistics.

Bronson, Jennifer, Laura M. Maruschak, and Marcus Berzofsky. 2015. *Disabilities among Prison and Jail Inmates, 2011–12*. Washington, DC: U.S. Department of Justice, Office of Justice Programs, Bureau of Justice Statistics.

Carson, E. Ann. 2015. *Prisoners in 2014*. Washington, DC: U.S. Department of Justice, Office of Justice Programs, Bureau of Justice Statistics.

Casey, Roy. 1954. "Catchall Jails." *The ANNALS of the American Academy of Political and Social Science* 293(1): 28–34.

Cornelius, Gary F. 2008. *The American Jail: Cornerstone of Modern Corrections*. Pearson/Prentice Hall.

Farbstein, Jay, Dennis R. Liebert, and Herbert Sigurdson. 1996. *Audits of Podular Direct Supervision Jails*. Washington, DC: National Institute of Corrections.

Fishman, Joseph Fulling, and Vee Perlman. 1923. *Crucibles of Crime: The Shocking Story of the American Jail*. No. 35. Patterson Smith.

Gollaher, David. 1995. *Voice for the Mad: The Life of Dorothea Dix*. New York: Free Press.

Hirsh, Adam J. 1992. *The Rise of the Penitentiary: Prisons and Punishment in Early America*. New Haven, CT: Yale University Press.

Irwin, John. 1985. "The Jail: Managing the Underclass in American Society." Berkeley, CA: University of California Press.

Kaeble, Danielle, Lauren Glaze, Anastasios Tsoutis, and Todd Minton. 2015. *Correctional Populations in the United States, 2014*. Washington, DC: U.S. Department of Justice, Office of Justice Programs, Bureau of Justice Statistics.

Lurigio, Arthur J. 2013. "Criminalization of the Mentally Ill: Exploring Causes and Current Evidence in the United States." *Criminologist* 38: 1–8.

Mattick, Hans W. 1969. Illinois Jails: Challenge and Opportunities for the 1970s. Chicago, IL: Center for Studies in Criminal Justice, University of Chicago.

Minton, Todd D., and Zhen Zeng. 2015. *Jail Inmates at Midyear 2014*. Washington, DC: U.S. Department of Justice, Office of Justice Programs, Bureau of Justice Statistics.

Morris, Norval. 1974. *The Future of Imprisonment*. Chicago, IL: University of Chicago Press.

Morris, Norval, and David Rothman. 1998. *The Oxford History of Prison: The Practice of Punishment in Western Society*. New York: Oxford University Press.

Olson, D.E. 2012. *Cook County Sheriff's Reentry Council Research Bulletin: Population Dynamics and the Characteristics of Inmates in the Cook County Jail*. Chicago, IL: Cook County Sheriff's Office.

Rothman, David J. 2011. *The Discovery of the Asylum: Social Order and Disorder in the New Republic.* New Brunswick, NJ: Transaction Press.
Schlanger, Margo. 2003. *Differences between Jails and Prisons*. Cambridge, MA: Prisons Seminar, Harvard Law School.
Subramanian, Ram. 2015. *Incarceration's Front Door: The Misuse of Jails in America.* New York: VERA Institute of Justice, Center on Sentencing and Corrections.
Subramanian, Ram, Christian Henrichson, and Jacob Kang-Brown. 2015. *In Our Own Backyard: Confronting Growth and Disparities in American Jails.* New York: VERA Institute of Justice, Center on Sentencing and Corrections. "The Ten Largest Jail Jurisdictions in the United States." Retrieved June 22, 2016 from correctionsone.com
Welsh, Wayne N. 1995. *Counties in Court: Jail-Overcrowding and Court-Ordered Reform.* Temple University Press.
Wener, Richard. 2006. "Effectiveness of the Direct Supervision System of Correctional Design and Management." *Criminal Justice and Behavior* 33: 392–410.
Zupan, Linda L. 1991. *Jails: Reform and the New Generation Philosophy*. Cincinnati, OH: Anderson.

11 Prisons in the United States

Vanessa H. Woodward and Dylan Pelletier

Prisons in the United States are an integral component of punishment within the United States' correctional system. While incapacitation (within prisons or jails) has often been viewed as the traditional form of punishment, within recent years, there has been an influx of alternatives to incarceration. In fact, as of 2014, only 22.7 percent of those under correctional supervision were incarcerated in prison (Kaeble, Glaze, Tsoutis, and Minton 2014). Yet, even with these alternative sanctions, rates of probation have not changed substantially, and the rate of incarceration has, on average, decreased only 0.3 percent annually (from 2000 to 2014). Further, America continues to have one of the highest rates of incarceration in the world. These rates are largely attributable to "get tough" policies that focused on extended sentences for various crimes, as well as mandatory imprisonment for certain drug-related offenses (Carlson and Garrett 2013).

Currently, there are almost 1300 American prisons, with at least one operating in every state. Almost half of facilities are located in the south, while all other regions (Midwest, West, and Northeast) run at or below 20 percent of all U.S. prisons (Clear, Reisig, Petrosino, and Cole 2016). As of 2014, there were 1,561,525 persons incarcerated, with 86.5 percent held in state prison facilities and the remaining 13.5 percent in federal facilities. These include offenders who were held in privately run institutions at both the federal and state level (19.0 percent and 6.8 percent, respectively) (Kaeble et al. 2014). Over half those incapacitated (54 percent) had been convicted of a violent crime, and almost 16 percent of inmates' most serious offense was drug related, including 3.6 percent being drug possession.

The Purpose of Prison

When an individual violates social norms and/or law to an extent that it causes disruption or harm, a desire to punish that person is, in part, reflexive (Travis III 2015). While community corrections (probation and other alternatives) is now the dominant form of punishment, prisons have maintained convention in the U.S. criminal justice system. This is largely because of their dual ability to punish those who have broken the law and protect both actual and potential victims from future crime as it "[destroys] the offender's capacity to reoffend" (McConville, 1994: 604). Further, the development of prisons during the early eighteenth century was motivated by the rationale of deterrence: that when a just punishment was imposed, it would regulate future crime. Specifically, proportionate punishment would prevent the specific offender whom it was punishing from committing that crime again (what Beccaria referred to as "specific deterrence"), as well as prevent others from committing the same crime, out of fear that they too would be given a similar punishment (referred to as general deterrence) (Lasker 1991). While prisons have changed drastically in the past two centuries, the same general mindset on prison and incapacitation remains: punish the offender, protect the public, and prevent future crime.

The History of Prisons in the United States

While prisons are regarded primarily as a function of punishment, this has not always been the case. Starting in the Middle Ages, the purpose of prisons was most often confinement; particularly, they were classified as houses of detention. Thus, the act of imprisonment was rarely implemented with the intention to punish (Langbein 1976). This remained commonplace in the U.S. through the late 1700s. For example, over an 85-year period (from 1691–1776), judges sentenced only 19 individuals to prison (Taylor 2008). Even in the early nineteenth century, most individuals in prisons had not committed serious offenses; instead, they had a debt they could not pay. This practice was abolished in 1831 (Barnes 1921).

Despite these more recent origins, the notion of imprisonment's utility as a mode of punishment is nothing novel. In his book, *Slavery and the Penal System*, Sellin (2016) described Plato's proposal of three prisons: one that would be public and heavily populated, located in close proximity to the people; a second for purposes of reforming inmates, and a third, that would be geographically isolated from the public—with an objective to (somehow) punish its offenders.

Historically, methods of imprisonment mirrored those of present-day jails: detaining individuals awaiting trial. Due to the transient inmate population, there were short time periods during gaol delivery when the jails would be emptied (Barnes 1921). For instance, in Pennsylvania, prior to the development of the penitentiary, the court was called "The Court of Quarter Sessions and Jail Delivery." As DePuy (1954) pointed out, it was a fitting name: four times annually, the jails would be briefly uninhabited.

Since the sixteenth century, imprisonment used for purposes of punishment has centered on two key objectives: hard labor and confinement. Banishment was a popular form of punishment in England, as it was a simple method of confinement—the convict was essentially quarantined without adding additional burdens or concerns on the state. Prior to the American revolution, the majority of banished convicts in England were sent to the U.S. colonies. Afterwards, Australia became the most popular destination of exiled, English convicts (Taylor 2008).

Using convicted offenders as labor has been a method of punishment used since (at least) the sixteenth century. The primary motivation behind implementing "penal servitude" has often lacked penological focus. For instance, in Europe, convicted offenders were sentenced to work as oarsmen on galleys (Taylor 2008). While easier to control than traditional ships, galleys were dangerous and required hundreds to row (Langbein 1976). Unable to find a sufficient number of workers to employ, it became common practice to sentence offenders to this work. Punishments of working on galleys changed in line with economic needs: once the need for galley oarsmen declined, convicts were then sentenced to work on construction. During the same period of time, and first developed in Holland (Barnes 1921), workhouses were used more as an effort to manage the poor and vagrants than to manage offenders who had committed serious crimes (Langbein 1976; Taylor 2008). There were some exceptions, with records indicating that some serious offenders had been sentenced to workhouses as well (DePuy 1951).

Within Europe and the Colonies, punishment typically focused on methods of corporal punishment and/or fines (Barnes 1921). Within the Colonies, there was little concern regarding why crime occurred. To the colonists, crime was another form of sin and thus normal and expected. Therefore, there was little regard to methods of punishment, as punishment was not considered in the context of a deterrent effect (Rothman 1971).

Prior to the American Revolution, the first prison was founded in the American colonies in 1773 in Simsbury, Connecticut. Used for purposes of detainment, it was also used to imprison loyalists during the war (Whitehead, Dodson, and Edwards 2012). Housed in an old copper mine, the prison was approximately 25 feet underground. There was little regard to separation by class, age, or sex—essentially creating chaos. The prison was closed in 1782 for a period of eight years, and was then replaced with a state prison in the 1820s (Welch 2013).

The creation of the American penitentiary arose in the late eighteenth century as a response to crime and prison reform, coupled with limitations of other methods of punishment. Specifically, banishment was no longer feasible, and the number of crimes classified as capital offenses had declined significantly. Maintaining the functions of hard labor and confinement, the first penitentiary was designed as an amalgamation of a workhouse and a jail (house of detention) (Barnes 1921).

The Pennsylvania System

After the American Revolution, there were a number of effects on social reform (Barnes 1921; Jenkins 1984). Specifically, during this time, there had been change in social philosophy and politics that focused more on rationalism (e.g., Beccaria's *On Crime and Punishment*; Bentham's *Utilitarianism*) (Clear, Reisig, and Cole 2016). The influence of enlightenment thinkers affected change in how people viewed punishment (Ignatieff 1981) in both Europe and the U.S.—particularly in Philadelphia. Essentially, there were two parties, who together, were primarily responsible for the impetus of punishment reform within the United States: Pennsylvania Quakers and European reformists and philosophers (Barnes 1921).

Starting in the seventeenth century, Quaker principles helped shape legal and social reform within the colonies. There was particular concern over the use of corporal punishment and an overabundance of offenses classified as capital crimes. William Penn, a Quaker, and the founder of the Pennsylvania Colony advocated for imprisonment as an alternative to severe corporal punishment (Stohr, Walsh, and Hemmens 2013). In 1682, his efforts became realized in "Penn's Great Law," which banned the practice of convicts paying for their own imprisonment. The penal code also outlined "the provision of jails to replace pillories and stocks" (Whitehead, Dodson, and Edwards 2012: 28). However, by 1718, progress made by Penn's laws were extinguished due to the reintroduction of England's traditional forms of corporal punishment (Sellin 1953).

During the late 1700s, Philadelphia was a prime environment to implement reform. There were a number of its inhabitants who were heavily influenced by French and English enlightenment philosophers and reformists. Deemed progressive, the city was populated with a number of Frenchmen during the revolution, many of whom were radical thinkers, influenced by the work of Voltaire and Montesquieu. Meanwhile, Thomas Jefferson traveled to Philadelphia shortly after spending time in France where he learned a great deal about enlightenment. Also residing in Philadelphia was Benjamin Franklin, a Founding Father and future governor of Pennsylvania, who, in 1776, became the first U.S. Ambassador to France. Concurrent with these events was John Howard's publication of *The State of the Prisons* (1777). An Englishman, John Howard had been imprisoned in France 12 years prior, which ostensibly motivated his concern for prisoner's rights. After becoming the High Sheriff of Bedfordshire in 1773, he was tasked with visiting prison institutions within Europe (Taylor 2008). These observations resulted in his published book, in which he provided a comprehensive review of prison conditions. Howard described the barbaric traditions of various institutions, such as Britain's gaols, in which there was no separation by age, crime, or sex and where "more prisoners died in sickness and disease than were executed by the very common practice of hanging" (Carlson and Garrett 2013: 5).

The Quaker influence continued in the late part of the century. Richard Wistar, a member of the Society of Friends, had seen the conditions of the local jails and began bringing the inmates homemade soup. In 1776, Wistar founded the Philadelphia Society for Assisting Distressed Prisoners (Vaux 1884). However, it dissolved within a year (due to the Philadelphia Campaign) (Post 1944). Eleven years later (in 1787), the society was resurrected and renamed The Philadelphia Society for Alleviating the Misery of Public Prisons. The Society's revival was partially attributable to the work of two Founding Fathers (Benjamin Rush and Benjamin Franklin), 13 members of the American Philosophical Society, as well as the resolve of a number of Quakers: half of the Society's members also belonged to the Society of Friends (Barnes 1921; Lasker 1991; Sellin 1953). The partnership between American reformers and Quakers was crucial to the development of the first state penitentiary in the U.S.: The Walnut Street Jail (Welch 2013). This effort was largely influenced by the work of John Howard; in fact, according to Barnes (1921), the society used Howard's description of a Bridewell in Norfolk to gain support for their proposed penitentiary design that separated convicts by crime seriousness and sex. The society's efforts were largely realized in an Act of 1789, in which debtors and other petty criminals were housed in the workhouse, and the prison became the home to felons and detainees. However, the society also campaigned for "solitary confinement at hard labor" (Sellin 1953: 328). These efforts were accomplished the following year, in an Act of 1790 that stipulated new requirements for the separation of offenders: workhouses were to be used solely for debtors, and renamed "The Debtor's Apartment" (Sellin 1953: 328). Petty criminals, convicted of misdemeanors were to be housed in the prison. A new addition was built in order to separately house the more serious felons, who would be confined in solitary and sentenced to hard labor, which became known as the "penitentiary house" (Sellin 1953: 329) and was supervised by 12 inspectors (Skidmore 1948).

The Walnut Street Jail became home to the first penitentiary and the establishment of the Pennsylvania System. Within the penitentiary, inmates were to be separated from other prisoners and occupy their time with hard, manual labor (Whitehead et al. 2012). There was little-to-no contact with the outside world. The only entity that inmates could turn to for solace was the Bible. In essence, the penitentiary was used to implement confinement as a method of punishment that would lead to individual reform. If those who had committed criminal acts were able to think about their wrongdoings in solitude devoid of external influences, then they could become aware of how their behavior was wrong and eventually transform into a productive member of society (Clear, Reisig, and Cole 2016; Rolston 2011).

While the ideals of the Quakers were quite prominent, it is somewhat of a misnomer that they were the dominant force of the establishment of the penitentiary. As Michael Welch explained:

> Although the influences of William Penn and the Quakers on penal reform in the 1780s cannot be easily dismissed, it is important to note that when the Walnut Street Jail opened, Episcopalians governed the Society. Whereas the Quakers were concerned with promoting penal reform, the Society was more interested in the establishment of the Walnut Street Jail as a state prison so that political power would be centralized.
>
> (2013: 58)

While there was strong speculation that the Walnut Street Penitentiary would be incredibly successful, there were a number of problems that had not been foreseen, most importantly, issues with classification and overcrowding (Barnes 1921; DePuy 1951). "Crude attempts" of classification of prisoners, such as one of four classes in 1791: "sentenced to confinement only, select class, probationary class, and old offenders" (DePuy 1954: 139) were problematic, due to limitations of housing structures, which resulted in frequent riots and escapes in the early 1800s. Despite these problems, there were still some indications that imprisonment with certain programs had the potential for some success as compared to other modes of punishment (DePuy 1954).

While the Pennsylvania system was first established at Walnut Street Jail, it evolved at two penitentiaries: The Eastern State Penitentiary and The Western State Penitentiary. The Western State Penitentiary, built in response to the recommendations of the Walnut Street Jail's Board of Inspectors, was designed in 1818 by William Strickland (Doll 1957). Built in 1826 with 190 cells, it was modeled after Bentham's *Panopoticon*, which proved faulty in its design (Barnes 1921; DePuy 1951; Welch 2013). Maintenance of the prison was much costlier than originally anticipated and the cells were small and dimly lit, making solitary manual labor impossible (Thibaut 1982).

William Strickland was originally the architect for the Eastern State Penitentiary; however, he was eventually replaced by John Haviland (DePuy 1951), who was acquainted with John Howard (Clear, Reisig, and Cole 2016). The Eastern State Penitentiary, located in Cherry Hill, Pennsylvania, near Philadelphia, was designed in 1821 and built in 1829. Its first Warden was Samuel R. Wood, who had served on the Board of Inspectors for the Walnut Street Prison (DePuy 1951). The Eastern State Penitentiary had a number of advantages, including that it was able to avoid past mistakes of both the Western State Penitentiary and the Walnut Street Jail. The design of the Eastern Penitentiary was unique; seven lines of cell blocks surrounded a circular hub that included a watchtower (Carlson and Garrett 2013). Although influenced from English prison designs, Haviland is credited with incorporating the radial design into American architecture (Johnston 1954). While prisoners were still in solitude, they were able to access a small prison yard twice daily (Welch 2013), yet were not able to have contact with other inmates. To ensure there was not contact, inmates were blinded when being escorted to the prison yard (Welch 2013). In response, inmates developed a "Morse code" type system to communicate with one another by "tapping noises over the plumbing pipes" (Whitehead et al. 2012: 29). While each cell had its own window, it could be easily blocked for purposes of further discipline (Clear, Reisig, and Cole 2016). Essentially, the only real human contact inmates had was with clergy (Whitehead et al. 2012).

Similar to its predecessors, the Eastern State Penitentiary's cost of maintenance was exorbitant, and the burden was simply too much to bear (Castle 2016). While the Pennsylvania system was implemented within a few other prisons outside the state, the system eventually died out. However, the implementation and design of this system remains relevant today for a myriad of reasons. Unsurprisingly, it has had substantial impact on the use of solitary confinement in penal institutions. Additionally, its effects on penal reform have been persistent (Skidmore 1948).

Auburn Model

Considering the downfalls of its predecessor, the Auburn (or New York) model of prisons implemented a variant approach: it maintained solitary confinement, but only at night (Rolston 2011). A call for a new prison in 1816 resulted in the Auburn Prison in Cayuga County, built in 1819. William Brittin was a carpenter who was put in charge of the project, and became the prison's first warden (Barnes 1921). The original intent of the Auburn system was to maintain continuous solitude; however, this was quickly abandoned and replaced with a modified method of confinement. Prisoners were allowed to congregate during the day; however, they were prohibited from interacting with one another, which became known as the "congregate but silent system" (Welch 2013). Within the prisons, the cells were quite small and lined up in rows, with each row containing a varying number of cells (depending on the population of prisoners within each classification), and each row having three levels (Carlson and Garrett 2013).

Two years after its founding, Elam Lynds became the second Warden of the prison. Lynds was crucial to the development of the Auburn System. His military background provided him with the idea to introduce the lockstep march within the prison. However, Lynds was also known for his use of physical discipline. Barnes and Teeter (1946: 522) wrote "In a perverse sense of logic, Lynds 'regarded flogging as the most effective and the most humane of all punishments, since it did no injury to the prisoner's health and in no wise impaired his physical strength'" (as cited in Welch 2013: 51). Similar to earlier use of inmate labor, prisoners worked daily for the dual purpose of individual reform and financial profit. Lynds, who scoffed at the idea of reforming convicts (Schwartz 1985), viewed the success of the prison from a macro perspective, focusing on the organization structure and gave little consideration to the individual (Clear, Reisig, and Cole 2016). Within the Auburn system, prisoners always were required to wear the classic black-and-white striped uniform. When it came time to replace the Newgate Prison at Mount Pleasant, Lynds was granted authority to supervise the building of the new prison, which was constructed by means of convict labor (Fiddler 2008; Welch 2013). Designed by John Carpenter, the design was unique and featured increased security: "The cells were positioned back to back in a freestanding, central core" (Fiddler 2008: 19). Similar to Auburn, the prisoners worked together in silence and were isolated at night. This prison eventually became what is known today as Sing-Sing (Taylor 2008).

Of the two systems, the Auburn System prevailed. Other states that had modeled the Pennsylvania system were quick to move towards replication of the Auburn style. Despite its controversies, the Auburn system was more popular than its predecessor, as it was seen as more manageable and economically feasible. In some form, the Auburn system continued as the dominant model of penitentiaries until after the Civil War (Castle 2016). During this time, there was grave concern regarding the corruption and brutality within prisons (Clear, Reisig, and Cole 2016), including the resignation of several wardens of Auburn-modeled institutions.

Correctional Reform and the Industrial Era

Most often, the historical development of U.S. prisons is predominantly attributable to institutions in the northeast; however, the development of prisons within both the south and west is also pertinent in understanding current correctional practices. It was not until the 1800s that the south developed any formal prison institutions; however, by 1820, four states operated Pennsylvania-model prisons: Georgia, Kentucky, Maryland, and Virginia (Clear, Reisig, and Cole 2016). By the mid 1800s, both Mississippi and Texas had built and operated Auburn-model institutions. After the Civil War, the south was met with multiple problems: the economy was in shambles, there was a need for more prisons, as well as a significant loss of labor due to the abolition of slavery. Many southerners were in dire need of workers, particularly considering their heavy reliance on farming (Whitehead et al. 2012). In effect, to replace a system of slavery, convicts were leased to local farmers, as well as large and small business owners. Convict leasing was nothing novel: it was first used in Massachusetts in the late 1700s, and many southern states already had implemented systems of leasing prior to the Civil War (Carleton 1967, 1984). While there was use of convict leasing prior to the civil war, it was scant in the public sector. As Gill (1931b) noted, inmate employment for "public works and ways" (p. 88), increased from 0.5 percent to 20 percent from 1885 to 1923. In exchange for paying off their fines, lessors gained temporary ownership of convicts to work in construction, farming, or other hard forms of labor (Welch 2013). While leasing was often done through individual cases, there were instances of mass convict leasing: Texas, Louisiana, and Alabama leased entire penitentiaries to contractors or firms for construction and farming (Clear, Reisig, Petrosino and Cole 2016; Dolovich 2005). This form of labor was relatively cheap. Further, policies were made to ensure that there was a continual influx of convicts. For instance, petty crimes once punishable by small fines were replaced with multi-year prison sentences, with particular targeting of African Americans (Dolovich 2005; Thompson 2010).

The shift from slavery to leasing was arguably slight—it was really just replacing one form of slavery with another. Since convicts were leased and not owned, there was no long-term investment; thus, there was little concern regarding their health, resulting in harsh punishments and brutal working conditions. This was seen as profitable and beneficial to prisons (leasing out its convicts) and business owners alike (Carlson and Garrett 2013). By no means was inmate labor isolated in the south; however, due to its distinct goals (of replacing slave labor for purposes of farming and construction) it led to the eventual creation of penal farms, which were first established in Louisiana, Mississippi, and Texas. Parchman farm, located in Mississippi, became known as the "model of southern penology" (Welch 2013). While there was copious criticism of the leasing system; many states did not outlaw the practice until the early 1900s, with Alabama being the last to follow suit (Taylor 1942).

Generally, the west saw little development of prisons until after the civil war, with the exception of San Quentin in 1852 (Dolovich 2005). Similar to the south, convict leasing was popular, as the primary concern was profit, not punishment. By 1879, a prison was built in Folsom, California to manage an overflow of inmates at San Quentin (MacCormick 1929).

Reformatory Era

The Elmira Reformatory (which opened in 1876) is most often associated with the reformatory era of imprisonment in the United States; however, there was already a foundation of reform. Almost 20 years prior (in 1857), Ohio had created a reform farm for first-time, young male offenders. The system was modeled after the ideologies of Sir Walter Crofton of Ireland and Alexander Maconochie, two penal reformers who each had made great strides in Ireland and Australia. Additionally, in the annual report of the New York Prison Association, Gaylord B. Hubell, a Crofton enthusiast, purported that the Irish prison system would serve great utility in the U.S. prison system (Lewis 1917; Putney and Putney 1962). This was followed by similar recommendations by two other Crofton enthusiasts: Enoch Cobb Wines and Theodore Dwight (Putney and Putney 1962). The aforementioned individuals, as well as Zebulon Brockway and Frank Sanborn, spoke at the Prison Congress of 1870, held in Cincinnati. Brockway purported that there was a need to reform prisoners for the good of society. If prisoners were released without reformation, then the institution was knowingly contributing to societal harm (Putney and Putney 1962). Zebulon, the would-be prison administrator of Elmira reformatory and a born-again Christian (Welch 2013), believed that individuals could be reformed, and that this change from "bad" to "good" was, in essence, permanent (Rolston 2011). The Declaration of Principles of the 1870 Congress emphasized the importance of two key factors for convict reform: self-respect and independence. The prison reform advocates also argued for the separation of inmates, with separate institutions for youth and for serious criminals (Gutterman 1992).

While the Act that authorized the building of the Elmira Reformatory in Elmira, NY was passed in 1869, it was not until 1876 that the reformatory opened its doors (Rolston 2011). In fact, the institution mirrored an Auburn system penitentiary until 1880 when its methods were more formally implemented (Putney and Putney 1962). The methods focused more on treatment, through an emphasis of indeterminate sentencing (Castle 2016), and was the first institution to implement parole (Bonta, Rugge, Scott, Bouorgon, and Yessine 2008). While inmates could be held no longer than a traditional sentence for a crime, the indeterminate sentencing structure allowed for a reward-centered system that had three classifications: all inmates entered the reformatory at a grade two, and, depending on their behavior, could either move "up" to a grade one or "down" to a grade three. In order to be reclassified as a grade-one inmate, one would have to earn 54 "marks" of good behavior, with a maximum of nine allowed monthly (Rothman 1980). To downgrade from a grade-two to a grade-one inmate, one had to commit one of three types of misconduct: crookedness, quarrelling, or total disregard for the rules (see Rothman, 1980). Additionally, simple acts of misconduct could negate any progress that one had made. For instance, if a convict committed three acts of misconduct each month, after three months all progress that had been made would be nullified, essentially requiring the inmate to start over. Changes in classifications were not meaningless. Those with grade-one status had a multitude of privileges that were not awarded to the lower grades (Putney and Putney 1962; Rothman 1980). Further, only those in grade one could be considered for release. While grade one inmates wore blue uniforms those who were classified as grade three wore bright red. There were three possible outcomes for incorrigible, grade-three inmates: placement in solitary, hard labor, or transfer to another institution (Rothman 1980).

The reformatory model also placed emphasis on education, vocational training, and religious instruction (Gutterman 1992; Welch 2013). While there was an emphasis on treatment, methods of discipline and punishment remained. Brockway used military methods, yet found maintaining control to be challenging. Although he had been outspoken regarding his opposition to corporal punishment, corporal punishment became a common form of discipline within the institution, with about one-third of the inmates receiving twice-weekly whippings. Brockway would also use solitary confinement combined with hand or feet shackling (Rothman 1980; Welch 2013).

In 1888, Brockway reported that 78.5 percent of its inmates had been released and were (in all likelihood) "reformed" (Gutterman 1992). While on their face these numbers sounded impressive, there were a number of problems with these statistics, and data to support these findings were gravely lacking (Rothman 1980). However, the seeming success of the system quickly faltered. In 1900, the International Penal and Penitentiary Congress was asked to endorse the reformatory model for all U.S. prisons. They failed to do so, arguing that there was simply not enough evidence to support such action. In that same time, *The New York World* published an article outlining Brockway's own use of corporal punishment (Gutterman 1992). Brockway blamed the downfall on the board, specifically issues of overcrowding. In that same year, Brockway and the board of managers partook in an argument that forced Brockway to resign. When reflecting on the outcome of the reformatory model, Gutterman identified the system's flaws.

> While Elmira had the important elements of reform, it failed to provide the right sort of psychological surroundings to implement its objectives. There was no grasp of the fundamental fact that a prisoner, to be prepared for a life of freedom, must be trained in some sort of social environment, which, as to his liberty and responsibility, has a fair resemblance to the society that he will reenter. There was no general recognition that the criminal must be dealt with as an individual, to assist him to lead a good and useful life on discharge. There was no encouragement to develop restraint born of character and responsibility. Basically, there was not attempt to develop in the prisoner a measure of self-development.
>
> (Gutterman 1992: 869)

What followed the reformatory era was the short-lived progressive era, which lasted only 20 years (Hanser 2016). During this time, there was an emphasis on what the reformatory model had lacked—social and psychological context. Progressives during this time worked to implement more educational and rehabilitative programs. While brief, the era helped to incorporate social and psychological staff in penological institutions (Hanser 2016). Progressives were of the mindset that crime reform had to be approached from the individual level, as each person's case varied; thus, there was no blanket program that could treat all offenders; there was a need for unique programs that were tailored to each inmate. Prior to the progressive era, behavior was typically thought of in the context of religion and morality. The progressives aided in reframing that context to incorporate other factors including economic, social, and psychological factors. Each individual's own history was pertinent to determining treatment (Welch 2013). Progressives were largely responsible for more widespread implementation of parole and probation (Clear, Reisig, and Cole 2016).

An emphasis on the therapeutic needs of the individual aided in the progression of the correctional system to the medical model. The medical model had a strong emphasis of positivism, and how inmates should be viewed as patients—diagnosing and treating each individually. The emergence of treatment was inevitable when considering changes in drug regulation and prohibition, which resulted in a wave of inmates sentenced for their substance use (Welch 2013). One of its chief advocates was Howard Gill, who was the superintendent of Norfolk State Prison in Massachusetts (Clear, Reisig, and Cole 2016). Gill believed in professionalizing the prison system (Gill 1962) by incorporating treatment staff, including social workers, educators, and psychologists (Gill 1931a; Prout and Ross 1988; Rothman 1980). Gill's work was largely criticized, and he was removed in 1934 after the escape of four inmates (Clear, Reisig, and Cole 2016).

Also of importance during this time period was the creation of the Federal Bureau of Prisons in 1930 (Bussert, Goldberger and Price 2006). While federal prisons had long been established—for instance, in 1891, Congress approved the building of three prisons (known as the "Three Prisons Act"); yet, until the 1920s, there were so few inmates that there was simply not a need for multiple federal institutions to house them, and the majority were housed in state prisons (see the Judiciary Act of 1789) (Roberts 1997). The national prohibition of alcohol changed that. As prisons became overcrowded, it was necessary to establish a more organized system with formal institutions. The Federal Bureau of Prisons, along with the Federal Prison Industry (established in 1934) aided in the creation of a more formal system with professional staff and emphasis on inmates being assigned to various work tasks. This was beneficial for multiple reasons: inmates' time was occupied, it deemphasized hard labor, it was economical (as inmates were essentially funding their own prison sentence), and inmates were able to develop employable skills that were useful upon their release (Clear, Reisig, and Cole 2016; Roberts 1997). The federal prison system also formalized the classification of prisoners, which aided in the movement towards treatment and rehabilitation (Clear, Reisig, and Cole 2016). The system received vast funding for various programs that were found to be effective. As Welch (2013) described, this was largely due to the characteristics of federal inmates—they tended to be less violent and more educated than state prisoners. The reverence of their programs was far-reaching: many states with limited funding tried to replicate both their programs and classification system (Roberts 1997).

Beginning in the early 1900s, there was stark awareness of the need for treatment. Penologists became mindful of the fact that the majority of inmates returned to society. In fact, in 1940, Gault (the editor of *Criminal Law and Criminology*, citing notes from the 1940 meeting of the Committee on Sentencing, Probation, Prisons, and Parole) concluded that all but 3 percent of inmates returned to society. Thus, in order for punishment to be justified and effective, it must consider how such punishment would affect the safety of the public. It became glaringly obvious that the safety of the public was dependent on the rehabilitation of most offenders. Findings indicated, however, that recidivism rates were high, and fault lay with more than prison officials: it was largely attributable to "partisan politics [preventing] progress in penology in many jurisdictions by making the prison a dumping ground for the spoilsman" (Gault 1940: 324). As a result of these findings, the committee made four recommendations; within them, "urging the bar to give greater attention to problems of penology and criminology" (p. 324).

Criticism of the treatment of inmates spread further in response to a string of prison riots in the early 1950s. One attribution to this problem was the increased use of probation: only the most serious offenders were now being sent to penal institutions, which gave the false impression that prisons were becoming more violent (Coulter and Korpi 1954). In a study on 176 penal institutions, Coulter and Korpi (1954: 615) found that rehabilitation in forms of vocational education, religion, and recreation were evident within most institutions. However, they noted that "some institutions seem not yet to have awakened to the new concept, the new method, the new function of correctional institutions: to prepare the inmate for reorientation into society."

Pushes toward rehabilitation generally continued through the 1960s and the first part of the 1970s. The ubiquity of the rehabilitative philosophy, however, was vastly different from its actual implementation. By 1970, there were over 4,600 detention facilities in the United States, and over 80 percent (including both prisons and jails) had no recreational or educational facilities (Axilbund 1976). It was the Riot at Attica in 1971 that reaffirmed the need to decrease violence within prisons. It was evident that prisons had become a place to better one's criminal skill, and were often referred to, as described by Edwards (1972), as "schools for crime." Determining how to transform an institution known for reinforcing criminality into a place with rehabilitative value was discernably challenging. Charles Tittle (1974: 385) remarked that prisons had "become the favorite 'whipping boys,'" as they were an easy target of criticism.

Robert Martinson's (1974) evaluation of correctional rehabilitation programs undoubtedly had a great impact on the downfall of the rehabilitation movement. A sociology professor in New York, Martinson's evaluation was the most comprehensive work yet on prison treatment programs. His results indicated no demonstrable evidence that rehabilitation was effective, at least in context of recidivism. This finding, along with others, led Martinson to the ever-famous conclusion that "nothing works." Remarking on the rise of a more punitive era, Holden (1975: 816), citing both Martinson (1974) and Norval Morris' work (1974), concluded:

> Both works have helped coalesce thinking along new lines, to wit: A prison can't set itself up as an agent for helping an individual (rehabilitation) when its reason for existing is to do violence (by robbing him of his freedom). Therefore, goes the thinking, let's cut out the hypocrisy and recognize prisons primarily as agents for "deterrence and incapacitation."

What followed was an era of crime control, that in some aspects, remains prominent in present-day penology (Clear, Reisig, and Cole 2016). While a more rehabilitative ideal has been prominent within methods of community correction, prison institutions, while different, still maintain a more crime-control perspective (Welch 2013).

Prison Designs and Inmate Classification

Prison Designs

Historically, changes in prison architecture coincided with changes in beliefs about inmates and punitiveness. As the U.S. became aware that many inmates were generally nonviolent and were low escape risks, the architecture changed to reflect this (Johnston 1961). Modern penal institutions are typically modeled after one of four designs: Radial Design, Telephone-Pole Design, Courtyard Style, or Campus Style (Clear, Reisig, and Cole 2016).

Radial-designed institutions resemble a traditional tire rim: a large center with spokes jutting out of it. The prison is managed from the center, and its halls "radiate" out from the center, allowing for efficient management and supervision of inmates (Waid and Clements 2001). Additionally, should one of the prison halls become disruptive or violent, the design allows for an efficient way to barricade those prisoners (Clear, Reisig, and Cole 2016). Radial designs were really a combination of traditional penal models, integrating the Auburn model into a traditional Pennsylvania-modeled prison (Beijersbergen, Dirkzwager, van der Laan, and Nieuwbeerta 2016; Carlson and Garrett 2013).

The Telephone-Pole Design, which originated in Europe, was designed for purposes of creating a high-security institution (Johnston 2009) Telephone-Pole institutions resemble a "t" with additional horizontal lines across one vertical line. The center is a long hallway that provides prisoners access to various parts of the prison. Like the radial design, the center is the supervision base, as it allows for easy surveillance (Clear, Reisig, and Cole 2016). While the Telephone-Pole Design looks quite different from the Radial design, its style and purpose are relatively similar (Carlson and Garrett 2013). The Telephone-Pole Design often does not bear a resemblance to a traditional penal institution, but provides effective security for maximum-security prisons. However, modified Telephone-Pole Designs are more often designed to "stress informality and a non-institutional appearance" (Johnston 1961: 18).

The Courtyard Style is square shaped, with separate buildings at each corner, and a centralized open area. The open area often has the congregate areas (dining, gymnasium, school, etc.) (Clear, Reisig, and Cole 2016). Courtyard-Style institutions are highly secure, but are also expensive, both in construction and maintenance (Beijersbergen et al. 2016).

Lastly, the Campus style differs in design, but most often resembles a college campus, with housing units intermixed with congregate areas for inmates. Supervision is not centralized, but they are typically fenced, making them secure (Clear, Reisig, and Cole 2016). Within the United States, campus-designed prisons were designed as an alternative to high-level secure prisons and are used for those offenders classified as medium or low-risk. Some of the first examples of campus-designed prisons were federal institutions, including the Federal Correctional Institutions in Seagoville, Texas (1940) and Tallahassee, Florida (1938) (Johnston 1961).

Prison Security and Inmate Classification

When inmates are sentenced, they are generally assessed by staff to determine what type of institution is appropriate for the inmate. For instance, most often, inmates are separated by gender and by age (juveniles and adults). Additionally, inmates are classified by their risk and needs to determine which level of security is appropriate for the individual. This is based upon demographic characteristics, criminal history, and social history, as well as their needs (treatment, education, social) (Carlson and Garrett 2013). Classification of inmates is somewhat novel, at least in regards to level of security. Historically, inmates were only classified by group (gender, age, and violent/nonviolent). Examining each inmate in context of the crime, his or her history, and his or her needs provides a more advanced system of classification that (ideally) leads to more effective supervision of inmates.

Prisons are classified by three or four levels of security, including maximum, medium, and minimum. In recent years, some states have also begun separating the most violent offenders into a higher level of security, called "supermax" (Clear, Reisig, and Cole 2016). Inmates are typically housed in supermax when they have demonstrated aggressive, uncontrollable violent behavior (Carlson and Garrett 2013). With some exception, prisons are usually classified as one security level. Those that are mixed are often women's prisons, as there are not enough inmates within an area to fill three institutions (minimum, medium, maximum). As of 2016, there are 355 maximum security prisons, 438 medium-security prisons, and 926 minimum-security (Clear, Reisig, and Cole 2016).

Conclusion

Although there have been tremendous changes in prison design and administration since the 1600s, many of the same problems remain in an era of mass incarceration. Yet, most of these issues revolve around one question: how can a penal institution be effectively managed to simultaneously punish and treat its inmates in order to prevent future crimes? Further, there continues to be a struggle to make institutions effective from a cost–benefit standpoint, while also maintaining acceptable inmate treatment.

References

Axilbund, Melvin T. 1976. "American Prisons and Jails." *Current History* 70(417): 265.

Barnes, Harry Elmer. 1921. "The Historical Origin of the Prison System in America." *Journal of the American Institute of Criminal Law and Criminology* 12(1): 35–60.

Beijersbergen, Karin A., Anja JE Dirkzwager, Peter H. van der Laan, and Paul Nieuwbeerta. 2016. "A Social Building? Prison Architecture and Staff–Prisoner Relationships." *Crime & Delinquency* 62(7): 843–874.

Bonta, James, Tanya Rugge, Terri-Lynne Scott, Guy Bourgon, and Annie K Yessine. 2008. "Exploring the Black Box of Community Supervision." *Journal of Offender Rehabilitation* 47(3): 248–270.

Bussert, Todd, Peter Goldberger, and Mary Price. 2006. "New Time Limits on Federal Halfway Houses." *Criminal Justice* 21: 20–26.

Carleton, Mark T. 1967. "The Politics of the Convict Lease System in Louisiana: 1868–1901." *Louisiana History: The Journal of the Louisiana Historical Association* 8(1): 5–25.

Carleton, Mark Thomas. 1984. *Politics and Punishment: The History of the Louisiana State Penal System*: Baton Rouge, LA: LSU Press.

Carlson, Peter M. and Judith S. Garrett. 2013. *Prison and Jail Administration: Practice and Theory*. Burlington, MA: Jones and Bartlett.

Castle, Tammy L. 2016. *Prison and Jail Systems*. Ipswich, MA: Salem Press.

Clear, Todd R., Michael D. Reisig, Carolyn Petrosino, and George F. Cole. 2016. *American Corrections in Brief*. Boston, MA: Cengage Learning.

Clear, Todd R., Michael D. Reisig and George F. Cole. 2016. *American Corrections*. Boston, MA: Cengage.

Coulter, Charles W. and Orvo E. Korpi. 1954. "Rehabilitation Programs in American Prisons and Correctional Institutions." *The Journal of Criminal Law, Criminology, and Police Science* 44(5): 611–615.

DePuy, LeRoy B. 1951. "The Walnut Street Prison: Pennsylvania's First Penitentiary." *Pennsylvania History: A Journal of Mid-Atlantic Studies* 18(2): 130–144.

DePuy, LeRoy B. 1954. "The Triumph of the 'Pennsylvania System' at the State's Penitentiaries." *Pennsylvania History: A Journal of Mid-Atlantic Studies* 21(2): 128–144.

Doll, Eugene E. 1957. "Trial and Error at Allegheny: The Western State Penitentiary, 1818–1838." *The Pennsylvania Magazine of History and Biography* 81(1): 3–27.

Dolovich, Sharon. 2005. "State Punishment and Private Prisons." *Duke Law Journal* 55(3): 437–546.

Edwards, George. 1972. "Foreword: Penitentiaries Produce No Penitents." *The Journal of Criminal Law, Criminology, and Police Science* 63(2): 154–161.

Fiddler, Michael. 2008. "Modernity, the New Republic and Sing Sing: The Creation of a Disciplined Workforce and Citizenry." Pp. 15–33 in *Punishment and Control in Historical Perspective*. New York: Springer.

Gault, Robert H. (Ed.). 1940. "Current Notes: Prisons." *Journal of Criminal Law and Criminology (1931–1951)* 31(3): 322–324.
Gill, Howard B. 1931a. "The Brief Contributions: Norfolk State Prison Colony at Massachusetts." *American Institute of Criminal Law & Criminology* 22: 107–112.
Gill, Howard B. 1931b. "The Prison Labor Problem." *The Annals of the American Academy of Political and Social Science* 157: 83–101.
Gill, Howard B. 1962. "Correctional Philosophy and Architecture." *The Journal of Criminal Law, Criminology, and Police Science* 53(3): 312–322.
Gutterman, Melvin. 1992. "Prison Objectives and Human Dignity: Reaching a Mutual Accommodation." *BYU Law Review* 4: 857–915.
Hanser, Robert. 2016. *Introduction to Corrections*. Thousand Oaks, CA: Sage.
Holden, Constance. 1975. "Prisons: Faith in 'Rehabilitation' Is Suffering a Collapse." *Science* 188(4190): 815–817.
Ignatieff, Michael. 1981. "State, Civil Society, and Total Institutions: A Critique of Recent Social Histories of Punishment." *Crime and Justice* 3: 153–192.
Jenkins, Philip. 1984. "Varieties of Enlightenment Criminology: Beccaria, Godwin, De Sade." *The British Journal of Criminology* 24(2): 112–130.
Johnston, Norman B. 1954. "Pioneers in Criminology V—John Haviland (1792–1852)." *Journal of Criminal Law, Criminology & Police Science* 45: 509–519.
Johnston, Norman. 1961. "The Changing Face of Correctional Architecture." *The Prison Journal* 41(1): 14–20.
Johnston, Norman. 2009. "Evolving Function Early Use of Imprisonment as Punishment." *The Prison Journal* 89(1 suppl): 10S–34S.
Kaeble, Danielle, Lauren E Glaze, Anastasios Tsoutis and Todd Minton. 2014. "Correctional Populations in the United States." Vol. *Bulletin*. Washington DC: U.S. Department of Justice.
Langbein, John H. 1976. "The Historical Origins of the Sanction of Imprisonment for Serious Crime." *Journal of Legal Studies* 5(1): 35–60.
Lasker, Morris E. 1991. "American Prisons and Prisoners in 1990." *Proceedings of the American Philosophical Society* 135(1): 30–40.
Lewis, Burdette G. 1917. *The Offender and His Relations to Law and Society*. New York: Harper & Brothers Publishing.
MacCormick, Austin H., Ed. 1929. *Handbook of American Prisons and Reformatories*. New York: Osborne Association.
Martinson, Robert. 1974. "What Works?-Questions and Answers About Prison Reform." *The Public Interest* 35: 22–54.
McConville, Sean D.M. 1994. "Punishment and Prisons." Pp. 603–606 in *Encyclopedia of Social Research*, edited by P.N. Stearns. New York: Garland Publishers.
Morris, Norval. 1974. "The Future of Imprisonment: Toward a Punitive Philosophy." *Michigan Law Review* 72(6): 1161–1180.
Post, Albert. 1944. "Early Efforts to Abolish Capital Punishment in Pennsylvania." *The Pennsylvania Magazine of History and Biography* 68(1): 38–53.
Prout, Curtis, and Robert N. Ross. 1988. *Care and Punishment: The Dilemmas of Prison Medicine*. Pittsburgh, PA: University of Pittsburgh Press.
Putney, Snell, and Gladys J. Putney. 1962. "Origins of the Reformatory." *The Journal of Criminal Law, Criminology, and Police Science* 53(4): 437–445.
Roberts, John W. 1997. "Federal Bureau of Prisons: Its Mission, Its History, and Its Partnership with Probation and Pretrial Services." *Federal Probation* 61: 53–57.
Rolston, Simon. 2011. "Conversion and the Story of the American Prison." *Critical Survey* (3): 103–118.
Rothman, David J. 1971. *The Discovery of the Asylum*. New Brunswick, NJ: Transaction Publishers.
Rothman, David J. 1980. *Conscience and Convenience: The Asylum and Its Alternatives in Progressive America*. New Brunswick, NJ: Transaction Publishers
Schwartz, Joel. 1985. "The Penitentiary and Perfectibility in Tocqueville." *The Western Political Quarterly* 38: 7–26.

Sellin, Thorsten. 1953. "Philadelphia Prisons of the Eighteenth Century." *Transactions of the American Philosophical Society* 43(1): 326–331.

Sellin, Thorsten. 2016. *Slavery and the Penal System*. New Orleans, LA: Quid Pro Books.

Skidmore, Rex A. 1948. "Penological Pioneering in the Walnut Street Jail, 1789–1799." *Journal of Criminal Law and Criminology (1931–1951)* 39(2): 167–180.

Stohr, Mary K., Anthony Walsh, and Craig Hemmens. 2013. *Corrections: A Text/Reader*. Thousand Oaks, CA: Sage.

Taylor, A. Elizabeth. 1942. "The Abolition of the Convict Lease System in Georgia." *The Georgia Historical Quarterly* 26(3/4): 273–287.

Taylor, Antony. 2008. *The Prison System and Its Effects: Wherefrom, Whereto, and Why?* New York: Nova Science Publishers.

Thibaut, Jacqueline. 1982. "To Pave the Way to Penitence: Prisoners and Discipline at the Eastern State Penitentiary 1829–1835." *The Pennsylvania Magazine of History and Biography* 106(2): 187–222.

Thompson, Heather Ann. 2010. "Why Mass Incarceration Matters: Rethinking Crisis, Decline, and Transformation in Postwar American History." *Journal of American History* 97(3): 703–734.

Tittle, Charles R. 1974. "Prisons and Rehabilitation: The Inevitability of Disfavor." *Social Problems* 21(3): 385–395.

Travis III, Lawrence F. 2015. "Criminal Sentencing: Goals, Practices and Ethics." Pp. 171–186 in *Justice, Crime, and Ethics*, edited by M. Braswell, B.R. McCarthy, and B.J. McCarthy. New York: Routledge.

Vaux, Richard. 1884. "The Pennsylvania Prison System." *Proceedings of the American Philosophical Society* 21(116): 651–664.

Waid, Courtney A., and Carl B. Clements. 2001. "Correctional Facility Design: Past, Present and Future." *Corrections Compendium* 26(11): 1–2.

Welch, Michael. 2013. *Corrections: A Critical Approach*. New York: Routledge.

Whitehead, John T., Kimberly D. Dodson, and Bradley D. Edwards. 2012. *Corrections: Exploring Crime, Punishment, and Justice in America*. New York: Routledge.

12 Women's Incarceration in the United States

Continuity and Change

Marilyn M. Brown and Meda Chesney-Lind

Introduction

Throughout more than 200 years of American correctional history, women have made up a small proportion of the total incarcerated population. Despite their low numbers and generally lesser offenses, incarcerated women have always received disparate and generally inferior treatment in correctional facilities (Bloom and Brown 2011; Owen and Bloom 1995; Rafter 1985). While dramatic increases in women's incarceration have occurred over the past four decades, rates of women's offenses have increased only slightly. In fact, arrest rates for females increased only a scant 3.4 percent between 2000 and 2009 compared to an increase of 24 percent in the incarceration rate during the same time period (Chesney-Lind and Pasko 2013). The nature of women's offending has remained remarkably consistent throughout American correctional history and, while women do commit violent crimes, their incarceration rates for violent offenses actually declined in the years between 1979 (49 percent) and 2006 (34 percent) (in Chesney-Lind and Pasko 2013: 122). The nature of women's offending has, in fact, been rather consistent since the eighteenth century, consisting primarily of morals charges such as prostitution, petty larceny, and theft, and, in the twentieth century, drug use (McCorkel 2013). In this chapter, we examine the history of women's incarceration in the United States with a focus on changing trends in correctional policies and their impact on women.

Women's unique trajectories to offending and their experiences of incarceration are informed by women's social status, the power dynamics inscribed on the family, racial and economic marginalization, and attitudes toward women's criminality. Crucial to the phenomenon of the modern mass incarceration of women are policies related to the war on drugs, mandatory minimum sentencing, as well as larger social policies related to the marginalization and economic subordination of women, especially women of color. We begin this discussion with a brief history of women's corrections in the United States, by highlighting how attitudes towards female deviance and race shaped, and continue to shape, their treatment in correctional systems.

History of Women's Prisons

Rafter's classic history of women's prisons in the United States reveals how, dating back to the inception of the American "experiment" with confinement, women have received disparate and generally inferior treatment. Eighteenth-century America found women prisoners crowded into large open spaces, segregated from prison wings where men were held. Whereas men in these early facilities were often made to work, women were left neglected and idle. The building of penitentiaries in the early nineteenth century initially left women's prison experiences unmarked. Under the nascent penitentiary regime, men were isolated in cells, under the discipline of keepers who insisted on religious reform and work. No matrons yet existed during the early penitentiary period, even in gender-segregated facilities, leaving women to fend off sexual exploitation by guards through their collective presence in cells. Indeed, according to Rafter, when women became imprisoned in isolated cells, their safety was much diminished. Early penitentiaries such as New York State's Auburn Penitentiary, refused female inmates, with authorities forced to place them in existing facilities with outmoded designs and practices. When penitentiaries were finally forced to accept females, they were often hidden away in areas of the prisons that had been repurposed as women's cells. Oftentimes, small buildings on the prison grounds, such as hospitals, were converted in part to house female inmates. It wasn't until the 1830s that women's special needs were somewhat recognized and female matrons came on the scene in penitentiaries such as Auburn. As Rafter (1985) notes, the treatment of women in corrections was dominated by their small numbers and informed by a reductionist view of women's nature.

Since early on in American corrections, beliefs about women's deviance intersected with racial attitudes, shaping women's punishment. In the nineteenth century, there were few challenges to the long-standing belief that women were not only a great deal more trouble than men but, in moral terms, were far more degraded and beyond reform (Dodge 1999). Prison officials viewed women as disruptive to the routine of prison, who, by their mere presence, often challenged the prevailing model of prison management based on the confinement of young men. Moreover, historians Rafter and Dodge both agree that women's experience of incarceration was racialized from the beginning, with African American women receiving longer sentences between 1860 and1890 (Dodge 1999). Dodge, in fact, argues that race was more central than gender in ideologies about female criminality and punishment. During the latter decades of the nineteenth century, in places such as Illinois, she notes that great numbers of former slaves migrating to the North led to increased female prison populations. Rafter points out that the reformatory movement in women's corrections further racialized prisons. White women received domestic training and other instruction as modes of rehabilitation while women of color continued to be "neglected" by the reformatory movement, treated badly, and punished as harshly as men (Rafter 1985).

Race and attitudes toward immigrants also played a profound role in the character of American punishment and sentencing law. Women's reformatories emerged in the context of the nineteenth century social purity movement along with heightened concerns about the influx of immigrants in an increasingly urban landscape. The desire to assimilate and control immigrant women marked a number of nineteenth century movements ranging from public education to the modes of discipline imposed upon women caught up in the criminal justice system. An early example of the nascent movement toward rehabilitating women through moral instruction and the domestic arts can be seen with the institution in 1868 of a women's facility in Detroit (Rafter 1985). The House of Shelter, as it was called, housed women convicted of misdemeanors and other crimes such as prostitution. The Michigan legislature passed the nation's first indeterminate sentencing law, called "the three-years law," which was applied exclusively to women (Colvin 1997). There were three women's reformatories established by 1900, which were eventually headed as well as staffed by women. Initially modeled on the custodial design of men's prisons, late nineteenth and early twentieth century reformatories adopted what became known as the cottage style (Colvin 1997; Rafter 1985). In these quasi-domestic spaces, female lawbreakers were taught domestic skills and often "paroled" to the households of middle-class white women to be servants.

The social purity crusade also reshaped notions of women's deviance and its remedies. However, this impulse, also, was informed by racial attitudes and the status of non-white women. Earlier attitudes that criminal women were beyond redemption gave way to the notion of women as victims of depraved moral and social environments. They were now "fallen" women (Freedman 1981) who were certainly worth redeeming. At least, this was the case for white women. Women of color were not expected to be paragons of true womanhood and appeared only sporadically in women's reformatories before the turn of the century (Rafter 1985). New sentencing laws weighed more heavily on non-white men and women. The post-Civil War South saw harsher penalties enacted for crimes such as stealing livestock, launching a war on property crime. These laws swept many blacks into penitentiaries and the convict lease system where custodialism and profit, rather than rehabilitation, were the *raison d'être* for punishment. If chivalry toward women offenders existed at all during the late nineteenth and early twentieth centuries, it was not directed toward African American women (Chesney-Lind and Pasko 2013; Rafter 1985).

Attitudes toward female offenders and racialized punishment continued to shape women's experience of incarceration in the twentieth century. Differential treatment of men and women in courts and in confinement continued to be defining aspects of the organization of punishment in the United States. In the early twentieth century, indeterminate confinement for women often meant that they served more time than men for the same offense. The underlying assumption was that women, at least white women, needed to be protected and required more time to achieve a rehabilitated state and be moved toward the feminine ideal (Colvin 1997).

Shifts in penal discourses about women's roles and the nature of feminine deviance continued to unfold in the twenty-first century. Gartner and Kruttschnitt (2004) traced developments in penal discourses and practices at the California Institute for Women (CIW) from the 1960s to the introduction of the get-tough era in the 1990s. In the beginning, CIW exemplified the reformative approaches of the rehabilitation era, staffed by matrons who often had social work training. Gendered discipline prevailed, however, with training classes in the domestic arts and the suppression of non-heterosexual behavior and appearance. As the rehabilitative era lost its support in favor of more punitive attitudes toward offenders, determinate sentencing (coupled with the war on drugs) caused the population at CIW to soar. Prison uniforms, guard towers, armed guards, and razor wire signified a more managerial and punitive approach to women's corrections. Although this account of CIW reveals more continuity than change in the day-to-day prison experiences of women themselves, the scope and rationalization of punishment has changed dramatically in California and the nation. There was no question that increased determinate sentencing along with reductions in the availability of rehabilitative programming made California a "bell weather" state for get-tough policies that placed unprecedented numbers of women in U.S. prisons.

Profile of Women Prisoners

By the end of the first decade of this century, more than one million women were under some form of correctional supervision. Of these, 205,000 women were incarcerated in local, state, and federal jails and prisons (Guerino, Harrison, and Sabol 2011). Beginning in the 1980s and through 2009, women's imprisonment in the United States increased 800 percent (West 2010). Women currently account for roughly 7 percent of the nation's total prison population (West and Sabol 2010). The war on drugs and trends in harsher determinate sentencing pushed the population of female prisoners in the nation's jails and prisons to levels that are only now beginning to plateau. Profiles of the incarcerated female population reveal that these women are disproportionately women of color, young, and convicted of a drug-related offense (Bloom and Brown 2011; Owen and Bloom 1995). Women in prison experience what Owen (1998) describes as multiple marginalization, which consists of intersecting forms of disadvantage that are racial, social, economic, psychological, and cultural in origin.

Incarcerated women come into the system with long-standing psychological, social, and economic challenges. Many have experienced a range of abusive and traumatic experiences, dating back to their childhoods and continuing into adulthood (Bloom, Owen and Covington 2003; McCorkel 2013; Pollock 2014). They often have disruptive and even violent family backgrounds. The majority are mothers, often having dependent children (Bloom and Brown 2011; Brown 2012). Profiles of incarcerated women indicate that this group has higher rates of childhood and adult trauma compared with women in the general population, and they have higher rates of mental health problems (Bloom et al. 2003; Bloom and Brown 2011; Bloom 2015; Owen and Bloom 1995). Additionally, they tend to have lower levels of education, job training, and low socio-economic status (Chesney-Lind and Pasko 2013). Data on incarcerated women reveal that they have lower educational levels and fewer employment skills than men entering prison (Greenfeld and Snell 2000). Despite the many gender-specific issues common to such women, it is less likely than ever that women will have access to the treatment and services they need. Mass incarceration in the United States has imposed unprecedented strains on nearly all correctional facilities, which ultimately reduces prison services and programming. In the following section, we review some of the determinants of mass incarceration and its impact on imprisoned women.

Mass Incarceration and Women's Prisons

The racial disparities that have marked women's incarceration since the nineteenth century continued into the twenty-first century. At the height of the war on drugs, from the mid 1980s through 1991, the number of African American females incarcerated for drug crimes increased by 828 percent, an increase nearly twice that of African American men and three times the number of white female drug offenders (Bush-Baskette 2013). Going back to the reformatory movement described previously, African American and other women of color have also been susceptible to disparate sentencing and treatment in prison.

The problems of women offenders are complex, but are beginning to be understood as linked to their social positions as women. This is especially true of women of color who are overrepresented in criminal justice populations. The war on drugs has been called a war against black women, fought by police, prosecutors, and courts in ways that position such women to be among those most arrested for drugs (Bush-Baskette 2013). As described by Michelle Alexander (2012) in her path breaking book, *The New Jim Crow*, policing and criminal justice processes have now become a racialized mechanism of social control of black and other minority communities already hit hard by structural changes of the twentieth century. The same dynamics of race and law described by Alexander, especially enforcement techniques associated with illegal drugs (crimes for which women are far more likely than men to be incarcerated), have created a racialized and gendered perfect storm of exclusion. This has, of course, taken place in a political climate whose punitive attitudes toward offenders has bled off into a number of social welfare policies including family supports, child welfare, education, and other institutional support for the poor (Haney 2010).

Recently, the proportion of African American women in prison has dropped; between 2000 to 2009 the rate of incarceration in state and federal prisons declined 9.8 percent for black men and 30.7 percent for black women (Mauer 2013). With that said, in 2014, the Bureau of Justice Statistics reports that Black females are still imprisoned at between two and three times the rate of white females (Carson 2015: 15).

The intersection of gender, race, and class continues to play out in mass incarceration. In 2014, the number of male prisoners showed an absolute decrease, while the number of females in state or federal prison who were sentenced to more than a year increased nearly 2 percent from a year earlier (Carson 2015: 7). Given these data, it appears that as a nation, we are replacing urban African American women drug users who used to be imprisoned in places such as New York, with rural, low-income white women convicted of the same offenses in places such as Oklahoma, Idaho, and Kentucky. Thus, while the overrepresentation of black women in prison continues, the war on drugs has exacerbated its impact on poor women for methamphetamine and prescription drug offenses (Mauer 2013)—with a growing incursion into the lives of poor, white women.

Gender-Specific Issues and Incarcerated Women

Crucial to understanding the phenomenon of the modern mass incarceration of women are policies related to the war on drugs, mandatory minimum sentencing, as well as broader social policies related to the marginalization and economic subordination of women, especially women of color. To a great extent, research into the pathways approach to women's offending has revealed the gender-specific issues that propel women into crime. Violence against girls and women and the ways in which this abuse is inscribed in the power-dynamics of the family are now understood as traumatic events that lead to offending. Status offenses such as running away, drug use, and other survival crimes pave the way for involvement in the juvenile justice system for girls. They are also very likely to become disengaged from social institutions such as school and work. Aggravating factors such as depression and other psychological disorders, in absence of community mental health and treatment, pave the way into illegal drug use and related offending.

Drugs and drug-related crime, coupled with economic disadvantage, are the origins of much of women's offending. All too often, the abusive relationships that shaped the early delinquency of girls lead to cycles of abuse and trauma that persist well into adulthood (Bloom et al. 2003; Owen 1998). Drug treatment and, to a certain extent, vocational programming for women in prison have been attempted. Gender-specific approaches to women's offending that are grounded in theories of women's abuse and marginalization have been attempted. However, with correctional budgets straining from the sheer numbers of incarcerated women, investment in these projects has been woefully insufficient (Villanueva 2009). Some of the limited remaining rehabilitation programs target addiction, but many times these consist of "soft skill approaches" that talk past the fundamental marginalization experienced by women who end up in prison (Brown 2012; McCorkel 2013). These programs, often discursively under the banner of women's empowerment, aim at encouraging women to make better choices in their lives. However, the onus for failure can then be placed on individual women whose choices are narrowly circumscribed by poverty, racism, and the damaging effects of violence (Haney 2010).

The gender-mediated factors that shape women's trajectories to prison often operate in the context of their roles as mothers. Mass incarceration's most profound impact on families occurs when mothers go to prison. Between 1991 and 2007, maternal incarceration rose 122 percent compared to a 77 percent increase in the incarceration of fathers. More than half (53 percent) of inmates in state and federal prisons in 2007 were parents of minor children who numbered some 1.7 million (Glaze and Maruschak 2008). Separation from children is one of the predominant pains of incarceration for women. In 2000, most imprisoned mothers lived with their children prior to their most current incarceration (Mumola 2000). Ties to children and family remain a central concern to incarcerated women. However, incarcerated mothers receive far fewer visits from children than incarcerated fathers according to a report by the General Accounting Office (1999). Despite the obstacles, women in prison go to great lengths to preserve relationships with their children, often having to rely on precariously situated care-givers (Enos 2001). Children without relatives or other care-givers are at risk of entering the foster care system. Changes in federal child welfare system regulations increase the chances that women serving sentences longer than 18 months will have their parental rights terminated and their children placed for adoption (Beckerman 1998).

A report prepared for the Women's Prison Association by Chandra Villanueva (2009) notes that the rising number of women being drawn into correctional systems has meant that pregnant women and women with dependent children are being incarcerated. Citing data from the Bureau of Justice Statistics, she notes that 4 percent of women incarcerated in state prisons and 3 percent of women in federal prisons were reported to be pregnant at time of entry into custody. Somewhat higher percentages (6 percent) of pregnant women enter jails. In general, the author notes, mothers and infants are separated at the time of birth. While experts disagree about the presence of infants in prison (Dwyer 2014), a number of states have established prison nursery programs to help mothers establish and sustain, for some limited period of time, a relationship with their newborn. These programs are generally open to only low-level, non-violent offenders. The report points out that neither the National Commission on Correctional Health Care nor the American Correctional Association has accreditation or standards for prison nursery programs, nor are there national standards for the treatment of pregnant women. Evaluations of these programs show positive results with lower recidivism rates for mothers and no adverse effects on babies. However, the report also finds that this population of low-level, non-violent prisoners (usually serving short sentences) could just as well be living in community programs with their children. Even for the handful of jurisdictions that still permit mothers to have their infant children with them in prison nurseries, women with long sentences will eventually be separated from their children (Arditti 2012).

Conclusion

The "get tough" era of American punishment, rationalized and fueled by the war on drugs, dramatically increased the numbers of women being held in jails and prisons in the United States. Many jurisdictions are rethinking the American experience with mass incarceration that dominated United States policy for the last 40 years. National attention has been paid to reducing sentences for drug use. Reentry programs to support prisoner reintegration are on the rise, but returning prisoners to their pre-prison environments proved to actually exacerbate crime in already disadvantaged communities (Clear 2007). Crucial to reducing women's imprisonment will be programs that employ gender responsive approaches to reentry. Specifically, women coming out of prison will need help in addressing their drug addiction, and support as they reunite with their children; they will also need to find safe and sober housing, and gainful employment with living wages. The lessons of the past tell us that both change and continuity in the nature of women's incarceration are rooted in the persistent inequalities of society.

References

Alexander, Michelle. 2012. *The New Jim Crow: Mass Incarceration in the Age of Colorblindness*. New York: The New Press.

Arditti, Joyce A. 2012. *Parental Incarceration and the Family: Psychological and Social Effects of Imprisonment on Children, Parents, and Care-Givers*. New York: NYU Press.

Beckerman, Adella. 1998. "Charting a Course: Meeting the Challenge of Permanency Planning for Children with Incarcerated Mothers." *Child Welfare* 77(5): 513–529.

Bloom, Barbara. 2015. *Meeting the Needs of Women in California's County Justice Systems*. Sacramento, CA: Californians for Safety and Justice.

Bloom, Barbara and Marilyn Brown. 2011. "Incarcerated Women: Motherhood on the Margins." Pp. 52–66 in *Razor Wire Women: Prisoners, Activists, Scholars and Artists*, edited by J.M. Lawston and A.E. Lucas. Albany, NY: SUNY.

Bloom, Barbara, Barbara Owen, and Stephanie Covington. 2003. *Gender-Responsive Strategies: Research, Practice, and Guiding Principles for Women Offenders*. Washington, DC: National Institute of Corrections.

Brown, Marilyn. 2012. "Rehabilitation, Risk, and the Carceral Mother: Subjectivity and Parenting Classes in Prisons." *Critical Criminology* 20(4): 359–375.

Bush-Baskette, Stephanie R. 2013. "The War on Drugs as a War against Black Women." Pp. 175–183 in *Girls, Women, and Crime: Selected Readings*, edited by M. Chesney-Lind and L. Pasko. Thousand Oaks, CA: Sage.

Carson, E. Ann. 2015. *Prisoners in 2014*. Washington, DC: Bureau of Justice Statistics, U.S. Department of Justice, Office of Justice Programs.

Chesney-Lind, Meda and Lisa Pasko, Eds. 2013. *The Female Offender: Girls, Women, and Crime*. Los Angeles, CA: Sage.

Clear, Todd R. 2007. *Imprisoning Communities: How Mass Incarceration Makes Disadvantaged Neighborhoods Worse*. New York: Oxford University Press.

Colvin, Mark. 1997. *Penitentiaries, Reformatories and Chain Gangs: Social Theory and the History of Punishment in Nineteenth-Century America*. Gordonsville, VA: Palgrave Macmillan.

Dodge, L. Mara. 1999. "'One Female Prisoner Is of More Trouble than Twenty Males': Women Convicts in Illinois Prisons, 1835–1896." *Journal of Social History* 32(4): 907–930.

Dwyer, James G. 2014. "Jailing Black Babies." *Utah Law Review: William & Mary Law School Research Paper No. 09–239* (3): Retrieved April 5, 2016 from http://ssrn.com/abstract=2231562

Enos, Sandra. 2001. *Mothering from the Inside: Parenting in a Women's Prison*. Albany, NY: SUNY.

Freedman, Estelle B. 1981. *Their Sisters' Keepers: Women's Prison Reform in America, 1830–1930*. Ann Arbor, MI: University of Michigan Press.

Gartner, Rosemary, and Candace Kruttschnitt. 2004. "A Brief History of Doing Time: The California Institution for Women in the 1960s and the 1990s." *Law & Society Review* 38(2): 267–304.

General Accounting Office. 1999. *Women in Prison: Issues and Challenges Confronting U.S. Correctional Systems*. Washington, DC: United States General Accounting Office.

Glaze, L., and L.M. Maruschak. 2008. *Parents in Prison and Their Minor Children*. Washington, DC: Bureau of Justice Statistics, U.S. Department of Justice, Office of Justice Programs.

Greenfeld, Lawrence A., and Tracy L. Snell. 2000. *Women Offenders: Bureau of Justice Assistance Special Report*. Washington, DC: U.S. Department of Justice, Office of Justice Programs.

Guerino, Paul, Paige M. Harrison, and William Sabol. 2011. *Prisoners in 2010*. Washington, DC: Bureau of Justice Statistics, U.S. Department of Justice, Office of Justice Programs.

Haney, Lynn A. 2010. *Offending Women: Power, Punishment, and the Regulation of Desire*. Berkeley, CA: University of California Press.

McCorkel, Jill. 2013. *Breaking Women: Gender, Race, and the New Politics of Imprisonment*. New York: New York University Press.

Mauer, Marc. 2013. *The Changing Dynamics of Women's Incarceration*. The Sentencing Project, Washington, DC.

Mumola, Christopher J. 2000. *Incarcerated Parents and Their Children*. Washington, DC: Bureau of Justice Statistics, U.S. Department of Justice, Office of Justice Programs.

Owen, Barbara. 1998. *In the Mix: Struggle and Survival in a Women's Prison*. New York: State University of New York.

Owen, Barbara and Barbara E. Bloom. 1995. *Profiling the Needs of California's Female Prisoners: A Needs Assessment*. Washington, DC.: National Institute of Corrections, U.S. Department of Justice.

Pollock, Joy. 2014. *Women's Crime, Criminology, and Corrections*. Long Grove, IL: Waveland Press.

Rafter, Nicole Hahn. 1985. *Partial Justice: Women in State Prisons, 1800–1935*. Boston, MA: Northeastern University Press.

Villanueva, Chandra Kring. 2009. *Mothers, Infants, and Imprisonment: A National Look at Prison Nurseries and Community-Based Alternatives*. Congress.
West, Heather C. 2010. "Prisoners at Midyear-Statistical Tables." Bureau of Justice Statistics, U.S. Department of Justice, Office of Justice Programs, Washington, DC.
West, Heather C., and S.J. Sabol. 2010. "Prisoners in 2009." Bureau of Justice Statistics, U.S. Department of Justice, Office of Justice Programs, Washington, DC.

13 Juvenile Corrections in the United States

O. Hayden Griffin III

Introduction

At the founding of the United States, most jurisdictions drew no distinctions between criminal offenders based upon age. As time went on, many people argued that juveniles should not receive the same treatment as adults within the criminal justice system and should be shielded from many of the harshest punishments that adults could receive. Furthermore, advocates of these reforms also argued that the punishment of juveniles should more often embrace a rehabilitative ideal and/or include diversion from official criminal justice processes and punishment, since juveniles' development is ongoing, making them less likely to recidivate if proper intervention occurs. Thus, beginning in the late 1800s, the juvenile justice system was born. Within this standalone system, juveniles received greater protections from many harsher criminal justice punishments, but also failed to receive the same constitutional rights as adult offenders. Beginning during the due process revolution of the 1960s, juvenile offenders began to receive many of the same protections as adults. However, while the overall juvenile justice system does not appear to be in any danger, many people have questioned whether the juvenile justice system is appropriate for all juvenile offenders. Indeed, juveniles with significant criminal histories and/or those who have committed serious violent crimes can often have their cases transferred to adult court. This chapter will discuss the evolution of the juvenile system and the various ways in which juveniles receive different or similar treatment to adult offenders.

The Creation of the Juvenile System

As mentioned previously, while the United States did not create a juvenile justice system until more than 100 years after its formation, the idea that juveniles had a different level of culpability or *mens rea* (criminal mind) was not exactly a novel idea. Indeed, the Code of Hammurabi (written approximately 4,000 years ago) had some references regarding the treatment of children, and the ancient Romans actually distinguished between adults and juveniles regarding the age at which a person could have criminal responsibility. Furthermore, many religious legal texts (such as those found in the Talmud and Koran), specifically addressed differential treatment for juveniles (Hanser 2017).

Since the United States was founded upon the principles of the common law that came from England, it comes as little surprise that some of the origins of the juvenile justice system also come from the common law. Indeed, the doctrine of *parens patriae*, which is the doctrine that controls American juvenile justice, was established in England and literally means "father of the country" (Champion, Hartley, and Rabe 2012). Along with this doctrine, which established that the government is essentially the parents of children, is the additional doctrine of *in loco parentis* that allows the government to act in place of juvenile's parents (Hanser

2017). This ethic of the government acting as a child's parents not only includes the legal authority to punish, but also includes the authority to act in the best interests of children. Many scholars have pointed to this legal authority as one of the foundations of the rehabilitative nature of the juvenile justice system. While *parens patriae* and *in loco parentis* did not necessarily create a formal justice system, the common law did place limits on when juveniles could be held criminally responsible for their actions. Children under the age of seven were not legally responsible for any crimes that they committed (Champion et al. 2012). Children between the ages of 7 and 14 were presumed to lack culpability, but if evidence was presented that the juvenile could form criminal intent, was able to understand the consequences of their actions, and able to distinguish right from wrong, then that juvenile could be held criminally responsible. Within the common law, juveniles over the age of 14 were tried as adults (Hanser 2017).

During the 1600s and 1700s, most juvenile offenders in England who were incarcerated served their time with adult convicts; some facilities segregated juvenile offenders from adults. The first facility dedicated to the incarceration and reform of juvenile offenders was created in Rome by the Catholic Church (Hanser 2017). This first facility, Hospice of St. Michael, kept juvenile offenders in a system similar to the Auburn System—solitary confinement at night and silent communal work by day. For those juveniles who did not follow the rules, they could expect corporal punishment and solitary confinement for such infractions. While well intended, the rehabilitative ideal of early juvenile facilities seemed to wane, and these facilities seemed to be increasingly punitive institutions. Indeed, much to the chagrin of famed prison reformer John Howard, not only was there an increasingly punitive tone to juvenile justice, the facility in England that housed juvenile offenders closed in 1827 (Jones and Johnstone 2012).

While European governments did not seem to embrace the funding of separate juvenile correctional facilities, there was ample support from private organizations and especially advocates of juvenile justice reform with educational backgrounds. These groups helped establish facilities that went by many different names, but among the most common monikers were "houses of refuge" and "training schools." Each facility was essentially equal part prison and school. Within Europe, the juveniles in these facilities often lived in cottages and an older male child would serve as a mentor. At the time, these facilities were seen as a great success and a welcome alternative to incarcerating juvenile offenders in adult prisons and jails.

Within the United States, a similar facility was first founded in New York City in 1826. The cities of Boston and Philadelphia founded similar facilities around the same time (Jones and Johnstone 2012). Many reformers viewed the establishment of houses of refuge as a worthwhile endeavor, but these facilities were not without their detractors. While houses of refuge were filled with juvenile offenders, these facilities were also dumping grounds for orphans and other youths who had committed no illegal behavior—they were simply poor. Furthermore, while many of these facilities were called training schools, since juveniles were able to learn various forms of vocational training, it was commonly argued that these facilities were training grounds for crime rather than for reformation (Friedman 1993). One of the great selling points of these juvenile facilities was that it allowed juveniles the chance to learn a work ethic and a job skill that could help to make it on their own once they were released from the facility. Indeed, through the process of "binding out," many juveniles were placed outside the facility and would live and work with law-abiding adults. Additionally, at the least, these facilities protected juveniles from more predatory adult offenders. While these facilities were initially hailed as reforming many juveniles, by the 1850s, it was widely accepted that these facilities did a poor job of rehabilitating juvenile offenders (Hanser 2017).

Considering the problems of the houses of refuge and training schools, many people started to advocate that rather than looking for new forms of punishment, juveniles needed alternative ways of being treated within the actual justice system. Perhaps the most vocal group of people who advocated such a position was the "child-savers," a group predominantly made up of upper- and middle-class women who believed that children had not yet properly developed their mental faculties and should receive different treatment in both court proceedings and punishment (Platt 1977). One of the ways in which some jurisdictions had reduced the possibility of juveniles being tried in adult courts and sent to adult correctional facilities was for police officers to treat juvenile offenders differently during the arrest process. These policies of informal diversion kept many juvenile offenders out of the adult system but seemed more of a stopgap than a permanent solution to the problem of juvenile crime. Thus, in 1899, the state of Illinois established the first juvenile court in Cook County, Illinois. By 1920, nearly every state in the United States established a juvenile court (Spillane and Wolcott 2013). Three states (Connecticut, New York, and North Carolina) set the maximum age that a juvenile could have their case heard in juvenile court at 15; eight states set the maximum age at 16; and the rest of the states and the federal government give juvenile courts jurisdiction over offenders who are under 18 (Champion et al. 2012).

Juvenile Courts and Punishment

While the most paramount concern of juvenile courts is diverting juveniles from both the adult courts and corrections systems, there are other important features that many believe lead to greater rehabilitation. Foremost is that juvenile courts are less confrontational than adult courts. One of the ways this is accomplished is by providing juvenile court judges with a wider latitude in diversionary tactics (Clear, Reisig, and Cole 2015). Although probation is the most frequent punishment for adult offenders, juvenile courts use this punishment at an even higher rate in an effort to ensure that most juveniles avoid the brutalizing effects of incarceration (Schlossman 1977). Perhaps one of the most striking differences between the adult and juvenile systems is the different terminology. Rather than being guilty of crimes, when juveniles are found guilty, they are declared "delinquent" (Clear et al. 2015).

To combat juvenile delinquency, Lundman (2001) noted that there are three different strategies. The first of these strategies is a focus on predelinquent interventions. In some instances, different juveniles who are deemed "at risk" may receive individual treatment. This can be done in a variety of ways from formal psychological or psychiatric treatment to more informal interventions, such as mentors for at-risk youth. In some instances, programs have been created to help prevent juvenile delinquency programs. One of the most commonly administered programs is Drug Abuse Resistance Education (DARE), a program taught by police officers to children while they are in school. Essentially, the program involves police officers telling students about the negative consequences of using drugs and/or alcohol. Overall, DARE is a relatively short intervention that does not take up too much of children's time. One of the more ambitious examples of predelinquent interventions was the Chicago Area Projects that were designed and administered by Clifford Shaw and Henry McKay. While entire articles and books have been written about the work of Shaw and McKay, Shaw specifically designed many programs in an attempt to foster greater community advocacy and cohesion to prevent social disorganization—a phenomenon that Shaw believed led to conditions that inevitably led to crime and juvenile delinquency.

The second strategy that the juvenile justice employs is diversion (Lundman 2001). The rationale behind diverting juveniles (or even adult offenders as well) from the criminal justice system is that the formal process will provide criminal labels on these offenders. Rather than providing deterrence from future criminal acts, many of the people who are labeled are more likely to commit future crimes. The prevention of juvenile delinquency by the avoidance of delinquent labels was developed by several leading criminologists including Tannenbaum (1938), Lemert (1951), and Schur (1971, 1973). Tannenbaum (1938), who never actually used the word "label," noted that juveniles may get "tagged" with a bad reputation when they engaged in petty juvenile crime. If left alone, most of these juveniles would simply grow out of these behaviors, but if these juveniles are too severely punished, it may lead them to commit future crime. Lemert (1951) developed these ideas further, purporting that there are two types of deviance: primary and secondary. Primary deviance is comprised of those crimes that people commit that are predicted by an assortment of different criminological theories. Secondary deviance is comprised of those crimes that people commit after they have been given and accepted a criminal label. Lastly, Schur (1973), who frequently discussed the dangers of labeling youths as delinquents, developed what he called a "radical non-intervention" whereby juveniles, especially those who are charged with minor crimes should be diverted from as much of the criminal justice process as possible.

One of the ways in which juvenile courts divert juveniles accused of crimes is through the use of intake hearings. While offenders in adult court will go through a first appearance before a judge (within 48 hours of arrest), juveniles will see an intake officer who is either a court-appointed official or a juvenile probation officer. This intake officer will consider a variety of factors (such as a juvenile's attitude, demeanor, age, the seriousness of the alleged offense, and the evidence against a juvenile) before making a determination, and in some cases interview an alleged juvenile offender's parents or neighbors. Some cases against juveniles may be dismissed with the option of a verbal or written warning accompanying the dismissal. In other instances, an intake officer may remand juveniles to their parents' custody (which may include orders to attend counseling or other services). In other cases, when appropriate, an officer may divert a youth to an alternative dispute resolution program. If an intake officer believes there is either enough evidence or the charges against a juvenile are serious enough, the officer may refer the case to a prosecutor for delinquency proceedings or begin the process of transferring the case to an adult court. This transfer, or what many people refer to as "waiver," can be one of four types: (1) waiver at the discretion of a prosecutor, (2) waiver by a judge, (3) a demand waiver in which a juvenile requests the case be moved to adult court, or (4) legislative or automatic waivers. The first two types of waiver (prosecutorial or judicial) are pretty self-explanatory, based upon some combination of the facts of the case and the characteristics of a particular juvenile defendant (such as criminal record or age of defendant), and a prosecutor or judge may elect to transfer a juvenile's case to an adult court. Different states have different procedures for these types of transfers. A demand waiver may seem odd to some people—why would a juvenile defendant want their case transferred to an adult court? In reality, this decision may be made if a juvenile believes they may receive greater rights or perhaps sympathy in an adult court. One of the most common incidents of such a request being made is in states that do not give juveniles the right to a jury trial. The last type of waiver, legislative or automatic, usually is determined by the crime charged. Such an example would be states that automatically transfer murder or sexual assault cases to adult courts (Champion et al. 2012).

As mentioned previously, one of the main purposes of the juvenile justice system was keeping juveniles out of adult prisons and jails. Two different federal laws, the Juvenile Justice and Delinquency Prevention Act of 1974 and the Prison Rape Elimination Act of 2003, both mandate that states do not incarcerate juveniles with adults. In most states the commingling of adult and juvenile offenders in the same correctional facilities was already forbidden before the passage of these acts. Yet, in most instances, just because a federal law is passed does not mean the states necessarily have to comply with such provisions. The main weapon that the federal government can levy against state governments is money. A few states have specifically turned down federal money in order to avoid compliance with these laws. As Lahey (2016) noted, on an average day, 10,000 juveniles are incarcerated in adult prisons and jails.

The third strategy of juvenile justice are postadjudication interventions. Essentially, as the name indicates, these are approaches that take place after juveniles have been found delinquent (Lundman 2001). Many of these approaches, such as probation, parole, boot camps, and incarceration are discussed in other chapters in this handbook. In general, if a juvenile is adjudged delinquent in a juvenile court, judges have one of three ways to dispose of the case. The first is through nominal dispositions. Among the most common of these dispositions is some form of verbal warning or reprimand to a juvenile. The second way is through conditional dispositions—the most common of which is juvenile probation. The third way that cases are disposed of is through custodial dispositions, which as the name implies, involves incarceration in one of several different types of facilities such as a group home, a boot camp, or a juvenile correctional facility that would closely resemble an adult prison (Champion et al. 2012).

Perhaps the most unique of juvenile justice programs (which can also be used for at-risk youth who have not been found delinquent) is Scared Straight. This program began at Rahway State Prison in New Jersey. It involved a group of at-risk and/or delinquent youth who visited the prison. In addition to the general intimidation factor of being brought into a prison, which usually includes barbwire, security checks, and a host of other intimidating factors, the juvenile visitors also had a session with inmates, many of whom were convicted of multiple serious and/or violent crimes. During the session, the inmates told stories about what "real" prison life is like and in many instances, the inmates would yell at the juvenile visitors and, in some cases, get within the juveniles' personal space. The purpose of the program was to confront these juveniles and show them what their future *could* be like if they did not desist from unlawful and/or delinquent behavior. If not for a massive intervention, Scared Straight may have been one of countless other programs aimed at reducing juvenile delinquency. However, a documentary called *Scared Straight* was made and broadcast on an independent television station in Los Angeles, California. Five months later, the same documentary was broadcast on national television. The next, *Scared Straight* won an Oscar for Best Documentary. In the wake of the publicity, scared straight programs were established in countless jurisdictions and thousands of school children, many of whom showed no potential for delinquency, were enrolled in these programs. This occurred without any evidence of the efficacy of these programs and some evidence suggesting that enrollment in scared straight programs actually made some juveniles *more* prone to future delinquency (Lundman 2001).

Status Offenses

One of the unique things about juvenile offenders is that they can be found delinquent of certain so-called "status offenses," behaviors that—had the juveniles been adults, would not have been criminal. One of the most common status offenses is running away from home. Juveniles who spend prolonged periods of time away from their parents' or guardians' homes can be found delinquent in juvenile court (Champion et al. 2012). Yet, one of the most frequent reasons that this occurs is due to physical or sexual abuse within juveniles' homes. This is especially true for juvenile girls (Chesney-Lind 1989). Another status offense is truancy, which is missing school without an excused absence. As Garry (1996) noted, students who are truant are more likely not only to drop out of school, but also to engage in other delinquent and/or criminal behavior. An additional status offense is curfew violations. Many places, especially urban areas, will have laws forbidding juveniles from being out past certain hours of the night unless they are engaging in an acceptable activity or under the accompaniment of an adult. One of the most common reasons cited for the creation of curfew laws is to prevent and control gang activity and juvenile crime. As Steinhart (1996) noted, among the many provisions of the Juvenile Justice and Delinquency Provision Act was the goal of status offender deinstitutionalization—the goal being to not incarcerate youth who are only convicted of status offenses.

The problem of status offenses is relative to a general critique of the juvenile system. As Friedman noted (1993), many people have credited the child-savers and the creation of the juvenile justice system as progressive actions by a group of people who were seeking to make the criminal justice system more humane and just. However, in a stunning critique of the child-savers, Platt (1977) argued that the creation of the juvenile justice system was another example of middle- and upper-class values enforcing their will over the impoverished. Many of the juveniles who commit status offenses or other crimes are members of impoverished and/or minority communities. Their general lack of resources is one of the primary reasons why these juveniles engaged in delinquency in the first place. According to Platt, "inventing delinquency" was just a way to further control problematic groups of people within the United States.

Juvenile Rights

While many people have viewed the juvenile justice system as protecting juveniles from brutal punishments and labeling and providing more opportunities for rehabilitation, the system began by essentially disregarding almost all of the constitutional rights of juveniles. Indeed, in a decision by the Pennsylvania Supreme Court in 1838 *Ex Parte Crouse*, a father attempted to obtain his daughter's release from the Philadelphia House of Refuge, since she was only from a poor family and had never been convicted of a crime. The Court ruled against the father and stated that the doctrine of *parens patriae* allowed the government to look out for the welfare of children and that any juvenile justice system did not need to follow the same constitutional safeguards that are reserved for adults since the government was looking out for the best interests of the children (Spillane and Wolcott 2013). Over one hundred years later, in 1955, the United States Supreme Court made a similar ruling in the case *In re Holmes*. The Court ruled that since juvenile courts were not criminal courts, the constitutional rights that defendants have in adult courts did not apply to the juvenile courts (Hanser 2017).

The complete lack of rights for juveniles in juvenile courts first began to erode in 1966 with the Supreme Court decision in *Kent v. United States*. In that case, Morris Kent had his case transferred to adult court without a hearing or committing a crime that legislatively mandated that the case be transferred to adult court. The Supreme Court ruled that such a process, transferring a case without a hearing, violated Kent's rights to due process. A year later, the Supreme Court went further in the protection of juveniles' rights in court proceedings. In the case *In re Gault*, Gerald Gault, who was 15 at the time, was taken into custody after allegedly making an obscene phone call to a neighbor. Gault, who had previously been placed on probation, was arrested while his parents were at work and the authorities failed to inform Gault's parents that he was being taken into custody. After proceedings before a juvenile court judge, Gault was sent to a state industrial school until he turned 21. Gault and his parents challenged multiple aspects within the processing of Gault's case. After reviewing the case, the Supreme Court ruled that multiple constitutional rights granted to adults should also be provided to juveniles in juvenile court proceedings. Included among these rights were that juveniles should be given adequate notice of the charges against them, notification of the right to counsel (including notice to the parents of a juvenile that their child has the right to counsel), the opportunity to confront and cross-examine witnesses during hearings and a trial, and that juveniles should be not only advised that they have the right to remain silent, but should have adequate protections and/or safeguards from being compelled to be a witness against themselves. In a later case in 1975, *Breed v. Jones*, the Supreme Court extended the protection against double-jeopardy to juveniles. Specifically, juveniles who were tried in juvenile court for an alleged crime could not be later charged with the same crime in adult court. However, while juveniles have gained many constitutional protections in juvenile court proceedings, one right that the Supreme Court was unwilling to provide to juveniles, in *McKeiver v. Pennsylvania*, was the right to a jury trial. Hanser (2017) does note that many states have given juveniles the right to a jury trial in juvenile court proceedings.

In addition to the greater informality and often more lenient punishment that juveniles are provided within the juvenile court system, juveniles are also afforded two protections in adult courts that adult offenders lack. In *Roper v. Simmons*, the Supreme Court ruled that it is cruel and unusual punishment to execute people who were under the age of 18 when they committed their crimes. Furthermore, in *Graham v. Florida*, the Supreme Court ruled that juveniles cannot be sentenced to life in prison without the possibility of parole unless they had committed murder. According to the Court in that case, since juveniles are more susceptible to rehabilitation, it stands to reason that juveniles should not be denied the chance from ever being reformed and obtaining their release from prison. Two years later, in *Miller v. Alabama*, the Supreme Court stated that even if a youthful offender commits murder, they should eventually receive the chance to be paroled.

Conclusion

Regardless of the motives for its origin, the juvenile justice system focuses on the needs of juvenile offenders, rather than solely punishment. The system was not, and is not without its issues: constitutional challenges were necessary in order to provide juveniles with the same rights as adult offenders. Additionally, problems remain regarding status offenses, treatment options, and diversion programs. It is the hope that through the use of evidence-based practices, coupled with the growth of alternative sanctions for adult offenders, that the juvenile justice system will continue to improve while maintaining its rehabilitative approach.

References

Breed v. Jones, 1975. 421 U.S. 519.

Champion, Dean John, Richard D. Hartley, and Gary A. Rabe. 2012. *Criminal Courts: Structure, Process, and Issues*, 3rd ed. Boston, MA: Pearson.

Chesney-Lind, Meda. 1989. "Girls' Crime and Woman's Place: Toward a Feminist Model of Female Delinquency." *Crime & Delinquency* 35(1): 5–29.

Clear, Todd R., Michael D. Reisig, and George F. Cole. 2015. *American Corrections*. 11th ed. Boston, MA: Cengage.

Friedman, Lawrence M. 1993. *Crime and Punishment in American History*. New York: Basic Books.

Garry, Eileen M. 1996. *Truancy: First Step to a Lifetime of Problems*. Washington, DC: United States Department of Justice.

Graham v. Florida, 2010. 560 U.S. 48.

Hanser, Robert D. 2017. *Introduction to Corrections*. 2nd ed. Thousand Oaks, CA: Sage.

In re Gault, 1967. 387 U.S. 1.

In re Holmes, 1955. 348 U.S. 973.

Jones, Mark, and Peter Johnstone. 2012. *History of Criminal Justice*, 5th ed. Waltham, MA: Anderson Publishing.

Kent v. United States, 1966. 382 U.S. 541.

Lahey, Jessica. 2016. "The Steep Costs of Keeping Juveniles in Adult Prisons," *The Atlantic*, January 8. Retrieved on December 2, 2016 from www.theatlantic.com/education/archive/2016/01/the-cost-of-keeping-juveniles-in-adult-prisons/423201/

Lemert, Edwin E. 1951. *Social Pathology*. New York: McGraw-Hill.

Lundman, Richard J. 2001. *Prevention and Control of Juvenile Delinquency*, 3rd ed. NewYork: Oxford University Press.

McKeiver v. Pennsylvania, 1971. 403 U.S. 528.

Miller v. Alabama, 2012. 567 U.S. 132 S. Ct. 2455.

Platt, Anthony M. 1977. *The Child Savers: The Invention of Delinquency*. Chicago, IL: University of Chicago Press.

Roper v. Simmons, 2005. 543 U.S. 551.

Schlossman, Steven. 1977. *Love and the American Delinquent: The Theory and Practice of "Progressive" Juvenile Justice, 1825–1920*. Chicago: University of Chicago Press.

Schur, Edwin M. 1971. *Labeling Deviant Behavior*. New York: Harper & Row.

Schur, Edwin M. 1973. *Radical Non-Intervention. Rethinking the Delinquency Problem*. Englewood Cliffs, NJ: Prentice Hall.

Spillane, Joseph F., and David B. Wolcott. 2013. *A History of Modern American Criminal Justice*. Thousand Oaks, CA: Sage.

Steinhart, David J. 1996. "Status Offenses." *The Future of Children* 6(3): 86–99.

Tannenbaum, Frank. 1938. *Crime and the Community*. Boston, MA: Ginn.

14 A Brief History of Private Prisons in the United States

Valerie A. Clark

Introduction

The role of private industry in U.S. correctional systems has ebbed and flowed since the eighteenth century, when public and private jailers would hold debtors and inmates awaiting trial in colonial America (Rothman 1971) to when low-cost prison labor was leased to private businesses in early New York penitentiaries and in the south during the post-Civil War reconstruction era (Sellin 1967). Since that time and up until the 1980s, for-profit entities had a limited stake in corrections, providing only contracted services such as healthcare, dining, and telephone services (Selman and Leighton 2010). The precipitous rise in prison populations since the 1970s introduced a larger venture for profit-driven corporations: privately owned and/or operated correctional facilities.

The massive influx of prisoners throughout the 1980s and 1990s—brought on by tough-on-crime sentencing laws and the decades-long "War on Drugs"—left state and federal governments unable to keep up with the demand for prison bed space (Austin and Coventry 2001; Selman and Leighton 2010). This period of time was also characterized by the public's disdain for the real and/or perceived wastefulness and incompetence of government organizations, as well as the admiration of real and/or perceived efficient and innovative private enterprises (Blakely and Bumphus 2004; Spivak and Sharp 2008). These combined circumstances led governments to rely on private corporations to manage and staff existing facilities and to build new facilities. This modern chapter of privatized corrections kicked off in 1984 when the state of Tennessee turned over management of the Tall Trees School, a juvenile detention facility, and the Silverdale Detention Center, an adult prison, to the Corrections Corporation of America (CCA) (CCA 2013a).

The Rise (and Fall?) of Private Prisons in the United States

The dramatic rise of U.S. prison populations throughout the 1980s and 1990s was rivaled only by the rise in private prison facilities. There were 110 privately owned or operated correctional facilities in 1995, little more than 10 years after CCA's takeover of Tall Trees and Silverdale (Stephan and Karberg 2003). By the year 2000 that number was 264, and 415 by year 2005 (Stephan 2008). Of the 153 new prison facilities built between years 2000 and 2005, 99 percent of them were private facilities. With more than 65 facilities nationwide, including some immigration detention centers, CCA has the largest share of private prison capacity in the U.S., as well as the fifth largest corrections system (CCA 2013b).

Despite the exponential growth of private facilities, the percentage of state and federal prisoners confined in private prisons has remained relatively stable since 1999, fluctuating between 5 and 9 percent of total prison populations (Carson 2015). The Federal Bureau of

Prisons (BOP), more than states, has relied heavily on private prisons to house their inmates. The percentage of federal inmates housed in private facilities rose from approximately 3 percent in 1999 to 19 percent in 2014. That is compared to state corrections systems, who housed about 5 percent of their populations in private facilities in 1999, and just under 7 percent in 2014 (Carson 2015). However, states can vary widely in the degree to which they use private prisons. As of 2014, 20 states did not have any state prisoners in private facilities, while seven states housed more than 20 percent of their state inmates in private prisons. New Mexico had the highest percentage of state inmates in private prisons, at 44 percent, followed closely by Montana at 39 percent (Carson 2015).

The national financial crisis of the late 2000s and the accompanying government budget crises forced several states to re-think their approaches to sentencing and incarceration (Reiman and Leighton 2015). Some states and the federal government have adjusted their sentencing laws, particularly for drug offenses, leading to fewer sentences of incarceration or reduced incarceration times (e.g., Chettiar and Gupta 2011; Martin and Van Dine 2008; Mauer and Ghandnoosh 2014; Pew Charitable Trusts 2011, 2014). States have also moved towards reserving prison space for offenders at high risk of recidivism and/or violent offenders, or they have adjusted how they penalize supervision violations, reducing short-term re-admissions to prison. While these changes have led to drastic reductions in prison admissions and overall populations sizes in a few states (e.g., Mississippi, New York, New Jersey), they have only stalled the growth of overall U.S. prison populations (Carson 2015). States that have traditionally had the lowest incarceration rates are still experiencing growth in their prison populations (e.g., Maine, Minnesota, North Dakota). Given that the U.S.'s approach to criminal justice has historically swung like a pendulum, shifting between punitive and rehabilitative ideals, more time is needed to tell whether or not overall prison populations have truly plateaued or are on a downward trend.

Trends in prison populations and incarceration rates, along with the public's uneasiness with for-profit corrections (Ball 2014), have led some states to be in a virtual game of tug-of-war over the degree to which they contract with private prison corporations. In the wake of the 2008 financial crisis, a handful of states either partially or completely ended contracts with private prison corporations, leaving large swaths of prison bed space unused, and even entire private prisons empty (e.g., Burnett 2011; Cook 2010; Porter 2013; Shelden 2010). Only a few years later, some states are re-opening once-shuttered private prisons. For example, after being closed for less than a year, the North Fork Correctional Facility in Sayre, Oklahoma, will re-open under a lease between CCA and the state in 2016 (Vicent 2016). Previously housing mostly out-of-state inmates, North Fork will now house Oklahoma inmates and be staffed by state employees. After Kentucky transferred its last state prisoners out of private facilities in 2013, the state recently passed a budget bill that will allow for the transfer of state inmates back into privately owned and operated prisons starting in 2016 (Cheves and Brammer 2016; French 2016).

Florida is another state conflicted over the use of private prisons. Elected as Florida Governor in 2010, Rick Scott vowed to cut one billion dollars in state corrections spending (Klas 2015a, 2015b). Central to this cost-cutting effort were plans to privatize several prisons and corrections services. Efforts to privatize more than two dozen state prisons encountered strong opposition by several legislators as well as labor unions, and failed in the state legislature in 2011 and in 2012. Governor Scott was able to privatize at least seven prisons via extra-legislative budget maneuvers, as well as enact large contracts with private companies for other services (e.g., healthcare, substance abuse treatment). After a few years in place, these moves now face new scrutiny due to the fact that corrections costs have risen to the point they may negate previously projected savings, and reports of unsafe and inhumane conditions in private facilities have risen.

In stark contrast to Florida, Minnesota has historically had one of the lowest rates of imprisonment within the nation. Minnesota has also been less reliant on private prisons than Florida. Minnesota's involvement in private prisons began in the late 1990s, when rapid prison population growth created a shortage of bed space in public facilities (Duwe and Clark 2013a). Minnesota's private prison population peaked in late 2007/early 2008 when 13 percent of the total state prison population was housed in the Prairie Correctional Facility, a CCA-owned and operated facility in the far western part of the state (Minnesota Department of Corrections 2008). Slowed growth in the state prison population, as well as the newly expanded capacity of a state-owned facility, led Minnesota to end its contract with CCA in 2010. Six years later, Minnesota state prison populations have exceeded the capacity of state-run facilities, and the prison population is still projected to grow. This turn of events has left the state legislature in a contentious debate over whether Minnesota should revert back to its contract with CCA, in which CCA owns, manages, and staffs the Prairie facility. Other compromises are on the table, including Minnesota purchasing the Prairie facility from CCA, making it a publicly owned and operated facility, or leasing the facility from CCA and staffing it with state employees. These options reflect a range of public–private compromises available to governments considering whether or not to privatize prisons.

Taken together, recent history has demonstrated that private prisons are following a similar trajectory to overall prison populations. That is, the growth of privately owned and/or operated prison facilities has at least stalled, if not fallen slightly. However, given the uncertainty of overall prison populations and incarceration rates, as well as the public control versus privatization debate that has become a fixture in state and federal governments, the future of prison privatization is at least uncertain. The following issues will likely shape the future private prisons.

Effects on Recidivism

Given that reduced recidivism rates is one of the primary goals of corrections, a bulk of the research on public versus private prisons has focused on recidivism outcomes. Only six comprehensive studies have compared the recidivism rates of prisoners released from public and private prisons (Bales, Bedard, Quinn, Ensley, and Holley 2005; Duwe and Clark 2013a; Farabee and Knight 2002; Lanza-Kaduce and Maggard 2001; Lanza-Kaduce, Parker, and Thomas 1999; Spivak and Sharp 2008). In two separate studies using the same data from Florida prisons, Lanza-Kaduce et al. (1999) and Lanza-Kaduce and Maggard (2001) found that offenders released from private prisons had a lower risk of recidivism compared to offenders released from public prisons. In the first study, approximately 200 male prisoners from medium-security public and private facilities were matched based on individual race, type of offense, prior record, and age. The prisoners released from private facilities were less likely to be arrested, convicted of a new offense, and sent back to prison for a new offense compared to public prisoners within 12 months of release. In the second study based on the same set of released prisoners after four years of follow-up time, Lanza-Kaduce and Maggard (2001) replicated the results of the previous study predicting only reincarceration using a relaxed standard of significance ($p < .10$) (Bales et al. 2005). The results indicated that private prisoners were less likely to be reincarcerated for either a new offense or a technical violation compared to public prisoners.

In another study using Florida data, Farabee and Knight (2002) examined public–private recidivism differences based on gender and age. The authors followed nearly 9,000 state prisoners released from public and private prisons between 1997 and 2000 for up to three years. Using new convictions and reincarcerations as the measures of recidivism, the researchers found that male prisoners released from public prisons did not have significantly different rates of recidivism for either measure of recidivism. Conversely, female prisoners released from private prisons were significantly less likely to be convicted of a new offense and less likely to be reincarcerated compared to their counterparts released from public prisons. These effects did not vary based on age.

Once again, using data from Florida, Bales and colleagues (2005) found that private prison confinement compared to state-run prison confinement had a null effect on recidivism. The researchers improved upon the methodologies employed in the previous studies, including more precise measurements of private prison exposure. Given that states often have a mix of public and private prisons, it is possible that prisoners will spend time in both types of facilities during a single sentence of incarceration. Thus, Bales et al. (2005) created multiple measures of private prison confinement, including the type of prisons prisoners were released from and the number of months prisoners spent at public versus private prisons. They followed a base sample of approximately 80,000 Florida inmates for up to 5 years after release. Based on several sets of analyses using varied measures of private prison incarceration, Bales and colleagues (2005) found that varying levels of private prison confinement did not significantly influence the likelihood of felony reconviction or reincarceration among adult males, adult females, and youthful offenders.

In a departure from Florida-based studies, Spivak and Sharp (2008) used data from Oklahoma to compare public and private prison recidivism rates. The authors replicated and expanded the private prison exposure measures used by Bales et al. (2005). More specifically, they measured the proportion of an inmate's confinement time spent at private prisons. Using data from more than 23,000 inmates 4 to 7 years after release from prisons in Oklahoma, the authors found that private prison confinement, relative to confinement in public prisons, was associated with an increased risk of recidivism. Regardless of how private prison exposure was measured, private prison confinement increased the risk of recidivism, and this relationship was significant in a majority of the analyses.

In the most recent study of recidivism outcomes between public and private prisons, Duwe and Clark (2013a) evaluated whether private prison confinement had an impact on recidivism among inmates released from Minnesota prisons between 2007 and 2009. Of the more than 9,500 male inmates released from Minnesota prisons during that period of time, 19 percent spent at least a portion of their confinement times at the CCA-owned Prairie facility described earlier. Because specific eligibility criteria determined whether or not inmates could be transferred to the Prairie facility, statistical matching techniques were used to ensure that the inmates that spent any time at the Prairie facility were comparable to the inmates that spent their entire incarceration sentences in state-run facilities. For example, the Prairie facility did not accept any inmates over the age of 60, or inmates with serious medical and/or mental health conditions. Further, the Prairie facility excluded offenders whose custody-level classification was either secure or maximum, accepting only offenders who had a medium or minimum custody level classification. Given that a prisoner's classification is determined largely by violent behavior within and outside of imprisonment, as well as risk of escape, minimum- and medium-level inmates tend to have less serious criminal histories and/or better behavior in prison than secure- and maximum-level offenders. Overall, Minnesota prisoners confined at the Prairie facility were relatively healthier (mentally and physically), more well-behaved, and had less serious criminal histories compared to Minnesota's overall male prison population.

Following the leads of Bales et al. (2005) and Spivak and Sharp (2008), Duwe and Clark (2013a) also used multiple measures of private prison exposure. The authors estimated the effects of 20 different levels of private prison confinement (e.g., any time spent in private prison, number of days spent in private prison, whether or not inmate spent more than one year in private prison) on the likelihood of rearrest, reconviction, reincarceration, and supervision revocation 1 to 4 years after release. The results revealed that all 20 levels of private prisons confinement were associated with a higher risk of recidivism, and this relationship was significant in eight of the models (Duwe and Clark 2013a).

Given that inmates who spent any time at the Prairie facility were almost identical to the comparison group inmates based on several key characteristics associated with recidivism risk (e.g., age, prior criminal history, institutional misconduct), what accounted for the observed differences in recidivism outcomes? The difference, the authors argue, may be due to access to reentry programs that have previously been linked to recidivism reduction (Duwe and Clark 2013a). Although confinement costs for inmates at the Prairie facility versus Minnesota state-run prisons were roughly the same, state-run facilities offered more programming options to the inmates. The Prairie facility inmates had access to chemical dependency treatment, adult basic education, and some types of vocational programming. That is compared to inmates in state-run facilities, who had access to employment reentry programming, sex offender treatment, community-based vocational training, and enhanced reentry planning programs, in addition to the programs offered at the Prairie facility.

Besides access to programming, it is also worth noting that the inmates at Prairie may have had more limited access to visits from friends and families than inmates at public facilities. The Prairie facility is located in Appleton, Minnesota, which is approximately 170 miles from the center of the Minneapolis–St. Paul metropolitan area, where more than half of the state's population reside and from which more than half of Minnesota's prisoners are committed. That amounts to approximately three hours of driving time between the metropolitan area and the Prairie facility. That is compared to eight out of nine of Minnesota's state-run facilities that are located 65 miles or less from Minneapolis–St. Paul, or approximately one hour's drive.

This difference in distance is important given that prison visits—and the frequency of those visits—from family and friends reduce an inmate's risk of recidivism (Bales and Mears 2008; Cochran 2014; Duwe and Clark 2013b; Mears, Cochran, Siennick, and Bales 2012). Increased distance between visitors and inmates' home communities and the prisons they are confined at reduces the likelihood and frequency of visitation (Acevedo and Bakken 2001; Cochran, Mears, Bales, and Stewart 2016; Clark and Duwe forthcoming; Schirmer, Nellis, and Mauer 2009; Tewksbury and DeMichele 2005). For example, Clark and Duwe (forthcoming) found that every increase of 100 miles between a would-be visitor and a prison decreased the frequency of visitation by 20 percent (Clark and Duwe forthcoming). Outside of Minnesota, there is evidence that private prisons concentrated their development efforts in rural areas, outside of city centers where most prisoners come from (Huling 2002). Interested in lowering costs and increasing profits, lower land values, taxes, and labor costs lured private prison corporations to rural areas.

Relative Costs

The most common argument in favor of private prisons is that private corporations can accomplish the same goals as public prisons (e.g., incapacitate dangerous offenders, maintain a safe environment for employees and inmates, reduce recidivism) at a lower cost. The motivation to minimize costs and maximize profits is expected to force private companies to operate more efficiently (Cheung 2004). Moreover, private prison employees are less likely to be represented by labor unions, allowing private prison administrators to maintain more control over labor costs. Labor costs account for more than two-thirds of most prison operation budgets (Kyle 2013). Given the rigid, unsavory, and potentially dangerous working conditions of corrections officers and other prison staff, public labor unions are typically able to bargain for more favorable wages, benefits, and retirement packages for these workers

(Obermueller 2010). Private corporations can more easily exclude labor union staff and offer whatever compensation the market will bear. More than 30 cash-strapped states have turned to private prisons under the assumption that they provide the same services and produce better recidivism rates for less money than public facilities (Oppel 2011). Proponents of private prisons have claimed as much as 20 percent in savings over state-run prisons.

Due to limited data availability, as well as the complex nature of calculating and comparing prison operation costs (Gaes 2010; Perrone and Pratt 2003), there are few methodologically sound evaluations of public versus private prison costs. However, a majority of the extant research on private versus public prison costs suggests that claims of cost savings are unfounded or over-stated (Cheung 2004; Mason 2012; Selman and Leighton 2010; U.S. General Accounting Office (GAO) 1996). At least two meta-analyses that examined private versus public prisons costs found mixed, minimal, or null differences in costs, concluding that there was no real guaranteed cost advantage in prison privatization (Pratt and Maahs 1999; Lundahl, Kunz, Brownell, Harris, and Van Vleet 2007). Perrone and Pratt (2003) found that the per diem for inmates at private prisons was on average U.S. $3.40 cheaper than at publicly run facilities, but given the data and methodological limitations, this finding should be taken with an abundance of caution. All of these findings together should be considered alongside the fact that private prisons generally accept only minimum- or medium-security offenders with few or no health and behavioral problems (Duwe and Clark 2013a; Arizona Department of Corrections 2011; Oppel 2011). In other words, an inmate population without chronically-ill or misconduct-prone inmates should be less expensive to manage than an average inmate population.

Few recent studies have empirically assessed the costs of private prisons relative to their state-run counterparts. Now more than 20 years ago, the GAO (1991; 1996) released two reports that examined whether private prisons save states and the federal government money. After reviewing several unpublished studies that compared public and private prison costs across several states, the GAO concluded that there is no evidence that private prisons save money. Many of the studies they reviewed did not have reliable data, and some offered misleading information. Of the few studies that have provided conclusive evidence that private facilities save money over public facilities, the savings were negligible. A study by the Bureau of Justice Assistance that compared the costs of private and public prisons found that, at best, private prisons provide a savings of only 1 percent compared to public facilities (Austin and Coventry 2001).

The most recent comprehensive analysis of public versus private prison costs came from the Arizona Department of Corrections (2011). The Arizona study found that the costs of private prisons are sometimes the same as, or greater than, the costs of running public facilities. Private prisons have either similar or higher costs in spite of the fact that in Arizona (and many other states) private prisons take only the healthiest and most well-behaved inmates (Oppel 2011). Moreover, as described earlier, private prisons usually offer fewer institutional programming and reentry services.

Confinement Quality

Besides recidivism and cost, another measure of prison performance is the quality of confinement. Generally, quality is captured using all or some of the following measures (Perrone and Pratt 2003): the upkeep of a facility; inmate involvement in programming; access to healthcare; inmate escapes from custody; assaults (including inmate-on-inmate and inmate-on-staff); documented misconduct incidents; and disturbances or riots (order). Much like research on public versus private costs, few studies have provided a comprehensive and/or fair comparison of institutional safety in private versus public prisons.

Again, like cost, this lacuna in the literature is likely due to limited data and the difficulty involved in comparing these measures (Perrone and Pratt 2003). In order to make a reasonable comparison, researchers must match facilities on several key characteristics that likely affect each of the above outcomes. These measures include the security level of the facility and the age of the facility, for example. Medium- and low-security prisons house lower-risk inmates and can therefore be expected to have fewer assaults, disturbances, and other types of adverse outcomes. Older prisons tend to come with more experienced staff who can better manage a facility than newer, less experienced staff. On top of these matching considerations, researchers must also consider that inmates in private facilities are more carefully selected. Privately run facilities can turn away unhealthy and troublesome inmates. Publicly run facilities may increase the security level of inmates that pose an escape risk or are a danger to themselves, other staff, or inmates, but they must still confine troublesome, mentally ill, and unhealthy inmates somewhere in their systems.

Austin and Coventry (2001) found a higher rate of inmate-on-inmate and inmate-on-staff assaults at privately run facilities compared to public facilities. However, private and public prisons were comparable on other measures of inmate misconduct, including riots and other inmate-led disturbances. Perrone and Pratt's (2003) review of nine studies that compared public versus private confinement quality based on all or some of the measures listed above found mixed and overall inconclusive results. The private prisons fared worse than public prisons in particular domains in a few studies, but better than public prisons in other studies. The same was true in Lundahl et al.'s (2009) meta-analysis of public–private prison comparisons. The authors of this last study concluded that there was no clear advantage for private prisons over public prisons, or vice versa. Where there were differences between public and private prisons, the effect sizes for each domain of confinement quality were so small in magnitude, no decisive conclusions could be drawn about the superior performance of one type of prison over the other.

Conclusion

After years of record-breaking growth, the size of the U.S. prison population and the number of private prison facilities have stalled, if not fallen slightly. While many state and federal governments are working to reduce their prison populations, low-incarceration states still have room for prison population growth, which could leave the door open for private prison expansion in the future. However, the public's growing uneasiness with for-profit corrections is sure to threaten this potential growth. Having the highest incarceration rate in the world is increasingly perceived as a scourge on the U.S., and many of its citizens are reluctant to promote and celebrate the financial success of private prison corporations.

Now that private prisons have been a part of U.S. corrections for more than 30 years, researchers have had time to evaluate whether claims of cost savings coupled with improved performance are real advantages of private prisons over their public counterparts, as many proponents of privatization have argued in the past. The most methodologically rigorous studies have produced mixed and inconclusive results on both counts. Data limitations, as well as the complex nature of prison operations, have made these questions of cost and efficiency difficult to answer. At the very least, it is safe to say that there is not a clear advantage of private prisons over public prisons or vice versa.

References

Acevedo, Karen Casey and Tim Bakken. 2001. "The Effects of Visitation on Women in Prison." *International Journal of Comparative and Applied Criminal Justice* 25(1): 49–70.

Arizona Department of Corrections. 2011. *FY 2010 Operating Per Capita Cost Report: Cost Identification and Comparison of State and Private Contract Beds*. Phoenix, AZ: Arizona Department of Corrections, Bureau of Planning, Budget and Research.

Austin, James and Garry Coventry. 2001. *Emerging Issues on Privatized Prisons*. Washington, DC: U.S. Department of Justice, Office of Justice Programs, Bureau of Justice Assistance.

Bales, William D., and Daniel P. Mears. 2008. "Inmate Social Ties and the Transition to Society: Does Visitation Reduce Recidivism?" *Journal of Research in Crime and Delinquency* 45: 287–321.

Bales, William D., Laura E. Bedard, Susan T. Quinn, David T. Ensley, and Glen P. Holley. 2005. "Recidivism of Public and Private State Prison Inmates in Florida." *Criminology and Public Policy* 4: 57–82.

Ball, Molly. 2014. "The Privatization Backlash." *The Atlantic*, April 23. Retrieved May 15, 2017 from www.theatlantic.com/politics/archive/2014/04/city-state-governments-privatization-contracting-backlash/361016/

Blakely, Curtis R., and Vic W. Bumphus. 2004. "Private and Public Sector Prisons—A Comparison of Select Characteristics." *Federal Probation* 68: 27–31.

Burnett, John. 2011. "Private Prison Promises Leave Texas Towns in Trouble." *National Public Radio, NPR News Investigates,* March 28. Retrieved May 15, 2017 from www.npr.org/2011/03/28/134855801/private-prison-promises-leave-texas-towns-in-trouble

Carson, E. Ann. 2015. *Prisoners in 2014*. Washington, DC: U.S. Department of Justice, Office of Justice Programs, Bureau of Justice Statistics.

Chettiar, Inimai M., and Vanita Gupta. 2011. *Smart Reform is Possible: States Reducing Incarceration Rates and Costs While Protecting Communities*. New York, NY: American Civil Liberties Union.

Cheung, Amy. 2004. *Prison Privatization and the Use of Incarceration*. Washington, DC: The Sentencing Project.

Cheves, John, and Jack Brammer. 2016. "General Assembly Gives Final Approval to State Budget." *Lexington Herald Leader*, April 15. Retrieved May 15, 2017 from www.kentucky.com/news/politics-government/article72123697.html

Clark, Valerie A. and Grant Duwe. (forthcoming). "Distance Matters: Examining the Factors that Impact Prisoner Visitation in Minnesota." *Criminal Justice and Behavior.*

Cochran, Joshua C. 2014. "Breaches in the Wall: Imprisonment, Social support, and Recidivism." *Journal of Research in Crime and Delinquency* 51: 200–229.

Cochran, Joshua C., Daniel P. Mears, William D. Bales, and Eric A. Stewart. 2016. "Spatial Distance, Community Disadvantage, and Racial and Ethnic Variation in Prison Inmate Access to Social Ties." *Journal of Research in Crime and Delinquency* 53(2): 220–254.

Cook, Nancy. 2010. "How the Recession Hurts Private Prisons." *Newsweek*, June 29. Retrieved May 15, 2017 from www.newsweek.com/how-recession-hurts-private-prisons-72961

Corrections Corporation of America. 2013a. *The CCA Story: Our Company History*. Retrieved May 15, 2017 from www.cca.com/our-history

Corrections Corporation of America. 2013b. *See CCA's Nationwide System of Correctional Centers*. Retrieved May 15, 2017 from www.cca.com/locations

Duwe, Grant, and Valerie Clark. 2013a. "The Effects of Private Prison Confinement on Offender Recidivism: Evidence from Minnesota." *Criminal Justice Policy Review* 24: 271–296.

Duwe, Grant, and Valerie Clark. 2013b. "Blessed be the Social Tie that binds the Effects of Prison Visitation on Offender Recidivism." *Criminal Justice Policy Review* 24: 271–296.

Farabee, David, and Kevin Knight. 2002. *A Comparison of Public and Private Prisons in Florida: During- and Post-prison Performance Indicators*. Los Angeles, CA: Query Research.

French, Jackson. 2016. "House-proposed Budget would Recommission Private Prisons: Would Increase State Spending on Corrections." *Bowling Green Daily News*, March 25. Retrieved May 15, 2017 from www.bgdailynews.com/news/house-proposed-budget-would-recommission-private-prisons/article_d9df467f-5726–553a-b3c9–8e5568158bed.html

Gaes, Gerry. 2010. "Cost, Performance Studies Look at Prison Privatization." *National Institute of Justice Journal* 259: 32–36.

Huling, Tracy. 2002. "Building a Prison Economy in Rural America." Pp. 197–213 in *From Invisible Punishment: The Collateral Consequences of Mass Imprisonment*, edited by M. Mauer and M. Chesney-Lind. New York, NY: The New Press.

Klas, Mary Ellen. 2015a. "Private Prison Vendors Could Face New Scrutiny in Florida." Tampa Bay Times, April 19. Retrieved May 15, 2017 from www.tampabay.com/news/politics/stateroundup/private-prison-vendors-could-face-new-scrutiny-in-florida/2226087

Klas, Mary Ellen. 2015b. "The 'Cannibalizing' of Florida's Prison System." Miami Herald, February 28. Retrieved May 15, 2017 from www.miamiherald.com/news/special-reports/florida-prisons/article11533064.html

Kyle, Peter H. 2013. "Contracting for Performance: Restructuring the Private Prison Market." *William & Mary Law Review* 54(6): 2087–2113.

Lanza-Kaduce, Lonn and Scott Maggard. 2001. "The Long-term Recidivism of Public and Private Prisoners." Unpublished paper presented at the National Conference of the Bureau of Justice Statistics and Justice Research and Statistics.

Lanza-Kaduce, Lonn, Karen Parker, and Charles W. Thomas. 1999. "A Comparative Recidivism Analysis of Releasees from Private and Public Prisons." *Crime & Delinquency* 45: 28–47.

Lundahl, Brad, Chelsea Kunz, Cyndi Brownell, Norma Harris, and Russ Van Vleet. 2007. *Privation Privatization: A Meta-analysis of Cost Effectiveness and Quality of Confinement Indicators*. Salt Lake City, UT: Utah Criminal Justice Center. Retrieved May 15, 2017 from www.cecilash.com/uploads/Univ_of_Utah_MetaAnalysis_of_private_prisons_vs_public.pdf

Martin, Brian and Steve Van Dine. 2008. *Examining the Impact of Ohio's Progressive Sanction Grid, Final Report*. Washington, DC: National Institute of Justice.

Mason, Cody. 2012. *Too Good to be True: Private Prisons in America*. Washington, DC: The Sentencing Project. Retrieved May 15, 2017 from: http://sentencingproject.org/wp-content/uploads/2016/01/Too-Good-to-be-True-Private-Prisons-in-America.pdf

Mauer, Marc and Nazgol Ghandnoosh. 2014. *Fewer Prisoners, Less Crime: A Tale of Three States*. Policy Brief. Washington, DC: The Sentencing Project.

Mears, Daniel P., Joshua C. Cochran, Sonja E. Siennick, and William D. Bales. 2012. "Prison Visitation and Recidivism." *Justice Quarterly* 29(6): 888–918.

Minnesota Department of Corrections (2008). *Adult Inmate Profile (January 1, 2008)*. St. Paul, MN: Minnesota Department of Corrections. Retrieved May 15, 2017 from www.doc.state.mn.us/PAGES/files/9913/8489/0056/2008_Jan_Adult_Profile.pdf

Obermueller, Andy. 2010. "Strapped States are Bullish for Private Prisons." *Forbes*, March 18. Retrieved from www.forbes.com/2010/03/18/corrections-corporation-america-private-prisons.html

Oppel, Richard. A. 2011. "Private Prisons Found to Offer Little in Savings." *The New York Times*. Retrieved May 15, 2017 from www.nytimes.com/2011/05/19/us/19prisons.html

Perrone, Dina, and Travis C. Pratt. 2003. "Comparing the Quality of Confinement and Cost-Effectiveness of Public Versus Private Prisons: What We Know, Why we do not Know More, and Where to go from Here." *The Prison Journal* 83(3): 301–322.

Pew Charitable Trusts. 2011. *Kentucky Reforms Cut Recidivism, Costs: Broad Bill Enacts Evidence-Based Strategies. Issue Brief*. Washington, DC: Pew Charitable Trusts.

Pew Charitable Trusts. 2014. *Mississippi's 2014 Corrections and Criminal Justice Reform: Legislation to Improve Public Safety, Ensure Certainty in Sentencing, and Control Corrections Costs*. Washington, DC: Pew Charitable Trusts.

Porter, Nicole D. 2013. *On the Chopping Block 2013: State Prison Closures*. Washington, DC: The Sentencing Project. Retrieved May 15, 2017 from www.sentencingproject.org/wp-content/uploads/2015/12/On-the-Chopping-Block-2013.pdf

Pratt, Travis C., and Jeff Maahs. 1999. "Are Private Prisons More Cost-effective than Public Prisons? A Meta-analysis of Evaluation Research Studies." *Crime & Delinquency* 45: 358–371.

Reiman, Jeffrey, and Paul Leighton. 2015. *The Rich Get Richer and the Poor Get Prison: Ideology, Class, and Criminal Justice*, 10th ed. New York: Routledge.

Rothman, David J. 1971. *The Discovery of the Asylum*. New Brunswick, NJ: Transaction Publishers.

Schirmer, Sarah, Ashley Nellis and Marc Mauer. 2009. *Incarcerated Parents and Their Children: Trends 1991–2007*. Washington, DC: The Sentencing Project.

Sellin, Thorsten. 1967. "A Look at Prison History." *Federal Probation* 31(3): 18–23.

Selman, Donna, and Paul Leighton. 2010. *Punishment for Sale: Private Prisons, Big Business, and the Incarceration Binge*. Lanham, MD: Rowman & Littlefield Publishers.

Shelden, Randall G. 2010. *The Prison Industry*. Research Brief. San Francisco, CA: Center on Juvenile and Criminal Justice. Retrieved May 15, 2017 from www.cjcj.org/uploads/cjcj/documents/the_prison_industry.pdf

Spivak, Andrew L., and Susan F. Sharp. 2008. "Inmate Recidivism as a Measure of Private Prison Performance." *Crime & Delinquency* 54: 482–508.

Stephan, James J. 2008. *Census of State and Federal Correctional Facilities, 2005*. Washington, DC: U.S. Department of Justice, Office of Justice Programs, Bureau of Justice Statistics.

Stephan, James J., and Jennifer C. Karberg. 2003. *Census of State and Federal Correctional Facilities, 2000*. Washington, DC: U.S. Department of Justice, Office of Justice Programs.

Tewksbury, Richard and Matthew DeMichele. 2005. "Going to Prison: A Prison Visitation Program." *The Prison Journal* 85(3): 292–310.

U.S. General Accounting Office. 1991. *Private Prisons: Cost Savings and BOP's Statutory Authority Need to be Resolved*. Report to the Chairman, Subcommittee on Regulation, Business Opportunities and Energy, Committee on Small Business, House of Representatives. Washington, DC: General Government Division, General Accounting Office.

U.S. General Accounting Office. 1996. *Private and Public Prisons: Studies Comparing Operational Costs and/or Quality of Service*. Report to the Subcommittee on Crime, Committee on the Judiciary, House of Representatives. Washington, DC: General Government Division, General Accounting Office

Vicent, Samantha. 2016. "State Reformatory Inmates Will Move to Leased Private Prison in July." *Tulsa World*, June 3. Retrieved May 15, 2017 from www.tulsaworld.com/news/government/state-reformatory-inmates-to-move-to-leased-private-prison-in/article_5a47b4b0-a8a0–58e0-b04f-f807adb90def.html

Section 3

Community Corrections and Alternative Sanctions

15 Probation in the United States

A Historical and Modern Perspective

Ryan M. Labrecque

On any given day, there are approximately 6.9 million adult offenders under some form of correctional supervision in the United States, with more than 4.7 million who are supervised in the community (Kaeble, Glaze, Tsoutis, and Minton 2016). Probation is the most commonly used criminal sentence, with probationers comprising 56 percent of the total correctional population and 82 percent of the total community supervision population (Kaeble, Maruschak, and Bonczar 2015). The total correctional population has steadily been declining for seven continuous years at a rate of approximately 1 percent per year. However, this decrease has largely been driven by the reduction in the use of probation, where in 2007 there were 4.3 million offenders on probation and in 2014 there were 3.9 million (Kaeble et al. 2016).

A similar trend exists in the juvenile justice system, where approximately 64 percent of all adjudicated delinquent cases and 56 percent of all adjudicated status offenses result in the disposition of probation as the most severe sanction ordered by the court (Hockenberry and Puzzanchera 2014). There are presently more than 500,000 juveniles on probation in the United States, which represents a nearly 30 percent reduction in the use of the practice since the late 1990s (Livsey 2012). Despite this widespread use of both adult and juvenile probation, however, there is little evidence that this practice is effective in reducing recidivism (Bonta, Rugge, Scott, Bourgon, and Yessine 2008).

This chapter reviews the historical development of probation in the United States, and highlights how the practice is used in the twenty-first century. This chapter also describes the process by which offenders are sentenced to probation, the types of offenders and offenses that lead to probation, the conditions of probation that are often imposed by the sentencing court, the process for dealing with technical violations of probation, and the effectiveness of probation in reducing crime. Finally, this chapter concludes by examining the status of emerging evidence-based attempts at redefining the function of probation in the modern era.

Probation

Probation is a court order through which a criminal defendant is placed under the control, supervision, and care of a probation officer in lieu of imprisonment; so long as the probationer maintains certain standards of conduct (American Probation and Parole Association 2013). In order for probation to be granted, the offender must agree to comply with the conditions of supervision imposed upon him or her by the sentencing court. General conditions of probation are placed upon all probationers regardless of individual circumstances. These mandatory conditions typically include that the probationer must obey all laws, submit to searches as ordered, report to the supervising probation officer as directed, notify supervising officer of any change in address or employment, not possess a firearm, associate with other known criminals, or leave the jurisdiction of the court without prior approval (Abadinsky 2014).

The sentencing court may also impose additional conditions of probation that are tailored in response to the offender's risk to the community and his or her individual rehabilitative needs. These specific conditions can include stipulations such as the probationer must remain confined to his or her house, submit to electronic monitoring, abide by a specific curfew, pay restitution or probation supervision fees, and participate in substance abuse, mental health, educational, vocational, or other treatment programs (Abadinsky 2014). The sentencing court retains the authority to supervise the offender in the community, modify the conditions of supervision, and revoke the probationary status of the offender (either in part or in full) based on his or her behavior while on probation (Allen, Latessa, and Ponder 2015). Probationers are presumed to be motivated to comply with the court's wishes because if one does not, he or she may face the possibility of being incarcerated (Latessa and Smith 2015).

It is the probation officer's responsibility to ensure that the conditions imposed by the court are met and, if necessary, to call the violation(s) to the attention of the court (Morgan 2016). As such, the probation officers' role is to serve as both a helper and a rule enforcer (Skeem and Manchak 2008). Assuming the probationer meets all of the court-imposed conditions, the term of probation will complete at the expiration of the sentence. Probation officers can also file a motion with the court to end a period of probation early if the offender has successfully satisfied all of the court's requirements (e.g., successfully completed a treatment program, paid off restitution) and it is believed that he or she has received the maximum benefit of supervision (Latessa and Smith 2015). In the United States, probationers spend an average of 22 months on probation (Kaeble et al. 2015), and the majority (68 percent) successfully completes his or her probation sentence (see Maruschak and Bonczar 2013).

If a probationer violates his or her conditions of probation (i.e., a technical violation), the probation officer must address the misbehavior with the offender. The court gives probation officers a great deal of discretionary power in responding to these situations. Officers are often free to choose in which instances a probationer should receive a stern warning and those that warrant an officer to bring the probationer back before the court for a formalized hearing (Abadinsky 2014). Ideally, the judge, probation officer, prosecutor, probationer and his or her defense counsel will collaborate during the revocation process to determine what course of action should be taken (Latessa and Smith 2015). Offenders may serve a portion of his or her initial underlying sentence in jail or prison, have additional conditions of supervision imposed upon him or her, or have his or her probationary term extended. In some cases the term of probation is unsatisfactorily terminated and the probationer may serve out the remainder of his or her sentence in custody (Maruschak and Bonczar 2013). Offenders incarcerated due to such revocations make up nearly half of all new intakes to state prisons in any given year (Taxman 2012), which has also contributed to the increase in the United States' inmate population (Austin and Irwin 2012).

Historical Development of Probation

The use of probation in the United States has a long history. John Augustus, a Boston shoemaker, is often credited with being the "father of probation" (Dressler 1970). Between 1841 and 1858, Augustus posted bail for nearly 2,000 men, women, and children—mostly minor offenders and alcoholics—who otherwise had no way of paying their fines (Taxman 2012). Augustus then aided these offenders in gaining employment and reported on their progress toward reformation when he or she was later brought before the court for sentencing

(Allen et al. 2015). It is no surprise that Augustus's home state of Massachusetts was the first to pass a probation statute in 1878; and by 1956, all 50 states and the federal government had adopted juvenile and adult probation laws (Petersilia 1997).

From its inception, probation emerged as a way to help offenders, which was largely supported by the correctional philosophy of rehabilitation (Rothman 1980). The use of probation was seen as an opportunity to divert the offender from imprisonment and give him or her another chance (Latessa and Smith 2015). By remaining in the community, the offender would be better able to support dependents, make restitution, retain employment, and participate in treatment programs (Morgan 2016). Public support for the practice remained relatively unchallenged until the early 1970s, when offender rehabilitation more generally came under attack (for more information see Cullen and Gilbert 1982). Robert Martinson's (1974: 25) review of the correctional treatment literature proclaimed "with few and isolated exceptions, the rehabilitative efforts that have been reported so far have had no appreciable effect on recidivism." The conclusion that "nothing works" dealt a devastating blow to the rehabilitative ideal (Allen 1981).

During this "get tough" era, it became increasingly more difficult for correctional administrators and policymakers to support rehabilitative strategies while the philosophy was being discredited (Cullen and Gendreau 2000). Throughout much of the 1980s and 1990s, a series of punitive sentencing policies were adopted in many federal, state, and local jurisdictions (e.g., mandatory minimum sentencing laws, three-strikes laws, truth-in-sentencing laws). Not surprisingly, these policy changes led to a drastic increase in the number of offenders in prison (Currie 1998). However, these policy changes also led to an increase in the number of offenders who were placed on probation (Austin and Irwin 2012). To illustrate, in 1980 there were slightly more than 1 million adult probationers in the United States; however, by the early 2000s, this number grew to 4 million (Maruschak and Parks 2012). This represents a 400 percent increase in the use of probation in two decades.

During this time, there was also a fundamental shift in the function of probation (see Taxman 2002). Probation departments began downplaying their officers' roles as social workers who aided in connecting probationers to resources and services in the community, and intensifying the use of controls over offenders (Taxman 2008). Whereas the first 150 years of probation were focused on rehabilitating and assisting offenders stabilize their lives, these changes led to probation officers emphasizing the law enforcement aspects of their job, with a particular emphasis on strictly enforcing the conditions of probation (e.g., reporting, drug testing, working, paying restitution, informing the officer of their whereabouts; Taxman 2012). This strategy was based on the assumption that technical violations of these conditions serve as a precursor to criminal behavior (see Campbell 2014). It was therefore reasoned that this strict enforcement strategy would deter offenders from engaging in such undesirable behavior (see e.g., Center for Civic Innovation 1999; Farabee 2005; and Hawken and Kleiman 2009).

Reaffirming Rehabilitation

In response to the growing movement of increasingly severe punishments (Clear 1994), there was a countermovement to "reaffirm rehabilitation" as the overarching goal of corrections (see Cullen and Gilbert 1982). Most notably, the Canadian school of rehabilitation led this effort to develop a viable theory of effective offender treatment (Cullen and Jonson 2011). The approach taken by this group of scholars was to search for the convergent validity across diverse empirical and theoretical literatures to demonstrate that certain types of treatment programs and strategies would benefit offenders and protect the public. As part of this process, the primary method used to summarize findings was to quantitatively synthesize the results (i.e., meta-analysis). Currently, there are more than 100 meta-analyses that have been conducted of the correctional treatment literature, which have been replicated with remarkable consistency (see McGuire 2013). Collectively, these findings are referred to as the *principles of effective intervention* (see Andrews and Bonta 2010 for a detailed review).

The three most important principles identified by Andrews and Bonta (2010) are those of risk, need, and responsivity (RNR). The *risk principle* asserts criminal behavior is predictable when valid risk assessment tools are used and treatment intensity is matched to level of risk, where higher risk offenders receive more services than lower risk offenders. The *need principle* suggests that in order to reduce recidivism, the dynamic (i.e., changeable) crime-producing risk factors—or criminogenic needs—should be the target of intervention (e.g., antisocial personality, antisocial cognition, antisocial associates). The *responsivity principle* describes how to best target criminogenic needs—with cognitive-behavioral interventions—and stresses the importance of matching offenders and treatment strategies in a manner that is most conducive to his or her learning style, motivation, abilities, and strengths (Andrews and Dowden 2006).

A growing body of research finds that stronger adherence to the principles of RNR is associated with more dramatic reductions in recidivism (increase of 2 percent recidivism with no adherence to the principles and decrease of 26 percent for adherence to all three principles; Andrews and Bonta 2010: 74). Further, research shows stronger treatment effects occur when interventions are applied in the community as opposed to the institutional setting (reductions of 40 percent compared to 30 percent; McGuire 2002). Regrettably, however, these principles have not yet been widely applied in probation settings (Bonta et al. 2011). Rather, the primary focus of probation officers remains on compliance monitoring and other law enforcement aspects of supervision (Bonta et al. 2008). This is rather unfortunate, given that it has been well documented that punitive-based supervision strategies (e.g., intensive supervision, electronic monitoring, house arrest) have no appreciable effects on recidivism, and under some circumstances may actually increase it (MacKenzie 2006; Petersilia and Turner 1993; Sherman et al. 1997).

In 2008, Bonta and his colleagues conducted a meta-analysis that has cast some doubt on the ability of the general practice of probation to effectively reduce recidivism. More specifically, Bonta et al. (2008) found that community supervision was associated with a 2 percent reduction in general recidivism and had no impact on violent recidivism. These weak findings seriously question the rationale of maintaining the current probation practices, when there are other potentially more viable options available that may be able to achieve better outcomes (Burrell 2012). In response, there has been a growing effort to nudge probation out of its focus on compliance monitoring and to better incorporate the use of evidence-based rehabilitation services in an effort to achieve better outcomes (see Bourgon, Gutierrez, and Ashton 2012).

New Approaches to Supervision

During the last decade, several formalized attempts have been made to improve the effectiveness of probation by incorporating the principles of effective intervention into practice (for a review see Trotter 2013; and Viglione and Taxman 2015). These new supervision strategies include the Proactive Community Supervision (PCS) model (Taxman 2008), the Strategic Training Initiative in Community Supervision (STICS) model (Bonta et al. 2011), the Effective Practices in Community Supervision (EPICS) model (Smith, Schweitzer, Labrecque, and Latessa 2012), and the Staff Training Aimed at Reducing Rearrest (STARR) model (Robinson et al. 2012). Each of these models seeks to teach probation officers how to more effectively apply the RNR principles within the context of the individual case management meetings with the offenders they supervise. More specifically, these initiatives seek to aid officers in targeting the criminogenic needs (*need principle*) of higher risk offenders (*risk principle*) with cognitive-behavioral based interventions, in a manner that is conducive to his or her learning style, motivation, abilities, and strengths (*responsivity principle*).

These new models of intervention further work to try and improve the nature of the relationship between the probation officer and the probationer. Inherent in these strategies is the notion that officers should develop quality relationships with the offenders they supervise, while balancing the goals of care (i.e., rehabilitating the offender) and control (i.e., protecting the community; Skeem and Manchak 2008). These models also attempt to increase the officer use of core correctional practices (CCPs), which are the core skills that have been shown to increase the therapeutic potential of correctional interventions (Dowden and Andrews 2004). There are eight CCPs identified by Gendreau, Andrews, and Thériault (2010):

anticriminal modeling—officer models prosocial behavior and reinforces the offender when he or she does the same;

effective reinforcement—officer reinforces a desirable behavior of the offender and discusses the short- and long-term benefits of its continued use with him or her;

effective disapproval—officer disapproves of an undesirable behavior of the offender, discusses the short- and long-term costs of its continued use with him or her, and demonstrates an alternative, prosocial behavior;

effective use of authority—officer guides offender toward compliance by focusing his or her message on the behavior exhibited, being direct and specific concerning his or her demands and specifying the offender's choices and attendant consequences;

structured learning—officer uses behavioral strategies to assist offender in developing prosocial skills to avoid or manage high-risk situations. Officer teaches skills in a structured manner by defining, modeling, and rehearsing the skill followed by providing constructive feedback. Officer encourages offender to practice the skill in increasingly difficult situations;

problem solving—officer teaches offender to address high-risk situations by exercising the steps of effective problem solving: identifying the problem, clarifying the goals, generating a list of alternative solutions, reviewing options, implementing the plan, and evaluating the outcome;

cognitive restructuring—officer helps offender generate descriptions of problematic situations and identify his or her related thoughts and feelings. Officer then helps offender to recognize risky thinking and practice prosocial alternatives;

relationship skills—effective officers possess several critical relationship skills including being warm, open, nonjudgmental, empathetic, flexible, engaging, solution-focused, and directive.

Support for these new models of supervision has begun to accumulate (see e.g., the reviews by Chadwick, Dewolf, and Serin 2015; Drake 2013; and Trotter 2013). Collectively, these new models have been found to enhance officer use of the CCPs (Bourgon, Bonta, Rugge, Scott, and Yessine 2010; Smith et al. 2012); improve the quality of the offender–officer relationship (Labrecque, Schweitzer, and Smith 2014), decrease offender antisocial attitudes (Labrecque, Smith, Schweitzer, and Thompson 2013); and reduce recidivism (Bonta et al. 2011; Latessa, Smith, Schweitzer, and Labrecque 2012; Labrecque, Smith, and Luther 2015; Lowenkamp, Holsinger, Robinson, and Alexander 2014). A recent meta-analysis conducted by Chadwick et al. (2015) reported that offenders supervised by officers trained in these new models were 1.5 times less likely to recidivate compared to the offenders supervised by officers not trained in these models.

Probation in the Twenty-first Century

Presently, there are more than 2,000 independent probation agencies in the United States that all operate under different state and federal laws (Abadinsky 2014). Under the umbrella of probation, there are six separate systems: juvenile probation, municipal probation, county probation, state probation, state combined probation and parole, and federal probation (Abadinsky 2014). Each state has more than one of these systems in operation simultaneously, which is administered either by a single, central agency; a variety of local agencies; or a bination of the two (Hanser 2014). Further, probation can be delivered through either the executive or judiciary branch of government. Probation agencies administered through the executive branch may exist as part of the larger state correctional system or may exist as their own separate system. Probation agencies administered through the judicial branch work for the court system itself. In both cases, the probation agency still oversees the compliance with the conditions of supervision (Hanser 2014).

In addition to its supervisory role, probation agencies also serve an investigatory function for the courts (Petersilia 1997). Under the direction of the criminal court, probation officers complete presentence investigation (PSI) reports in order to provide the sentencing court with information about the offender and the facts surrounding his or her case (Latessa and Smith 2015). A PSI typically includes information on the offender's background, past criminal behavior, offense situations, personal and family circumstances, personality, need, risk level, a summary of permissible sentencing options, and a recommendation for disposition (Allen et al. 2015). If incarceration is recommended, the probation officer recommends a sentence length; and if probation is recommended, the officer recommends sentence length and the conditions to be imposed (Petersilia 1997). In general, judges have a wide range of options in the disposition of a criminal case including suspending a sentence, imposing a fine, requiring restitution, imposing community supervision, and incarcerating an offender. The PSI is thus designed to help the judge make a more informed decision by taking into account the needs of the offender, as well as the safety of the community (Latessa and Smith 2015).

The use of probation supervision is no longer reserved for first-time and less serious offenders, as it was during the Augustus era (Taxman 2012). A Bureau of Justice Statistics report found that nearly half of all sentenced probationers had a prior criminal conviction (Mumola and Bonczar 1998). In 2014, 56 percent of adult offenders were on probation for a felony offense (Kaeble et al. 2015). Although the majority of probationers are sentenced for non-violent offenses, 19 percent of adults (Kaeble et al. 2015) and 26 percent of juveniles are sentenced to probation for violent (i.e., personal) offenses (Hockenberry and Puzzanchera 2014). Approximately, three-fourths of all juvenile and adult probationers are males who are also represented by a disproportionately higher rate of ethnic/minority offenders. Further, more than one-third of juvenile probationers are also under the age of 16 (Hockenberry and Puzzanchera 2014). These changes in the probationer characteristics have made this population more difficult to manage, especially when coupled with shrinking departmental budgets and increasing officer to offender ratios (see DeMichele 2007; and Petersilia 1997).

Conclusion

Probation has many advantages over imprisonment, including lower operational costs, increased opportunities for rehabilitation, and reduced risk of criminal socialization (Latessa and Smith 2015). However, there is increasing evidence to suggest that probation strategies that focus on compliance monitoring and other law enforcement aspects of supervision are not effective in reducing recidivism, and may even increase it (Bonta et al. 2008; MacKenzie 2006; Petersilia and Turner 1993; Sherman et al. 1997). There is also a growing body of literature that indicates the effectiveness of probation is contingent upon the extent to which the principles of effective intervention are adhered (Andrews and Bonta 2010). As Judge Burton Roberts—the Administrative Judge of the Bronx Supreme and Criminal Courts—explains: "Nothing is wrong with probation. It is the *execution* of probation that is wrong" (as cited in Klein 1997: 72).

It has been well documented that the effectiveness of any correctional intervention is greatly diminished if careful attention is not paid to how the program is implemented in practice (Gendreau, Goggin, and Smith 1999). Prior research has demonstrated that incompetent use of treatment strategies can have the unintended consequence of increasing, rather than decreasing, recidivism (see e.g. Lowenkamp, Latessa, and Smith 2006). Despite the efforts of the new supervision models to increase the officer adherence to the RNR principles and use of CCPs, there is evidence that even trained officers do not consistently apply these skills in their interactions with offenders during follow-up evaluations (Robinson et al. 2012).

This is unfortunate because research suggests there is a relationship between adherence to the model and offender outcomes. For example, Smith and Labrecque (2016) found that offenders supervised by EPICS trained officers who used the models' skills with high fidelity had lower recidivism rates than those supervised by officers who used the skills with less fidelity. This result stresses the importance of ensuring that probation officers adhere to the models' skills with fidelity. One strategy for improving the use of these skills is to monitor officer performance (e.g., audio-record officer–offender interactions) and provide officers with coaching opportunities and booster training sessions. Labrecque and Smith (2017) found that coaching officers over a period of 18 months led to increased use of CCPs throughout the duration. It is therefore critical that probation agencies not only adopt such models of supervision and train their officers in these curricula, but these organizations must also ensure these skills are being used in practice with fidelity (e.g., monitor officer performance, provide coaching, and booster sessions).

Probation agencies have a responsibility to protect the community. Although many intra-agency commonalities exist, the administration of probation is not uniform across the United States; rather it varies widely from jurisdiction to jurisdiction (Taxman 2012). Likewise, these correctional agencies are free to enforce different strategies of supervision. It is no longer adequate for organizations and officers to focus exclusively on controlling and punishing probationers. The incorporation of the principles of effective intervention into probation settings is therefore crucial to better serve the millions of probationers in the United States and to achieve better societal outcomes (i.e., lower recidivism rates; Viglione and Taxman 2015). Fortunately, there are several new models of supervision available that seek to increase the use of these principles in probation settings (e.g., PCS, STICS, EPICS, STARR), which have shown very promising results. The attempts undertaken thus far are a great first step in generating meaningful changes in probation organizations, but there is still much work to be done in this area.

References

Abadinsky, Howard. 2014. *Probation and Parole: Theory and Practice*, 12th ed. Upper Saddle River, NJ: Prentice Hall.

Allen, Francis A. 1981. *The Decline of the Rehabilitative Ideal: Penal Policy and Social Purpose*. New Haven, CT: Yale University Press.

Allen, Harry E., Edward J. Latessa, and Bruce S. Ponder. 2015. *Corrections in America: An Introduction*, 14th ed. Upper Saddle River, NJ: Prentice Hall.
American Probation and Parole Association. 2013. *Probation & Parole Directory*. Lexington, KY: American Probation and Parole Association.
Andrews, Don A., and Craig Dowden. 2006. "Risk Principle of Case Classification in Correctional Treatment: A Meta-Analytic Investigation." *International Journal of Offender Therapy and Comparative Criminology* 50(1): 88–100.
Andrews, Don A., and James Bonta. 2010. *The Psychology of Criminal Conduct*, 5th ed. Newark, NJ: LexisNexis.
Austin, James, and John Irwin. 2012. *It's About Time: America's Imprisonment Binge*, 4th ed. Belmont, CA: Wadsworth, Cengage Learning.
Bonta, James, Guy Bourgon, Tanya Rugge, Terri-Lynne Scott, Annie K. Yessine, and Leticia Gutierrez. 2011. "An Experimental Demonstration of Training Probation Officers in Evidence-Based Community Supervision." *Criminal Justice and Behavior* 38(11): 1127–1148.
Bonta, James, Tanya Rugge, Terri-Lynne Scott, Guy Bourgon, and Annie K. Yessine. 2008. "Exploring the Black Box of Community Supervision." *Journal of Offender Rehabilitation* 47(3): 248–270.
Bourgon, Guy, James Bonta, Tanya Rugge, Terri-Lynne Scott, and Annie K. Yessine. 2010. "The Role of Program Design, Implementation, and Evaluation in Evidence-Based 'Real World' Community Supervision." *Federal Probation* 74(1): 2–15.
Bourgon, Guy, Leticia Gutierrez, and Jennifer Ashton. 2012. "The Evolution of Community Supervision Practice: The Transformation from Case Manager to Change Agent." *Federal Probation* 76(2): 27–35.
Burrell, William D. 2012. *Community Corrections Management: Issues and Strategies*. Kingston, NJ: Civic Research Institute.
Campbell, Christopher M. 2014. "It's Not Technically a Crime: Investigating the Relationship Between Technical Violations and New Crime." *Criminal Justice Policy Review*. Advance online publication.
Center for Civic Innovation. 1999. *"Broken Windows" Probation: The Next Fight in Fighting Crime*. New York, NY: Manhattan Institute.
Chadwick, Nick, Angela Dewolf, and Ralph Serin. 2015. "Effectively Training Community Supervision Officers: A Meta-Analytic Review of the Impact on Offender Outcome." *Criminal Justice and Behavior* 42(10): 977–989.
Clear, Todd R. 1994. *Harm in American Penology: Offenders, Victims, and Their Communities*. Albany, NY: State University of New York Press.
Cullen, Francis T., and Paul Gendreau. 2000. "Assessing Correctional Rehabilitation: Policy, Practice, and Prospects." Pp. 109–175 in *Criminal Justice 2000: Volume 3—Changes in Decision Making and Discretion in the Criminal Justice System*, edited by J. Horney. Washington, DC: Department of Justice.
Cullen, Francis T., and Karen E. Gilbert. 1982. *Reaffirming Rehabilitation*. Cincinnati, OH: Anderson Publishing.
Cullen, Francis T., and Cheryl L. Jonson. 2011. "Rehabilitation and Treatment Programs." Pp. 293–344 in *Crime and Public Policy*, edited by J.Q. Wilson and J. Petersilia. New York, NY: Oxford University Press.
Currie, Elliott. 1998. *Crime and Punishment in America: Why the Solutions to America's Most Stubborn Social Crisis Have Not Worked—and What Will*. New York: Henry Holt.
DeMichele, Matthew T. 2007. *Probation and Parole's Growing Caseloads and Workload Allocation: Strategies for Managerial Decision Making*. Lexington, KY: American Probation and Parole Association.
Dowden, Craig, and Don A. Andrews. 2004. "The Importance of Staff Practice in Delivering Effective Correctional Treatment: A Meta-Analytical Review of Core Correctional Practice." *International Journal of Offender Therapy and Comparative Criminology* 48(2): 203–214.
Drake, Elizabeth. 2013. *Inventory of Evidence-Based and Research-Based Programs for Adult Corrections*. Olympia, WA: Washington State Institute for Public Policy.
Dressler, David. 1970. *Practice and Theory of Probation and Parole*. New York: Columbia University Press.

Farabee, David. 2005. *Rethinking Rehabilitation: Why Can't We Reform Our Criminals?* Washington, DC: AEI Press.

Gendreau, Paul, Don A. Andrews, and Yvette Thériault. 2010. *Correctional Program Assessment Inventory—2010 (CPAI-2010).* Saint John, Canada: University of New Brunswick.

Gendreau, Paul, Claire Goggin, and Paula Smith. 1999. "The Forgotten Issue in Effective Correctional Treatment: Program Implementation." *International Journal of Offender Therapy and Comparative Criminology* 43(2): 180–187.

Hanser, Robert D. 2014. *Community Corrections*, 2nd ed. Thousand Oaks, CA: Sage.

Hawken, Angela, and Mark Kleiman. 2009. *Managing Drug Involved Probationers With Swift and Certain Sanctions: Evaluating Hawaii's HOPE.* Washington, DC: National Institute of Justice.

Hockenberry, Sarah, and Charles Puzzanchera. 2014. *Juvenile Court Statistics, 2011.* Pittsburg, PA: National Center for Juvenile Justice.

Kaeble, Danielle, Lauren Glaze, Anastasios Tsoutis, and Todd Minton. 2016. *Correctional Populations in the United States, 2014.* Washington, DC: Bureau of Justice Statistics.

Kaeble, Danielle, Laura M. Maruschak, and Thomas P. Bonczar. 2015. *Probation and Parole in the United States, 2014.* Washington, DC: Bureau of Justice Statistics.

Klein, Andrew R. 1997. *Alternative Sentencing, Intermediate Sanctions, and Probation.* Cincinnati, OH: Anderson.

Labrecque, Ryan M., Myrinda Schweitzer, and Paula Smith. 2014. "Exploring the Perceptions of the Offender-Officer Relationship in a Community Supervision Setting." *Journal of International Criminal Justice Research* 1(1): 31–46.

Labrecque, Ryan M., Paula Smith, and Jennifer D. Luther. 2015. "A Quasi-Experimental Evaluation of a Model of Community Supervision." *Federal Probation* 79(3): 14–19.

Labrecque, Ryan M., Paula Smith, Myrinda Schweitzer, and Cara Thompson. 2013. "Targeting Antisocial Attitudes in Community Supervision Using the EPICS Model: An Examination of Change Scores on the Criminal Sentiment Scale." *Federal Probation* 77(3): 15–20.

Labrecque, Ryan M., and Paula Smith. 2017. "Does training and coaching matter? An 18-month evaluation of a community supervision model." *Victims and Offenders*, 12(2): 233–252.

Latessa, Edward J., and Paula Smith. 2015. *Corrections in the Community*, 6th ed. New York: Routledge.

Latessa, Edward J., Paula Smith, Myrinda Schweitzer, and Ryan M. Labrecque. 2012. *Evaluation of the Effective Practices in Community Supervision Model (EPICS) in Ohio.* Cincinnati, OH: University of Cincinnati.

Livsey, Sarah. 2012. *Juvenile Delinquency Probation Caseload, 2009.* Washington, DC: Office of Juvenile Justice and Delinquency Prevention.

Lowenkamp, Christopher T., Alexander M. Holsinger, Charles R. Robinson, and Melissa Alexander. 2014. "Diminishing or Durable Treatment Effects of STARR? A Research Note on 24-Month Re-arrest Rates." *Journal of Crime and Justice* 37(2): 275–283.

Lowenkamp, Christopher T., Edward J. Latessa, and Paula Smith. 2006. "Does Correctional Program Quality Matter? The Impact of Adhering to the Principles of Effective Intervention." *Criminology and Public Policy* 5(3): 575–594.

MacKenzie, Doris L. 2006. *What Works in Corrections: Reducing the Criminal Activities of Offenders and Delinquents.* New York, NY: Cambridge University Press.

Martinson, Robert. 1974. "What Works?-Questions and Answers About Prison Reform." *The Public Interest* 35: 22–54.

Maruschak, Laura M., and Thomas P. Bonczar. 2013. *Probation and Parole in the United States, 2012.* Washington, DC: Bureau of Justice Statistics.

Maruschak, Laura M., and Erika Parks. 2012. *Probation and Parole in the United States, 2011.* Bureau of Justice Statistics Bulletin. Washington, DC: Bureau of Justice Statistics.

McGuire, James. 2002. "Integrating Findings from Research Reviews." Pp. 3–38 in *Offender Rehabilitation and Treatment: Effective Programmes and Policies to Reduce Re-Offending*, edited by J. McGuire. Chichester: John Wiley.

McGuire, James. 2013. "'What Works' to Reduce Reoffending: 18 Years On." Pp. 20–49 in *What Works in Offender Rehabilitation: An Evidence-Based Approach to Assessment and Treatment*, edited by L.A. Craig, L. Dixon, and T.A Gagnon. Chichester, UK: Wiley-Blackwell.

Morgan, Kathryn. 2016. *Probation, Parole, and Community Corrections Work in Theory and Practice: Preparing Students for Careers in Probation in Parole Agencies*. Durham, NC: Carolina Academic Press.
Mumola, Christopher J., and Thomas P. Bonczar. 1998. *Substance Abuse and Treatment of Adults on Probation, 1995*. Rockville, MD: Bureau of Justice Statistics.
Petersilia, Joan. 1997. "Probation in the United States." Pp. 149–200 in *Crime and Justice: A Review of the Research*, vol. 22, edited by M. Tonry. Chicago, IL: University of Chicago Press.
Petersilia, Joan, and Susan Turner. 1993. "Intensive Probation and Parole." Pp. 281–335 in *Crime and Justice: A Review of the Research*, edited by M. Tonry. Chicago, IL: University of Chicago Press.
Robinson, Charles R., Christopher T. Lowenkamp, Alexander M. Holsinger, Scott VanBenschoten, Melissa Alexander, and J. C. Oleson. 2012. "A Random Study of Staff Training Aimed at Reducing Re-Arrest (STARR): Using Core Correctional Practices in Probation Interactions." *Journal of Crime and Justice* 35(2): 167–188.
Rothman, David J. 1980. *Conscience and Convenience: The Asylum and Its Alternatives in Progressive America*. Boston, MA: Little, Brown.
Sherman, Lawrence W., Denise C. Gottfredson, Doris L. MacKenzie, John Eck, Peter Reuter, and Shawn D. Bushway. 1997. *Preventing Crime: What Works, What Doesn't, What's Promising*. Washington, DC: National Institute of Justice.
Skeem, Jennifer L., and Sarah Manchak. 2008. "Back to the Future: From Klockars' Model of Effective Supervision to Evidence-Based Practice in Probation." *Journal of Offender Rehabilitation* 47(3): 220–247.
Smith, Paula, and Ryan M. Labrecque. 2016. Assessing the Importance of Program Fidelity in Reducing Recidivism: An Evaluation of the Effective Practices in Community Supervision (EPICS) Model. Manuscript in preparation.
Smith, Paula, Myrinda Schweitzer, Ryan M. Labrecque, and Edward J. Latessa. 2012. "Improving Probation Officers' Supervision Skills: An Evaluation of the EPICS Model." *Journal of Crime and Justice* 35(2): 189–199.
Taxman, Faye S. 2002. "Supervision: Exploring the Dimensions of Effectiveness." *Federal Probation* 66(2): 14–27.
Taxman, Faye S. 2008. "No Illusions: Offender and Organizational Change in Maryland's Proactive Community Supervision Efforts." *Criminology & Public Policy* 7(2): 275–302.
Taxman, Faye S. 2012. "Probation, Intermediate Sanctions, and Community-Based Corrections." Pp. 363–385 in *The Oxford Handbook of Sentencing and Corrections*, edited by J. Petersilia and K.R. Reitz. New York: Oxford University Press.
Trotter, Chris. (2013). "Reducing Recidivism Through Probation Supervision: What We Know and Don't Know from Four Decades of Research." *Federal Probation* 77(2): 43–48.
Viglione, Jill, and Faye S. Taxman. 2015. "Probation and Parole." Pp. 363–383 in *APA Handbook of Forensic Psychology, Vol. 2: Criminal Investigation, Adjudication, and Sentencing Outcomes*, edited by B.L. Cutler and P.A. Zapf. Washington, DC: American Psychological Association.

16 Parole Process and Practice

Kathryn Morgan

Introduction

In a recent publication, researchers at the Sentencing Project reported that 2.2 million people are incarcerated in the nation's jails and prisons making the United States the world's leader in incarcerating its citizens (Sentencing Project 2016: 1). While the United States incarcerates 700 individuals per 100,000 population (Sentencing Project 2016: 1), 95 percent of those incarcerated will return to the community through a prison release program at the rate of 600,000 per year or 1600 per day (Petersilia 2004: 4). Historically, discretionary parole has been the most common correctional strategy for releasing offenders and returning them back into the community. Parole, birthed by the rehabilitative ideal, is a correctional strategy that grants early release to an inmate prior to the expiration of the prison term. After release, the parolee serves the remainder of the sentence under supervision in the community. Parole allows offenders to avoid long prison terms that increase the likelihood of recidivism.

Historically, the emergence of parole is associated with the emphasis on rehabilitation and the development of the indeterminate sentence. Under this sentencing structure, the sentencing judge imposes a minimum and maximum sentence, leaving it up to the parole board to determine the actual length of the sentence. Parole functioned to release the inmate at a time when conditional release was most beneficial, prevent further internalization of the prison subculture thus reducing the likelihood that the former inmate would return to a life of crime, and assist in the rehabilitation and reintegration of the offender back into society. Parole officers were first volunteers, then clinical agents of rehabilitation who used their expertise to assist the parolee. Although used mainly as a rehabilitation technique for the offender, parole has also served other functions. As early as 1893, California used parole for non-rehabilitative functions, such as minimizing the use of clemency and correcting for sentences that were considered excessive (Messinger 1985). Recent studies have examined the changing parole process and the non-rehabilitative functions of parole. Simon (1993) found that the transformation of the parole process has been related to the political and economic changes of society. He concluded that rehabilitation interests have been replaced by management concerns. Institutional and political efforts have taken priority over rehabilitation issues, including efforts to control prison population overcrowding (Champion 2002: 272), as well as efforts to remedy disparate sentencing of inmates because of their race/ethnicity, gender, and/or social class (Hofer 1999).

Release from Prison

Inmates may be released from prison through discretionary release, mandatory release, or unconditional release. *Discretionary release* is conditional release granted by a state's parole board after inmates have served at least one-third of their sentence. When the parole board decides to release the inmate on parole, the newly released inmate is given a parole order that identifies the rules governing the conditional release. The parole order is a contractual agreement between the State's parole-granting agency and the parolee; it specifies the board's conditions governing conditional freedom. Parolees who violate the conditions of parole are subject to revocation and return to prison.

Mandatory release requires the inmate to be released after serving the entire sentence minus good time. When several states and the federal government made the legislative shift to a determinate sentencing structure, mandatory release became the primary form of release (Clear and Cole 2000: 348). When inmates enter prison, classification personnel calculate a "mandatory release date," which includes good time and other credits. The mandatory release date is specified by law, and inmates must be released on that date. Justice Department data revealed that in 2000, mandatory releases had surpassed discretionary releases. During that year, 39 percent of those released from prison were discretionary releases compared to 41 percent of percentage of the inmates granted a mandatory release (Bureau of Justice Statistics 2001). Consistent with mandatory release is *truth-in-sentencing*, which requires convicted offenders serve 65–100 percent of their court-imposed sentences. Truth-in-sentencing laws reduce the power and discretion of the parole board because they mandate inmates serve all or a substantial portion of the sentence (Ditton and Wilson 1999). Critics of truth-in-sentencing have pointed out that this mandate for tougher sentencing increases the prison population, escalates already high prison costs, and removes the incentive of early release. Judges and correctional administrators have argued that this approach leaves the judge little or no discretion and shifts sentencing decisions from the judge to the legislature.

Unconditional release is granted to offenders who are released from prison with no further correctional supervision; they have completed their sentences, received a pardon, or had their sentences commuted (Clear and Cole 2000: 349).

Despite the increase in mandatory releases and recent attempts to abolish parole, parole populations have continued to increase annually. As incarceration rates increased, probation populations have been decreasing. Probation and parole trend data indicate that probation populations have seen a steady decline since 2002 (Maruschak and Parks 2012). While there has been a declining probation population, the parole population has shown slight increases especially since 2008. California and Texas were the largest contributors to the increase in the parole population (Maruschak and Parks 2012: 7). Although federal parole was phased out by 1992, federal offenders may be granted supervised release by the federal courts. The number of federal offenders under supervised release also contributed to the increase in the parole population (Maruschak and Parks 2012: 7).

History of Parole

The historical development of parole can be traced to the transportation programs to America and Australia. In the early seventeenth century, Great Britain experienced high unemployment rates, an increase in crime rates, and prison overcrowding. When given a choice of execution or being transported to the American colonies where there was a labor shortage, most of the English prisoners chose the more humane alternative of transportation to America. After being pardoned by the English government, prisoners were transported by independent contractors to America to work as indentured servants (Abadinsky 1997: 209). Initially, there were no conditions attached to the pardon, but felons would completely avoid transportation and remain in England or would escape and return to England prior to the expiration of the prison term (Abadinsky 1997: 209). The Transportation Act of 1718 imposed conditions and specified that the pardon would be nullified if convicts failed to comply with the rules and regulations (Champion 2005). When the Revolutionary War ended the transportation to American program, the English government again searched for a solution to its increasing crime rate and overcrowded convict population. This search resulted in the implementation of the transportation to Australia program under the leadership of Superintendent Alexander Maconochie. Maconochie instituted many reforms, the most important being the "mark system" where inmates could accumulate marks for hard work and good behavior and use those marks to earn early release (Abadinsky 1997: 210). Under Maconochie's leadership and service as superintendent, over 1,400 convicts were released; many of them did not reoffend. He is known in corrections as the "Father of Parole" (Champion 2005).

In 1853, England passed the Penal Servitude Act, which allowed convicts to be released on a ticket-of-leave under the supervision of police. Sir Walter Crofton became the administrator of the Irish Prison System. Similar in philosophy to Maconochie, Crofton believed that sentences and time served in some way should be related to rehabilitation (Abadinsky 2009: 210). In 1854, he implemented the ticket-of-leave program in Ireland. This Irish system consisted of four stages that culminated in release of the prisoner: (1) strict imprisonment and forced solitary confinement; (2) placement in a special prison to work with other inmates earning marks to progress to the third stage; (3) transportation to an open institution where he could earn release on a ticket-of-leave; and (4) release on the ticket-of-leave under the supervision of police who would help them seek employment (Champion 2008).

In the United States, the first parole system was implemented at the Elmira Reformatory that opened in 1876 under Zebulon Brockway, Elmira's first superintendent (Abadinsky 2009: 212). Zebulon Brockway, a penologist from Detroit, Michigan, previously attempted to implement the indeterminate sentence for Michigan first-time offenders. Even though the Michigan Legislature passed the statute, the courts later reversed the legislation. At the Elmira Reformatory for adult males in New York, he introduced the indeterminate sentence and recommended that young male offenders be given indeterminate sentences not to exceed the maximum recommended by law. Additionally, he introduced the "mark system" where the accumulation of marks could be used for early release. Once the inmate accumulated enough marks, the inmate was conditionally released and supervised in the community for six-month parole periods by appointed guardians. Parolees were required to report to the guardian once monthly and give an account of their conduct and situation. If there was actual or potential criminal behavior, the parolee could be returned to prison. By 1900, the foundation for parole in the United States had been laid with three underlying principles: (a) indeterminate sentences, (b) reduction of prison sentences based on good behavior, and (c) release of the parolee and supervision in the community. The use of parole as a correctional practice spread throughout the United States in the early 1900s, and by 1944, all states had implemented some form of conditional release (Abadinsky 2009: 212).

Parole was the most common form of release until the 1970s, when criminologists, policymakers, and legislators questioned the effectiveness of rehabilitation programs, rejected indeterminate sentencing in favor of determinate sentencing structures, and introduced the idea of "just deserts"—criminals deserve punishment for their crimes and harm that they have caused society. These challenges resulted in many states abolishing parole as a rehabilitative strategy. With the passage of the Federal Sentencing Reform Act of 1984, the federal government abolished parole and implemented truth-in-sentencing for federal offenders that required convicted federal offenders to serve 85 percent of their court-imposed sentences. By 1999, 15 states had completely abolished discretionary parole board release for all offenders (Arizona, Delaware, Maryland, Florida, Illinois, Indiana, Kansas, Maine, Minnesota, Mississippi, North Carolina, Ohio, Oregon, Washington, Wisconsin) (Ditton & Wilson, 1999). Currently, 16 states have abolished discretionary parole for all offenders and four additional states have abolished it for violent offenders (Hughes, Wilson, and Beck 2001). Possible reasons for abolishing discretionary parole are: (a) the failure of indeterminate sentencing and rehabilitation to reduce recidivism rates; (b) abolition of parole fits the ideology of the get tough on crime movement; and (c) the lack of transparency in the parole board process (Abadinsky 2009: 212).

Parole Process

An inmate may be considered for parole after serving one-third of the sentence if that inmate is not prohibited from parole. Inmates who have been sentenced under a determinate sentencing structure have a sentence of life in prison without the possibility of parole, and former death row inmates whose sentences have been commuted to life in prison are not eligible for parole consideration (Champion, 2008: 376). Some states give incoming inmates a presumptive parole date. All offenders who are not excluded by law from getting parole are given advance notice of parole. The inmate will be released, unless there are major problems (Clear and Dammer 2000: 199). When the Comprehensive Crime Control Act of 1984 was passed (Public Law 98–473, October 12, 1984), one provision mandated the elimination of parole at the federal level by 1992. The legislation also specified that offenders sentenced under a determinate sentencing structure would be granted a 15 percent reduction in sentence for good behavior, and post-release supervision would be called supervised release rather than parole (United States Parole Commission 2003).

The State parole board is an important part of the parole process. Although the number of board members and the length of service on the board vary across states, board membership is a political appointment and board members serve at the pleasure of the Governor. The parole board functions to award good time, set initial and subsequent dates for parole hearings, and make decisions about granting or denying parole. Critics of parole boards have cited the lack of transparency regarding the decision-making process and the limited knowledge and education of parole board members to make informed decisions as contributors to the skepticism about parole board effectiveness (Gottfredson and Ballard 1966).

The parole process begins when the inmate's name appears on a computer-generated list indicating eligibility for parole consideration. Victims and trial officials are notified and the list is sent to the institutional parole officer. Institutional parole officers interview the inmate, prepare case files for board members' review and assist inmates in the preparation of the pre-parole release plan. The pre-parole release plan is an important component of parole release consideration. It details the inmate's plans for employment, living arrangements, and treatment if released. Before the plan can be included as a part of the case file for review, field parole services must verify the information. Parole boards often will not approve release if there is no pre-parole plan that has been verified by field parole services. In addition to reviewing the information contained in the inmate's case file, the parole board schedules a parole release hearing where the inmate, the inmate's family and supporters, the victim, the victim's family, and others who may oppose or support parole release will speak to the parole board. These hearings are not adversarial and the inmate is not entitled to counsel. The inmate does not have interests that must be protected by the presence of an attorney. Therefore, since it is not required that an attorney is present to represent the inmate, most jurisdictions do not permit legal counsel. During the release hearing, parole board members consider several things, such as the seriousness of the crime, the length of time served, inmate's age, prior criminal history, alcohol and drug use, and the institutional record. They also consider opposition from police, the district attorney, and/or the victim or victim's family (Morgan 2016: 112). If the parole board votes to release, a release certificate is prepared, victims are notified and the inmate is released within two weeks of the decision. If the vote is to deny parole release, the reason for denial is not given to the inmate. Instead, the inmate may be provided with a new case review date or an order to "serve all" of the sentence (Abadinsky 2003: 247). Once inmates are released on parole, they are given conditions of parole and are supervised by Field Parole Services. Violation of parole conditions may result in revocation of parole and a return to prison to serve the remainder of the sentence.

Current Issues in Parole

Parole Board Decision Making

Parole boards are composed of members who are politically appointed or selected based on a state's selection criteria. Gottfredson and Gottfredson (1988) point out that parole boards exercise a great deal of discretion and make a number of decisions including determining the length of the prison sentence, awarding good time, setting the date for the first parole consideration, setting dates for subsequent parole hearings, granting or denying parole, and considering special conditions for parole. The sentencing judge may set the minimum and the maximum term of the sentence but the parole board may decide how much time the inmate actually spends in prison. Sometimes the parole board may even waive the minimum term (Gottfredson and Gottfredson 1988). In instances of overcrowding, the court may order emergency releases to relieve prison overcrowding. Under these circumstances, court orders override parole board decisions (Champion 1994: 58).

Given the amount of discretion exercised by the parole board, there has been some concern with *how* parole release decisions are made. Criminologists have agreed that there has been a lack of knowledge regarding how parole boards make release decisions (Bonham 1986; Gottfredson and Gottfredson 1978). Critics have identified four major problems associated with parole board's decision-making process. The first problem has been the lack of accurate offender information on which to base their decisions (Bonham 1986). Parole board members often do not have access to accurate data regarding offender characteristics, how decisions may be related to criminal justice system goals, or consequences of parole decisions (Bonham 1986). A second problem is related to the lack of knowledge regarding significant variables related to parole decisions (Bonham 1986). Often, it is difficult to identify these variables, never mind understand the nature of their relationship with parole decisions. A third problem is the difficulty associated with trying to determine criteria used for parole decision making and the quality of those criteria. A fourth problem is related to the statistical prediction instruments used by paroling authorities to predict the probability of recidivism among prospective parolees. Although critical to decision making, risk assessment using forecasting models is prone to error. As a result, there will be false positives and false negatives causing some to be erroneously classified as high risk and subjected to further imprisonment while high-risk offenders (e.g. Willie Horton) may be classified as low risk and released to inflict more harm on society (Champion 1994). Critics of parole boards also maintain that the major responsibility for determining the amount of time served has been shifted from the judge to an administrative board whose decisions are often viewed as arbitrary, capricious, and ambiguous, and leave the inmate in a state of uncertainty (Clear and Cole 2000). Supporters have argued that parole boards can often make release decisions that are objective and unaffected by the public pressure that may affect legislatures and judges. In response to criticism of parole decision making, the U.S. Board of Parole devised administrative guidelines that would result in more rational decision making by parole boards. Although these guidelines were developed to structure and guide parole decisions, they were not designed to eliminate the discretion of the parole board in decision making (Gottfredson and Gottfredson 1988). Paroling guidelines identify the three variables that should take precedence in parole decisions: *time served*, *offense seriousness*, and *risk of recidivism*.

According to paroling guidelines, *the amount of time served* is an important legislative guideline for parole decisions. Although parole boards may exercise discretion in unusual cases, laws in most states require that an inmate serve at least one-third of the minimum sentence before being considered for parole release. In some instances, the parole board may refuse to consider the inmate even after the one-third has been served. In others, the board may consider an inmate prior to the completion of the one-third requirement.

Seriousness of the offense is also a major factor for parole consideration. Parole boards rate offense seriousness from low seriousness (simple theft) to high seriousness (planned and deliberate killing). Parole board members are likely to treat highly serious offenses more severely and are less likely to grant parole for these serious offenses (Gottfredson and Gottfredson 1988).

Parole guidelines also recommend that parole boards assess the risk of recidivism or the likelihood of parole success. The salient factor score predicts the likelihood of the inmate's success on parole. This assessment is based on the inmate's criminal history, prior imprisonment, prior probation, prior parole, previous drug use, and pre-prison unemployment. The lower scores indicate a higher risk for recidivism and may result in the inmate being denied parole (Abadinsky 2003: 246).

Despite paroling guidelines, questions remain about the factors that influence decisions and the discretion exercised by parole boards. Only 30 states currently make the votes of the parole board release hearing public. In the remaining states using discretionary parole, votes of the parole board members are not public but kept private (Schmallenger and Smykla 2011).

Victim Participation in Parole Release Hearings

A major goal of many victim groups has been to influence offender sanctioning. Victims potentially may have an effect on the severity of punishment at two points in the judicial process: sentencing and parole release hearings. Victim impact statements (VIS), designed to influence case outcomes, allow victims the opportunity to speak directly to the court regarding the consequences of the crime on their lives. Research has indicated that the victim impact statement has had little effect on sentence severity and disposition. These statements do not influence decisions to sentence defendants to probation or prison (Erez and Tontodonato 1992).

Victims may also affect outcomes at parole release hearings. Although the research that examines victim impact on parole release decisions has been minimal, there is evidence that victims may have significant influence on parole release outcomes. Victims may participate by protesting the release at the parole release hearing or they might choose to write letters of protest that will be read by board members considering the inmate's release. McLeod (1989) found that when no victim impact statements are available for board review, 40 to 50 percent of parole applications are denied; when statements are submitted, the rate of parole denial rises sharply to approximately 80 percent (McLeod 1989). Morgan and Smith (2005) found that when victims write letters, it is unlikely that inmates will receive parole. When victims attend hearings, it is almost certain that parole will be denied because victims' oral participation has great impact on decisions made by parole board members (Morgan and Smith 2005). The extent to which parole boards will consider victim input and not inmate rehabilitation as the most important variable is a concern and policy issue. How far are decision makers willing to go to appease victims of crime? Are prison officials and parole boards willing to keep offenders locked up even when they present a low risk of recidivism simply because victims oppose the release? A disturbing pattern suggests that victim influence, not institutional behavior or participation in rehabilitation programs, is the important factor in the decision to grant or deny parole. The question is to what extent will parole boards allow victim influence to override the concerns for the inmate? Is it fair to further punish an inmate who presents a low risk of recidivism for future criminal behavior because victims show up at hearings to protest the release? Should victim input and participation become the most significant consideration or simply one of many variables to be considered in these decisions? (Morgan and Smith 2005).

Race and Parole

One of the most important controversies in criminal justice and criminology today focuses on whether or not there are racial disparities in the criminal justice system. This controversy has raised questions about the impact of race on decision making. It has been suggested that there is racial disparity at every level of processing where criminal justice authorities have the power to make discretionary decisions. Police are more likely to arrest, verbally and physically abuse, harass, and profile racial and ethnic minorities; prosecutors are more likely to charge and prosecute minorities for felonies; courts are more likely to convict and sentence minorities to a term of incarceration (Petersilia 1983; Walker, Spohn, and DeLeon 2004).

By year-end in 2014, Bureau of Justice Statistics data reported that there were 2.2 million being supervised in state and federal prisons in the United States. Approximately 60 percent of those incarcerated were Blacks and Hispanics (Carson 2015). Correctional data for 2014 reported that were 856,900 adults were under parole supervision. Forty-three percent of the parole population was white; Blacks comprised 39 percent of the parole population, and 16 percent of those on parole were Hispanics (Kaeble, Maruschak and Bonczar 2015). The controversy has recently focused on the issue of racial disparity in granting probation and parole. Are offenders of color less likely to be granted probation or selected for parole release?

Empirical findings are ambiguous regarding the impact of race on discretionary parole decisions. Some studies conclude that race significantly influences parole release decisions. Results of Petersilia's study of racial discrimination in three states revealed three significant findings: (a) Black and Hispanic defendants received more severe sentences than White defendants who had similar criminal records and were convicted of similar crimes; (b) Blacks and Hispanics also consistently served longer sentences than Whites sentenced to prison; and (c) Black inmates serve longer sentences, are less likely to receive parole, and often have additional criteria to satisfy. Other studies reported similar findings. These studies concluded that Black inmates serve longer sentences before being considered for parole, are often required to show proof of participation in institutional treatment programs, are less likely than White inmates to receive positive recommendations for parole from the Senior Parole Officer and Warden, and are less likely to be chosen by the parole board for release even though they have met the criteria (Carroll and Mondrick 1976; Hughes, Wilson and Beck 2001; Morgan and Smith 2005).

Other studies indicate that race does not influence parole release decisions. These studies note that legal, social, and institutional variables are the most significant predictors of parole release decisions, and parole boards make no distinctions between races in decisions to release. Although these studies acknowledge that Black inmates serve a larger portion of their sentences than Whites do, researchers attribute these differences to social, legal, and institutional variables and not race (Elion and Megargee 1978; Scott 1974). Wilbanks (1987) attributes the disparity in sentencing and parole releases to legal variables rather than racial discrimination. Blacks and Hispanics have more severe criminal histories and commit crimes that are more serious; therefore, they are often not eligible for shorter sentences or placement in community correctional programs (Wilbanks 1987).

Reentry and Parole

In this period of mass imprisonment with 2.2 million incarcerated in our state and federal prisons, reentry is reality. It is also a fact that 95 percent of those entering prison will be released back into the community. Some will be released unconditionally or under mandatory release guidelines without the benefit of pre-release risk assessment or post-release custody and supervision (Petersilia 2004).

It is commonly accepted knowledge that parole failure rates are high. It is estimated that only 46 percent of parolees complete parole supervision without absconding or committing a new offense (Glaze and Palla 2005). Unfortunately, the numbers are more dismal for parole failures. In 1983, the Bureau of Justice Statistics reported that 63 percent of released offenders were rearrested within three years (Beck and Shipley 1989). Data reported by Bureau of Justice Statistics in 1994 revealed that 68 percent of released prisoners were rearrested within three years (Lanagan and Levin 2005). In 2004, 187,000 parolees were revoked and returned to prison as the result of violating parole rules or commission of a new offense. The numbers of parolees returning to prison each year continues to rise. Recent statistics indicate that nationally parolees constitute 35 percent of all prison admissions (Glaze and Palla 2005). Those released from prison are likely to be over age 35, have served longer prison terms, have previous criminal convictions and probation and parole terms, and be addicted to drugs and alcohol. Many did not participate in educational or vocational programs to prepare them for jobs after release (Lynch and Sabol 2001). Some of the parolees who reenter society are churners—parolees who have failed at reentry for previous releases from prison (Lynch and Sabol 2001: 15).

Parolees returning to the community face many challenges. Parolees may return with physical and mental health problems. Although treated for these illnesses while incarcerated, they lack access to services and treatment after release. Often diagnosed with depression and drug addiction, inmates fail to seek help for mental health problems because of their distrust for the mental health system (Bureau of Justice Statistics 1999; Hammett, Roberts and Kennedy 2001; Morgan 2013). Employment is the toughest challenge for parolees who have dismal prospects for securing gainful employment. The lack of skills and prospective employers' unwillingness to hire "ex-cons" make obtaining and maintaining employment a major issue. Family violence, crime, and substance abuse may be related to the offender's frustration with the lack of employment and economic status. Returning prisoners may experience homelessness, loss of political rights, and exclusion from housing areas and professions. Many return to socially disorganized neighborhoods plagued with high crime rates and ample criminal opportunities. According to Petersilia, many prisoners lack the motivation while in prison to participate in programs that address employment, educational, and vocational needs once they leave prison (Petersilia 2004: 4).

Of those released on discretionary parole, approximately 80 percent of parolees are placed on regular parole caseloads where they receive less than adequate supervision. As parole caseload sizes increase, caseloads may have as many as 70 parolees for one officer, which exceeds the ideal size of 35 parolees for each officer. This means one or two 15-minute face-to-face visits per month (Petersilia 2004). More parolees are violating parole conditions and absconding from supervision. Many parolees return to criminal behavior and return to prison. The public is more fearful of parolees and the likelihood of being victimized.

To address the reentry problem and promote public safety, some communities are strengthening supervision of parolees through supervision teams; implementing state and federal reentry programs and collaborating with police departments to assist in finding and providing services to inmates while making parolees accountable (Morgan 2016; Schmalleger and Smykla 2011).

Parole Legal and Liability Issues

In recent years, legal and liability issues have affected parole supervision and practice. Parole officers may be held criminally and civilly liable in their interactions with clients or a third party. They may be held criminally liable if an officer commits a criminal act under federal or state law, such as assaulting, harassing, or threatening a client or a member of the client's family; injuring a client by using excessive force with malice; and/or participating in criminal behavior with a client, such as allowing a drug dealer to continue in criminal behavior in exchange for a percentage of the profits (Watkins 1989: 29). A parole officer may be held civilly liable and sued in state court if it is believed that the officer's negligence in the performance of duties resulted in harm to the parolee or a third party. The majority of civil lawsuits filed against parole officers are filed by third parties who have been injured by parolees when they believe that the officer failed to control the parolee as a part of their supervisory responsibilities. A parole officer may be sued for negligence if the officer has (a) a duty to supervise and control the parolee's behavior and/or (b) a duty to warn a third party about the potential dangers posed by the parolee and failure in those duties resulted in injury to the victim (Watkins 1989: 29). As the parolee's supervisor, the parole officer has a legal duty to protect victims. The injured party may sue the individual officer, the parole department, or the state parole board for damages if the victim believes that the board or officer's negligence in the performance of legal duties is the cause of injury (Morgan, Belbot, and Clark 1997). In the case *Taggart v. State* (822 P.2d 243, 1992), the Washington State Supreme Court found a supervising parole officer negligent in her duty to supervise and control parolee Lou Brock, who assaulted Victoria Taggart, causing serious injuries. The parolee, who had convictions for sexual and alcohol related offenses, was released from prison with the conditions that he seek drug counseling and submit to random drug testing. The supervising officer failed to make sure that the parolee submitted to random drug testing or continue substance abuse counseling, did not make collateral contacts, and did not follow up on information provided by his girlfriend that he was drinking on a regular basis and had assaulted his ex-wife's new husband. The court ruled that there existed a special relationship between the parole officer and the parolee where the supervising officer had a duty to exercise reasonable and responsible control over the parolee's behavior but failed in that responsibility.

Some lawsuits have focused on the officer's failure to warn a victim about the potential dangers posed by the parolee. The officer has a duty to warn a third party of the possible dangers posed by an offender under supervision. One of the earliest cases that was based on failure to warn is *Goergen v. State* (1959). The New York State court determined that a parole officer was liable for failure to disclose information about a violent parolee that he recommended for employment. The female employer, who had no knowledge of the parolee's violent tendencies, was assaulted by the parolee. In its decision for the plaintiff, the Court ruled that the parole officer was negligent because he recommended the parolee for employment but failed to disclose information about the inmate's violent tendencies (Morgan, Belbot, and Clark 1997: 216). The most well-known case of third-party liability in parole supervision is *Reiser v. District of Columbia* (1977). Rebecca Reiser, a female apartment manager, was killed by a parolee whom she employed as a maintenance man at the apartment complex. The parole officer assisted the parolee in securing employment but failed to disclose information about the parolee's violent history or the fact that he was a suspect in two rapes and a third rape and murder of a little girl. One night, the parolee entered the female manager's apartment and raped and murdered her. The victim's family sued the parole department, alleging that the parole officer had a duty to inform management of the parolee's prior violent sex offenses in order to prevent harm to the tenants of the apartment complex. According to the court's ruling, since the parole officer assisted the parolee in securing employment at the apartment complex, there was a "duty" to disclose the offender's prior criminal record (Morgan, Belbot, and Clark 1997: 216).

Aside from legal and liability issues affecting officers' responsibilities and the failure to fulfill those obligations, there have been several Appellate and U.S. Supreme Court decisions that have modified the parole process. Because parole is viewed as more administrative than judicial, the parole process had functioned for many years without any interference from the judiciary. That changed in the 1970s, when landmark decisions regarding parole release and parole revocation hearings were handed down by the New York Court of Appeals and the U.S. Supreme Court.

In 1970, the case of *Menechino v. Oswald* (1970) was brought before the New Court of Appeals. Joseph Menechino was paroled for a murder conviction after spending time in prison. His parole was revoked after 16 months and he was returned to prison. The basis of revocation was association with criminals and giving the parole officer misleading information. Two years later, he appeared before the parole board seeking release but was denied. He appealed, claiming that his rights had been violated because he was denied representation by counsel at the revocation and parole release hearings. The Court addressed the issue of representation by counsel in both hearings. Regarding the parole release hearing, the court ruled that because the inmate was already in prison, there was no "present private interest" that needed to be protected. There were no rights to be protected; he was in prison seeking the privilege of early release. The parole release hearing is not a fact-finding hearing but an evaluation hearing where the parole board makes its decision based upon many different sources of information and the parole release hearing makes up a very small part of the process. The inmate is not entitled to representation by legal counsel in the release hearing. In addressing the presence of counsel in the parole revocation hearing, the Court ruled that at this stage, an inmate does have a present private interest to be protected—conditional freedom. Therefore, some procedural safeguards must be provided. The Court of Appeals ultimately ruled against Menechino because he initiated actions regarding both the release hearing and the revocation hearings. If he had initiated actions regarding only the revocation hearing, he would have won (*Menechino v. Oswald New York Court of Appeals*, 1970) (Abadinsky 1997).

In 1972, the U.S. Supreme Court handed down the landmark ruling in *Morrissey v. Brewer* (1972), marking the first intervention by the Supreme Court in the parole process. John Morrissey was sentenced to a seven-year prison term for forgery; he was paroled after serving one year. Seven months later, he was arrested after violating several conditions of parole and was returned to prison without a preliminary or revocation hearing. The supervising officer justified the return by saying that Morrissey failed to justify the violations adequately. In its ruling, the Supreme Court ruled that a number of parolees (30–40 percent) are being revoked and returned to prison each year. Because these numbers are high, there must be some protection of parolees' rights. Further, the Court ruled that there should be a two-stage revocation process: the arrest of the parolee and preliminary hearing and the revocation hearing. The preliminary hearing should be informal and presided over by a hearing officer who is not involved with the case. The parolee should be given a written notice of charges. Witnesses who have given unfavorable testimony should be questioned in the parolee's presence (*Morrissey v. Brewer*, 1972).

The Future of Parole

As we entered the twenty-first century, the downward trend in crime rates that began in the 1990s continued. Despite decreasing crime rates, incarceration rates continued to increase. This mass incarceration trend has led to an increase in the number of inmates being released on parole.

The primary challenges to parole during the twenty-first century have been the increased workload with limited resources and increasing gun violence. As probation and parole populations have increased over the years, workloads for officers have also increased. The "get tough" era of criminal justice resulted in changes in sentencing and more offenders being sentenced to prison. As "get tough" policies strained budgets and cost billions of dollars in criminal justice spending, many states began to rethink those policies. Escalating prison costs forced corrections departments to develop alternatives to prison. Many of these programs were based in probation and parole departments, causing caseload sizes and workloads to increase while resources diminished. Probation and parole agencies are often called on to "do more with less." The expectation is effective management and supervision with fewer resources (Morgan 2016: 268).

In the twenty-first century, gun violence continues to be a problem in the United States and a major challenge for parole officers. As a social problem that costs billions of dollars annually, gun violence affects all members of society both directly and indirectly. Although violent crime has been decreasing since the mid 1990s, gun violence continues to be a problem. Probation and parole professionals are often at risk for violent attacks or have been threatened by gun violence as they make unannounced field visits and serve warrants. In a recent study of probation and parole officers killed in the line of duty, data indicated that over 80 percent of those killed were killed with a firearm (Thornton 2005: 9). Firearm violence continues to be a social and public health epidemic that poses a challenge to parole officers in their supervision responsibilities.

Emphasis has been placed on strategies that work in parole supervision or evidence-based practice. One of the effects of evidence-based strategies for parole supervision has been the use of supervised caseloads. This approach involves placing parolees with special needs in a single caseload that is much smaller than regular caseloads. Offenders that may be better served through specialized caseloads include mental health offenders, drug and alcohol offenders, sex offenders, and domestic violence offenders. Officers supervising these specialized caseloads target the special needs of the offenders. However, the specialized caseloads go beyond simply placing offenders with similar problems into one caseload. Many of these officers supervising special caseloads develop expertise over time and engage in partnerships with professionals and treatment specialists to provide the offender more comprehensive services (Burrell 2005).

There are three trends likely to define both probation and parole in the twenty-first century: the reemergence of rehabilitation, community partnerships, and community justice.

Re-emergence of rehabilitation. A growing awareness in the 1990s, the awareness that some offenders had special mental health and substance abuse needs and the reentry of prisoners who were addicted to drugs, mentally ill, and lacking vocational skills fueled an interest in rehabilitation in an attempt to improve and return people to society (Reisig 1998: 172). Reentry programs were implemented to facilitate prisoners' return to the community, and drug courts, mental health courts, and specialized caseloads emerged to address offenders' special needs (Reisig 1998: 173).

Community Partnerships. While parole agencies have always collaborated with community resources such as police departments, drug treatment centers, employment agencies, and mental health counselors, those partnerships have recently become formal. Collaborations with drug courts and mental health courts serve as good examples of formal partnerships (Burrell 2005: 3). A recent collaboration between probation and parole departments and law enforcement has been Project Safe Neighborhoods. Project Safe Neighborhoods is an initiative that promotes collaborations between local, state, and federal law enforcement agencies, corrections, the prosecutor, and the community, with the goal of reducing gun crime and violence (Thornton 2005: 9).

Community Justice. Realizing that a brief monthly visit with probationers and parolees is not sufficient to reduce risk and promote public safety, officers are encouraged to engage in the community and involve the community in the supervision process. Officers are encouraged to use community-oriented strategies to supervise offenders where they live, work, and have recreation (Reinventing Probation Council 2000).

References

Abadinsky, Howard. 1997. *Probation and Parole.* Upper Saddle River, NJ: Prentice Hall.

Abadinsky, Howard. 2003. *Probation and Parole.* Englewood Cliffs, NJ: Prentice Hall.

Abadinsky, Howard. 2009. *Probation and Parole.* Upper Saddle River, NJ: Prentice Hall.

Beck, Allen, and Bernard Shipley. 1989. *Recidivism of Prisoners Released in 1988.* Washington, DC: Bureau of Justice Statistics.

Bonham, Gene. 1986. "Predicting Parole Decisions in Kansas via Discriminant Analysis." *Journal of Criminal Justice* 14(2): 123–133.

Burrell, William Burrell. 2005. "Trends in Probation and Parole in the States." Pp. 595–600 in *Book of the States.* Lexington, KY: Council of State Governments.

Bureau of Justice Statistics. 1999. *Mental Health and Treatment of Prisoners and Probationers.* Washington, DC: US Department of Justice, Office of Justice Programs, Bureau of Justice Statistics.

Bureau of Justice Statistics. 2001. *Trends in State Parole. 1990–2000.* Washington, DC: U.S. Department of Justice: Office of Justice Programs.

Carroll, Leo, and Margaret Mondrick. 1976. "Racial Bias in the Decision to Grant Parole." *Law and Society Review* 11(Fall): 93–107.

Carson, E. Anne. 2015. *Prisoners in 2014.* Washington, DC: Bureau of Justice Statistics.

Champion, Dean. 1994. *Measuring Offender Risk: A Criminal Justice Sourcebook.* Westport, CT: Greenwood Press.

Champion, Dean J. 2002. *Probation, Parole, and Community Corrections.* Upper Saddle River, NJ: Prentice Hall.

Champion, Dean. 2005. *Corrections in the United States: A Contemporary Perspective.* Upper Saddle River, NJ: Prentice Hall.

Champion, Dean. 2008. *Probation, Parole and Community Corrections.* Upper Saddle River, NJ: Prentice Hall.

Clear, Todd, and George Cole. 2000. *American Corrections.* Belmont, CA: Wadsworth.

Clear, Todd, and Harry Dammer. 2000. *The Offender in the Community.* Belmont, CA: Wadsworth.

Ditton, Paula, and Doris Wilson. 1999. *Truth in Sentencing in State Prisons.* Washington, DC: U.S. Department of Justice.

Elion, Victor, and Edward Megargee. 1978. "Racial Identity, Length of Incarceration, and Parole Decision-Making," *Journal of Research in Crime and Delinquency* 16: 233–245.

Erez, Edna, and Pamela Tontodonato. 1992. "Victim Participation in Sentencing and Satisfaction with Justice." *Justice Quarterly* 9(3): 393–417.

Glaze, L.E., and Palla, S., 2005. Probation and Parole in the United States in 2004. Washington, DC: *Bureau of Justice Statistics.*

Gottfredson, Don, and Kelly Ballard. 1966. "Differences in Parole Decisions Associated with Decision-makers." *Journal of Research in Crime and Delinquency* 3(2): 112–119.

Gottfredson, Michael, and Don Gottfredson. 1988. *Decision-Making in Criminal Justice: Towards the Rational Exercise of Discretion.* New York: Plenum Press.

Hammett, Theodore, Cheryl Roberts, and Sofia Kennedy. 2001. "Health- Related Issues in Prisoner Reentry." *Crime & Delinquency* 47(3): 390–409.

Hofer, Paul. 1999. "The Effect of the Federal Sentencing Guidelines on Inter- Judge Disparity." *Journal of Criminal Law and Criminology* 90: 239–321.

Hughes, Timothy, Doris Wilson, and Alan Beck. 2001. *Trends in State Parole: 1990–2000.* Washington, DC: U.S. Department of Justice, Office of Justice Programs, Bureau of Justice Statistics.

Kaebele, Daniel, Laura M. Maruschak, and Thomas P. Bonczar. 2015. *Probation and Parole in the United States, 2014.* Bureau of Justice Statistics. U.S. Department of Justice: Office of Justice Programs.

Lanagan, Patrick, and David Levin. 2005. *Recidivism of Prisoners Released in 1994.* Washington, DC: Bureau of Justice Statistics Bulletin.

Lynch, James, and William Sabol. 2001. "Prisoner Reentry in Perspective." *Crime Policy Report 3.* Washington, DC: The Urban Institute.

Maruschak, Laura, and Erika Parks. 2012. *Probation and Parole in the United States, 2011.* Washington, DC: U.S. Department of Justice, Office of Justice Programs.

McLeod, Maureen. 1989. Getting Free: Victim Participation in Parole Board Decisions. *Criminal Justice Policy Review* 4(1): 41–43.

Messinger, Sheldon. 1985. "The Foundations of Parole in California." *Law and Society Review* 19: 69–106.

Morgan, Kathryn. 2013. "Issues in Female Inmate Health: Results from a Southeastern State." *Women & Criminal Justice* 23(2): 121–142.

Morgan, Kathryn. 2016. *Probation, Parole, and Community Corrections Work in Theory and Practice.* Charlotte, NC: Carolina Press.

Morgan, Kathryn, Barbara Belbot, and John Clark. 1997. "Liability Issues Affecting Probation and Parole Supervision." *Journal of Criminal Justice* 25(3): 211–222.

Morgan, Kathryn, and Brent Smith. 2005. "Victims, Punishment, and Parole: The Effects of Victim Participation on Parole Hearings." *Criminology and Public Policy* 4(2): 333–360.

Petersilia, Joan. 1983. *Guideline-Based Justice: Implications for Racial Minorities.* A report prepared for the National Institute of Corrections. Santa Monica, CA: Rand Corporation.

Petersilia, Joan. 2004. "What works in Prisoner Reentry? Reviewing and Questioning the Evidence." *Federal Probation* 68(2): 4–8.

Reisig, Martin. 1998. "Rediscovering Rehabilitation: Drug Courts, Community Corrections and Restorative Justice." *Michigan Bar Journal* 172: 172–176.

Reinventing Probation Council. 2000. *Transforming Probation through Leadership: The Broken Windows Model.* New York: The Manhattan Institute.

Schmallenger, Frank, and John Smykla. 2011. *Corrections in the 21st Century.* New York: McGraw-Hill.

Scott, Joseph. 1974. "The Use of Discretion in Determining the Severity of Punishment for Incarcerated Offenders." *Journal of Criminal Law and Criminology* 65: 214–224.

Sentencing Project. 2016. *Criminal Justice Facts: Trends in U.S. Corrections.* Washington, DC: The Sentencing Institute.

Simon, Jonathan. 1993. *Poor Discipline Parole and the Social Control of the Underclass, 1980–1990.* Chicago, IL: University of Chicago Press.

Thornton, Robert. 2005. *Guns, Safety and Proactive Supervision.* Washington, DC: American Probation and Parole Association.

United States Parole Commission. 2003. *History of the Federal Parole System.* Washington, DC: U.S. Department of Justice.

Walker, Samuel, Cassia Spohn, and Miriam DeLeon. 2004. *The Color of Justice.* Belmont, CA: Wadsworth.

Watkins, Robert. 1989. "Probation and Parole Malpractice in a Noninstitutional Setting: A Contemporary Analysis." *Federal Probation* 73(3): 29–34.

Wilbanks, William.1987. *The Myth of a Racist Criminal Justice System.* Monterrey, CA: Brooks/ Cole.

Cases Cited

Goergen v. State, 718N.Y.2d, 193 (1959).
Menechino v. Oswald New York Court of Appeals, 430 F2d 403 (1970).
Morrissey v. Brewer, 408 US. 471, 485–486 (1972).
Reiser v. District of Columbia, 563 F.2d 462 (1977).
Taggart v. State, 822 P.2d 243 (1992).

17 Community Supervision Officers

An Overview and Discussion of Contemporary Issues

Eric J. Wodahl and Brett Garland

Probation and Parole: A Brief History of the Profession

Probation and parole officers have one of the most important and difficult jobs in the criminal justice system. With over 4.7 million adults under correctional supervision in the community (Kaeble, Maruschak, and Bonczar 2015), supervision officers have the dual responsibility of managing this population in a manner that both enhances public safety and promotes rehabilitation. The roles and responsibilities of the modern day probation and parole officer are complex and have evolved over a century and a half. As such, it seems necessary to begin this chapter with an overview of the profession's history and development. As the old adage goes, you don't know where you're going until you know where you've been.

The history of parole as an institution is most commonly traced back to the efforts of Captain Alexander Maconochie, who was named superintendent of the British penal colony on Norfolk Island in 1840 (Cromwell, Killinger, and Kerper 1974). As part of his efforts to humanize the conditions at Norfolk Island, Maconochie established a mark system that allowed inmates to progress through graduated levels of confinement as well as earn time off their sentences through good behavior and steady employment. Once an inmate earned enough marks, he became eligible for a ticket of leave, which was an order signed by the colonial governor releasing him from confinement (Dressler 1969). Upon release the inmate was required to remain within the jurisdiction and "check-in" with police; however, no formal conditions of release were imposed (Doherty 2013). Maconochie's reforms proved to be short-lived, however, as he was relieved of his duties after only four years, due primarily to the perception that his methods were too soft on criminals (Morris 2002).

Maconochie's ideas were later embraced by Sir Walter Crofton, who was named administrator of the Irish prison system in 1854. Crofton is credited with implementing the Irish system, which was very similar to Machonochie's mark system. Inmates progressed through a three-stage system of incarceration, which culminated with release to serve the remainder of their sentence in the community. Unlike Maconochie's ticket of leave system, inmates released under the Irish system were subjected to more specific conditions of release closely resembling modern parole. In addition, released inmates were subject to more formal supervision. While much of this supervision fell to the responsibility of the police, in 1856, James P. Organ was hired as the Inspector of Released Prisoners in Dublin, essentially making him the first parole officer (Paparozzi and Guy 2014; Smith 1990). Organ's caseload consisted of 140 released inmates, and according to Paparozzi and Guy, he "spent the majority of his time trying to secure employment for his charges" (2014: 15).

The pioneering reforms of Maconochie and Crofton proved to be major influences on the American correctional system, and directly influenced the development of probation and parole supervision in this country. The first use of parole in the U.S. coincided with the opening of the Elmira Reformatory in New York in 1876 (Pisciotta 1994). Elmira, under the leadership of Warden Zebulon Brockway, implemented an indeterminate sentencing model in which inmates who were deemed to have been rehabilitated were released to the supervision of a "guardian," a citizen volunteer who took on the responsibility of assisting the offenders' return to the community. Following New York's lead, other states, including Massachusetts, Pennsylvania, and Minnesota, adopted indeterminate sentencing and parole practices, and by the early twentieth century, all states and the federal government had parole systems in place (Wodahl and Garland 2009).

Probation, unlike parole, can be considered an American innovation. While some trace the roots of probation to early methods of suspending punishment such as benefit of clergy or judicial reprieve, the origination of modern probation is most commonly attributed to John Augustus and his pioneering efforts with the Boston Police Court (Augustus 1972; Linder and Saverse 1984). Augustus, a Boston shoemaker, began visiting the Boston Police Court in 1841. On one of these occasions, Augustus became convinced that he could assist a man who was charged with being a "common drunkard" (Augustus 1972: 5). Augustus persuaded the judge to release the man on bail to his care. The judge agreed on the condition that the man would return to court in three weeks for sentencing. When they returned to court, "his whole appearance was changed and no one, not even the scrutinizing officers, could have believed that he was the same person who less than a month before, had stood trembling on the prisoner's stand" (Augustus 1972: 5). The judge, pleased with the results, fined the man one cent plus court costs. Over the next 18 years, Augustus assisted an estimated 1,100 defendants, only one of whom was reported to have forfeited his bond.

In 1878 Massachusetts became the first state to pass laws formally authorizing probation, which is not surprising considering the pioneering efforts of John Augustus in that state. In Massachusetts, like most of the other states that followed, statutes authorizing the use of probation for juveniles preceded those for adults (Dressler 1969). It was not until 1901, in the state of New York, that the first adult probation statutes were approved. It did not take long for other states to follow suit, and by 1925, all states had laws authorizing the use of probation for juveniles, and by 1938, 37 states, along with the federal government and the District of Columbia, authorized the use of probation for adults (Wodahl and Garland 2009).

The role of volunteers during the emergence of probation and parole supervision in the U.S. cannot be understated. Early probation statutes, for example, failed to authorize money for probation officer salaries. This was not simply an oversight or a measure to save money; rather, it was in large part a reflection of what early advocates aspired community supervision to be. Initially the role of the supervision officer was conceived as providing friendship and advocacy, which many believed would be eroded if they received compensation (Linder and Saverse 1984; Rothman 1980). As probation and parole evolved in the early 1900s and the correctional system adopted a more medical model approach, the role of the volunteer diminished and the trained, professional supervision officer emerged (Wodahl and Garland 2009).

The Work of Probation and Parole Supervision

Modern probation and parole officers are charged with completing a number of diverse tasks associated with the management of offenders on their caseloads, ranging from collecting urine samples to testifying in court. In this section we examine issues surrounding the work of supervision officers. We begin with a discussion of caseloads, followed by a look at the common tasks undertaken by officers in their day-to-day activities. Finally, we look at research that explores the amount of time officers spend on particular types of activities. Before proceeding, it is important to acknowledge that supervision officers are often assigned duties that extend beyond the supervision of their caseloads (Petersilia 2002). Probation officers, for example, are often responsible for completing presentence investigations and the supervision of defendants released under pretrial release programs. Similarly, parole officers often work with inmates before their release, helping them prepare for reentry or completing prerelease investigations for the parole board or other release-granting authority to determine the suitability of the offender's parole plan. Thus, while the following discussion will focus on activities associated with caseload supervision, it is recognized that probation and parole officers often play a larger role in the criminal justice system.

The work of the supervision officer is normally centered on his or her caseload, which refers to the collection of individuals under the officer's control. The workload and responsibilities of the officer can vary greatly depending on both the size and the composition of the caseload being supervised. Recent statistics on caseload sizes of supervision officers are limited; however, the information that is available reveals that caseload sizes vary greatly by both jurisdiction and caseload type (Bonzcar 2008; Camp 2003; DeMichele 2007). A national survey of state parole agencies in 2006 found that while the average caseload for supervising parole officers was 38, averages varied greatly across states with Tennessee coming in with a high of 141 and Wyoming with a low of 4 (Bonzcar 2008). While these numbers should be interpreted with caution,[1] they do highlight the high variation in caseload sizes across jurisdictions; a finding that is likely influenced by both economic and political factors.

Caseload size is also often influenced greatly by the composition of offenders being supervised. Caseloads are generally broken down into two types: traditional and specialized. Traditional caseloads are caseloads made up of diverse offenders, which are normally assigned to officers on a rotating basis. Specialized caseloads, by contrast, concentrate on specific offender qualities, such as their risk level, offense type, or treatment needs. Specialized caseloads generally target offender populations who present a greater risk to the community or who have struggled under traditional supervision (Klein and Crowe 2008). One type of specialized caseload is an intensive supervision (ISP) caseload, which is comprised of high-risk offenders. Other examples of specialized caseloads include sex offender caseloads, domestic violence caseloads, and mental health caseloads. Specialized caseloads generally have fewer offenders than traditional caseloads, as the offenders are generally considered to need greater attention. In addition to having lower caseload sizes, a benefit of specialized caseloads is the capacity to assign offenders to supervision officers who have the temperament, abilities, and training to work with a specialized group (Hamblin and Rhyne 2010).

The day-to-day tasks required of supervision officers in the management of their caseloads are very diverse, and include a variety of surveillance, treatment, and administrative activities. Surveillance tasks refer to those activities that are most closely associated with monitoring and enforcing the conditions of supervision, including collecting court fines and costs, drug testing, investigating possible violations, and conducting home visits and other community surveillance activities. Treatment-related tasks are those that focus on rehabilitating the offender, including conducting risk/needs assessments, making treatment referrals, and providing individual and group counseling to offenders. Administrative tasks refer to those activities associated with completing the required documentation and reports associated with the supervision of caseload; in other words, paperwork! Agents are normally required to maintain case notes on all activities they undertake in the supervision of their caseload. In addition, they are often required to complete a variety of reports and other paperwork, such as violation reports to the court or parole board when offenders violate their conditions of supervision.

How much time do supervision officers spend on the various types of activities associated with the supervision of their caseloads? This is a good, but difficult question to answer given the diversity of caseloads and supervision environments where officers work. Despite these difficulties, there has been some research that provides us insight into this question. A study by West and Seiter (2004) surveyed probation and parole officers in Missouri and Kentucky to examine how much time they spent on surveillance as opposed to treatment related activities. Their study found that supervision officers spent a greater amount of time on treatment or casework activities (54 percent) compared to surveillance activities (42 percent) (West and Seiter 2004). A report from the American Probation and Parole Association presented findings from information collected from a survey of community corrections professionals that asked how much time they spent each month on various supervision-related activities (DeMichele, 2007). While the report clearly points out that the generalizability of these findings is limited due to the non-probability sampling procedures, findings revealed that officers spent the most time each month on administrative tasks (36 hours). Other tasks that consumed a large amount of the officers' time included conducting home visits (20 hours), engaging in motivational interviewing (18 hours), and spending time in court (13 hours).

The Role of the Probation and Parole Officer

Since the emergence of the professional probation and parole officer, the profession has struggled with defining the "proper" role of community supervision. At the risk of over-simplifying the issues, debates generally center on how to most appropriately balance the seemingly conflicting authoritarian and therapeutic roles supervision officers are required to undertake. An officer who adopts an authoritarian or law enforcement role emphasizes those job tasks that are associated with the monitoring and enforcement of supervision conditions, such as drug testing and conducting home visits or other surveillance of the offender in the community, while an officer who embraces a more therapeutic or social work role emphasizes those tasks that promote treatment and reintegration such as helping the individual secure employment and connecting the person to treatment programs and other available resources.

A substantial body of research has been undertaken over the years to better understand the degree to which supervision officers emphasize authoritarian versus therapeutic roles in their supervision practices. This research has found that supervision roles are not static; rather, they change over time and are influenced by the broader correctional policy environment. For example, research conducted in the 1960s and 1970s revealed a strong proclivity among supervision officers for the treatment-oriented approach (Glaser 1964; Klockars 1972; Van Laningham, Taber, and Dimants 1966). Glaser's (1964) study of United States Probation Officers (USPOs), for example, discovered that USPOs emphasized counseling or surveillance in their supervision practices. This emphasis on treatment over surveillance reflected the dominance of the rehabilitative climate, which guided correctional policy and practice at this time (Wodahl and Garland 2009).

By the 1980s, evidence indicated that supervision officers began to shift their priorities to reflect a more law enforcement orientation (Burton, Latessa, and Barker 1992; Clear and Latessa 1992; Harris, Clear, and Baird 1989). Harris and colleagues' study of probation officers in three states revealed that "concern for authority among community supervision officers has increased, and that authority is not a more meaningful concept in supervision than either assistance or treatment" (1989: 242). In hindsight, this shift should have been expected as it corresponded with the transition away from rehabilitation as the dominant correctional goal. At this time, the U.S. had adopted a get tough on crime stance that dominated criminal justice policy throughout much of the 1980s and 1990s (Wodahl and Garland 2009).

More contemporary study findings suggest another shift in supervision orientation toward a hybrid or synthetic approach (Miller 2015; Skeem and Manchak 2008; Taxman, 2008). The concept of a synthetic approach to community supervision can be traced back to

Klockars' (1972) seminal ethnographic study of an urban probation officer. Klockars utilized the term synthetic office to describe a hybrid style of supervision in which the officer integrates both therapeutic and surveillance activities into her supervision practices. A recent study by Miller (2015), utilizing data from a national survey of community corrections practitioners, found strong support for the existence of synthetic supervision in contemporary probation and parole supervision. Based on his analysis of over 1,700 survey responses asking about probation and parole officers' supervision practices, Miller concluded that "the conventional narrative of probation supervision that contrasts law enforcers with social workers seems outdated . . . the field now appears dominated, or at least substantially populated, by synthetic officers" (p. 331). Additional research suggests that synthetic approaches to supervision lead to better outcomes when compared to traditional treatment or surveillance supervision styles (Kennealy, Skeem, Manchak, and Eno Louden 2012; Paparozzi and Gendreau 2005; Skeem, Eno Louden, Polaschek, and Camp 2007). Kennealy and colleagues' (2012: 501) study, for example, found that a hybrid supervision approach "characterized by a firm, fair, and caring approach help protect against rearrest among general offenders."

The emergence of the hybrid supervision approach in contemporary community corrections practices reflects a changing policy environment that recognizes the importance of integrating evidence-based practices into offender management. Beginning in the 1990s and gaining steam throughout the first two decades of the twenty-first century, the correctional system has been transformed by the amalgamation of new practices guided by the mantras of "what works" and "evidence-based practices," including risk and needs assessments, cognitive-behavioral treatments, and motivational interviewing (Latessa, Listwan, and Koetzle 2014). These largely treatment-oriented strategies, which are grounded in sound research, have created a policy environment in which both therapeutic and surveillance approaches can coexist. In the next section, we explore in more detail the effect this evidence-based movement has had on probation and parole supervision and the supervision officer.

The Supervision Officer in the Era of Evidence-Based Supervision

In a relatively short time span the term evidence-based practices (EBPs) has become common nomenclature in probation and parole organizations. EBPs refer to those programs, practices, and treatments that have been found, through scientific study and evaluation, to be effective in reducing recidivism and improving offender outcomes. The entrenchment of EBPs in contemporary correctional practices can be traced back to Martinson's (1974) now infamous conclusion that "nothing works" in offender treatment and rehabilitation. While Martinson's proclamation is largely credited with moving correctional ideology and policy on a destructive and costly path that embraced incapacitation and retribution over traditional rehabilitative values, it also invigorated efforts to corroborate what many correctional scholars knew—some programs and practices are effective in reducing recidivism (Gendreau 1996). These efforts were aided in large part by the adoption of meta-analysis techniques, which gave correctional researchers the ability to look inside the "black box" of correctional programs and begin to develop a set of core correctional practices that helped usher in the era of evidence-based supervision (Latessa et al. 2014).

Perhaps the most well-known and influential of the core correctional practices has been the risk, needs, responsivity (RNR) model. The RNR model asserts that correctional interventions are most effective when they adhere to the principles of risk, needs, and responsivity (Andrews, Bonta, and Hoge 1990). The risk principle maintains that the intensity of correctional interventions should be scaled to the risk of the offender. More specifically, higher risk offenders should be targeted for more intense levels of treatment and supervision, while low-risk offenders "do as well or better with minimal as opposed to more intensive service" (Andrews et al. 1990: 20). The needs principle asserts that correctional interventions need to address criminogenic needs. Criminogenic needs are those needs such as criminal peers, antisocial attitudes and beliefs, and substance abuse that have been scientifically proven to correlate with reoffending (Latessa et al. 2014). Finally, the responsivity principle refers to the practice of matching the "styles and modes of service" to the "learning styles and abilities of offenders" (Andrews et al. 1990: 20).

One of the most significant developments in probation and parole supervision materializing from the RNR model has been the mass implementation of risk and needs assessments. Risk and needs assessments refer to scientifically validated assessment tools that utilize "statistical algorithms to establish risk profiles of individuals that share certain characteristics" (Zhang, Roberts, and Farabee 2014: 169). Given the emphasis of risk and needs in the RNR model, the need to incorporate tools to guide supervision officers in making informed decisions is paramount. It is important to note that assessment tools in offender management practices are not novel; they have been around for decades, dating back to the Burgess scale in 1928 (Bonta 1996; Wright, Clear, and Dickson 1984). These early assessment tools, while utilized in probation and parole agencies, were integrated on a more superficial level and not given the same level of salience they are today. It was not until the emergence of the RNR model that the assimilation of these instruments as a necessary component of probation and parole supervision occurred.

Perhaps not surprisingly, this action has been met with resistance from officers, who are likely concerned by both a perceived loss of discretion in decision making about the supervision of their caseloads and skepticism about the capacity of these instruments to accurately measure risk (Harris 2006; Miller and Maloney 2013; Schneider, Ervin, and Snyder-Joy 1996). To a large degree, practitioner concerns about risk and needs assessments have been quelled by an abundance of research showing the superiority of actuarial assessment tools compared to gut-level or clinical assessments that rely solely on human judgment (Harris 2006). Additionally, the acceptance of these tools by community supervision officers has likely been enhanced by advancements in assessment technology. Early generation assessment tools focused primarily on static or unchangeable risk factors, such as prior criminal history and age at first arrest. While these tools were fairly effective in predicting risk, they provided little guidance into identifying and addressing criminogenic needs. More recent assessment tools, often referred to as third and fourth generation assessments, have remedied this shortcoming by incorporating dynamic or changeable factors into the assessment process, thus giving officers a valuable tool in developing case plan interventions that have the capacity to improve offender outcomes (Andrews, Bonta, and Wormith 2006).

In many jurisdictions, the RNR model has led to even more substantial changes in the daily routines of probation and parole officers. These shifts have come about in large part due to efforts to align supervision practices with the third leg of the RNR model—responsivity. Responsivity can be conceived of as consisting of two subtypes, general and specific. *General responsivity* refers to the understanding that offender change is best accomplished through programs and interventions that are grounded in social learning theory and cognitive behavioral approaches, while *specific responsivity* is the acknowledgment that one-size treatment approaches are of limited value and efforts should be made to tailor the delivery of interventions to the individual characteristics of the offender (Latessa et al. 2014).

In many supervision agencies, efforts to adhere to these principles have led to a shift in the underlying responsibility of supervision officers from service brokers to change agents (Bourgon, Gutierrez, and Ashton 2012; Taxman 2008). When it comes to facilitating offender treatment and change, probation and parole officers traditionally have taken on primarily a service broker function, meaning that their efforts to facilitate change have generally been limited to connecting offenders to appropriate treatments in the community, such as mental health or substance abuse treatment. Under this framework, agent interactions with offenders were generally superficial and focused on making referrals and monitoring compliance with those referrals. In the era of evidence-based supervision, however, supervision officers are called upon to be change agents by taking an active role in the treatment process (Bourgon et al. 2012; Taxman 2008).

One way in which probation and parole officers take an active role in the treatment process is through the direct delivery of treatment programs. For example, it is now common practice for supervision officers to be trained in delivering cognitive behavioral treatment (CBT) groups such as Thinking for a Change (T4C) or Moral Recognition Therapy (MRT). A second, and perhaps more comprehensive way officers take an active role in the treatment process is through their one-on-one interactions with offenders under their supervision. In the evidence-based supervision era, interactions between officers and offenders such as office meetings or home visits, which have traditionally been viewed as opportunities to monitor compliance, are viewed as opportunities to help bring about behavioral change.

Toward this end, officers commonly receive training in motivational interviewing (MI) techniques to utilize in their interactions with their clients to help decrease offender resistance to change (Clark 2005). Officers in many locales have been given the capacity to administer sanctions (e.g. community service hours, written assignments, and short jail stays) and incentives (e.g. monetary rewards, certificates of achievement, and reductions in supervision conditions) as tools to facilitate change (Wodahl, Garland, Culhane, and McCarty 2011). Additionally, a number of jurisdictions have taken a more comprehensive approach through the implementation of training programs such as the Effective Practices in Community Supervision program (EPICS), Strategic Training Initiative in Community Supervision (STICS), and Staff Training Aimed at Reducing Rearrest (STARR), which provide structured training and coaching to supervision officers on the use of CBT and other evidence-based approaches in their one-on-one interactions with offenders (Bonta, Bourgon, Rugge, Gress, and Gutierrez 2013; Robinson et al. 2012; Smith, Schweitzer, Labrecque, and Latessa 2012). The purpose of these programs, as well as a variety of other initiatives that have been undertaken in the evidence-based supervision era, has been to engage the supervision officer in the change process, which has fundamentally shifted the functions and responsibilities of the supervision officer from service broker to change agent.

Probation and Parole Officers and the use of Discretion

Probation and parole officers, like other criminal justice professionals, enjoy a high level of discretion in the fulfillment of their daily activities, and their use of this discretion can greatly affect case outcomes. Community supervision officers, for example, often have high levels of discretion when making recommendations to judges and other court personnel concerning pretrial release decisions, sentencing outcomes (normally as part of the completion of the presentence investigation), and revocation outcomes (Jones and Kerbs 2007). Additionally, officers have traditionally enjoyed a great deal of freedom in making decisions about the supervision of individuals on their caseload, such as the intensity of monitoring (e.g. number of drug tests or frequency of office visits), treatment referrals, and the fervor through which supervision conditions are enforced. Finally, and maybe most importantly, supervision officers often enjoy wide discretion in deciding how to respond when offenders violate the conditions of their supervision (Kerbs, Jones, and Jolley 2009). In this section we explore the research on officers' use of discretion and look at some recent policy actions that have sought to limit or control this discretion.

Research on the use of discretion in community supervision has focused almost exclusively on officer discretion in responding to offenders who violate the conditions of their supervision. Probation and parole officers generally have two options when they discover an individual has violated the terms of his supervision. The first is to handle the violation internally, which means the officer does not initiate revocation proceedings and responds to the violation with some other response. Internal responses might include increasing supervision intensity such as increased office visits or drug testing, imposing an administrative sanction such as community service hours, or increasing treatment requirements. The second option is to handle the violation externally by initiating revocation proceedings. When revocation is pursued, the case is referred back to the release-granting authority, normally the judge or parole board, where if the violation behavior is substantiated the offender could likely be returned to custody. Not surprisingly, the decision between responding to violations internally versus externally can have huge consequences for both the offender and criminal justice system.

Research suggests that officer discretion in responding to violations is influenced by a variety of factors, including offender/violation related factors, organizational/caseload factors, and officer characteristics (Harris, Petersen, and Rapoza 2001; Kerbs et al. 2009; Lowe, Dawson-Edwards, Minor, and Wells 2008; McCleary, 1975; Slabonik and Simms 2002; Steiner, Makarios, Travis, and Meade 2011). Offender/violation related factors, such as the severity of the violation, the dangerousness of the offender, and the frequency of misconduct, have generally been found to have the largest effect on supervision officers' decisions to handle violations internally versus externally (Harris et al. 2001; Lowe et al. 2008; Steiner et al. 2011). A study by Steiner and colleagues (2011) of parole officer decision making in Ohio, for example, found that offenders who committed more serious violations, had a history of previous misconduct, and who had been incarcerated for more serious crimes were at higher risk of facing revocation as opposed to having their misconduct handled internally.

Organizational and caseload factors, such as agency policy, supervisor expectations, and caseload size, have also influenced how probation and parole officers respond to offender violations (Kerbs et al. 2009; McCleary 1975; Steiner et al. 2011). For instance, Kerbs, Jones, and Jolley's (2009) study of 332 probation officers found that officers with higher caseload sizes were more likely to respond to violations externally. McCleary's (1975) qualitative study of probation officers in Cook County, Illinois found that officer decisions are influenced in part by their loyalty to the organization and a desire not to make their supervisors look bad. Finally, there is some evidence that discretion in the handling of offender misconduct is influenced by certain characteristics of the supervising officer (Kerbs et al. 2009; McCleary 1975). Kerbs and colleagues (2009) found that some officer characteristics such as gender, years of experience, and race impacted how officers responded to certain types of violations. It should be emphasized, however, that the influence of officer characteristics appears to be limited and secondary to the offender/violation and organization/caseload factors previously discussed.

Certain policy changes have taken place in recent years that have sought, at least in part, to limit the level of discretion enjoyed by probation and parole officers. The two most noticeable examples are the incorporation of risk/needs assessments and policies that limit discretion in the handling of probation and parole violations. Since risk/needs assessments have already been addressed, we focus our attention on policies aimed at limiting discretion in officer responses to misconduct. Motivations for these policies have generally centered on issues of fairness and the desire to better manage correctional resources. Given the large amount of discretion officers have when responding to violations, it is not surprising that there are often great disparities in how officers respond to transgressions, which raises questions about equity and fairness in the system (Burke 1997; Taxman, Soule, and Gelb 1999). Additionally, it has been recognized that probation and parole violators have been a major contributor to prison and jail growth and crowding. In several states, probation and parole failures account for over half of all new prison admissions (Wodahl, Ogle, and Heck 2011). In response to these issues, many jurisdictions have enacted policies to structure how officers respond to violations in hopes of limiting revocations, and thus limiting the costs associated with incarcerating community supervision failures.

A common approach has been the implementation of response grids that structure officer discretion (Burke 1997; Steiner et al. 2011). Response grids are very similar to sentencing guidelines that were enacted to limit judicial discretion in sentencing. Response grids provide officer guidance in the handling of violations by providing officers a menu of acceptable responses based on the severity of the transgression, the risk level of the offender, and the frequency of violation behavior. It should be noted that these response grids do not eliminate officer discretion; rather, they structure discretion to improve consistency and give organizations more control over which offenders are subject to revocation and incarceration. Limited research suggests that response grids have been effective in decreasing revocations and increasing consistency in decision making (Steiner et al. 2011).

Supervision Officer Stress and Burnout

Probation and parole officers have one of the most difficult jobs in the criminal justice field. As Lewis (2013: 56) notes:

> whereas most helping professionals assist motivated clients in physically and psychologically safe environments, probation and parole officers work with involuntary clients, are repeatedly exposed to a variety of potentially traumatic incidents, must maintain heightened and sustained levels of mental vigilance for officer safety and have the due (and at times conflicting) responsibility for both offender rehabilitation and control.

Given the nature of this work, it is not surprising that supervision officers experience high levels of stress and burnout, an issue that is important to consider for several reasons. First, elevated levels of stress and burnout can lead to high turnover rates, which are both costly to the agency and can place an undue burden on remaining officers who are forced to pick up the slack until new officers can be hired and trained (Lee, Joo, and Johnson 2009). High stress and burnout levels have also been associated with increased levels of mental and physical ailments, such as depression, sleep problems, and substance abuse (Oginska-Bulik 2005; Sinha 2001). There is also good reason to believe that supervision officers who experience greater levels of stress are less effective in their jobs, which can likely limit the effectiveness of supervision and ultimately place the community at risk (Garland 2002). In this section we take a closer look at the issue of stress and burnout by reviewing the research on correlates of stress and burnout for probation and parole officers, followed by a discussion of the ways in which individuals and agencies address the issue.

Research reveals that officer stress and burnout is associated with a combination of factors related to the organizational environment, job experiences, and personal characteristics. For example, role conflict has consistently been found to be associated with a number of negative outcomes associated with stress and burnout among community supervision officers (Gayman and Bradley 2013; Holgate and Clegg; 1991; Whitehead 1989; Whitehead and Lindquist 1985). Role conflict refers to the internal conflict that arises when an officer perceives an expectation to fulfill incompatible roles (e.g. law enforcer v. social worker). Other organizational climate factors that have contributed to stress and burnout include role ambiguity (a perceived lack of clarity concerning job goals) and role overload (the feeling of being unable to complete job expectations within reasonable timeframes) (Holgate and Clegg 1991; White, Gasperin, Nystrom, Ambrose, and Esarey 2005).

Certain job experiences also impact stress and burnout. A study by Lewis, Lewis, and Garby (2013) of adult probation officers in three states, for example, found that officers who experienced certain negative job experiences (often referred to as secondary trauma), such as having an offender on their caseload engage in violent or sexual recidivism or commit suicide, is associated with elevated levels of stress and burnout. In addition, being assaulted or threatened with violence was also associated with stress and burnout; a finding that is consistent with prior research focusing on institutional corrections personnel (Garland 2004; Lambert and Paoline 2005). It also appears that the levels of stress and burnout experienced on the job vary among certain personal characteristics, such as race, gender, age, time on the job, and health (Gayman and Bradley 2013; Rhineberger-Dunn, Mack, and Baker 2016; Whitehead and Lindquist 1985). A recent study focusing on community corrections officers in Iowa found that female officers, those in poorer health, and officers with more years of experience were more likely to experience dimensions of burnout (Rhineberger-Dunn et al. 2016).

Given the high level of stress and burnout experienced by supervision officers and the negative outcomes associated with it, there is a clear need for strategies to help probation and parole officers deal with the rigors of the job. One mechanism that supervision officers use to cope with stress is to utilize self-care strategies (Finn and Kuck 2003; White et al. 2005). A study by White and associates (2005) asked officers in Illinois about the importance of various self-care strategies. The strategies identified as most important included cultivating a sense of humor, having healthy intimate and family relationships, and having enjoyable hobbies and leisure activities. In addition to self-care strategies, a number of supervision agencies have implemented formal programs to assist officers in dealing with stress (Finn and Kuck 2003). While these programs vary, there are certain components that are considered "ideal," including providing training and education to new and existing staff, access to counseling services, peer support, and services to assist officers in dealing with critical incidents (for a good review see Finn and Kuck 2003).

Conclusion

Probation and parole are relatively new mechanisms for dealing with criminal offenders, considering that their beginnings date back only to the mid 1800s. Nonetheless, probation and parole are now the dominant forms of correctional supervision in the U.S. The modern community supervision officer manages a diverse set of roles and functions, is often responsible for a sizeable caseload, and is afforded considerable discretion regarding how offender misconduct is handled. In recent decades, probation and parole have begun to absorb and employ principles and practices from a growing EBP literature, which has led to the integration of risk and need assessments in daily operations and increased use of cognitive-behavioral and motivational interviewing techniques. Many organizational and job-related forces, such as role conflict and secondary trauma, have the potential to generate stress and burnout for probation and parole officers, which, in turn, can lead to high turnover, mental and physical impairments, and diminished job performance. Undoubtedly, probation and parole will remain prominent components of correctional systems in future decades, and correctional authorities and agencies will need to continuously reevaluate and readjust policies and practices to meet new and changing demands associated with community supervision work.

Note

1. States at the extreme low end of the caseload sizes are most likely agencies that have the combined responsibilities to supervise both probations and parolees. Thus, while supervision officers in these states might have a low number of parolees on their caseloads, they likely supervise a higher density of probationers.

References

Andrews, D.A., James Bonta, and R.D. Hoge. 1990. "Classification for Effective Rehabilitation: Rediscovering Psychology." *Criminal Justice and Behavior* 17: 19–52.

Andrews, D.A., James Bonta, and J. S. Wormith. 2006. "The Recent Past and Near Future of Risk and/or Need Assessment." *Crime & Delinquency* 52: 7–27.

Augustus, John. 1972. *John Augustus: First Probation Officer*. Montclair, NJ: Patterson Smith.

Bonczar, Thomas, P. 2008. *Characteristics of State Parole Supervising Agencies, 2006*. Bureau of Justice Statistics. Washington, DC: U.S. Department of Justice. Retrieved September 6, 2016 from www.bjs.gov/content/pub/pdf/cspsa06.pdf

Bonta, James. 1996. "Risk-Needs Assessment and Treatment." Pp. 18–32 in *Choosing Correctional Options that Work: Defining the Demand and Evaluating the Supply*, edited by A.T. Harland. Thousand Oaks, CA: Sage Publications.

Bonta, James, Guy Bourgon, Tanya Rugge, Carmen Gress, and Leticia Gutierrez. 2013. "Taking the Leap: From Pilot Project to Wide-Scale Implementation of the Strategic Training Initiative in Community Supervision (STICS)." *Justice Research and Policy* 15: 17–35.

Bourgon, Guy, Leticia Guitierrez, and Jennifer Ashton. 2012. "The Evolution of Community Supervision Practice: The Transformation from Case Manager to Change Agent." *Federal Probation* 76: 27–35.

Burke, Peggy B. 1997. *Policy-Driven Responses to Probation and Parole Violations*. Washington, DC: U.S. Department of Justice. Retrieved August 26, 2016 from http://static.nicic.gov/Library/013793.pdf

Burton, Velmer S., Edward J. Latessa, and Troy Barker. 1992. "The Role of Probation Officers: An Examination of Statutory Requirements." *Journal of Contemporary Criminal Justice* 8: 273–282.

Camp, Camille G. 2003. *The 2002 Corrections Yearbook: Adult Corrections*. Middletown, CT: Criminal Justice Institute.

Clark, Michael D. 2005. "Motivational Interviewing for Probation Staff: Increasing the Readiness to Change." *Federal Probation* 69: 22–28.

Clear, Todd R., and Edward J. Latessa. 1992. "Probation Officers' Roles in Intensive Supervision: Surveillance Versus Treatment." *Justice Quarterly* 10: 441–462.

Cromwell, Paul F., George Killinger, and Hazel Kerper. 1974. "The History and Concept of Parole." Pp. 233–241 in *Corrections in the Community: Alternatives to Imprisonment Selected Readings*, edited by G. Killinger and P.F. Cromwell. St. Paul, MN: West Publishing.

DeMichele, Matthew T. 2007. *Probation and Parole's Growing Caseloads and Workload Allocations: Strategies for Managerial Decision Making*. Lexington, KY: American Probation and Parole Association. Retrieved August 29, 2016 from www.appa-net.org/eweb/docs/appa/pubs/SMDM.pdf

Doherty, Fiona. 2013. "Indeterminate Sentencing Returns: The Invention of Supervised Release." *New York University Law Review* 88: 958–1030.

Dressler, David. 1969. *Practice and Theory of Probation and Parole*. New York, NY: Columbia University Press.

Finn, Peter, and Sarah Kuck. 2003. *Addressing Probation and Parole Officer Stress*. Washington, DC: U.S. Department of Justice. Retrieved September 1, 2016 from www.ncjrs.gov/pdffiles1/nij/grants/207012.pdf

Garland, Brett. 2002. "Prison Treatment Staff Burnout: Consequences, Causes, and Prevention." *Corrections Today* 67(4): 116–121.

Garland, Brett. 2004. "The Impact of Administrative Support on Prison Treatment Staff Burnout: An Exploratory Study." *The Prison Journal* 84: 452–471.

Gayman, Mathew D., and Mindy S. Bradley. 2013. "Organizational Climate, Work Stress, and Depressive Symptoms among Probation and Parole Officers." *Criminal Justice Studies* 26: 326–346.

Gendreau, Paul. 1996. "The Principles of Effective Intervention with Offenders." Pp. 117–130 in *Choosing Correctional Options that Work: Defining the Demand and Evaluating the Supply*, edited by A.T. Harland. Thousand Oaks, CA: Sage Publications.

Glaser, Daniel. 1964. *The Effectiveness of a Prison and Parole System*. Indianapolis, IN: The Bobbs-Merrill Company.

Hamblin, Lailah, and Charlene Rhyne. 2010. *What Makes a Specialized Caseload Special? Portland, OR: Multnomah County Department of Community Justice*. Retrieved September 6, 2016 from https://multco.us/file/27861/download

Harris, Patricia M. 2006. "What Community Supervision Officers Need to Know About Actuarial Risk Assessment and Clinical Judgment." *Federal Probation* 70(2): 8–14.

Harris, Patricia M., Todd R. Clear, and S. C. Baird. 1989. "Have Community Supervision Officers Changed Their Attitudes Toward Their Work?" *Justice Quarterly* 6: 233–246.

Harris, Patricia M., Rebecca D. Petersen, and Samantha Rapoza. 2001. "Between Probation and Revocation: A Study of Intermediate Sanctions Decision-Making." *Journal of Criminal Justice* 29: 307–318.

Holgate, Alina M., and Ian Clegg, J. 1991. "The Path to Probation Officer Burnout: New Dogs, Old Tricks." *Journal of Criminal Justice* 19: 325–337.

Jones, Mark, and John J. Kerbs. 2007. "Probation and Parole Officers and Discretionary Decision-Making: Responses to Technical and Criminal Violations." *Federal Probation* 71: 9–15.

Kaeble, Danielle, Laura M. Maruschak, and Thomas P. Bonczar. 2015. *Probation and Parole in the United States, 2014*. Washington, DC: U.S. Department of Justice. Retrieved September 6, 2016 from www.bjs.gov/content/pub/pdf/ppus14.pdf

Kennealy, Patrick J., Jennifer L. Skeem, Sarah S. Manchak, and Jennifer Eno Louden. 2012. "Firm, Fair, and Caring Officer–Offender Relationships Protect Against Supervision Failure." *Law and Human Behavior* 36: 496–505.

Kerbs, John J., Mark Jones, and Jennifer M. Jolley. 2009. "Discretionary Decision Making by Probation and Parole Officers: The Role of Extralegal Variables as Predictors of Responses to Technical Violations." *Journal of Contemporary Criminal Justice* 25: 424–441.

Klein, Andrew R., and Ann Crowe. 2008. "Findings from an Outcome Examination of Rhode Island's Specialized Domestic Violence Probation Supervision Program: Do Specialized Supervision Programs of Batterers Reduce Reabuse?" *Violence Against Women* 14: 226–246.

Klockars, Carl B. Jr. 1972. "A Theory of Probation Supervision." *Journal of Criminal Law and Criminology* 63: 550–556.

Lambert, Eric G., and Eugene A. Paoline. 2005. "The Impact of Medical Issues on the Job Stress and Job Satisfaction of Jail Staff." *Punishment & Society* 7: 259–275.

Latessa, Edward J., Shelly J. Listwan, and Deborah Koetzle. 2014. *What Works (and Doesn't) in Reducing Recidivism*. Waltham, MA: Anderson Publishing.

Lee, Won-Jae, Hee-Jong Joo, and W.W. Johnson. 2009. "The Effect of Participatory Management on Internal Stress, Overall Job Satisfaction, and Turnover Rate among Federal Probation Officers." *Federal Probation* 73: 33–40.

Lewis, Kristen. 2013. "Secondary Trauma: The Personal Impact of Working with Criminal Officers." *Perspectives* 37(1): 50–63.

Lewis, Kirsten R., Ladonna S. Lewis, and Tina M.Garby. 2013. "Surviving the Trenches: The Personal Impact of the Job on Probation Officers." *American Journal of Criminal Justice* 38: 67–84.

Linder, Charles, and Margaret R. Saverse. 1984. "The Evolution of Probation: Early Salaries, Qualifications, and Hiring Practices." *Federal Probation* 48(1): 3–10.

Lowe, Nathan C., Cherie Dawson-Edwards, Kevin I. Minor, and James B. Wells. 2008. "Understanding the Decision to Pursue Revocation of Intensive Supervision: A Descriptive Survey of Juvenile Probation and Aftercare Officers." *Journal of Offender Rehabilitation* 46: 137–169.

Martinson, Robert. 1974. "What Works? Questions and Answers about Prison Reform." *The Public Interest* 35: 22–54.

McCleary, Richard. 1975. "How Structural Variables Constrain the Parole Officer's Use of Discretionary Powers." *Social Problems* 23: 209–225.
Miller, Joel. 2015. "Contemporary Modes of Probation Officer Supervision: The Triumph of the 'Synthetic' Officer?" *Justice Quarterly* 32: 314–336.
Miller, Joel, and Carrie Maloney. 2013. "Practitioner Compliance with Risk/Needs Assessment Tools: A Theoretical and Empirical Assessment." *Criminal Justice and Behavior* 40: 716–736.
Morris, Norval. 2002. *Maconochie's Gentlemen: The Story of Norfolk Island and the Roots of Modern Prison Reform*. New York: Oxford University Press.
Oginska-Bulik, Nina. 2005. "Emotional Intelligence in the Workplace: Exploring the Effects on Occupational Stress and Health Outcomes in Human Service Workers." *International Journal of Occupational Medicine and Environmental Health* 18: 167–775.
Paparozzi, Mario A., and Paul Gendreau. 2005. "An Intensive Supervision Program that Worked: Service Delivery, Professional Orientation, and Organizational Supportiveness." *The Prison Journal* 85: 445–466.
Paparozzi, Mario, and Roger Guy. 2014. "Reentry: Parole by Any Other Name." Pp. 7–22 in *Offender Reentry: Rethinking Criminology and Criminal Justice*, edited by M.S. Crow and J.O. Smykla. Burlington, MA: Jones & Bartlett Learning.
Petersilia, Joan. 2002. *Reforming Probation and Parole*. Lanham, MD: American Correctional Association.
Pisciotta, Alexander W. 1994. *Benevolent Repression: Social Control and the American Reformatory-Prison Movement*. New York: New York University Press.
Rhineberger-Dunn, Gayle, Kristin Y. Mack, and Kimberly M. Baker. 2016. "Comparing Demographic Factors, Background Characteristics, and Workplace Perceptions as Predictors of Burnout among Community Corrections Officers." *Criminal Justice and Behavior* 44(2): 205–225.
Robinson, Charles R., Christopher T. Lowenkamp, Alexander M. Holsinger, Scott VanBenschoten, Melissa Alexander, and J.C. Oleson. 2012. "A Random Study of Staff Training Aimed at Reducing Re-arrest (STARR): Using Core Correctional Practices in Probation Interactions." *Journal of Crime and Justice* 35: 167–188.
Rothman, David J. 1980. *Conscience and Convenience: The Asylum and its Alternatives in Progressive America*. Boston, MA: Little, Brown.
Schneider, Anne L., Laurie Ervin, and Zoann Snyder-Joy. 1996. "Further Exploration of the Flight from Discretion: The Role of Risk/Need Instruments in Probation Supervision Decisions." *Journal of Criminal Justice* 24: 109–121.
Skeem, Jennifer L., Jennifer Eno Louden, Devon Polaschek, and Jacqueline Camp. 2007. "Assessing Relationship Quality in Mandated Community Treatment: Blending Care with Control." *Psychological Assessment* 19: 397–410.
Skeem, Jennifer L., and Sarah Manchak. 2008. "Back to the Future: From Klockars' Model of Effective Supervision to Evidence-Based Practice in Probation." *Journal of Offender Rehabilitation* 47: 220–247.
Sinha, Rajita. 2001. "How Does Stress Increase Risk of Drug Abuse and Relapse?" *Psychopharmacology* 158: 343–359.
Slabonik, Maria L., and Barbara Sims. 2002. "Controlling Discretion in Bureaucratic Agencies: A Survey of Adult Probation Officers." *Corrections Compendium* 27(9): 1–5, 22, 23.
Smith, Beverly. 1990. "The Female Prisoner in Ireland, 1855–1878. *Federal Probation* 54: 69–81.
Smith, Paula, Myrinda Schweitzer, Ryan M. Labrecque, and Edward J.Latessa. 2012. "Improving Probation Officers' Supervision Skills: An Evaluation of the EPICS Model." *Journal of Crime and Justice* 35: 189–199.
Steiner, Benjamin, Matthew D. Makarios, Lawrence F. Travis, and Benjamin Meade. 2011. "Short-Term Effects of Sanctioning Reform on Parole Officers' Revocation Decisions." *Law & Society Review* 45: 371–400.
Taxman, Faye S. 2008. "No Illusions: Offender and Organizational Change in Maryland's Proactive Community Supervision Efforts." *Criminology and Public Policy* 7: 275–302.
Taxman, Faye S., David Soule, and Adam Gelb. 1999. "Graduated Sanctions: Stepping into Accountable Systems and Offenders." *The Prison Journal* 79: 182–204.
Van Laningham, Dale E., Merlin Taber, and Ruta Dimants. 1966. "How Adult Probation Officers View Their Job Responsibilities." *Crime and Delinquency* 12(2): 97–108.

West, Angela D., and Richard P. Seiter. 2004. "Social Worker or Cop? Measuring the Supervision Styles of Probation & Parole Officers in Kentucky and Missouri." *Journal of Crime & Justice* 27: 27–57.

White, William L., David L. Gasperin, Judi L. Nystrom, Charles T. Ambrose, and Carol N. Esarey. 2005. "The Other Side of Burnout: An Ethnographic Study of Exemplary Performance and Health among Probation Officers Supervising High-Risk Offenders." *Perspectives* 29(2): 26–31.

Whitehead, John T. 1989. *Burnout in Probation and Corrections*. New York: Praeger.

Whitehead, John T., and Charles Lindquist. 1985. "Job Stress and Burnout among Probation/Parole Officers: Perceptions and Causal Factors." *International Journal of Offender Therapy and Comparative Criminology* 29: 109–119.

Wodahl, Eric J., and Brett Garland. 2009. "The Evolution of Community Corrections: The Enduring Influence of the Prison." *The Prison Journal* 89: 81S–104S.

Wodahl, Eric J., Brett Garland, Scott E. Culhane, and William P. McCarty. 2011. "Utilizing Behavioral Interventions to Improve Supervision Outcomes in Community-Based Corrections." *Criminal Justice and Behavior* 38: 386–405.

Wodahl, Eric J., Robbin Ogle, and Cary Heck. 2011. "Revocation Trends: A Threat to the Legitimacy of Community-Based Corrections." *The Prison Journal* 91: 207–226.

Wright, Kevin N., Todd R. Clear, and Paul Dickson. 1984. "Universal Applicability of Probation Risk-Assessment Instruments." *Criminology* 22: 113–134.

Zhang, Sheldon X., Robert E. L. Roberts, and David Farabee. 2014. "An Analysis of Prisoner Reentry and Parole Risk Using COMPAS and Traditional Criminal History Measures." *Crime & Delinquency* 60: 167–192.

18 Halfway Houses and House Arrest

Jason Rydberg and Elias Nader

Introduction

There were more than 1.56 million men and women in United States state and federal correctional facilities at year-end 2014, an increase of more than 400 percent since 1980 (Cahalan and Parsons 1986; Carson 2015). With the explosive growth of mass incarceration since the onset of the crime control era (Garland 2001), criminal justice practice has placed increased emphasis on community corrections to serve as a mechanism to release pressure on the bloated correctional population. In particular, since the 1980s, community corrections practitioners have experimented with and become increasingly reliant on intermediate sanctions, which allow for sanctions that are more severe than traditional probation but do not contribute to the prison population, or allow for offenders to exit prison sooner than they would have otherwise (Caputo 2004). This chapter will review and discuss two particular intermediate sanctions—*halfway houses* and *electronically monitored house arrest*. Both community corrections programs are designed to restrict the activities of offenders in the community, structuring activity during the day and requiring the offender to be at a particular location during the night. Specifically, for each of these programs this chapter will consider their effectiveness in reducing recidivism, with special attention on adherence to the principles of effective correctional interventions, and the potential unintended consequences on offenders and the criminal justice system.

Halfway Houses

The term *halfway house* (HWH) refers to a community-based residential correctional facility operating with the purpose of providing transitional housing towards a variety of community corrections goals. These facilities are typically small, can be privately or publicly maintained, and are most often situated within or close to urban communities (Caputo 2004; Hamilton and Campbell 2014). As correctional institutions, HWHs can vary in the level of security provided, ranging from converted private residences with a 24-hour security guard, up to and including lock-down style facilities with security mechanisms similar to that of a prison (Kras, Pleggenkuhle, and Huebner 2016). However, even with relatively higher levels of security, offenders residing at HWHs are able (and often required) to enter the community to work or to find work, to attend school, and to attend community-based treatment services, but must return to the residence for the evening (Olgoff 2006). HWHs represent an intermediate sanction positioned between prison and community supervision in multiple senses.

For instance, HWHs can be utilized as a non-custodial sanction that provides more structure than traditional probation supervision, but avoids incarceration in prison by allowing the offender to continue to reside in the community. This positioning of a HWH as an intermediate sanction between probation and prison entails utilizing them to provide sanctioning or supervision as a *halfway-in* strategy (Thalheimer 1975). More common, though, is the utilization of HWHs as a *halfway-out* strategy (Caputo 2004). That is, rather than requiring an offender to serve the entirety or a relatively larger proportion of their sentence in prison prior to release, individuals released on parole can reside at a HWH as a transitional step back into community life.

Hamilton and Campbell (2014) note further differentiation in the halfway-out functioning of HWHs. Parolees can be placed in a HWH as an *early release* mechanism, where the offender is released from prison and spends a specified period of time in residence before they are permitted to live with family or on their own (Caputo 2004). A second mechanism is to use the HWH as a form of *pre-release* supervision. That is, offenders are sent to a HWH as a trial run for parole supervision, and are technically considered inmates until they can complete a specified set of programming, upon which they are granted traditional parole supervision (Caputo 2004; Hamilton and Campbell 2014). Finally, HWH can be used as a *back-end diversion program* to remand parole violators to increased supervision or services, in lieu of returning them to prison. For instance, in order to avoid returning too many parolees to prison, parole agents in Michigan utilize several forms of residential placement to manage parolees with chronic violations while under supervision (Rydberg and Grommon 2016).

The use of HWHs contributes to several community corrections goals. Both halfway-in and halfway-out utilizations act as an alternative to incarceration, enabling the criminal justice system to reduce costs (Latessa and Allen 1982) and allowing offenders to avoid negative consequences associated with prolonged exposure to incarceration (Listwan, Sullivan, Agnew, Cullen, and Colvin 2013). Primarily, a key purpose of utilizing HWHs as a halfway-out step between prison and the community is to provide structure and stability to the reintegration of former prisoners into society. Indeed, although HWHs have existed in the United States for nearly 200 years (Cohen 1973), they did not become widely utilized until the 1950s during the height of the medical model, when rehabilitation was the dominant paradigm of correctional interventions (Garland 2001). To this extent, service provision is a central component of HWH programs (Hamilton and Campbell 2014), and the growth of HWH utilization over the previous 50 years is largely a function of the expansion of services provided to offenders in residence (Latessa and Smith 2015). In a comprehensive review of HWH programs across Ohio, Lowenkamp and Latessa (2002) observed that the most common services linked to HWH programs included substance use treatment (95 percent of HWH programs), and employment programming (81 percent), while over half of facilities offered educational classes (62 percent), financial skills classes (59 percent), and cognitive behavioral treatment groups (54 percent).

The manner in which HWHs provide these services to participants can also vary (Caputo 2004; McCarthy, McCarthy, and Leone 2001). *Supportive* programs are those that provide little or no services in-house and instead act as a broker, maintaining connections with treatment and services within the community and referring participants to those services. These HWH programs primarily provide shelter and food, and employ few staff (Latessa and Smith 2015). On the other hand, HWH programs that *intervene* in the reintegration of participants deliver a number of services in-house and employ a specialized staff in order to do so. For instance, the Kalamazoo Probation Enhancement Program (KPEP) employs trained counselors to provide cognitive behavioral treatment for sex offenders following their release from prison, but prior to the beginning of their parole supervision in the community. Rather than strictly aligning with one mode of service provision over another, most HWH programs fall between the supportive and intervening models, providing some services in-house and making referrals to others (Hamilton and Campbell 2014). Despite the worthy goals of improving the capacity of offenders to reintegrate to the community, an empirical question remains as to how effective they are in accomplishing these goals. The following sections will review the research concerning the effectiveness of HWH programs in reducing recidivism, and the conditions in which HWHs are the most effective towards this goal.

Correctional Effectiveness

Although HWH programs can theoretically impact a number of different outcomes, such as reducing negative incarceration effects or reducing criminal justice system operating costs (Latessa and Allen 1982), recidivism remains the bottom line in determining whether a given program is effective (Grommon and Rydberg 2016). Indeed, Latessa (2012: 91) states:

> When asked whether a correctional program "works," most do not care whether the offenders or staff like the program, if participants feel better about themselves, or even if they completed the program. They want to know whether the program helped change their behavior and whether those who completed are less likely to recidivate than those that did not complete or go to the program.

In this regard, there have been numerous evaluations of the impact of participation in HWH programs on recidivism in a variety of contexts. However, the diversity of HWH programs, including the types of offenders served and services provided, make the generalization of findings from the evaluation of any given program difficult. One of the primary issues for impact evaluations to consider is what offenders should serve as a control group for comparison to the HWH participants. For instance, Hartmann, Friday, and Minor (1994) observed lower recidivism rates for individuals who completed probation-focused HWH programming at KPEP relative to those who did not successfully complete the programming. This should only be considered weak evidence of a beneficial effect for HWHs, given that those offenders who do not complete the programming may differ from those who do in a number of meaningful ways, and thus provide only a weak counterfactual (i.e., what the outcome *would* have been for the program completers had they not finished the KPEP program).

Indeed, early meta-analyses systematically examining outcomes from dozens of parole-focused HWH evaluations suggested that there was little evidence indicative of HWHs systematically reducing recidivism (Latessa and Allen 1982; Seiter, Carlson, Bowman, Grandfield, and Beran 1977). A meta-analysis by Seiter and colleagues (1977) observed a nearly equal number of studies suggesting that HWHs improve recidivism outcomes for parolees as those suggesting that they either have no effect or a criminogenic effect. A follow-up by Latessa and Allen (1982) produced similar conclusions, but highlighted the lack of appropriate counterfactuals in the inability of research to draw strong conclusions about HWH effects (Hamilton and Campbell 2014).

More recently, high-quality research focused on New Jersey HWH programs has produced promising results regarding effectiveness in reducing recidivism. Ostermann (2009) employed a quasi-experimental design to compare multiple recidivism outcomes (rearrest, reconviction, reincarceration) across four groups of offenders following their release from prison—parolees who participated in a HWH program, parolees who participated in a day reporting center program, offenders on parole who did not participate in either program, and offenders who maxed out of their sentence and were released with no supervision. He observed that while offenders subject to parole and day reporting centers were less likely to experience reconviction and reincarceration, only HWH parolees were less likely to experience all recidivism outcomes (including rearrest). Similarly, Hamilton and Campbell (2014) evaluated the impact of 18 privately owned New Jersey HWHs on recidivism by comparing participants to a matched sample of parolees who were released directly to the community. The authors found that HWH participants were significantly less likely than eligible controls to be returned to prison on a technical violation (a difference of about 8 percentage points after a 3-year follow-up), but were not significantly less likely to experience rearrests, reconvictions, and/or reincarcerations. In all, these studies suggest some reason for optimism—in at least some circumstances, HWHs can significantly reduce some indicators of recidivism in some settings.

The question of the circumstances under which HWHs are most effective was considered by Lowenkamp and Latessa's (2002, 2005) systematic review of Ohio HWH programs. Using a quasi-experimental design, Lowenkamp and Latessa (2002) compared recidivism outcomes for ~3,700 HWH participants with ~3,000 comparison offenders. Overall, they observed small reductions in recidivism (~3 percentage points) for HWH offenders relative to comparisons for reincarcerations on technical violations and new offenses. Across 19 individual HWH programs, 14 boasted lower recidivism rates relative to controls, ranging from 2 to 21 percentage points. However, when the results were disaggregated by the recidivism risk level of the sample, the results were more dramatic. Lowenkamp and Latessa (2002) found consistently large recidivism reductions for offenders at the highest risk of recidivism, with 14 of 19 programs delivering recidivism reductions for high-risk offenders. Conversely, low-risk offenders participating in HWHs had consistently higher recidivism rates than low-risk comparison offenders, with controls outperforming HWH participants in 12 of 19 sites. That is, assigning low-risk offenders to HWHs appeared to consistently make them *worse*.

This patterning of findings across HWHs can be explained by the *risk principle* of correctional effectiveness (Andrews et al. 1990). The correctional programs that consistently result in the largest reduction in recidivism will be those that reserve the most intense treatment and services for those offenders at the highest risk of recidivism. Taking the opposite approach—providing intense treatment to low-risk offenders or failing to distinguish levels of intervention between recidivism risk levels—will tend to result in a net increase in recidivism. Intense services tend to produce the strongest effects with high-risk offenders because they have the most to gain from participation in treatment, while low-risk offenders tend to become worse since relegation to residential treatment (such as a HWH) can disrupt pro-social ties or other factors that contribute to their low risk of recidivism (Andrews and Bonta 1998). As such, although evaluations have found modest recidivism reductions for HWHs on aggregate offender populations, they will be most effective when focusing on offenders at the highest risk of recidivism, with recidivism risk classifications determined by validated, actuarial assessments (Andrews and Bonta 1995).

Collateral Consequences

Despite goals that are largely consistent with the ideal of rehabilitating offenders and facilitating community reintegration, as with any correctional intervention, the best intentions can produce unintended consequences. First, for the offenders themselves, even though HWHs attempt to act as an alternative to incarceration, they may operate in a fashion that actually *increases* the likelihood of a return to prison. Hamilton and Campbell (2013) observed that participation in HWH programs creates unique opportunities for prison returns based on increased levels of surveillance. For instance, assignment to a HWH creates a wide variety of new supervision conditions with which parolees must comply, including abiding by curfew, submitting to substance use tests, or attending various treatments—each of which has the potential to return a parolee to prison if they fail to comply. Indeed,

Rydberg and Grommon (2016) observed that for a cohort of parolees over a period of two years, chronic parole violators were those who were assigned to and repeatedly walked out of HWH-based substance use treatment. In this respect, HWHs may introduce new ways for reentry to fail, when it would not have otherwise. As this is especially a concern with lower-risk offenders, assigning offenders to HWHs on the basis of recidivism risk will lower the likelihood of this consequence being realized.

Second, qualitative research has examined the experiences of individual offenders within HWHs, observing that these experiences are not always aligned with the rehabilitative ideal. Kras and colleagues (2016) interviewed registered sex offenders staying at a mandatory, post-release transitional housing facility in Missouri, observing that offenders experienced the HWH as an extension of the prison. Depending on the level of security at the facility (e.g., guards, surveillance, walls), extended stays at HWH facilities serve to replicate the incarceration experience. To this extent, HWHs may fall short of achieving the "halfway out" objective, instead serving as an extension of prison and a disruption to the reentry process (Kras et al. 2016; Rydberg 2014).

House Arrest

The confinement of offenders within their own residences, or house arrest, has been utilized as a flexible alternative to incarceration since the early 1970s, but has grown increasingly prevalent since the mid 1980s (Renzema 1992). The flexibility and popularity of house arrest is an extension of how it can be applied as an intermediate sanction at various points of criminal justice system processing (Caputo 2004). That is, house arrest can be used as a *front-end diversion program*, allowing offenders to serve periods of pre-trial supervision in the community, rather than in jail custody. It can also be utilized as *a back-end diversion program* following sentencing, in which offenders serve periods of home confinement as a dedicated sanction, or following their early release from prison (Payne and Gainey 2004). Additionally, house arrest can be utilized to *enhance* existing supervision regimes (e.g., as a condition of probation or parole), increasing the intensity of community supervision in lieu of a custodial sanction.

House arrest is utilized as an intermediate sanction towards several goals. On a practical basis, house arrest is used to restrict the activities of offenders by requiring them to be at their place of residence during specified blocks of time (e.g., a curfew from 6pm to 9am), or away from their residence at other points during the day (e.g., when they should be at work or attending treatment) (Austin, Johnson, and Weitzer 2005). Implementing these restrictions ideally provides benefits for criminal justice system processing and for the offender themselves. Concerning criminal justice system processing, a primary driver of the rapid spread of house arrest in the United States was the explosive growth of the incarceration rate since the onset of the crime control era (Garland 2001). As correctional facilities became increasingly overcrowded, "desperate" criminal justice officials turned to house arrest as a mechanism to alleviate pressure caused by the mushrooming correctional population (Maxfield and Baumer 1990: 521). By avoiding incarceration in prison or jail entirely, or by providing a means by which to release offenders from custody early, confining offenders within their own homes avoids contributing to the institutional population and is a significantly less costly alternative to incarceration (Padgett, Bales, and Blomberg 2006).

Concerning benefits to the offender, house arrest avoids or reduces the negative social consequences associated with incarceration, such as prolonged exposure to deleterious prison conditions (Massoglia 2008) or the loss of employment and deprivation of prosocial community contacts (Gendreau, Cullen, and Goggin 1999; Petersilia 2009). Simultaneously, by allowing the offender to be supervised in the community, house arrest realizes some of the primary benefits of community-based sanctions, enabling the offender to continue working or searching for employment, and continue caring for his or her family (Andersen and Andersen 2014).

When house arrest was initially implemented as an intermediate sanction, frequent home or telephone contacts between the offender and their supervising agent were necessary in order to determine whether the offender was at home for the prescribed period of confinement (Gowen 2000). The practicality of enforcing house arrest was dramatically improved by the advent and proliferation of electronic monitoring technology since the late 1980s (Maxfield and Baumer 1990). Indeed, the use of electronic monitoring in home detention applications grew so rapidly that after they were first utilized for criminal justice purposes in Florida in 1985 (Beck, Klein-Saffran, and Wooten 1990), as many as 21 states were supervising offenders using some form of electronic monitoring by 1987 (Gable and Gable 2005). More recently, growth has been substantial, with the number of active electronic monitoring devices growing from 75,000 to over 200,000 between 1999 and 2009 (DeMichele and Payne 2009).

There are two primary forms of electronic monitoring for the purposes of enforcing house arrest. Radio frequency (RF) tethers are typically tamper-proof devices worn on the ankle and communicate with a transmitter located at the offender's place of residence. This technology enables the enforcement of house arrest because the RF device is capable of telling supervision agents when the offender is within a particular distance from the transmitter. However, RF devices can only relay information about whether the offender is close enough to the transmitter, and does not include the capacity to track offender movements in the community (Button, DeMichele, and Payne 2009). In order to gain this functionality, global positioning system (GPS) monitoring combines with RF tethering to track the movements of offenders in three dimensional space utilizing satellite monitoring (Brown, McCabe, and Wellford 2007). This review will focus on the use of RF tethering, as this is the most common technology for enforcing house arrest sanctions (Padgett et al. 2006). The following sections will consider the research examining the effectiveness of electronically monitored house arrest (EMHA) for community corrections, and the potential unintended consequences of its use.

Correctional Effectiveness

As with HWH programs, the benchmark for determining whether EMHA is "effective" is if it reduces recidivism, compared to the available alternatives (Grommon and Rydberg 2016). Evaluations of the effectiveness of EMHA have been unable to keep pace with its rapid proliferation through U.S. and international criminal justice systems (Gainey, Payne, and O'Toole 2000; Padgett et al. 2006). In particular, reviews of the research on the effectiveness of EMHA have found very few trials in which offenders are randomly assigned to EMHA conditions (Renzema and Mayo-Wilson 2005), allowing the possibility that any observed effects are an artifact of pre-existing differences between the EMHA and comparison groups. Of those reviews that have been conducted, the results have not been overly promising.

For instance, a review of six studies covering 1,414 offenders by Gendreau and colleagues (2000) found that those assigned to EMHA demonstrated similar recidivism rates to offenders assigned to traditional probation supervision. A meta-analysis by Renzema and Mayo-Wilson (2005) that focused on moderate- to high-risk adult offenders identified only three studies published between 1986 and 2002 that were of sufficient quality for valid conclusions to be drawn. Taken individually, none of the three studies suggested a systemic difference in recidivism between the EMHA groups and various comparisons, leading Renzema and

Mayo-Wilson (2005: 230) to describe the results as "grim," suggesting "no overall impact on recidivism."

More recent quasi-experimental research has provided somewhat more promising evidence in a variety of contexts. Examining recidivism outcomes for over 75,000 Florida probationers placed on house arrest, Padgett and colleagues (2006) found that adding electronic monitoring (either RF or GPS) resulted in a significant decrease in technical violations or returns to prison. Marklund and Holmberg (2009) compared Swedish offenders conditionally released under a back-end diversion EMHA program to a matched comparison who served their entire sentence. Their results suggested a 12 percentage point decrease in reconvictions for the EMHA group, and suggest the most positive effects for older offenders with less extensive criminal histories. A randomized experiment in Switzerland (Killias, Gillieron, Kissling, and Villettaz 2010) compared offenders assigned to EMHA to those serving community service sanctions. The study suggested that the EMHA offenders demonstrated lower reconviction rates than the community service comparison, but the differences were not statistically significant ($p = 0.08$).

To date, the empirical literature has produced little systematic evidence for EMHA generating a noticeable reduction in recidivism. Research on the most effective means of reducing recidivism can shed some light on these unimpressive findings. First, EMHA is most often utilized with offenders at a low risk of recidivism (Renzema and Mayo-Wilson 2005). This makes sense, where in practice both front-end and back-end diversion programs are likely to be reserved for those who pose relatively less risk to public safety, while those at higher risk tend to receive custodial sanctions. However, this arrangement is in opposition to the *risk principle*, in which the most intense services and supervision should be reserved for the offenders at the highest risk of recidivism (Andrews et al. 1990). Previous research has found that programs that focus on high-risk offenders tend to produce larger reductions in recidivism than those that do not (Lowenkamp, Latessa, and Holsinger 2006). One reason for this effect is that high-risk offenders tend to have more to gain from the application of programming, while low-risk offenders do not (i.e., there is a reason they are at a low risk of recidivism!) (Latessa, Listwan, and Koetzel 2013). Indeed, in Germany Schwedler and Woessner (2017) found little differences in psychological and psychosocial functioning between offenders randomly assigned to EMHA or a custodial sanction because those eligible for EMHA already had good psychological characteristics to begin with (i.e., there was little potential for improvement). As such, Schwedler and Woessner (2017) suggest that if EMHA is to produce rehabilitative outcomes, a good starting point is to actually target offenders who are in need of rehabilitation.

Second, evaluations of EMHA have produced unimpressive results because there is little direct connection between such programming and the risk factors that are correlated with recidivism, giving little reason to expect such programs to produce a reduction in recidivism. Indeed, the *needs principle* suggests that the most effective correctional programs will directly address multiple risk factors correlated with recidivism, and the *responsivity* principle suggests that cognitive behavioral programming is the most effective means to change these risk factors (Smith, Gendreau and Swartz 2009). On its own, house arrest only marginally adheres to these principles. For instance, Hucklesby (2008) noted that EMHA reduces an offender's anti-social capital by limiting contact with situations, persons, and places conducive to reoffending. However, such opportunity restriction only acts as incapacitation unless the EMHA is paired with treatments designed to change the offender's thinking and behavior. To this extent, little recidivism reduction should be expected unless the EMHA programming is paired with treatments or services specifically designed to target criminogenic needs (Latessa and Lowenkamp 2006; Renzema and Mayo-Wilson 2005). In other words, practitioners should expect little change in offender behavior on the average unless specific effort is taken to address the underlying correlates of recidivism risk, and on its own EMHA cannot deliver in this respect.

Collateral Consequences

Outside of reducing recidivism, EMHA schemes are applied to achieve a variety of other goals, with varying levels of success. As an alternative to incarceration, EMHA is utilized to reduce financial costs to the criminal justice system, with research suggesting that the per-diem costs of house arrest using RF tethering being much lower than that of prison (Padgett et al. 2006). Further, recent research in Denmark observed that younger offenders (under 25 years old) sentenced to EMHA had lower levels of social welfare dependence than those serving custodial sanctions (Andersen and Andersen 2014), suggesting that EMHA helps to avoid some of the negative consequences of incarceration.

As with any correctional intervention, the best intentions can produce unintended consequences. Even since the early days of its implementation, criminologists have examined the potential for EMHA to produce collateral consequences for the offenders assigned to it. One of these consequences is referred to as "net-widening," in which programs meant to divert offenders from deep criminal justice system processing instead wind up *increasing* the number of offenders under criminal justice system supervision (Mainprize 1992). In the case of EMHA, net-widening occurs when offenders are sentenced to EMHA when they instead would likely have received a sentence with less supervision (e.g., fines) or no other sentence at all (DeMichele and Payne 2009). This increase in the number of offenders within the criminal justice system is linked to an increase in the punitiveness of the system (Di Tella and Schargrodsky 2013).

Researchers have drawn mixed conclusions about the relationship between EMHA and net-widening. For example, Bonta, Wallace-Capretta, and Rooney (2000) compared several types of EM community programs with inmates and probationers and found that EM contributes minimally to the reduction of recidivism and instead supplements net-widening. However, another study identified a sample in which offenders on EMHA, when compared to those who are not, had more serious offenses, thus contradicting the effect of net-widening in the justice system (Padgett et al. 2006). Additionally, the effects of EM on net-widening may vary according to offender characteristics (e.g., by racial group) and across communities (e.g., due to local decision making) (Payne, May, and Wood 2014).

Despite these mixed results, the continual development of and ease of access to technology is likely to drive the growing usage of EMHA (DeMichele and Payne 2009). Specifically, the motivation and criteria for applying EMHA as a sanction for offenders may influence the usage of EMHA. For example, private and for-profit companies may benefit from an increased number of offenders on EM. These companies may persuade the criminal justice system and policymakers that the application of EM devices is beneficial, allowing the continued monitoring of all types of offenders, such as a lifelong monitoring of sex offenders (Payne et al. 2014). Thus, the "crime control industry" may influence the continued growth of offenders on EMHA and net-widening (Jones 2014: 484). The utilization of this technology must be carefully considered and applied to strengthen criminal justice supervision, and not applied because EMHA is "trendy" (DeMichele and Payne 2009: 208).

Additionally, research has considered the extent to which EMHA itself can act as a potentially noxious intervention. In particular, Payne and Gainey (1998, 2000, 2004) have examined offenders' perceptions of the experience of EMHA using RF tethers. This research has observed that even though offenders view EMHA as less punitive than a custodial sanction, living with it on a day-to-day basis produces social isolation experiences similar to that of imprisonment. For instance, Payne and Gainey (1998, 2004) found that a sample of electronically monitored offenders were unprepared for the extent to which the supervision would restrict autonomy and control their day-to-day activities. Similarly, Martin, Hanrahan, and Bowers (2009) note that offenders experience EMHA as a punitive sanction to the extent that it restricts activities at home and in the community. This is an important consideration in terms of the potential for recidivism reduction. Qualitative research by Deuchar (2012) in Scotland observed that even though youth gang members subject to EMHA experienced reduced contacts with sources of anti-social capital, the social isolation experienced by the sample may ultimately produce a criminogenic strain effect. This research reinforces the need to pair EMHA interventions with treatment and services designed to build pro-social capital and address anti-social thinking and behavior.

Conclusion

In the wake of mass incarceration brought about by the crime control era of correctional philosophy, community corrections practice has found renewed interest in implementing interventions that reduce the burden on institutional corrections. Simultaneously, corrections research in the previous decades has devoted significant effort to understanding the characteristics of correctional interventions that will be the most effective in reducing recidivism. The research reviewed in this chapter suggests that correctional programs designed to achieve the former (reducing burden on prisons), do not necessarily achieve the latter (reducing recidivism). This is especially important to consider in light of research that suggests that even the best intended interventions can have collateral consequences for offenders. Ultimately, we suggest that the implementation of HWHs and EMHA schemes strongly consider adherences to the principles of effective correctional interventions—or the conditions under which these programs will produce the most beneficial results for offenders, public safety, and the criminal justice system. Finally, there is a continuing need for research utilizing strong counterfactuals to better understand the impact of these programs on recidivism and collateral consequences. The use of randomized control trials (RCTs) would be especially helpful in producing valid conclusions about the characteristics of programs that are the most effective in reducing recidivism.

References

Andersen, Lars H., and Signe H. Andersen. 2014. "Effect of Electronic Monitoring on Social Welfare Dependence." *Criminology & Public Policy* 13: 349–379.

Andrews, Donald A., and James Bonta. 1995. *Level of Service Inventory-Revised*. Toronto: Multihealth Systems.

Andrews, Donald A., and James Bonta. 1998. *The Psychology of Criminal Conduct*. Cincinnati, OH: Anderson Publishing.

Andrews, Donald A., Ivan Zinger, Robert D. Hoge, James Bonta, Paul Gendreau, and Francis T. Cullen. 1990. "Does Correctional Treatment Work? A Clinically Relevant and Psychologically Informed Meta-analysis." *Criminology* 28: 369–404.

Austin, James F., Kelly D. Johnson, and Ronald J. Weitzer. 2005. *Alternatives to the Secure Detention and Confinement of Juvenile Offenders*. Washington, DC: U.S. Department of Justice.

Beck, James L., Jody Klein-Saffran, and Harold B. Wooten. 1990. "Home Confinement and the Use of Electronic Monitoring with Federal Parolees." *Federal Probation* 54: 22–33.

Bonta, James, Suzanne Wallace-Capretta, and Jennifer Rooney. 2000. "Can Electronic Monitoring Make a Difference? An Evaluation of Three Canadian Programs." *Crime & Delinquency* 46: 61–75.

Brown, Tracy M.L., Steven A. McCabe, and Charles F. Wellford. 2007. *Global Positioning System (GPS) Technology for Community Supervision: Lessons Learned*. Falls Church, VA: Noblis.

Button, Deeanna M., Matthew DeMichele, and Brian K. Payne. 2009. "Using Electronic Monitoring to Supervise Sex Offenders: Legislative Patterns and Implications for Community Corrections Officers." *Criminal Justice Policy Review* 20: 414–436.

Cahalan, Margaret W., and Lee A. Parsons. 1986. *Historical Corrections Statistics in the United States, 1850–1984*. Washington DC: U.S. Department of Justice, Office of Justice Programs, Bureau of Justice Statistics.

Caputo, Gail A. 2004. *Intermediate Sanctions in Corrections*. Denton, TX: University of North Texas Press.

Carson, E. Ann. 2015. *Prisoners in 2014*. Washington DC: U.S. Department of Justice, Office of Justice Programs, Bureau of Justice Statistics.

Cohen, J. 1973. *A Study of the Community-based Correctional Needs in Massachusetts*. Boston, MA: Massachusetts Department of Corrections.

DeMichele, Matthew, and Brian K. Payne. 2009. *Offender Supervision with Electronic Technology: A User's Guide*, 2nd ed. Washington, DC: U.S. Department of Justice, Bureau of Justice Assistance.

Deuchar, Ross. 2012. "The Impact of Curfews and Electronic Monitoring on the Social Strains, Support and Capital Experienced by Youth Gang Members and Offenders in the West of Scotland." *Criminology and Criminal Justice* 12: 113–128.

Di Tella, Rafael, and Ernesto Schargrodsky. 2013. "Criminal Recidivism after Prison and Electronic Monitoring." *Journal of Political Economy* 121: 28–73.

Gable, Ralph K., and Robert S. Gable. 2005. "Electronic Monitoring: Positive Intervention Strategies." *Federal Probation* 69: 21–25.

Gainey, Randy R., Brian K. Payne, and Mike O'Toole. 2000. "The Relationships between Time in Jail, Time on Electronic Monitoring, and Recidivism: An Event History Analysis of a Jail-based Program." *Justice Quarterly* 17: 733–752.

Garland, David. 2001. *The Culture of Control: Crime and Social Order in Contemporary Society*. Oxford, UK: Oxford University Press.

Gendreau, Paul L., Francis T. Cullen, and Claire Goggin. 1999. *The Effects of Prison Sentences on Recidivism*. Ottawa, ON: Solicitor General Canada.

Gendreau, Paul L., Claire Goggin, Francis T. Cullen, and Donald A. Andrews. 2000. "The Effects of Community Sanctions and Incarceration on Recidivism." *Forum on Corrections Research* 12: 10–13.

Gowen, Darren. 2000. "Overview of the Federal Home Confinement Program 1988–1996." *Federal Probation* 64: 11–18.

Grommon, Eric, and Jason Rydberg. 2016. "Correctional interventions and outcomes." Pp. 351–376 in *Handbook of Measurement Issues in Criminology and Criminal Justice*, edited by Beth M. Huebner, and Timothy Bynum. Hoboken, NJ: John Wiley.

Hamilton, Zachary K., and Christopher M. Campbell. 2013. "A Dark Figure of Corrections: Failure by Way of Participation." *Criminal Justice and Behavior* 40: 180–202.

Hamilton, Zachary K., and Christopher M. Campbell. 2014. "Uncommonly Observed: The Impact of New Jersey's Halfway House System." *Criminal Justice and Behavior* 41: 1354–1375.

Hartman, David J., Paul C. Friday, and Kevin I. Minor. 1994. "Residential Probation: A Seven-year Follow-up Study of Halfway House Discharges." *Journal of Criminal Justice* 22: 503–515.

Hucklesby, Anthea. 2008. "Vehicles of Desistance? The Impact of Electronically Monitored Curfew Orders." *Criminology and Criminal Justice* 8: 51–71.

Jones, Richard. 2014. "The Electronic Monitoring of Offenders: Penal Moderation or Penal Excess?" *Crime, Law and Social Change* 62: 475–488.

Killias, Martin, Gwladys Gilleron, Izumi Kissling, and Patrice Villettaz. 2010. "Community Service versus Electronic Monitoring—What Works Better? Results of a Randomized Trial." *British Journal of Criminology* 50: 1155–1170.

Kras, Kimberly R., Breanne Pleggenkuhle, and Beth M. Huebner. 2016. "A New Way of Doing Time on the Outside: Sex Offenders' Pathways in and out of a Transitional Housing Facility." *International Journal of Offender Therapy and Comparative Criminology* 60: 512–534.

Latessa, Edward J. 2012. "Why Works is Important, and How to Improve the Effectiveness of Correctional Reentry Programs that Target Employment." *Criminology & Public Policy* 11: 87–91.

Latessa, Edward J., and Harry E. Allen. 1982. "Halfway Houses and Parole: A National Assessment." *Journal of Criminal Justice* 10: 153–163.

Latessa, Edward J., Shelley J. Listwan, and Deborah Koetzle. 2013. *What Works (and doesn't) in Reducing Recidivism*. Boston, MA: Routledge.

Latessa, Edward. J., and Christopher Lowenkamp. 2006. "What Works in Reducing Recidivism." *University of St. Thomas Law Journal* 3: 521–535.

Latessa, Edward J., and Paula Smith. 2015. *Corrections in the Community*, 6th ed. New York, NY: Routledge.

Listwan, Shelley J., Christopher J. Sullivan, Robert Agnew, Francis T. Cullen, and Mark Colvin. 2013. "The Pains of Imprisonment Revisited: The Impact of Strain on Inmate Recidivism." *Justice Quarterly* 30: 144–168.

Lowenkamp, Christopher T., and Edward J. Latessa. 2002. *Evaluation of Ohio's Community Based Correctional Facilities and Halfway House Programs: Final report*. Cincinnati, OH: University of Cincinnati.

Lowenkamp, Christopher T., and Edward J. Latessa. 2005. "Increasing the Effectiveness of Correctional Programming through the Risk Principle: Identifying Offenders for Residential Placement." *Criminology & Public Policy* 4: 263–290.

Lowenkamp, Christopher T., Edward J. Latessa, and Alexander M. Holsinger. 2006. "The Risk Principle in Action: What Have We Learned from 13,676 Offenders and 97 Correctional Programs?" *Crime & Delinquency* 52: 77–93.

Mainprize, Stephen. 1992. "Electronic Monitoring in Corrections: Assessing Cost Effectiveness and the Potential for Widening the Net of Social Control." *Canadian Journal of Criminology* 34: 161–180.

Marklund, Fredrik, and Stina Holmberg. 2009. "Effects of Early Release from Prison Using Electronic Tagging in Sweden." *Journal of Experimental Criminology* 5: 41–61.

Martin, Jamie S., Kate Hanrahan, and James H. Bowers Jr. 2009. "Offenders' Perceptions of House Arrest and Electronic Monitoring." *Journal of Offender Rehabilitation* 48: 547–570.

Massoglia, Michael. 2008. "Incarceration as Exposure: The Prison, Infectious Disease, and Other Stress-related Illnesses." *Journal of Health and Social Behavior* 49: 56–71.

Maxfield, Michael G., and Terry L. Baumer. 1990. "Home Detention with Electronic Monitoring: Comparing Pretrial and Postconviction Programs." *Crime & Delinquency* 36: 521–536.

McCarthy, Belinda R., Bernard J, McCarthy Jr., and Matthew C. Leone. 2001. *Community-based Corrections*. Belmont, CA: Wadsworth Group.

Ogloff, James R.P. 2006. *Effective Reintegration through Halfway House Programs: The Important Influence of Service Location*. Victoria, Australia: Monash University Centre for Forensic Behavioral Science.

Ostermann, Michael. 2009. "An Analysis of New Jersey's Day Reporting Center and Halfway Back Programs: Embracing the Rehabilitative Ideal through Evidence Based Practices." *Journal of Offender Rehabilitation* 48: 139–153.

Padgett, Kathy G., William D. Bales, and Thomas G. Blomberg. 2006. "Under Surveillance: An Empirical Test of the Effectiveness and Consequences of Electronic Monitoring." *Criminology & Public Policy* 5: 61–91.

Payne, Brian K., and Randy R. Gainey. 1998. "A Qualitative Assessment of the Pains Experienced on Electronic Monitoring." *International Journal of Offender Therapy and Comparative Criminology* 49: 49–63.

Payne, Brian K., and Randy R. Gainey. 2000. "Electronic Monitoring: Philosophical, Systemic, and Political Problems." *Journal of Offender Rehabilitation* 31: 93–112.

Payne, Brian K., and Randy R. Gainey. 2004. "The Electronic Monitoring of Offenders Released from Jail or Prison: Safety, Control, and Comparisons to the Incarceration Experience." *The Prison Journal* 84: 413–435.

Payne, Brian K., David C. May, and Peter B. Wood. 2014. "The 'Pains' of Electronic Monitoring: A Slap on the Wrist or Just as Bad as Prison?" *Criminal Justice Studies* 27: 133–148.

Petersilia, Joan. 2009. *When Prisoners Come Home: Parole and Prisoner Reentry*. New York: Oxford University Press.

Renzema, Marc. 1992. "Home Confinement Programs: Development, Implementation, and Impact." Pp. 41–53 in *Smart Sentencing: The Emergence of Intermediate Sanctions*, edited by J.M. Byrne, A.J. Lurigio, and J. Petersilia. Newbury Park, CA: Sage Publications.

Renzema, Marc, and Evan Mayo-Wilson. 2005. "Can Electronic Monitoring Reduce Crime for Moderate to High-risk Offenders?" *Journal of Experimental Criminology* 1: 215–237.

Rydberg, Jason. 2014. *Sex Offender Reentry: The Negotiation of Treatment and GPS Monitoring Following Release from Prison*. East Lansing, MI: Michigan State University.

Rydberg, Jason, and Eric Grommon. 2016. "A Multi-method Examination of the Dynamics of Recidivism during Reentry." *Corrections: Policy, Practice, and Research* 1: 40–60.

Schwedler, Andreas, and Gunda Woessner. 2017. "Identifying the Rehabilitative Potential of Electronically Monitored Release Preparation: A Randomized Controlled Study in Germany." *International Journal of Offender Therapy and Comparative Criminology* 61(8): 839–856.

Seiter, Richard P., Eric W. Carlson, Helen H. Bowman, James J. Grandfield, and Nancy J. Beran 1977. *Halfway Houses*. Washington, DC: U.S. Department of Justice.

Smith, Paula, Paul Gendreau, and Kristin Swartz. 2009. "Validating the Principles of Effective Intervention: A Systematic Review of the Contribution of Meta-analysis in the Field of Corrections." *Victims & Offenders* 4: 148–169.

Thalheimer, Donald J. 1975. *Halfway Houses*. Washington, DC: Law Enforcement Assistance Administration, National Institute of Law Enforcement and Criminal Justice.

19 Day Reporting Centers and Work Release Programs

Lee Michael Johnson

Day Reporting Centers

Overview

Day reporting is a community-based (non-residential) sanction that combines intensive rehabilitation programming with punishment and control through a structured environment and increased supervision. It also offers a cost-efficient alternative to incarceration. Participants spend their evenings at home and are allowed, sometimes required, to do other essential activities such as work and attend school. Day reporting is considered to be an "intermediate sanction," as it is less restrictive than prison or jail but more restrictive than traditional probation (Marciniak 2000; Martin, Lurigio, and Olson 2003; Roy and Grimes 2002).

Day reporting services are delivered at a center—a facility to which participants must report frequently and regularly (e.g. daily) as a condition of probation, parole, or release. Since day reporting involves frequent attendance and other limitations of freedom, it potentially serves the purposes of punishment and public safety, while avoiding much of the damaging effects of imprisonment upon a person's socialization. Day reporting is similar to, and may even be used in tandem with, other intermediate sanctions such as intensive supervision probation (ISP), house arrest, and electronic monitoring. However, what sets the *day reporting center* (DRC) apart is its emphasis on rehabilitative services. These services include a variety of counseling, education, and training activities. Services may be delivered on site or by agencies outside of the center. DRCs vary widely in participant eligibility and functioning, but ideally, services are tailored to the individual offender; center staff conduct assessments to determine which programs and services each individual needs (Marciniak 2000).

DRC is a "generic term." Specific programs may also be called "day treatment centers, day incarceration centers, restorative justice centers, community resource centers, and the like" (Craddock 2004: 71). Operated by either public (e.g. state or county) or private agencies, DRCs are intended to serve offenders who are at high risk of reoffending but may benefit from not being incarcerated—more often those with substance abuse issues. These offenders are assessed to have a strong need for treatment services that are more available in a highly structured community context, as compared to other environments such as standard probation or jail. In addition to substance abuse, DRCs may offer other types of individual and group counseling including family interventions. They may also offer a variety of educational/vocational programs and other services including life skills (e.g. anger and stress management), health skills (e.g. HIV education and mental health services), cultural awareness and diversity training, and courses on the harms of crime (Roy and Grimes 2002).

DRCs are generally reserved for non-violent offenders. They may focus on populations such as probation violators, parolees and others who are re-entering, or pre-trial defendants.

A DRC can be used as a sentencing alternative to incarceration or to re-integrate ex-prisoners into the community. The types of services offered by DRCs are helpful in facilitating re-entry, and compared to halfway houses (which are more residential), they can be more cost-effective at monitoring persons in need of less supervision (Boyle, Ragusa-Salerno, Lanterman, and Marcus 2013). DRC programs range in length from about three to 12 months. Longer ones are usually divided into phases that gradually decrease supervision levels, which likely means that participants report to the center less often. DRCs' program rules also vary, but often participants must provide daily itineraries, adhere to curfews, submit to random drug tests, attend school or work, participate in treatment activities, and perform community service and/or pay restitution. Participants in longer term programs are especially susceptible to revocation for violating these rules (Martin et al. 2003; Roy and Grimes 2002).

DRCs were developed in Great Britain beginning in the early 1970s, as a way to manage probationers and meet the needs of nonviolent chronic offenders with substance abuse problems. By the late 1980s, DRCs had become well established in Great Britain and were beginning to be used in the United States. Early advocates sought a sanction that would maintain offenders' social ties that discourage reoffending, primarily those with family members and employers. Incarceration threatens to sever these kinds of ties. In the U.S., DRCs may have appeared more as a solution to jail and prison overcrowding (Marciniak 2000; Martin et al. 2003). Cost-savings may also have been a major motive, as DRC use reduces expenses from incarceration, and programs may charge participants fees to offset some operational costs. The number of DRCs grew steadily in the U.S. during the 1990s, although critics charged that their popularity was not grounded enough in evaluative research (Roy and Grimes 2002).

Compared to standard probation, the increased strictness and surveillance by DRCs (and other intermediate sanctions such as ISP) may have an "ironic effect": they seem more likely to detect non-compliance and revoke probation, sending more offenders to jail or prison. It is hoped that the intensive treatment offered by DRCs will overshadow this risk. Further, perhaps increased interaction may lead to closer bonds between participants and their probation officers and center staff, and these bonds motivate participants to do well in their programs and refrain from offending. Still, these advantages may do no more than counter-balance increased surveillance and control. If so, it is difficult to justify the use of DRCs in addition to, or instead of, other intermediate sanctions such as ISP (Marciniak 2000).

It is also questionable whether cost-effectiveness validates DRCs. First, the highest potential for cost savings lies in the effectiveness of rehabilitation. If DRCs are better at making offenders desist, then much money would be saved by avoiding harm to victims and deeper involvement with the justice system. DRCs are typically cheaper to operate than jails and prisons, but these cost savings will only be momentary if participants reoffend and continue system involvement. Thus it must be shown that DRCs significantly reduce recidivism. Examining one DRC, Roy and Grimes (2002) found that participants placed in lieu of jail were less likely than others to successfully complete the program. Another issue is more philosophical. DRCs have punitive aspects but are typically less punitive than incarceration. One may question whether cost-savings outweigh the consideration that DRCs may not be "just punishment" for more serious offenders (Roy and Grimes 2002). It is important, then, to examine research on the effectiveness of DRCs.

Research

The Hampden County, Massachusetts Sheriff's Department created the first DRC in the U.S. in 1986, which served both sentenced offenders and pre-trial detainees. The program was largely a success, boasting a 78 percent completion rate from 1986 to 1996, one-year recidivism rates much lower compared to research on other offenders in the county (e.g. 22 percent vs. 65–70 percent), and cost-savings estimated to be as much as 75 percent of traditional incarceration (Boyd 1998). However, research conducted since this time tends to offer more tentative support.

Generally, DRC *completion* rates are rather low (Craddock 2009). Rates can be high for short programs (e.g. about 80 percent for 3–4 months) and very low for long programs (e.g. less than 20 percent for one year) (Roy and Grimes 2002). Because DRCs have more control and behavioral expectations, they may be more difficult to complete compared to other community sanctions. Roy and Barton (2006) found that in one county, the DRC program had a lower successful exit rate (51 percent) compared to the electronic monitoring program (76 percent).

Research has identified risk factors for DRC program incompletion. These include *unemployment* (Marciniak 1999), *lack of education* (Kim, Spohn, and Foxall 2007; Marciniak 1999), *severe substance abuse* (Craddock 2009; Roy, 2004; Roy and Barton 2006; Roy and Grimes 2002), *seriousness of offense* (e.g. felony) (Craddock 2009; Kim, Spohn, and Foxall 2007; Roy 2004; Roy and Barton 2006; Roy and Grimes 2002), *severe criminal history* (Roy 2004; Roy and Barton 2006; Roy and Grimes 2002), and *non-independent home living* (Marciniak 1999; Roy and Grimes 2002). Craddock (2009) also identified *younger age, ethnic minority status, having primarily criminal companions*, and *poor living situation* (unsafe, unstable housing/high-crime neighborhood).

This research generally shows that offenders who are the most difficult to treat—those with high criminogenic needs and longer histories of offending and system involvement—are less likely to complete DRC programs, which has implications for placement decisions. Caution must be taken when basing decisions upon program termination risk factors however. There is a dilemma in selecting participants most likely to finish while excluding those who are in the most need of the program's services (Marciniak 1999). These factors may suggest that programs be modified to better meet criminogenic needs, not that certain groups be excluded. Still, selectivity is central to the utility of DRCs. These programs are intended for offenders who appear to be on a *pathway toward* imprisonment (Marciniak 1999).

Thus, it is important to refine risk assessment and classification procedures for DRC programs. Kim, Joo, and McCarty (2008) evaluated one DRC procedure. An eight-category classification system based on type of offense, education, and completion of a relapse prevention course compared probabilities of program termination. Another eight-category classification system based on age, criminal history, and employment compared probabilities of recidivism. One interesting result is that undereducated felons had the highest overall termination rate (70 percent) but also showed the greatest reduction (51 percent) from an early to a late stage in the program, after completing a relapse prevention course. Such matrices can better pinpoint individuals' future chances of failing the program and/or reoffending and inform decisions concerning supervision, resource allocation, and release eligibility (Kim et al. 2008).

Caution must also be taken when basing the value of DRCs upon completion rates. First, a participant may benefit from the program even if one does not complete it. After a "relapse," one may be better prepared for success in a later program. Here it is important to note that DRCs target persons who may have strong addiction problems. Also, one cannot assume that successful program completion equals success in general. Many participants complete a program but still reoffend. In fact, short-term programs may not be potent enough to impact the lives of persistent offenders (Boyle et al. 2013), but they have higher completion rates (Roy and Grimes 2002). Long-term programs may be more effective at changing behavior (controlling for offender risk level). Thus, although they have lower completions rates, long-term DRC programs may be more effective at changing the behavior of those who do complete them. It may be more important, then, for research to determine whether DRCs reduce recidivism.

Most of the relatively few published *recidivism* studies of DRCs used rather small samples and simple designs. However, they usually control for demographic and other potentially confounding variables such as criminal history. To begin, three early studies evaluated Chicago's Cook County DRC, one of the largest programs in the U.S., for drug-using pretrial defendants (Lurigio and Olson 2000; Lurigio, Olson, and Sifferd 1999; McBride and VanderWaal 1997). Together these studies found that: about 4–5 percent of unsuccessful discharges were due to arrests for new crimes and about 1–2 percent of participants failed to appear in court, which are very low rates in comparison to past research on pretrial defendants; the percentage of those testing positive for drugs declined over time in the program; and generally, participants reported favorable perceptions of the program and DRC staff reported positive interactions with clients. These studies favorably evaluated the DRC but did not examine post-program recidivism.

However, Martin et al. (2003) evaluated the Chicago/Cook County DRC for longer-term recidivism. They found that participants who spent at least 30 days in the program were less likely to be rearrested or reincarcerated, and took longer to recidivate when they did, compared to participants released from the DRC for non-performance related reasons (e.g. made bail or charges dropped) prior to ten days in the program. However, the study suggests only that full DRC participation is better than discontinued DRC participation, as the program was not compared to other interventions.

Craddock and Graham (2001) studied probationers at two locations—one rural, one urban. They found that DRC program completers were less likely than non-completers to be rearrested within 12 months. Further, DRC completers had lower rearrest rates compared to other probationers, but the only significant difference appeared specifically at the rural location between completers and their risk-level equivalents within the comparison group. A subsequent analysis of DRC completers and high-risk/need other probationers showed that factors other than DRC program completion significantly predicted rearrest. Thus, the study may offer slight support for DRCs but also suggests that lower recidivism may not be due to qualities of DRC participation itself, although the authors warn of the possible impact of small sample size.

Ostermann (2009) studied four groups of re-enterers in New Jersey. Compared to "maxed-out" ex-prisoners (completed their sentences in prison and were not under community supervision), DRC participants were significantly less likely to be rearrested, reconvicted, and reincarcerated, but so too were participants in a halfway house program. Also, non-program parolees were significantly less likely to be rearrested (but not reconvicted or reincarcerated) compared to maxed-out ex-prisoners. These results suggest that community programs are needed for reenterers, but not necessarily that a DRC is their best option.

Champion, Harvey, and Schanz (2011) studied 36-month recidivism among convicted offenders in a Western Pennsylvania county. They found that those sentenced to a DRC had a significantly lower mean rearrest rate compared to a matched group of offenders incarcerated or under electronic monitoring or house arrest. This study directly suggests that DRCs are relatively effective at reducing reoffending, but the sample size was quite small (63 in each group).

Two studies failed to offer even tentative support for DRCs. Marciniak (2000) compared rearrest rates of persons in ISP-only to persons in ISP and a DRC in North Carolina and found no significant difference in rearrests. However, the study suggests only that adding day reporting to ISP, not the DRC itself, is ineffective. In a rare randomized-controlled trial experiment, Boyle et al. (2013) studied male parolees in New Jersey. They found that

DRC participants were less likely to be arrested for violating parole but more likely to be arrested for committing a new offense. There were no significant differences in the follow-up periods except that DRC participants were *more* likely to be reconvicted within six months of program completion. DRC participants also had a shorter median time to rearrest (by almost 100 days) but this difference was not statistically significant, which could have been due to small sample size. This study suggests that a DRC may *increase* recidivism. However, it did not compare DRC use among probationers or to incarceration.

Reduced recidivism is essential to program cost-effectiveness. DRCs are not likely to reduce recidivism among minor offenders who will likely desist on their own or with light sanctions. DRCs are also not likely to reduce recidivism among serious violent offenders, because they require more extensive control and treatment. DRCs are cheaper to operate than incarceration (Boyd 1998; Champion, Harvey, and Schanz 2011) but usually more expensive than some other community sanctions such as traditional probation (Boyle et al. 2013). Craddock (2004) conducted net cost–benefit analyses of two DRCs and found that lower rearrests among DRC probationers translated into criminal justice system cost-savings benefits for at least one of the programs. Although limited and exploratory, the study suggests it is possible for DRCs to eventually reduce net costs through lower recidivism.

Moving Forward

Research thus far has not provided convincing evidence that DRCs are effective, but this does not mean that the DRC is a fundamentally flawed correctional strategy—that it "just doesn't work." First, methodological limitations may have prevented some studies from accurately detecting the utility of programs. Most used fairly basic quasi-experimental designs, with data drawn retrospectively from official records (Boyle et al. 2013). Second, some evaluated DRC programs may not have been implemented properly.

Steiner and Butler (2013) believe that some of the New Jersey DRCs that provided subjects for Boyle et al.'s (2013) study may have been flawed in terms of providing evidence-based treatment and targeting offenders with the right risk level. In fact, during site visits to the DRCs, Boyle et al. (2013) reported observing considerable participant socializing during unstructured time, which could result in a contagion effect ("networking" among antisocial individuals). As opposed to discontinuing the use of DRCs for medium–high-risk paroles, Ostermann (2013) recommends (1) proactively directing programmatic resources away from low-risk parolees toward high-risk parolees, (2) performing actuarial assessments of program quality, providing training to correct for service gaps, and then analyzing participant outcomes in conjunction with assessed program quality, (3) regularly re-assessing program quality and improving or eliminating programs that repeatedly fail to meet evidence-based standards, and (4) analyzing and tracking parolee compliance and parole officer responses to noncompliance to determine how to better use diversionary resources.

If DRCs are an alternative to incarceration, then perhaps they should be reserved for medium–high-risk offenders who are likely to become incarcerated. Steiner and Butler (2013) point out that placing low–moderate-risk offenders in environments that expose them to influences from higher-risk offenders, and subjecting them to intensive programming that may disrupt their prosocial bonds, could increase their tendency to reoffend. DRC use potentially "widens the net" of criminal justice—increases the capacity to sanction more minor offenders. Marciniak (1999) found that judges occasionally sentenced less serious offenders, who according to their classification should have received a standard community sanction, to a DRC, while they often chose not to sentence more serious but still eligible offenders to a DRC. This limited the use of the DRC as a cost-effective diversion from incarceration.

Although they have existed for about three decades, DRCs are still works-in-progress. It is important that operations and services are periodically examined to see if they are being carried out correctly, to identify areas in need of improvement, and make changes accordingly. Brunet (2002) conducted an implementation evaluation of two DRCs. A review of records, interviews with staff and service providers, direct observations, and a telephone survey of overseers were used to compare planned and actual operations. Brunet (2002) concluded four main "lessons learned." First, implementation can be a continuous process; managers may modify or abandon some planned operations, which is warranted if improvements result. Second, despite support from some justice authorities, managers are challenged with overcoming resistance to the program by others (participant referrals may be low). Third, services and surveillance must be balanced to achieve public safety, cost-savings goals, and thus program survival. Fourth, while managers may not be able to assess long-term recidivism, they should use intermediate measures of participant outcomes to assess program effectiveness, which may uncover areas in need of remedy.

There is also room for improvement in the DRC paradigm. Kim et al. (2007) argue that more attention needs to be paid to the DRC's potential to reintegrate offenders into the community by boosting informal social control. Intensive treatment programs should have the effect of strengthening participants' social ties, such as those to family members and employers. They recommend a two-level DRC strategy. The first, short-term, strategy is to specifically design programs, such as a relapse prevention class, that help participants avoid or control the situations that drive them to offend and thus remain in the program. Rehabilitative programming may take a long time to effect change in a person, while in the meantime participants may "slip up" and be terminated from the program. The researchers found that DRC participants in a relapse prevention class were more likely to graduate. The second, long-term, strategy is to reduce post-program recidivism by boosting participants' social capital. This would require extended treatment and collaboration with the community, as enhancing education and employability (for example) requires more time than the typical duration of a DRC program, especially among participants who are younger, unemployed, or otherwise high risk (Kim et al. 2007). Craddock (2009) found that having more contact hours in employment services increased DRC program completion. Integrating DRC services with other community services for participants after they leave can be difficult, so special efforts are needed here (McBride and VanderWaal 1997).

To date, little literature focuses on inequality issues in DRCs, for example whether they are designed or implemented in race, class, and gender biased ways. However, the empirical studies reviewed herein often controlled for race, gender, and socioeconomic variables. Only one study found that racial minorities were less likely to complete a DRC program (Craddock 2009), and gender was not found significant in any of the completion studies. Marciniak (1999) found that the unemployed were less likely to complete, and Marciniak (1999) and Kim et al. (2007) found that the less educated were less likely to complete. Race and employment differences could not be adequately explored in three studies that had predominately white, employed samples (Roy 2004; Roy and Barton 2006; Roy and Grimes 2002).

Very few studies explored demographic differences in recidivism among DRC program completers. Craddock and Graham (2001) found that low income predicted recidivism among DRC participants, controlling for program completion, in their predominately white, male sample. In their more diverse sample, Kim et al. (2007) found that unemployment but not race or gender predicted rearrest. However, most DRC recidivism studies would not have been able to explore demographic differences due to predominately white, predominately non-white, or all or predominately male samples. More research is needed to test whether demographic variables predict chances of receiving a DRC placement as opposed to other intermediate sanctions or incarceration, and to explore how well DRCs meet the needs of women and minorities.

To conclude, the value of day reporting centers is not yet determined. To properly assess them as a correctional strategy, more thorough studies must be conducted on programs that are provided with adequate resources, implemented properly, target the appropriate offender population, and meet the diverse needs of participants.

Work Release Programs

Overview

Correctional work release programs attempt to use employment as a buffer against recidivism. Criminology has long recognized that persons who are employable or employed, especially gainfully, are less likely to offend. Incarceration, especially long term, often results in lost jobs or prospects and offers a very limited environment under which one may retain and improve employment capabilities. Work release (WR) is a strategy to provide educational and vocational programming to offenders who are at higher risk of reoffending due to inadequate education, income, and job experience. WR also helps ease overcrowding and financial expenses, and participants may even be required to pay reimbursement for confinement costs (Duwe 2015; Jung 2014; Turner and Petersilia 1996).

WR is often given to prisoners near the end of their sentences, and may be followed by parole. While some travel back and forth between work and a prison facility on a daily basis, others may be released from prison to reside in a local jail or other residential facility (e.g. halfway house or secure transition center). Early WR helps ex-prisoners earn money, acquire positive living habits, and in general transition back into the community. However, since many prisoners do not have their own job prospects, WR programs typically offer some type of work training and job search assistance. Programs may even work with area employers to place participants (Duwe 2015; Jung 2014; Turner and Petersilia 1996).

WR is well established, existing in some form in the U.S. since the beginning of the twentieth century, and programs expanded considerably as a rehabilitative approach to corrections during the 1970s (Turner and Petersilia 1996). Today, most states operate a prison WR program. However, the proportion of state or federal correctional facilities with WR programs declined after the 1970s (Jung 2014), which was likely due to the termination of federal funding and the political shift from the rehabilitation ideal back to the punishment ideal (imprisonment) during the 1980s (Turner and Petersilia 1996).

Highly publicized and sensationalized extreme cases of failure may have negatively impacted the use of WR, such as the case of Willie Horton used in a 1988 campaign against presidential candidate Michael Dukakis. Horton committed serious and violent crimes while on a weekend *furlough* in Massachusetts, and Dukakis was the Governor of the state at the time. Work furlough is different from work release and appears to have a vaguer meaning, although the two terms are often used interchangeably (Turner and Petersilia 1996). Perhaps work "release" refers more specifically to a reduction or easing of a sentence into a transitional or halfway back environment that allows participants to work regularly, whereas "furlough" may include more brief and temporary visits to work sites.

WR is offered more as a privilege than a right, which seems to be the position of at least three federal court rulings. In *Weller v. Grant County Sheriff* (1999), a U.S. District Court ruled that an Indiana jail inmate was justifiably removed from a temporary WR program for rule violations, and that his due process rights were not violated when removed from the program prior to a hearing (to the extent that it did not impact his length of incarceration) (Miller and Walter 2010). In *Kitchen v. Upshaw* (2002), a U.S. Appeals Court upheld that a former Virginia jail inmate's due process rights were not violated when he was denied participation in a WR program. In *Domka v. Portage County* (2008), a U.S. District Court ruled that a Wisconsin jail inmate's WR and home detention privileges granted in a plea bargain were justifiably revoked because he violated the terms of the plea agreement (Miller and Walter 2010). Of course, these decisions do not mean that a prisoner can be denied or removed from WR for any reason, nor that one can be subjected to discrimination on the basis of race, sex, religion, etc.

Research

While it may seem obvious that it has at least short-term financial benefits, there is a lack of evidence, especially from methodologically sound studies, that WR reduces recidivism (Duwe 2015). The body of published research, especially recent studies, on work release programs is rather small. A few published studies done in the 1970s and 1980s suggested that WR was either modestly or not effective, but not that WR increased recidivism or other problems (Duwe 2015; Jung 2014). The body of more recent studies suggests about the same.

To begin, little coverage is given to WR *completion* rates and risk of program failure. Turner and Petersilia (1996) found that about 70 percent of male participants completed a WR program in Washington without being returned to prison for a serious violation. Further, of those who returned to prison, most did so because of some kind of program or release violation; 3.6 percent committed new crimes or law violations, most of which were nonviolent. Bivariate analyses showed that participants who were older, white, had no prior criminal record, and, interestingly, were convicted of person crimes (compared to property or drug) were more likely to be successful. Duwe (2015) found a similar success rate among WR ex-prisoners in Minnesota: 76 percent completed the program, and not all of those who failed the program returned to prison (45 percent returned within 60 days of placement into WR). Like other alternative correction programs, however, the success rate may vary widely depending on population and program characteristics.

Two studies suggest that WR indeed improves *employment* among transitioning prisoners. Duwe (2015) found that WR increased odds of finding post-program employment, total hours worked, and total wages earned among ex-prisoners in Minnesota. Jung (2014) found that males who finished a WR program at "adult transition centers" in Illinois were better employed and had higher earnings compared to program dropouts and ex-prisoners released from minimum-security prisons who were WR eligible but did not participate. However, improving one's employment situation does not automatically mean that one will not reoffend (reduced recidivism cannot be assumed).

The few WR *recidivism* studies published since 1990 utilized fairly strong research methodologies that included experimental or rigorous quasi-experimental designs. This research offers only slight support for WR. First, using base expectancy tables to control for individual characteristics, LeClair and Guarino-Ghezzi (1991) found in Massachusetts that male inmates at pre-release centers, most of whom were employed, had lower reincarceration rates compared to nonparticipants, especially those who previously received prison furloughs. Also, as part of their study, Turner and Petersilia (1996) conducted a randomized experiment using a small sample of WR-eligible male prisoners in Seattle. They found that compared to a similar group of those not assigned to WR, a smaller portion of participants were rearrested (22 percent vs. 30 percent) but the difference was not statistically significant. Also, participants were significantly much more likely to commit infractions (58 percent vs. 4.7 percent) and return to prison (about 25 percent vs. 1 percent).

Later, Butzin, O'Connell, Martin, and Inciardi (2006) found in a sample of prisoners given WR in Delaware that those who dropped out were more likely to be reincarcerated than graduates, but a non-WR comparison group was not used in the study. Thus, the study does not judge whether WR is better than serving a full sentence or another type of early release program. Two very recent studies used propensity score matching to devise suitable comparison groups. Duwe (2015) found in a sample of released prisoners in Minnesota that those on work release were more likely to return to prison for technical violations but less likely to reoffend, compared to a group of ex-prisoners on regular supervised release. Routh and Hamilton (2015) analyzed data from a large sample of released prisoners in New Jersey. They did not find significant differences in rearrests, reconvictions, or reincarcerations specifically, but they did find that those in work release halfway houses were less likely to have parole revoked or be sent back to prison, *for any reason*, compared to a group of ex-prisoners released directly into the community (WR-eligible but not placed due to time or space limits).

Research on WR *cost effectiveness* tends to be inconsistent, although there does not seem to be evidence that WR is more expensive than serving full sentences in prison. In their study, Turner and Petersilia (1996) estimated that correctional costs were similar between work releases and non-work releases in Washington. While the daily cost of work release was cheaper than imprisonment, the sizeable minority of WR participants who returned to prison due to program and rule violations generated re-processing costs (from going back through the system) that negated the cost-saving potential of WR. Accounting for release savings, reimbursements by participants, revocation costs, and recidivism costs, Duwe (2015) on the other hand estimated that Minnesota's prison work release program produced cost avoidance savings of $1.25 million ($700 per participant) between 2007 and 2010.

Moving Forward

Work release participants usually present multiple risk factors. Employment only counters one or a few of them. Thus, it is important that residential placements do more than just house participants. They also require full risk/need assessments and other services such as cognitive behavioral programming and drug treatment (Duwe 2015). Butzin et al. (2006) view WR as an important secondary stage in reintegrating prisoners with drug issues. They recommend that the therapeutic community (TC) model traditionally used in prisons be adapted to meet the supervisory and support needs of participants in WR centers, and that participants receive aftercare. In their study, Butzin et al. (2006) found that compared to a similar group of regular WR center residents, those in a TC drug treatment program were significantly less likely to recidivate. Further, interaction results suggest that the treatment was particularly beneficial for those with more extensive criminal histories (e.g. higher number of arrests).

It is important that WR programming be responsive to the behaviors and environmental contexts of specific populations, such as women. Although women make up a small portion of the incarcerated, the number of incarcerated women has grown considerably in recent decades. Thus, there are more women who need transitional programming such as WR. While they may share some with men, women have different rehabilitation needs that correctional program designs must meet. For example, sexual abuse and domestic violence victimization and its impact upon self-esteem and coping skills is a major part of women's risk histories that could make transitional experiences such as WR more difficult. Feelings of hopelessness and being overwhelmed can be obstacles to reintegration (Dickow, Robinson, and Copeland 2007).

Dickow et al. (2007) describe a women's WR program in Hawaii. Its model is based on original quantitative and qualitative research, as well as behavioral and social science theory. The model recognizes five stages through which women must negotiate to successfully reenter the community: *adjustment* from the regimented prison environment to the community-based WR environment; *stabilization* in the program (acquire employment and/or schooling, develop a routine); *destabilization or derailing* due to experiencing challenges, frustrations, and crises; *re-stabilization* upon resolving these problems and being able to proceed; and *moving on* from the structure of the program to integration into the community. Each stage presents different challenges, and individuals proceed through them at their own pace depending on their personal and social resources. The program aims to tailor tools, activities, classes, and other interventions to each individual and each stage, rather than to a fixed time period.

Another issue is how well WR works for disabled persons (e.g. mentally, intellectually, or physically). Employment and financial barriers to reintegration such as discrimination, inability to perform some tasks, and loss of welfare benefits while incarcerated can be especially severe for disabled prisoners (Mawhorr 1997). Mawhorr (1997) found in a small group of physically or mentally impaired residents in a community-based WR facility that about half remained unemployed throughout residence, those who were employed were not necessarily gainfully employed, and all but one owed rent upon release. Because of these kinds of problems, and that residents may not receive welfare benefits while confined to the facility, another community-based placement such as day treatment may better meet the employment and financial needs of the disabled.

In another study, Way, Abreu, Ramirez-Romero, Aziz, and Sawyer (2007) found that mental illness reduced program completion among female WR inmates in prison for parole violations, but that mental illness was not a predictor among males. Mentally ill men even had a higher success rate than their non-mentally ill WR counterparts, although the difference was not quite statistically significant. The authors concluded that more mentally ill men should participate in WR but that mentally ill women who have experienced trouble with parole should receive more intensive services. Clearly, more research and program development are needed to meet the needs of disabled WR participants.

The WR literature deals very little with social inequality. Other than the two disability studies just discussed, none of the studies reviewed in this chapter directly examined inequality, short of including demographic controls. Turner and Petersilia (1996) found that 25 percent of white compared to over 40 percent of Hispanic and Black participants failed WR (returned to prison), but this was just a bivariate relationship that could reflect the general higher risk of (re)incarceration for racial minorities. They did not find race, prior employment, nor high school education to interact with WR participation in a logistic regression analysis of recidivism in their small sample. Routh and Hamilton (2015) found that compared to their nonwhite counterparts, white WR halfway house participants were less likely to be rearrested but more likely to return to prison for any reason. Butzin et al. (2006) found among WR participants that African American race did not predict recidivism, but that females were less likely to be reincarcerated.

Finally, charging WR participants fees can be controversial. Care must be taken to ensure that such practices do not misappropriate workers' earnings or interfere with rehabilitation goals. Local agencies cannot simply choose to charge participants; fees are usually allowed under state law (Feldschreiber 2003). Making offenders pay for the cost of living in a facility, rather than taxpayers, may seem fair, and some may believe that fees help serve as a deterrent to crime. However, the practice raises some important questions. Is it fair and beneficial to single out those who have gained employment? What about those who do not participate in WR and simply serve out their sentences in prison: will they have to pay an equitable amount for their confinement? Do fees punish prisoners for engaging in a productive, prosocial activity? Do they also put economic strain on workers that interferes with their ability to reintegrate into the community and refrain from reoffending?

WR reimbursement fees may be charged according to a per-diem rate, a flat fee, or a percentage of salary (Feldschreiber 2003). When a percentage of salary is used, a cap may be established that prevents overcharging. However, in the 1990s, New York State charged WR participants an uncapped fee—20 percent of their net salaries, which meant that participants with higher earnings would pay more than others for the same services. Also, in some cases participants were charged more than the actual cost of stay in the program, which could be seen as a violation of constitutional property rights (Takings Clause of the Fifth Amendment). However, this may have been an extreme, atypical case. Perhaps the obligation to pay living costs accompanies the privilege of having more freedom while working in the community, and it may be difficult to offer prisoners WR as an option without the funding that comes from fees. Since the fees at issue are reimbursements for living costs, not fines (official punishments), courts have not interpreted them as cases of excessive fine or double jeopardy. Thus, WR fees may be good for all involved (prisoners, the public, and the justice system) as long as they are reasonable and appropriate to the costs of confinement (Feldschreiber 2003).

As with day reporting centers, the ability of WR to reduce crime is yet to be determined. However, at minimum, it gives an ex-prisoner the opportunity to be a productive contributing community member, eases overcrowding, and potentially reduces correctional costs. At this point it does not appear that WR increases offending, which suggests that it is not a major threat to public safety. Since no intervention is perfect, offenders will at times commit serious crimes while on WR, but so too will those who completed their entire sentence in prison or even persons who have never before been incarcerated. Regardless, more work release research and program development is needed, including that which addresses fairness in offering WR and meeting the needs of diverse populations.

References

Boyd, Lorenzo M. 1998. "Day Reporting Centers: A Safe and Cost Effective Way of Reducing Prison Overcrowding." *The Discourse of Sociological Practice* 1(1): 8–9.

Boyle, Douglas J., Laura M. Ragusa-Salerno, Jennifer L. Lanterman, and Andrea F. Marcus. 2013. "An Evaluation of Day Reporting Centers for Parolees: Outcomes of a Randomized Trial." *Criminology & Public Policy* 12(1): 119–143.

Brunet, James R. 2002. "Day Reporting Centers in North Carolina: Implementation Lessons for Policymakers." *The Justice System Journal* 23(2): 135–156.

Butzin, Clifford A., Daniel J. O'Connell, Steven S. Martin, and James A. Inciardi. 2006. "Effect of Drug Treatment during Work Release on New Arrests and Incarcerations." *Journal of Criminal Justice* 34: 557–565.

Champion, David R., Patrick J. Harvey, and Youngyol Y. Schanz. 2011. "Day Reporting Center and Recidivism: Comparing Offender Groups in a Western Pennsylvania County Study." *Journal of Offender Rehabilitation* 50: 433–446.

Craddock, Amy. 2004. "Estimating Criminal Justice Costs and Cost-Savings Benefits of Day Reporting Centers." *Journal of Offender Rehabilitation* 39(4): 69–98.

Craddock, Amy. 2009. "Day Reporting Center Completion: Comparison of Individual and Multilevel Models." *Crime & Delinquency* 55(1): 105–133.

Craddock, Amy, and Laura A. Graham. 2001. "Recidivism as a Function of Day Reporting Center Participation." *Journal of Offender Rehabilitation* 34(1): 81–97.

Dickow, Alice, Lorraine Robinson, and Kristina Copeland. 2007. "A New Paradigm: Stage-Based Change in Work Release Programs for Women." *Corrections Today* 69(4): 52–55.

Duwe, Grant. 2015. "An Outcome Evaluation of a Prison Work Release Program: Estimating Its Effects on Recidivism, Employment, and Cost Avoidance." *Criminal Justice Policy Review* 26(6): 531–554.

Feldschreiber, Sara. 2003. "Fee at Last? Work Release Participation Fees and the Takings Clause." *Fordham Law Review* 72(1): 2017–2250.

Jung, Haeil. 2014. "Do Prison Work-Release Programs Improve Subsequent Labor Market Outcomes? Evidence from the Adult Transition Centers in Illinois." *Journal of Offender Rehabilitation* 53(5): 384–402.

Kim, Dae-Young, Hee-Jong Joo, and William P. McCarty. 2008. "Risk Assessment and Classification of Day Reporting Center Clients: An Actuarial Approach." *Criminal Justice and Behavior* 35(6): 792–812.

Kim, Dae-Young, Cassia Spohn, and Mark Foxall. 2007. "An Evaluation of the DRC in the Context of Douglas County, Nebraska." *The Prison Journal* 87(4): 434–456.

LeClair, Daniel P., and Susan Guarino-Ghezzi. 1991. "Does Incapacitation Guarantee Public Safety? Lessons from the Massachusetts Furlough and Prerelease Programs." *Justice Quarterly* 8(1): 9–36.

Lurigio, Arthur J., and David E. Olson. 2000. "An Evaluation of the Cook County Sheriff's Office's Day Reporting Center: A Pretrial Surveillance and Service Program for Drug Using Defendants." *The ICCA Journal* May: 16–25.

Lurigio, Arthur J., David B. Olson, and Katrina Sifferd. 1999. "A Study of the Cook County Day Reporting Center." *The Journal of Offender Monitoring* Spring: 5–11.

Marciniak, Liz M. 1999. "The Use of Day Reporting as an Intermediate Sanction: A Study of Offender Targeting and Program Termination." *The Prison Journal* 79(2): 205–225.

Marciniak, Liz M. 2000. "The Addition of Day Reporting to Intensive Supervision Probation: A Comparison of Recidivism Rates." *Federal Probation* 64(1): 34–39.

Martin, Christine, Arthur J. Lurigio, and David E. Olson. 2003. "An Examination of Rearrests and Reincarcerations among Discharged Day Reporting Center Clients." *Federal Probation* 67(1): 24–30.

Mawhorr, Tina L. 1997. "Disabled Offenders and Work Release: An Exploratory Examination." *Criminal Justice Review* 22(1): 34–48.

McBride, Duane, and Curtis Vanderwaal. 1997. "Day Reporting Centers as an Alternative for Drug Using Offenders." *Journal of Drug Issues* 27(2): 379–397.

Miller, Rod, and Donald J. Walter. 2010. "Cases Addressing Inmate Work and Work Release." *American Jails* July/August: 87–89.

Ostermann, Michael. 2009. "An Analysis of New Jersey's Day Reporting Center and Halfway Back Programs: Embracing the Rehabilitative Ideal through Evidence Based Practices." *Journal of Offender Rehabilitation* 48(2): 139–153.

Ostermann, Michael. 2013. "Using Day Reporting Centers to Divert Parolees from Revocation." *Criminology & Public Policy* 12(1): 163–171.

Routh, Douglas, and Zachary Hamilton. 2015. "Work Release as a Transition: Positioning Success via the Halfway House." *Journal of Offender Rehabilitation* 54(4): 239–255.

Roy, Sudipto. 2004. "Factors Related to Success and Recidivism in a Day Reporting Center." *Criminal Justice Studies* 17(1): 3–17.

Roy, Sudipto, and Shannon Barton. 2006. "Convicted Drunk Drivers in Electronic Monitoring Home Detention and Day Reporting Centers: An Exploratory Study." *Federal Probation* 70(1): 49–55.

Roy, Sudipto, and Jennifer N. Grimes. 2002. "Adult Offenders in a Day Reporting Center—A Preliminary Study." *Federal Probation* 66(1): 44–50.

Steiner, Benjamin, and H. Daniel Butler. 2013. "Why Didn't They Work? Thoughts on the Application of New Jersey Day Reporting Centers." *Criminology & Public Policy* 12(1): 153–162.

Turner, Susan, and Joan Petersilia. 1996. "Work Release in Washington: Effects on Recidivism and Corrections Costs." *The Prison Journal* 76(2): 138–164.

Way, Bruce B., Dan Abreu, Doris Ramirez-Romero, David Aziz, and Donald A. Sawyer. 2007. "Mental Health Service Recipients and Prison Work Release: How Do the Mentally Ill Fare Compared to Other Inmates in Prison Work Release Programs?" *Journal of Forensic Sciences* 52(4): 965–966.

20 Boot Camp Prisons in an Era of Evidence-Based Practices

Faith E. Lutze and Jenny L. Lau

Boot Camp Prisons in an Era of Evidence-Based Corrections

Boot camp prisons are institutions steeped in a traditional military training model designed to instill discipline, establish order, and encourage responsiveness to authority. Boot camp prisons (BCP), also known as shock incarceration programs,[1] emerged during a "get tough" crime control era (1970–present) that emphasized punishment and retribution in an attempt to deter offenders from committing crime. The quick embrace and popularity of this correctional method to "shock" offenders into compliance and to restore them to a prosocial, law-abiding lifestyle was promoted as a panacea by supporters and as an over simplistic and abusive approach doomed to failure by critics (Stinchcomb 2005). In spite of relatively consistent scientific findings showing BCPs to be ineffective in reducing recidivism, the programs continue to persist 30 years beyond their inception in 1984. Over time, the paramilitary core has remained constant, but the design has morphed from sole reliance on military drill, exercise, labor, and corporal punishment to include education, treatment, support, and aftercare programming. In this review, we present the evolution of BCPs over time and discuss how this correctional practice continues to be controversial within an evolving era of evidence-based corrections.

The War on Drugs and the Rise of Boot Camp Prisons

By the end of the 1970s the guiding philosophy of corrections would clearly shift away from rehabilitation and become firmly entrenched in a conservative crime control era grounded in retribution, punishment, and incapacitation (see Cullen and Gilbert 1982; Cullen and Jonson 2012; Curry 1985; Garland 2001). The criminal justice system would commence "wars" on crime and drugs. These wars, even as early as the 1980s, began to have a significant impact on corrections (Alexander 2012; Austin and Irwin 1997; Reiman 2004). Federal and state legislators began to pass laws resulting in longer sentences, mandatory minimums for specific crimes involving firearms or drugs, civil penalties excluding drug offenders from access to public housing, student loans, state-licensed occupations, social service benefits, and the right to vote (Mele and Miller 2005). These policies, especially those targeting drug offenders, had a disparate impact on racial minorities and the poor, and quickly began to increase the jail and prison population, creating severe overcrowding and the need to build new prisons at a rate and expense unprecedented in United States' history (Alexander 2012; Austin and Irwin 1997). It is within this social and political context that BCPs were created and deemed the latest correctional panacea destined to solve system-level challenges related to prison crowding and correctional costs as well as the ability to instill discipline in young, streetwise, out of control, offenders (see Benda 2005a; Stinchcomb 2005).

Symbolically BCPs were a natural outcome supporting the war analogies created to inspire the criminal justice system's response to crime, drug use, and social disorder (see Kraska 2001; Lutze 2006). Shock incarceration provided the perfect juxtaposition to images of traditional prisons portrayed as "holiday inns" providing "three hots and cot" with the imagery of tough military-like drill instructors yelling in the face of young offenders who are uniformly dressed with shaved heads, performing drills, participating in group exercise or hard labor, and stripped of all basic comforts (see Benda 2005a; Lutze and Brody 1999; MacKenzie and Hebert 1996). Politically, BCPs served as a visual presentation easily consumed by the public as an example of corrections officials "getting tough" on crime and providing politicians positive press as proactive crime fighters working to protect the public.

In more practical terms, proponents viewed boot camps as an opportunity to reduce recidivism by being tough on crime while simultaneously shortening prison sentences, reducing prison costs, and serving as a way to reduce overcrowding by moving nonviolent offenders destined for longer prison sentences out of the system more quickly (see Benda 2005a; MacKenzie and Piquero 1994). Proponents also argued that a strict, highly disciplined, military correctional environment would enhance prosocial behavior, improve self-esteem, increase self-control, instill a positive work ethic, and translate the lessons learned in boot camp into success upon return to the community.

Critics of boot camp prisons, however, raised numerous concerns about the use of coercive tactics that included emotional and physical abuse, the use of aggression to gain compliance, and the use of summary punishments without due process giving staff absolute power over inmates (see Benda 2005a; Lutze and Bell 2005; Lutze and Brody 1999; Morash and Rucker 1990). Critics also had concerns that BCPs would not reduce prison crowding but instead would widen the "correctional net"[2] by incarcerating offenders who would have otherwise been placed on probation or diverted from the system. Before this debate would be resolved, boot camps would spread quickly across federal, state, and local jurisdictions including both adult and juvenile populations (see Benda 2005a; Wilson, MacKenzie, and Mitchell 2005).

In spite of early criticism and unimpressive performance from initial process and outcome evaluations, the number of BCPs increased from 65 in 1995 to 95 in 2000 with 86 percent of programs located in minimum or medium security facilities and 71 percent serving only male offenders (Stephan and Karberg 2003). The number of BCPs appear to be declining in the last 15 years, however, no census has been conducted since 2000 to confirm this trend. Although the military training has remained a core element, BCP design has changed over time. The first wave of boot camps focused solely on basic military drill, work, exercise, and corporal punishment to correct behavior. Second-wave BCPs retained the military discipline and physical challenges, but began to integrate programing such as education, treatment, and life skills. Third-wave BCPs tended to build upon second-wave designs by providing aftercare to assist graduates of the program with reentry to the community. Aside from the general reliance on a basic military structure there is a great deal of variation across settings (see Benda and Pallone 2005; MacKenzie and Hebert 1996). For instance, differences exist regarding the target populations served (adults, juveniles, women); the age of participants (juveniles, young adults 18–25, adults up to 40); physical and mental health; the type of offender (criminal history, type offender, risk to reoffend, etc.); and the length of original sentences. Differences also exist across programs related to the duration of the program (60, 90, or 180 days); the emphases placed on physical training and labor versus education, treatment, and life skills; whether the program serves as an alternative to probation or prison; who has control over admission and release from the program; and whether programs possess an aftercare component for graduates (see Benda 2005a; Duwe and Kerschner 2008; MacKenzie and Piquero 1994; Wilson et al. 2005).

The Successes and Failures of Boot Camp Prisons

The rapid development and implementation of boot camp prisons during the late 1980s outpaced scientific evaluations to determine their effectiveness. Thus, like many popular programs in criminal justice, BCPs were implemented without a strong theoretical basis guiding their development or scientific evidence that they would achieve the goals set forth by reformers (see Benda 2005a; Corriea 1997; Stinchcomb 2005). Initial implementation appeared to be driven by a commonsense belief that subjecting disobedient young offenders to military discipline would transform them into mature and contributing citizens much like traditional military boot camps turn immature boys into men (Cullen, Blevins, Trager and Gendreau 2005). Reformers were confident that BCPs would help to solve multiple problems confronting individual offenders, prison disorder, and the need for system level expansion. Thus, studies of shock incarceration programs tend to focus on three areas: (1) system-level outcomes such as reductions in overcrowding and costs; (2) institutional-level effects such as changing prison environments; and (3) individual-level outcomes such as attitudinal change, institutional adjustment, and recidivism. Nearly three decades of research has shown that, in general, outcomes did not support the broad claims made by proponents nor totally fulfill the overarching concerns of critics.

System-Level Outcomes

Boot camp prisons came about during a period when the capacity of many state corrections systems could not meet the demand for the number of offenders being sentenced to prison. During the early 1980s more than half of the states were under court order or confronting litigation due to overcrowding, and corrections leaders were seeking solutions to manage the prison population while remaining true to the public and political pressure to be tough on crime (see Benda 2005a). The increasing prison population and the need for additional prisons to meet demand also created a financial burden for many states that was unsustainable. Therefore, an argument was made that boot camps could serve as an intermediate sanction that would reduce prison populations and save money through several different mechanisms of offender management.

There were primarily three perspectives about how boot camps could reduce prison overcrowding (see Duwe and Kerschner 2008; MacKenzie and Piquero 1994; Parent 1996). One view was that BCPs could decrease traditional prison populations by changing offenders' desire to recidivate either through rehabilitation or deterrence. Another mechanism to reduce overcrowding was for prison administrators to use boot camps as an early release option for nonviolent offenders already serving time in traditional prisons, resulting in a shorter sentence and the ability to transition offenders back to the community more quickly. Finally, was the opportunity for judges to divert nonviolent offenders destined for traditional prison to BCP instead, thus reserving prison beds for more serious violent offenders. Embedded within each potential path to reduce crowding and costs was the overarching concern that BCPs target only offender populations that would have been admitted to prison instead of probation and that BCPs have a capacity large enough to significantly impact existing prison populations (Parent 1996). Without an adequate target population or program capacity, BCPs would have the unintended consequence of increasing the prison population and correctional costs.

Multi-site studies of BCPs implemented through the early 1990s show that programs with an admissions process in place that target offenders already incarcerated or those bound for prison have a positive impact on reducing prison overcrowding and costs (MacKenzie and Parent 1991; MacKenzie and Piquero 1994; Parent 1996). Similarly, a more contemporary longitudinal study of a mature BCP (10 years old) in Minnesota shows cost savings over time once the program transitioned from early implementation into full operation. Costs were reduced by providing early release and reducing the time offenders later spent in prison (Duwe and Kerschner 2008; also see Kempinen and Tinik 2011). The results of process evaluations, as well as statistical simulations, however, show several threats to BCPs' ability to reduce overcrowding (MacKenzie and Parent 1991; MacKenzie and Piquero 1994; Parent 1996).

As Parent (1996: 265) observes, in order for boot camp programs to reduce overcrowding they must target offenders whose probability of imprisonment is very high, participants must get a substantial and real reduction in their sentence, program failure rates must be low, and boot camp programs must operate at a large enough scale to have a meaningful impact on the need for prison bed space (also see Duwe and Kerschner 2008; Kempinen and Tinik 2011). It appears that BCPs do have the potential to successfully reduce the need for additional prison bed space and reduce costs, but there are critical threats to achieving these goals. Contemporary implementers must be mindful of the decisions made throughout the process, from beginning to end (sentencing, selection, admission, retention, graduation) and integrate quality assurances to guide decisions to enhance positive outcomes or to prevent implementation drift from occurring that may sabotage outcomes over time. It is also possible that other system-level factors, such as increases in prison admission rates greater than the reductions accomplished through boot camps, could overwhelm the capacity of boot camp programs to have an effect on the general prison population (Parent 1996). The importance of conducting process and outcome evaluations to ensure program integrity over time is essential (see Duwe and Kerschner 2008).

Institutional-Level Effects

In addition to system level goals, reformers also expressed one of the objectives for BCPs was to modify the institutional environment to support positive change and to reduce the negative effects of exposing young, first-time offenders, to traditional prisons often portrayed as "schools of crime," resulting in hardening inmates within a criminal lifestyle. Thus, BCPs were envisioned as an opportunity to isolate young impressionable offenders from the negative effects of adapting to a negative environment found in many traditional prisons. This vision was aligned with research conducted in traditional prisons where inmates were found to actively develop routines and to grow relationships with others that distance them from the harsher aspects of doing time in contemporary prisons.

The study of prison environments identifies the organization and climate within the institution and how it serves to enhance or sabotage the efforts of staff and inmates to achieve positive outcomes through rehabilitation.

> A rehabilitative environment should possess attributes that support internal change and should provide external controls that inhibit negative behavior. External environmental controls relate to those attributes of the environment which create a place where rehabilitation may occur.
>
> (Lutze 1998: 548)

For example, inmates in traditional prisons express a need for safety, structure, support, emotional feedback, activity, social stimulation, privacy, and freedom to achieve psychological and physical wellbeing (Johnson 2002; Toch 1977; Wright and Goodstein 1989). Lutze (1998, 2002) proposes that safety, structure, support, and emotional feedback are key elements to designing a prison environment, especially in BCPs, likely to be supportive of rehabilitation and offender change. Prisons that provide these environmental attributes allow inmates to maturely adjust and cope with their prison experience, reducing harm to themselves and others (Johnson 2002; Lutze 1998).

Therefore, there is support in the traditional prison literature for redesigning prison environments in ways reflected in BCP designs (see Lutze 2002). For example, with the exception of the concerns voiced by critics, most BCP designs attempt to assure safety by targeting and separating first-time, non-violent offenders from hardened, repeat offenders found in traditional prisons; creating a highly structured prison environment with a stable and predictable daily routine; providing various support for positive change through mandatory participation in military decorum, exercise, work, education, and life skills programs; and promoting emotional feedback through positive peer pressure via cohorts or platoons of inmates led by staff who work as a team to accomplish goals together as they move toward successful completion of the program (see Lutze 1998, 2002; MacKenzie and Hebert 1996). Although many have questioned the original intentions of BCP reformers immersed in a conservative crime control era (see Cullen et al., 2005;Lutze 2006; Lutze and Bell 2005; Lutze and Brody 1999; Morash and Rucker 1990), what was accomplished by design or by accident, was to radically create a new prison niche that may promote "mature coping" (see Johnson 2002 for a full discussion in traditional prison) and offender change through highly regulated and intensive program designs instituted across entire prison settings (see Duwe and Kerschner 2008; Lutze 1998, 2002).

Only a few studies have considered to what degree BCP environments differ from traditional prisons and how inmates perceive the boot camp environment according to key elements of its programmatic design and implementation. Many scholars have described how BCPs differ from traditional prisons, but most do not extend the analyses to how inmates review the environment as meeting their needs. Lutze's (1998) study of the Federal Bureau of Prison's Intensive Confinement Center (ICC) shows that the boot camp group, as compared to those serving time in a traditional minimum security prison camp, were significantly more likely to define the environment as safe, but no more likely than the traditional prison group to define the boot camp as possessing structure, support, or emotional feedback. Lutze and Murphy's (1999) further study of the ICC intended to follow-up on critics concerns about the aggressive, coercive, militaristic and masculine emphasis in BCPs (see Morash and Rucker 1990), shows that regardless of the prison setting, inmates who perceive the prison climate as hyper-masculine also define the institution as providing less safety, support, and emotional feedback and as being more coercive. Unfortunately, Lutze's (1998, 2001; Lutze and Murphy 1999) research did not compare how inmates defined the institutional environment with their success within the program or post release.

Wilson, MacKenzie, and Mitchell's (2005) meta-analyses of 43 independent BCPs lends insight to the importance of institutions providing rehabilitative environments by showing that BCPs with a stronger rehabilitative focus, especially those with some form of counseling, performed slightly better than those programs relying more heavily on military drill and ceremony. Yet, a study to determine whether the military milieu enhanced outcomes in changing antisocial attitudes by comparing the effects of a treatment-oriented BCP to a treatment-oriented transition center showed no significant differences between groups over time, indicating that the military-based prison environment does not appear to enhance treatment outcomes (Mitchell, MacKenzie, and Perez 2005). These studies suggest for the most part BCPs provide environments that are safer than traditional prisons, but struggle to provide the more complex elements related to structure, support, and emotional feedback that are posited as being supportive of rehabilitation. These mixed findings are similarly reflected in the research evaluating the effects of BCPs on individual-level offender change.

Individual-Level Outcomes

The primary purpose of boot camp prisons is to transform individual attitudes and behavior to reduce recidivism. A full schedule each day steeped in military order and strict discipline is to, "build self-esteem, positive values and beliefs, thinking and problem-solving skills, and prosocial attitudes," as well as instill self-discipline, control, and strong bonds with others (Clark and Aziz 1996: 42). Indicators of individual-level success and failure are measured through self-reported attitudes, adjustment to prison, program graduation rates, and recidivism post release.

Attitudinal Change and Institutional Adjustment. In general, it is expected that programs that have a positive effect on changing antisocial attitudes will also be effective in reducing recidivism and increasing participation in prosocial activities related to long term success after release. Similarly, those who experience positive adjustment to the program are expected to be more likely to internalize changes to their beliefs and behaviors. Overall, research on inmate attitudinal change shows positive outcomes for boot camp participants. The results for inmate adjustment to BCPs, however, are mixed, indicating both positive and negative adjustment to the intense military prison environment compared to traditional prison.

Inmates participating in BCPs tend to experience positive prosocial change overtime and these findings are consistent across multiple research settings and periods of boot camp implementation. In general, research shows that inmates in BCPs are significantly more likely than those in traditional prison settings to become less impulsive, become more positive about themselves and others, hold less oppositional attitudes, hold a positive work ethic, and believe the boot camp will be beneficial in reducing their future criminality and supporting a prosocial lifestyle (Burton, Marquart, Cuvelier, Alarid, and Hunter 1993; Kempinen and Tinik 2011; Lutze 2001; MacKenzie and Souryal 1995; McCorkle 1995; Millkey 2005). Attitudes toward BCPs' staff and programs also tend to be positive with participants reporting greater respect for staff, viewing staff as role models, and being generally supportive of rehabilitation (Burton et al. 1993; Lutze 2001; MacKenzie and Shaw 1990; MacKenzie and Souryal 1995). Boot camp participants also tend to show positive attitudes related to treatment outcomes such as educational skills, relationships, and work (Burns, Anderson, and Dyson 1997; Burton et al. 1993; Ethridge and Sorensen 1997) with the exception of attitudinal change toward alcohol and drug use.

Attitudes toward alcohol and drug use appears to be where BCPs have the least influence and produce the most inconsistent findings (Cowles and Castellano 1996; Lutze and Marenin, 1997; MacKenzie and Shaw 1990; Millkey 2005; Shaw and MacKenzie 1991). One of the most in-depth studies of BCP participants and their attitudes toward alcohol and drug use shows that the BCP group when compared to a traditional prison group had the greatest effect on attitudes toward alcohol, but had little to no effect on attitudes toward the use of soft- or hard-illicit drugs (Lutze and Marenin 1997; also see Millkey 2005; Shaw and MacKenzie 1991). In addition, this same study showed that, regardless of prison setting, nonusers, casual users, and alcohol-only users were more likely to experience positive change while soft-illicit users (alcohol and marijuana) and hard-illicit drug users remained unchanged in their attitudes toward hard-drug use. Most disturbing was the finding that both groups of inmates, boot camp and traditional prison, who were heavy alcohol or heavy soft-illicit users became more supportive in their attitudes toward hard drugs over time (Lutze and Marenin 1997). These findings across studies may be due to the fact that BCPs were not originally designed to target substance abusing offenders, and often by default these types of offenders became dominant in BCP populations because they were the most likely to meet the admission criteria restricted to non-violent incarcerated offenders. In addition, BCPs, due to their duration, often focused on substance abuse education instead of treatment, thus not meeting the needs of those with addiction (also see Benda 2005a).

Unlike the generally consistent positive attitudinal findings in BCPs, offender adjustment to BCPs is mixed. Many of the differences appear to be related to boot camps' intensity and military discipline compared to traditional prisons. For example, inmates in BCPs, when compared to traditional prisons, tend to report greater levels of conflict, isolation, feelings of helplessness, stress, and conflict with other inmates and staff. Yet, within the same studies boot camp inmates also report less aggressive attitudes, opposition to staff and programs, and levels of prisonization (Lutze 2001; Lutze and Murphy 1999; MacKenzie and Shaw 1990; MacKenzie and Souryal 1995). Lutze and Murphy's (1999) research shows that these findings may be due to masculine sex-role stereotypes within prisons generally and that men and women who view the environment as hyper-masculine are more likely to have negative experiences due to increased feelings of isolation, helplessness, and victimization (also see MacKenzie, Elis, Simpson, and Skroban 1996; MacKenzie and Donaldson 1996; Benda 2005a, 2005b).

Interestingly, in spite of the overall positive attitudinal changes and the mixed findings on multiple measures of prison adjustment, BCP inmates are more likely to experience positive changes in their beliefs about the legitimacy (fairness) of the criminal justice system after completing boot camp than those serving time in traditional prison (Franke, Bieirie, and MacKenzie 2010). However, the differences between facility type and legitimacy of the system disappear when the quality of programming, treatment by staff, and interactions with other inmates were taken into consideration with those having a more positive experience viewing the system as possessing increased legitimacy generating greater respect, faith, and confidence in the justice system (Franke et al. 2010). These findings strongly suggest that program design and interactions between inmates and between inmates and staff are crucial to building positive outcomes.

Graduation Rates. Another line of research considers what type of offenders are most likely to be successful in completing the program. Understanding who is successful in BCPs is important to inform policymakers about whether the appropriate population is being targeted for inclusion in BCPs and whether modifications are necessary to achieve intended outcomes. Remember, in order to achieve the system-level goals to reduce crowding and costs, BCPs must successfully move enough offenders through the programs to have a significant impact. Thus, achieving individual level goals has an effect on achieving system-level goals.

Success *within* BCPs is measured by identifying who drops out, is dismissed, or graduates (Benda, Toombs, and Peacock 2006). Dropouts are those who self-select to leave the program prior to completion and will finish their sentence through the traditional system of incarceration. Dismissals are those returned to traditional prison because staff decided they were not worthy of completing the program due to a failure to comply or participate at an acceptable level. Finally, graduates are those who complete all of the required elements of the program while demonstrating appropriate attitudes and behaviors signaling their potential to be successful post release. Nationally, it appears that those who fail to complete boot camp programs range from as low as 3 percent to as high as 62 percent (see MacKenzie and Hebert 1996).

The most detailed study about who is most likely to complete a boot camp program was conducted by Benda and colleagues (2006) on male participants of a BCP. Using life-course theory and elements of social learning theory, they considered the entirety of boot camp participants' lives such as family, work history, religiosity, peer affiliations, drug use, personality traits, and psychological wellbeing. The results of their study show that nearly a quarter of those who begin the boot camp program dropped out or were dismissed and that clear differences existed between graduates, dropouts, and dismissals. Dropouts were more likely to have a history of drug use and treatment, possess low self-control, and have criminal peers (Benda et al. 2006). Dismissals were identified as having a history of sexual and physical abuse, emotional problems including anger, alienation, and suicidal attempts (Benda et al. 2006). Interestingly Benda and colleagues (2006) found two distinct groups of graduates—those who were older with preexisting conventional ties to family, work, education and those who were gang members.

These findings are important because they suggest BCPs serve those who already have the coping skills necessary to withstand or embrace the demands of a physically and psychologically stressful environment (Benda et al. 2006). Those recovering from drug addiction, histories of abuse, and assorted emotional problems appear to experience the greatest challenges in coping with or adapting to the coercive environment. These findings also appear to be true for women offenders in BCP (MacKenzie and Donaldson 1991; MacKenzie, Elis, Simpson, and Skroban 1996). This may be because the BCP environment replicates the same coercive and emotionally abusive conditions that are known to be highly correlated with crime and substance abuse and thus difficult for those with such histories to endure (see Benda et al. 2006; Lutze 2006; Lutze and Bell 2005; Marcus-Mendoza, Klein-Saffran, and Lutze 1998; Morash and Rucker 1990). These findings are important and may explain why BCPs generally produce positive attitudinal change, but mixed results for institutional adjustment and recidivism.

Recidivism Outcomes. Ultimately the utility of boot camp prisons was promoted as a means to reduce recidivism and readmission to prison. Therefore, most research on BCPs has focused on measuring the likelihood of success for those released from boot camp compared to those released from traditional prisons. The results of meta-analyses consistently show that BCPs do not reduce recidivism at a rate significantly greater than those released from traditional prison (see Aos, Phipps, Barnoski, and Lieb 2001; Lipsey and Cullen 2007; Wilson et al. 2005). Stronger predictors for women's failure post release are having experienced recent sexual or physical abuse, adverse feelings, living with a criminal partner, and drug use; conversely the number of children and caring relationships significantly increase women's time in the community (Benda 2005b). For men, those most likely to return to prison are those who are younger, with criminal peer associations, carrying a weapon, alcohol abuse, and aggressive feelings; conversely those with satisfying work and education are more likely to remain in the community longer (Benda 2005b).

It is important to note, however, that findings embedded within many outcome evaluations of BCPs show elements of success depending on program design with BCPs inclusive of greater levels of rehabilitative programming and intensive supervision or aftercare during reentry showing the greatest reductions in recidivism (Duwe and Kershner 2008; Kempinen and Tinik 2011; Kurlychek and Kempinen 2006; MacKenzie and Souryal 1996). Even findings within these more positive outcome studies are mixed and lend to the continued consternation about whether BCPs should be modified to achieve intended outcomes or be abandoned as a correctional approach (Cullen et al. 2005; Lutze 2002, 2006; Lutze and Bell 2005; Stinchcomb 2005).

For example, many of the more positive findings for BCPs are found in second and third generation programs that include military drill, a greater emphasis on rehabilitation programs, and aftercare (Clark and Aziz 1996; Duwe and Kerchner 2008; Kurlychek and Kempinen 2006). An instance of how complex BCPs outcomes are to measure is reflected in Minnesota's well established Challenge Incarceration Program (CIP). The CIP significantly reduces the rate at which offenders commit a new crime, but supervised release violators return to prison at roughly the same rate as the comparison group, thus showing no significant difference for prison readmission (Duwe and Kerschner 2008). Yet, the CIP offenders who did return to prison spent 40 fewer days in prison than the comparison group, thus reducing the costs of the program. In addition, the CIP group was significantly less likely to commit a new crime against a person than the comparison group. The authors indicate that this study emphasizes the need to conduct longitudinal studies that are inclusive of multiple outcome measures and an understanding of why and how offenders fail, and not just whether they fail (Duwe and Kerschner 2008). Similarly, a study of Pennsylvania's Quehanna Motivational Boot Camp, when only considering the incarceration period of the boot camp program, researchers found no significant differences in recidivism except for those with a longer criminal record (Kempinen and Kurlychek 2003), but after the program added a reentry aftercare component the program showed a significant reduction in recidivism overall (Kurlychek and Kampinen 2006).

The culmination of 30 years of findings on BCPs' effects on institutional crowding, costs, attitudes, adjustment, program completion, and recidivism shows support for both proponents and critics of BCPs; when strategically implemented programs appear to significantly shorten sentences, reduce crowding and system-level costs. They also appear to have a positive effect on attitudinal change, but are stressful environments that are embraced by some and create greater emotional and psychological hardships for others. Finally, the cumulative evidence is that they do not significantly reduce recidivism and when they do minimize post-release failure it is because they incorporate rehabilitation and other life skills programs followed by aftercare support for graduates during reentry.

Aligning Boot Camp Prisons with Core Correctional Practices

Since the implementation of the first boot camp prison in 1984, a lot has been learned about core correctional practices and the principles of effective interventions (PEI) that may help to explain the successes and failures of boot camp prions (see National Institute of Corrections (NIC) 2013, 2016). The advent of research on "what works" in corrections lends powerful insight about using BCPs as an intervention to address offender change. We argue that BCPs should be restructured where necessary to adhere to well-established and evidence-based core correctional practices. If BCPs fail to meet and sustain these professional standards then they should be abandoned as a correctional intervention.

There are eight principles of effective interventions including: assessing offenders' risk/needs; enhancing intrinsic motivation; targeting meaningful interventions to offenders; providing cognitive-behavioral strategies with well trained staff; increasing positive reinforcement; engaging prosocial support systems; measuring relevant processes/practices; and providing measurable feedback (NIC 2016). Research shows that interventions with greater levels of adherence to these principles significantly reduce recidivism and those programs that do not adhere to these principles risk having the unintended consequence of increasing recidivism (Andrews and Bonta 2010). Although not framed in terms of core correctional practices, MacKenzie and colleagues' extensive research based on multi-site studies of BCPs shows differences across programs based on the integrity of their implementation and the inclusion of attributes that reflect these principles. When these findings are placed in context of the principles of effective interventions the mixed results found in the BCP literature become more understandable.

First, important elements of the principles of effective interventions focus on offender risk and needs assessments and the targeting of appropriate populations. Most BCPs target lower-risk, young, non-violent, offenders exchanging a longer term in prison for a shorter more intense prison experience. Although this is effective for accomplishing system level goals of reducing prison populations and costs, according to the PEI, intensive programs should be reserved for high-risk offenders, address criminogenic needs, and be of a duration to fully address risks and needs through programming. Military drill, exercise, and labor are not designed to address criminogenic needs (antisocial attitudes, antisocial peers, chemical dependency, etc.) and many boot camps severely limit the time dedicated to cognitive-behavioral programming that is proven to be effective. Thus, it is not surprising that BCPs with more time devoted to programming were more effective in reducing recidivism. Finally, the type and duration of programming, also known as dosage, matters. Subjecting low-risk offenders to intensive interventions with little to no attention given to cognitive-behavioral programs risks increasing recidivism versus reducing it (see NIC 2013).

Second, the principles of effective interventions indicate that it is important to use communication techniques that enhance intrinsic motivation (versus persuasion) and emphasize positive re-enforcements to bring about lasting change (NIC 2013, 2016). Boot camps steeped in military drill and ceremony, depending upon how it is implemented, may support or violate these principles. If boot camp military environments are implemented in accordance with the concerns of critics by using humiliation, aggression, and coercion to persuade offenders to change, then boot camps are likely to fail and potentially increase recidivism and other negative outcomes for offenders. Conversely, if BCP programs are implemented within a military philosophy that builds people up through motivating internal change and reinforcing positive behavior through maximizing the recognition of accomplishments, versus overemphasizing personal failures, than BCPs may ultimately create a prison environment that is safe, structured, supportive, and provides the emotional feedback necessary to transition short-term attitudinal change to long-term behavioral change necessary to reduce recidivism (see Kurlychek 2010, for a related discussion).

Third, interventions must be responsive to participants' temperament, learning styles, motivation, gender, and culture (NIC 2016). Boot camp prisons, due to the rigid military-based training environment, tends to be restricted in its ability to adjust to different types of individual level offenders' needs and styles of learning. Therefore, it is not surprising that participants who had histories of sexual and physical abuse, substance abuse, and emotional problems were more likely to be dismissed or dropped out of the program. Subjecting offenders to a hyper-masculine, militaristic prison environment designed by men to subject young men to intense discipline and control fails to consider the unique needs of women or young men who may need support in transitioning out of controlling and abusive environments into self-sustainability and independence. This is especially true given men and women graduating from BCPs are not transitioning to a welcoming profession in the military where the lessons learned in boot camp are applicable, but instead into families and communities challenged by economic, social, and political contexts (see Lutze 2014); thus, the apparent success of aftercare programs that provide a continuum of care to assist graduates to decompress from their intensive boot camp experience and transition successfully back into families and the community.

Finally, the principles of effective treatment recognize the importance of well-trained and professional staff and the ability to measure outcomes that can inform effective policy and practice. Corrections is a complex profession and requires a professional and skilled staff to safely manage offender populations, effectively implement interventions, and achieve system and institutional level goals (see Lutze 2014, 2016). Correctional interventions such as BCPs, although appearing simple in their symbolism, are extremely complex as they attempt to effect change in human behavior through the simultaneous use of coercion, treatment, support, and accountability within a unique correctional environment. Expertise or personal experience in military training alone is not enough to successfully implement such a complex intervention inclusive of understanding the social, psychological, physical, and emotional baseline for each individual; especially in an offender population that is often challenged by learning deficits, poor coping skills, and antisocial attitudes. Therefore, program integrity through evaluation and quality assurance procedures are crucial to assuring success over time. Given the complexity of what BCPs attempt to do within a short period of time, it is no wonder that the findings are mixed and not always complimentary.

Conclusion

The future of BCPs is dependent on their ability to adhere to evidence-based practices and their potential to achieve long-term offender change as measured through reducing recidivism. Although there was an explosion of research on BCPs in the two decades following their implementation, there is a scarcity of research focused on contemporary boot camp programs. The optimism for success surrounding third-wave implementation of BCPs including military ceremony/drill, increased programming, and aftercare programs suggest that these programs may be gravitating toward enhanced implementation considerate of the principles of effective interventions. Based on current research, however, it is uncertain whether most contemporary BCPs in operation are stagnated replicas of early failures or advancing according to evidence-based practices that will enhance the system-, institutional-, and individual-level goals envisioned by the original reformers.

Notes

1. Shock incarceration was originally used to describe short, harsh, punitive periods of jail or prison time designed to scare offenders away from committing future crime by developing an aversion to imprisonment. As boot camp prisons became popular they too became known as shock incarceration programs due to their intensity.
2. Net widening refers to the practice of implementing policies or practices that sweep more people into the criminal justice system who otherwise would have been diverted from the system or treated through the least controlling mechanism possible to achieve intended outcomes.

References

Alexander, Michelle. 2012. *The New Jim Crow: Mass Incarceration in the Age of Colorblindness*. New York, NY: The New Press.

Andrews, Donald, and James Bonta. 2010. *The Psychology of Criminal Conduct*, 5th ed. Cincinnati, OH: Anderson Publishing.

Aos, Steve, Polly Phipps, Robert Barnoski, and Roxanne Lieb. 2001. *The Comparative Costs and Benefits of Programs to Reduce Crime: Version 4.0*. Olympia, WA: Washington State Institute for Public Policy.

Austin, James, and John Irwin. 1997. *It's About Time: America's Imprisonment Binge*. Belmont, CA: Wadsworth.

Benda, Brent. 2005a. "Boot Camps Revisited: Issues, Problems, Prospects." *Journal of Offender Rehabilitation* 40(3/4): 1–25.

Benda, Brent. 2005b. "Gender Differences in Life-course Theory of Recidivism: A Survival Analysis." *International Journal of Offender Therapy and Comparative Criminology* 49(3): 325–342.

Benda, Brent, and Nathaniel J. Pallone, Eds. 2005. *Rehabilitation Issues, Problems, and Prospects in Boot Camp*. Binghamton, NY: The Haworth Press.

Benda, Brent, Nancy Toombs, and Mark Peacock. 2006. "Distinguishing Graduate from Dropouts and Dismissals: Who Fails Boot Camp?" *Journal of Criminal Justice* 34: 27–28.

Burns, Jerald, James F. Anderson, and Laronistine Dyson. 1997. "What Disciplinary Rehabilitation Unit Participants are Saying about Shock Incarceration." *Journal of Contemporary Criminal Justice* 13(2): 172–183.

Burton, Velmer, James W. Marquart, Steven J. Cuvelier, Leanne Fiftal Alarid, and Robert J. Hunter. 1993. "A Study of Attitudinal Change among Boot Camp Participants." *Federal Probation* 57(3): 46–52.

Clark, Cheryl L., and David W. Aziz. 1996. "Shock Incarceration in New York State: Philosophy, Results, and Limitations." Pp. 39–68 in *Correctional Boot Camps: A Tough Intermediate Sanction*, edited by D. MacKenzie, and E. Hebert. Washington, DC: U.S. Department of Justice.

Correia, Mark. 1997. "Boot Camps, Exercise, and Delinquency: An Analytical Critique of the Use of Physical Exercise to Facilitate Decreases in Delinquent Behavior." *Journal of Contemporary Criminal Justice* 13: 94–113.

Cowles, Ernest L., and Thomas C. Castellano. 1996. "Substance Abuse Programming in Adult Correctional Boot Camps: A National Overview." Pp. 207–232 in *Correctional Boot Camps: A Tough Intermediate Sanction*, edited by D. MacKenzie, and E. Hebert. Washington, DC: U.S. Department of Justice.

Cullen, Francis T., and Karen E. Gilbert. 1982. *Reaffirming Rehabilitation*. Cincinnati, OH: Anderson Publishing.

Cullen, Francis, and Cheryl Lero Jonson. 2012. *Correctional Theory: Context and Consequences*. Thousand Oaks, CA: Sage.

Cullen, Francis, Kristie R. Blevins, Jennifer S. Trager, and Paul Gendreau. 2005. "The Rise and Fall of Boot Camp Prisons." *Journal of Offender Rehabilitation* 40(3–4): 53–70.

Curry, Elliott. 1985. *Confronting Crime: An American Challenge*. New York: Panteon Books.

Duwe, Grant, and Deborah Kerschner. 2008. "Removing a Nail from the Boot Camp Coffin: An Outcome Evaluation of Minnesota's Challenge Incarceration Program." *Crime & Delinquency* 54(4): 614–643.

Ethridge, Philip A., and Jonathan R. Sorensen. 1997. "An Analysis of Attitudinal Change and Community Adjustment among Probationers in a County Boot Camp." *Journal of Contemporary Criminal Justice* 13(2): 139–154.

Franke, Derrick, David Bierie, and Doris MacKenzie. 2010. "Legitimacy in Corrections: A Randomized Experiment Comparing a Boot Camp Prison with a Prison." *Criminology & Public Policy* 9(1): 89–117.

Garland, David. 2001. *The Culture of Control: Crime and Social Order in Contemporary Society*. Chicago, IL: The University of Chicago Press.

Johnson, Robert. 2002. *Hard Time: Understanding and Reforming the Prison*, 3rd ed. Belmont, CA: Wadsworth.

Kempinen, Cynthia A., and Megan C. Kurlychek. 2003. "An Outcome Evaluation of Pennsylvania's Boot Camp: Does Rehabilitative Programming within a Disciplinary Setting Reduce Recidivism?" *Crime & Delinquency* 49(4): 581–602.

Kempinen, Cynthia, and L. Tinik. 2011. *Pennsylvania's Motivational Boot Camp Program: What Have We Learned Over the Last Seventeen Years?* Harrisburgh, PA: Pennsylvania Commission on Sentencing.

Kraska, Peter, Ed. 2001. *Militarizing the American Criminal Justice System: The Changing Roles of the Armed Forces and the Police*. Boston, MA: Northeastern University Press.

Kurlychek, Megan. 2010. "Transforming Attitudinal Change into Behavioral Change: The Missing Link. *Criminology & Public Policy* 9(1): 119–125.

Kurlychek, Megan, and Cynthia Kempinen. 2006. "Beyond Boot Camp: The Impact of Aftercare on Offender Reentry." *Criminology & Public Policy* 5(2): 363–388.

Lipsey, Mark W., and Francis T. Cullen. 2007. "The Effectiveness of Correctional Rehabilitation: A Review of Systematic Reviews." *Annual Review of Law and Society* 3: 297–320.

Lutze, Faith E. 1998. "Are Shock Incarceration Programs more Rehabilitative than Traditional Prisons? A Survey of Inmates." *Justice Quarterly* 15(3): 547–563.

Lutze, Faith. 2001. "The Influence of a Shock Incarceration Program on Inmate Adjustment and Attitudinal Change." *Journal of Criminal Justice* 29(3): 255–267.

Lutze, Faith. 2002. "Conscience and Convenience in Boot Camp Prison: An Opportunity for Success." *The Journal of Forensic Psychology Practice* 2(4): 71–81.

Lutze, Faith E. 2006. "Boot Camp Prisons and Corrections Policy: Moving from Militarism to an Ethic of Care." *Journal of Criminology and Public Policy* 5(2): 389–400.

Lutze, Faith. 2014. *The Professional Lives of Community Corrections Officers: The Invisible Side of Reentry*. Thousand Oaks, CA: Sage.

Lutze, Faith. 2016. "Corrections Education at the Nexus of Science and Practice: A History of Conscience and Convenience in Achieving Professionalization." *Journal of Criminal Justice Education* 27(4): 509–534.

Lutze, Faith E., and Cortney Bell. 2005. "Boot Camp Prisons as Masculine Organizations: Rethinking Recidivism and Program Design." *Journal of Offender Rehabilitation* 40(3/4): 133–152.

Lutze, Faith, and David C. Brody. 1999. "Mental Abuse as Cruel and Unusual Punishment: Do Coot Camp Prisons Violate the Eighth Amendment?" *Crime and Delinquency* 45(2): 242–255.

Lutze, Faith E., and Otwin Marenin. 1997. "The Effectiveness of a Shock Incarceration Program and a Minimum Security Prison on Changing Attitudes Towards Drugs." *The Journal of Contemporary Criminal Justice* 13(2): 106–130.

Lutze, Faith, and David W. Murphy. 1999. "Ultra-masculine Prison Environments and Inmate Adjustment: It is Time to Move Beyond the 'Boys will be Boys' Paradigm." *Justice Quarterly* 16(4): 709–733.

MacKenzie, Doris Layton, and Heidi Donaldson. 1996. "Boot Camp for Women Offenders." *Criminal Justice Review* 21(1): 21–43.

MacKenzie, Doris L., and Eugene E. Hebert, Eds. 1996. *Correctional Boot Camps: A Tough Intermediate Sanction*. National Institute of Justice. Washington, DC: U.S. Department of Justice.

MacKenzie, Doris, and Dale G. Parent. 1991. "Shock Incarceration and Prison Crowding in Louisiana." *Journal of Criminal Justice* 19: 225–237.

MacKenzie, Doris, and Alex Piquero. 1994. "The Impact of Shock Incarceration Programs on Prison Crowding." *Crime and Delinquency* 40(2): 222–249.

MacKenzie, Doris Layton, and James W. Shaw. 1990. "Inmate Adjustment and Change During Shock Incarceration: The Impact of Correctional Boot Camp Programs." *Justice Quarterly* 7(1): 125–150.

MacKenzie, Doris Layton, and Claire Souryal. 1995. "Inmate's Attitude Change During Incarceration: A Comparison of Boot Camp with Traditional Prison." *Justice Quarterly* 12(2): 324–353.

MacKenzie, Doris Layton, and Claire Souryal. 1996. "Multisite Study of Correctional Boot Camps." Pp. 287–296 in *Correctional Boot Camps: A Tough Intermediate Sanction*, edited by D. MacKenzie and E. Hebert. Washington, DC: U.S. Department of Justice.

MacKenzie, Doris Layton, Lori A. Elis, Sally S. Simpson, and Stacy B. Skroban. 1996. "Boot Camps as an Alternative for Women." Pp. 233–244 in *Correctional Boot Camps: A Tough Intermediate Sanction*, edited by D. MacKenzie and E. Hebert. Washington, DC: U.S. Department of Justice.

Marcus-Mendoza, Susan T., Jody Klein-Saffran, and Faith Lutze. 1998. "A Feminist Examination of Boot Camp Prison Programs for Women." *Women & Therapy* 21(1): 173–185.

McCorkle, Richard C. 1995. "Correctional Boot Camps and Change in Attitude: Is All this Shouting Necessary? A Research Note." *Justice Quarterly* 12(2): 365–375.

Mele, Christopher, and Teresa Ann Miller, Eds. 2005. *Civil Penalties, Social Consequences*. New York: Routledge.

Millkey, Alexander Millkey. 2005. "Comparison of Attitudes Related to Substance Abuse in Male Inmates Following Treatment in Boot Camps and Therapeutic Communities." PhD Dissertation, School of Professional Psychology, Forest Grove, Pacific University.

Mitchell, Ojmarrh, Doris L. MacKenzie, and Deanna M. Perez. 2005. "A Randomized Evaluation of the Maryland Correctional Boot Camp for Adults: Effects on Offender Antisocial Attitudes and Cognitions." *Journal of Offender Rehabilitation* 40(3/4): 71–86.

Morash, Merry, and Lila Rucker. 1990. "A Critical Look at the Idea of Boot Camp as a Correctional Reform." *Crime and Delinquency* 36: 204–222.

National Institute of Corrections. 2013. *Evidence-based Practices in the Criminal Justice System*. National Institute of Corrections. Washington, DC: U.S. Department of Justice.

National Institute of Corrections. 2016, June 29. *The Principles of Effective Interventions*. Retrieved May 3, 2017 from http://nicic.gov/theprinciplesofeffectiveinterventions

Parent, Dale. 1996. "Boot Camps and Prison Crowding." Pp. 263–274 in *Correctional Boot Camps: A Tough Intermediate Sanction*, edited by D. MacKenzie, and D. Parent. Washington, DC: U.S. Department of Justice.

Reiman, Jeffrey. 2004. *The Rich Get Richer and the Poor Get Prison: Ideology, Class, and Criminal Justice*, 7th ed. Boston, MA: Allyn & Bacon.

Shaw, James W., and Doris Layton MacKenzie. 1991. "Shock Incarceration and its Impact on the Lives of Problem Drinkers." *American Journal of Criminal Justice* 16: 64–96.

Stephan, James J., and Jennifer C. Karberg. 2003. *Census of State and Federal Correctional Facilities, 2000*. Bureau of Justice Statistics. Washington, DC: U.S. Department of Justice.

Stinchcomb, Jeanne B. 2005. "From Optimistic Policies to Pessimistic Outcomes: Why Won't Boot Camps Either Succeed Pragmatically or Succumb Politically." *Journal of Offender Rehabilitation* 40(3/4): 27–52.

Toch, Hans. 1977. *Living in Prison: The Ecology of Survival*. New York: Free Press.
Wilson, David B., Doris L. MacKenzie, and Fawn Ngo Mitchell. 2005. *Effects of Correctional Boot-Camps on Offending: A Campbell Collaboration Systematic Review*. Retrieved May 3, 2017 from www.campbellcollaboration.org
Wright, Kevin, and Lynne Goodstein. 1989. "Correctional Environments." Pp. 253–270 in *The American Prison*, edited by L. Goodstein, and D. Makenzie. New York: Plunum.

21 Specialty Courts

Brittany Hood and Bradley Ray

Specialty Courts, also known as problem-solving courts or therapeutic courts, are criminal courts that attempt to divert specific types of offenders out of further involvement in the criminal justice system, by linking them into community-based treatments or services designed to address the underlying causes of these offenders' criminal behavior. The most common type of specialty court is the drug court, though as specialty courts continue to evolve, the model has been applied to a growing number of social issues such as mental illness, domestic violence, veterans, juvenile delinquency, and homelessness. One of the key factors that is often cited as distinguishing specialty courts from traditional criminal courts is the emphasis placed on therapeutic jurisprudence, a philosophy that suggests if the law is administered properly, it can be used as a therapeutic agent to promote the mental health and physical wellbeing of defendants (Wexler and Winick 1991). Thus, specialty courts do not focus on establishing guilt and the appropriate punitive response, but instead attempt to leverage the authority of the court to have a positive effect on the defendant's wellbeing.

Brief History of Specialty Courts

The juvenile court system of the late nineteenth century is perhaps the earliest example of a specialty court (Nolan 2001; Winick 2002; Winick and Wexler 2003). The juvenile court movement began in Cook County (Chicago), Illinois in the late 1800s and was an attempt to address the criminal behavior of minors. These early juvenile courts originated from *parens patriae*, which suggests the government has the right to impose on the life of a child when there is a threat of potential harm (Hahn, O'Conner, and Chimsky 1978; Sullivan 1997). Juvenile courts were a response to increasing rates of juvenile delinquency during this time and championed by policymakers who were seeking an intervention that would teach adolescents law-abiding behaviors (Colomy and Kretzmann 1995; Sullivan 1997). The juvenile court model was considered successful in reducing juvenile delinquency by seeking rehabilitation in place of incarceration (Handler 1965). This was accomplished through evaluations of individual circumstances in each case rather than equally punishing youths as adults for their offenses. As a result of this specialty court model's perceived success, by 1925 nearly all states in the U.S. had a juvenile court. However, critics of the juvenile court movement suggested that judges made decisions based on little evidence; that children were automatically removed from parental custody for as little as truancy; that juvenile intervention disproportionately affected lower-class families; and that facilities meant to house juvenile delinquents were overcrowded and lacked qualified staff (Elroy and Ryder 1999; Wizner 1971). By the 1950s, many also came to question the ability of the juvenile court to successfully rehabilitate delinquent youth as a growing number of juveniles were being institutionalized, but also because these youth were not afforded constitutional legal rights in their juvenile court cases. Therefore, following a 1967 U.S. Supreme Court decision

(*In re Gault* 387, U.S. 1), youth offenders in juvenile court cases were given constitutional rights such as protection against self-incrimination, rights to notice of the charges, and to have an attorney. Consequently, juvenile courts were required to follow more moral criminal court proceedings.

While juvenile courts represent an early attempt to create a specialized docket, the modern specialty court movement is more commonly associated with the first drug court in Dade County, Florida in 1989 (Goldkamp 1999; Nolan 2001). Following the "war on drugs" policies of the 1980s, there were vast increases in the arrest, prosecution, and incarceration of drug-related offenses, which led to overcrowding in jails and prisons (Clear and Frost 2015; Glass, Perron, Ilgen, Chermack, Ratliff, and Zivin 2010). This mass incarceration of drug-related offenses resulted in the implementation of various diversion programs, including drug courts. Like juvenile courts, the first drug court maintained a separate docket for defendants who were arrested. However, the drug court focused specifically on those defendants with drug charges or those who had a history of substance of abuse. Moreover, unlike juvenile courts, participation in drug court was voluntary and presented as an alternative to the traditional criminal court process. Observers lauded the drug court model for its innovation and success and it was quickly emulated in other jurisdictions. In 1997, drug court stakeholders convened to determine the "key components" of the drug court model (National Association of Drug Court Professionals 1997). These components stated that drug courts should provide a continuum of drug treatment that is integrated with criminal justice case processing; use a nonadversarial court team made up of criminal justice, legal, and addiction specialists; monitor defendants using drug testing as well as continued judicial supervision, and utilize sanctions and incentives to obtain compliance from defendants. These guidelines helped gain federal funds for implementation of these courts nationwide, and ten years after the creation of the Dade County court there were over 500 drug courts in the U.S.

Specialty courts have continued to proliferate and recent estimates suggest that there are over 4,000 specialty courts in the United States (Huddleson and Marlowe 2011). Moreover, the key components identified in the early drug courts have continued to serve as guiding framework as the speciality court movement has progressed to serve specific offender populations; with the intent of focusing on ongoing judicial supervision, a nonadvisarial team approach, the use of sanctions and incentives, and case management. As specialty courts have evolved there are now both post-adjudication courts, where participants are required to enter a guilty plea or be convicted prior to enrollment and upon successful completion the sentence is reduced or the charges are expunged; as well as pre-adjudication model where criminal charges are held in limbo pending outcome. Today there are specialty courts that address a wide range of social issues such as drug addiction, mental illness, prostitution, homelessness, domestic violence, and community reentry from custody, just to name a few.

The Specialty Court Process

While specialty courts vary in many details, there are several unique commonalities to note. To discuss these, we rely primarily on the process for two of the most popular specialty court models: drug courts and mental health courts. Specialty courts generally operate under a separate docket from traditional courts and develop policies and procedures that the court operates by, but also expectations for defendants who opt into the process. In developing these policies and procedures, the specialty court model must also develop a team that generally consists of a judge, criminal justice personnel, and community-based treatment or service providers. These specialty court teams often use screening and assessments to identify appropriate individuals based on court eligibility. For example, drug courts screen offenders to determine whether they have a history of substance abuse or a substance abuse diagnosis. The specialty court team then develops a process to determine which clients are eligible for admittance into the program; for example, the judge may serve as the final decision maker, or the final decision might be based on a consensus from the team (see Belenko, Fabrikant, and Wolff 2011).

A key procedural component of specialty courts is their voluntariness; that is, defendants choose to be in the specialty court and can opt out at any time. If a defendant opts into the court process, they must agree to comply with the rules set out by the court. Another important aspect of the specialty court process is the use of extended judicial supervision. Defendants must attend regularly scheduled status hearings where they meet with the judge; these supervision periods vary by court and can be anywhere from a few months to more than one year. As part of this extended judicial supervision, specialty court teams meet on the days between status hearings to discuss changes in each defendant's progress, or lack thereof. The specialty court team uses a nonadversarial approach; therefore, defense and prosecuting attorneys do not dispute innocence or guilt, but rather work as part of a team to develop individualized treatment plans for defendants. For example, treatment personnel on the team work with criminal justice personnel to identify community-based treatments and services that address the underlying causes of each defendant's behavior. The team might also assign additional requirements for defendants, such as meeting with treatment providers, attending appointments, or checking in with criminal justice personnel. Collaboration between a specialty court and community treatment and services agencies provides opportunities to promote successful outcomes and criminal desistance.

Each specialty court has its own program structure, often consisting of phases that mark consistent compliance and successes. For example, phase progress might require employment, completing treatment, and following additional court mandates. In some specialty courts defendants are required to pay for drug tests and court fines; if these fees are not paid, sanctions can be implemented that may interfere with progression to the next phase. When defendants act against the court or violate rules, sanctions are imposed, which might include jail days, bench warrants, increased treatment, increased drug testing, and extension of the defendant's time in the program. If the defendant abides by court mandates, incentives are handed down to positively reinforce compliance. Incentives might include verbal praise, certificates, graduation to higher program phase, and less frequent court or intervention requirements. If the defendant remains compliant for the required period of time, criminal charges are dismissed or the sentence is reduced. However, if consistently noncompliant, the defendant is terminated from the program and the case is sent back to traditional criminal court for sentencing.

While similarities exist in the specialty court process, there are several factors that differentiate these courts from one another. Of these differences, the most notable are eligibility requirements. For example, some specialty courts accept only misdemeanor charges, others also accept felony offenses, and some accept *only* felony offenses. Specialty courts also differ in whether they accept defendants prior to their plea (deferred prosecution) or only after a guilty plea and sentencing (post-adjudication). When a court operates under post-adjudication methods, the defendant is required to first plead guilty to charges and the court either suspends or defers charges until completion. If the defendant is terminated or opts out of the program, they will be charged in traditional court. When the defendant completes the diversion program successfully, they will have their charges dropped, reduced, or expunged from their criminal record. Alternatively, in the case of the deferred prosecution model, defendants are diverted to specialty court awaiting completion of their criminal sentence. If the defendant is successful, their charges are dropped, whereas unsuccessful completion would result in being returned to the traditional court for adjudication.

Specialty Court Types

Drug courts are the most common of all specialty courts, yet there is a myriad of specialty court typologies that focus on specific types of offenses or offenders. For example, most drug courts are adult drug courts (described above), but there are also juvenile drug courts that work with youth who have drug or alcohol problems; campus drug courts that focus on drug use in the college environment; DWI courts that focus on repeat offenders arrested for driving while impaired; family drug treatment courts that focus on situations where there is parental substance abuse; and reentry drug courts that focus on the reintegration of drug-involved offenders released from correctional facilities. Moreover, within each of these various specialty drug court models there is also variation in the judicial process. Most early drug courts used deferred prosecution methods (pre-plea) and were considered diversion programs, while drug courts today are often post-adjudication (post-plea) or allow both types of cases (Justice Policy Institute 2011). As mentioned previously, eligibility requirements can also vary by drug court; the majority of courts allow for drug possession and non-violent offenses, require a positive drug test, or have a history of substance abuse at the time of arrest.

Following the success of drug courts, the nation's first mental health court was established in 1997 in Broward County (Florida), where local judges observed the county's rapidly increasing number of misdemeanor cases involving mental illness that led to overburdened court dockets and overcrowded jails (Boothroyd, Poythress, McGaha, and Petrila 2003; McGaha, Boothroyd, Poythress, Petrila, and Ort 2002). Many suspect that deinstitutionalization (which refers to closing psychiatric hospitals and releasing former patients to be served in the community) contributed to increases in the incarceration of persons with mental illness; because persons with mental illness were no longer held in hospitals, there were greater numbers of them in the community who were at risk of arrest (see Teplin 1984 for discussion). This first mental health court adapted the drug court model to serve mentally ill offenders, and proposed that judges who preside over the court's docket should "possesses a unique understanding and ability to expeditiously and efficiently move people from an overcrowded jail system into the mental health system" (Boothroyd et al. 2003: 16). However, the key components of the drug court model—e.g., voluntariness, a separate docket, judicial supervision, sanctions, and incentives—continued to serve as the foundation for the mental health court model. In November 2000, the government approved the Law Enforcement and Mental Health Project that enacted legislation to develop and fund 100 pilot mental health courts. Today there are over 300 mental health courts, making them the second most prevalent type of specialty court.

Another specialty court model that has continued to proliferate in the U.S. is the domestic violence court. Following recognition of domestic violence as criminal behavior in the 1970s, and experimentation by police and prosecutors with new approaches towards this issue, various court-based domestic violence programs were developed in the following decade (Casey and Rottman 2003). However, it was not until the mid 1990s, following the Violence Against Women Act, that funding was made available for specialty court programs to focus on domestic violence. The first courts dedicated to domestic violence exerted efforts towards protection of the victim and mediating familial issues between partners while concurrently adjudicating other family cases. It is estimated that there are over 200 domestic violence courts in the United States, and almost equal numbers across Canada and England (Gover, MacDonald, and Alpert 2003; Karan, Keilitz, and Denaro 1999), and that over 300 courts have incorporated specialized processing for domestic violence cases (Keilitz 2000; Levey, Steketee, and Keilitz 2001). These domestic violence courts share six goals, including informed decision making; offender accountability; collaboration between therapeutic agencies, community services, and the court; and reductions in recidivism. Judges, prosecutors, and law enforcement are more likely to receive training in specialized areas pertaining to intimate-partner violence, and to accept cases between non-partner disputes (Tsai 2000). However, it is important to note that there are many aspects of domestic violence courts that distinguish them from other specialty courts. For example, domestic violence courts accept only violent criminal cases; because of this the court proceedings are often more adversarial. Moreover, because the defendant's behavior is learned, rather than a treatable addiction or illness, domestic violence court teams often focus less on therapy and more on monitoring the defendant and promoting accountability for actions.

As noted previously, early juvenile courts were designed to address all legal problems committed by minors and relied on little information when supervising participants; however, modern juvenile courts have much more stringent proceedings and due process (National Juvenile Court Data Archive Online 2010). Courts now accept referrals and rely on reports from police, school administration, and concerned adults. Cases are adjudicated or referred to a waiver hearing which is the court's opportunity to remove the juvenile from the court's docket and transfer him/her to criminal adult court. During adjudication within the juvenile court, an individual will be judged as either a "delinquent" or as a "status offender," and in some instances, cases can be dismissed or continued in contemplation. Once a minor is under the jurisdiction of the court, they follow adult court proceedings.

While not as common as drug courts or mental health courts, one recent application of the specialty court model is reentry court, which focuses on helping offenders reintegrate back into the community post-incarceration. Thus, the goal of reentry courts is to decrease or remove barriers that recently released offenders traditionally experience, that are predictive of reoffending, and increase access to services and therapeutic interventions to reduce recidivism. The reentry court team acts as an additional parole component, intervening in the months prior to offender release to ease the transition back into the community and foster compliance while on parole. Reentry court is voluntary; though in a contractual sense, returning inmates often have to agree to intense judicial supervision and drug testing, usually for 12 to 18 months, in return for a reduced parole period. As with other specialty courts, reentry courts link participants to needed substance abuse treatment, mental health services, employment and education services, healthcare, childcare, and parenting skills courses; there are also court-ordered sanctions and incentives for court mandates.

A final specialty court model worth noting is veterans courts. The first veterans court was established in Buffalo, New York in 2008 in response to the growing number of veterans with post-traumatic stress disorder, traumatic brain disorder, and substance abuse or mental health issues. Following therapeutic jurisprudence principles, the veteran court aimed to combine elements of drug court and mental health court to link active-duty or military veterans to substance abuse or mental health treatment, as an alternative to incarceration. Moreover, veterans often face additional barriers such as psychological, employment, and housing issues that might increase the likelihood to engage in criminal *behavior* (Walls 2010). One of the unique elements of the veterans court experience is their use of a mentoring program. Each defendant is paired with a mentor who works with them throughout the court process. This mentor serves in a similar role as a case manager would, in that they help defendants to navigate the process but also provide moral and motivational support. As with other specialty court types, one aspect of the veterans court process that varies by jurisdiction is eligibility. Some courts only accept misdemeanants and exclude offenders with a felony or crimes of violence. This can be an especially important criterion, as offenders charged with inter-family violence may be excluded from the veterans court process. Sizeable research literature demonstrates support for the utilization of veterans specialty courts to reduce veteran-defendant recidivism and encourage psychological healing through applications of therapeutic jurisprudence (Walls 2010).

Empirical Research on Specialty Courts

The vast majority of empirical research on specialty courts has focused on the goal of increasing public safety by reducing criminal activity. From this research, there is little debate that participation in a drug court or mental health courts can reduce a defendant's subsequent involvement in the criminal justice system. While much more research has been done on drug courts than mental health courts, meta-analyses of available empirical evidence consistently suggests that defendants participating in these courts have lower rates of recidivism during court supervision (and following court completion) than similar defendants in regular court (GAO 2005; Mitchell, Wilson, Eggers, and MacKenzie 2012; Sarteschi, Vaughn, and Kim 2011; Wilson, Mitchell, and MacKenzie 2006). Within this literature, researchers frequently use administrative data to examine criminal justice outcomes to determine whether those who participate in a specialty court are less likely to be rearrested, have fewer rearrests, or serve fewer jail days than groups of similar defendants who were not in specialty court. Comparison groups most often come from quasi-experimental designs, as few studies have been able to use random assignment.

It is not surprising that so much of the specialty court research has focused on recidivism as a measure of success, as this is consistent with the key goals of practitioners who work in these programs (Almquist and Dodd 2009; National Association of Drug Court Professionals 1997). However, far fewer studies have examined participant perspectives of the specialty court process or the theoretical mechanisms associated with positive criminal justice outcomes. As legal perspectives, therapeutic jurisprudence and restorative justice have been pivotal in the growing number of problem-solving courts. Both perspectives shine a critical light on the criminal justice system's "get tough" approach to crime and highlight the ability of the legal system to address social problems. However, they offer little help to researchers attempting to examine what is working inside the so-called "black box" of the specialty court process (Gottfredson, Kearley, Najaka, and Rocha 2007). The theory most often attributed to specialty court's success with criminal justice outcomes is procedural justice theory which postulates that making fair decisions and having respectful relationships with defendants (giving them both voice and validation), lead to increased compliance with court mandates and the law (McIvor 2009; Tyler 2009; Tyler and Fagan 2008; Tyler, Sherman, Strang, Barnes, and Woods 2007). Researchers note various important elements in explaining these reduced recidivism rates (Carey, Finigan, and Pukstas 2008; Cissner, and Rempel 2005), but procedural justice has been emphasized as an essential factor in explaining success among these courts (see Marlowe 2010; Rossman, Roman, Zweig, Rempel, and Lindquist 2011).

Literature indicates the presence of procedural justice results in greater compliance with legal authorities and engaging in law abiding behaviors (Lind and Tyler 1988; Tyler 2006). Procedural justice processes are present when defendants perceive being treated with respect and dignity, having an opportunity to voice their side of the dispute, and fair decision making of court personnel. The concept of coercion is expected to be inversely related to procedural justice as defendants should ideally perceive the process to be both voluntary (non-coercive) and procedurally just (Munetz, Ritter, Teller, and Bonfine 2014; Poythress, Petrila, McGaha, and Boothroyd 2002; Redlich and Han 2014). There is an extensive body of literature suggesting that defendants perceive greater procedural justice and less coercion in drug courts and mental health courts as compared to traditional court or community-based treatments (Munetz et al. 2014; Poythress et al. 2002). In addition, defendant outcomes are enhanced when defendants perceive the process to be more procedurally just and voluntary (Kopelovich, Yanos, Pratt, and Koerner 2013; Redlich and Han 2014; Rossman, Roman, Zweig, Rempel, and Lindquist 2011; Young and Belenko 2002).

Critiques of the Specialty Court Model

Specialty courts have proliferated for over a century, and while they have improved in a number of ways, some critiques remain. In most specialty courts, eligibility requirements restrict participation to individuals who are low risk in comparison to higher-risk individuals as indicated by a risk-assessment tool. Specialty court scholars assert that it would be more beneficial to focus efforts and invest resources into higher-risk individuals. These defendants tend to have a higher need for therapeutic intervention, and would be less likely to have their charges dismissed in traditional cases (Broner, Lattimore, Cowell, and Schlenger 2004; Case, Steadman, Dupius, and Morris 2009; Hartford, Carey, and Mendonca 2006; Ray, Hood, and Canada 2015; Steadman and Naples 2005). Other literature suggests that defendants of specialty courts sometimes are unaware of the voluntariness associated with supervision of diversion courts. Individuals who feel coerced into being under the jurisdiction of the court, are less likely to successfully complete their program (Munetz et al. 2014; Poythress et al. 2002; Redlich, Hoover, Summers, and Steadman 2010; Tyler 2003). Study results support full disclosure to defendants prior to opting into the court, so they are made aware of all requirements for participation and completion when deciding to divert to specialty court programs in lieu of traditional adjudication.

While specialty courts show promise in their ability to reduce recidivism post successful completion, some critics of diversion programs such as these emphasize the length of time an offender spends in court in comparison to being traditionally adjudicated. Defendants who choose to have their cases adjudicated in a specialty court spend longer in the court system than they would have if they had instead chosen to pursue the traditional court process, or would have if sentenced to jail (Bazelon Center for Mental Health Law 2003; Petrila, Poythress, McGaha, and Boothroyd 2001; Ray et al. 2015). In cases where defendants are unsuccessful in specialty court, and therefore returned to traditional court for adjudication, oftentimes their charges are dismissed (Ray et al. 2015). Relatedly, literature suggests post-adjudication models, which require the defendant to make a plea of guilty prior to entering under the jurisdiction of the court, would foster successful completion instead of termination and charges being dropped in traditional court. This calls into question whether specialty courts are the best use of resources and defendants' time. Finally, there are a growing number of studies that suggest disparities in the specialty court process both in terms of who is accepted into the court and who completes them (Belenko et al. 2011; Luskin and Ray 2015; Ray and Dollar 2013; Wolff, Fabrikant, and Belenko 2011). Specifically, these studies suggest that White and female specialty participants are more likely to successfully complete the process than Black or male defendants (Dannerbeck, Harris, Sundet, and Lloyd 2006; Krebs, Lindquist, Koetse, and Lattimore 2007; Listwan, Sundt, Holsinger, and Latessa 2003; Taxman and Bouffard 2005).

Conclusion

The number of specialty courts continues to grow, as do the types of problems they address, and they are steadily becoming a standard part of the U.S. criminal justice system. However, there are still many questions and concerns that need to be addressed. Evaluating criminal justice outcomes of specialty court defendants has been a crucial part of their success; given the ethical implications of denying services to those not selected for participation, random design has been difficult so researchers will have to continue improving how they generate control groups. Moreover, specialty court personnel and researchers will need to critically examine disparities in who is referred to and admitted into the program while also targeting those offenders who are best-suited for these programs. The risk-needs-responsivity model—

which suggests low-risk offenders should receive lower levels of supervision and treatment and more intense supervision should be reserved for high-risk and high-need offenders—has been suggested as an ideal framework for specialty courts (Bonta and Andrews 2007; Marlowe 2012). However, to adopt this model specialty courts will need to modify how they target offenders in order to accurately identify risk but also assure that there are not disparities or exclusions of certain groups. There are similar concerns with disparities and selection bias in terms of program completion. Graduation specialty court is one of the best predictors of reduced involvement in the criminal justice system; yet, research suggests that Black males are often less likely to be accepted into and complete the specialty court process (Dannerbeck et al. 2006; Ray and Dollar 2013). Establishing specialty courts can reduce crime and increase public safety; however, we must also be mindful to provide fair and just legal practices that provide equal opportunities for all those who might benefit from these programs.

References

Almquist, Lauren, and Elizabeth, Dodd. 2009. *Mental Health Courts: A Guide to Research-informed Policy and Practice*. New York: Council of State Governments Justice Center.

Bazelon Center for Mental Health Law. 2003. "Criminalization of People with Mental Illnesses: The Role of Mental Courts in System Reform." *Jail Suicide/Mental Health Update* 12: 1–11.

Belenko, Steven, Nicole Fabrikant, and Nancy Wolff. 2011. "The Long Road to Treatment Models of Screening and Admission into Drug Courts." *Criminal Justice and Behavior* 38(12): 1222–1243.

Bonta, James, and D.A. Andrews. 2007. *Risk-Need-Responsivity Model for Offender Assessment and Rehabilitation*. Ottawa, ON: Public Safety Canada.

Boothroyd, Roger A., Norman G. Poythress, Annette McGaha, and John Petrila. 2003. "The Broward Mental Health Court: Process, Outcomes, and Service Utilization." *International Journal of Law and Psychiatry* 26(1): 55–71.

Broner, Nahama, Pamela K. Lattimore, Alexander J. Cowell, and William E. Schlenger. 2004. "Effects of diversion on adults with co-occurring mental illness and substance use: Outcomes from a national multi-site study." *Behavioral Sciences and the Law* 22: 519–541.

Carey, Shannon, Michael Finigan, and Kimberly Pukstas. 2008. *Exploring the Key Components of Drug Courts: A Comparative Study of 18 Adult Drug Courts on Practices, Outcomes and Costs*. Portland, OR: NPC Research.

Case, Brian, Henry J. Steadman, Seth A. Dupuis, and Laura S. Morris. 2009. "Who Succeeds in Jail Diversion Programs for Persons with Mental Illness? A Multi-Site Study." *Behavioral Sciences and the Law* 27: 661–674.

Casey, P.M., and Rottman, D.B. 2003. *Problem-solving Courts: Models and Trends*. Williamsburg, VA: National Center for State Courts

Cissner, Amanda B., and Michael Rempel. 2005. *The State of Drug Court Research: Moving Beyond "Do They Work?"*. New York: Center for Court Innovation.

Clear, Todd R., and Natasha A. Frost. 2015. *The Punishment Imperative: The Rise and Failure of Mass Incarceration in America*. Ithaca, NY: New York University Press.

Colomy, Paul, and Martin Kretzmann. 1995. "Projects and Institution Building: Judge Ben B. Lindsey and the Juvenile Court Movement." *Social Problems* 42(2): 191–215.

Dannerbeck, Anne, Gardenia Harris, Paul Sundet, and Kathy Lloyd. 2006. "Understanding and Responding to Racial Differences in Drug Court Outcomes". *Journal of Ethnicity in Substance Abuse* 5(2): 1–22.

Elroy, Preston, and R. Scott Ryder. 1999. *Juvenile Justice, a Social, Historical, and Legal Perspective*. Gaithersburg, MD: Aspen.

Glass, Joseph E., Brian E. Perron, Mark A. Ilgen, Stephen T. Chermack, Scott Ratliff, and Kara Zivin. 2010. "Prevalence and Correlates of Specialty Substance Use Disorder Treatment for Department of Veterans Affairs Healthcare System Patients with High Alcohol Consumption." *Drug and Alcohol Dependence* 112: 150–155.

Goldkamp, John S. 1999. "The Origin of the Treatment Drug Court in Miami" Pp. 19–42 in *The Early Drug Courts: Case Studies in Judicial Innovation*, edited by C. Terry. Thousand Oaks, CA: Sage Publications.

Gottfredson, Denise C., Brook W. Kearley, Stacy S. Najaka, and Carlos M. Rocha. 2007. "How Drug Treatment Courts Work an analysis of Mediators." *Journal of Research in Crime and Delinquency* 44(1): 3–35.

Gover, Angela R., John M. MacDonald, and Geoffrey P. Alpert. 2003. "Combating Domestic Violence: Findings from an Evaluation of a Local Domestic Violence Court." *Criminology and Public Policy* 3(1): 109–132.

Government Accountability Office (GAO). 2005. *Adult Drug Courts: Evidence Indicates Recidivism Reductions and Mixed Results for Other Outcomes*. Report to Congressional Committees (GAO-05-219). Washington, DC: GAO.

Hahn, Paul H., John P. O'Connor, and Mark E. Chimsky. 1978. *The Juvenile Offender and the Law*. Cincinnati, OH: Anderson Publishing.

Handler, Joel F. 1965. "The Juvenile Court and the Adversary System: Problems of Function and Form." *Wisconsin Law Review*, 7–51.

Hartford, Kathleen, Robert Carey, and James Mendonca. 2006. "Pre-arrest Diversion of People with Mental Illness: Literature Review and International Survey." *Behavioral Sciences and the Law* 24: 845–856.

Huddleson, C. West, and Douglas Marlowe. 2011. *Painting the Current Picture: A National Report on Drug Courts and Other Problem-Solving Court Programs in the United States*. Alexandria, VA: National Drug Court Institute.

Justice Policy Institute. 2011. "Addicted to Courts: How a Growing Dependence on Drug Courts Impacts People and Communities". March 2011. Retrieved November 20, 2015 from www.justicepolicy.org/uploads/justicepolicy/documents/addicted_to_courts_finalpdf

Karan, Amy, Susan Keilitz, and Sharon Denaro. 1999. "Domestic Violence Courts: What are they and How Should We Manage Them?" *Juvenile and Family Court Journal* 50: 75–86.

Keilitz, Susan L. 2000. *Specialization of Domestic Violence Case Management in the Courts: A National Survey*. Washington, DC: National Center for State Courts.

Kopelovich, Sarah, Phillip Yanos, Christina Pratt, and Joshua Koerner. 2013. "Procedural Justice in Mental Health Courts: Judicial Practices, Participant Perceptions, and Outcomes Related to Mental Health Recovery." *International Journal of Law and Psychiatry* 36(2): 113–120.

Krebs, Christopher P., Christine Lindquist, Willem Koetse, Willem, and Pamela K. Lattimore. 2007. "Assessing the Long-term Impact of Drug Court Participation on Recidivism with Generalized Estimating Equations." *Drug and Alcohol Dependence* 91(1): 57–68.

Levey, Lynn S., Martha Wade Steketee, and Susan L. Keilitz, Susan L. 2001. *Lessons Learned in Implementing an Integrated Domestic Violence Court: The District of Columbia Experience*. Williamsburg, VA: National Center for State Courts.

Lind, E. Allen, and Tom R. Tyler. 1988. *The Social Psychology of Procedural Justice*. New York: Springer Science & Business Media.

Listwan, Shelley J., Jody L. Sundt, Alexander M. Holsinger, and Edward J. Latessa. 2003. "The Effect of Drug Court Programming on Recidivism: The Cincinnati Experience." *Crime and Delinquency* 49(3): 389–411.

Luskin, Mary L., and Bradley Ray. 2015. "Selection into Mental Health Court: Distinguishing Among Eligible Defendants." *Criminal Justice and Behavior* 42(11): 1145–1158.

McGaha, Annette, Roger A. Boothroyd, Norman G. Poythress, John Petrila, and Rhonda Ort. 2002. "Lessons from the Broward County Mental Health Court Evaluation" *Evaluation and Program Planning* 25: 125–135.

McIvor, Gill. 2009. "Therapeutic Jurisprudence and Procedural Justice in Scottish Drug Courts." *Criminology & Criminal Justice*, 9(1): 29–49.

Marlowe, Douglas B. 2010. *Research Update on Adult Drug Courts*. Retrieved on June 23, 2017 from https://jpo.wrlc.org/bitstream/handle/11204/2346/Research%20Update%20on%20Adult%20Drug%20Courts.pdf?sequence=3

Marlow, Douglas B. 2012. "Targeting the Right Participants for Adult Drug Courts." National Drug Court Institute, Volume VII, No. 1.

Mitchell, Ojmarrh, David B. Wilson, Amy Eggers, and Doris L. MacKenzie. 2012. "Assessing the Effectiveness of Drug Courts on Recidivism: A Meta-analytic Review of Traditional and Non-traditional Drug Courts. *Journal of Criminal Justice* 40: 60–71.

Munetz, Mark R., Christian Ritter, Jennifer L. Teller, and Natalie Bonfine. 2014. "Mental Health Court and Assisted Outpatient Treatment: Perceived Coercion, Procedural Justice, and Program Impact." *Psychiatric Services* 65(3): 352–358.

National Association of Drug Court Professionals. 1997. *Defining Drug Courts: The Key Components*. Washington, DC: U.S. Department of Justice, Drug Court Programs Office.

National Juvenile Court Data Archive Online. 2010. "Juvenile Court Statistics 2006–2007." March 2010. Retrieved November 23, 2015 from www.ncjj.org/PDF/jcsreports/jcs2007.pdf

Nolan, James L. 2001. *Reinventing Justice: The American Drug Court Movement*. Princeton, NJ: Princeton University Press.

Petrila, John, Norman G. Poythress, Annette C. McGaha, and Roger A. Boothroyd. 2001. "Preliminary Observations from an Evaluation of the Broward County Florida Mental Health Court." *Court Review* 37(4): 14–22.

Poythress, Norman G., John Petrila, Annette McGaha, and Roger Boothroyd. 2002. "Perceived Coercion and Procedural Justice in the Broward Mental Health Court." *International Journal of Law and Psychiatry 25*(5): 517–533.

Ray, Bradley, and Cindy Brooks Dollar. 2013. "Examining Mental Health Court Completion: A Focal Concerns Perspective." *Sociological Quarterly* 54(4): 647–669.

Ray, Bradley, Brittany J. Hood, and Kelly E. Canada. 2015. "What Happens to Mental Health Court Noncompleters?" *Behavioral Sciences and the Law* 33(6): 801–814.

Redlich, Allison D., and Woojae Han. 2014. "Examining the links between Therapeutic Jurisprudence and Mental Health Court Completion." *Law and Human Behavior* 38(2): 109–118.

Redlich, Allison D., Steven Hoover, Alicia Summers, and Henry J. Steadman. 2010. "Enrollment in Mental Health Courts: Voluntariness, Knowingness, and Adjudicative Competence." *Law and Human Behavior* 34(2): 91–104.

Rossman, Shelli B., John K. Roman, Janine M. Zweig, Michael Rempel, and Christine H. Lindquist. 2011. *The Multi-site Adult Drug Court Evaluation: Executive Summary*. Washington, DC: Urban Institute.

Sarteschi, Christine M., Michael G. Vaughn, and Kevin Kim. 2011. "Assessing the Effectiveness of Mental Health Courts: A Quantitative Review." *Journal of Criminal Justice* 39: 12–20.

Sullivan, Frank. 1997. "Indiana as a Forerunner in the Juvenile Court Movement." *Indiana Law Review* 30: 279–303.

Steadman, Henry J., and Michelle Naples. 2005. "Assessing the Effectiveness of Jail Diversion Programs for Persons with Serious Mental Illness and Co-Occurring Substance Use Disorders." *Behavioral Sciences and the Law* 23: 163–170.

Taxman, Faye S., and Jeffrey A. Bouffard. 2005. "Treatment as Part of Drug Court: The Impact on Graduation Rates." *Journal of Offender Rehabilitation* 42(1): 23–50.

Teplin, Linda A. 1984. "Criminalizing Mental Disorder: The Comparative Arrest Rate of the Mentally Ill." *American Psychologist* 39(7): 794–803.

Tsai, Betsy. 2000. "Trend Toward Specialized Domestic Violence Courts: Improvements on an Effective Innovation." *Fordham Law Review* 68: 1285–1327.

Tyler, Tom R. 2003. Procedural Justice, Legitimacy, and the Effective Rule of Law. *Crime and Justice* 30: 283–357.

Tyler, Tom R. 2006. "Psychological Perspectives on Legitimacy and Legitimation." *Annual Review of Psychology* 57: 375–400.

Tyler, Tom R. 2009. "Legitimacy and Criminal Justice: The Benefits of Self-regulation." *Ohio State Journal of Criminal Law* 7: 307–359.

Tyler, Tom R., and Jeffery Fagan. 2008. "Legitimacy and Cooperation: Why Do People Help the Police Fight Crime in Their Communities?" *Ohio State Journal of Criminal Law* 6(1): 231–275.

Tyler, Tom R., Lawrence Sherman, Heather Strang, Geoffrey C. Barnes, and Daniel Woods. 2007. "Reintegrative Shaming, Procedural Justice, and Recidivism: The Engagement of Offenders' Psychological Mechanisms in the Canberra RISE Drinking-and-Driving Experiment." *Law and Society Review* 41: 553–586.

Walls, Samantha 2010. "Need for Special Veterans Courts." *The Denver Journal of International Law and Policy* 39: 695–729.

Wexler, David B., and Bruce J. Winick. 1991. *Essays in Therapeutic Jurisprudence*. Durham, NC: *Carolina Academic Press*.

Wilson, David B., Ojmarrh Mitchell, and Doris L. MacKenzie. 2006 "A Systematic Review of Drug Court Effects on Recidivism." *Journal of Experimental Criminology* 2(4): 459–487.

Winick, Bruce J. 2002. "Therapeutic Jurisprudence and Problem Solving Courts." *Fordham Urban Law Journal* 30(3): 1055–1103.

Winick, Bruce J., and David B. Wexler. 2003. *Judging in a Therapeutic Key: Therapeutic Jurisprudence and the Courts*. Durham, NC: Carolina Academic Press.

Wizner, Stephen. 1971. "Juvenile Justice and the Rehabilitative Ideal: A Response to Mr. Stapleton." *Yale Review of Law and Social Action* 1(2): 82–85.

Wolff, Nancy, Nicole Fabrikant, and Steven Belenko. 2011. "Mental Health Courts and their Selection Processes: Modeling Variation for Consistency." *Law and Human Behavior* 35(5): 402–412.

Young, Douglas, and Steven Belenko. 2002. "Program Retention and Perceived Coercion in Three Models of Mandatory Drug Treatment." *Journal of Drug Issues* 32(1): 297–328.

Section 4

Issues Affecting Corrections and Punishment

22 The War on Drugs and American Corrections

Ojmarrh Mitchell

Introduction

The United States has declared several drug wars since approximately 1900 (Musto 1999). The latest and most intense of these wars was declared in the mid 1980s and largely continues to this day but with waning enthusiasm. Unlike previous drug wars, the primary tactic in the latest drug war has been to use the criminal justice system to arrest, prosecute, and incarcerate even low-level drug offenders including drug users (Boyum and Reuter 2005). This punitive change in drug enforcement has had a tremendous effect on American corrections, apprehended drug offenders, particularly African American drug offenders, and inner-city communities. However, this punitive shift in drug enforcement has not achieved its stated goals of reducing drug use and inflating drug prices (see e.g., MacCoun and Reuter 2001). On the other hand, the punitive policies implemented as part of the war on drugs have had serious, negative collateral consequences on those convicted of drug crimes and disproportionately affected racial/ethnic minorities—particularly African Americans.

This chapter provides an overview of the war on drugs, its legacy, and its impact on American corrections. As a starting point, this chapter sketches the policies implemented as part of the war on drugs and their stated goals. This is followed by a discussion of the drug war's effects on American correctional populations and costs. This discussion will demonstrate that the war on drugs was a key contributing factor to the explosion in the prison population and racial disparities in drug sanctioning. Next, the evidence evaluating the effectiveness of the war on drugs in achieving its stated goals as well as its collateral consequences is discussed. The chapter concludes by noting that there is considerable dissatisfaction with drug enforcement in America; this dissatisfaction fuels a growing movement to discard the war on drugs' punitive drug policies and tactics and replace them with less punitive, more treatment-oriented approaches.

The War on Drugs

"The war on drugs" refers to a set of drug control policies adopted largely in the mid 1980s, which continue to dominate drug enforcement to the present. Earlier drug control strategies concentrated on reducing illicit drug crops, disrupting international drug distribution networks, interdicting drugs at U.S. borders, and apprehending high-level drug dealers. For example, methods of drug enforcement during President Nixon's drug war included spraying Mexico's drug fields, convincing Turkey to reduce opium production, and breaking up the so-called "French Connection" that imported heroin into the United States (Boyum and Reuter 2005; Musto 1999). Domestically, President Nixon successfully pushed for the creation of a network of methadone maintenance clinics; in fact, under Nixon the majority of federal drug enforcement funds went to drug treatment—not law enforcement. Yet, the mid 1980s' war on drugs expanded the focal points of drug enforcement to include mid-level drug dealers (e.g., drug wholesalers), low-level dealers (e.g., retail/street drug dealers), and even drug users. Lawmakers adopted policies that called for law enforcement to aggressively target and prosecute drug offenders, even minor offenders such as those in possession of small amounts of illicit drugs. And this punitive shift towards targeting the numerous but relatively minor drug offenders was accompanied by a movement away from drug treatment.

The legislative centerpieces of this latest drug war were the Anti-Drug Abuse Acts of 1986 and 1988. These Acts contained many individual laws and components. Without a doubt the best known of these components was the creation of long, mandatory, minimum prison terms for those convicted of federal drug offenses, especially offenses involving crack cocaine. The most astonishing feature of these mandatory minimum sentences was that they applied not only to drug dealers, but also to minor players in drug distribution (e.g., someone who introduced a minor dealer to a major dealer could be convicted of drug conspiracy and sentenced to a term of imprisonment equal in length to the drug dealers) and even those convicted of simple possession of small amounts of crack cocaine.

While these punitive policies are the best-known components of the Anti-Drug Abuse Acts, perhaps the most important component of these laws was the billions of dollars in federal funding allocated to state and local law enforcement for drug enforcement. The receipt of these federal funds was contingent on the jurisdiction adopting policies/practices consistent with the war on drugs. Through these funds, the *federal* Anti-Drug Abuse Acts, in effect changed *state* drug enforcement; and thus, the war on drugs became national policy.

The stated goal of this punitive shift in drug policy was to reduce drug consumption. The first National Drug Control Strategy explained this philosophy unambiguously:

> To prevent people from using drugs, drug enforcement activities must make it increasingly difficult to engage in any drug activity with impunity . . . That's why we need a national drug law enforcement strategy that casts a wide net and seeks to ensure that all drug users—whatever its scale—face the risk of criminal sanction.
>
> (ONDCP 1989: 18)

Further, the same document called for the criminal justice system to accommodate the influx of drug offenders by growing markedly: "Making streets safer and drug users more accountable for their actions requires the criminal justice system to expand and reform in an unprecedented way. Effective street-level enforcement means dramatically increasing the number of drug offenders arrested" (ONDCP 1989: 24).

To achieve the goal of dramatically increasing the number of drug offenders arrested, law enforcement adopted a set of practices focused on low-level drug offenders. These tactics included the use of place-based drug crackdowns, place-based street sweeps, buy-busts, reverse stings, controlled buys, and the use of drug courier profiles. These tactics were highly effective in apprehending low-level drug dealers and drug users.

The best evidence of these tactics' effectiveness in capturing low-level drug offenders is the explosion in the number of drug arrests after the war on drugs was declared. For instance, in 1980, prior to the drug war, there were approximately 581,000 drug arrests reported to the FBI. Yet, in 1989, that number ballooned to 1,362,000 and continued to grow in the 1990s and into the new millennium (Snyder and Mulako-Wangota 2012). Further, large shares of these arrests were for possession offenses and offenses involving marijuana, which illustrates that many of those arrested were low-level drug offenders.

Consequences of the War on Drugs for American Corrections

The dramatic rise in drug arrests unsurprisingly had major implications for American corrections. Simply stated, the policy changes enacted as part of the war on drugs not only caused the number of drug offenders under correctional control to explode, these policies also were a key cause of overall growth in the prison population. For instance, the proportion of prison inmates serving time in state prisons for a drug offense went from 8 percent in 1980 to more than 20 percent in the 1990s, and to roughly 17 percent currently. Additionally, approximately 50 percent of inmates in federal facilities are currently serving time due to a drug offense (National Research Council 2014). Perhaps more telling is the fact that the state incarceration rates for drug offenses went from 15 per 100,000 in 1980 to more than 150 by 2000 and just below 150 in 2010 (National Research Council 2014).

This dramatic growth in drug incarceration was a key-contributing factor to the overall growth in prison population. There was a general increase in punitiveness in the 1980s and 1990s for nearly all kinds of crimes, which pushed correctional populations upward. Yet, this shift in punitiveness was most pronounced for drug offenses—leading to the rise in drug offenders pushing prison populations to unprecedented heights (National Research Council 2014). In fact, Blumstein and Beck (1999) estimate that 45 percent of the overall growth in the total incarceration rates between 1980 and 1996 was attributable to the influx of drug offenders. These figures demonstrate that the drug war dramatically affected correctional populations, particularly in the 1990s, and, while these effects have eased in recent years, the number of drug prisoners and the rate of drug imprisonment is still elevated in comparison to before the drug war.

Contrary to popular belief, the primary reason for the explosion in the drug prisoner population is not a lengthening of prison sentences. In fact, the average time served by state drug offenders increased only modestly from 1.6 years in 1980 to 1.9 years in 2010 (National Research Council 2014). Instead, the rise in the number of imprisoned drug offenders is attributable to a combination of the previously discussed growth in drug arrests and a steep increase in the likelihood of imprisonment. For example, for every 100 drug arrests there were two state prison commitments for a drug offense in 1980, ten state prison commitments in 1990, and nine state prison commitments in 2010 (National Research Council 2014). Thus, drug offenders apprehended after the war on drugs began have a much higher likelihood of imprisonment than those arrested before the drug war.

What's truly remarkable about this growth in the number of drug arrests and drug prisoners is the fact that drug use was generally declining in this time period. In fact, drug use had been declining even before the war on drugs was declared in earnest in the mid 1980s. For example, past month illicit drug use for those 12 and over dropped from 14 percent in 1979 to 12.1 percent in 1985 (Substance Abuse and Mental Health Data Archive 2012). Drug use continued to drop after the drug war; by 1988, past month drug use was 7.7 percent of those 12 and over, 5.9 percent by 1993, before rebounding and then stabilizing at approximately 8.5 percent (Substance Abuse and Mental Health Data Archive 2012). Thus, while there was variation in illicit drug use over time, generally, there has been a downward trend in drug use—even prior to the drug war. This finding makes it clear that changes in drug enforcement and drug sanctioning produced the growth in drug arrests and drug prisoners—not increases in the number of illicit drug users.

The Effectiveness of the War on Drugs

The primary intended consequence of declaring a war on drugs was to reduce the availability of drugs, drug use, and drug-related violence. This section briefly reviews evidence of the general effectiveness of the war on drugs and the effectiveness of specific drug war components (e.g., drug treatment, drug use prevention). This review finds limited and, at best, modest evidence of the war's general effectiveness in reducing drug use and drug-related crime. Further, the strongest evidence of effectiveness comes from evaluations of "demand reduction" strategies, which have served as a secondary component of the war on drugs.

According to the drug war's proponents, the policies and practices put in place would reduce drug consumption. Specifically, illicit drugs are overwhelmingly produced outside of the United States; hence, the supply of drugs would be suppressed by destroying these crops in the fields and helping drug farmers produce alternative cash crops (i.e., source control); preventing illicit drugs from crossing into the United States (interdiction); breaking up drug distribution networks by targeting international drug distributors; and, punishing domestic drug offenders. Second, preventing first-time drug use and preventing casual drug users from becoming addicts, as well as treating existing addicts will reduce the demand for illicit drugs. These supply-and-demand reduction strategies were supposed to increase drug prices, reduce drug consumption, and by extension drug-related crime.

The findings from the empirical research, however, largely contradict the expressed rationale for the drug war. First, both source control and interdiction efforts in absolute terms have been modestly successful in destroying drug crops and seizing drugs around the borders; however, the relative scale of the overall drug trade simply has dwarfed these successes. MacCoun and Reuter (2001) find that the land necessary to grow the world's supply of illicit drugs is compact and these drugs can be grown in many different parts of the world. As a result of these factors, source control has had limited success in controlling the supply of illicit drugs because drug growing operations can simply relocate to another location if detected. Likewise, and second, border control agencies have seized remarkable amounts of illicit drugs at and near the border, but access to illicit drugs has not been reduced. One common measure of access to illicit drugs is an annual survey of high school students (the Monitoring the Future study) that asks twelfth graders how difficult it would be to obtain a particular illicit drug. From 1975 until 2005 the proportion of twelfth graders reporting that it would be "very easy" or "fairly easy" to obtain marijuana remained stable at 85 to 90 percent, and these percentages do not differ meaningfully before or after the drug war (Johnston, O'Malley, Miech, Bachman, and Schulenberg 2016). The same study reaches similar conclusions about other drugs such as cocaine and heroin. Access to these drugs is more difficult and more volatile than marijuana; but again, the proportion of students reporting easy or fairly easy access to these drugs did not drop meaningfully in this time period. Interestingly, however, access to these drugs has fallen since 2005—a period in which the drug war de-escalated. These findings do not support the contention that the drug war's policies reduce access to illicit drugs.

Third, punitive drug sanctions do not have a general or specific deterrent effect on offending. A sizable body of research using aggregate data examines the general deterrent effects of punitive drug control policies, and typically finds that punitive law enforcement approaches can have at least temporary effects on drug markets but have little sustained effect on drug consumption (see e.g., Abt 2001; Bushway, Caulkins, and Reuter 2003; MacCoun and Reuter 2001; Mazerolle, Soole, and Rombouts 2007). Similarly, punitive sanctions such as arrest for a drug offense and imprisonment do not reduce subsequent offending (specific deterrence). As an illustration of this finding, Mitchell (2016) examined the effect of drug arrest on subsequent drug offending. This research found that in comparison to similar drug offenders who were not arrested, drug arrest did not reduce subsequent marijuana use, hard drug use, or involvement in drug distribution. Likewise, Mitchell, Cochran, Mears, and Bales (2017) examined the effect of imprisonment for a drug offense on the likelihood of reconviction for drug and non-drug offenses. Again, this study did not find a specific deterrent effect; in fact, in comparison to similar drug offenders who were sentenced to community sanctions (e.g., probation, home confinement) imprisoned drug offenders had slightly higher rates of reconviction, but this difference was not statistically significant.

Most distressingly, illicit drug prices have dropped markedly in comparison to the prices in the mid 1980s. A national data set called STRIDE (System To Retrieve Information on Drug Evidence) records illicit drug prices. These data find that the price of marijuana, cocaine, heroin, and methamphetamine are all lower in recent years in comparison to the mid 1980s (see e.g., Abt 2001). This drop in drug prices appears to be attributable to drug dealers finding economies of scale that brought down retail drug prices in spite of mounting efforts to curtail drug production and distribution.

The key measure of the war on drugs' effectiveness is drug use. Here again, the evidence does not support the efficacy of the drug war. Drug use dropped in the mid 1980s, but it is not clear that the drug war caused this decline because drug use had been declining consistently since 1979. Perhaps more important is the fact that both of the key national measures of drug use (i.e., the Monitoring the Future study and the National Survey of Drug Use and Health) indicate that drug use in recent years is virtually identical to drug use in the late 1980s.

Taken together, the evidence assessing the effectiveness of supply-side drug-control tactics finds many small-scale successes but there is little evidence to suggest that these tactics have been successful in increasing drug prices and reducing drug consumption. Despite this limited evidence of effectiveness, most of the resources allocated to drug control under the latest drug war have gone to supply-side tactics. In fact, approximately two-thirds of the annual drug enforcement resources have focused on supply-side tactics in the vast majority of years since the war on drugs commenced (see e.g., Mitchell 2009).

Interestingly, demand reduction strategies, which have been a secondary component of the war on drugs, have considerable evidence of effectiveness in reducing drug offending. To be clear, not all demand reduction strategies have proven effective; drug prevention programs such as D.A.R.E. (the most commonly used drug prevention program in the U.S.) have repeatedly been found to be ineffective in preventing illicit drug use (Ennett, Tobler, Ringwalt, and Flewelling 1994; Rosenbaum 2007). Yet, both community- and incarceration-based drug treatment programs have been found to be modestly successful in reducing subsequent drug offending and use. Drug courts have emerged as the most prominent community-based drug treatment for those involved in the criminal justice system. Scores of evaluations have found that drug court participants are less likely to reoffend and relapse into drug use than similar offenders who did not participate in a drug court (Mitchell, Wilson, Eggers, MacKenzie 2012). Evaluations of incarceration-based programs, such as therapeutic communities, have also found that participants in such programs are less likely to reoffend than similar offenders who did not participate (Mitchell, Wilson, and MacKenzie 2007).

Overall, the strategies adopted under the war on drugs have had limited success, particularly the supply-side strategies emphasizing punitive sanctions. When weighed against the considerable financial costs associated with these policies, the limited success of the war on drugs makes it one of the largest boondoggles in recent U.S. history. In recent years, federal expenditures on drug control have been in the realm of $30 billion (ONDCP 2015) and while total state expenditures are not available, they are estimated to be at least as large in total as federal expenditures (U.S. Bureau of Census 1993). Thus, a conservative estimate is that the United States currently spends approximately $60 billion on largely ineffective drug control, which is considerably less than the $134 billion (in constant dollars) spent in 1988 towards the height of the drug war (Boyum and Reuter 2005). The available evidence strongly suggests that these expenditures have not achieved their stated goals of reducing drug consumption. Simply put, the war on drugs has been a public policy failure and a very expensive one.

Collateral Consequences of the War on Drugs

As previously discussed, the war on drugs has been ineffective in achieving its stated goals; however, the war on drugs has had significant collateral consequences on individual life chances and community wellbeing. Drug convictions can have serious, negative collateral consequences on employment and educational opportunities. Drug convictions in 27 states led to an automatic suspension of drivers' licenses (Legal Action Center 2004), which constrains employment and educational opportunities via restricted mobility. Also, drug convictions trigger prohibitions preventing access to federally funded student grants, loans, or work assistance for drug offenders—but not for other kinds of offenders. Further, many states allow employers to deny employment to those convicted of a crime if the crime has implications for the position. Given that drug use has a multitude of potential implications such as absenteeism, inattentiveness, theft, and violence, a drug conviction could be used to exclude an applicant from a host of positions. Further still, given that drug enforcement activities are concentrated in inner-city areas, these collateral consequences on education and employment can negatively affect neighborhood stability by removing largely males of working and child rearing ages via incarceration and, as a result, reduce said neighborhoods' social and economic wellbeing.

Empirical research notes the negative effects of official sanctions generally and drug sanctions specifically, particularly on employment outcomes. Research using a variety of different methodologies demonstrates that individuals convicted of crimes have higher unemployment rates, more difficulty obtaining work, and lower incomes than otherwise similar individuals (see e.g., Apel and Sweeten 2010; Pager 2003; Western 2006). Mitchell (2016) finds that drug arrest without necessarily a conviction did not affect educational attainment but had a negative effect on weeks worked and income.

Importantly, these collateral consequences disproportionately have affected racial/ethnic minorities, especially African Americans, due to the fact that the war on drugs exacerbated racial disparities in drug sanctions and minorities' marginalized social status (Alexander 2010). Like prior drug wars, politically and socially marginalized groups have been most affected, particularly African Americans. For instance, prior to the war on drugs, the drug arrest rate for African Americans was three times higher than that of whites. Yet, at the height of the latest drug war (1989), this disparity in drug arrest rates rose to approximately 6 to 1 and subsequently stabilized at approximately 4 to 1. In turn, the growth in racial disparities in drug arrests has worsened preexisting racial disparities in imprisonment for drug offense. As evidence of this, note that in 1980 the imprisonment rate of African Americans was 6.5 times higher than that of whites and in 1990, near the height of the war on drugs, this ratio grew to 6.8.

What's more, the collateral consequences of drug sanctions appear to be more detrimental to minorities than whites. Again, Mitchell (2016) found that while drug arrest had negative effects on weeks worked and income, this effect was only statistically significant among African American drug arrestees. Sabol and Lynch (2003.3) find similar results at the community level; specifically, these authors find that communities with higher levels of incarceration have lower employment but this effect was only statistically significant among black men—not white men.

Clearly, the existing evidence indicates that the punitive shift in drug policy has had unanticipated, collateral consequences on drug offenders. Employment outcomes such as stability of employment and income have the clearest evidence of being negatively affected—both at the individual level and at the community level. The extant literature also demonstrates that these collateral consequences are strongest among African Americans.

Conclusion

The policies enacted as part of the war on drugs have not achieved their stated goals. Crop eradication and interdiction have had many successes, and the criminal justice system has arrested, prosecuted, and incarcerated countless drug offenders. Yet, illicit drugs are not higher priced or less accessible than before the war on drugs. In fact, current drug use is not meaningfully lower than in the late 1980s, at the height of the drug war. Not only have these policies proven to be ineffective, they also have been financially expensive, unfair (in that African American drug offenders have disproportionately been affected), deeply racially divisive, and destructive to the life chances of those caught in their web.

Remarkably, in spite of these policies' many failures, the policies implemented under the war on drugs still dominate drug policy in most jurisdictions (Reuter 2013). The best evidence of this continued adherence to the war's policies is the sustained high number of drug arrests and drug imprisonments, particularly of low-level drug offenders.

At the same time, there is a growing movement to abandon these policies in favor of less punitive and more just policies. In fact, political support for the war on drugs' policies has crumbled in recent years. For example, a 2008 national poll found that 76 percent of likely voters believe that the "war on drugs is failing" and just 11 percent of Americans believe that it "is working" (Zogby 2008). And political support for less punitive and treatment-oriented drug policies appears to be growing. A 2014 national survey conducted by the Pew Research Center found that 67 percent of Americans support providing treatment instead of prosecuting drug users and 63 percent believe that moving away from mandatory prison sentences is a "good thing."

In response to this growing backlash against the war on drugs, the federal government under the Obama administration rejected "the law enforcement-only 'war on drugs'" approach to drug control (ONDCP 2013: 1). Instead, the Obama administration adopted and promoted a "21st century approach to drug policy that balances public health programs, effective law enforcement, and international partnerships" (ONDCP 2013: 1). These federal policy statements represent significant departures from the federal drug control strategies adopted under the war on drugs.

At the same time, several state and local jurisdictions forcefully rejected some elements of the war on drugs, particularly concerning marijuana enforcement. Notably, New York softened its long-standing Rockefeller drug sentencing laws and Michigan repealed its mandatory minimum drug sentencing laws. Other jurisdictions have recently decriminalized marijuana (i.e., fines instead of jail time) or made marijuana offenses the "lowest priority" of law enforcement. Most prominently, Colorado, Washington, Alaska, Oregon, and Washington, DC have legalized personal use amounts of marijuana via voter initiatives. And still other jurisdictions have mandated treatment instead of incarceration for drug offenders with limited criminal histories.

These policy changes seem to be a harbinger of larger changes in drug policies. It is difficult at this point in time to predict the exact nature of these policy changes; yet, it seems likely that the new paradigm in drug policy will focus less on punitive sanctions (especially towards marijuana), focus more on drug treatment, and promote greater racial fairness.

References

Abt Associates Inc. 2001. *The Price of Illicit Drugs: 1981 through the Second Quarter of 2000.* Washington, DC: U.S. Office of National Drug Control Policy.

Alexander, Michelle. 2010. *The New Jim Crow: Mass Incarceration in the Age of Colorblindness*. New York: The New Press.

Apel, Robert, and Gary Sweeten. 2010. "The Impact of Incarceration on Employment during the Transition to Adulthood." *Social Problems* 57(3): 448–479.

Blumstein, Alfred, and Allen J. Beck. 1999. "Population Growth in US Prisons, 1980–1996." *Crime and Justice* 26: 17–61.

Boyum, David, and Peter Reuter. 2005. *An Analytic Assessment of U.S. Drug Policy*. Washington, DC: AEI Press.

Bushway, Shawn, Jonathan Caulkins, and Peter Reuter. 2003. *Does State and Local Drug Enforcement Raise Drug Prices?* College Park, MD: University of Maryland: Unpublished manuscript.

Ennett, Susan T., Nancy S. Tobler, Christopher L. Ringwalt, and Robert L. Flewelling. 1994. "How Effective is Drug Abuse Resistance Education? A Meta-analysis of Project DARE Outcome Evaluations." *American Journal of Public Health* 84(9): 1394–1401.

Johnston, Lloyd D., Patrick M. O'Malley, Richard A. Miech, Herald G. Bachman, and John E. Schulenberg. 2016. *Monitoring the Future National Survey Results on Drug Use, 1975–2015: Overview, Key Findings on Adolescent Drug Use*. Ann Arbor, MI: Institute for Social Research, The University of Michigan.

Legal Action Center. 2004. *After Prison: Roadblocks to Reentry*. New York: Legal Action Center.

MacCoun, Robert, and Peter Reuter. 2001. *Drug War Heresies: Learning from Other Vices, Times, and Places*. New York: Cambridge University Press.

Mazerolle, Lorraine, David Soole, and Sacha Rombouts. 2007. "Drug Law Enforcement: A Review of the Evaluation Literature." *Police Quarterly* 10(2): 115–137.

Mitchell, Ojmarrh. 2009. "Ineffectiveness, Financial Waste, and Unfairness: The Legacy of the War on Drugs." *Journal of Crime & Justice* 32(2): 1–19.

Mitchell, Ojmarrh. 2016. "The Effect of Drug Arrest on Subsequent Drug Offending and Social Bonding." *Journal of Crime and Justice* 39(1): 174–188.

Mitchell, Ojmarrh, Joshua C. Cochran, Daniel P. Mears, and William D. Bales. 2017. "Examining Prison Effects on Recidivism: A Regression Discontinuity Estimate of the Effect of Prison Effects on Drug Offender Recidivism." *Justice Quarterly* 34(4): 571–596.

Mitchell, Ojmarrh, David B. Wilson, Amy Eggers, and Doris L. MacKenzie. 2012. "Assessing the Effectiveness of Drug Courts on Recidivism: A Meta-analytic Review of Traditional and Non-traditional Drug Courts." *Journal of Criminal Justice* 40: 60–71.

Mitchell, Ojmarrh, David B. Wilson, and Doris L. MacKenzie. 2007. "Does Incarceration-based Drug Treatment Reduce Recidivism? A Meta-analytic Synthesis of the Research." *Journal of Experimental Criminology* 3(4): 353–375.

Musto, David F. 1999. *The American Disease: Origins of Narcotic Control*, 3rd ed. New York: Oxford.

National Research Council. 2014. *The Growth of Incarceration in the United States: Exploring Causes and Consequences*. Washington, DC: The National Academies Press.

Office of National Drug Control Policy (ONDCP). 1989. *National Drug Control Strategy*. Washington, DC: Office of National Drug Control Policy.

ONDCP. 2015. *National Drug Control Budget: FY 2016 Funding Highlights*. Washington, DC: Executive Office of the President.

ONDCP. 2013. *National Drug Control Strategy, 2013*. Washington, DC: ONDCP.

Pager, Devah. 2003. "The Mark of a Criminal Record." *American Journal of Sociology* 108(5): 937–975.

Pew Research Center. 2014. *America's New Drug Policy Landscape: Two-thirds Favor Treatment, Not Jail, for Use of Heroin, Cocaine*. Washington, DC: Pew Research Center.

Reuter, Peter. 2013. "Why Has US Drug Policy Changed So Little over 30 Years?" Pp. 75–140 in *Crime and Justice*, edited by M. Tonry. Chicago, IL: University of Chicago.

Rosebaum, Dennis P. 2007. "Just Say No to D.A.R.E." *Criminology and Public Policy* 6(4): 815–824.

Sabol, William J., and James P. Lynch. 2003. "Assessing the Longer-run Consequences of Incarceration: Effects on Families and Employment." *Contributions in Criminology and Penology* 55: 3–26.

Snyder, Howard N., and Joseph Mulako-Wangota. 2012. *Drug Arrest Rates of Juveniles by Race, 1980–2009*. Generated Using the Arrest Data Analysis Tool. Washington, DC: Bureau of Justice Statistics.

Substance Abuse and Mental Health Data Archive. 2012. *National Household Survey on Drug Abuse* (August 11, 2012). Generated using the Analyze Online Tool (www.icpsr.umich.edu/icpsrweb/SAMHDA/). Rockville, MD: Substance Abuse and Mental Health Services Administration.

U.S. Bureau of Census. 1993. *State and Local Expenditures on Drug Control Activities*. Washington, DC: Government Printing Office.

Western, Bruce. 2006. *Punishment and Inequality in America*. New York: Russell Sage Foundation.

Zogby International. 2008. *Zogby Interactive Likely Voters 9/23/08 thru 9/25/08*. Retrieved August 19, 2009 from www.zogby.com/news/X-IAD.pdf.

23 Mass Incarceration

Travis C. Pratt

Prison. Jail. The clink, the big house, the pokey, the slammer, the joint. Whatever you want to call these kinds of places, here in the United States we like to use them. A lot. Indeed, American prisons and jails currently hold 2.2 million people behind bars (Glaze and Kaeble 2014). Just to put this figure into perspective, this is roughly the same number of people that populate the Canadian cities of Edmonton Alberta, Ottawa Ontario, and Halifax Nova Scotia—combined. This group of incarcerated citizens would also be large enough to fill the seats of the nation's largest college football stadium at the University of Michigan—twenty times. The term "mass incarceration" is therefore not at all an exaggeration.

Accordingly, in this chapter I focus on the nature of mass incarceration in the United States. Specifically, I begin by outlining the nature of mass incarceration in the United States. This section presents the current state of incarceration in both cross-national and historical terms within the United States. I then trace the key social and political factors—particularly those that have developed over the last four decades—that led to our current state institutional punishment. The discussion then shifts toward outlining the wide array of consequences (mostly negative) that have emerged as a result of mass incarceration. Finally, I discuss some of the key recent trends in the philosophy and application of punishment that may provide insight into the future of mass incarceration in America.

How "Mass" Is It?

One of the ways that we can tell just how "mass" our rate of incarceration is, is to make some international comparisons. For example, the United States incarceration rate per 100,000 citizens is estimated at roughly 738 (Hartney 2006). Russia was once close to us, but they let a bunch of people out of prison over concerns about things such as diseases and poor living conditions, so now they are down to a distant second-place finish at 607. Even our nearest geographic neighbors incarcerate only a fraction of their citizens compared to us, with Mexico at 196 and Canada at a measly 107. Put a little differently, the state of California locks up almost ten times as many people than the entire nation of Australia—a country that started out as a prison colony (Hartney 2006).

While these figures are disturbing all on their own, it is important to note that the odds of being incarcerated are not randomly distributed throughout all segments of the American population. African Americans are incarcerated at a rate nearly six times that of whites, and Hispanics are twice as likely to be incarcerated as whites—patterns that hold when examining incarceration rates for women as well and seem to have gotten much worse over time (Mauer and King 2007; Western and Wildeman 2009). Viewed in this way, some have even argued that the term "mass" incarceration is a bit of a misnomer because it turns out that incarceration rates are—and have always been—a lot more "mass" for some groups of people than they are for others (Wacquant 2014). And while an effective argument could be made to that effect, the bottom line is that, as a nation, we spend around 70 billion dollars a year incarcerating our offenders—a price tag far too hefty to be attached to anything other than a massive problem (Austin et al. 2013).

Sources of Mass Incarceration

Of course, incarceration in the United States was not always "mass." American incarceration rates were instead relatively modest and stable for most of our nation's history (Jacobs and Helms 1996). There was, of course, some fluctuation, but the general trend was one characterized by a pretty flat trajectory of growth over time (Porter, Bushway, Tsao, and Smith 2016).

All of that changed in the 1960s—a time period characterized by two simultaneous developments that had important implications for how, as a nation, we came to see punishment differently. The first development was a rather sharp increase in the crime rate in the late 1960s (Blumstein 1998). In retrospect, the "crime wave" that occurred during this time could be traced in large part to a demographic shift in the age structure of the population of the country: the post-World War II "baby boom" had produced a sizable swelling of the population that had entered their prime "crime prone" years (Fox and Piquero 2003). This explanation was not, however, a very popular one. Accordingly, the second development was a declining level of confidence in the ability of the state to control rising crime via the current method and philosophy of punishment: correctional rehabilitation (Cullen and Gilbert 1982). This declining confidence meant that the rise in crime was attributed in the policy arena to lenient punishments that failed to deter would-be offenders (Beckett and Western 2001).

It was this shift in the thinking about the "problem" of crime that provided the ideological legitimacy for a new approach to the "solution" to crime—one where the punishments for virtually all crimes got stiffer (Pratt, Maahs, and Stehr 1998). The primary goal of punishment thus drifted away from rehabilitation toward a more hard-lined focus on deterrence and incapacitation (Clear 1994; Pratt 2009). And when this new "get tough" philosophy met the "war on drugs" in the 1980s, our incarceration rates really started to skyrocket (Pratt, Franklin, and Gau 2011).

And they have never really come down in any significant way since. But how could they, when this new faith in the power of punishment gave us so many of the things we thought we wanted, such as mandatory minimum sentences, three strikes-laws, boot-camp prisons, private prisons, scared straight programs, chain gangs, and the prison industrial complex (Cullen and Jonson 2017; Maahs and Pratt 2017; Pratt and Maahs 1999)? The reality is that our current state of mass incarceration was driven by a series of political decisions—decisions that put more people behind bars and kept them there for a longer period of time than ever before. The million-dollar-question, then (or perhaps the 70-billion-dollar question), is: what have we gotten out of this investment?

Consequences of Mass Incarceration

The big question—at least the one that has typically been viewed as most important by both policymakers and the public at large—is whether mass incarceration has reduced crime. And as could be expected, there has been considerable disagreement among the voices providing answers to that question—voices that also disagree considerably with respect to how much the empirical evidence matters to them when they formed their opinions (see, e.g., Conklin 2003; Liedka, Piehl, and Useem 2006). But if we were to take a careful look at the evidence, we see that a rather clear picture starts to emerge. Early estimates of the famed "crime drop" of the 1990s, for example, claimed that increased incarceration rates were responsible for a large portion of the drop (Spelman 2000). But when other scholars noted that certain methodological problems still needed to be considered (e.g., such as taking into account the simultaneous effect of crime on incarceration rates), the portion of the crime drop that could be attributed to the increased use of incarceration started to steadily dwindle (Fagan, West, and Holland 2002). The general consensus now is that the effect of mass incarceration on crime is not zero—you cannot lock up over two million offenders and expect it to have *no* effect on crime—but that the effect is not very strong either (Pratt and Cullen 2005).

So, there is a benefit—even if a rather modest one—to mass incarceration in terms of crime. But there are also costs, and not just those confined to the public price tag of maintaining our incarcerated population. To be sure, the American way of incarceration has taken a toll on the families of those incarcerated—particularly the children of incarcerated parents and those who are charged with their care (Tasca, Turanovic, White, and Rodriguez 2014; Turanovic and Rodriguez 2017; Turanovic, Rodriguez, and Pratt 2012). In short, when a family member—especially a parent—is sent to prison, those left behind often have a tough time coping with their absence (Arditti 2005; Clear 2007). In addition, there is mounting evidence that shifting more public resources toward incarceration has undermined the effectiveness of other public institutions. Education has been hit really hard (Blomberg, Bales, Mann, Piquero, and Berk 2011)—a reality that seems to have exacerbated racial disparities in economic deprivation over the last few decades (Wakefield and Uggen 2010). To put it bluntly, there has been a substantial "hidden cost" to mass incarceration that is becoming less and less hidden.

Nowhere is this more clearly visible than when we take another look at the incarceration–crime link through a more long-term lens. Indeed, while there is evidence of a short-term incapacitation effect associated with mass incarceration, given the "collateral costs" noted above it should come as no surprise that there are some pretty serious signs that, down the road, mass incarceration has done more harm than good when it comes to crime. This idea was set forth explicitly by Rose and Clear (1998), who argued that offenders who are sent to prison come disproportionately from economically deprived, minority neighborhoods. These offenders typically have complex relationships with the communities they live in—they contribute both negatively (their crime) and positively (their roles as fathers and income providers) to community life. And when they are removed *en masse* from these communities, their positive contributions are removed as well, which tends to result in even greater economic deprivation and social disorganization. Enhancing social disorganization, in turn, leads to higher rates of community crime and victimization. And this process is no longer seen as speculation, as empirical research has affirmed the mass incarceration–community crime link (Lynch and Sabol 2004).

Recent Trends

The current state of mass incarceration was not inevitable, and there is no reason to believe that the size of our incarcerated population will continue to stay the same as time goes on. To be sure, we are already starting to see a leveling off of incarceration rates in certain key states such as New York and California (Goode 2013). At the same time, the broader field of corrections is experiencing a renaissance of sorts with respect to embracing the philosophy and practice of rehabilitation—an approach that, at its heart, is opposed to the kind of punitiveness that gave us mass incarceration in the first place (Thielo, Cullen, Cohen, and Chouhy 2015; Wright, Pratt, Lowenkamp, and Latessa 2012).

Even so, while these developments are promising, we must be careful not to speak too soon about the end of the "grand experiment" in punishment (Clear and Frost 2014).

As prison admissions have taken a bit of a dip in recent years, the populations of local jails have swelled in an effort to pick up the slack (Minton and Zeng 2015). And there are certain segments of the American population—most notably, Hispanics—who continue to see their incarceration rates rise at a steady rate (Warren, Chiricos, and Bales 2012).

So, to put it simply, our love affair with mass incarceration is far from over. Political change tends to come slowly, and even a concerted effort among states to reduce the prison population will likely feel like trying to turn the *Titanic* around. And there is no evidence that such a concerted effort is even on the horizon. There is instead a lingering faith in punishment among American citizens that is still quite punitive—a portion of whom have grown increasingly vocal about reviving some of the more bloodthirsty policy approaches from our country's dubious past when it comes to the immigration–incarceration link (Stewart, Martinez, Baumer, and Gertz 2015). So even though it is always dangerous to make predictions about the future, I still think that it is pretty safe to say this: if mass incarceration is on its way out, it will not happen any time soon.

References

Arditti, Joyce A. 2005. "Families and Incarceration: An Ecological Approach." *Families in Society* 86(2): 251–258.

Austin, James, Eric Cadora, Todd R. Clear, Kara Dansky, Judith Greene, Vanita Gupta, Marc Mauer, Nicole Porter, Susan Tucker, Malcolm C. Young. 2013. *Ending Mass Incarceration: Charting a New Justice Reinvestment.* Washington, DC: The Sentencing Project.

Beckett, Katherine, and Bruce Western. 2001. "Governing Social Marginality: Welfare, Incarceration, and the Transformation of State Policy." *Punishment and Society* 3(1): 43–59.

Blomberg, Thomas G., William D. Bales, Karen Mann, Alex R. Piquero, and Richard A. Berk. 2011. "Incarceration, Education and Transition from Delinquency." *Journal of Criminal Justice* 39(4): 355–365.

Blumstein, Alfred. 1998. "U.S. Criminal Justice Conundrum: Rising Prison Populations and Stable Crime Rates." *Crime and Delinquency* 44(1): 127–135.

Clear, Todd R. 1994. *Harm in American Penology*. Albany, NY: State University of New York Press.

Clear, Todd R. 2007. *Imprisoning Communities*. New York: Oxford University Press.

Clear, Todd R., and Natasha A. Frost. 2014. *The Punishment Imperative: The Rise and Failure of Mass Incarceration in America.* New York: New York University Press.

Conklin, John E. 2003. "Why Crime Rates Fell." *Crime and Justice International* 19(72): 17–20.

Cullen, Francis T., and Karen E. Gilbert. 1982. *Reaffirming Rehabilitation*. Cincinnati, OH: Anderson.

Cullen, Francis T., and Cheryl Lero Jonson. 2017. *Correctional Theory: Context and Consequences.* Thousand Oaks, CA: Sage.

Fagan, Jeffrey, Valerie West, and Jan Holland. 2002. "Reciprocal Effects of Crime and Incarceration in New York City Neighborhoods." *Fordham Urban Law Journal* 30(5): 1551–1599.

Fox, James Alan, and Alex R. Piquero. 2003. "Deadly Demographics: Population Characteristics and Forecasting Homicide Trends." *Crime and Delinquency* 49(3): 339–359.

Glaze, Lauren E., and Danielle Kaeble. 2014. *Correctional Populations in the United States, 2013.* Washington, DC: Bureau of Justice Statistics Bulletin.

Goode, Erica. 2013. "U.S. Prison Populations Decline, Reflecting New Approach to Crime." *New York Times*, July 25.

Hartney, Christopher. 2006. *US Rates of Incarceration: A Global Perspective.* Oakland, CA: National Council on Crime and Delinquency.

Jacobs, David, and Ronald E. Helms. 1996. "Toward a Political Model of Incarceration: A Time-Series Examination of Multiple Explanations for Prison Admission Rates." *American Journal of Sociology* 102(2): 323–357.

Liedka, Raymond V., Anne Morrison Piehl, and Bert Useem. 2006. "The Crime-Control Effect of Incarceration: Does Scale Matter? *Criminology and Public Policy* 5(2): 245–276.

Lynch, James P., and William J. Sabol. 2004. "Assessing the Effects of Mass Incarceration on Informal Social Control in Communities." *Criminology and Public Policy* 3(2): 267–294.

Maahs, Jeff, and Travis C. Pratt. 2017. "'I Hate These Little Turds!': Science, Entertainment, and the Enduring Popularity of *Scared Straight* Programs." *Deviant Behavior*, 38(1): 47–60.

Mauer, Marc, and Ryan S. King. 2007. *Uneven Justice: State Rates of Incarceration by Race and Ethnicity*. Washington, DC: The Sentencing Project.

Minton, Todd D., and Zhen Zeng. 2015. *Jail Inmates at Midyear 2014*. Washington, DC: Bureau of Justice Statistics.

Porter, Lauren C., Shawn D. Bushway, Hui-Shien Tsao, and Herbert L. Smith. 2016. "How the U.S. Prison Boom Has Changed the Age Distribution of the Prison Population." *Criminology* 54(1): 30–55.

Pratt, Travis C. 2009. *Addicted to Incarceration: Corrections Policy and the Politics of Misinformation in the United States*. Thousand Oaks, CA: Sage.

Pratt, Travis C., and Francis T. Cullen. 2005. "Assessing Macro-Level Theories and Predictors of Crime: A Meta-Analysis." *Crime and Justice: A Review of Research* 32: 373–450.

Pratt, Travis C., Travis W. Franklin, and Jacinta M. Gau. 2011. *Key Ideas in Criminology and Criminal Justice*. Thousand Oaks, CA: Sage.

Pratt, Travis C., and Jeff Maahs. 1999. "Are Private Prisons More Cost-Effective than Public Prisons? A Meta-Analysis of Evaluation Research Studies." *Crime and Delinquency* 45(3): 358–371.

Pratt, Travis C., Jeffrey Maahs, and Steven D. Stehr. 1998. "The Symbolic Ownership of the Corrections 'Problem': A Framework for Understanding the Development of Corrections Policy in the United States." *The Prison Journal* 78(4): 451–464.

Rose, Dina R. and Todd R. Clear. 1998. "Incarceration, Social Capital, and Crime: Implications for Social Disorganization Theory." *Criminology* 36(3): 441–480.

Spelman, William. 2000. "What Recent Studies Do (and Don't) Tell Us about Imprisonment and Crime." *Crime and Justice: A Review of Research* 27: 419–494.

Stewart, Eric A., Ramiro Martinez, Eric P. Baumer, and Marc Gertz. 2015. "The Social Context of Latino Threat and Punitive Latino Sentiment." *Social Problems* 62(1): 68–92.

Tasca, Melinda, Jillian J. Turanovic, Clair White, and Nancy Rodriguez. 2014. "Prisoners' Assessments of Mental Health Problems Among Their Children." *International Journal of Offender Therapy and Comparative Criminology* 58(2): 154–173.

Thielo, Angela J., Francis T. Cullen, Derek M. Cohen, and Ceclia Chouhy. 2015. "Rehabilitation in a Red State: Public Support for Correctional Reform in Texas." *Criminology and Public Policy* 15(1): 1–34.

Turanovic, Jillian J., and Nancy Rodriguez. 2017. "Mental Health Service Needs in the Prison Boom: The Case of Children of Incarcerated Parents." *Criminal Justice Policy Review* 28(5): 415–436.

Turanovic, Jillian J., Nancy Rodriguez, and Travis C. Pratt. 2012. "The Collateral Consequences of Incarceration Revisited: A Qualitative Analysis of the Effects on Caregivers of Children of Incarcerated Parents." *Criminology* 50(4): 913–959.

Wacquant, Loic. 2014. "Class, Race and Hyperincarceration in Revanchist America." *Socialism and Democracy* 28(3): 35–56.

Wakefield, Sara, and Christopher Uggen. 2010. "Incarceration and Stratification." *Annual Review of Sociology* 36: 387–406.

Warren, Patricia, Ted Chiricos, and William Bales. 2012. "The Imprisonment Penalty for Young Black and Hispanic Males: A Crime-Specific Analysis." *Journal of Research in Crime and Delinquency* 49(1): 56–80.

Western, Bruce, and Christopher Wildeman. 2009. "The Black Family and Mass Incarceration." *Annals of the American Academy of Political and Social Science* 621(January): 221–242.

Wright, Kevin A., Travis C. Pratt, Christopher T. Lowenkamp, and Edward J. Latessa. 2012. "The Importance of Ecological Context for Correctional Rehabilitation Programs: Understanding the Micro- and Macro-Level Dimensions of Successful Offender Treatment." *Justice Quarterly* 29(6): 775–798.

24 Religion in Correctional Settings and Faith-Based Programming

Kent R. Kerley and Llynea Sherwin

Penal systems worldwide have incorporated religious programs into their systems of correctional treatment. In the United States, religious adherents (e.g., Quakers) developed the first penitentiaries, such as the famous Eastern State Penitentiary that opened in 1829. The Quakers championed the cause of more humane treatment of inmates, and included religious studies as part of their overall approach to reformation and rehabilitation.

While the Quakers and other faith groups focused primarily on the logistics and purposes of confinement, there was no formal data collection to measure the impact of faith and faith-based programs for inmates. Only since the 1980s have scholars begun to measure this impact with empirical studies. The important empirical question is this: to what extent does the practice of religion in correctional settings impact the attitudes, identities, behaviors, and criminal careers of inmates?

The most accepted conclusion by religion scholars is religious involvement, under certain conditions, may create social networks, emotional support, and accountability structures that constrain many deviant and criminal behaviors. As informal social controls influence the attitudes and behaviors of religious individuals, firm bonds often are established with religious institutions. Thus, individuals who consider themselves very religious often claim that their attitudes and behaviors are guided by concern for a higher power and by the supernatural punishments and rewards outlined in religious texts.

Religion may also act as a shield against deviant and criminal behaviors by creating and reinforcing social networks and social bonds. To the extent that religious beliefs promote prosocial behaviors, they may simultaneously discourage offenders from engaging in negative behaviors. According to Christopher Ellison (1992), religiosity—defined as an attitudinal and behavioral commitment to organized religion—is linked with prosocial behaviors for two reasons. First, those with high levels of religiosity often view their lives and interaction with others in context of how they perceive what is expected by a "divine other." Second, religious individuals may internalize religious norms regarding compassion, kindness, and civility. As religious adherents read and internalize scriptural stories, such as the story of the Good Samaritan, they learn a model and structure for relationships with others (Ellison 1992).

Empirical Studies

Many researchers have studied possible connections between religion and various attitudes and behaviors in correctional settings. Byron Johnson (1987) was the first to do so. In his study of recently released inmates in Florida between 1978 and 1982, he found that inmate religious attendance, inmate religiosity, and chaplains' assessment of inmate religiosity did not affect the amount of prison misconduct or time spent in disciplinary confinement.

Johnson, Larson, and Pitts (1997) then conducted the first major study of a faith-based prison program, which was developed by Prison Fellowship Ministries (PFM). The early signature program by PFM involved inmates meeting one or more times per week for intensive Bible study and periodically for brief seminars. Johnson and colleagues measured inmates' participation in various religious programs as well as the length of time they were involved in an activity. A convenience sample of 201 male prisoners from four different New York state prisons was identified and split almost equally between PFM participants and a matched control group. The key measures of religiosity were how often inmates participated in religious programs and the total length of time they were involved. Those categorized as "highly active" participated in ten or more activities per year, "medium activity" was indicated by activity in one to ten programs, and those who did not attend at least one were considered "inactive." Incident records of incarcerated participants were evaluated, as well as arrest records for up to one year after release.

The results were not favorable for the PFM program. Johnson and colleagues found that participation in PFM activities did not reduce prison misconduct. In fact, the authors found that inmates most active in PFM activities were slightly more likely to have a record of serious infractions. Although the cause was unclear, there is a chance that the inmates surveyed may have committed the infractions and then turned to religion to make amends. In terms of long-term impact of involvement in PFM programs, the results showed that the sample of inmates involved in PFM activities did not have a reduced likelihood of recidivism when compared with the control group.

Although some researchers have criticized them for doing so, Johnson and colleagues (1997) conducted supplementary analyses in which they compared the criminal outcomes of only PFM "graduates"—those who were enrolled continuously until the end of the program—with control group inmates. The researchers found that inmates most heavily involved in PFM activities were much less likely to have been arrested one year after release when compared with individuals in the control group. Because this comparison produced a very different result than the true quasi-experimental comparison of all PFM inmates to all control group inmates, it suggested that long-term involvement was the key to faith-based programs having any significant impact on future behaviors.

Johnson (2004) then expanded his data collection efforts and published a follow-up study. In particular, he modified the definition of "active participation" in religious programs, and also increased the amount of time in which inmates were tracked after release. He found that it was more effective to lower the number of PFM activities in which inmates participated to determine the effect of involvement in PFM activities more thoroughly. In the new study, high participation was considered five or greater, instead of ten, and he increased the time after release from one to eight years. Despite these changes, Johnson found little to no difference in the median arrest times and reincarceration rates between PFM inmates and inmates in the control group. The rate at which inmates were arrested after release, known as the survival rate, was only slightly lower for the PFM group after eight years. The only real differences appeared when PFM graduates were compared to low-active inmates and to control group members.

Rather than a prospective study of future recidivism, Jensen and Gibbons (2002) took a different approach. They identified a group of 20 ex-prisoners who had stayed out of prison for at least six years and explored via in-depth interviews how the individuals were able to avoid a return to prison. The 20 participants were former inmates in Oregon correctional facilities. The average length of incarceration was about 12 years, and the range was 5 to 25 years. They were asked a series of questions about their pre- and post-incarceration experiences, and in particular asked to explain key factors in their desistance.

Ten of the 20 offenders interviewed mentioned religion as providing some motivation for staying out of prison. Seven of the interviewees who identified as religious reported feeling shame, and three who remained neutral or possessed negative views towards religion mentioned shame as a motivating factor. While it may be reasonable to conclude that feelings of shame accompany religious beliefs, the study design did not allow the researchers to determine an exact time order. The authors speculated that there could be an inverse relationship, in which offenders turn to religion after experiencing feelings of guilt for their crimes. One offender experienced guilt after observing the pain caused to her victims and their joy when the prison sentence was announced. Another inmate outlined the importance of introspection and the ability to accept outside help, "First of all, you have to see your own evil before you can really share it" (Jensen and Gibbons 2002: 222). This personal revelation was key in experiencing the redemption associated with many forms of religion. The most important result of this study was that no offender interviewed who associated with both key variables, religion and shame, committed a new offense (Jensen and Gibbons 2002: 223).

Clear and Sumter (2002) studied the value of religion in prison, in particular they focused on the relationship between inmate religiousness, adjustment to prison, and amount of disciplinary infractions or other problematic behaviors. With the use of a self-report questionnaire, the authors surveyed a sample of 769 inmates from 20 different prisons across 12 states to measure what effect, if any, inmates' religiousness had on their ability to adjust to prison and on their conduct. The sample was non-representative, but chosen to distinguish the most genuinely religious inmates from individuals who were not truly involved. The authors found that inmates with higher levels of religiousness tended to report a lower frequency of disciplinary confinements.

Kent Kerley and colleagues (2005) conducted a study to determine whether religiosity had an effect on arguments and fights within a Mississippi prison. Their study included the first representative sample survey about inmates' current religiosity, religious background, personal background, and prison deviance. The authors found that higher levels of religiosity directly reduced the likelihood of inmates getting into serious arguments. Religiosity did not directly reduce combat between inmates; however, it was shown to reduce the frequency of arguments that typically precede fights.

Kerley, Allison, and Graham (2006) then conducted a follow-up study, and found that religiosity had no significant impact on the emotional status of inmates, such as sadness, stress, anger, bitterness, depression, and worry. Due to the debilitating nature of being held in a captive context, religiosity was not enough to reduce inmates' experience of negative emotions. The authors concluded that religion may be viewed by inmates as more of a tool for solving external problems, such as conflicts with other inmates, than for overcoming the emotional difficulties of prison life.

Camp and colleagues (2006) conducted a survey of inmates participating in a faith-based program called Life Connections Program (LCP). The survey reached 407 inmates from five different treatment prisons and compared those participants with 592 inmates at five other prisons in the area. The results showed that inmates who previously had a religious identity before incarceration were less likely to be involved in religious programs available within their prison. Only those who reported high involvement in religious programs showed a reduction in prison deviance, as those programs proved to be ineffective for inmates with only moderate or low involvement. Similarly, Camp (2008) found in a follow-up study that participation in LCP reduced the likelihood of inmates committing serious violations within the prison, but there was again no effect of LCP participation concerning minor infractions of prison rules.

As part of a multi-site study, Grant Duwe and colleagues (2015) analyzed prison misconduct in a maximum-security Texas prison. In the Darrington prison facility, inmates may enroll in a Bible College program that culminates in a Bachelor of Science degree in biblical studies. Organizers of this program consider it a way for offenders to spend their free time constructively without reverting to nefarious behaviors. The Bible College participants live together and are required to spend 15 hours in class per week, and another 25–45 hours studying outside the classroom setting. The end goal of the program is to deploy graduates as ministers throughout the Texas Department of Criminal Justice system. The authors found that program participants showed a significant decrease (65 to 80 percent) in major misconduct when compared with a control group of inmates who volunteered for the program but were not selected.

The second study site is the Louisiana State Penitentiary in Angola, where a similar seminary-style program is offered to inmates. Graduates of the program, while serving the remainder of their sentences, are allowed to establish churches, officiate funerals, and serve in a variety of ways including cellblock visitation and hospice. These activities are not only cost-effective, but allow inmates on good behavior to gain training and experience while incarcerated and provide a constructive outlet for idle time. Michael Hallett and colleagues (2015) conducted in-depth interviews with 107 graduates of the seminary program, as well as with 19 staff members over a two-year period. The interviewees identified four key themes that they claimed were critical to program success and to inmate satisfaction: building trusting relationships, respectful treatment by correctional administrations, restoration through intervention, and religious content.

Kerley and colleagues (2011) used data on Iowa parolees to conduct the first study of religiosity, self-control, and deviant behavior in a correctional setting. The authors found a declining level of statistical significance for religion on prison deviance. They found that several measures of religiosity were significant predictors of prison deviance; however, with the addition of criminal history and demographic measures the effect of religion was down to only two measures. After the authors controlled for inmates' level of self-control, they found that only one measure of religiosity was significant, which was frequency of attendance at religious services. The authors concluded that both religiosity and self-control were important theoretical constructs in explaining prison deviance.

Finally, in perhaps the most comprehensive scholarly work on faith and faith-based prison programs in the United States, Kerley (2014) provided an analysis of a decade of research on Protestant-based prison programs. For his book, *Religious Faith in Correctional Contexts*, Kerley interviewed 103 inmates, 30 prison ministry workers, and 70 residents of a halfway house to understand how faith works in captive contexts. Among the many findings, Kerley found key differences in how men and women experienced faith in prison; that is, men generally preferred to practice faith in group-based settings, while women chose solitude or very small-group settings. A key factor in successful adjustment was social support networks provided by chaplains, local religious volunteers, and other religious inmates. Finally, Kerley found that a strong focus on redemption and compassion from religious leaders provided a more stable environment for adjustment than other mentoring styles, such as a justice- or security-based style (Kerley, Bartkowski, Matthews, and Emond 2008; Kerley, Matthews, and Shoemaker 2009).

Women, Religion, and Correctional Settings

Although researchers have studied religion in correctional settings since the 1980s, only a handful of those studies have been conducted in women's prisons or in co-residential prisons. This neglect of women's experiences with faith and faith-based programs in prison is unfortunate, especially as rates of incarceration have increased dramatically for women as part of the "get tough on crime" movement since the 1970s. Women increasingly have also received long-term sentences, including life sentences.

Aday and colleagues (2014) chose a population of women serving life sentences for their study of religion in the prison context. The authors conducted a study of 21 women serving life sentences at a maximum-security women's facility in Tennessee. Twenty of the women surveyed were serving life sentences for homicide. They found that religious activities provided a positive avenue for channeling stress and the negative emotions associated with incarceration. With an alternative way to spend idle time, inmates often refrained from committing prison infractions or disturbing the routine. All 21 inmates referenced their religious beliefs when asked how they coped with their life sentences. At least 20 percent reported a significant loss in faith since their incarceration, but the majority mentioned the struggle to believe as a hardship they were able to overcome. Failure to recover from religious discontentment, the authors found, was challenging emotionally and could lead to increased feelings of depression or anxiety, and in extreme cases, suicide.

The authors conducted a follow-up study with the same population in which they explored the effects of religious involvement on prison adjustment. Dye, Aday, Farney, and Raley (2014) noted that in past studies, it was found that women struggle internally when facing incarceration because of issues with low self-esteem, depression, and anxiety. These factors may be influenced by personal histories of abuse, addiction, or victimization. Religious programs, on the other hand, seek to relieve or at least mitigate the stressors of incarceration. Dye and colleagues invited 303 inmates serving life sentences in a Southern state penitentiary to complete a survey regarding the effects of religion on imprisonment. The authors asked a range of questions about religious importance (coded as 0–2) and religious participation (coded as 0–4). A total of 214 women completed the survey. The authors found that 87 percent of respondents used religion to cope with their life sentences, and 84 percent claimed that religion was "very important" to them.

Kerley, Deitzer, and Leban (2014) studied the impact of faith on the process of recovery from drug addiction for women in a Southern faith-based halfway house. They conducted in-depth interviews with 30 women residents at the facility. The authors explored the issue of how drug-addicted women attempt to regain control of their lives via a newfound or renewed religious faith. In particular, the authors sought to understand how women were taught to recover control over their lives by relinquishing control to a higher power. The authors found that the most common way that participants did this was to adopt a "collaborative" coping style in which individuals perceived themselves to be in partnership with God and committed to a new life. Even though these women lost their own sense of control over their lives, their experience with religion allowed them to bear the burden of recovery. Many of the women interviewed by Kerley (2014) claimed to have a positive relationship with a higher power that enabled them to break free of their debilitating addictions to drugs.

Severance (2004) conducted a unique study of women inmates in which she asked about their prospects and expectations for successful entry after release. The author conducted 40 in-depth interviews with women inmates classified as: (1) newly admitted inmates, (2) general population inmates, and (3) inmates approaching release. The major areas of concern for the inmates upon release included employment and education, relapse and recidivism, children, food, clothing, and shelter. In addition to the stigma of having a criminal record, several other concerns arose about obtaining and keeping employment. Some inmates were concerned with changes in technology that occurred while they were in prison. Aside from the physical and financial needs mentioned by inmates, some claimed that faith and prayer would help them once they were released. A few noted that they planned to use their faith as a basis for successful reentry, and would simply put their futures "in God's hands."

"Other" Religions in Correctional Settings

Although the phrase "religion in prison" seemingly connotes a broad and inclusive area, nearly all of the empirical research in U.S. prisons has focused on Christian faith traditions, in particular on Protestant faith traditions (Kerley 2014, 2017; Kerley, Bartkowski, Matthews, and Emond 2008; Kerley, Matthews, and Shoemaker 2009). Although this is understandable given the faith backgrounds of early prison designers and the current religious composition of U.S. prisons, it is important that researchers also explore the practice of Buddhism, Hinduism, and Islam, for example, in correctional settings.

Todd Clear and colleagues (2000) conducted one of the only studies that included non-Christian inmates. The authors gathered survey and ethnographic data on inmates involved in Muslim and Christian religious activities. Their focus was on the "value of religion," which they characterized as intrinsic or extrinsic. The authors found strong evidence of intrinsic value, in that being outwardly religious helped inmates to cope with confinement. Inmates who chose to be active in religious programs were more likely than others to report positive emotional health and prosocial behaviors. In some cases, inmates claimed that their Christian or Muslim faith provided a "mental escape" from the drudgery of prison life. By believing in a higher power, the inmates found hope that their lives could be changed for the better upon release from prison.

Although not as prevalent a theme, the authors also found evidence of extrinsic value. Inmates who regularly attended religious services interacted with others who shared a similar mindset. Over time, those interactions could create positive relationships with other inmates and staff members in the facility. For inmates practicing Islam, in particular, religious services often created a sense of physical safety and protection. The meeting places were thought of as "safe havens" where inmates could retreat from illegitimate activities. Both Muslim and Christian inmates claimed that they could better avoid disciplinary infractions than their non-religious counterparts. Finally, since most of the faith-based programs were coordinated by local faith congregations (e.g., churches, mosques) inmates had the opportunity to forge new relationships outside the prison walls. This contact with those from the free world gave inmates a sense that they had not been "forgotten" (Clear et al. 2000; Clear and Sumter 2002).

Santos and Lane (2014) recently expanded the study by Clear and colleagues (2000) to include the value of religion *after* prison. They used convenience and snowball sampling techniques to recruit participants at six halfway houses or transitional programs. Out of 106 males surveyed, about 75 percent claimed that religion was important or very important to them after incarceration. Moreover, about 40 percent of the former inmates reported attending religious services on a regular basis, which is much higher than the national average in free society. As in the Clear et al. study (2000), Santos and Lane (2014) found much greater evidence of the intrinsic value of religion than extrinsic value. The authors concluded that incarcerated offenders place greater importance on religion than those in free society, and thus religious programs should remain available to inmates as part of a comprehensive approach to successful rehabilitation and reentry (Lane 2009).

O'Connor and Duncan (2011) conducted a review of various humanist, spiritual, and religious programs in prisons that are designed to reduce recidivism. First, the most widely known of these, religious programs, have been used since the inceptions of the U.S. prison system. Many stories of prison conversion have been viewed as anomalies; however, the pattern of religious conversion followed by improvements in inmates' attitudes and behaviors has been observed routinely over time and in many contexts. One of the more popular stories of dramatic change after conversion was of Malcolm X, who reportedly ceased violating prison rules after converting to Islam. The Oregon Department of Corrections, for example, currently employs staff members from diverse religious backgrounds, including Zen Buddhist, Presbyterian, Sunni Muslim, Greek Orthodox, Unitarian, and Latter-day Saints.

Second, the authors categorized programs as humanist if they aimed to give inmates a sense of meaning related to life itself, and were not tied to an alternative reality or to a transcendental being. Humanists usually include atheist, agnostic, and other belief systems categorized as no religious preference. Many volunteers in Oregon prisons identify best with humanist groups. One such group, known as the Inside-Out Prison Exchange Program, works with incarcerated offenders as well as students from a local university. This helps to encourage collaboration with peers outside of the prison and is thought to help with the reentry process. The authors suggest the importance of offering humanist programs as part of an overall approach to correctional treatment and rehabilitation.

Third, O'Connor and Duncan (2011) then described a new category of prison programming, which is focused on helping inmates who want to identify as "spiritual" but not as "religious." A few examples in Oregon prisons include: Wiccans, some Native American groups, and some Buddhist groups.

Legal and Political Considerations

Under the Religious Land Use and Institutionalized Persons Act (RLUIPA) of 2000, those incarcerated in the United States have the freedom to exercise any religious rite or practice, so long as it does not pose a significant threat to safety or security in the facility. Since passage of this act, many prisons have reported instances in which inmates have used religious practice requests to obtain special accommodations and treatment, even though there was no clear religious intent.

Moustafa (2014) recently explored the contours of this situation, and argued that federally funded prisons must implement more effective ways to test the sincerity of inmates' religious beliefs. The RLUIPA does not specify treatment based on any specific religion, but allows prisoners to petition for any exception necessary for their beliefs. The act does permit scrutiny into the sincerity of inmates' beliefs, thus allowing prisons the ability to remove prisoners from preferential treatment if found to be insincere. The problem lies in the application of such scrutiny, as safeguards must be taken to ensure that prisons do not engage in unconstitutional acts. According to Moustafa (2014), the solution may be to define clearly the permissible scope of sincerity testing so that inmates may retain the freedom to practice religion, while prisons may avoid being taken advantage of.

Not surprisingly, the study of religion in prison has become politicized, and thus strongly opposing viewpoints have emerged (Lane 2009). In a recent special issue of the journal, *Religions*, Hallett and Johnson (2014) provided an insightful overview of the political considerations associated with faith-based prison programs, and suggested several strategies for uniting those whose views may differ. Most faith-based prison programs are supported via donation of funds and time by members of local faith congregations and other volunteers. This appeases not only conservatives, who generally desire limited government involvement in social programming, but also liberals that desire extensive inmate programming in prisons. Hallett and Johnson suggest two reasons for continuing, or even expanding, faith-based programming in U.S. prisons: (1) provision of services at a low cost and (2) provision of services where a government agency lacks the ability to perform effectively.

References

Aday, Ronald H., Jennifer J. Krabill, and Dayron Deaton-Owens. 2014. "Religion in the Lives of Older Women Serving Life in Prison." *Journal of Women & Aging* 26(3): 238–256.

Camp, Scott D. 2008. "The Effect of Faith Program Participation on Prison Misconduct: The Life Connections Program." *Journal of Criminal Justice* 36(5): 389–395.

Camp, Scott D., Jody Klein-Saffran, Okyun (Karl) Kwon, Dawn Daggett, and Victoria Joseph. 2006. "An Exploration into Participation in a Faith-based Prison Program." *Criminology and Public Policy* 5: 529–550.

Clear, Todd R., Patricia L. Hardyman, Bruce Stout, Karol Lucken, and Harry R. Dammer. 2000. "The Value of Religion in Prison: An Inmate Perspective." *Journal of Contemporary Criminal Justice* 16: 53–74.

Clear, Todd R., and Melvina T. Sumter. 2002. "Prisoners, Prison, and Religion: Religion and Adjustment to Prison." *Journal of Offender Rehabilitation* 35: 127–159.

Duwe, Grant, Michael Hallett, Joshua Hays, Sung J. Jang, and Byron R. Johnson. 2015. "Bible College Participation and Prison Misconduct: A Preliminary Analysis." *Journal of Offender Rehabilitation* 54(5): 371–390.

Dye, Meredith. H., Ronald H. Aday, Lori Farney, and Jordan Raley. 2014. "'The Rock I Cling to': Religious Engagement in the Lives of Life-sentenced Women." *The Prison Journal* 6(17): 1–21.

Ellison, Christopher G. 1992. "Are Religious People Nice People? Evidence from the National Survey of Black Americans." *Social Forces* 71(2): 411–430.

Hallett, Michael, and Byron Johnson. 2014. "The Resurgence of Religion in America's Prisons." *Religions* 5(3): 663–683.

Hallett, Michael, Joshua Hays, Byron Johnson, Sung J. Jang, and Grant Duwe. 2015. "'First Stop Dying': Angola's Christian Seminary as Positive Criminology." *International Journal of Offender Therapy and Comparative Criminology* 8(4): 1–19.

Jensen, Kenneth D., and Stephen G. Gibbons. 2002. "Shame and Religion as Factors in the Rehabilitation of Serious Offenders." *Journal of Offender Rehabilitation* 35(3–4): 209–224.

Johnson, Byron R. 1987. "Religiosity and Institutional Deviance: The Impact of Religious Variables upon Inmate Adjustment." *Criminal Justice Review* 12: 21–30.

Johnson, Byron R. 2004. "Religious Programs and Recidivism among Former Inmates in Prison Fellowship Programs: A Long-term Follow-up Study." *Justice Quarterly* 21: 329–354.

Johnson, Byron R., David B. Larson, and Timothy C. Pitts. 1997. "Religious Programs, Institutional Adjustment, and Recidivism among Former Inmates in Prison Fellowship Programs." *Justice Quarterly* 14: 145–166.

Kerley, Kent R. 2014. *Religious Faith in Correctional Contexts*. Boulder, CO: First Forum Press/Lynne Rienner Publishers.

Kerley, Kent R. 2017. "Protestantism in Prisons." *The Encyclopedia of Corrections*, edited by Kent R. Kerley. Hoboken, NJ: Wiley-Blackwell.

Kerley, Kent R., Marisa C. Allison, and Rachelle D. Graham. 2006. "Investigating the Impact of Religiosity on Emotional and Behavioral Coping in Prison." *Journal of Crime and Justice* 29(2): 69–93.

Kerley, Kent R., John P. Bartkowski, Todd L. Matthews, and Tracy L. Emond. 2008. "From the Sanctuary to the Slammer: Exploring the Narratives of Evangelical Prison Ministry Workers." *Sociological Spectrum* 30: 504–525.

Kerley, Kent R., Heith Copes, Richard Tewksbury, and Dean A. Dabney. 2011. "Examining the Relationship between Religiosity and Self-control as Predictors of Prison Deviance." *International Journal of Offender Therapy and Comparative Criminology* 55: 1251–1271.

Kerley, Kent R., Jessica R. Deitzer, and Lindsay Leban. 2014. "Who Is in Control? How Women in a Halfway House Use Faith to Recover from Drug Addiction." *Religions* 5(3): 852–870.

Kerley, Kent R., Todd L. Matthews, and Troy C. Blanchard. 2005. "Religiosity, Religious Participation, and Negative Prison Behaviors." *Journal for the Scientific Study of Religion* 44: 443–457.

Kerley, Kent R., Todd L. Matthews, and Jessica Shoemaker. 2009. "A Simple Plan, A Simple Faith: Chaplains and Lay Ministers in Mississippi Prisons." *Review of Religious Research* 51: 87–103.

Lane, Jodi. 2009. "Faith-Based Programming for Offenders." *Victims & Offenders: An International Journal of Evidence-based Research, Policy, and Practice* 4: 327–333.

Moustafa, Noha. 2014. "The Right to Free Exercise of Religion in Prisons: How Courts Should Determine Sincerity of Religious Belief Under RLUIPA." *Michigan Journal of Race & Law* 20(1): 213–244.

O'Connor, Tom P., and Jeff B. Duncan. 2011. "The Sociology of Humanist, Spiritual, and Religious Practice in Prison: Supporting Responsivity and Desistance from Crime." *Religions* 2: 590–610.

Santos, Saskia D., and Jodi Lane. 2014. "Expanding Clear et al.'s Value of Religion Ideas: Former Inmates' Perspectives." *Deviant Behavior* 35: 116–132.

Severance, Theresa A. 2004. "Concerns and Coping Strategies of Women Inmates Concerning Release: 'It's Going to Take Somebody in my Corner.' *Journal of Offender Rehabilitation* 38: 73–97.

25 Drug Treatment Trends and the Use of Criminal Justice to Address Substance Use Disorder

Jada N. Hector and David N. Khey

It is no secret that the American criminal justice system has become the de facto hub for managing substance use disorders and mental illness. Just in 2010, the National Center on Addiction and Substance Abuse issued a report that documented that almost two-thirds of inmates in American correctional facilities met the criteria to be diagnosed with a substance use disorder. Further, this report detailed another set of inmates who did not meet the diagnostic criteria for substance use disorder, yet reported substantial drug abuse and/or misuse histories. Specifically, these inmates were under the influence at the time they committed the crimes that got them incarcerated, committed these crimes to score money for drugs, or were put in jail/prison for an alcohol or drug crime (or any combination of these). Taken together, these two groups account for 85 percent of people behind bars. While this report documented that only 11 percent of inmates with substance abuse disorder received treatment, the bigger picture was detailed in an older Bureau of Justice Statistics report; that is, roughly half of federal inmates and 40 percent of state inmates receive some form of drug programming (Mumola and Karberg 2006). This programming heavily relies on self-help and peer counseling groups, both of which provide zero to marginal reductions of problem behaviors in isolation. For inmates in 2004, 15 percent of state and 17 percent of federal inmates received treatment from professionals, even indicating a possible decline in treatment rates when comparing these two reports. Regardless of the true rate of treatment today, it can be plainly stated that not much headway has been made in providing treatment to those who need it while under justice supervision overall.

Not surprisingly perhaps, the same could be said about "free" Americans. The latest data from the Substance Abuse and Mental Health Services Administration (SAMHSA) indicate that 21.2 million people aged 12 and older needed substance abuse treatment at some time in 2014, yet only roughly 10 percent of them actually received any help (Hedden et al. 2015). This vast amount of unmet need can easily translate into criminal problems for many, especially among the vulnerable who lack the access to quality treatment, the money to pay for it, and/or the supports it takes to seed successful recovery. To better understand drug treatment in correctional settings, this chapter focuses on barriers to and stigma of treatment, the pathways to treatment, the rise of evidence-based programming, the major treatment modalities used in correctional settings, and the newest problem on the horizon—dealing with prescription drug abuse and the collateral problems caused by two decades of liberal use of opioid medication by the American populous.

Barriers to and Stigma of Treatment

Drug treatment in the United States can be broken down into two major categories: public and government run, and private or for-profit. This is important, because each of these categories is very different in both access to and success for individuals, and each comes with its own barriers to treatment. There is also an insinuation in the differences in the level of quality across these two domains; however, the outcomes of both are typically the same: eventual relapse and need for additional care. These barriers also present a primary driver for the flow of individuals needing treatment into the criminal justice system.

Within the private sector of drug treatment, costs can be quite high, making it impossible for the average person to have access to care and has been cited as a primary barrier to seeking help for many people regardless of age, gender, or race/ethnicity (Xu, Rapp, Wang, and Carlson 2008). For example, Passages Malibu offers a "luxury" rehabilitation environment on the beach. Costs can range from $60,000 to well over $100,000 *per month*, according to a 2013 *New York Times* exposé on Passages and the "Passages Model" (Haldeman 2013). The center does accept most health insurance providers, but the costs far exceed what insurance plans cover. Even though Passages is an extreme example, private and "luxury" treatment centers do have the capacity to offer more options for treatment. For instance, options such as acupuncture therapy, equine-assisted therapy, and meditation are offered at private facilities. While many of these types of therapies have been shown to offer a more well-rounded experience for patients, they have not been proven to be necessary in the treatment of substance use disorders. Passages boasts a 70 percent success rate, or what Passages materials call a "cure rate," which well surpasses the typical average success rate of most other drug treatment centers. Critics first argue that this success is overinflated and not supported by evidence, and second, argue that the clientele who can afford these options have different life circumstances than average individuals with drug problems.

Evidence-based programs such as the ones offered at Hazeldon in Minnesota (in recent news coverage due to the proximity to pop star Prince when he died at his home) are more typical and may be more accessible to the middle class, but remain quite expensive to most Americans. Costs at Hazeldon can run over $30,000 per month without insurance coverage or reimbursement; this seems to be the going rate to provide clients with a holistic array of services scientifically proven to optimize the likelihood of lasting sobriety. The proper balance of individualized treatment services offers success rates that hover around 50 percent, lending further credence to the disease model. In most circumstances, the family is included to assist with social supports and aftercare to help insure lasting sobriety.

Conversely, the public sector offers a very different experience for each patient and family. Often, with government-based programs, finding a "bed" in a center can be difficult enough to begin the process. For many, simply the decision to enter into drug treatment is a major hurdle; consider, then, the effect of being asked to be placed on a waitlist, which can be weeks, if not months long. Thus, the enrollment process can be seen as another primary barrier to entering treatment. Policymakers at the federal level have only recently addressed both cost and unnecessary delay of substance use disorder treatment in the last few years with limited success. Most important of their efforts was part of the Affordable Care Act—also known as Obamacare. Essentially, lawmakers sought to increase the capacity of private sector substance use disorder treatment by requiring all health care plans to cover this treatment to be authorized to receive any federal subsidies. In other words, since part or all of the premiums paid to insurance companies may be subsidized by the federal government for individuals who sign up for health insurance under the Affordable Care Act, any insurance company that wishes to offer their plans to this segment of America are legally mandated to cover drug treatment. The idea is that the waitlist for treatment would be eliminated and the cost of private care dramatically reduced for those who have successfully enrolled in private insurance—these individuals would be able to enter the private care system, which has a greater capacity to help patients, given its level of resources. Even those who remain uninsured would benefit—these individuals would face shorter waits as the number of uninsured Americans would be greatly reduced. At the time of this writing, it is unclear just how many Americans have benefited from this requirement, and all evidence suggests that our criminal justice system remains the primary care system for addiction and mental illness. It is important that, if successful, these policy shifts could dramatically reduce the pressure on the criminal justice system and/or alter its role in recovery for the people who become involved with the system via probation, diversion, jails, prisons, et cetera. Until then, a large flow of people will continue to be referred to some form of education and/or treatment by the criminal justice system that lacks the capacity to handle these problems.

Stigma with drug treatment can often be difficult to overcome for individuals suffering from addiction. Society as a whole lends to the thought process that drug addiction directly correlates with criminal activity. In fact, as more recent studies have shown, more factors come into play such as "adverse childhood experiences" or ACE, trauma, mental health, and lack of coping skills. Each of these concerns also comes with a stigma, only expanding the issue. People are often riddled with guilt surrounding their drug addiction, especially since success rates of drug treatment are so low. Friends and families struggle with their own guilt while watching their loved ones fail. Yet, most importantly, the stigma of addiction and criminal history can do lasting damage when considering its effect on seeking treatment, relapse, employment prospects, and so on. One particular impact that is tantamount to lasting success is on social support, which can be frayed, given the levels of stigma and guilt associated with both substance abuse and criminal histories. Research has suggested that certified peer support specialists can assist in bridging this gap in social support by assisting those with substance abuse problems with health and wellness ideation; hope; communication with spouses/partners, family, friends, and care providers; illness management; and stigma (Salzer, Schwenk, and Brusilovskiy 2010). For this reason and because peer support specialists do not command high salaries, there has been a sharp increase of these individuals serving justice-involved men, women, and adolescents. And while investigations into stigma and its impact has a robust history, much more work needs to be done to understand best practices in dealing with stigma and guilt for individuals who are afflicted and those around them who can be sources of social support.

Pathways to Treatment

The primary referral sources of substance use disorder treatment typically consist of the following: criminal justice (a form of coerced treatment via court order or condition of probation/parole), employer (another form of coerced treatment with a possible threat of termination), health care provider (voluntary), family and/or friends (voluntary), and self (voluntary). Since the turn of the century, research has shown that successful treatment completion is highly dependent on the referral source (Arndt, Acion, and White 2013). Coerced treatment referrals from criminal justice and employers have been consistently associated with greater levels of successful treatment completion overall (Sahker, Toussaint, Ramirez, Ali, and Arndt 2015) relative to any other source. Importantly, longer periods of sobriety and prosocial outcomes (e.g., furthering educational attainment, reduced levels of criminal activity and arrest, exhibiting healthier behaviors, including sexual behaviors, and so on) are contingent on successful treatment completion. Getting people through the treatment process from start to finish is therefore a primary concern for most practitioners. This issue can become complicated when considering the different needs of all of the kinds of people receiving care. "Individualized treatment planning" has become an important mantra for practitioners in the twenty-first century with hopes in boosting success rates for all.

With the rise in the interest of reducing health disparities across race, ethnicity, gender, and sexual orientation, research has recently explored treatment success by referral source across groups. For example, Ethan Sahker and his colleagues (2015) explored the importance of referral source for successful treatment completion for white and black Americans using a nationally representative data source. This study found that employment referral predicted greatest levels of successful treatment completion among black clients while criminal justice referral predicted the same for white clients. The underlying cultural differences may be driving these differences; that is, white Americans may be responding to the coercive force of criminal justice that drive their treatment success to a greater degree than black Americans. On the other hand, an employer willing to work with black Americans through treatment via an employee assistance program (EAP) and/or private health insurance in order to retain their employment or face termination seems to offer a powerful incentive to this group in particular. Perhaps ironically, in a twisted fashion, white Americans tend to have greater access to employee assistance programs and/or private health insurance than black Americans, while black Americans tend to be processed through all aspects of the criminal justice system at greater rates than white Americans. This highlights the need for multicultural approaches to treatment and a greater need for understanding cultural differences in the perception of treatment, incentives involved during the course of treatment, and much more.

Modern treatment in correctional settings is driven by scientific risk and needs assessment, typically performed by a mental health professional (Drake 2014). In essence, risk and need assessment is an actuarial tool that predicts future behavior, given static (e.g., family history, prior criminal/substance use history, treatment history, et cetera) and dynamic factors (e.g., peer associations, current substance abuse, current attitudes, et cetera). These assessments can also predict potential for substance use disorder, which should be further diagnosed by a licensed health professional using the current Diagnostic and Statistical Manual (DSM-V) criteria and referred to appropriate treatment. These risk and needs assessment tools are used in various stages of criminal justice processing, using what is called the Sequential Intercept Model (Munetz and Griffin 2006). The goal of this particular model is to attempt to provide mental health services—including substance use disorder treatment services—to individuals caught up in the criminal justice system as early as possible to get people the help they need. Thus, justice professionals (primarily a judge, prosecutor, and defense counsel) can be well-informed if *clients* should be referred to drug court (described elsewhere in this book), day reporting centers as a condition of probation that may offer an array of substance abuse education and treatment programming, intensive outpatient treatment as a condition of probation, diversion programming, and other programs. Risk and needs assessment tools (and further diagnoses) can also inform jail and prison professionals on which forms of programming may be conducive to inmate success and potential success upon release and reentry into the community. However, it should be reemphasized that drug education programming and not true treatment remain the norm for those who are incarcerated. Community-based treatment has grown extensively with the expanded use of drug courts, and at this point in time, a growing array of reentry programming is featuring true treatment either upon reentering the community or just before release.

Steps of Treatment and the Language Associated with Them

Based on information collected in the 1970s by the National Institute of Health's (NIH) National Institute on Drug Abuse (NIDA), "no single treatment is right for everyone." In addition, "effective treatment addresses all of the patients' needs, not just drug abuse" (NIDA 2016). Keeping this in mind, substance users often need multiple modalities to be successful in treatment—even across multiple treatment episodes for longer lasting success. This fits neatly in the ideology of the majority of experts in substance use and abuse, also known as the disease model—that addiction is a chronic disease of the brain, often prone to exhibit relapse. The disease model is also typically dominant among professionals who work in a criminal justice setting or who treat justice-involved individuals in the community.

Often the first step in drug treatment is detox or detoxification and medically assisted withdrawal, also known as drying out or cleaning up. Depending upon the substance (alcohol, opioids, cocaine, etc.), the detox stage can take a few days or last up to several weeks. Detox usually takes place in a hospital or jail infirmary setting—or at least medically supervised treatment facility—in order to maintain a safe and healthy environment for the individual to remove the drug(s) from their system. Critically, withdrawing from alcohol can be very dangerous and may lead to seizures or delirium tremens (DTs), even death in some cases. Jail and treatment facilities will then create treatment plans for individuals depending on available resources. A treatment plan is created by a team of professionals including: psychiatrists, medical doctors, counselors, therapists, nurses, and other medical, mental health, and substance use professionals. An individual's past drug use history, physical health, mental health, and family support should be included in a treatment plan as well.

Upon completion of medical detox, individuals should then enter into an inpatient treatment facility, if appropriate. Inpatient treatment can be either long term or short term. Typically, short-term treatments last 28 days but some long-term programs offer 3, 6, or 12 month options. During inpatient treatment, the person lives within the center and maintains a full schedule of programming including group therapy, individual therapy, recreation time, reflection/meditation, and medication monitoring if needed. Most correctional settings have limited access to true inpatient treatment programming for individuals both pre-trial and post-conviction. This issue becomes incredibly important in that substance abuse patterns can persist even in total institutions designed to keep licit or illicit "contraband" to a minimum (Plourde and Brochu 2002). While estimates of extent of use in jails and prisons are difficult to come by, one study of male and female inmates in a maximum security prison setting estimated use to be 7 percent via self-report (Rowell-Cunsolo, Sampong, Befus, Mukherjee, and Larson 2016). This likely is an underestimate of the level of substance use in incarcerated settings.

Other treatment options include outpatient, intensive outpatient (IOP) and entering into a halfway house, typically after 28-day inpatient treatment. All of these options can be linked with criminal justice processing, depending on local availability. Outpatient treatment differs in that the patient/client is much more responsible for their treatment. The individual attends treatment programs during an allotted period of time but is not living inside of a center. Instead, their programming of individual, group, et cetera, takes place at a facility during scheduled times each week. One of the main struggles with outpatient treatment for "free individuals" comes in the lack of supervision and accountability for those in dire need. For those involved in the criminal justice system, supervision and accountability can be appended by criminal justice system representatives, such as a probation or parole officer, judge, or court-appointed personnel (such as a case manager)—thus, making outpatient programming a viable option if these resources are available in the community.

Intensive outpatient, or IOP, is just that, a very intense version of outpatient treatment. Typically, an individual is required to attend meetings, group sessions, individual sessions, et cetera for hours at a time daily or weekly, but without actually living on the grounds of the facility. This type of programming can be used in lieu of halfway houses if better housing options are available with a support system in place, particularly for those reentering the community from a jail or prison setting. This decision should be made on an individualized basis, and, again, depends on the local availability of this type of programming. Alternatively, halfway houses have specifically been used as an effort to transition a person from an inpatient facility, jail, or prison back into society and daily living. Within a house, individuals live with others who have recently "graduated" from an inpatient program and begin working on returning to work, school, while still having some contact with treatment. This environment provides support while empowering someone to regain control of their lives, which offers obvious advantages for those reentering society from jail or prison settings.

In almost all of the aforementioned settings, the language of treatment is largely the same. Participants are taught about "triggers," avoiding persons, places, or things that may trigger drug use cravings, and to have a plan in place in case cravings occur. In addition to all types of treatment, many suffering from drug/alcohol addiction participate in Alcoholics Anonymous (AA) or Narcotics Anonymous (NA), which continue to dominate the language and discourse used in recovery. In fact, almost *all* individuals referred to treatment by the criminal justice system are required to participate in this type of programming, thus knowledge of the language of AA or NA is almost ubiquitous among those with previous jail or prison sentences. This language is full of easy-to-remember acronyms such as ABCs (acceptance, belief, change) and ASK (ass-saving kit) and slogans such as "I'm an addict," "easy does it," "but for the grace of God," and the serenity prayer, "God grant us the serenity to accept the things we cannot change, the courage to change the things we can, and the wisdom to know the difference." Also, given the nature of recovery requiring multiple treatment episodes to ensure lasting success, most Americans who have entered treatment are very familiar with this language at some point in their lives.

AA and NA groups are part of a national organization created in 1935 and operate throughout the country. In any given community, there are AA or NA groups taking place daily at local community centers, churches, hospitals, treatment centers, and so on. The groups can be open to the public or closed and may also incorporate a specific group within the population. For example, there is often a women-only group in most areas. Al-Anon or Alateen are also two groups for family and friends affected by a loved one's use of drugs or alcohol. Finding support from others can be beneficial to the healing of family and friends as much as the individual immersed in drug addiction. Within the AA or NA system, the use of the "12 steps" is the main method of recovery. Each step creates a goal for the individual to work toward and achieve in order to remain sober. The process of completing these steps requires the individual to find a sponsor, which is very similar to a mentor who has been in recovery for a length of time. A sponsor guides an individual in the process of recovery and remaining sober by using the 12-step model. While these groups are mainstays in recovery, it should be noted that true treatment cannot occur without professional help for the vast majority of individuals with addiction.

Major Modalities, Evidenced-Based Programming and Practices

There are many different modalities of true treatment for substance use disorders, each with pros and cons. Yet, the trend for providers receiving some form of government funding is to only offer vetted, evidence-based models that have proven track records of success. Two major modalities that have been proven to be successful and backed with evidence include cognitive-behavioral therapy or CBT and motivational interviewing. Both of these can be used individually or in tandem, depending on client need.

Cognitive-behavioral therapy (CBT) is a technique used in individual behavioral counseling sessions with a client and mental health professional. The National Alliance on Mental Illness (NAMI) explains CBT as "the exploration of a person's thoughts, feelings and behaviors" (2016). The goal for each client is to discover unhealthy thought patterns in order to decrease self-destructive behaviors. Identifying false or negative beliefs and restructuring those beliefs are the basic principles of CBT. At this time, CBT and modifications of CBT tend to dominate the approach of practitioners, particularly in criminal justice settings. Non-licensed providers can be utilized to supplement CBT programming through the use of a curriculum that utilizes a CBT approach, making it more accessible in places where cost limits the number of clinicians available to treat people with addiction (NAMI 2016).

Motivational interviewing (MI), much like CBT, is a clinical approach to treatment of substance use disorders as well as mental illness. SAMHSA describes MI as a way to "help people with mental illness and substance use disorder make positive behavioral changes to support better health" (SAMHSA 2016a). MI uses four principles; expressing empathy and avoiding arguing, developing discrepancy, rolling with resistance, and supporting self-efficacy as the basis for developing positive change. A major advantage of MI is that it is readily accessible to licensed professionals as well as non-licensed justice professionals such as probation and parole officers, case managers, peer support specialists, and so on. Therefore, a larger subset of individuals whose daily responsibilities include managing individuals with histories of substance abuse can readily benefit from this evidence-based approach with proven results. Further, non-licensed personnel can become certified MI instructors, which can greatly improve the rate of dissemination of this approach in justice settings. Over the past few years, this practice has expanded rapidly as a result (SAMHSA, 2016a).

To supplement these modalities, evidence-based services can be utilized on an individualized basis to ensure success. One such service that has been increasing in use is medication-assisted treatment (MAT) (SAMHSA, 2016b). While not new, the growing use of MAT has been important, given the expanding level of opioid addiction in the United States since the 1990s and into the 2000s. MAT utilizes medication under strict supervision in order to assist individuals with relapse prevention, manage withdrawal, or both. For example, a drug such as methadone can be used to replace an opioid drug of choice while going through treatment with the eventual hope of weaning off use to self-sustained sobriety, as appropriate. Other drugs, such as naltrexone, can be used to help prevent relapse by rendering any opioid ingestion useless by blocking its effects, equating relapse to essentially a waste of drugs, money, and time. These services cannot be used in isolation—research has proven time and time again that MAT in conjunction with counseling and behavioral therapy is required for success in treating opioid and alcohol dependency. MAT has only recently been acceptable for use in criminal justice settings, broadly, due to entrenched ideology of popular abstinence-based approaches of prominent criminal justice practitioners. As this ideology begins to shift with a more progressive approach, and with the federal government shifting resources to jurisdictions that utilize MAT services or at least make them available, MAT will continue to flourish.

Behavioral counseling continues to be the most common treatment used for substance use disorders. Inpatient, outpatient, and IOP all use behavioral counseling as part of the overall treatment plan for patients/clients. The two ways counseling is used is individual and group-based therapy sessions. An individual therapy session is conducted between a trained mental health professional and a patient or client. Group therapy consists of a mental health professional leading the group with between five and 15 clients.

A Special Note—on an Opioid State of Emergency

One of the most widespread drug problems currently affecting the United States is opioid addiction. These opioids include heroin and prescription drugs such as hydrocodone, OxyContin(r), fentanyl, morphine, and others used to treat pain, but can often be as dangerous as street drugs. From 1991 to 2013, the number of prescribed pain medications dispensed by retail pharmacies has almost tripled from 76 million to 207 million prescriptions by 2013 (Volkow 2014). This has led to a few key trends that will continue to impact American society well into the future: (1) the increasing level of opioid use in the United States has led to an increasing level of opioid addiction, (2) tightening access to opioids on the primary or diverted markets in conjunction with the increased availability of heroin from the Far East and Mexico has led to an increase in heroin use in the United States, (3) the number and rates of individuals who have experienced overdose and/or death due to drug use is rising, and (4) the rates of individuals in criminal justice supervision with opioid abuse problems is rapidly increasing. These trends also have an impact on drug treatment in all settings. For example, researchers at Hazelden (2016) are exploring the impact of the increase of individuals with opioids as their drug of choice in inpatient treatment. This was in response to the alarm Hazelden clinicians sounded as they were noticing increased problems with their patients overall as the numbers of people with opioid problems grew. To address these issues, Hazelden designed a new approach to take with their individuals with opioid addiction and decided to keep these individuals segregated from others in inpatient treatment. Research is under way to determine whether this increases success for patients overall and, specifically, those who have a history of abusing opioids. If it is the case that a certain "tipping point" of patients with opioid addiction sours the level of success for everyone in treatment, this finding will have a major impact on treatment in correctional settings as the ability to create specialized treatment for opioid users will remain contingent on scant resources and funding.

Obstacles

A substance use disorder can be very difficult to overcome alone. Statistically, most who enter drug treatment for a substance use disorder will not remain drug-free. Often, individuals enter into treatment multiple times across their lifetime. One major obstacle to success in drug treatment is accountability. This can be seen with the guilty, hiding, lying, and other behaviors included with substance use, and could be behind one of the reasons why criminal justice can be such a powerful motivating source to remain "clean" for many. As mentioned before, individuals suffering from substance use disorders may have undiagnosed mental illness, past traumas, or unresolved personal struggles. The substance use can be a way of "self-medicating" or masking true feelings and not feeling pain. Without appropriate and healthy coping skills, resisting the urge to use substances is a major hurdle. Talk therapy, or behavioral counseling (both individual and group) can be a great resource to explore the negativity feelings and develop positive coping skills. Unfortunately, again, cost and accountability can be factors. Access to mental health professionals and services without health insurance or income to pay for the services is often a struggle of individuals with substance use disorder. In addition, discussing past trauma can be intimidating and uncomfortable for most people. Individuals can have difficulty with attending sessions regularly and really working toward the goal of healing.

Addressing and treating mental illness is crucial in the success of an individual suffering from a substance use disorder. After ridding the body of substances, mental illness symptoms can appear that may have been masked before. At this point, revisiting and possibly restructuring a treatment plan is needed to reassess any changes. Mental illness brings its own stigma and obstacles, but can also be successfully treated to allow an individual to function in a positive manner. Until the availability of resources of the criminal justice system is increased and improved to handle the current level of need within its supervised population, problems—including criminal problems—will continue to occur. In the twenty-first century, there has been an increased level of community-based criminal justice programming that addresses these issues and the momentum for continued expansion is present. It may take a generation to see notable gains; however, we are at a point in which the system seems to be pointed in a positive direction after years of cuts, an unsuccessful drug war, and a deterioration of mental health service capacity.

References

Arndt, Stephan, Laura Acion, and Kristin White. 2013. "How the States Stack Up: Disparities in Substance Abuse Outpatient Treatment Completion Rates for Minorities." *Drug and Alcohol Dependence* 132(3): 547–554.

Drake, Elizabeth. 2014. *Predicting Criminal Recidivism: A Systemic Review of Offender Risk Assessments in Washington State*. Olympia, WA: Washington State Institute for Public Policy.

Haldeman, Peter. 2013. "An Intervention for Malibu." *The New York Times*: September 13, 2013.

Hazelden. 2016. Butler Center for Research Updates. Retrieved May 6, 2017 from www.hazelden.org/web/public/researchupdates.page

Hedden, Sarra L., Joel Kennet, Rachel Lipari, Grace Medley, Peter Tice, Elizabeth A.P. Copello, and Larry A. Kroutil. 2015. *Behavioral Health Trends in the United States: Results from the 2014 National Survey on Drug Use and Health*. Washington, DC: Substance Abuse and Mental Health Services Administration.

Mumola, Christopher, and Jennifer C. Karberg. 2006. *Drug Use and Dependence, State and Federal Prisoners, 2004*. Washington, DC: Bureau of Justice Statistics.

Munetz, Mark R., and Patricia A. Griffin. 2006. "Use of the Sequential Intercept Model as an Approach to Decriminalization of People with Serious Mental Illness." *Psychiatric Services* 57(4): 544–549.

National Alliance on Mental Illness. 2016. *Psychotherapy*. Retrieved May 6, 2017 from www.nami.org/Learn-More/Treatment/Psychotherapy

National Center on Addiction and Substance Abuse. 2010. *Behind Bars II: Substance Abuse and America's Prison Population*. New York: The National Center on Addiction and Substance Abuse at Columbia University.

National Institute on Drug Abuse. 2016. *Principles of Drug Treatment*. Retrieved May 6, 2017 from www.drugabuse.gov/publications/principles-drug-addiction-treatment-research-based-guide-third-edition/principles-effective-treatment

Plourde, Chantal, and Serge Brochu. 2002. "Drugs in Prison: A Break in the Pathway." *Substance Use & Misuse* 37(1): 47–63.

Rowell-Cunsolo, Tawandra L., Stephen A. Sampong, Montina Befus, Dhritiman V. Mukherjee, and Elaine L. Larson. 2016. "Predictors of Illicit Drug Use Among Prisoners." *Substance Use & Misuse* 51(2): 261–267.

Sahker, Ethan, Maisha N. Toussaint, Marizen Ramirez, Saba R. Ali, and Stephan Arndt. 2015. "Evaluating Racial Disparity in Referral Source and Successful Completion of Substance Abuse Treatment." *Addictive behaviors* 48(September): 25–29.

Salzer, Mark S., Edward Schwenk, and Eugene Brusilovskiy. 2010. "Certified Peer Specialist Roles and Activities: Results from a National Survey." *Psychiatric Services* 61(5): 520–523.

Substance Abuse and Mental Health Services Administration. 2016a. *Motivational Interviewing*. Retrieved May 6, 2017 from www.integration.samhsa.gov/clinical-practice/motivational-interviewing

Substance Abuse and Mental Health Services Administration. 2016b. *Medication Assisted Treatment*. Retrieved May 6, 2017 from www.integration.samhsa.gov/clinical-practice/mat/mat-overview

Volkow, Nora D. 2014. "America's Addiction to Opiates: Heroin and Prescription Drug Abuse." National Institute of Drug Abuse. Retrieved May 6, 2017 from www.drugabuse.gov/about-nida/legislative-activities/testimony-to-congress/2016/americas-addiction-to-opioids-heroin-prescription-drug-abuse

Xu, Jiangmin, Richard C. Rapp, Jichuan Wang, and Robert G. Carlson. 2008. "The Multidimensional Structure of External Barriers to Substance Abuse Treatment and Its Invariance Across Gender, Ethnicity, and Age." *Substance Abuse* 29(1): 43–54.

26 Law of Corrections

Christopher E. Smith

Introduction

For much of American history, law had little relevance for corrections. Law was at the heart of the processing of criminal cases. Laws of criminal procedure shaped the processing of criminal suspects' cases after they were arrested for violating criminal laws. Upon conviction and sentencing, prisoners were typically placed under the control of correctional authorities' discretionary decisions in prisons and other contexts. Officials' rules and discretion, rather than law, ruled prisoners' lives. In the 1960s, by contrast, the Civil Rights Movement and the Warren Court's "rights revolution," as well as decisions by lower court judges, expanded the reach of law and constitutional rights throughout American society, including behind the walls of correctional institutions. Ultimately, judicial directives and legal rules were major influences in reforming and professionalizing prisons' policies and practices. However, the actual nature and number of legally protected rights for convicted offenders remained limited.

The Development of Prisoners' Rights

Prior to the 1960s, a few state judges issued rulings providing specific protections for convicted offenders within their own states' correctional systems (Wallace 1994). More typically, judges took what has been characterized as a "hands-off" approach by expressing deference to the decisions of corrections officials. Such judges often quoted a Virginia court's language referring to incarcerated offenders as "slaves of the state" (*Ruffin v. Commonwealth* 1871). The absence of judicial definition and protection for convicted offenders' rights enabled officials to use whippings and other forms of coercive violence. In addition, living conditions for prisoners often fell below basic standards for human health and survival. Indeed, southern corrections systems in the late nineteenth and early twentieth centuries effectively perpetuated slavery by incarcerating innocent African Americans and then leasing them to business owners as workers for dangerous jobs in mining, manufacturing, agriculture, and railroad building (Blackmon 2008). The dearth of legal protections for these prisoners is starkly illuminated by the fact that they were treated worse than antebellum slaves. Prior to the Civil War, plantation slaves were a form of financial investment and source of wealth for their owners. By contrast, industrial enterprises felt free to work the prisoners literally to death with the knowledge that they could be replaced at little cost by other imprisoned workers (Friedman 1993).

By the mid-twentieth century, most states' prisons had developed into secure custodial institutions whose operations and treatment of offenders were not visible to the outside world. In southern states, scandals concerning corruption and violence associated with the leasing of prison labor to outside businesses had pushed prison systems to a plantation model of using prison labor for the states' own purposes, including prison farms and state road maintenance. With the dawn of the 1960s, prisons were increasingly affected by the Civil Rights Movement, as activist lawyers looked to use law to reform correctional practices. Changes in corrections were also affected by prisoners' rising expectations about rights and the entry of college-trained officials with ideas about the application of public administration principles to prison management (Jacobs 1977). Imprisoned African Americans who joined the Nation of Islam and other Muslim sects inside prisons were especially important in asserting legal claims about rights to religion, speech, and humane living conditions. They presented their claims despite facing punitive retaliation from prison officials and limited support in the initial decisions of lower court judges (Rosenbaum and Kossy 1976; Schaich and Hope 1977; Smith 1993).

The U.S. Supreme Court—the court whose decisions impact the entire nation—played a very limited role in the earliest stages of developing the law of corrections. In *Ex parte Hull* (1941), the Supreme Court ruled that prison officials cannot block prisoners from mailing petitions to a courthouse. The case established the basis for recognizing a right of access to the courts for imprisoned offenders. However, it did not define all of the contours of that right beyond barring officials from blocking prisoners' submissions to courts. Two decades later, in its brief opinion in *Cooper v. Pate* (1964), the Court approved convicted offenders' ability to sue state officials by using Title 42, section 1983 of the United States Code, a key federal civil rights statute. The *Cooper* decision officially opened the doors of the federal courts for consideration of prisoners' claims about the existence and violation of constitutional rights in the context of corrections. Many lower federal courts had already begun examining prisoners' claims about constitutional rights. Indeed, the *Cooper* decision cited as authority two federal court of appeals decisions concerning imprisoned Nation of Islam members' claims for religious rights and equal treatment (*Pierce v. LaVallee* 1961; *Sewell v. Pegelow* 1961). The *Cooper* decision contributed to widespread litigation about prisoners' rights throughout the country. This litigation led to many lower court decisions ordering prisons to reform their policies and practices (Feeley and Rubin 1998).

Later in the 1960s, the Supreme Court applied its concern about the eradication of government-sponsored racial discrimination to corrections. In *Lee v. Washington* (1968), the Court endorsed a lower court order that prohibited Alabama from engaging in racial segregation in its prisons. The decision in *Lee* represented the beginning of the Supreme Court's active involvement in the identification and definition of constitutional rights in correctional contexts. During the 1970s, the Supreme Court made important rights-defining decisions concerning such matters as procedural rights during parole revocation (*Morrissey v. Brewer* 1972) and prison disciplinary proceedings (*Wolff v. McDonnell* 1974), the right to medical care inside prisons (*Estelle v. Gamble* 1976), and the right of access to law books for preparing legal cases (*Bounds v. Smith* 1977).

Although "Section 1983" lawsuits provide the primary vehicle for prisoners to seek vindication of federal constitutional rights, there can be other legal bases for lawsuits, depending on the circumstances of a particular case. Section 1983 enables prisoners to sue state and local officials as well as local agencies, such as county jails, for violations of constitutional rights. In a judicial decision, the Supreme Court created a parallel means to file these lawsuits against federal officials, including federal prison officials, through so-called "Bivens actions" (*Bivens v. Six Unknown Named Agents of the Federal Bureau of Investigation* 1971). Prisoners may be able to file lawsuits in state courts for personal injuries and negligent damage to property through regular state tort laws about such matters. In certain circumstances, federal prisoners can use the Federal Tort Claims Act for personal injury actions against prison officials (*Millbrook v. United States* 2013). In addition, prisoners may have opportunities to pursue legal actions through other statutes, such as disability discrimination claims under the

Americans with Disabilities Act (*Pennsylvania Department of Corrections v. Yeskey* 1998). When governments contract with private companies to hold prisoners in privately owned prisons, prisoners may need to use regular tort laws for lawsuits concerning injuries and damage to property. Civil rights statutes, such as Section 1983, are not typically available for legal actions against private businesses and their employees (*Minneci v. Pollard* 2012). Section 1983, the civil rights statute used most frequently by prisoners for their lawsuits, is specifically intended to remedy rights violations by state and local officials.

The Right of Access to the Courts

The Supreme Court's decision in *Ex parte Hull* (1941) confirmed the principle that convicted offenders, including those serving terms in prison, are entitled to have access to the courts. In *Johnson v. Avery* (1969), the Court expanded its definition of the right of access beyond *Hull*'s initial prohibition on corrections officials' actions that blocked prisoners from mailing documents to a courthouse. In *Johnson*, the Court recognized that incarcerated offenders face challenges in attempting to prepare and file their own legal documents. While the Sixth Amendment in the Constitution's Bill of Rights grants a right to "assistance of counsel," the state's obligation to provide attorneys for indigent people only applies to *criminal* prosecutions, including plea bargaining, trials, and initial appeals (*Argersinger v. Hamlin* 1972). By contrast, civil rights lawsuits by prisoners that assert claims about constitutional rights violations in corrections contexts are *civil* cases and therefore the Sixth Amendment right to counsel does not apply. Thus, prisoners who cannot afford to hire their own attorneys must be "*pro se* litigants," the term for people who represent themselves in court processes. Despite the fact that large percentages of convicted offenders have limited formal education, struggle with developmental disabilities or mental illness, lack literacy skills, or do not speak English fluently, they must conduct their own legal research and prepare their own documents in order to pursue civil rights lawsuits or habeas corpus petitions (Smith 1987). In *Johnson*, the Supreme Court declared that prison officials must permit prisoners to seek help from other prisoners in preparing legal petitions unless the prison itself provides an alternative means of legal assistance for *pro se* litigants.

In *Wolff v. McDonnell* (1974), the Supreme Court endorsed the protection of correspondence between prisoners and their attorneys. Because prison officials have a strong interest in preventing contraband from entering institutions, they can open mail marked as coming from attorneys, but only in the presence of the prisoners. The prison officials cannot read the legal mail. By opening each envelope and pouring the contents on a table in front of the prisoner, they can check to be sure no drugs or weapons are inside the envelopes and prisoners can see that officials are not reading the mail from attorneys.

In *Bounds v. Smith* (1977), the Supreme Court expanded the legal entitlement underlying the right of access to the courts by declaring that prison officials must provide prisoners with access to a law library unless the prison provides alternative assistance, such as legal advice through attorneys or paralegals. Subsequently, as the Court's composition changed through the appointment of new justices who were less supportive of protecting prisoners' rights, new decisions limited the potential for further expansion of the right of access to the courts. In *Lewis v. Casey* (1996), in particular, the Court placed a heavy burden on prisoners who sought judicial orders requiring additional assistance beyond the availability of a law library. In order for prisoners to seek special assistance because of claimed inability to use a law library effectively due to problems with literacy, mental illness, or fluency in English, they would have to show a court clear proof of their lack of ability. This poses the dilemma of requiring people who are unable to effectively make presentations to a court to actually make an effective presentation to a court in order to prove their asserted lack of effectiveness.

In practice, prisoners who truly need assistance are unlikely to be able to gain that assistance without the help of interest group lawyers who volunteer to prove the existence of the prisoner's disability. Thus, the *Lewis* decision may, in effect, block access to the courts for those who lack the requisite education and skills to make use of law libraries.

Search and Seizure

In 1984, the Supreme Court rejected Fourth Amendment protections for the living spaces and possessions of those inside correctional institutions. According to Chief Justice Warren Burger's majority opinion:

> [W]e hold that society is not prepared to recognize as legitimate any subjective expectation of privacy that a prisoner might have in his prison cell and that, accordingly, the Fourth Amendment proscription against unreasonable searches does not apply within the confines of the prison cell.
>
> (*Hudson v. Palmer* 1984: 525–526)

The categorical rejection of legal protections against unreasonable searches and seizures of prisoners' property does not, however, mean that the Fourth Amendment has no application in correctional contexts. Instead, the focus of Fourth Amendment disputes is body searches of arrestees, detainees, and convicted offenders. Typical of Fourth Amendment analysis in other contexts, courts balance the interests of the institution against the level of intrusion on individuals' reasonable expectations of privacy. In the jail context, for example, this has led to the conclusion that society's interests in keeping weapons and contraband out of jails outweigh privacy interests, even for presumptively innocent, unconvicted detainees. Thus, arrestees can be subjected to strip searches and body cavity inspections upon entering jails even if there is no specific basis to believe that an individual is concealing contraband (*Florence v. Board of Chosen Freeholders* 2012). However, some states have statutes that protect arrestees accused of minor offenses from being strip searched unless there is a specific reasonable suspicion concerning the behavior of an individual or the circumstances of the arrest.

Legal protections within corrections institutions seek to ensure that invasive body searches are not done for purposes of harassment or sexual abuse. As a result, there are usually specific policies created by states, counties, and cities that corrections officials must follow in prisons and jails. These guidelines often spell out specific circumstances that justify strip searches and body cavity inspections, such as after there has been a contact visit with a friend or family member in the visiting room (*Bell v. Wolfish* 1979). Contact visits create concerns that visitors will pass drugs or other contraband to prisoners and detainees who will then hide these forbidden items inside their body cavities. Very invasive searches that probe, rather than just visually inspect, inside body cavities often must be undertaken only by medically trained personnel rather than by corrections officials. Invasive searches often have record-keeping requirements that specify which forms must be filled out in order to keep track of how often such searches are done as well as the justifications for such searches. Policies also spell out the circumstances under which body searches can be carried out by corrections personnel who are not of the same sex as the individual who is subjected to the search. If these searches go beyond a frisk of the outer clothing, there may be rules that permit cross-gender searches only in urgent situations or with supervisors' approval.

Search and seizure issues are important for people serving criminal sentences in the community on probation and parole. In deciding cases concerning convicted offenders under supervision in the community, the Supreme Court has generally demonstrated great awareness of corrections officials' interest in detecting whether these individuals have committed new crimes or are otherwise violating their conditions of probation or parole. In *Griffin v. Wisconsin* (1987), the Supreme Court approved the warrantless search of a probationer's home that was conducted under the authority of a state law that authorized such warrantless searches when there were "reasonable grounds" to justify the search. The Court approved a warrantless search of another probationer's home because the individual had signed a form acknowledging that the terms of his probation required him to be subject to warrantless searches when police or probation officers had "reasonable cause" to conduct such searches (*United States v. Knights* 2001). A similar justification was used by the Supreme Court to approve a police officer's suspicionless search of a parolee who was walking down the sidewalk (*Samson v. California* 2006). Under the California law that guided the Court's decision, parolees must agree to be subject to searches "at any time of the day or night, with or without a search warrant and with or without cause" (*Samson v. California* 2006: 846). In effect, the Supreme Court's decisions instructed states on how they can maximize their authority to search probationers and parolees without a warrant or, in the case of parolees, without any suspicion at all. States can make susceptibility to searches a condition of probation and parole or enact statutes that provide specific authority for officials to conduct searches.

Conditions of Confinement

After the Supreme Court's decision in *Cooper v. Pate* (1964) clearly opened opportunities for prisoners to file civil rights lawsuits, lower court judges increasingly considered claims about conditions of confinement within prisons. Federal judges moved forward with examining whether prison conditions violated the Eighth Amendment prohibition on "cruel and unusual punishments" and issued many orders requiring prisons to change their facilities and policies (Crouch and Marquart 1989; Yackle 1989).

The use of the Eighth Amendment to find violations in prisons' conditions of confinement reached the Supreme Court in 1976. The case of *Estelle v. Gamble* (1976) specifically concerned whether prisoners possess any right to medical care under the Eighth Amendment. In reviewing this issue and ruling that prisoners have a limited right to medical care, the Supreme Court simultaneously applied the Eighth Amendment to conditions of confinement. Thus, the medical rights case clarified and expanded the authority of judges to make rulings about food, sanitation, ventilation, overcrowding, and other conditions of confinement. The actual right to medical care announced in *Estelle* was quite narrow: the right was only violated when prison officials were "deliberately indifferent" to serious medical needs. The lone dissenter, Justice John Paul Stevens, complained that the Court did not go far enough in clearly establishing a strong right to medical care. In his view, the Court had placed an inappropriate and unnecessary burden on prisoners. They were required to prove what prison officials were thinking rather than just present evidence for an objective examination of whether there was a deprivation of needed medical treatment (Smith 2015).

Two years later in *Hutto v. Finney* (1978), Justice Stevens wrote the Court's majority opinion that endorsed the authority of lower court judges to order remedies for prison conditions that were so deficient as to constitute "cruel and unusual punishment." In *Hutto*, dozens of prisoners were crammed into a small punishment cell and fed fewer calories than were necessary to keep an average adult healthy and alive. For two decades after these seminal decisions, federal judges issued numerous remedial orders requiring changes in prison conditions in nearly every state. Southern states were affected in the most significant way because their plantation model often placed discretionary authority and coercive power in the hands of "trusty" inmates who supervised other prisoners at prison farms and in prison living quarters (Crouch and Marquart 1989). Reforms ordered by judges to remedy Eighth

Amendment rights violations required very expensive changes through expansions of living quarters, construction of medical facilities, and the hiring and training of corrections officers to take over the supervisory tasks previously undertaken by "trusty" inmates.

Later, a Supreme Court decision made it more difficult for prisoners to challenge successfully the conditions of confinement in correctional institutions. In *Wilson v. Seiter* (1991), a narrow majority of justices took the "deliberate indifference" standard that applied to prisoners' medical care claims and said that it should apply in all conditions of confinement cases. As a result, prisoners were required to provide evidence about corrections officials' knowledge and intentions in order to prove Eighth Amendment violations concerning excessive use of force, nutrition, overcrowding, sanitation, and other matters. The concurring justices in *Wilson* complained about the new standard. They said inadequate prison conditions would be beyond judicial remedies if prison officials merely expressed concern about the substandard conditions but claimed not to have enough money from the legislature to correct problems.

Despite the increased difficulty in proving conditions of confinement cases, prisoners remain able to use lawsuits to claim violations of Eighth Amendment rights concerning a variety of issues. The precedent in *Wilson* reduced opportunities for federal judges to examine prison conditions, yet there are individual cases in which prisoners' lawyers are able to show "deliberate indifference" in order to gain judicial protection and remedial action. For example, prisoners can sue for excessive use of force even when they did not suffer serious injuries as a result (*Hudson v. McMillian* 1992). They can also sue for potential future harms to their health, such as the risk to non-smokers from being housed in a small cell with a chain smoker (*Helling v. McKinney* 1993). In 2011, for example, the Supreme Court endorsed lower court decisions that required California to significantly reduce its prison population because overcrowded conditions had led to deficiencies in the provision of medical and mental health care (*Brown v. Plata* 2011). However, the Supreme Court has declined to support some Eighth Amendment claims, such as the assertion that it is "cruel and unusual" to punish prisoners by forbidding them from seeing visitors for extended periods of time as a means to sanction them for rule infractions (*Overton v. Bazzetta* 2003). The Supreme Court has never defined a right for prisoners to have visitors, although a permanent ban on visitors could lead a prisoner to pursue a new Eighth Amendment claim or a claim under the First Amendment right to association.

The Supreme Court limited the Eighth Amendment's prohibition on "cruel and unusual punishments" to only those individuals experiencing "punishment," namely people convicted of crimes. Thus, pretrial detainees awaiting trial must file lawsuits claiming deprivation of "due process" in order to challenge conditions of confinement in jails. As a result, the protection of rights under the Fourteenth Amendment's Due Process Clause provides the basis for lawsuits challenging issues within jails, such as excessive use of force (*Kingsley v. Hendrickson* 2015) and unsanitary, illness-causing conditions (*Duvall v. Dallas County* 2011).

As federal judges throughout the country ordered states to make changes to their facilities, services, and policies in response to prisoners' lawsuits about conditions of confinement, governors complained that the federal courts were too involved in telling states how to run correctional institutions. After years of lobbying by governors, state attorneys general, and mayors, Congress enacted the Prison Litigation Reform Act (PLRA) in 1996 (Sandler and Schoenbrod 2003). The PLRA affects litigation concerning conditions of confinement as well as other constitutional rights issues. The PLRA makes it more difficult for prisoners to file lawsuits, especially by changing the prior practice of routinely waiving court costs when prisoners claim that they cannot afford to pay the usual fees to initiate litigation. The PLRA requires prisoners to make partial payments from whatever funds they have in their prison accounts and precludes waiver of fees for any prisoners who have had three previous lawsuits dismissed as "frivolous" (Schlanger and Shay 2008). The PLRA also requires prisoners to exhaust administrative remedies through prison grievance processes before constitutional rights lawsuits can be filed. These administrative processes typically favor prison officials' versions of events and make prisoners' grievances vulnerable to dismissal if they fail to follow all of the steps in each level of the internal grievance processes (Calavita and Jenness 2015). In addition, the PLRA prevents individual federal judges from ordering the release of prisoners in order to reduce overcrowding. After the PLRA, such orders can only be issued by multi-judge panels. Moreover, judges can no longer maintain control over the implementation of prison reform orders for years after the initial litigation. Instead, judges' orders face mandatory expiration dates unless new litigation demonstrates the continuing existence of constitutional rights violations. Overall, the PLRA caused a significant decline in prisoners' constitutional rights lawsuits. It also makes such litigation much more difficult for prisoners to win (Schlanger 2015).

First Amendment Rights: Speech, Press, and Association

In the 1960s and thereafter, prisoners filed lawsuits claiming First Amendment rights to correspond with others, receive publications, and marry. The Supreme Court initially recognized limited rights related to these matters (*Procunier v. Martinez* 1974). In a major First Amendment decision that influenced many prisoners' rights cases afterward, the Supreme Court, in *Turner v. Safley* (1987), presented a four-part test for evaluating whether prison officials' actions violated certain constitutional rights. In the case itself, the Court upheld prison restrictions on correspondence between prisoners in different prisons. At the same time, the Court rejected strict regulations that prevented prisoners from marrying while in prison without the approval of prison officials. The essential element of the four-part test is an emphasis on judges' deferring to rational policy decisions by prison officials, even if those policies are not essential to the operation of the institution. In the words of the Court's majority opinion, "there must be a 'valid, rational connection' between the prison regulation and the legitimate governmental interest put forward to justify it" (*Turner v. Safley* 1987: 89). In many instances, if prison officials claim that a policy is useful for the preservation of order and security inside a prison, judges will automatically reject the prisoner's constitutional challenge to the policy. Judges throughout the country have subsequently applied the so-called "Turner test" to many First Amendment issues. In *Beard v. Banks* (2006), for example, the majority of justices applied the "Turner test" by deferring to prison officials' decisions and thereby rejecting claims by prisoners in a high-security housing unit that their First Amendment rights were violated when they were deprived of access to newspapers, magazines, and family photos.

Freedom of Religion

The First Amendment provides two aspects of religious freedom. The protection against "an establishment of religion" provides Americans with freedom from the imposition of religion upon them by government. The protection is also supposed to prevent taxpayers' money from being spent in support of particular religions. The guarantee of "free exercise" of religion seeks to protect people's freedom to engage in religious practices without improper interference by government. In contemporary times, the "establishment" aspect of religion arises only in specific situations in corrections while claims about the "free exercise" of religion arise with regularity in prisoners' lawsuits.

The earliest American prisons of the nineteenth century were founded amid expectations that isolating convicted offenders would enable them to use Bible study and prayer to reform themselves. By the late twentieth century, Supreme Court decisions had made clear that government could typically not provide support for religious institutions nor impose religious services and prayer on Americans, including prisoners. Thus, contemporary litigation concerning the "establishment" issue is relatively infrequent and generally concerns prison systems' support for churches' programs inside prisons in contexts in which there is pressure for prisoners to participate. In one case, Iowa gave a Christian religious group control over rehabilitation programs within one prison. A federal appeals court found that Iowa's support for these church-run programs violated the First Amendment by providing government financial support to one particular religion and by forcing prisoners seeking to benefit from the prison's rehabilitation programs to participate in religious practices (*Americans United for Separation of Church and State v. Prison Fellowship Ministry* 2007).

With respect to the free exercise of religion, the development of prisoner litigation in the 1960s was shaped by religious freedom claims, as well as assertions about other constitutional rights, put forward by members of the Nation of Islam and other Muslims. Eventually, federal judges recognized that Muslims, as well as Buddhists and others, received unequal treatment from prison officials who typically permitted Christian religious practices but not practices by members of other religions.

In 1987, the Supreme Court applied its newly-created "Turner test" to a free exercise of religion claim by minimum-security Muslim prisoners who were assigned to work outside the prison's walls on weekdays (*O'Lone v. Estate of Shabazz* 1987). The Muslim prisoners wanted to return to the prison at midday on Fridays for an important religious service, but the Supreme Court accepted prison officials' claim that any midday return to the prison would pose administrative problems for staffing and security. Thus, the deference that the Supreme Court showed to prison officials under the "Turner test" denied these prisoners access to a religious ceremony that even the majority opinion conceded was of "central importance" to their religious beliefs and practices (*O'Lone v. Estate of Shabazz* 1987: 351).

A few years later, the Supreme Court applied a similarly deferential approach in a non-corrections case to limit the judicial protection for free exercise of religion for all Americans (*Employment Division of Oregon v. Smith* 1990). Congress reacted against that decision by enacting laws to provide greater protection for religious practices than that applied by the Supreme Court. The new laws provided more protection for prisoners' religious rights than prisoners received under the "Turner test." The Religious Freedom Restoration Act (RFRA) increased protection for federal prisoners and the Religious Land Use and Institutionalized Persons Act (RLUIPA) increased protection for people held in state prisons and local jails. Under these laws, instead of deferring to rational reasons given by corrections officials for policies that clash with free exercise of religion, judges must demand that officials show a "compelling governmental interest" for the policies and demonstrate that the policy is the "least restrictive" means to advance the compelling interest. This standard requires judges to look closely at and question the justifications provided by corrections officials for their policies. As a result, prisoners have greater opportunities to prevail with free exercise of religion claims than with claims concerning many other constitutional rights. In 2015, for example, by applying the standard of the RLUIPA, a unanimous Supreme Court ruled that a Muslim prisoner in Arkansas could grow a short, religiously required beard despite prison officials' claims that the beard posed the danger of permitting the prisoner to change his appearance and potentially hide contraband (*Holt v. Hobbs* 2015).

Procedural Due Process

In *Morrissey v. Brewer* (1972), the Supreme Court set forth limited procedural protections for parolees when officials sought to revoke parole and send them back to prison for parole violations. Previously, lower court judges typically assumed that prisoners, parolees, and probationers had temporarily forfeited the Due Process Clause's constitutionally-protected "liberty" interests by being placed under the restrictive conditions of correctional supervision. The *Morrissey* decision presented the Supreme Court's first clear acknowledgment that convicted offenders retain elements of "liberty" that deserve due process protections (Stevens 2011). Parole revocation proceedings need not be full-blown adversarial trials in the manner of criminal prosecutions. Instead, parolees are entitled to specific procedural elements that are intended to enhance fair decision making without requiring complete trials. Parole revocation proceedings must include the following: notice to the parolee of alleged violations; an opportunity to present information to support the parolee's side of the story; a neutral decision maker; and a report describing the reasons for the ultimate decision concerning parole revocation. Previously, parole could be revoked based solely on discretionary decisions by parole officers. The Supreme Court subsequently imposed the same due process protections for probation revocation (*Gagnon v. Scarpelli* 1973) and prison disciplinary proceedings that will result in the loss of "good time" credits (*Wolff v. McDonnell* 1974). The convicted offender is not entitled to representation by counsel in any of these proceedings, although there may be specific circumstances, such as a probationer or parolee affected by mental illness or developmental disabilities, that might require assistance from an advocate. In addition, a "neutral decision maker" does not mean someone from outside the corrections system. The Supreme Court accepts parole officers not involved in a particular parolee's supervision and committees made up of prison officials as neutral decision makers for these disciplinary purposes.

These basic due process requirements do not apply to all punitive and administrative actions in the context of corrections. For example, without holding hearings that permit prisoners to object to these actions, prison officials can place prisoners in administrative segregation (*Sandin v. Conner* 1995) or transfer prisoners to more restrictive prison settings (*Meachum v. Fano* 1976) and to prisons in other states (*Olim v. Waikinekona* 1983).

Conclusion

In the realm of constitutional rights, Americans often think of the U.S. Supreme Court as leading the development and definition of legal protections under the U.S. Constitution. With respect to the law of corrections, rights received recognition and definition through the combined actions of lower courts, Congress, and the Supreme Court. Constitutional rights had little applicability to people being punished for criminal convictions until the 1960s and thereafter. Lower court judges led the way in examining prisoners' claims about rights violations. Indeed, certain aspects of the law of corrections, such as the abolition of whipping in prisons (*Jackson v. Bishop* 1968) and court orders to improve prison conditions (*Pugh v. Locke* 1976), are directly attributable to innovative decisions in the federal lower courts. In the 1970s, the Supreme Court issued a series of decisions that established important baseline rights with respect to access to the courts, due process rights, and the application of Eighth Amendment rights to conditions-of-confinement and use-of-force issues in prisons. Subsequently, political backlash against judicial decisions led to two important actions by Congress. Through the enactment of the Prison Litigation Reform Act (PLRA), Congress made it more difficult for prisoners to file civil rights lawsuits and limited lower court judges' authority to impose and supervise reforms in prisons' facilities and policies. In contrast to the litigation-limiting effects of the PLRA, Congress increased protection for prisoners' right to free exercise of religion through the federally focused Religious Freedom Restoration Act and the state-focused Religious Land Use and Institutionalized Persons Act. The Supreme Court remains important. Advocates for either the expansion or contraction of constitutional rights in corrections continue to bring cases to the highest court with the hope of spurring decisions that will have national impact. Yet, the development of the law of corrections shows how the actions and reactions of various lawmaking institutions can influence both the definition of constitutional rights and the extent of judicial authority to enforce those rights.

References

Blackmon, Douglas A. 2008. *Slavery by Another Name: The Re-Enslavement of Black Americans from the Civil War to World War II.* New York: Anchor Books.

Calavita, Kitty, and Valerie Jenness. 2015. *Appealing to Justice: Prisoner Grievances, Rights, and Carceral Logic.* Berkeley, CA: University of California Press.

Crouch, Ben M., and James W. Marquart. 1989. *Appeal to Justice: Litigated Reform of Texas Prisons.* Austin, TX: University of Texas Press.

Feeley, Malcolm M., and Edward L. Rubin. 1998. *Judicial Policy Making and the Modern State: How the Courts Reformed America's Prisons.* New York: Cambridge University Press.

Friedman, Lawrence M. 1993. *Crime and Punishment in American History.* New York: Basic Books.

Jacobs, James B. 1977. *Stateville: The Penitentiary in Mass Society.* Chicago, IL: University of Chicago Press.

Rosenbaum, Lorrin P., and Judith Kossy. 1976. "A Question of Justice." *Index on Censorship* 5(3): 3–9.

Sandler, Ross, and David Schoenbrod. 2003. *Democracy by Decree: What Happens When Courts Run Government.* New Haven, CT: Yale University Press.

Schaich, Warren L., and Diane S. Hope. 1977. "The Prison Letters of Martin Sostre: Documents of Resistance." *Journal of Black Studies* 7: 281–300.

Schlanger, Margo. 2015. "Trends in Prisoner Litigation as PLRA Enters Adulthood." *UC-Irvine Law Review* 5: 153–178.

Schlanger, Margo, and Giovanna Shay. 2008. "Preserving the Rule of Law in America's Jails and Prisons: The Case for Amending the Prison Litigation Reform Act." *University of Pennsylvania Journal of Constitutional Law* 11: 139–154.

Smith, Christopher E. 1987. "Examining the Boundaries of Bounds: Prison Law Libraries and Access to the Courts." *Howard Law Journal* 30: 27–44.

Smith, Christopher E. 1993. "Black Muslims and the Development of Prisoners' Rights." *Journal of Black Studies* 24: 131–146.

Smith, Christopher E. 2015. *John Paul Stevens: Defender of Rights in Criminal Justice.* Lanham, MD: Lexington Books.

Stevens, John Paul. 2011. *Five Chiefs: A Supreme Court Memoir.* Boston, MA: Little, Brown.

Wallace, Donald. 1994. "The Eighth Amendment and Prison Deprivations: Historical Revisions." *Criminal Law Bulletin* 30: 3–29.

Yackle, Larry W. 1989. *Reform and Regret: The Story of Federal Judicial Involvement in the Alabama Prison System.* New York: Oxford University Press.

Cases Cited

Argersinger v. Hamlin, 407 U.S. 25 (1972).

Americans United for Separation of Church and State v. Prison Fellowship Ministry, 509 F.3d 406 (2007).

Beard v. Banks, 548 U.S. 521 (2006).

Bell v. Wolfish, 441 U.S. 520 (1979).

Bivens v. Six Unknown Named Agents, 403 U.S. 388 (1971).

Bounds v. Smith, 430 U.S. 817 (1977).

Brown v. Plata, 131 S.Ct. 1910 (2011).

Cooper v. Pate, 378 U.S. 546 (1964).

Duvall v. Dallas County, 631 F.3d 203 (5th Cir. 2011).

Employment Division of Oregon v. Smith, 494 U.S. 872 (1990).
Estelle v. Gamble, 429 U.S. 97 (1976).
Ex parte Hull, 312 U.S. 546 (1941).
Florence v. Board of Chosen Freeholders, 132 S.Ct. 1510 (2012).
Gagnon v. Scarpelli, 411 U.S. 778 (1973).
Griffin v. Wisconsin, 483 U.S. 868 (1987).
Helling v. McKinney, 509 U.S. 25 (1993).
Holt v. Hobbs, 135 S.Ct. 853 (2015).
Hudson v. McMillian, 503 U.S. 1 (1992).
Hudson v. Palmer, 468 U.S. 517 (1984)
Hutto v. Finney, 437 U.S. 678 (1978).
Jackson v. Bishop, 404 F.2d 571 (8th Cir. 1968).
Johnson v. Avery, 393 U.S. 483 (1969).
Kingsley v. Hendrickson, 135 S.Ct. 2466 (2015).
Lee v. Washington, 390 U.S. 333 (1968).
Lewis v. Casey, 518 U.S. 343 (1996).
Meachum v. Fano, 427 U.S. 215 (1976).
Millbrook v. United States, 133 S.Ct. 1441 (2013).
Minneci v. Pollard, 132 S.Ct. 617 (2012).
Morrissey v. Brewer, 408 U.S. 471 (1972).
Olim v. Waikinekona, 461 U.S. 238 (1983).
O'Lone v. Estate of Shabazz, 482 U.S. 342 (1987).
Overton v. Bazzetta, 539 U.S. 126 (2003).
Pennsylvania Department of Corrections v. Yeskey, 524 U.S. 206 (1998).
Pierce v. LaVallee, 293 F.2d 233 (2d Cir. 1961).
Procunier v. Martinez, 416 U.S. 396 (1974).
Pugh v. Locke, 406 F. Supp. 318 (M.D. Ala. 1976).
Ruffin v. Commonwealth, 62 Va. 790 (1871).
Samson v. California, 547 U.S. 843 (2006).
Sandin v. Conner, 515 U.S. 472 (1995).
Sewell v. Pegelow, 291 F.2d 196 (4th Cir. 1961).
Turner v. Safley, 482 U.S. 78 (1987).
United States v. Knights, 534 U.S. 112 (2001).
Wilson v. Seiter, 501 U.S. 294 (1991).
Wolff v. McDonnell, 418 U.S. 539 (1974).

27 Evidence-Based Practices in Sentencing and Corrections

Faye S. Taxman

The evidence-based practices label implies that there is accumulated research (i.e. more than two studies) to confirm the validity of a practice, policy, or intervention. The research is used to document that there are certain desired outcomes that are likely to occur. It is also the buzz word in sentencing and corrections that is associated with the "new punishment practices" or a cadre of tools, curriculums, procedures, and policies that are considered part of a platform that should generate better, more positive client[1] outcomes. But, front-line staff question the validity, utility, and effectiveness of these toolkits, and they question the supporting research for the evidence-based practice (EBP). A degree of skepticism may be warranted given that the generic EBP may be based on research, or at least the best available research, but it does not mean that the assorted tools or practices that are associated with the EBP are also based on research, or that the tools even reflect a research foundation. In this essay, this quagmire will be examined, and the impact on research, policy, and practice. The essay ends with a call for more research to better understand EBPs.

Research Foundation for EBPs

A research base refers to the collection or body of research studies, varying in terms of study design and quality, to support a practice, policy or intervention (treatment whether it be social control or therapeutic). This body of research is an accumulation of knowledge about "something" that can generate a conclusion regarding its effectiveness. But a research base is not something to sneeze about—it requires numerous (at least ten) studies on similar topics, generally on similar type of individuals, that can be synthesized. One study is not sufficient because it does not allow for the variations in study location, type of participating organization(s), normal variations in the characteristics of the program, similar populations, variations in the staff delivering the practice/treatment, and generally a host of other variables that may impact the outcomes. In field studies, there are variations in how studies are conducted, and many factors that cannot be controlled such as the characteristics of jurisdictions or organizations or the degree of implementation of a practice. Two studies on the same topic are more useful; but again, this is generally insufficient given the normal variations in the intervention, the organizations, the clients, or the processes. Ten studies are generally recommended to make a consensus.

To become an EBP, there is generally the need for a convergence of research regarding the effectiveness of different practices, policies or interventions. In the field of science, the preferred method for assessing the collective knowledge from research studies is to use systematic review or meta-analysis methods. In general, there should be at least ten studies to warrant a synthesis using systematic reviews and meta-analyses. These are the favored tools for synthesizing across studies, which generates an average or mean effect that one is likely to achieve if practice/policy/intervention mirrors what was studied. The Campbell Collaboration (social sciences, www.campbellcollaboration.org/) and the Cochrane Collaboration (health and medical, www.cochrane.org/) are two hosting organizations for systematic reviews and/or meta-analyses. The advantage of a meta-analysis or systematic review is that there are sound scientific principles that guide how information is synthesized, and that they provide numbers—the mean effect size and confidence intervals—by which we can have faith in our efforts.

But, like other research methods, a meta-analysis or systematic review may not always fill in the knowledge gap. The limitation associated with the mean effect size is that the factors that affect variation are often not identified, measured, or reported. First, meta-analyses or systematic reviews are subject to information documented in the primary published studies or often-called gray material (i.e. unpublished papers, reports, and other documentation of a study) studies. Many studies do not document the practice/policy/intervention that is tested, which means that it is unclear which are the core components that define a practice in that study, what is the specific population involved in the study, how did the staff deliver the intervention, and what are the implementation issues. For example, in one drug court study that examined moderators of the drug courts, they could not identify drug court participant characteristics, drug court interventions or practices (such as frequency of drug testing), and drug court features that defined more effective drug courts because most of the information was not available in the primary studies. They did find that the method of disposal had a difference with pre-plea being slightly more effective (mean = 1.74 compared to post pleas of 1.60), minimum time to graduate with 12 to 15 months being more effective than under 12 months or over 15 months (1.77 compare to 1.58 or 1.61), and minor criminal history (1.80 compared to 1.51 for not having a minor criminal history) (see Mitchell, Wilson, Eggers, and MacKenzie 2012).

Second, some of the contextual information regarding setting, organization, justice actors, system capacity issues that affect the degree to which innovations can be implemented and sustained, are infrequently reported in published studies or gray studies, and they are seldom accounted for in the meta-analyses or systematic reviews. Most importantly, some contextual differences are *not* reported in the original study which precludes the ability to analyze these factors (or conduct moderator analyses). Thus, one does not have a good understanding of the factors that affect the degree to which that effect size can be replicated in different environments, actors, program components, or other typical variations that occur in the real world. This is a limitation of understanding the transportability of an EBP into new settings since the underlying differences among organizations implementing change are seldom documented.

Third, the number of studies used in a systematic review or meta-analysis to document an "evidence-based" practice, policy, or treatment varies considerably. The systematic review or meta-analysis process includes a process of identifying all studies on a given topic and then selecting the studies that meet certain core criteria (i.e. document certain outcomes, certain key variables, certain populations, etc.). That is, the researcher often defines the eligible studies, which means that some studies, for whatever reason, are not included in the analyses. Students of syntheses need to explore the study inclusion and/or exclusion criteria that affect the reported findings in a meta-analysis or systematic review. That is, the meta-analyses and systematic reviews synthesize research studies but, like other research studies, decisions are made about what is included and not included. In this end, this can also affect the findings, and may be important to understand when reviewing the evidence pool.

Best Practices Based on Consensus/Expert Panels and Clinical Knowledge

Besides research studies, there are a number of other means that are used to identify desired practices/policies/interventions. The two other common techniques are: (1) consensus or experts' panels where experts and/or practitioners of various backgrounds gather together to review the research studies, practices, and collective knowledge about a topic; and (2) clinical knowledge with standards of quality care. The importance of these techniques is that they tend to "fill in" what is available in research studies, and also infuse standards of care and moral and/or ethical issues along with the identification of research-based "evidence." For example, Taxman and Ainsworth (2009) identify the importance of working relationships and rapport as important factors in correctional milieux, even though the evidence regarding the importance of this information is still being tested. The working relationship is identified as a good clinical practice that is important in a correctional setting to facilitate trust that is needed in treatment settings. Andrews and Bonta (2010) also discuss the importance of a human service environment to facilitate quality treatment programming because they recognize that behavioral change is unlikely to occur if the individual is coerced or not vested in changing behavior. Both of these are examples of incorporating environmental or setting factors that serve to facilitate the achievement of the research-based recommendations where there may be insufficient evidence to do a meta-analysis or systematic review.

The language that is used—consensus panel, expert panel, clinical experts—is important to consider since it signifies how the evidence was acquired to define a best practice or even an evidence-informed practice. The consensus or expert panel uses the expertise of a wide range of individuals to review the current state of knowledge, to garner their own professional experience, and to highlight the clinical issues that affect study outcomes and uptake of different practices. The best practices designation is often confused with an evidence-based approach due to too few studies, conflicting findings, or inconsistent research and practice experience.

Evidence-Based or Evidence-Informed Practices

A variety of evidence-based (or informed) practices have been identified for the field of corrections, and there is a general consensus that the EBPs cover the major components of managing individuals in the justice system. The key decision points that are included are: (1) intake including screening and assessment; (2) case planning; (3) interventions including treatment and social controls; (4) graduated responses to address compliance; and (5) working relationship or therapeutic milieu. The following sections will review what aspect of the policy and practice is evidence-based and then discuss the frequently under-researched factors that affect solid, quality implementation and the ability for an EBP to be effective. That is, the research defines the "evidence" but there are important factors how that EBP is translated into operational practice. And, the operational practice affects the goals.

Intake Processes Including Screening and Assessment

The use of a standardized risk and need assessment tool is one of the most important EBPs. The standardized risk and need assessment instrument is used to identify those factors that affect the likelihood that an individual will be successful on supervision. There are a number of standardized risk and need assessment tools—generally they are referred to in terms of generations or the era of development from static risk (history) to tools that assess risk and needs (where needs refers to the factors that affect involvement in criminal behavior).

The invention of the risk *and* need assessment tool is that the tool can be used not only for assessment of severity of behavior but also for case planning.

The research that establishes this principle is that a standardized risk and need assessment tool improves the accuracy of the prediction of the desired outcome as compared to clinical judgment—in other words, the use of a risk and need assessment tool improves decision making. The use of a standardized tool is justified by the ability to remove bias from decision making, and to frame decisions in terms of the individual's likelihood for future involvement in the justice system. As cited in a number of studies, the use of a standardized tool reduces bias, improves accuracy, and standardizes the information used in the decision calculus across staff. And, the risk assessment is based on statistical factors, not individual interpretation of a person's prior criminal history. Statistical techniques are used to predict reoffending or reincarceration, which improves solely clinical decision making. The statistical analyses in terms of what ingredients are in the assessment tool define the EBP.

But, just having a risk and need assessment tool is not sufficient to achieve the desired results. That is, most of the literature is focused on a few factors: (1) the tool must be standardized; (2) the tool must be validated on the population; (3) the tool must measure key constructs related to risk and needs and these constructs must be statistically validated; and, (4) the tool should be used in decision making regarding key factors. The issue is not which tool to use but: (1) how to use the tool in decisions and (2) what decisions should the tool be used in. The "how tos" are not articulated in the research literature since it is assumed that individuals will use the tools if they are provided with the tool. The "how tos" are generally not part of the research evidence for this EBP.

The gaping hole in our knowledge is how best to use the RNA (Risks and Needs Assessment) tool in practice. Many organizations use a screener to identify who is to use the full instrument whereas others self-select individuals to apply the tool. All of these practices have an impact on the perception of the RNA tool as an "effective practice." That is, if the tool is designed for overall use but then is only used on select clients or at various points in the process, then the RNA is considered to be of less value to the organization. Another area that undermines the use of the tool is that the staff believe that it replaces their decision, instead of augmenting or informing their decision. Wider applications increase the belief in the tool as being compatible with the organization and work processes.

Borrowing from the clinical literature, there are several pointers that can inform the "how to" use the RNA tool to achieve the desired outcomes. In fact, the "how to" integrates the actuarial with clinical with a structured clinical judgment (SCJ). SCJ addresses the "how tos" by emphasizing that the tool is part of a process and the process includes using the RNA tool to inform decision making. First, the tool requires the individual and the officer/representative of the state to have a trusting relationship. This relationship is needed to ensure that the individual is open and honest in terms of answering sensitive or confidential questions, and that the individual trusts that the officer will understand the circumstances of the risk behaviors. As part of this interview, it is important that there is transparency where the officer of the state details the risk behaviors of the individual. That is, the person must inform the individual of the state's decision—the person should not find out about it by reading a piece of paper but good communication is needed to ensure that the individual is aware of the state's assessment. Second, SCJ leads to transparency of the officer of the state informing the individual of the implications of their results of their risk and need assessment. This means that the individual is aware of how the information is being used, and also what role they have in the decisions that are going to be made. Third, the individual should acknowledge that they agree to the risk and need assessment information. SCJ as a tool reinforces that the RNA tool is a decision-support tool instead of a definitive purpose.

Case Planning

Case planning per se is not an evidence-based practice, especially since most studies of case management do not appear to have an impact on positive outcomes. The lack of evidence in case planning/management is primarily due to the emphasis on developing a paper plan that primarily refers to services. Case management is more effective when the process ends with placement in appropriate services (Taxman 2012). The emphasis is on *appropriate* services which means that the information obtained from the structured clinical interview and standardized risk and need assessment tool should drive the decisions about the type of services and controls that are needed.

Many agencies lack specific policies and procedures to assist officers to determine the appropriate services and controls, or what type of results from the RNA should be translated into different types of programs and services. Taxman, Pattavina, and Caudy (2014) offer some conceptual matching criteria based on the risk and needs that the individual presents. These conceptual criteria are as follows:

- Substance Dependence Treatment including residential treatment, drug treatment courts, or other programs that are more than six months in duration are for those individuals that, according to the DSM-V, are tolerant to substances such as opioids, cocaine, and methamphetamines. This is regardless of the risk level for reoffending.
- Cognitive restructuring programs that address criminal thinking, criminal lifestyle, or criminal subculture are for those that have three or more needs that are linked to criminal behavior and are moderate to high risk for reoffending. The emphasis is on identifying individuals that are engaged in persistent criminal lifestyle as an adult.
- Self-management and improvement is designed for those that have two factors that are directly linking offending behavior but also have other life factors (i.e. mental illness, homelessness, etc.) that affect stability in the community. These individuals are moderate to low-moderate risk for reoffending.
- Interpersonal skill development is designated for those that have no more than two factors that affect involvement in criminal behavior and are moderate risk for offending. These services are designated for those that have social or interpersonal skills that need attention to reduce the involvement in criminal behavior.
- Life skills are designated for individuals that are low to moderate risk that do not have any major criminogenic need but lack financial skills, vocational skills, did not complete high school, or could generally use some skills to better advance stability.
- Other programs address restorative justice, retribution, or repayment for the criminal behavior.

These conceptual models are built on the premise that the more serious behaviors (substance dependence and cognitive restructuring) should be addressed first and then other needs (i.e. self management, interpersonal skills, life skills) should be addressed. Those with serious mental illness will need to be stabilized before being placed into other treatment in order to prepare the individual to be receptive for the treatment programming. Also, individuals with mental challenges or low literacy will need to have the intervention provided at a slower pace to allow for the individual to absorb the material.

The next question is how to distribute social controls. Social controls are designed to exercise physical or psychological limits on an individual. The most prevalent social controls are drug testing, house arrest or curfews, and financial restrictions (i.e. fines, fees, and restitution payments). The social controls, for the most part, have been shown to not be effective in reducing recidivism because they are generally punitive. But, in combination with different programming, the social controls can provide structure that is important to facilitate behavioral changes especially impulse or regulation control.

The other misnomer is that the case plan is static—it is completed at the onset of criminal justice control. But, in fact, the case plan is dynamic, which requires constant revision based on the progress of the individual. The case plan should be revised to indicate progress made during each phase of the process to reflect the progress of the individual.

Treatment from a Therapeutic Approach

For nearly 40 years, the preferred treatments are cognitive or cognitive-behavioral therapy, therapeutic communities, or group therapy that uses cognitive-behavioral approaches (Andrews and Bonta 2010). These interventions have the largest effect sizes with the greatest potential to reduce recidivism (Lipsey and Cullen 2007). The treatments are designed to assist the individual in learning new options in terms of how to think through problems and situations, how to handle situations and respond with more prosocial behaviors, and how to use different resources to accomplish and meet one's needs. The emphasis is on socialization, restructuring responses, and providing a prosocial support system.

It is not enough to subscribe to a cognitive, cognitive-behavioral or therapeutic community approach. The "how to" practices associated with effective treatments or programs are many, and have an impact on the likelihood of successful outcomes. In other words, effective treatments are not just about the approach but also about the components of the program, staffing, goals and objectives, and integration with the criminal justice system.

Treatment Components. Evidence-based treatments are typically associated with the use of a manual to guide the treatment curriculum. This is referred to as a manualized approach that serves to specify which are the goals and objectives for each treatment session. There are a number of manualized curriculums available—some are proprietary, some are in the public domain, and some are developed specific to certain programs. Landenberger and Lipsey (2005) examined whether the type of curriculum had an impact on the results in a meta-analysis of the key components of effective programing. In this study, six curriculums were analyzed and the study found that the curriculum was not an effective moderator (noting that some curriculums had few evaluations) but rather some components were more important in impacting outcomes. That is, no one curriculum results in improved outcomes. Landenberg and Lipsey (2005) identified that effective CBT programs tend to occur in community settings, target moderate- to high-risk offenders, include an anger-management component, include a cognitive restructuring component, provide supplementary individual sessions, are of sufficient duration, and are well-implemented. Treatment needs to include elements of interpersonal problem solving, anger control, victim impact, and behavior modification that appear to approach or be statistically significant moderators of CBT treatment elements. CBT is considered a key factor in core correctional practices since it creates a social learning environment.

But, the manualized approach has gained traction because it provides a uniform approach to the treatment sessions, it guides the staff as to the core components, it is standardized and therefore it is possible to ascertain how the program is facilitating individual change, and the curriculum provides the ability to conduct quality assurance with more ease because there are clear objective criteria to assess whether the staff are adhering to the curriculum. Quality implementation is related to improved outcomes. Quality needs to be maintained and it requires a commitment to strategies to observe treatment sessions (delivered in person, not on paper) and provide feedback to the counselors or facilitators of the treatment. CBT and therapeutic communities are more than workbooks that the individual participants use in the treatment sessions; CBT involves using the workbook and activities to assist the individual in processing, role-playing, and providing feedback on strategies to respond to typical situations that affect their negative behavior. How these sessions are administered is critically important—the sessions need to be interactive instead of didactic. The sessions should provide opportunities for participants to be active learners and guide responses as a means to advance their acquisition of new skills.

Dosage or Program Length. Dosage, or the amount of programming that is needed to achieve desirable results, is an area that is under-researched. Three studies exist that highlight the need for longer duration of involvement in treatment with recommendations for 100 hours for low-risk individuals, 200 hours for moderate-risk individuals, and 300 hours for high-risk individuals (Bourgon and Gutierrez 2012; Sperber, Latessa, and Makarios 2013a, 2013b). However, it is unclear from these studies as to what is included in the recommended dosage amounts, whether it includes group sessions, individual counseling sessions, aftercare, support services, or any intervention. This is an area that is under-researched but it is clear from Landenberger and Lipsey's study that it is important to augment the core programming with individual sessions, anger management, and some aspects of cognitive restructuring.

Staffing. Staffing is critical to effective programming. Staffing includes both the credentials of the counselors or those delivering the treatment as well as the training to use the manualized curriculum. Essentially, staff that have a Master's degree in some clinical practice (i.e. psychology, social work, counseling, etc.) are preferred because they have a better command of the processing components (i.e. interactive sessions, role-playing, practice sessions, etc.) of a curriculum. Staff with a Master's degree are also more likely to be receptive to evidence-based treatments (Kirby, Benishek, Dugosh, and Kerwin 2006). Another issue related to the staffing is the training in the curriculum. Training is considered critical to understand the mechanisms of action embedded in the treatment curriculum, and also to focus attention on key components that facilitate the mechanisms of action. Most training consists of one or two days on the curriculum (Friedmann, Taxman, and Henderson 2007; Grella et al. 2007) without giving attention to certification of the individual in the use of the curriculum.

Criminal Justice Interface. While treatment programming can be independent of justice involvement, the integrated model of care modeled after problem solving courts or therapeutic communities has the most efficacy in terms of client outcomes. In the problem-solving court model, the probation officer or some representative of case management is part of the problem-solving court team (i.e. judge, prosecutor, defender, case manager/probation officer, treatment provider, other court actors) involved in monitoring the progress of the client and providing feedback. Frequent status hearings are required to monitor the progress and make adjustments to the plan of action. Problem-solving courts are one of the most effective justice interventions (Mitchell et al. 2012). Another intervention that integrates care is therapeutic communities. This model has the justice actor involved in monitoring progress with consistent feedback from the treatment provider and/or group. In the therapeutic community, the role of the individual actor is an indicator of the progress of the individual.

Compliance Management

Within the justice system, there is a focus on client accountability to the requirements of the punishment and/or assigned to programs. Generally, the justice emphasis has been on using negative reinforcers (more punishment) to ensure that the individuals uphold their requirements. The process of managing compliance is to give feedback to the individual on their progress in their case plans and/or programming. Feedback is important to reinforce gains and address any mishaps. There are a number of different approaches to providing feedback with an emphasis on either punishment or rewards.

The justice system usually focuses attention on punishment or the use of sanctions to address negative behaviors. The notion is that a punishment should be given for violations of probation conditions or requirements. The punishment should be close to the event, the type of punishment will be certain (the individual is aware of the consequences), and the response should be fair and proportionate to the behavior. Sometimes the punishment is administered by the probation or correctional staff; generally, the use of incarceration or residential treatment requires the judge to make that decision. In the justice system, there have been a number of attempts to develop graduated sanctions matrices that identify the nature of certain behaviors and the appropriate response. Studies have generally found that graduated sanction matrices are not effective in changing behavior, and there are a number of challenges to officers using the matrices (Makarios, McCafferty, Steiner, and Travis 2012; Rudes 2012; Turner, Braithwaite, Kearney, and Hearle 2012). And, a recent replication of the Hawaii Hope model in four jurisdictions, with good adherence to the swift and certain sanctions including the use of short periods of incarceration (shock incarceration) found that the effort did not have an impact on recidivism, and was not cost-effective (Lattimore et al. 2016).

Another approach is the use of incentives that are more likely to result in lasting change (NIDA 2009). In particular, contingency management is the preferred strategy because it identifies a small set of desired behaviors and then provides swift and certain incentives to reinforce the desired behavior(s). Contingency management is one of the most effective interventions for drug users to reduce drug use and to stay in treatment (Griffith, Rowan-Szal, Roark, and Simpson 2000; Lussier, Heil, Mongeon, Badger, and Higgins 2006; Prendergast, Podus, Finney, Greenwell, and Roll 2006). Within the justice system, rewards are an effective tool to shape behavior (Wodahl, Gardland, Culhane, and McCarty 2011). Contingency management is a tool for reinforcement of positive behaviors as compared to punishment which is a response to negative behaviors. The emphasis on desired behaviors draws attention to the importance of clearly identifying the set of behaviors that are preferred to allow the individual to focus attention on this set of behaviors.

In the justice system, there is often a need to use sanctions and rewards (incentives) with a preference for sanctioning negative behavior. The clash between sanctions and incentives that coexist results in sanctions undermining incentives. Therefore, it is important to have some principles about how to do both simultaneously. The JSTEPS project piloted this approach and used a few basic principles. First, the sanctions were confined to the most serious behaviors—rearrest for a new crime and positive drug (alcohol) test. The sanctions were used to address these undesirable behaviors, and to signify to the client that the behaviors are those the justice system is trying to diminish (see Rudes et al. 2012 for a discussion of JSTEPS).

Second, rewards should focus on principles that affect positive behaviors that facilitate behavior change: attending treatment and other appointments and having a stable environment. Taxman and colleagues (2010) identified the key principles of rewarding behaviors:

- provide rewards immediately after the behavior occurs;
- be specific about behaviors that should be rewarded;
- keep it simple;
- make it relevant to the target behaviors that need to be changed;
- craft rewards meaningful to the client—allow for different rewards for different types of people;
- respond with rewards early in the supervision process; put in place a tapering approach with heavy rewards in the beginning and spreading out over time;
- share information between sites regarding "effective" rewards.

The key to a good reward scheme is to ensure that the rewards are clear to the client (transparency) and that the emphasis is on desired behaviors. A preliminary study found that agencies that rewarded early tended to have reductions in recidivism (Sloas, Wooditch, Murphy, and Taxman 2016).

Working Relationships

A fifth EBP is that there is a need to have a working relationship with criminal justice actors that is positive. The nature of the working relationship is yet to be determined but a few studies have found that a therapeutic relationship that is trustworthy and caring is important to achieving client outcomes (Blasko, Friedmann, Rhodes, and Taxman 2015). But questions have been raised as to whether it is the therapeutic relationship or the sense of fairness (procedural justice) (Taxman and Ainsworth 2009). However, as noted by Andrews and Bonta (2010: 47), the crux of core correctional practice is to be a human service environment by introducing that focus on "high quality relationship skills in combination with high quality structuring skills." That is, the notion should be that the environment needs to support the correctional staff and individuals in a process whereby they can be caring, trusting, fair, and appropriate. This is an emerging area, but part of the training on core correctional practices focuses on building a positive interaction between the individual and the correctional staff.

Evidence-Based Practices or Programming

In sum, EBPs are evidence-based or evidence-informed, which means that there is a solid research foundation. To clarify, EBPs are the foundation. But, it is the contextual factors that affect the "how to" or the most important feature to transport. In each area, this essay identifies the information that is typically not stated or provided as part of the definition of an EBP. More importantly, many pointers are from the clinical science literature or experience of the agencies. More research is needed to identify the core mechanisms that define an EBP. That is, if risk assessment is an EBP, does transparency of the decisions that result from using a standardized risk and need assessment tool make a difference in the results from risk assessment? There is a tension between disclosing the risk level to an individual and helping the person understand the implications of their risk level. It can create a dialogue about the risk level that may be difficult for officers to navigate.

EBPs are relevant in an era when the pendulum is swinging from punitive or retributive punishments to rehabilitative sanctions. In some ways, EBPs contributed to this pendulum swing by validating that the EBPs are research-based, therefore adding credibility to the EBP. But even more so, the EBPs are compatible with the process of managing individuals from assessment through compliance. The consistency with management of individuals reinforces that the EBPs are compatible with the goals and work processes of correctional (institutional and community corrections) agencies. And, the EBPs add value to the existing work processes to generate better outputs and outcomes.

Overall, EBPs provide important benchmarks for agencies since they define a preferred set of domains that, if achieved, should arguably change the outcomes. They also transform the organization by focusing attention on critical benchmarks that reflect the importance of core components at each stage in the process. The value laden associated with "evidence-based" serves to reassure staff and stakeholders that these are important steps to put in place. Even more, it signifies that the organization is doing business in such a way to generate better outcomes. The lack of research foundations for many of the "how to" or "why are we doing this, this way" limit the persuasiveness of EBPs. That is the challenge ahead.

Note

1. Clients is preferred over offenders since clients is less stigmatizing. Offenders indicates the person has a second-class status. Current efforts are to reduce the stigma and labeling of individuals in the justice system to further efforts of reintegration into society.

References

Andrews, Donald Arthur, and James Bonta. 2010. *The Psychology of Criminal Conduct*. Newark, NJ: Anderson.

Blasko, Brandy L., Peter D. Friedmann, Anne Giuranna Rhodes and Faye S. Taxman, F.S. 2015. "The Parolee–Parole Officer Relationship as a Mediator of Criminal Justice Outcomes." *Criminal Justice & Behavior* 42(7): 722–740.

Bourgon, Guy, and Leticia Gutierrez. 2012. "The General Responsivity Principle in Community Supervision: The Importance of Probation Officers Using Cognitive Intervention Techniques and its Influence on Recidivism." *Journal of Crime and Justice* 35(2): 149–166.

Friedmann, P.D., F.S. Taxman, and C.E. Henderson. 2007. "Evidence-based Treatment Practices for Drug-involved Adults in the Criminal Justice System. *Journal of Substance Abuse Treatment*, 32, 267–277.

Grella, C.E., L. Greenwell, M. Prendergast, D. Farabee, E. Hall, J. Cartier, and W. Burdon. 2007. "Organizational Characteristics of Drug Abuse Treatment Program for Offenders." *Journal of Substance Abuse Treatment*, 32, 291–300.

Griffith, James D., Grace A. Rowan-Szal, Ryan R. Roark, and D. Dwayne Simpson. 2000. "Contingency management in outpatient methadone treatment: a meta-analysis." *Drug and Alcohol Dependence* 58(1): 55–66.

Kirby, Kimberly C., Lois A. Benishek, Karen Leggett Dugosh, and MaryLouise E. Kerwin. 2006. "Substance Abuse Treatment Providers' Beliefs and Objections Regarding Contingency Management: Implications for Dissemination." *Drug and Alcohol Dependence* 85: 19–27.

Lattimore, Pamela K., Debbie Dawes, Stephen Tueller, Doris L. MacKenzie, Gary Zajac, and Elaine Arenault. 2016. *Summary Findings from the National Evaluation of the Honest Opportunity Probation with Enforcement Demonstration Field Experiment: The HOPE DFE Evaluation*. Research Triangle Park, North Carolina: RTI, International.

Landenberger, Nana A. and Mark W. Lipsey. 2005. "The Positive Effects of Cognitive-behavioral Programs for Offenders: A Meta-analysis of Factors Associated with Effective Treatment." *Journal of Experimental Criminology* 1: 451–476.

Lipsey, Mark W. and Francis T. Cullen. 2007. "The Effectiveness of Correctional Rehabilitation: A Review of Systematic Reviews." *Annual Review of Law and Social Science* 3: 297–320.

Lussier, Jennifer Plebani, Sarah H. Heil, Joan A. Mongeon, Gary J. Badger, and Stephen T. Higgins. 2006. "A Meta-Analysis of Voucher-based Reinforcement Therapy for Substance Use Disorders." *Addiction* 101(2): 192–203.

Makarios, Matthew D., James McCafferty, Benjamin Steiner, and Lawrence F. Travis. 2012. "The Effects of Parole Officers' Perceptions of the Organizational Control Structure and Satisfaction with Management on their Attitudes toward Policy Change." *Journal of Crime and Justice* 35(2): 296–316.

Mitchell, Ojmarrh, David B. Wilson, Amy Eggers, and Doris L. MacKenzie. 2012. "Effectiveness of Drug Courts on Recidivism: A Meta-analytic Review of Non-traditional Drug Courts." *Journal of Criminal Justice* 40: 60–71.

National Institute on Drug Abuse (NIDA). 2009. *Principles of Drug Addiction Treatment: A Research-Based Guide*, 3rd ed. Bethesda, MD: NIDA.

Prendergast, Michael, Deborah Podus, John Finney, Lisa Greenwell, and John Roll. 2006. "Contingency Management for Treatment of Substance Use Disorders: A Meta-analysis." *Addiction* 101(11): 1546–1560.

Rudes, Danielle S. 2012. "Getting Technical: Parole Officers' Continued Use of Technical Violations under California's Parole Reform Agenda." *Journal of Crime & Justice* 35(2): 249–268.

Rudes, Danielle S., Faye S. Taxman, Shannon Portillo, Amy Murphy, Anne Rhodes, Maxine Stitzer, Peter F. Luoungo, and Peter D. Friedmann. 2012. "Adding Positive Reinforcement in Justice Settings: Acceptability and Feasibility." *Journal of Substance Abuse Treatment* 42: 260–270.

Sloas, Lincoln, Alese Wooditch, Amy Murphy, and Faye Taxman. 2016. "Assessing the use and impact of points and rewards across four federal probation districts: A contingency management approach." Unpublished manuscript.

Sperber, Kimberly Gentry, Edward J. Latessa, and Matthew D. Makarios. 2013a. "Establishing a Risk-dosage Research Agenda: Implications for Policy and Practice." *Justice Research and Policy* 15: 123–141.

Sperber, Kimberly Gentry, Edward J. Latessa, and Matthew D. Makarios. 2013b. "Examining the Interaction between Level of Risk and Dosage of Treatment." *Criminal Justice and Behavior* 40: 338–348.

Taxman, Faye S. 2012. "Probation, Intermediate Sanctions, and Community-based Corrections." Pp. 363–388 in *Oxford Handbook on Sentencing and Corrections*, edited by J. Petersilia and K. Reitz. New York: Oxford University Press.

Taxman, Faye S., and Stephanie Ainsworth. 2009. "Correctional Milieu: The Key to Quality Outcomes." *Victims & Offenders* 4(4): 334–340.

Taxman, Faye S., April Pattavina, and Michael Caudy. 2014. "Justice Reinvestment in the United States: An Empirical Assessment of the Potential Impact of Increased Correctional Programming on Recidivism." *Victims & Offenders* 9(1): 50–75.

Taxman, Faye S., D. Rudes, M. Stitzer, A. Murphy, P. Loungo, and A. Rhodes. 2010. *JSTEPS Manual: Implementation of Contingency Management in Justice Settings*. Fairfax: Center for Advancing Correctional Excellence. Retrieved May 6, 2017 from www.gmuace.org/documents/research/jsteps/JSTEPS_manual.pdg

Turner, Susan F., Helen Braithwaite, Lauren Kearney, and Darin Hearle. 2012. "Evaluation of the California Parole Violation Decision-Making Instrument (PVDMI)." *Journal of Crime and Justice* 35(2): 269–295.

Wodahl, Eric J., Brett Gardland, Scott E. Culhane, and William P. McCarty. 2011. "Utilizing Behavioral Interventions to Improve Supervision Outcomes in Community-based Corrections." *Criminal Justice and Behavior* 38: 386–405.

28 Race/Ethnicity, Sentencing, and Corrections

Michael J. Leiber and Maude Beaudry-Cyr

In this chapter, a brief description, differentiated by race/ethnicity, of the number of offenders who fall within each type of sanction is provided. The discussion centers first on juvenile delinquents involved in the correctional system followed by adult involvement. Next, theoretical explanations for involvement in corrections is provided followed by a discussion on empirical assessments of the relationship between race/ethnicity and correc-tions. The chapter concludes with a discussion of additional causes for race/ethnic disparities in corrections and implications for those who are subjected to correctional supervision and/or incarceration.

Number of Delinquents/Criminals under Corrections

The most severe sanction that a juvenile court can dispense on youth is an outcome involving an out-home placement such as in a residential facility. Typically, such an outcome occurs following being found guilty, or more accurately, an adjudication of delinquency. Youth may also be held in secure detention after arrest, during court proceedings, or as a judicial disposition (Leiber 2013). Most cases in the juvenile court, however, result in probation of some form, either as a diversionary outcome at the stages of intake/petition or as a judicial disposition outcome following an adjudication of delinquency (Puzzanchera and Hockenberry 2015). For example, in 2013, a total of 283, 900 youth were diverted, 205,300 received formal probation, 221,600 were detained, and 78,700 were placed in a residential facility (Puzzanchera and Hockenberry 2015). A breakdown of all juvenile delinquents under correctional supervision differentiated by race is presented in Table 28.1. Keep in mind when looking at these numbers Whites comprised 25,234,700 (76 percent) of the youth population at risk (age 10 through 17); Blacks made-up 5,430,600 (16 percent) (Puzzanchera and Hockenberry 2015). Thus, considerable Black youth overrepresentation exists in juvenile corrections and among those who transfer to adult court (Leiber and Rodriguez, 2011; Puzzanchera and Hockenberry 2015).

Similar to minority overrepresentation in the juvenile justice system, Blacks and to a lesser extent Hispanics comprise a significant percentage of those in adult corrections. First, it is important to note that while there are 2.2 million people in prison and jail and although the overall population is declining, the United States is the World's leader in incarceration (The Sentencing Project 2016). Of those incarcerated, in 2012, 744,579 were in local jails (Bureau of Justice Statistics 2014). In 2014, 2,094,100 people were on probation while 856,900 people were on parole (Bureau of Justice Statistics 2015). In terms of race/ethnicity, one out of every 13 Black males age 30 through 34 was in prison in 2011; one of 36 Hispanic males in this age group and one of 90 for similar White males (Bureau of Justice Statistics 2014). Another way to show these disparities is to look at the likelihood in their life time of serving time in prison: 32 percent for Black males, 17 percent for Hispanics males, and

Table 28.1 Racial Breakdown of Juvenile Offenders under Correctional Supervision, 2013

	White		*Black*	
Type of Correctional Supervision	*N*	*(%)*	*N*	*(%)*
Diversion	195,200	69	81,000	29
Probation	127,400	62	71,000	35
Secure Detention	121,600	59	93,000	42
Out-of-home Placement	44,800	57	31,600	40
Waiver to Adult Court	2,100	53	1,800	45

Source: Puzzanchera and Hockenberry 2015.

Table 28.2 Racial/Ethnic Breakdown of Adult Offenders under Correctional Supervision, 2011

Type of Correctional Supervision	*White* %	*Black* %	*Hispanic* %
Prison	35	38	21
Probation	54	30	13
Parole	43	41	16

Source: Bureau of Justice Statistics 2014; 2015.

6 percent for White males (Bureau of Justice Statistics 2014). A racial/ethnic breakdown of adult offenders within the prison system, as well as those under supervised probation and parole is presented in Table 28.2.

Theoretical Explanations for Understanding Race/Ethnic Disparities in Sentencing and Corrections

According to the consensus tradition, law, punishment, and treatment derive from a broad consensus of societal norms and values (Durkheim 1964). State intervention into individual liberty and the incarceration of an individual results primarily from the occurrence, distribution and severity of delinquent behavior. In the juvenile justice system, due to the *parens patriae* foundation of the juvenile court, extralegal factors such as age (younger youth may be viewed differently than older youth), school (conduct problems or not attending) and the family (assessments about the ability of the youth's family to effectively supervise and socialize their child), also enter into decision-making process and outcomes (e.g., Bishop, Leiber and Johnson 2010; Leiber, Peck and Beaudry-Cyr 2016; Rodriguez, Smith, and Zatz 2009). Under a consensus perspective, differences in case outcomes for Whites and minorities are therefore attributed to differential involvement in crime (i.e., more crime, more serious crime) and/or problematic school or family situations when discussing juvenile court proceedings. Accordingly, when these factors are considered, race/ethnicity is not expected to be a significant predictor of sentencing and correction decisions, but rather factors such as crime severity and prior record are believed to explain differences in case outcomes (Caudill, Morris, Sayed, Yun, and Delisi 2013; Tracy 2005; Wilbanks 1987).

The conflict approach is a more traditional theory of differential selection to understand why Blacks, and to some degree Hispanics, are overrepresented in both the juvenile and criminal justice systems and are the recipients of greater social control than Whites. According to conflict theory, majority groups (e.g. Whites) exercise social control over more powerless groups (e.g. minorities) to maintain the status quo and protect their own interests. This is done through the majority group's ability to control the law, law enforcement, and the court system, ultimately resulting in minorities becoming labeled as outsiders, deviants, delinquents, and criminals, and in turn subjected to harsher punishment in the criminal justice system. Refinements to the conflict perspective, and in general the differential selection bias explanation, have centered on the contexts or conditions linked to when race/ethnicity matters (Leiber 2003; Spohn 2000; Stewart, Martinez, Baumer, and Gertz 2015; Ulmer and Johnson 2004).

Various theoretical explanations have taken into consideration structural contextual factors in the form of community and neighborhood-level characteristics to explain sentencing outcomes. For example, levels of impoverishment, minority representation, crime rates, court contexts, and political orientation are some of the factors incorporated within these perspectives (e.g., Sampson and Laub 1993; Steffensmeier, Ulmer, and Kramer 1998; Wang and Mears 2010). One example of a macro-level theory of differential selection is Blalock's minority group power-threat thesis, which argues that as the minority group population grows within a community, the White majority population becomes threatened (Blalock 1967). This perceived threat comes in the form of competition for economic resources (e.g. jobs, money, and property), and increased income and wealth by the minority group. From this, prejudicial, discriminatory attitudes and practices are employed by Whites to diffuse this threat, which results in increased social control and harsher outcomes for minorities in the juvenile and adult court systems.

A more recent contextual and structural theory is Sampson and Laub's (1993) macro-level perspective, which argues that the poor, underclass, and minorities are perceived by juvenile justice decision makers as threatening and in need of increased social control. This is due, in part, to the concentration of minorities who reside in communities with high levels of economic and racial inequality. Sampson and Laub proposed that juvenile justice decision makers encompass beliefs of minority youth as aggressive, sexual, lacking discipline, and suggest that they pose symbolic threats to public safety and middle-class standards. Also important to this perspective is the interrelationship between the War on Drugs of the 1980s, stereotyping, and the prevalence of disadvantaged communities that leads to the typecast of minority males as drug users and dealers. Central to Sampson and Laub's argument is that as a result of these three situations, poor, Black men (especially those involved with drugs) are subjected to increased social control by the juvenile justice system (also see Sutton 2013 who applied the perspective to the sentencing of adult felons).

The focal concerns perspective has also been applied as an organizational approach to explain why minorities receive more severe sentencing outcomes in the juvenile and adult justice system. Steffensmeier and colleagues (1998) argued that judges have a limited amount of time and information about defendants and therefore may rely on three focal concerns or attributions involving race, gender, and class stereotypes when making criminal justice outcome decisions. The three focal concerns include: (1) the defendant's blameworthiness and culpability; (2) society's concern to protect the community; and (3) organizational considerations involving available correctional resources. While the three focal concerns are interrelated, it is argued that judges do not have complete information about each component and end up exercising their own discretion by relying on the offender's age, race, gender, and social class to reach decisions. In other words, judges develop a "perceptual shorthand" where they rely on both legal factors (crime severity, prior record) and racial stereotypes to determine case outcomes. Young, poor, Black males are theorized to be perceived or stereotyped by judges as dangerous and not suitable for rehabilitation but rather in need of incarceration. More recently, Bishop and colleagues (2010) have applied a revised focal concerns perspective to help explain sentencing of youth, especially Black youth, in juvenile court proceedings.

An attempt to identify the types of perceptions and attributions used by court officials to understand how minorities and Whites are treated within the juvenile justice system is presented by Bridges and Steen (1998). The analysis of juvenile probation officers' predisposition reports by Bridges and Steen provides evidence of racial stereotyping and of its influence on recommendations for final disposition by judges. In these accounts, probation officers made attributions about the causes of crime and the risk of reoffending that were shown to be linked closely to race. They often attributed offending among Whites to external and alterable causes (e.g., delinquent peers, problems at school), while attributing offending among Blacks to internal and enduring character traits (e.g., aggressiveness, lack of remorse). These causal attributions corroborated the probation officers' views of minority offenders as more dangerous than Whites, which in turn provided the basis for more punitive recommendations.

Empirical Studies of Race/Ethnicity in Sentencing and Corrections

Sentencing

Similar to decision making at other stages in juvenile justice proceedings, legal factors are often the strongest predictors of dispositional outcomes (Bishop and Leiber 2011). Prior record and previous dispositions, for example, are highly influential determinants of case outcomes, sometimes even more so than the current offense (Henretta, Frazier and Bishop 1986; Leiber 2016). Where this is true, it is consistent with the conclusion that judges are most concerned about community protection (predictions of risk) and treatment (e.g., what interventions have already been utilized). Emerson (1969) suggested that at disposition, judges are especially interested in assessing the moral character of youth. If a juvenile reappears in court multiple times, he or she is generally perceived as a hardened delinquent with criminal values. Multiple previous (and, by definition, unsuccessful) dispositions ultimately lead judges to conclude that the youth is not amenable to treatment. Unfortunately, prior record and previous dispositions, although seemingly race neutral, are contaminated to unknown degrees (Farrell and Swigert 1977; Leiber 2016). Minority youth are more vulnerable to arrest and formal processing than otherwise similar Whites. Compared to White youth engaged in the same behaviors, minorities more readily accumulate offense histories and dispositions from which inferences are drawn about their character and capacity for reform.

Research has shown that race additionally has a significant direct effect on dispositional outcomes once legal variables are taken into consideration (Bishop and Leiber 2011). Family considerations have often been reported to also play a role at judicial disposition in ways that often work to the disadvantage of minority offenders. Youth from single-parent families and youth experiencing (or perceived to be experiencing) family problems often receive more severe dispositions (Leiber and Mack 2003). Other evidence of the importance of the family (and of the intersection of race, class, and family) is provided in an inquiry by Sanborn (1996), who interviewed 100 court officials in three eastern communities regarding factors that influence judicial disposition. When asked what characteristics should be taken into consideration at judicial disposition, court officials most often cited the family. In addition, when asked whether the juvenile court in fact discriminated against any particular type of youth, 87 percent of respondents answered positively, most often identifying Black males from dysfunctional families in lower class neighborhoods as those most likely to be targeted.

Two recent studies have brought attention to the ways by which judicial disposition is measured to capture race effects. Most past research has operationalized judicial disposition as community-based sanctions versus out-of-home placement (e.g., Bishop et al. 2010; Leiber and Mack 2003). While this body of research can reach conclusions as to whether Blacks or Hispanics are more likely to receive out-of-home placement than alike Whites, effects may be masked since the range of sanctions within the community-based corrections outcome and the out-of-home placement is not delineated. Fader, Kurlychek, and Morgan (2014), for example, differentiated among residential placement facilities according to three categories (i.e., traditional reform schools, therapeutic programs, programs emphasizing physical regimen) to provide insights into the relationship between race and juvenile dispositional decision making. Results from this inquiry revealed higher rates of placement in facilities emphasizing physical regimen for Black youth, while therapeutic treatment programs were significantly more common among outcomes for White youth (Fader et al. 2014).

Cochran and Mears (2015) also offered a nuanced inquiry into the multiple interventions available to juvenile court decision makers. They did this by using a five-category measure of general disposition, a three-category measure of diversion, a two-category probation measure, and a three-category commitment placement measure. The authors found that Black youth were at a considerably higher likelihood of being the recipients of more severe sanctions across five disposition groups (dismissal, diversion, probation, commitment, transfer). Minority youth were also less likely to receive rehabilitation-oriented services and more likely to receive judicial warnings when diverted. A lower likelihood of receiving intensive probation was noted among Blacks as a whole, while minority males were shown as less likely to be placed in medium-security facilities. Leiber and Stairs (1999) and Leiber (1994) have made similar arguments concerning the measurement of intake decision making by breaking out the outcomes of release from probation, diversion, and referral for further court proceedings.

Recall that minority youth, especially Blacks, are also disproportionately subjected to waiver to adult court (Soler 2010). Legal factors as well as race itself have been reported to predict the waiver decision. McNulty (1996), for example, examined the likelihood of receiving incarceration or probation in adult court among a sample of White, Black, and Hispanic juveniles. Findings from this inquiry indicated that Blacks were three times more likely to be incarcerated than Whites, while Latinos were almost twice as likely as Whites to be incarcerated. Jordan and Freiburger (2010) focused specifically on race and the sentencing of youth in adult court in nineteen of the nation's largest counties and also found that Black youth were more likely than similarly situated White youth to be sentenced to both prison and jail compared to probation. Hispanic youth were also more likely to receive prison sentences over jail compared to Whites. In addition, Blacks with a prior record were characterized as having increased chances of receiving a prison sentence compared to their White counterparts. The authors concluded that judges' perception and interpretation of prior record may differ on the basis of the offender's race and argued that Blacks with a prior record may be perceived as more dangerous than similarly situated Whites. Lastly, Jordan (2014) examined a national sample of over 35,000 offenders convicted in adult court. Only 240 of the sample consisted of youth and of this number, the author discovered that Blacks and Hispanics were more likely to receive a jail sentence and prison sentence than similarly situated Whites. In addition, Blacks were given lengthier jail sentences than Whites. Hispanic offenders received longer incarceration in the form of both jail and prison sentences than Whites.

Involvement in probation violations and in particular technical violations has been increasing as a means of re-entry into the juvenile justice system, especially for Blacks and Hispanics (Austin, Johnson, and Weitzer 2005; Gies, Cohen, and Villarruel 2009). Technical violations typically involve non-compliance with conditions stipulated as part of probation (e.g., not passing a drug test, failure to appear for a scheduled appointment). There also appears to be a link between being a minority and involvement in a probation violation with the likelihood of placement in secure detention (Holman and Ziedenberg 2006).

Especially true among minorities, being detained has been shown to create a path toward cumulative disadvantage by having an indirect effect on case outcomes. That is, detained youth are more likely to move further into court proceedings (i.e. from intake to adjudication to judicial disposition). This in turn leads to more severe case outcomes compared to youth who were not previously detained. Concomitantly, minorities are increasingly impacted since these youth are more likely to be detained than similarly situated White youth (Leiber and Fox 2005; Rodriguez 2010).

Results from Leiber (2013) found that very few youth who were charged with a probation violation were referred to pre-adjudication detention, while involvement in a probation violation was predictive of post-adjudication detention. Specifically, this inquiry revealed that all but one youth involved in a probation violation within the inquiry's sample was held in detention following post-adjudication. Results also indicated that technical violations in the form of missing curfew and failing drug urinalyses (rather than being charged with a delinquent act) comprised a significant percentage of the court violations. Within the court violations, 29 of the referrals involved new crimes, most of which were non-serious offenses (e.g. disorderly conduct). Race was not shown to be significantly associated with technical violations.

In another study, and consistent with the findings reported by Leiber (2013), Leiber and Peck (2013a) found that technical violations comprised a significant percentage of the probation violations among the sampled youth. Yet, neither involvement in a new crime nor technical violations were shown to have an impact on case outcomes for Blacks and Hispanics. Probation violation as a whole resulted in severe case outcomes. While probation violation was not tied to race/ethnicity or increased social control of minority youth, Blacks and Hispanics as a whole did receive disadvantaged outcomes relative to comparable Whites.

Jail and Prison

Although prior research has failed to show race as a consistent determinant of decision making in sentencing and correctional outcomes in the criminal justice system as in the juvenile justice system (Gabbidon and Tayler Greene 2016), similar contextual effects have been reported in the literature (Spohn 2000; Stewart et al. 2015). First, prior studies have shown the manner according to which the dependent variable is measured has implications for assessing race/ethnic differences in the treatment of adult offenders. More specifically, research points to the importance of distinguishing between sentencing decisions resulting in incarceration in jail versus those involving prison sentencing, as collapsing the two outcomes into a single incarceration variable could potentially obscure possible race differences. For example, studies generally have generally shown that Blacks are less likely to receive a jail sentence than similarly situated Whites, but more likely to receive an outcome of prison (Leiber, Reitzel, and Mack 2011; Holleran and Spohn 2004). Some research has also reported that Blacks receive lengthier sentences than their White counterparts (e.g., Albonetti 1991; Feldmeyer and Ulmer 2011).

Past studies have also shown that race/ethnic relationships with case outcomes acts in combination with demographic characteristics of the offender (e.g., gender, age), victim characteristics (e.g., race of the victim), legal considerations (e.g., crime type, prior record), and case-processing factors (e.g., pretrial detention) to influence judicial decision making (Albonetti and Hepburn 1997; Spohn 2000; Spohn and Holleran 2001; Steffensmeier et al. 1998). As in the juvenile justice system, family considerations seem to influence judicial sentencing of adult offenders. According to Steffensmeier and colleagues (1998: 787) "the 'ability to do time' and the costs of incarceration appear linked to race/gender and age-based perceptions and stereotypes." Prior research has revealed that women offenders with children often receive more lenient sentences than men as a result of judges attempting to preserve the family unit (Daly 1987, 1994). Furthermore, White women with children are perceived by judges as "good mothers," but judges often need to be convinced of this before extending leniency to Black women for the purpose of not breaking up the family unit (Bickle and Peterson 1991).

Based on Blalock's (1967) minority group threat perspective, Wang and Mears (2010) examined the macro-level characteristics of counties (e.g., size of the race/ethnic population, economic and political indicators) in an effort to identify potential predictors of incarceration. Overall, the authors found greater support for the racial threat argument as higher concentrations of Black population within a county increased the odds of receiving a prison sentence but not a jail sentence. Ethnic threat (i.e. Hispanics), on the other hand, was linked to increased jail sentences. To account for these findings, Wang and Mears (2010) concluded that Blacks and Hispanics may be perceived differently due to their own unique historical contexts and the ways in which crime has been racialized; Blacks being perceived as more dangerous than Hispanics. Thus, the research by Wang and Mears suggests that the minority group threat perspective either applies to Blacks only or may only be applicable to other minorities in a more nuanced way (citing Stults and Baumer 2007; cf., Ulmer and Johnson 2004).

Probation and Parole

There have been a number of studies that have examined probation revocation and probation recidivism or probation failure involving technical violations as well as new crimes (Albonetti and Hepburn 1997; Rodriguez and Webb 2007; Stalans, Juergens, Seng, and Lavery 2004; Taxman and Cherkos 1995). Recall that while Blacks comprise 13 percent of the population, they make up 30 percent of those on probation. Some studies have reported that minority offenders are more likely to have a violation of probation filed against them than White offenders (Gray, Fields, and Maxwell 2001). More specifically, in a study of probation revocation in four sites across the nation (Dallas County, Texas, Iowa's Sixth Judicial District, Multnomah, Oregon, and New York City), probation revocation was noted at significant higher rates among Black probationers than Hispanic and White probationers (Jannetta, Breaux, Ho, and Porter 2014). Hispanic probationers' revocation was lower than Whites in the Iowa site, higher in New York City, and no differences between the two race/ethnic groups were reported in the other two sites. Further analyses yielded additional insights into the race/ethnic disparities in probation revocation. Although Black probationers on the whole had higher risk scores and more extensive criminal histories, once these factors were taken into account, Black probationers evidenced a higher likelihood of revocation than Hispanics and Whites. The odds of probation revocation for Blacks ranged from 18 percent to 39 percent after taking into consideration relevant legal and extralegal factors. Conversely, in three of the four sites studied, Hispanic probationers were less likely to be subjected to revocation. It should be noted that a shortcoming of this research is the failure to assess whether the revocation was based on a new crime or a technical violation.

An inquiry of parole decisions is offered by Huebner and Bynum (2008) who evaluated a sample of incarcerated offenders in a single state. The results reveal race/ethnic variation in parole decisions. Consistent with the focal concerns perspective, attribution theory and prior research, Huebner and Bynum (2008) found that parole decision makers seem to be concerned with community protection; heavily taking into consideration the current offense, institutional behavior, and the official parole guidelines score. Their research found that in addition to the previously mentioned factors, race also emerged as a significant predictor of parole. Black offenders spent a longer time in prison awaiting parole compared to White offenders, even after controlling for legal and individual demographic and community characteristics. Hispanics as a whole served shorter terms in prison than comparable Whites and Blacks. Huebner and Bynum therefore conclude that being Black is a proxy for dangerousness that impacts parole outcomes.

Additional Factors Contributing to Race/Ethnic Disparities in Sentencing and Corrections

Beginning in the early 1980s and lasting into the 2000s, a "get tough" movement on crime and the War on Drugs led to a dramatic growth in arrests and incarceration of offenders, and in particular drug offenders (Mauer and King 2007). The impact was especially felt by minorities, particularly African Americans from impoverished communities (Mauer 2009; Tonry 1995). Porter (2016) gave a more specific explanation, suggesting that a combination of rising crime rates and changes in legislative and administrative policies fueled an era of mass incarceration. Some of these sentencing practices that resulted in lengthier prison sentences included mandatory minimums, three-strike laws or habitual offender laws, an increased use of life without parole, and restrictions on judicial discretion (Porter 2016). One example is the passage of the Anti-Drug Abuse Act of 1986 and the Anti-Drug Abuse Act of 1988, which aided this movement by requiring minimum sentencing laws for certain drug offenses (Mauer and King 2007). As a result, the number of offenders incarcerated for drug-related infractions rose from 41,000 in 1980 to nearly a half million in 2014 (The Sentencing Project 2015). At the federal level, people incarcerated on a drug conviction comprised half the prison population. Most of those imprisoned were not high-level actors in the drug trade; most had no prior criminal record for a violent offense (The Sentencing Project 2015). In fact, from 1980 through 1992, the number of White male drug offenders incarcerated increased by 143 percent, while the prevalence for Black male drug offenders increased by 186 percent (The Sentencing Project 2015; Tonry 1995).

Emerging from the War on Drugs was the mandatory minimum penalty tied to crack cocaine versus that of powder cocaine. As a result of these strict policies, a person found to be in possession of 5 grams of crack cocaine would receive a minimum mandatory sentence of five years; the same sentence as that which would be delivered to an individual found in possession of 500 grams of powder cocaine. This 100-to-1 crack cocaine-to-powder cocaine sentencing differential had a tremendous influence on the incarceration of Black and Hispanic crack cocaine offenders (Gabbidon and Taylor Greene 2016). As pointed out by Mauer and King (2007), Blacks made up 14 percent of regular drug users, yet comprised 37 percent of those arrested for drug offenses and 56 percent of those in state prison for drug offenses. Furthermore, the average length of incarceration in federal prison for Blacks with a drug offense (58.7 months) was almost the same as that of White offenders imprisoned for a violent offense (61.7 months). Mauer and King argue that these results are "largely due to racially disparate sentencing laws such as the 100-to-1 crack-powder cocaine disparity" (2007: 2).

Recently, several legislative acts (The Fair Sentencing Act of 2010; The Fair Sentencing Clarification Act of 2015) have been crafted and implemented to reduce such disparities in sentencing. Included among these are efforts to reduce sentencing for individuals subjected to lengthy minimum mandatory sentences prior to the passage of The Fair Sentencing Act in 2010. Further analysis of the impact of the Fair Sentencing Act of 2010 by the United States Sentencing Commission suggests that five years following its implementation, the Act had successfully lowered the disparity between crack and powder cocaine sentences from a 100-to-1 ratio down to an 18-to-1 crack-to-powder drug quantity ratio, reduced the federal prison population, as well as reducing the number of federal prosecutions for crack cocaine (United States Sentencing Commission 2015).

Collateral Consequences of Imprisonment for Minorities

Recent works have placed a focus on the unintended effects of state intervention on communities as a whole and in particular, the impact that mass incarceration and the War on Drugs have had on poor minority communities (Clear 2008; Mauer 2016; Wildeman and Wakefield 2014). Another area of concern, although not as widely discussed, involves the long-term consequences associated with the use of life without the parole (LWOP) sentencing for juvenile offenders. In this concluding section to follow, the focus will first be on the latter, followed by a discussion of the larger impact of incarceration on minority communities and family relations.

According to new research by The Sentencing Project, an estimated 2,500 individuals nationwide have been identified as serving LWOP sentences for homicides they committed while under the age of 18 (Rovner 2016). Of those, as many as 2,100 (84 percent) might have been sentenced according to a mandatory sentencing rule and 73 were age 14 or younger at the time of the offense (Rovner 2016; The Sentencing Project 2010). Nationwide, 77 percent of LWOP prisoners are minorities (Nellis and King 2009; Rovner 2016). In 17 states, more than 60 percent of the LWOP population is Black (Rovner 2016). The overrepresentation of minority youth, and in particular Black youth, as LWOPs, parallels their disproportionate presence in the juvenile justice system as a whole (Leiber and Peck 2013b).

In a series of Supreme Court decisions (i.e., *Graham v. Florida* 2010; *Miller v. Alabama*, and *Jackson v. Hobbs* 2012; *Montgomery v. Louisiana* 2016) the sentencing of juveniles to mandatory life without parole was found to violate the Eighth Amendment. Thus, life without the opportunity of parole for juveniles has since been deemed unconstitutional. As Rovner (2016) discusses, these decisions allow individuals who were sentenced to LWOP as juveniles the opportunity for release, although not guaranteed. Rather, these Supreme Court decisions require states to provide a review for parole after a reasonable time of incarceration has been completed. At the hearing, the unique circumstances of each defendant must be taken into consideration.

While the granting of a review hearing provides possible release for the defendants sentenced for crimes committed as a youth, a number of problematic concerns still remain with regards to juvenile LWOP sentencing. For example, the placement of youth in adult jail and/or prison involves not only the loss of freedom, but also increases exposure to criminal influences, as well as emotional, physical, and sexual harm (Fagan 2010). Further, continued involvement in the system leads to a mortgaging of these youths' life chances in terms of educational attainment, access to quality employment, marriage, effective parenting, and overall, the ability to escape a life of impoverishment upon release (Laub and Sampson 2003). Additional support for this rather bleak portrait comes from the results of a national survey of 1,579 juveniles serving life sentences in 2010/2011 (Nellis 2012). The author found that for the most part, the respondents came from environments that involved exposure to home and neighborhood violence, educational deficits, engagement with delinquent peers, and family members in prison.

Across the literature addressing the effects of mass incarceration, some attention has been paid to the negative impact of parental imprisonment on children, families, and communities, as well as the numerous barriers ex-offenders themselves encounter upon reintegration into society (Clear 2008; The Annie Casey Foundation and Kids Count 2016; Western and Wildeman 2009). In all, it has been estimated that nearly 5 million children have been affected by having one of their parents imprisoned at some point in their lives (The Annie Casey Foundation and Kids Count 2016: 1). Black children are over seven times more likely than their White counterparts to have an incarcerated parent while Hispanic children are twice as likely (The Sentencing Project 2009). In addition to dealing with family instability, children with an absent parent(s) have an increased likelihood of experiencing impoverishment, educational difficulties, and health issues, and in general reside in communities that lack collective efficacy and social/cultural capital (The Annie Casey Foundation and Kids Count 2016).

Some of the obstacles faced by ex-offenders when returning home include gaining access to and maintaining employment and housing, as well as the ability to participate in civic activities such as voting (Hlavka, Wheelock, and Cossyleon 2015; Uggen, Manza, and Thompson 2006). Difficulty with reintegration into society emerges as a result of laws and policies that restrict access and further augment imageries and stereotyping of persons with a prior record as "lazy," "unreliable," and "dangerous" (Alexander 2010; Pager 2007). It is these restrictions, combined with the overall overrepresentation of Blacks with a prior record and in particular, ex-felons, and the resulting stereotyping of these populations that lead collateral consequences of incarceration to be most profound for Blacks (e.g., Pager 2007; Western and Wildeman 2009). These barriers have been described by some as a form of "invisible punishment" (Wheelock 2005) or an example of "The New Jim Crow" (Alexander 2010).

As stated in the Annie Casey Foundation and Kids Count report, ex-offenders "lack training or work experience and an interrupted or illegitimate employment history . . . close the doors to most family supporting jobs" (2016: 4). Research has also shown that disclosing a criminal record or "checking the box" when completing a job application further decreases the likelihood of successfully gaining employment (Pager 2007; Vallas, Boteach, West, and Odum 2015). The denial of employment on the basis of having a prior record is especially heightened for Black ex-offenders. In an experimental study, Pager (2007) found that Blacks with a prior record had a lesser chance of securing employment than Whites with a similar criminal record. In fact, the research further suggests that Whites with a prior record were more likely to get a job than Black applicants with no prior criminal record (Pager 2007). In an effort to remedy such disparaging practice, there has been a number of recent initiatives to "ban the box" on job applications (see Gabbidon and Taylor Greene 2016: 271–274).

In addition to facing barriers to employment, ex-offenders are further disenfranchised by the inability to secure housing (The Annie Casey Foundation and Kids Count 2016) and to exercise their constitutional right to vote (Uggen et al. 2006). In all but two states, Maine and Vermont, voting rights are restricted for anyone with a felony conviction, including those in prison at the time of the election (Chung 2016). Approximately, 5.85 million ex-offenders convicted of felony offenses are currently unable to vote due to such laws in the United States (Chung 2016). An estimated 2.6 million people are disenfranchised in states that restrict voting rights even after completion of sentence (probation, parole). A significant number of these individuals are minorities and in particular, Black. As stated by Chung, "Black Americans of voting age are four times more likely to lose their voting rights than the rest of the adult population, with one of every 13 black adults disenfranchised nationally" (2016: 2). An active effort to change these disenfranchisement voting laws has been occurring and is crucial to the effective reentry of ex-felons as productive members of society (Chung 2016; Gabbidon and Taylor Greene 2016). For example, in the spring of 2016, the Governor of Virginia restored the rights of Virginians with a prior felony conviction for those having successfully completed the terms of their incarceration and had been released from supervised probation or parole (Thomason 2016). The effect of this change means that 200,000 ex-felony offenders will soon have the right to vote in the state of Virginia (Horwitz and Portnoy 2016). Only through similar and continued efforts will the racial and ethnic disparities in sentencing and corrections in both the juvenile and criminal justice systems slowly begin to decrease and disappear.

Conclusion

In sum, while racial and ethnic minorities have been and continue to be overrepresented at almost all stages of both the juvenile and criminal justice systems, a certain level of progress has been made in recent years towards identifying and addressing some of the factors that contribute to the disparate treatment of minorities across sentencing and corrections. With guidance from theoretical frameworks and empirical research, policymakers have begun to seek change by implementing more comprehensive programs and initiatives to ensure more equitable treatment of all racial and ethnic groups involved in the judicial and correctional systems. Much work still remains in narrowing the racial/ethnic gap in sentencing and corrections, but recent efforts suggest that there is movement in the right direction.

References

Albonetti, Celesta A. 1991. "An Integration of Theories to Explain Judicial Discretion." *Social Problems* 38(2): 247–266.

Albonetti, Celesta A., and John R. Hepburn. 1997. "Probation Revocation: A Proportional Hazards Model of the Conditioning Effects of Social Disadvantage." *Social Problems* 44(1): 124–138.

Alexander, Michelle. 2010. *The New Jim Crow: Mass Incarceration in the Age of Colorblindness*. New York: The New Press.

Austin, James, Kelly Dedel Johnson, and Ronald John Weitzer. 2005. *Alternatives to the Secure Detention and Confinement of Juvenile Offenders*. Washington, DC: U.S. Department of Justice, Office of Justice Programs, Office of Juvenile Justice and Delinquency Prevention.

Bickle, Gayle S., and Ruth D. Peterson. 1991. "The Impact of Gender-Based Family Roles on Criminal Sentencing." *Social Problems* 38(3): 372–394.

Bishop, Donna, and Michael J. Leiber. 2011. "Race, Ethnicity, and Juvenile Justice: Racial and Ethnic Differences in Delinquency and Justice System Responses." Pp. 445–484 in *The Oxford Handbook of Juvenile Crime and Juvenile Justice*, edited by B. Feld and D. Bishop. New York: Oxford University Press.

Bishop, Donna M., Michael J. Leiber, and Joseph Johnson. 2010. "Contexts of Decision Making in the Juvenile Justice System: An Organizational Approach to Understanding Minority Overrepresentation." *Youth Violence and Juvenile Justice* 8(3): 213–233.

Blalock, Hubert M. 1967. *Toward a Theory of Minority-Group Relations*. New York: Wiley.

Bridges, George S., and Sara Steen. 1998. "Racial Disparities in Official Assessments of Juvenile Offenders: Attributional Stereotypes as Mediating Mechanisms." *American Sociological Review* 63(4): 554–570.

Bureau of Justice Statistics. 2014. "Correctional Populations in the United States, 2012." Retrieved June 10, 2016 from www.bjs.gov/content/pub/pdf/cpus12.pdf

Bureau of Justice Statistics. 2015. "Probation and Parole in the United States, 2014." Retrieved June 10, 2016 from www.bjs.gov/content/pub/pdf/ppus14.pdf

Caudill, Jonathan W., Robert G. Morris, Sarah E. Sayed, Minwoo Yun, and Matt Delisi. 2013. "Pathways through the Juvenile Justice System: Predictors of Formal Disposition." *Youth Violence and Juvenile Justice* 11(3): 183–195.

Chung, June. 2016. "Felony Disenfranchisement: A Primer." *The Sentencing Project*. Retrieved June 10, 2016 from www.sentencingproject.org/publications/felony-disenfranchisement-a-primer/

Clear, Todd R. 2008. "The Effects of High Imprisonment Rates on Communities." *Crime and Justice* 37(1): 97–132.

Cochran, Joshua C., and Daniel P. Mears. 2015. "Race, Ethnic, and Gender Divides in Juvenile Court Sanctioning and Rehabilitative Intervention." *Journal of Research in Crime and Delinquency* 52(2): 181–212.

Daly, Kathleen. 1987. "Structure and Practice of Familial-Based Justice in a Criminal Court." *Law & Society Review* 21(2): 267–290.

Daly, Kathleen. 1994. *Gender, Crime, and Punishment*. New Haven, CT: Yale University Press.

Durkheim Emile. 1964. *The Division of Labor in Society*. New York: Free Press.

Emerson, Robert M. 1969. *Judging Delinquents; Context and Process in Juvenile Court*. Chicago, IL: Aldine Publishing.

Fader, Jamie J., Megan C. Kurlychek, and Kirstin A. Morgan. 2014. "The Color of Juvenile Justice: Racial Disparities in Dispositional Decisions." *Social Science Research* 44: 126–140.

Fagan, Jeffrey. 2010. "The Contradictions of Juvenile Crime & Punishment." *Daedalus* 139(3): 43–61.

Farrell, Ronald A., and Victoria Lynn Swigert. 1977. "Prior Offense Record as a Self-Fulfilling Prophecy." *Law & Society Review* 12(3): 437–453.

Feldmeyer, Ben, and Jeffery T. Ulmer. 2011. "Racial/Ethnic Threat and Federal Sentencing." *Journal of Research in Crime and Delinquency* 48(2): 238–270.

Gabbidon, Shaun L., and Helen Taylor Greene. 2016. *Race and Crime*, 4th ed. Sage Publications.

Gies, Stephen, Marcia Cohen, and Francisco Villarruel. 2009. "Intervention." in *Disproportionate Minority Contact: Technical Assistance Manual*. Washington, DC: U.S. Department of Justice, Office of Justice Programs, Office of Juvenile Justice and Delinquency Prevention.

Graham v. Florida, 130 s. Ct. 2011 (2010)

Gray, Kevin M., Monique Fields, and Sheila R. Maxwell. 2001. "Examining Probation Violations: Who, What, and When." *Crime & Delinquency* 47(4): 537–557.

Henretta, John C., Charles E. Frazier, and Donna M. Bishop. 1986. "The Effect of Prior Case Outcomes on Juvenile Justice Decision-Making." *Social Forces* 65(2): 554–562.

Hlavka, Heather R., Darren Wheelock, and Jennifer E. Cossyleon. 2015. "Narratives of Commitment: Looking for Work with a Criminal Record." *The Sociological Quarterly* 56(2): 213–236.

Holleran, David, and Cassia Spohn. 2004. "On the Use of the Total Incarceration Variable in Sentencing Research." *Criminology* 42(1): 211–240.

Holman, Barry, and Jason Ziedenberg. 2006. "The Dangers of Detention: The Impact of Incarcerating Youth in Detention and Other Secure Facilities." *Justice Policy Institute*. Retrieved June 9, 2016 from www.justicepolicy.org/research/1978

Horwitz, Sari and Jenna Portnoy. 2016. "About 200,000 Convicted Felons in Virginia will Now Have the Right to Vote in November." *The Washington Post*. Retrieved June 10, 2016 from www.washingtonpost.com/news/post-nation/wp/2016/04/22/about-200000-convicted-felons-in-virginia-will-now-have-the-right-to-vote-in-november/

Huebner, Beth M. and Timothy S. Bynum. 2008. "The Role of Race and Ethnicity in Parole Decisions." *Criminology* 46(4): 907–938.

Jannetta, Jesse, Justin Breaux, Helen Ho, and Jeremy Porter. 2014. "Examining Racial and Ethnic Disparities in Probation Revocation: Summary Findings and Implications from a Multisite Study." *Urban Institute*. Retrieved June 8, 2016 from www.urban.org/research/publication/examining-racial-and-ethnic-disparities-probation-revocation

Jordan, Kareem L. 2014. "Juvenile Status and Criminal Sentencing: Does It Matter in the Adult System?" *Youth Violence and Juvenile Justice* 12(4): 315–331.

Jordan, Kareem L., and Tina L. Freiburger. 2010. "Examining the Impact of Race and Ethnicity on the Sentencing of Juveniles in the Adult Court." *Criminal Justice Policy Review* 21(2): 185–201.

Laub, John H., and Robert J. Sampson. 2003. *Shared Beginnings, Divergent Lives: Delinquent Boys to Age 70*. Cambridge, MA: Harvard University Press.

Leiber, Michael J. 1994. "A Comparison of Juvenile Court Outcomes for Native Americans, African Americans, and Whites." *Justice Quarterly* 11(2): 257–279.

Leiber, Michael J. 2003. *Contexts of Juvenile Justice Decision Making: When Race Matters*. Albany, NY: State University of New York Press.

Leiber, Michael J. 2013. "Race, Pre- and Postdetention, and Juvenile Justice Decision Making." *Crime & Delinquency* 59(3): 396–418.

Leiber, Michael J. 2016. "Race, Prior Offending, and Juvenile Court Outcomes." *Journal of Crime and Justice* 39(1): 88–106.

Leiber, Michael J., and Kristan C. Fox. 2005. "Race and the Impact of Detention on Juvenile Justice Decision Making." *Crime & Delinquency* 51(4): 470–97.

Leiber, Michael J., and Kristin Y. Mack. 2003. "The Individual and Joint Effects of Race, Gender, and Family Status on Juvenile Justice Decision-Making." *Journal of Research in Crime and Delinquency* 40(1): 34–70.

Leiber, Michael J., and Jennifer H. Peck. 2013a. "Probation Violations and Juvenile Justice Decision Making: Implications for Blacks and Hispanics." *Youth Violence and Juvenile Justice* 11(1): 60–78.

Leiber, Michael J., and Jennifer H. Peck. 2013b. "Race in Juvenile Justice and Sentencing Policy: An Overview of Research and Policy Recommendations." *Law & Inequality* 31: 331–368.

Leiber, Michael J., Jennifer H. Peck, and Maude Beaudry-Cyr. 2016. "The Likelihood of a 'Youth Discount' in Juvenile Court Sanctions: The Influence of Offender Race, Gender, and Age." *Race and Justice* 6(1): 5–34.

Leiber, Michael, John Reitzel, and Kristin Mack. 2011. "Probation Officer Recommendations for Sentencing Relative to Judicial Practice: The Implications for African Americans." *Criminal Justice Policy Review* 22(3): 301–329.

Leiber, Michael J., and Nancy Rodriguez. 2011. "The Implementation of the Disproportionate Minority Confinement/Contact (DMC) Mandate: A Failure or Success?" *Race and Justice* 1(1): 103–124.

Leiber, Michael J., and Jayne M. Stairs. 1999. "Race, Contexts, and the Use of Intake Diversion." *Journal of Research in Crime and Delinquency* 36(1): 56–86.

Mauer, Marc. 2009. *The Changing Racial Dynamics of the War on Drugs*. Washington, DC: The Sentencing Project.

Mauer, Marc. 2016. "Voting Rights for Individuals with Felony Convictions." The Sentencing Project. Retrieved June 10, 2016 from www.sentencingproject.org/news/people-felony-convictions-vote/

Mauer, Marc, and Ryan S. King. 2007. *A 25-Year Quagmire: The War on Drugs and Its Impact on American Society*. Washington, DC: The Sentencing Project.

McNulty, Elizabeth. 1996. *Arizona Juvenile Transfer Study: Juveniles Transferred to Adult Court, 1994.* Phoenix, AZ: Arizona Supreme Court, Administrative Office of the Courts.

Miller v. Alabama and Jackson v. Hobbs, 132 s. Ct. 2455 (2012)

Montgomery v. Louisiana, 577 U.S. (2016)

Nellis, Ashley. 2012. *The Lives of Juvenile Lifers: Findings from a National Survey*. Washington, DC: The Sentencing Project.

Nellis, Ashley, and Ryan S. King. 2009. *No Exit: The Expanding Use of Life Sentences in America.* Washington, DC: The Sentencing Project.

Pager, Devah. 2007. *Marked: Race, Crime, and Finding Work in an Era of Mass Incarceration*. Chicago, IL: University of Chicago Press.

Porter, Nicole D. 2016. "Unfinished Project of Civil Rights in the Era of Mass Incarceration and the Movement for Black Lives." *Wake Forest Journal of Law & Policy* 6(1): 1–34.

Puzzanchera, Charles, and Sarah Hockenberry. 2015. "National Disproportionate Minority Contact Databook." Retrieved June 8, 2016 from www.ojjdp.gov/ojstatbb/dmcdb/index.html

Rodriguez, Nancy. 2010. "The Cumulative Effect of Race and Ethnicity in Juvenile Court Outcomes and Why Preadjudication Detention Matters." *Journal of Research in Crime and Delinquency* 47(3): 391–413.

Rodriguez, Nancy, Hilary Smith, and Marjorie S. Zatz. 2009. "Youth Is Enmeshed in a Highly Dysfunctional Family System: Exploring the Relationship among Dysfunctional Families, Parental Incarceration, and Juvenile Court Decision Making." *Criminology* 47(1): 177–208.

Rodriguez, Nancy, and Vincent J. Webb. 2007. "Probation Violations, Revocations, and Imprisonment: The Decisions of Probation Officers, Prosecutors, and Judges Pre- and Post-Mandatory Drug Treatment." *Criminal Justice Policy Review* 18(1): 3–30.

Rovner, Joshua. 2016. "Juvenile Life without Parole: An Overview | The Sentencing Project." The Sentencing Project. Retrieved June 10, 2016 from www.sentencingproject.org/publications/juvenile-life-without-parole/

Sampson, Robert J., and John H. Laub. 1993. "Structural Variations in Juvenile Court Processing: Inequality, the Underclass, and Social Control." *Law & Society Review* 27(2): 285–311.

Sanborn, J.B. 1996. "Factors Perceived to Affect Delinquent Dispositions in Juvenile Court: Putting the Sentencing Decision into Context." *Crime & Delinquency* 42(1): 99–113.

Soler, Mark. 2010. "Missed Opportunity: Waiver, Race, Data, and Policy Reform." *Louisiana Law Review* 71(1): 17–33.

Spohn, Cassia. 2000. "Thirty Years of Sentencing Reform: The Quest for a Racially Neutral Sentencing Process." Pp. 427–501 in *Criminal Justice 2000*, edited by J. Horney. Washington, DC: U.S. Dept. of Justice, Office of Justice Programs, National Institute of Justice.

Spohn, Cassia, and David Holleran. 2001. "The Imprisonment Penalty Paid by Young, Unemployed Black and Hispanic Male Offenders." *Criminology* 38(1): 281–306.

Stalans, Loretta J., Rebecca Juergens, Magnus Seng, and Timothy Lavery. 2004. "Probation Officers' and Judges' Discretionary Sanctioning Decisions about Sex Offenders: Differences between Specialized and Standard Probation Units." *Criminal Justice Review* 29(1): 23–45.

Steffensmeier, Darrell, Jeffery Ulmer, and John Kramer. 1998. "The Interaction of Race, Gender, and Age in Criminal Sentencing: The Punishment Cost of Being Young, Black, and Male." *Criminology* 36(4): 763–798.

Stewart, Eric A., Ramero Martinez, Eric P. Baumer, and Marc Gertz. 2015. "The Social Context of Latino Threat and Punitive Latino Sentiment." *Social Problems* 62(1): 68–92.

Stults, Brian J., and Eric P. Baumer. 2007. "Racial Context and Police Force Size: Evaluating the Empirical Validity of the Minority Threat Perspective." *American Journal of Sociology* 113(2): 507–546.

Sutton, John R. 2013. "Structural Bias in the Sentencing of Felony Defendants." *Social Science Research* 42(5): 1207–1221.

Taxman, Faye, and Robert Cherkos. 1995. "Intermediate Sanctions: Dealing with Technical Violators." *Corrections Today*, 46–57.

The Annie E. Casey Foundation and Kids Count. 2016. "A Shared Sentence—The Annie E. Casey Foundation." The Annie E. Casey Foundation. Retrieved June 10, 2016 from www.aecf.org/resources/a-shared-sentence/

The Fair Sentencing Act of 2010, Pub. L. No. 111–220, 124 Stat. 2372 (2010) (codified at 21 U.S.C. §§ 841, 844, 960).

The Fair Sentencing Clarification Act of 2015. 2015. "H.R.1252—114th Congress (2015–2016)." Congress.gov. Retrieved June 10, 2016 from www.congress.gov/bill/114th-congress/house-bill/1252

The Sentencing Project. 2009. "Incarcerated Parents and Their Children (Trends 1991–2007)." Retrieved June 10, 2016 from www.sentencingproject.org/wp-content/uploads/2016/01/incarcerated-parents-and-their-children-trends-1991–2007.pdf

The Sentencing Project. 2010. "Juvenile Life without Parole: An Overview." Retrieved June 10, 2016 from www.sentencingproject.org/wp-content/uploads/2015/12/juvenile-life-without-parole.pdf

The Sentencing Project. 2015. "Trends in U.S. Corrections." Retrieved June 10, 2016 from http://sentencingproject.org/wp-content/uploads/2016/01/trends-in-us-corrections.pdf

The Sentencing Project. 2016. "Criminal Justice Facts". Retrieved June 8, 2016 from www.sentencingproject.org/criminal-justice-facts/

Thomasson, Kelly. 2016. "Secretary of the Commonwealth Kelly Thomasson." Commonwealth of Virginia. Retrieved June 10, 2016 from https://commonwealth.virginia.gov/judicial-system/restoration-of-rights/

Tonry, Michael H. 1995. *Malign Neglect: Race, Crime, and Punishment in America*. New York: Oxford University Press.

Tracy, Paul. 2005. "Race, Ethnicity, and Juvenile Justice." Pp. 245–269 in *Our Children, Their Children: Confronting Racial and Ethnic Differences in American juvenile justice*, edited by D.F. Hawkins and K. Kempf-Leonard. Chicago, IL: University of Chicago Press.

Uggen, Christopher, Jeff Manza, and Melissa Thompson. 2006. "Citizenship, Democracy, and the Civic Reintegration of Criminal Offenders." *The ANNALS of the American Academy of Political and Social Science* 605(1): 281–310.

Ulmer, Jeffery T., and Brian Johnson. 2004. "Sentencing in Context: A Multilevel Analysis." *Criminology* 42(1): 137–178.

United States Sentencing Commission. 2015. "2015 Report to the Congress: Impact of the Fair Sentencing Act of 2010." United States Sentencing Commission. Retrieved June 10, 2016 from www.ussc.gov/research/congressional-reports/2015-report-congress-impact-fair-sentencing-act-2010

Vallas, Rebecca, Melissa Boteach, Rachel West, and Jackie Odum. 2015. "Removing Barriers to Opportunity for Parents with Criminal Records and Their Children: A Two-Generation Approach." *CSG Justice Center*. Retrieved June 10, 2016 from https://csgjusticecenter.org/reentry/publications/removing-barriers-to-opportunity-for-parents-with-criminal-records-and-their-children-a-two-generation-approach/

Wang, Xia, and Daniel P. Mears. 2010. "A Multilevel Test of Minority Threat Effects on Sentencing." *Journal of Quantitative Criminology* 26(2): 191–215.

Western, Bruce, and Christopher Wildeman. 2009. "The Black Family and Mass Incarceration." *The ANNALS of the American Academy of Political and Social Science* 621(1): 221–242.

Wheelock, Darren. 2005. "Collateral Consequences and Racial Inequality: Felon Status Restrictions as a System of Disadvantage." *Journal of Contemporary Criminal Justice* 21(1): 82–90.

Wilbanks, William. 1987. *The Myth of a Racist Criminal Justice System*. Monterey, CA: Brooks/Cole.

Wildeman, Christopher, and Sara Wakefield. 2014. "Long Arm of the Law: The Concentration of Incarceration in Families in the Era of Mass Incarceration." *Journal of Gender Race & Justice* 17: 367–515.

29 Corrections and Mental Illness

Susan Jones, Risdon N. Slate, and W. Wesley Johnson

> The enormously increased presence of persons with mental illness in the criminal justice system is one of the great problems of our time.
>
> (H. Richard Lamb in Slate, Buffington-Vollum, and Johnson 2013: xv)

In the mid 1800s, Dorothea Dix successfully lobbied for the creation of state hospitals to treat the mentally ill. As a result, the state hospital system expanded to the point that it held 559,000 patients by 1955 (Slate, Buffington-Vollum, and Johnson 2013). This system seemed to be fulfilling a need in this country, but the hospitals quickly became overcrowded, which resulted in horrendous abuses of patients and budget-breaking fiscal pressures. As the era of de-institutionalization evolved, many persons with mental illnesses were released from the hospitals but then were unable to find and maintain resources in the community to help them live independently. In hindsight, it is easy to declare that the warehousing of the mentally ill in state hospitals was a disaster. Predictably, many of the former mentally ill patients became mentally ill inmates.

Today there are ten times more mentally ill Americans behind bars than being treated in state hospitals. There are approximately 350,000 people with mental illness in either jail or prison and about 35,000 in state hospitals (Torrey et al. 2014). Rep. Tim Murphy, R-PA, claims "we have replaced the hospital bed with the jail cell, the homeless shelter, and the coffin." (Human Rights Watch 2015). Correctional institutions have become de facto mental health facilities (Slate et al. 2013). It is time to declare the warehousing of the mentally ill in state prisons an even greater disaster and move toward reform.

While there have been improvements in the treatment of the mentally ill since the deinstitutionalization of state hospitals in the 1970s, specifically, psychotropic drug therapy, many of the improvements in treatment have not been made available to mentally ill inmates. It is easy to say that the jails and prison systems were not funded to provide mental health treatment and medication, but this issue is more complicated than simply lamenting a lack of funds. The corrections profession did not realize the fact that the demographics of their clientele had changed and that more inmates had serious mental health issues. The failure to respond to this change was exacerbated by the failure of the corrections profession to embrace a treatment philosophy. For years, the needs of mentally ill inmates were given low priority as politicians and correctional executives retained a "get tough" posture and blamed other entities for failing to treat individuals living with mental illness. In essence, the mounting issues surrounding the growing number of mentally ill offenders was a problem that politicians and correctional executives failed to address in a proactive manner. Many corrections systems delayed even asking for funding for persons with mental illnesses because they were afraid that if they did so it would be the same as claiming the problem as their own.

However, the condition of mentally ill inmates in prison was not being ignored by outside stakeholders. Recent rulings by the United States Supreme Court and investigations by Human Rights Watch, the Southern Poverty Law Center, and the American Civil Liberties Union have revealed horrid cases of mistreatment of offenders living with mental illness (see Slate et al. 2013). These investigators may understand that these institutions were not designed with mental health treatment in mind, but they are firm in their stance that the lack of treatment in our prisons and jails is a serious constitutional and ethical issue. According to Dr. E. Torrey, founder of the Treatment Advocacy Center, the treatment of these incarcerated inmates is reminiscent of practices used over 170 years ago (Culp-Ressler 2014).

The legitimacy of incarcerating mentally ill individuals, in large part due to behaviors that can be directly attributed to their mental illness, is questionable on both fiscal and moral grounds. Contrary to popular opinion, "most people who are mentally ill are not violent and most people who are violent are not mentally ill" (Vogel 2014: 344). Mental illnesses in most cases can be treated successfully, but prison and jail environments often exacerbate symptoms of mental illnesses and, as noted by Lurigio (2012) treating mental illness alone without addressing other risk factors can increase the chances of recidivating for those returning to the community from custody.

Prisons

The physical design of prisons and jails can be a difficult place for any individual to live. The noise levels, large congregate housing units, community shower and toilet facilities, and the need to manage the day while dealing with large groups of diverse people are typical in many settings. These institutions often include the possibility of violent confrontations. Inmates often have to worry about their interactions and relationships with others on a daily basis. This environment is complicated by the fact that many correctional systems have a constantly changing population within and between institutions. When an individual has a mental illness, the ability to function appropriately in this type of environment can be unachievable. Even though many institutions offer services to mentally ill inmates, such as group therapy or individual counseling, often these services fall short of fulfilling the actual need.

If a mentally ill inmate is originally placed in a lower security facility, they may be moved or regressed into more and more secure facilities. Inmates with mental health problems are more likely to be charged with rule violations, including being charged with verbally and physically assaulting correctional staff. This type of aggression is often a direct result of the lack of mental health treatment coupled with the debilitating atmosphere of the prison environment. This type of disruptive behavior can result in reclassification to high security facilities and may result in criminal convictions that lead to longer prison sentences (Human Rights Watch 2015). It is not uncommon for a mentally ill inmate to be sentenced to prison on a relatively minor crime with a corresponding relative short sentence but actually accumulate more and more time so that realistically he or she may never be released from prison.

Segregation/Supermax

The end of the line for the movement or regression for inmates in most prison and jail systems is a highly structured, very restrictive, control unit. In some jurisdictions, these segregation units have been labeled as supermax, administrative segregation, or solitary confinement. The irony is that once mentally ill offenders are moved to these types of environments some may actually experience more peace and feel more in control of their surroundings.

Mentally ill inmates may experience a brief relief of symptoms, but eventually the totality of the circumstances from their surrounding environment begins to cause symptoms to increase (Metzner and O'Keefe 2011).

As indicated by Human Rights Watch (2015), in Pennsylvania, prisoners with mental illnesses are twice as likely to be placed in segregation as other inmates; in South Carolina, inmates with mental illnesses are three times more likely to be assigned to their most restrictive form of security detention. This type of segregation usually involves solitary confinement for 23 hours a day, with three to five hours out of cell time a week for recreation (Human Rights Watch 2105). The psychological effects of segregation and social isolation are difficult for any individual, but many research studies have found that the impact of this type of housing is more profound on inmates with mental illnesses (Metzner and Dvoskin 2006).

The most common form of treatment for mental illness is psychotropic medication, but even medication can be limited in facilities due to cost containment strategies and, more often, due to lack of psychiatric staff. In a report published by the ACLU that detailed the conditions of confinement for the severely mentally ill in Colorado's supermax prison, Dr. Joel Dvoskin was quoted as saying: "One of the most significant threats to the [Colorado Department of Corrections] CDOC's success in managing its mentally ill population is its severe shortage of psychiatrists" (American Civil Liberties Union of Colorado 2013: 17).

Treatment sessions with clinicians occur infrequently (Human Rights Watch 2015: 24). Institutions may offer individual treatment to high security inmates, but often those sessions are limited to once every 90 days. The American Correctional Association's Standards for Adult Correctional Institutions requires that all inmates held in segregation for more than 30 days are to be personally interviewed by a mental health clinician who then must prepare a written report regarding their status. If the inmate continues to be confined in segregation, then a mental health assessment must be performed once a quarter (American Correctional Association 2003). The reality in many segregation units is that these interviews and assessments take place as a clinician walks from cell to cell as they converse, very briefly, with the inmate on the other side of the door. This type of "drive-by" mental health treatment has been heavily criticized, but it is still the reality in many institutions. The results of this type of management can be seen in reports of abuse and neglect.

One example of such an incident occurred, February 18, 2008, when Jerome Laudman was placed in South Carolina's Special Management Unit (a super maximum security facility). Jerome Laudman had a documented history of mental illness and had been hospitalized 13 times in the previous five years. A nurse reported that Laudman "was down." When he was moved from his cell he was found naked, lying on the floor in feces, urine and vomit. He was taken to the emergency room. His core body temperature was 80.6 degrees, indicating hypothermia. He died a few hours later (Human Rights Watch 2015).

Correctional systems are reacting to the incidents of abuse, self-harm, violence, and neglect of the mental health needs by designing programs that can provide more appropriate treatment options, while maintaining the safety of the staff and inmates. Many jurisdictions have designed barriers that allow for modified group therapy sessions. These barriers differ in appearance, but most people refer to them as therapy cages. Many experts doubt the ability to conduct meaningful treatment with individuals who are lined up in cages, placed far enough apart as to protect all involved. However, corrections professionals counter that this type of option is sound practice in that it protects the inmates and staff from possible violence.

Segregation of inmates with mental illness is a prescription for failure: it worsens the mental condition of the inmate, and it endangers the offender and correctional staff. This type of confinement and lack of "real" treatment has been the subject of much litigation. Recent rulings by the Department of Justice in Georgia mandate that an inmate "shall not remain in segregation absent extraordinary and exceptional circumstances" (Human Rights Watch 2015: 25). Similarly, another settlement with the Massachusetts Department of Correction has replaced segregation with two maximum security mental health units; in 2014, the Colorado General Assembly passed a law that required the removal of all mentally ill inmates from segregation.

The recent court decisions and actions of legislators to remove the mentally ill from all forms of segregation or solitary confinement suggest a shift in correctional philosophy. The message that it is cheaper to treat proactively than to punish reactively is beginning to be heard in many different arenas and jurisdictions.

Mental Health Prisons or Treatment Programs

Correctional systems have been trying to manage the ever-increasing numbers of mentally ill inmates since the late 1980s. More than one jurisdiction has responded by building or retrofitting facilities for the specific mission of housing and providing treatment to mentally ill inmates. The Federal Bureau of Prisons currently has six medical and psychiatric referral centers throughout the nation. Additionally, many states, including Massachusetts, Colorado, and Kansas, have facilities dedicated to treating mentally ill inmates. In essence, these prison systems have built secure state hospital settings.

Unfortunately, even in these settings, compassionate treatment and supervision have been found to be lacking. The report from Human Rights Watch, *Callous and Cruel*, details the type of confinement and abuse that mentally ill inmates endure, even in these specialized prison settings. One case they describe resulted in the death of an inmate in Colorado's prison for the mentally ill, San Carlos Correctional Facility, while the inmate was on the most secure and most closely supervised type of mental health watch (Human Rights Watch 2015).

Jails

The percentage of incarcerated persons with mental illness has been found in research studies to be five to eight times greater than persons with mental illness in free society, with prevalence rates of mental illness for both state prisons and jails hovering around 16 percent of those populations (Slate et al. 2013). The plight of mentally ill inmates in prisons is grim, but often the services and treatment options in jails are even scarcer. Jails are by far the most used facilities to hold persons in custody within the criminal justice system, and jail populations are much more transient than prison populations (Anderson and Slate 2011). The fact that prisons generally have offenders for longer periods of time as opposed to jails may explain the lack of resources in jails, but the need for these resources is just as critical for jails. The stress of the initial incarceration and risk for self-injury or suicide is very high. Couple this stress with the fact that jails detain people from a few days up to a year or more, the management of mentally ill inmates can be very complex. It is no coincidence that the three largest in-patient psychiatric facilities in this country are jails (Slate et al. 2013: 7).

We know that people with mental illnesses are more likely to be arrested and jailed; with their conditions worsening while in custody, they are more likely to be victimized, violate rules, be placed in isolation, and have longer jail stays than persons in custody without mental illnesses. With limited prospects of treatment in jails, persons with mental illnesses who are released from custody are more likely to recidivate after their return to the community. This is compounded by the fact that discharge planning for persons with mental illnesses released into the community is considered one of the most needed yet least provided services (Steadman and Veysey 1997).

Community Corrections (Probation and Parole)

As states downsize prisons, greater pressure is placed on probation and parole to supervise/treat offenders in the community. Probation officers supervise those offenders who were convicted but not sent to prison. Parole officers supervise offenders, generally, after they have been released from prison. In some jurisdictions, community supervision officers have caseloads with probationers and parolees.

The individual caseloads for probation and parole officers continue to increase as their clients present with ever-increasing needs. While institutional staff have specific challenges managing mentally ill inmates, the challenges of trying to supervise a client in a community that does not have adequate resources to support the needs of the individual can be just as daunting. It is no secret that the range of community support resources promised at the time of the closing of the state hospitals does not exist in most places.

There is a myriad of reasons for the lack of services. Under the leadership of President John F. Kennedy, a significant amount of funds was appropriated for community mental health centers. However, Kennedy was assassinated, and the funds were never appropriated. The decline in funding for mental health was exacerbated by the increasing costs for our military involvement in Vietnam and a "not in my backyard" mentality towards community mental health centers in communities across America (Slate et al. 2013). The reality is that those with mental illnesses who encounter the criminal justice system are often put at the bottom of the priority list for the precious few resources that do exist unless some entity intervenes; these individuals that are under community supervision often return to the same communities who originally dealt with them by sending them to prison. Only recently have states begun to provide funds and local mental health treatment to assist mentally ill offenders prior to and following their incarceration or while they are on probation.

Staff Preparation for This Population

Not only is the corrections environment not conducive to good mental health treatment, often the staff who work in these environments are not adequately prepared to manage the mentally ill inmate. The security employees working in correctional institutions often have no specific education related to corrections, other than agency provided training. The agency training spends little, if any time, educating employees about the management of the mentally ill inmate. This is particularly troubling because the line officers have far more contact with individual inmates than any other correctional employee.

The lack of education and preparation for the correctional environment also frequently extends to the clinical staff. Educational preparation and licensure programs for clinicians rarely include information on working with inmates or in confined facilities. Recruiting licensed providers to even apply at correctional facilities is difficult but retaining them in the position is more difficult. Often the providers who do seek employment in correctional facilities are new to the profession and are not prepared for the highly structured and potentially dangerous environment. The fact that these professionals are entering an environment for which they were not prepared and then find themselves directed to conduct treatment in very unusual settings can be a reason to seek work elsewhere. During an exit interview, one provider told the warden that she was leaving because "this wasn't treatment I was doing, it was something I didn't sign up for." She went on to explain that she felt pressure to make clinical decisions based on the needs of the staff and not on the clinical needs of the inmate (S. Jones, personal communication, May 29, 2012).

Historically, correctional systems have not provided staff with the tools and resources to deal with mentally ill inmates, especially those in crisis. One of the most effective new approaches to dealing with offenders living with mental illness is Crisis Intervention Team (CIT) training, which emerged within the policing field. In recent years, CIT has been implemented in training jail and prison personnel. The core component of CIT is de-escalation—a proactive approach to defusing volatile situations. The central tenant of CIT is not force but effective communication. CIT training typically involves role playing among participants who are faced with various crisis scenarios, identification of available resources, and includes persons with mental illnesses who are not in crisis as trainers during part of the training protocol (see Slate et al. 2013).

Probation agencies have even been found to incorporate many of the key elements of CIT with officers. A number of probation offices around the country have established mental health caseloads for specially trained officers, and recommendations have been made that such caseloads should be significantly smaller than normal caseloads due to the special needs of this population (Slate, Feldman, Roskes, and Baerga 2004).

Another specially trained group of professionals that has been used to supervise persons with mental illnesses in the community can be found in assertive community treatment (ACT) teams, and, if these teams exclusively supervise persons with mental illnesses involved with the criminal justice system, they are typically referred to as forensic assertive community treatment (FACT) teams. Team members generally consist of a psychiatrist, psychiatric nurse, licensed clinical social worker, peer counselor (someone with a mental illness in recovery who can serve as an example/mentor to others), and even a probation officer on FACT teams (see Lamberti, Weisman, and Faden 2004). Such teams seek to link persons to appropriate treatment, ensure medication compliance of participants, see that transportation and supportive housing are available, and those to be supervised by the teams may be placed there by the court, such as mental health courts, for monitoring.

Fiscal Costs Versus Human Suffering

While it may be politically correct to debate whether the primary mission of prisons is to incapacitate or to rehabilitate, the reality is that prison programs of all varieties have been underfunded or eliminated. The most basic medical and mental health services are often a fraction of the amount needed to provide treatment that is equitable to the community standard of care. Where services are offered they often suffer from inadequate staffing and adverse working conditions that leave mental health staff burned out and cynical or leaving the systems.

Inmates have died from the lack of mental health care and these deaths have resulted in multi-million dollar lawsuits (Human Rights Watch 2015). Jurisdictions can avoid lawsuits and save money by providing adequate, proactive treatment, but this funding for these treatment programs must come from lawmakers. However, according to Blevins and Soderstrom (2012), while the majority of chief correctional mental health administrators they surveyed agreed that treating offenders with mental illnesses is one of the greatest correctional challenges in America, the researchers found that the majority of these administrators reported that legislators were not adequately funding this objective.

Conclusion

Treatment in correctional facilities can work. According to Steve Cambra, former Warden of the California Department of Corrections and Rehabilitation, treatment does work. If the nation's response to treating the mentally ill is to treat them in prison, prisons must be funded accordingly (Human Rights Watch 2015). Of course, proper funding of mental health treatment within free society could go a long way towards linking persons with mental illnesses to proper health care and could serve as a deterrent to incarceration on the front end. Furthermore, the Affordable Care Act (ACA), also known as Obamacare, has been touted for linking persons with mental illnesses to treatment after their encounters with the criminal justice system as seen with example programs at jails in San Francisco and Chicago, with probation administrators in Chicago, and the Ohio Department of Rehabilitation and Correction; projected savings, as persons adequately treated are believed to be less likely to return to the criminal justice system, are in the millions of dollars (Slate and Usher 2014).

In addition to inadequate funds, stigma has been identified as a significant impediment to persons with mental illnesses seeking mental health treatment in America. As such many persons with mental illnesses have gone without treatment due to the potential shame of being ostracized for seeking such help. The ACA is also aimed at extending parity in funding for the treatment of mental illnesses so that they can be treated on par with physical illnesses. We as a society do not look at persons with diabetes and single them out and blame them for their illnesses, nor should we persons with mental illnesses. Insuring that mental illnesses are covered on par with physical illnesses helps to send a message to the general public that each of us has one body and that there should not be second-class illnesses that are stigmatized (see Slate et al. 2013).

A prominent advocacy organization aimed at destigmatizing mental illnesses is the National Alliance on Mental Illness (NAMI), which can be located at nami.org. This organization is also a good resource for family members and friends who have loved ones with mental illness, and for consumers of mental health services. This organization is also a good resource for collaborating with criminal justice practitioners for training endeavors. Other organizations worthy of note regarding information concerning the interface of mental illness and the criminal justice system include the Substance Abuse and Mental Health Services Administration (samhsa.gov), the Council of State Governments (csgjusticecenter.org/mental-health), Policy Research Associates (prainc.com), the National Institute of Corrections (nicic.gov), the Bureau of Justice Assistance (bja.gov), and the Treatment Advocacy Center (treatment advocacycenter.org).

Corrections is often the place of last resort for offenders living with mental illness. The ability to affect positive change among mentally ill offenders is constrained by a variety of factors including public opinion, fiscal resources, institutional design and operation, as well as the seriousness of the mental illness. While there is much that has been done to improve services for offenders living with mental illness there is still much work needed.

Crime is a multifaceted phenomenon that is driven by a variety of factors—mental illness is one of those factors. Responses that address improving the incapacitation of offenders living with mental illness are needed immediately. The permanent long-term answers to the mentally ill in prison, jails, and on probation or parole are to be found outside of the criminal justice system, in the legislative decision-making process, in budget allocations, in churches, communities, and the medical profession. In a perfect world, correctional personnel would not need to know how to properly interact with persons with mental illnesses. Since that utopia does not exist, the need for properly funding and training those in the corrections profession engaged in this endeavor is paramount.

References

American Civil Liberties Union of Colorado. 2013. *Out of Sight, Out of Mind: Colorado's Continued Warehousing of Mentally Ill Prisoners in Solitary Confinement*. Denver, CO: American Civil Liberties Union of Colorado.

American Correctional Association. 2003. *Standards of Adult Correctional Institutions*, 4th ed. Alexandria, VA: American Correctional Association.

Anderson, Patrick R., and Risdon N. Slate. (2011). *The Decision-making Network: An Introduction to Criminal Justice*. Durham, NC: Carolina Academic Press.

Blevins, Kristie, and Irina Soderstrom. 2012. "Examining Regional Differences in States' Approaches to the Treatment of Offenders with Mental Illness." Paper presented at the Southern Criminal Justice Conference, Atlantic Beach, FL, September 28.

Culp-Ressler, Tara. 2014. "There are 10 Times More Mentally Ill Americans behind Bars than State Hospitals." *LA Progressive*, April 8. Retrieved May 6, 2017 from https://thinkprogress.org/there-are-10-times-more-mentally-ill-americans-behind-bars-than-being-treated-in-state-hospitals-42cb00d98812#.1l44ftwex

Human Rights Watch. 2015. *Callous and Cruel: Use of Force Against Inmates with Mental Disabilities in US Jails and Prison*. New York, NY: Human Rights Watch. Retrieved May 6, 2017 from www.hrw.org/report/2015/05/12/callous-and-cruel/use-force-against-inmates-mental-disabilities-us-jails-and

Lamberti, J. Steven, Robert Weisman, and Dara I. Faden. 2004. "Forensic Assertive Community Treatment: Preventing Incarceration of Adults with Severe Mental Illness." *Psychiatric Services* 55(11): 1285–1293.

Lurigio, Arthur. 2012. "Responding to the Needs of People with Mental Illness in the Criminal Justice System: An Area Ripe for Research and Community Partnerships." *Journal of Crime and Justice* 35(1): 1–12.

Metzner, Jeffrey, and Joel Dvoskin. 2006. "An Overview of Correctional Psychiatry." *Psychiatric Clincs of North America* 29: 761–772.

Metzner, Jeffrey L., and Maureen O'Keefe. 2011. "Psychological Effects of Administrative Segregation: The Colorado Study." *Correctional Mental Health Report* 13(1): 1–16.

Slate, Risdon N., Jacqueline K. Buffington-Vollum, and W. Wesley Johnson. 2013. *The Criminalization of Mental Illness: Crisis and Opportunity for the Justice System*. Carolina Academic Press, Durham, NC.

Slate, Risdon N., Richard Feldman, Erik Roskes, and Migdalia Baerga. 2004. "Training Federal Probation Officers as Mental Health Specialists." *Federal Probation* 68(3): 9–15.

Slate, Risdon N., and Laura Usher. 2014. "Health Coverage for People in the Justice System: The Potential Impact of Obamacare." *Federal Probation* 78(2): 19–23.

Steadman, Henry J., and Bonita M. Veysey. 1997. *Providing Services for Jail Inmates with Mental Disorders* (Research in brief). Washington, DC: National Institute of Justice.

Torrey, E. Fuller, Mary T. Zdanowicz, Aaron D. Kennard, H. Richard Lamb, Donald F. Eslinger, Micahel C. Biasoitti, and Doris A. Fuller. 2014. *The Treatment of Persons with Mental Illness in Prisons and Jails. A State Survey*. Arlington, VA: Treatment Advocacy Center.

Vogel, Matt. 2014. "Mental Illness and Criminal Behavior." *Sociology Compass* 8(4): 337–346.

30 Sex Offenders

Sean Maddan and Lynn Pazzani

Introduction

Sex offenders pose a unique challenge for the correctional system. Sex offenders engage in a wide variety of behaviors (contact and non-contact acts) and cross a myriad of different demographic characteristics. These offenders are generally driven by either biological urges for sexual gratification or psychological urges for power or dominance over victims. In either case, there are limits to any criminal sanction's ability to deter sex offenders from future offending. Herbert Packer (1968) indicated that the effectiveness of any punishment can be limited. In the case of sex offenders, it is arguable that punishments are largely incapable of meeting the correctional goal of deterrence. Effective sanctions for sex offenders should be a balance of punishment (retribution/incapacitation) and treatment (rehabilitation).

While sex offenses happen for a variety of reasons, Lippke (2011: 163) stated that some sex offenses are committed as a result of paraphilias that cannot be satisfied in any other way, and therefore argued that the long-term "control of such desires is difficult, perhaps exceedingly so." Lippke (2011) suggested that corrections are left with only four possible policy choices: psychological treatment, chemical or surgical castration, monitoring, or quarantine. Psychological treatment focuses on trying to help the offender; this is closely tied to the correctional goal of rehabilitation. Castration (chemical or surgical) is an attempt to "reduce the strength or intensity of illicit sexual desires" (Lippke, 2011: 163). This policy is linked primarily to rehabilitation, but has strong links to retribution as well. Closer monitoring of sex offenders revolves around limiting the movement of offenders via intensive parole/probation, registries, or residence restrictions (deterrence). Quarantine would focus on the long-term imprisonment of sex offenders, which would align with the goal of incapacitation.

This chapter will examine the punishment and treatment of sex offenders in the United States. We begin by providing an overview of the primary punishments convicted sex offenders receive; primarily we focus on incarceration and castration. In addition, this chapter will evaluate the pseudo punishment of sex offenders via sex offender registration and notification (SORN) policies; other policies directed at sex offenders, such as residence restrictions and civil commitments are discussed in other chapters of this sourcebook. Lastly, this chapter will address the rehabilitation of sex offenders in the U.S.

Sex Offenders and Modern Corrections

Historically, most forms of punishment have been used against sex offenders. These corrective actions have included capital punishment, corporal punishment, and incarceration. While corporal punishment for criminals was abandoned in the 1960s, capital punishment remained an alternative to punishing sex offenders into the twenty-first century. Various courts across the twentieth century evaluated whether juveniles, the mentally handicapped, and sex offenders should be subjected to the death penalty as a viable punishment strategy. In *Coker v. Georgia* (1977), the Court concluded that a "sentence of death is grossly disproportionate and excessive punishment for the crime of rape and is therefore forbidden by the Eighth Amendment as cruel and unusual." The *Coker* decision only applied to rape cases where victims were adults. A case in Louisiana over 30 years later would determine the Constitutionality of the death penalty in cases where the victim of a sex offender was a child.

In 2008, the Supreme Court heard *Kennedy v. Louisiana* (2008). In this case, the Court determined that the death penalty cannot be applied to rape cases where there was no murder, even in cases pertaining to child victims. As with the rape of adult females, the Court found that a death sentence in response to the rape of children was a violation of the Eighth Amendment's ban on cruel and unusual punishment. The Court's rationale for this was twofold. First, statistics indicated that the death penalty has not been used to punish a sex offender since 1964. Louisiana is the only state that had attempted to execute an individual for child rape since then. Second, of the 37 jurisdictions (federal and states) with the death penalty at the time, only six states offered the death penalty for child rape; in 45 states, a child rapist could not be executed.

Today, the use of the death penalty for sex offenders is a historical artifact. Unless the sex offense results in the death of a victim, sex offenders cannot be put to death. Convicted sex offenders will likely receive some term of incarceration as punishment for their crimes. In some cases, a sex offender may be punished through castration. This section will explore these forms of punishment.

Incarceration

The punishment that many sex offenders will receive upon their conviction for a sex crime is incarceration in either a prison or a jail. The key goal of punishment associated with institutional corrections is both deterrence and incapacitation. Greenfield (1997) noted that 240,000 sex offenders were under the control of the correctional system on any given day. Just under half of these sex offenders were incarcerated; the remaining sex offenders were under community correctional control (Greenfield 1997). In 2012, 160,900 sex offenders were serving time in prisons for rape or sexual assault, which accounted for 12.2 percent of all inmates under state jurisdictions; the federal level rarely prosecutes the crime of rape, or most other sex crimes, so the total number of prisoners in federal prisons is not reported (Carson 2014). These numbers also do not account for less serious sex offender classes. As with the UCR and other official data sources, lesser sex offenses are only counted within an overall category of "other sex offenses." As such, the sex offenders we know are in custody are the most serious of these offenders.

The serious sex offender inmates were predominantly male (98.7 percent) and white (48.8 percent); Hispanics accounted for 22.3 percent of all sex offender inmates. In 2012, the median time served for inmates convicted of sexual assault was 48 months (4 years). This was an increase of 10 months served since 2002 for those convicted of sexual assault or rape. Other than murderers, sex offenders tend to serve the longest sentences in prison (Carson 2014).

Castration

Castration is one of the most interesting punishments for sex offenders as it falls in the nexus of punitive and rehabilitative sanctions. Castration clearly has an "eye-for-an-eye" quality; offenders who have sexually victimized others are rendered incapable of sexual urges or fulfilling those sexual urges. Despite this logic, the practice of castration has largely been conducted under the aegis of a rehabilitative philosophy. The belief is that if the sexual drive is muted by castration, this will also result in the decrease of sexual recidivism. This effectively "cures" a sex offender of being a sex offender.

Meyer and Cole (1997: 2) indicated the oldest form of castration was the physical castration (removal) of the testes; this had been done for centuries for a myriad of reasons. The removal of the testes decreases the production of testosterone which affects "the libido and reduces sexual behavior in the male of the species." In animals, this creates docile creatures. In the earliest times, slaves were castrated by monarchs to guard the king's harem; it was believed that castrated males would not desire their charges or impregnate them even if they did (Meyer and Cole 1997). Meyer and Cole (1997: 2) indicated the first use of castration as a therapeutic technique was done in Switzerland to treat an "imbecile for hypersexuality."

Using castration as a method of managing sexual misbehaviors began in Europe in the early 1900s. Le Maire (1956) indicated that a Dr. Sharp, in 1899, was one of the first to castrate prisoners in Indiana. Meyer and Cole (1997) noted that castration was also used in the south when authorities suspected that black offenders had raped white women. During the first wave of U.S. sex crime legislation (late 1800s to World War II), sterilization became a mechanism to deal with sex offenders, other types of offenders, the mentally ill, and the mentally incapacitated.

Letourneau and Caldwell (2013) attributed the use of castration to the emerging fields of sexology and eugenics; both of these views greatly, if wrongly, still have a profound impact on how sex offenders are seen today. Sexologists suggested that even minor forms of sexual misbehavior could result in later sexual violence and, possibly, sexual homicide (Letourneau and Caldwell 2013). Eugenicists suggested crime was a function of genetic determination (Letourneau and Caldwell 2013); eugenics was effectively selective breeding with the sterilization of "defective" individuals (criminals, insane, handicapped, etc.). Between these two views, sex offenders are deviant criminals who are incapable of change and highly likely to escalate in their criminal behaviors. Sterilization programs were designed to address this ideal of the sex offender. Only anecdotal evidence suggested these programs were effective.

The courts have largely permitted the use of castration for sex offenders. The underlying basis for the various court conclusions focused on the rehabilitative nature of castration; if castration was used punitively, courts did not support the practice. In *Buck v. Bell* (1927), the Supreme Court upheld the use of sterilization in cases where proper Eugenics, not punishment, was the goal. This decision was reversed in 1942 (*Skinner v. Oklahoma*), when castration was differentially used for equally serious crimes (white-collar crimes vs. street level crimes). The courts today support castration provided there is a rehabilitative intent to the laws and practices.

Physical castration today is used primarily for stemming the advance of cancer, especially prostate cancer; however, it is still a sentencing option for sex offenders in a few states. The modern day form of castration is actually referred to as chemical castration. In 1944, chemical castration was argued to control the sexual drive of sex offenders. Chemical castration requires the use of pharmaceutical drugs to either reduce or entirely eliminate the sexual drives of offenders. Chemical castration requires the injection of Depo-Provera, a testosterone-reducing drug, into subjects. Under this policy, the drugs must be continually administered to achieve the desired end; if not continually administered, the effect can diminish. In addition to the permanence of the procedure, physical castration is argued to be more effective than chemical castration at reducing sexual desire and recidivism (Chisum 2013).

Chemical castration is used in several states for both repeat and first-time rapists. Wilson (2004) indicated that California adopted the first modern castration policy in 1996; it was soon adopted in Florida, Michigan, Massachusetts, Missouri, Texas, Washington, and New York. As of 2013, seven states still used some form of chemical castration (California, Florida, Iowa, Louisiana, Montana, Texas, and Wisconsin); Georgia and Oregon repealed their castration policies in 2006 and 2011 respectively (Chisum 2013).

There are reasons for both support for and opposition to castration. Proponents of chemical castration suggest that the practice is both justified and proper; the continued used of pharmaceutical drugs allow the sex offender to be released back into the public without endangering the public. According to Wilson (2004), opponents to chemical castration invoke two primary rationales. First, legislatures do not have the expertise to enact such legislation. Second, chemical castration violates the Eighth Amendment's ban on cruel and unusual punishment. Physical castration causes an irreversible loss to the offender (Meyer and Cole 1997). Meyer and Cole (1997) indicated that it was questionable whether an offender could give consent to castration if the alternative was imprisonment. In addition, if a sex offender has a "medical problem," this inherently means they cannot take responsibility for their so-called medical disorder (Meyer and Cole 1997). Wilson (2004: 383) argued that "such laws demonstrate the difficulty in combining rigid and formalistic laws with complex medical treatments."

Both physical and chemical castration are very physically intrusive techniques. Even so, society is largely okay with the practice of castration on sex offenders. The sex offender committed a crime and deserved to lose all their rights, including procreation. Comartin, Kernsmith, and Kernsmith (2009) argued that support for severe policies against sex offenders, such as castration, was associated with lower income, less education, being a parent of children under the age of five, and general fear of sex offenders. In multiple regression models, general fear of sex offenders was the most important variable in determining support for severe sex offender policies.

Thus, the practice of castration inherently contains a retributive goal. The retributive philosophy argues an "eye for an eye" approach to punishment. Castration, even if it is done to treat a sex offender still echoes the retributive spirit. If an individual commits a serious sex offense, that individual is stripped of their ability to procreate as well as their sexual drive. With the exception of the death penalty (death for a death), no other correctional practice is inherently so retributive (loss of sexuality for a rape). Unfortunately, it is not known what the incidence of castration for sex offenders actually is due to the fact that it is rarely imposed.

Sex Offender Registration and Notification (SORN)

Sex offender registration laws date back to the 1950s in California. While this law was quickly dismissed, the 1980s saw a revival of the registration of offenders. These habitual offender registries were not focused on sex offenders per se, but on offenders who had recidivated multiple times. To this point it is important to recognize that while there were registration policies for sex offenders, there was no semblance of community notification with the exception of law enforcement agencies and courts. Registration is merely the collection of names and information into a database. Notification is the process of disseminating information contained in a registry. While registration efforts had generally been problematic up to the early 1990s, the addition of notification during that time would have been disastrous. Considering the limited technology of that time, notification would have significantly increased the workload of officers and would have been largely ineffectual as data collection and distribution would have lagged significantly. Technology in the form of more advanced computers would make the process of registration and notification more attainable.

In 1994, the U.S. began a movement to better protect its citizens from the threat of sex offenders. There are several federal statutes that have governed the states in developing, implementing, and maintaining a sex offender registry and guidelines on how to release the information contained in the registry to other agencies and the public. These codes are the Jacob Wetterling Crimes Against Children Act of 1994, Megan's Law of 1996, the Pam Lychner Sexual Offender Tracking and Identification Act of 1996, and the Adam Walsh Child and Safety Protection Act of 2006. These laws "focus principally on sex offenders due to their perceived high rate of re-offending" (Hebenton, Thomas and Webb 1997: 22). Of these statutes, Megan's Law is the key to current SORN policies. Megan's Law, in 1996, amended the notification guidelines of the Jacob Wetterling Act. Megan's Law eliminated confidentiality of the registration data collected by the states and mandated the release of sex offender information to the public (Semel 1997: 21). The goal of Megan's Law was to give the public the ability to protect itself from convicted sex offenders residing in an area.

The Efficacy of SORN Policies

Research that seeks to determine how effective sex offender registries and notification are at curbing sex offending has raised serious questions about the ability of SORN to reduce sex offending and recidivism. Numerous studies have evaluated the success of SORN policies. Research has indicated support from those in law enforcement and the community. Individuals tend to like SORN policies and the perceived benefits they provide. Likewise, research indicates that SORN policies have adverse consequences for sex offenders on registries; sex offenders listed on registries face harassment, depression, lack of employment, and potential victimization by vigilantes. While these lines of research have evaluated SORN tangentially, other research has examined the influence of SORN on general sex offending patterns and sex offender recidivism.

Vásquez, Maddan, and Walker (2008) conducted the first time-series study to evaluate whether sex offender registration and notification laws impact the incidence of rape as counted in the Uniform Crime Report (UCR). While they set out to evaluate all 50 states, data constraints limited their study to only ten states: Arkansas, California, Connecticut, Hawaii, Idaho, Nebraska, Nevada, Ohio, Oklahoma, and West Virginia. Pre and follow-up periods of data ranged from three to five years. Vásquez et al.'s results indicated that only three states (Idaho, Ohio, and Hawaii) had statistically significant decreases in the incidence of rape after the implementation of SORN; one state, California, actually had a statistically significant increase in the incidence of rape. For the remaining six states, there was no difference before and after the implementation of SORN. Since this first time-series analysis, there has been little support illustrating SORN impacts general sex offending patterns. Sandler, Freeman, and Socia's (2008) study in New York, Maurelli and Ronan's (2013) research from 1960–2008, and Ackerman, Sacks, and Greenberg's (2012) research from 1970–2002 indicated SORN was not effective in curbing rape across the U.S. Time-series analyses illustrate that SORN has no general deterrent effect on sex offending.

The most important line of research on SORN policies comes in the form of recidivism studies. One of the earliest evaluations of sex offender registration and notification laws occurred in Washington State in 2005. The Washington State Institute for Public Policy examined recidivism rates of Washington sex offenders (N = 8,359) during three periods, before the 1990 initial notification act, after the 1990 act, and after the 1997 amendments of sex offender notification. This report indicated that general, non-sex offense felony recidivism remained the same, while both sex and violent felony recidivism decreased substantially. To date, this is the best evidence supporting the utility of sex offender registration and notification laws.

In Minnesota, the Minnesota Department of Correction (2008; Duwe and Donnay 2008) released a report that suggested sex offender notification policies were having a deterrent effect, and that sex offenses were the least likely offenses perpetrated by those who did recidivate. Research from New Jersey (Zgoba, Witt, Dalessandro, and Veysey 2008: 2) utilizing a similar design (*N* = 550) concluded that sex offender registration and notification policies had no impact on sexual reoffending and argued that the "growing costs may not be justifiable." These results were further validated by the work of Tewksbury, Jennings, and Zgoba (2012), Jennings, Zgoba, and Tewksbury (2012), in Wisconsin by Zevitz, (2006), in Iowa by Tewksbury and Jennings (2010), in Arkansas by Maddan, Miller, Walker, and Marshall (2011), and in England by Piquero, Farrington, Jennings, Diamond, and Craig (2012).

As can be seen, the impact of current sex offender registration and notification is highly questionable. As Levenson and D'Amora (2007: 172) noted, "Law makers designed registration as a tool to assist law enforcement agents to track sexual criminals and apprehend potential suspects." Notification served to increase public awareness, thereby strengthening community members' ability to protect themselves from potential victimization. What is clear from this review of SORN is that sex offenders are not recidivating to the degree imagined by the public or the public is not utilizing sex offender registries to their fullest benefit.

Rehabilitating Sex Offenders

Attempts to cure sex offenders have been going on for hundreds of years. In the 1930s to 1950s, also known as the sexual psychopath era in the U.S., sex offenders were considered to be mentally and/or physically different from non-offenders; treatment in this era focused on psychiatric and medical treatment (London and Caprio 1950). Indeed, Sheldon Glueck considered that:

> the aggressive sex offender is more a problem for psychopathology than for criminal justice. Sometimes he is feeble-minded; sometimes he suffers from some epileptic condition; frequently he is a chronic alcoholic; often his uninhibited impulses are related to premature senility.
>
> (Glueck 1937: 319)

Both the fields of psychology and criminal justice are utilized in responding to sex offenders and in treating them. For most of the twentieth century, castration, drug therapy, lobotomy, and electroshock were used to deal with the "sexual psychopath." While some of these treatment strategies are still used today (in modified fashions), modern approaches to rehabilitating sex offenders tend to lose their retributive philosophy of punishment.

Contemporary sex offender treatments include therapeutic communities, behavioral therapy, cognitive-behavioral therapy, relapse prevention, and drug therapies. Each method has shown some degree of success in reducing reoffending, sexual reoffending, or deviant sexual interests, although there is no clear choice in terms of what is the most effective treatment. The common myth that sex offenders cannot be treated seems to be not entirely true, but perhaps the type of treatment that is effective for one may not be the best treatment for another. This section will explore these modern rehabilitative approaches to treating sex offenders and the effectiveness of rehabilitation in dealing with sex offenders.

Therapeutic Communities

A therapeutic community (TC) in a prison environment is a treatment program that involves a small community of inmates. These inmates live together and go through treatment together (Baker and Prete 2011). These communities were initially developed for individuals with substance abuse problems, both in and out of prison, and showed some promising results related to recovery and recidivism reduction. TCs have been modified now to treat a variety of populations, including sex offenders (Baker and Prete 2011). The goal of TCs is rehabilitation for those who have had positive community interactions in the past and habilitation for those who have not. This is done by socializing the inmates in a small community of other similar inmates, where inmates who have completed more treatment influence the newer members and help them develop appropriate social skills (Jensen and Kane 2012). These communities must be places where the inmates can develop relationships and hold each other accountable for individual actions. While TCs vary somewhat from prison to prison, important factors in their success include the degree of support from correctional staff and administration, the effectiveness of treatment staff, and the design of the prison facility itself (Baker and Prete 2011).

There are a number of components of a TC that are standard, despite variation by prison. TCs will have primary therapy groups, where inmates meet in smaller groups and are guided by one or more therapists (Baker and Prete 2011). They will also have psychoeducational classes, where inmates learn coping skills appropriate to their needs, and specialty groups where inmates with particular conditions or situations, such as the need for remedial education, their own victimization, or substance abuse treatment needs, can meet in small groups to address these issues that will be associated with their individual treatment success (Baker and Prete 2011). Finally, TCs have community meetings where all members of the TC and the staff group come together to address any problems within the community. Community meetings are initially held by staff, but the inmates may elect officers and later take control of the meetings themselves, which shows community development (Baker and Prete 2011).

Ware, Frost, and Hoy (2010) argued that there is limited empirical evidence that TCs are successful in the treatment of sexual offenders, although some studies do find lower rearrest rates for TC-treated sexual offenders than non-treated sexual offenders. Ware et al. (2010) suggested the real benefit of TCs is creating a treatment-friendly environment in areas such as prisons, which would ordinarily not be conducive to receiving treatment. There is potential that openness regarding discussing inappropriate sexual desires that is encouraged in a TC may help enhance the content of specific types of treatment, as opposed to a typical prison environment where disrespect and secretiveness are more common reactions to this topic (Ware et al. 2010). The types of treatment discussed hereafter could be conducted as part of a TC, or in a different environment.

Behavioral Treatment

If sexual offending is associated with deviant sexual arousal, changing the offender's pattern of arousal could stop his offending. Using behavioral therapy to change deviant sexual arousal as a treatment for sexual offending relies upon sexual offenders having deviant sexual interests and relies upon sexual interests being malleable (Marshall, O'Brien, and Marshall 2009). While not all sex offenders display arousal to deviant sexual interests, for those that do there is no definitive evidence that behavioral treatment methods are successful. Regardless, these methods are used in a majority of programs that treat sexual offenders, both adult and juvenile (Marshall et al. 2009).

There are a number of forms of aversion therapy that can be used to change sexual arousal patterns, including shame aversion, ammonia aversion, faradic (electrical) aversion, and olfactory (smell) aversion. The basic idea behind each of these techniques is that the offender should come to associate his deviant arousal with something unpleasant and will therefore reduce deviant sexual fantasies (Marshall et al. 2009). Shame aversion is the most ethically questionable and least researched of these treatments. In this technique, treatment staff watch an offender in treatment act out deviant behavior and stare at him, causing him to experience shame. There is evidence that offenders going through this treatment experience nightmares and anxiety; and, there is only anecdotal evidence that this form of treatment is successful. Despite the potential problems with this treatment, it is still practiced in approximately 20 percent of treatment facilities, including those for adolescents and children (Marshall et al. 2009).

Ammonia and olfactory aversion are often conflated, although inhaling ammonia really triggers the pain system of the body rather than the olfactory system (Marshall et al. 2009). Both forms of aversion therapy require the offender in treatment to inhale either ammonia or some other foul smelling substance (such as rotten meat) in response to deviant fantasies or being exposed to simulations of their deviant interest (Marshall et al. 2009). Ammonia can be particularly unpleasant, causing not just a reaction to the smell, but watering of the eyes and coughing (Laws 2001). Over the course of a few weeks, an offender in treatment will watch films or see pictures with their deviant interest featured and will then inhale the unpleasant substance. The offender's erectile response to the deviant sexual stimuli can be tracked over time to determine whether the treatment is causing a reduction in arousal to deviant sexual interests.

Faradic shock has been used to treat a number of different problem behaviors, most notably alcoholism. While it appears that for alcoholism specifically, inducing vomiting as the negative stimulus is more successful than giving an electrical shock in reducing alcohol consumption (Cannon and Baker 1981), electric shock aversion therapy has been applied with some success to people with negative sexual behaviors (Kilmann, Sabalis, Gearing, Bukstel, and Scovern 1982). For electric shock to be most effective at reducing deviant sexual arousal, it should be applied only when there is evidence that such arousal is occurring. This can be done by monitoring erectile response and only applying electric shock when the offender undergoing treatment has an erection in response to deviant sexual stimuli. Electric shock is applied to the fingers of the offender undergoing treatment. When an erection is present in response to appropriate sexual stimuli, no shock is applied (Callahan and Leitenberg 1973). In Callahan and Leitenberg's (1973) study of electrical shock, they found that subjects did reduce erectile response to deviant sexual stimuli, but also noted that this does not necessarily mean that they reduced their arousal, they could have just learned to inhibit their erection.

Cognitive-behavioral Therapy

Behavioral therapies set the stage for the development of cognitive-behavioral therapy (CBT; Marshall and Laws 2003); CBT has become the most popular form of treatment (Shaffer, Jeglic, Moster, and Wnuk 2010). This type of therapy takes a cognitive-behavioral approach to changing problems that are associated with sexual offending. For instance, cognitive distortions, or false thought processes and beliefs, have been shown to be associated with sexual offending. These include "beliefs that children are sexual beings, that individuals are entitled to sex, that sexual activity does not harm children, that society's rules and norms may be disregarded, and that women are game-playing, deceitful, and/or hurtful individuals" (Shaffer et al. 2010: 95). Another problem associated with sexual offending is emotional dysregulation, "which may be defined as a propensity to experience negative affect, a slow return to baseline after emotional arousal, and/or non-normative emotional reactions to stimuli" (Shaffer et al. 2010: 96). Additionally, deficits in interpersonal skills, preoccupations with deviant sexual behavior, and a lack of empathy are also associated with sexual offending. Each of these issues can be addressed using CBT.

In CBT, a therapist will address cognitive distortions by discussing the incorrect belief in a group setting and identifying alternative interpretations. A therapist may also use role playing where the offender plays the role of a victim in order to address some of their cognitive distortions regarding victims (Shaffer et al. 2010). Emotional dysregulation can be addressed by labeling emotions and learning about the functions of emotions, and then working to find the underlying cause of emotions that precede sexual offending. CBT for interpersonal skills deficits can include training and role-playing in social situations and discussions regarding age-appropriate friends and relationships (Shaffer et al. 2010). Deviant sexual behaviors are usually treated using the behavioral techniques described previously, while a lack of empathy can be treated in a CBT context by examining victim reactions in videos or letters to help the offender understand the victim's perspective (Shaffer et al. 2010).

Most studies of cognitive behavior treatment for sex offenders have been done by treating incarcerated offenders and tracking them after their release. For instance, participants in a Vermont sexual offender treatment program during a 12-year period were followed for an average of just over five years to determine whether they committed sexual, violent but non-sexual, non-violent offenses, and/or parole violations. The specialized treatment group, which was a cognitive-behavioral group program, focused on accepting responsibility, modifying cognitive distortions, developing victim empathy, controlling sexual arousal, improving social competence, and developing relapse prevention skills (McGrath, Hoke, and Vojtisek 1998). One control group consisted of offenders who received peer-group therapy and individual therapy and the other control group received no treatment. Although the number of sexual reoffenders was quite small, it was still determined that the specialized treatment group had the lowest rate of sexual reoffending (McGrath et al. 1998), indicating that CBT was effective in treating sexual offenders. A similar study was conducted using a group of sex offenders in a CBT treatment program in California; this study found that sex offenders in the CBT treatment were less likely to commit new sex offenses than offenders who did not wish to (and did not) receive treatment (Marques, Day, Nelson, and West 1994).

Relapse Prevention

Relapse prevention is a strategy used after other treatment has already been applied; this strategy teaches the offender methods of preventing himself from reoffending. It is based on treatment used in the case of "indulgent" behaviors, such as alcoholism, gambling addiction, and drug addiction (Pithers, Marques, Gibat, and Marlatt 1983). While similar to CBT, it has a different structure and different terminology that make it distinct (Laws 1999). In relapse prevention, the therapist takes the perspective that while relapse (committing another sexual offense) is not to be expected, it should be planned for. Even after undergoing treatment, an offender should not expect to never have urges or fantasies associated with their offending again. Learning how to prevent acting on such urges will reduce the incidence of relapse (Pithers et al. 1983).

In the relapse prevention model, high-risk situations, which generally involve negative emotional states or interpersonal conflict, are identified. High-risk situations can lead to fantasizing about the inappropriate behavior, which can lead to developing a plan and engaging in the inappropriate behavior (Pithers et al. 1983). Reoffending, or relapse, can occur due to an "apparently irrelevant decision" (AID) that results in the offender being exposed to a high-risk situation. Using a coping strategy during high-risk situations can reduce the likelihood of relapse. If a treated offender successfully avoids committing an offense in such a situation, his confidence about the next high-risk situation increases; whereas, if an offender does not avoid committing an offense he believes he cannot control his urges and the likelihood of continuing to offend increases (Pithers et al. 1983). An offender's belief that he cannot control his offending and that he will always be a sex offender is known as the "abstinence violation effect" (AVE). The offender who has failed and attributed it to his always being a sex offender will continue to fulfill that role (Pithers et al. 1983).

Because avoiding all risk is not practical, the offender is taught coping strategies for when he does find himself in such situations. He outlines a "problem-solving procedure" (Pithers et al. 1983: 231) by fully describing a risky situation and how he can best react. He describes these situations to a therapist as practice for encountering them and to receive feedback to modify coping strategies if necessary. He is taught to cope with urges by imagining himself as something disgusting if he considers acting out an urge. He is also taught to avoid situations and behaviors, to the extent possible, that put him at risk of feeling deviant sexual urges (Pithers et al. 1983). Research has supported relapse prevention programs as a viable treatment for sex offenders.

Drug Therapies

There are several types of drug therapies that have been used to attempt to reduce deviant sexual activity, including anti-androgen drugs and drugs used as anti-depressants. The most studied of these drugs is Medroxyprogesterone acetate, also known as Depo-Provera. Depo Provera is most commonly used as a contraceptive injection for women. It is administered for this purpose in a dose of 150 mg every 13 weeks as an intramuscular injection. At this dose, the manufacturer warns that Depo-Provera has been shown to reduce bone density in users and should not be used for more than two years ("Depo-Provera" n.d.). As noted earlier, Depo-Provera has also been used to attempt to reduce reoffending in sexual offenders. In studies of sex offenders, the dose given is as high as 400 mg every week (Meyer, Cole, and Emory 1992).

The mechanism by which Depo-Provera should work to reduce sexual offending is that it will reduce testosterone levels, which is the source of sexual arousal. Depo-Provera also has a tranquilizing effect on individuals (Kiersch 1990). The effect of the Depo-Provera injection was tested in a study at Atascadero State Hospital in California using eight volunteer sex offenders, four of whom completed the entire study. Each subject was given 16 weeks of the Depo-Provera injection and 16 weeks of a saline injection, in four rotations, so each subject served as his own control. With this small sample size, the researchers did not find a consistent difference in arousal to deviant sexual stimuli during the saline injection phases and the Depo-Provera injection phases. They do suggest that this is possibly because it took several weeks for subjects to return to their pre-treatment testosterone levels after the last Depo-Provera injection, thus weakening any impact that might have been seen (Kiersch 1990). Other research with larger sample sizes and more rigorous scientific methodologies seems to indicate that using Depo-Provera to treat sex offenders can be successful, at least for those that are recommended to receive the treatment.

Conclusion

This chapter has evaluated the formal corrections, punishments, and treatment of sex offenders. The majority of the approaches enumerated here work under the myth that sex offenders are likely to specifically recidivate. This misperception is present in all correctional approaches revolving around sex offenders. While there are many approaches to dealing with convicted sex offenders, these strategies fall on a continuum that focuses on public safety from the threat of sex offenders. While there are many promising treatments, the public is largely unwilling to pay for these rehabilitative efforts based on the notion that sex offenders are atypical recidivists. Thus, corrections for sex offenders will continue to be punitive (especially incarceration), with the argument for such punishment techniques being that they are employed for the purposes of community safety.

References

Ackerman, Alissa R., Meghan Sacks, and David F. Greenberg. 2012. "Legislation Targeting Sex Offenders: Are Recent Policies Effective in Reducing Rape?" *Justice Quarterly* 29: 858–887.

Adam Walsh Child Protection and Safety Act. *United States Code*. Vol. 42, Section 16911, 2006.

Baker, Debra, and Malee Prete. 2011. "Developing Therapeutic Communities for Sex Offenders." Pp. 30.1–30.10 in *Handbook of Sex Offender Treatment*, edited by B. Schwartz. Kingston, NJ: Civic Research Institute.

Callahan, Edward J., and Harold Leitenberg. 1973. "Aversion Therapy for Sexual Deviation: Contingent Shock and Covert Sensitization." *Journal of Abnormal Psychology* 81(1): 60–73.

Cannon, Dale S., and Timothy B. Baker. 1981. "Emetic and Electric Shock Alcohol Aversion Therapy: Assessment of Conditioning." *Journal of Consulting and Clinical Psychology* 49(1): 20–33.

Carson, E. Ann. 2014. *Prisoners in 2013*. Washington, DC: Bureau of Justice Statistics.

Chisum, Laura S. 2013. "Case for Castration: A 'Shot' towards Rehabilitation for Sex Offenders." *Law and Psychology Review* 37: 193–209.

Comartin, Erin B., Poco D. Kernsmith, and Roger M. Kernsmith. 2009. "Sanctions for Sex Offenders: Fear and Public Policy." *Journal of Offender Rehabilitation* 48: 605–619.

Depo-Provera-medroxyprogesterone acetate injection, suspension. n.d. Retrieved May 8 2017 from labeling.pfizer.com/ShowLabeling.aspx?id=522

Duwe, Grant, and William Donnay. 2008. "The Impact of Megan's Law on Sex Offender Recidivism: The Minnesota Experience." *Criminology* 46: 411–446.

Glueck, Sheldon. 1937. "Sex Crimes and the Law." *The Nation* 145(13): 319–320.

Greenfield, Lawrence A. 1997. *Sex Offense and Offenders: An Analysis of Data on Rape and Sexual Assault*. Washington, DC: Bureau of Justice Statistics.

Hebenton, Bill, Terry Thomas, and Barry Webb. 1997. Keeping Track? Observations on Sex Offender Registers in the U.S. *Crime Detection and Prevention Series* 83.

Jacob Wetterling Crimes Against Children and Sexually Violent Offender Registration Program Act. *United States Code*. Vol. 42, Section 14071 (1994).

Jennings, Wesley G., Kristin M. Zgoba, and Richard Tewksbury. 2012. "A Comparative Longitudinal Analysis of Recidivism Trajectories and Collateral Consequences for Sex and Non-sex Offenders Released Since the Implementation of Sex Offender Registration and Community Notification." *Journal of Crime and Justice* 35: 356–364.

Jensen, Eric, and Stephanie L. Kane. 2012. "The Effects of Therapeutic Community on Recidivism Up to Four Years after Release from Prison: A Multisite Study." *Criminal Justice and Behavior* 39(8): 1075–1087.

Kiersch, Theodore A. 1990. "Treatment of Sex Offenders with Depo-Provera." *Bulletin of the American Academy of Psychiatry and the Law* 18(2): 179–187.

Kilmann, Peter, Robert F. Sabalis, Milton L. Gearing, Lee H. Bukstel, and Albert W. Scovern. 1982. "The Treatment of Sexual Paraphilias: A Review of the Outcome Research." *The Journal of Sex Research* 18(3): 193–252.

Laws, Richard D. 1999. "Relapse Prevention: The State of the Art." *Journal of Interpersonal Violence* 14(3): 285–302.

Laws, D.R. 2001. "Olfactory Aversions: Notes on Procedure, with Speculations on its Mechanism of Effect." *Sexual Abuse: A Journal of Research and Treatment* 13(4): 275–287.

Le Maire, Louis. 1956. "Danish Experience Regarding Treatment of Sex Offenders." *Journal of Criminal Law and Criminology* 473: 274–310.

Letourneau, Elizabeth J., and Michael F. Caldwell. 2013. "Expensive, Harmful Policies that Don't Work or How Juvenile Sexual Offending is Addressed in the U.S." *International Journal of Behavioral Consultation and Therapy* 8: 23–29.

Levensen, Jill S., and David A. D'Amora. 2007. "Social Policies Designed to Prevent Sexual Violence: The Emperor's New Clothes?" *Criminal Justice Policy Review* 18: 168–199.
Lippke, Richard L. 2011. "Why Sex (offending) is Different." *Criminal Justice Ethics* 30: 151–172.
London, Louis, and Frank S. Caprio. 1950. *Sexual Deviations*. Washington, DC: Linarce Press.
Maddan, Sean, J. Mitchell Miller, Jeffrey T. Walker, and Ineke Haen Marshall. 2011. "The Efficacy of Sex Offender Registration and Notification Laws in Arkansas: Utilizing Criminal History Information to Explore Sex Offender Recidivism." *Justice Quarterly* 28(2): 303–324.
Marques, Janice K., David M. Day, Craig Nelson, and Mary Ann West. 1994. "Effects of Cognitive-behavioral Treatment on Sex Offender Recidivism: Preliminary Results of a Longitudinal Study." *Criminology & Penology* 21(1): 28–54.
Marshall, William L., and D.R. Laws. 2003. "A Brief History of Behavioral and Cognitive Behavioral Approaches to Sexual Offender Treatment: Part 2. The Modern Era." *Sexual Abuse: A Journal of Research and Treatment* 15(2): 93–120.
Marshall, William L., Matt D. O'Brien, and Liam E. Marshall. 2009. "Modifying Sexual Preferences." Pp. 311–327 in *Assessment and Treatment of Sex Offenders: A Handbook*, edited by A. Beech, L. Craig, and K. Browne. Chichester, UK: Wiley-Blackwell.
Maurelli, Kimberly, and George Ronan. 2013. "A Time-series Analysis of the Effectiveness of Sex Offender Notification in the USA." *Journal of Forensic Psychiatry and Psychology* 24: 128–143.
McGrath, Robert J., Stephen E. Hoke, and John E. Vojtisek. 1998. "Cognitive-behavioral Treatment of Sex Offenders: A Treatment Comparison and Long-term Follow-up Study." *Criminal Justice and Behavior* 25(2): 203–225.
Meyer, Walter J., and Collier M. Cole. 1997. "Physical and Chemical Castration of Sex Offenders: A Review." *Journal of Offender Rehabilitation* 25: 1–16.
Meyer, Walter J., Collier Cole, and Evangeline Emory. 1992. "Depo Provera Treatment for Sex Offending Behavior. An Evaluation of Outcome." *Bulletin of the American Academy of Psychiatry and the Law* 20(3): 249–259.
Minnesota Department of Corrections. 2008. *Megan's Law in Minnesota: The Impact of Community Notification on Sex Offender Recidivism*. St. Paul, MN: Minnesota Department of Corrections.
Packer, Herbert L. 1968. *The Limits of the Criminal Sanction*. Stanford, CA: Stanford University Press.
Pam Lychner Sexual Offender Tracking and Identification Act. *United States Code*. Vol. 42, Section 13701 (1996).
Piquero, Alex R., David P. Farrington, Wesley G. Jennings, Brie Diamond, and Jessica Craig. 2012. "Sex Offenders and Sex Offending in the Cambridge Study in Delinquent Development: Prevalence, Frequency, Specialization, Recidivism, and (Dis)Continuity over the Life-course." *Journal of Crime and Justice* 35: 412–426.
Pithers, William D., Janice K. Marques, Cynthia C. Gibat, and G.A. Marlatt. 1983. "Relapse Prevention with Sexual Aggressives: A Self-control Model of Treatment and Maintenance of Change." Pp. 214–239 in *The Sexual Aggressor: Current Perspectives on Treatment*, edited by J. Greer and I. Stuart. New York: Van Nostrand Reinhold.
Sandler, Jeffrey C., Naomi J. Freeman, and Kelly M. Socia. 2008. "Does a Watched Pot Boil? A Time-series Analysis of New York State's Sex Offender Registration and Notification Law." *Psychology, Public Policy, and Law* 14: 284–302.
Schaffer, Megan, Elizabeth Jeglic, Aviva Moster, and Dorota Wnuk. 2010. "Cognitive-behavioral Therapy in the Treatment and Management of Sex Offenders." *Journal of Cognitive Psychotherapy: An International Quarterly* 24(2): 92–103.
Semel, Elisabeth. 1997. "Megan's Law is a Knee-jerk Reaction to a Senseless Personal Tragedy." *Corrections Today*, October, 21.
Tewksbury, Richard, and Wesley G. Jennings. 2010. "Assessing the Impact of Sex Offender Registration and Community Notification on Sex-offending Trajectories." *Criminal Justice and Behavior Policy Review* 37: 570–582.
Tewksbury, Richard, Wesley G. Jennings, and Kristen M. Zgoba. 2012. "A Longitudinal Examination of Sex Offender Recidivism Prior to and Following the Implementation of SORN Sex Offenders and Recidivism." *Behavioral Sciences and the Law* 30: 308–328.

Vásquez, Bob Edward, Sean Maddan, and Jeffrey T. Walker. 2008. "The Influence of Sex Offender Registration and Notification Laws in the United States: A Time Series Analysis." *Crime and Delinquency* 54(2): 175–192.
Ware, Jayson, Andrew Frost, and Anna Hoy. 2010. "A Review of the Use of Therapeutic Communities with Sexual Offenders." *International Journal of Offender Therapy and Comparative Criminology* 54(5): 721–742.
Washington State Institute for Public Policy. 2005. *Sex Offender Sentencing in Washington State: Has Community Notification Reduced Recidivism*. Olympia, WA: Washington State Institute for Public Policy.
Wilson, Franklin T. 2004. "Out of Sight, Out of Mind: An Analysis of *Kansas v. Crane* and the Fine Line between Civil and Criminal Sanctions." *The Prison Journal* 84: 379–394.
Zevitz, Richard G. 2006. "Sex Offender Community Notification: Its Role in Recidivism and Offender Reintegration." *Criminal Justice Studies* 19: 193–208.
Zgoba, Kristen, Philip Witt, Melissa Dalessandro, and Bonita Veysey. 2008. *Megan's Law: Assessing the Practical and Monetary Efficacy*. Washington, DC: U.S. Department of Justice.

Cases Cited

Buck v. Bell, 240 U.S. 200, (1927).
Coker v. Georgia, 433 U.S. 584, (1977).
Kennedy v. Louisiana, 554 U.S. 407, (2008).
Skinner v. Oklahoma, 316 U.S. 535, (1942).

Section 5

Issues Affecting Incarceration

31 Correctional Facility Overcrowding

Benjamin Steiner and Sara Toto

Correctional facility overcrowding occurs when the inmate population in a prison or jail exceeds its design capacity (Steiner and Wooldredge 2008).[1] Overcrowding is associated with a number of health and safety problems for inmates and correctional staff, not to mention heightened correctional costs that are absorbed by taxpayers (Steiner and Wooldredge 2008). The incarcerated population in the United States (U.S.) experienced unprecedented growth between 1973 and the early 2000s that contributed to overcrowding in many prisons and jails (Blumstein and Beck 2005; Glaze and Parks 2012; Steiner and Wooldredge 2009a; Travis and Western 2014; Western 2006). Despite some declines in the incarcerated population nationally, prison populations in 26 states and the Federal Bureau of Prisons still exceed their available design capacity; prison populations in most other states exceed 90 percent of their design capacity (Carson 2015). Inmate populations in nearly 28 percent of the jails in the U.S. are at or exceed their design capacity, while an additional 17 percent of jails confine inmate populations that are at or exceed 90 percent of their design capacity (Bureau of Justice Statistics 2014).

The increase in the U.S. incarcerated population, corresponding correctional facility overcrowding, and problems that result from prison and jail crowding have generated a considerable amount of research pertaining to the influences of prison or jail population size, facility crowding, or the consequences thereof. In this chapter, we provide an overview of the scientific evidence pertaining to these topics.

Influences of Correctional Facility Crowding

Few studies have focused on determining the influences of correctional facility crowding (e.g., Steiner and Wooldredge 2008; Wooldredge 1991, 1996); most studies have focused on the sources of prison or jail population size. Findings from these studies are still relevant, however, since they provide information pertaining to the influences of the numerator in the correctional facility crowding equation.

The simplest explanation for growth in the U.S. prison population that occurred between 1970 and the early 2000s is that the crime rate increased, and so did the corresponding incarceration rate. However, researchers have determined that growth in the U.S. prison population was primarily attributable to increases in the incarceration rate for drug offenses, prison sentences per arrest, time served in prison, and recommitments for parole violations (e.g., Blumstein and Beck 2005; Travis and Western 2014). The incarceration rate for drug offenses alone increased tenfold between 1980 and 2001 (Blumstein and Beck 2005). In other words, the growth in the U.S. prison population was attributable to changes in how the states responded to crime, rather than changes in the crime rate.

Researchers who have conducted state-level studies of the influences of correctional facility populations or incarceration rates have typically focused on evaluating the effects of state sentencing policies such as sentencing guidelines or truth in sentencing on prison or jail populations (e.g., D'Alessio and Stolzenberg 1995; Marvell and Moody 1996; Nicholson-Crotty 2004; Sorenson and Stemen 2002; Spelman 2013; Stemen and Rengifo 2011). Findings from these studies have revealed that state sentencing policies have modest, albeit significant, effects on prison and jail populations. Results of a state-level study of the effects of four sentencing policies—presumptive sentences, presumptive sentencing guidelines, voluntary sentencing guidelines, and determinate sentencing—enacted between 1977 and 2000 on state incarceration rates conducted by Stemen and Rengifo (2011) are illustrative.[2]

Stemen and Rengifo (2011) examined the main and moderating effects of the four policy variables previously mentioned, while controlling for other potentially relevant crime (e.g., violent crime rate), socioeconomic (e.g., poverty rate), and political (e.g., government ideology) factors. They observed that states that enacted determinate sentencing experienced lower incarceration rates. Implementing presumptive sentences, presumptive sentencing guidelines, or voluntary sentencing guidelines did not significantly affect incarceration rates; however, states that enacted both determinate sentencing and presumptive guidelines experienced lower incarceration rates. Specifically, states that put both of these policies in place reduced their incarceration rate by approximately 20 persons per 100,000 residents. Moreover, states that had both of these policies in place at the same time reduced their incarceration rates by an additional 18 persons per 100,000. Based on their findings, Stemen and Rengifo (2011) argued that reducing or removing the discretion of release authorities via determinate sentencing is an effective way to reduce prison populations, whereas the effect of placing constraints on sentencing authorities (i.e., presumptive guidelines) on incarceration rates depends on whether release authorities are similarly constrained. Other researchers have found that states that enacted certain types of sentencing guidelines had lower prison populations or incarceration rates (e.g., Marvell 1995; Nicholson-Crotty 2004; Sorenson and Stemen 2002; Spelman 2013), while truth in sentencing and three-strikes laws either did not affect prison populations or incarceration rates, or were associated with increases in them (e.g., Sorenson and Stemen 2002; Spelman 2013; Turner, Greenwood, Chen, and Fain 1999).

In a state-level study of prison crowding, Wooldredge (1996) found that states with longer minimum sentences for felony offenders, more mandatory prison terms, parole guidelines, and states with larger populations had more inmates serving longer sentences, which contributed to greater levels of crowding. However, in a subsequent study, Steiner and Wooldredge (2008) observed that focusing exclusively on states might ignore potential differences in crowding between facilities operating in the same state. Their bi-level analysis uncovered significant variation in crowding levels both within and between states. Steiner and Wooldredge (2008) found that states with a greater number of drug arrests had higher levels of crowding, while states with mandatory sentencing guidelines had lower levels of crowding. Neither voluntary sentencing guidelines, truth in sentencing, nor abolishing parole affected crowding levels. Steiner and Wooldredge (2008) also found that facilities within states that confined a greater density of medium security inmates had higher levels of crowding, whereas facilities with larger design capacities and facilities with a higher annual cost per inmate had lower levels of crowding.

Most of the extant research has focused on the influences of prison population or crowding; however, a few studies have assessed the predictors of jail crowding (e.g., D'Alessio and Stolzenberg 1995, 1997; Wooldredge 1991). Although these studies are limited in number and dated, several of them have uncovered that states with higher levels of prison crowding also have higher levels of crowding in the jails located in that state (e.g., D'Alessio and Stolzenberg 1997:). For instance, Wooldredge (1991) examined crowding in U.S. jails in 1983 and 1988. In addition to jails located in more urban areas and jails located in counties with larger court caseloads, he found that jails with a larger proportion of inmates awaiting transport to prison (presumably because of prison crowding) were more likely to be crowded. He also found that the degree of prison crowding in a state was associated with higher levels of jail crowding in 1988, owing to the increases in the degree of prison crowding that occurred between 1983 and 1988 (Wooldredge 1991).

Taken together, the evidence pertaining to the influences of correctional facility crowding suggests that changes in crime rates have little to no effect on correctional facility crowding. Increases in prison populations and crowding are primarily the result of changes in how states respond to crime, such as incarcerating a greater number of drug offenders, sentencing more people to prison per arrest, and imprisoning people for longer periods. Policies that restrict sentencing authorities (e.g., presumptive sentencing guidelines) and/or release authorities (e.g., determinate sentencing) have small, but not insignificant, effects on prison and jail populations. Prisons within states vary in their level of overcrowding, and states that experience higher levels of prison crowding also experience population increases, or crowding in their jails.

Consequences of Correctional Facility Crowding

The growth in the incarcerated population between 1970 and the early 2000s forced researchers and practitioners to consider correctional facility overcrowding as a potential environmental inhibitor to institutional safety (e.g., Camp, Gaes, Langan, and Saylor 2003; Gaes and McGuire 1985; Harer and Steffensmeier 1996; Steiner and Wooldredge 2009a; Wooldredge and Steiner 2009a). Overcrowding could be an environmental condition of a prison or jail that deprives inmates of satisfying particular needs (Camp et al. 2003; Steiner and Wooldredge 2009a). Inmates placed in such an environment may experience stress, anxiety, and/or seek illegitimate alternatives to satisfy needs (Paulus, McCain, and Cox 1985; Sykes 1958). Crowding might also promote opportunities for inmate misconduct (offending in prison and jail) and self-harm by interfering with staff supervision and limiting access to programs and resources that restrict inmates' exposure to situations conducive to offending, victimization, or self-harm (Steiner and Wooldredge 2009a). Reduced, or less effective, supervision could also increase stress and the risk of victimization among staff (Steiner and Wooldredge 2015; Steiner and Wooldredge 2017).

The bulk of the extant research pertaining to potential consequences of correctional facility crowding has focused on the link between crowding and inmate misconduct. Empirical findings across these studies are mixed, with studies finding positive, negative, and nonsignificant crowding effects on misconduct (e.g., Camp et al. 2003; Gaes and McGuire 1985; Harer and Steffensmeier 1996; Steiner and Wooldredge 2009b; Steiner, Butler, and Ellison 2014; Wooldredge, Griffin, and Pratt 2001; Wooldredge and Steiner 2009a). Recent meta-analyses of the crowding–misconduct relationship have also yielded different findings. Gendreau, Goggin and Law (1997) and Franklin, Franklin, and Pratt (2006) found a positive relationship between crowding and misconduct, whereas Goncalves, Goncalves, Martins, and Dirkwager (2014) found a negative relationship. The authors of each meta-analysis found that crowding had a relatively small effect on misconduct; however, the authors also found between-study heterogeneity in crowding effects (see also Steiner et al. 2014).

Differences across studies in the facility crowding–inmate misconduct relationship could be attributable to differences in the samples examined (e.g., inmates housed in federal facilities versus state facilities), the different levels of analysis at which these studies were conducted (individual versus aggregate), or differences in the measures of crowding or misconduct examined. Researchers have uncovered between-study variation in each of the aforementioned items (Steiner and Wooldredge 2009a). For instance, some researchers have measured crowding with objective measures such as a facility's population divided by its design capacity, while other researchers have measured inmates' perceptions of whether a facility was crowded. There are certainly advantages to each measurement strategy, but the effect of inmates' perceptions of whether a facility is crowded is likely to vary across studies; such perceptions are linked to inmates' background characteristics and institutional routines, each of which varies across the inmate populations confined in different facilities (e.g., Wooldredge 1997). Objective measures of crowding, on the other hand, are easier to replicate across studies, which reduces the possibility that differences in the characteristics of the inmate samples examined in these studies will contribute to differences in findings across studies using these measures.

Differences in how researchers have measured misconduct could also be causing the between-study differences in the facility crowding–inmate misconduct relationship. For instance, researchers typically measure misconduct using official or self-report data. Each approach has its strengths and limitations (see Steiner and Wooldredge 2014 for an overview), but the choice of measure could determine the direction and magnitude of the crowding–misconduct relationship. For example, Steiner and Wooldredge (2009a) hypothesized that crowding affects the level of supervision in a facility, which in turn, could affect the level of officially detected misconduct. In support of this idea, Steiner and Wooldredge (2014) found that crowding was positively related to self-reported assaults, but inversely related to officially detected assaults.

Researchers have also hypothesized that facility crowding may not have direct effects on inmate misconduct, but that crowding may have conditioning or indirect effects on misconduct (Steiner and Wooldredge 2009; Wooldredge and Steiner 2009). We have already discussed how crowding may indirectly affect misconduct via its effect on supervision, available programming, and so forth, though it is worth noting that we are unaware of any studies that have included an analysis of these potential indirect effects. Crowding could also condition the effect of other facility or individual characteristics. For instance, crowding could amplify the facility-level effect of a higher concentration of violent inmates on misconduct rates; this is because more volatile inmates (i.e., those incarcerated for violent offenses) might offend more frequently in crowded environments where they are more likely to be exposed to other antagonistic inmates in the absence of adequate supervision (owing to the crowding). Crowding might also amplify the effects of individual (inmate) characteristics on misconduct. If, for example, crowded environments provide greater opportunities for misconduct, then higher risk inmates might be more likely to offend in such environments. A handful of researchers have found evidence that the magnitude of the effects of risk factors such as age, prior criminal history, and prior abuse on misconduct are greater in prisons that are more crowded (e.g., Gillespie 2005; Wooldredge et al. 2001; Wooldredge and Steiner 2009), though further investigation of the possible conditioning effects of crowding is certainly needed.

Researchers have also examined consequences of facility crowding beside inmate misconduct, albeit to a lesser extent. Several studies have found that higher levels of crowding are associated with higher rates of suicide or natural deaths, while other studies have not found a relationship between crowding and these outcomes (e.g., Cox, Paulus, and McCain 1984; Dye 2010; Huey and McNulty 2005; Paulus, Cox, and McCain 1988; Wooldredge and Winfree 1992). A few researchers have found that inmates exposed to more crowded environments experience elevated levels of stress, blood pressure, and psychiatric commitments (e.g., Cox et al. 1984; Paulus et al. 1988). Evidence is mixed concerning the effects of crowding on officer stress; some studies have revealed that crowding is associated with higher levels of officer stress, while others have not found a relationship between crowding and stress (e.g., Martin, Lichtenstein, Jenkot, and Forde 2012; Steiner and Wooldredge 2015).

In sum, the extant research pertaining to the consequences of prison and jail crowding is inconclusive. Although a considerable amount of research has focused on determining the relationship between crowding and inmate misconduct, findings across these studies are mixed. Moreover, there are differences across these studies in the measures of crowding and misconduct examined that could be generating the heterogeneity in the study findings. Very few studies have examined potential indirect or conditioning effects of crowding on misconduct. Similarly, too few studies have examined the effect of crowding on other outcomes to draw any meaningful conclusions.

Discussion and Conclusion

After 50 years of relative stability, the U.S. incarceration rate increased five-fold between 1973 and 2007. Although the rate of incarceration has declined to some extent, the U.S. incarceration rate remains well above the previously stable rate for 1972 (Travis and Western 2014). The unparalleled growth in the number of persons entering prisons and jails in the U.S. contributed to overcrowding in many correctional facilities (Glaze & Parks 2012; Steiner and Wooldredge 2009a), and the inmate populations of many of these facilities are still above their design capacities (Bureau of Justice Statistics 2014; Carson 2015). In this chapter, we reviewed the scientific evidence pertaining to the influences of prison and jail populations, facility crowding, and consequences of overcrowding.

We found evidence that the increases in prison and jail populations and corresponding facility overcrowding were primarily due to changes in how states and the federal criminal justice system responded to crime. Specifically, the growth in the U.S. prison population was almost entirely attributable to increases in the incarceration rate for drug offenses, prison commitments per arrest, the length of prison sentences, and recommitments for parole violations (e.g., Blumstein and Beck 2005; Travis and Western 2014). We also found that policies that restrict the discretion of sentencing authorities (e.g., presumptive sentencing guidelines) and/or release authorities (e.g., determinate sentencing) have modest effects on levels of prison crowding. Finally, we observed that there is variation in the crowding levels of prisons within the same state, and states with higher levels of prison crowding also have higher inmate populations or levels of crowding in their jails.

Regarding the consequences of correctional facility crowding, we found inconclusive evidence pertaining to the effect of crowding on inmate misconduct (offending in prison or jail), though the between-study heterogeneity in crowding effects could be due to researchers' decisions related to the measurement of crowding or misconduct (see also Steiner and Wooldredge 2009). We also found some evidence that crowding may indirectly affect misconduct or condition the effects of other facility or inmate characteristics on misconduct, but too few studies have examined these potential indirect or conditioning effects of crowding on misconduct to draw meaningful conclusions. Finally, we found a handful of studies that have examined the effects of crowding on other outcomes (e.g., inmate and staff stress, suicide), but this evidence base is also too small to draw any conclusions.

Our review also uncovered a number of gaps and future directions for research pertaining to the causes and consequences of correctional facility crowding, but we think there are three focus areas that are most critical for both research and practice. First, researchers should determine whether specific levels of crowding correspond to different severity levels of problems resulting from crowding. Klofas, Stojkovic, and Kalinich (1992) found that crowding begins to affect facility operations when an inmate population reaches 80 percent of its design capacity. The U.S. Supreme Court recently determined that overcrowding could constitute cruel and unusual punishment by limiting a facility's ability to provide adequate medical and mental health care to the inmates (*Brown v. Plata* 2011). In rendering their decision, the Court ordered the state of California to reduce its prison population to 137.5 percent of its design capacity. It is not completely clear how the Court arrived at the 137.5 percent of design capacity threshold, but the figure has become a benchmark for other states. Future studies should investigate whether the 137.5 percent threshold or other crowding levels are meaningful standards for correctional administrators, and whether problems stemming from crowding lessen significantly once facility populations drop below those levels.

Second, researchers should continue to investigate the direct, indirect, and conditioning effects of facility crowding on different outcomes. Despite the size of the evidence base pertaining to the direct effect of crowding on misconduct, there are simply too many differences across these studies in terms of the levels of analysis at which these studies were conducted and the measures of crowding or misconduct examined in these studies to draw any conclusions. Future researchers should seek to develop a more consistent and reliable evidence base in order to inform policy and practice related to managing crowding levels. Steiner and Wooldredge (2009a) have offered some recommendations in this regard. Future researchers should also examine the indirect or conditioning effects of crowding on misconduct; too few studies have examined these effects to date. Finally, researchers should examine whether crowding impacts other outcomes beside misconduct. A handful of studies have examined crowding effects on inmate stress, self-harm, and other health problems, and a few studies have assessed crowding effects on staff. More research pertaining to these potential consequences of crowding is needed, however.

Third, the growth in prison populations and corresponding levels of crowding has leveled off in a number of states, and some states are experiencing reductions in their inmate populations (Carson 2015). Much of the research we discussed in this chapter focused on the influences of prison population growth. An equally important line of inquiry for future research is determining the factors that predict reductions in prison populations and corresponding crowding levels. A number of states have undertaken reforms designed to reduce their prison and jail populations (e.g., JFA Institute 2007; Mauer and Ghandnoosh 2014), but there have been few evaluations of whether any of these reforms work in both the short and long term. Future research should conduct rigorous examinations of the reform efforts that have commenced in some states in order to provide other states with an evidence base regarding what works to reduce facility crowding, and what does not.

Correctional facility overcrowding is a problem for at least some prison and/or jails in most states. Although we argued that the three focus areas that were previously mentioned are the most central to both research and practice in the immediate future, there are certainly other areas of research related to the influences of prison or jail populations, facility crowding, or the consequences of crowding that are worth pursuing. By providing this overview of the research related to these topics, we hope to stimulate further interest in the subject. It is only by continuing to study the causes and consequences of correctional facility crowding that we can get a better handle on the problem and inform the development of strategies designed to reduce crowding levels or ameliorate crowding effects.

Notes

1. Design capacity refers to the number of inmates that the prison architects intended for the facility. Overcrowding has also been determined using rated capacity—the number of inmates intended for a facility assigned by a rating official—instead of design capacity, but some prison and jail administrators have historically manipulated the former to give the impression that facilities can house more inmates than they were designed to accommodate (Rothman, 1980; Wooldredge, 1996; Zimring and Hawkins, 1991). The United States Supreme Court used design capacity when

they determined problems stemming from overcrowding violated inmates' Eighth Amendment rights (*Brown v. Plata* 2011).

2. Presumptive sentences provide a single recommended prison sentence within a range for each felony offense. The recommended sentence is based solely on the offense committed. Sentencing guidelines provide multiple recommended sentences for each offense class and a set of sentencing procedures designed to guide sentencing decisions. Recommended sentences under sentencing guidelines are typically determined by the severity of the offense and prior criminal history of the defendant. Presumptive guidelines require judges to impose the recommended sentence, whereas voluntary guidelines do not have formal legal authority to ensure that judges impose the recommended sentences. Determinate sentencing refers to the abolishment of discretionary parole (Stemen and Rengifo 2011).

References

Blumstein, Alfred, and Allen Beck. 2005. "Reentry as a Transient State Between Liberty and Recommitment." Pp. 50–79 in *Prisoner Reentry and Crime in America*, edited by Jeremy Travis and Christy A. Visher. New York: Cambridge University Press.

Brown v. Plata, 131 S. Ct. 1910, 1931 (2011).

Bureau of Justice Statistics. 2014. *Annual Survey of Jails, ICPSR36274-v1*. Ann Arbor, MI: Inter-university Consortium for Political and Social Research.

Camp, Scott D., Gerald G. Gaes, Neil P. Langan, and William G. Saylor. 2003. "The Influence of Prisons on Inmate Misconduct: A Multilevel Investigation." *Justice Quarterly* 20(3): 501–533.

Carson, E. Ann. 2015. *Prisoners in 2014*. Washington, DC: U.S. Department of Justice.

Cox, Vernon C., Paul B. Paulus, and Garvin McCain. 1984. "Prison Crowding Research: The Relevance for Prison Housing Standards and a General Approach Regarding Crowding Phenomena." *American Psychologist* 39(10): 1148–1160.

D'Alessio, Stewart J., and Lisa Stolzenberg. 1995. "The Impact of Sentencing Guidelines on Jail Incarceration in Minnesota." *Criminology* 33: 283–302.

D'Alessio, Stewart J., and Lisa Stolzenberg. 1997. "The Effect of Available Capacity on Jail Incarceration: An Empirical Test of Parkinson's Law." *Journal of Criminal Justice* 25(4): 279–288.

Dye, Meredith Huey. 2010. "Deprivation, Importation, and Prison Suicide: Combined Effects of Institutional Conditions and Inmate Composition." *Journal of Criminal Justice* 38(4): 796–806.

Franklin, Travis W., Cortney A. Franklin, and Travis C. Pratt. 2006. "Examining the Empirical Relationship between Prison Crowding and Inmate Misconduct: A Meta-Analysis of Conflicting Research Results." *Journal of Criminal Justice* 34(4): 401–412.

Gaes, Gerald G., and William J. McGuire. 1985. "Prison Violence: The Contribution of Crowding Versus Other Determinants of Prison Assault Rates." *Journal of Research in Crime and Delinquency* 22(1): 41–65.

Gendreau, Paul, Claire E. Goggin, and Moira A. Law. 1997. "Predicting Prison Misconducts." *Criminal Justice and Behavior* 24(4): 414–431.

Gillespie, Wayne. 2005. "A Multilevel Model of Drug Abuse inside Prison." *The Prison Journal* 85(2): 223–246.

Glaze, Lauren E., and Erika Parks. 2012. *Correctional Populations in the United States, 2011*. Washington, DC: U.S. Department of Justice.

Gonçalves, Leonel C., Rui A. Gonçalves, Carla Martins, and Anja J. E. Dirkzwager. 2014. "Predicting Infractions and Health Care Utilization in Prison: A Meta-Analysis." *Criminal Justice and Behavior* 41(8): 921–942.

Harer, Miles D., and Darrell J. Steffensmeier. 1996. "Race and Prison Violence." *Criminology* 34(3): 323–355.

Huey, Meredith P., and Thomas L. McNulty. 2005. "Institutional Conditions and Prison Suicide: Conditional Effects of Deprivation and Overcrowding." *The Prison Journal* 85(4): 490–514.

JFA Institute. 2007. *Unlocking America: Why and How to Reduce America's Prison Population*. Washington, DC: The JFA Institute.

Klofas, John, Stan Stojkovic, and David Kalinich. 1992. "The Meaning of Correctional Crowding: Steps toward an Index of Severity." *Crime and Delinquency* 38(2): 171–188.

Martin, Joseph L., Bronwen Lichtenstein, Robert B. Jenkot, and David R. Forde. 2012. "'They Can Take Us Over Any Time They Want': Correctional Officers' Responses to Prison Crowding." *The Prison Journal* 92(1): 88–105.

Marvell, Thomas B. 1995. "Sentencing Guidelines and Prison Population Growth." *Journal of Criminal Law and Criminology* 85(3): 696–709.

Marvell, Thomas B., and Carlisle E. Moody. 1996. "Determinate Sentencing and Abolishing Parole: The Long-Term Impacts on Prisons and Crime." *Criminology* 34(1): 107–128.

Mauer, Marc, and Nazgol Ghandnoosh. 2014. *Fewer Prisoners, Less Crime: A Tale of Three States.* Washington, DC: The Sentencing Project.

Nicholson-Crotty, Sean. 2004. "The Impact of Sentencing Guidelines on State-Level Sanctions: An Analysis over Time." *Crime & Delinquency* 50(3): 395–411.

Paulus, Paul, Garvin McCain, and Vernon Cox. 1985. "The Effects of Crowding in Prisons and Jails." Pp. 113–134 in *Reactions to Crime: The Public, the Police, Courts, and Prisons*, edited by Judith Gunn and David Farrington. New York: John Wiley & Sons.

Paulus, Paul B., Vernon C. Cox, and Garvin McCain. 1988. *Prison Crowding: A Psychological Perspective.* New York: Springer-Verlag.

Rothman, David. 1980. *Conscience and Convenience: The Asylum and Its Alternatives in Progressive America.* Boston, MA: Little Brown.

Sorensen, Jon, and Don Stemen. 2002. "The Effect of State Sentencing Policies on Incarceration Rates." *Crime & Delinquency* 48(3): 456–475.

Spelman, William. 2013. "Prisons and Crime, Backwards in High Heels." *Journal of Quantitative Criminology* 29(4): 643–674.

Steiner, Benjamin, H. Daniel Butler, and Jared Ellison. 2014. "Causes and correlates of prison inmate misconduct: A systematic review of the evidence." *Journal of Criminal Justice* 42(6): 462–470.

Steiner, Benjamin, and John Wooldredge. 2008. "Comparing State-Versus Facility-Level Effects on Crowding in US Correctional Facilities." 54(2): 259–290.

Steiner, Benjamin, and John Wooldredge. 2009a. "Rethinking the Link between Institutional Crowding and Inmate Misconduct." *The Prison Journal* 89(2): 205–233.

Steiner, Benjamin, and John Wooldredge. 2009b. "Individual and Environmental Effects on Assaults and Nonviolent Rule Breaking by Women in Prison." *Journal of Research in Crime and Delinquency* 46(4): 437–467.

Steiner, Benjamin, and John Wooldredge. 2015. "Individual and Environmental Sources of Work Stress among Prison Officers." *Criminal Justice and Behavior* 42(8): 800–818.

Steiner, Benjamin, and John Wooldredge. 2017. "Individual and Environmental Influences on Prison Officer Safety." *Justice Quarterly* 34(2): 324–349.

Stemen, Don, and Andres Rengifo. 2011. "Policies and Imprisonment: The Impact of Structured Sentencing and Determinate Sentencing on State Incarceration Rates, 1978–2004." *Justice Quarterly* 28(1): 174–201.

Sykes, G.M. 1958. *Society of Captives: A Study of a Maximum Security Prison.* Princeton, NJ: Princeton University Press.

Travis, Jeremy, and Bruce Western. 2014. *The Growth of Incarceration in the United States: Exploring Causes and Consequences.* Washington, DC: The National Academies Press.

Turner, Susan, Peter Greenwood, Elizabeth Chen, and Terry Fain. 1999. "The Impact of Truth-in-Sentencing and Three Strikes Legislation: Prison Populations, State Budgets, and Crime Rates." *Stanford Law and Policy Review 11*(1): 75–91.

Western, Bruce. 2006. *Punishment and Inequality in America.* New York: Russell Sage Foundation.

Wooldredge, John D. 1991. "Identifying Possible Sources of Inmate Crowding in Us Jails." *Journal of Quantitative Criminology* 7(4): 373–386.

Wooldredge, John D. 1996. "Research Note: A State-Level Analysis of Sentencing Policies and Inmate Crowding in State Prisons." *Crime & Delinquency* 42(3): 456–466.

Wooldredge, John. 1997. "Explaining Variation in Perceptions of Inmate Crowding." *The Prison Journal* 77(1): 27–40.

Wooldredge, John, Timothy Griffin, and Travis Pratt. 2001. "Considering Hierarchical Models for Research on Inmate Behavior: Predicting Misconduct with Multilevel Data." *Justice Quarterly* 18(1): 203–31.

Wooldredge, John D., and L. Thomas Winfree. 1992. "An Aggregate-Level Study of Inmate Suicides and Deaths Due to Natural Causes in U.S. Jails." *Journal of Research in Crime and Delinquency* 29(4): 466–479.

Zimring, Franklin and Gordon Hawkins. 1991. *The Scale of Imprisonment*. Chicago, IL: University of Chicago Press.

32 Inmate Code and Prison Culture

Eileen M. Ahlin, Don Hummer, and Daniela Barberi

Introduction

Inmate violence and adaptations to prison life via the inmate code are depicted quite vividly in popular culture, including movies (e.g., *Shawshank Redemption, Attica*), television shows (e.g., *Orange is the New Black*), and first-person accounts (e.g., *In the Belly of the Beast*). Scholarly literature on the topic is equally powerful, detailing the inter-workings of prison life often through the qualitative narratives of inmates and correctional officers that demonstrate how prisons—a total institution where all aspects of inmates' lives are governed by the state or federal government (see Goffman 1961)—operate and routinely maintain order among those who were convicted of violating the social contract. Some of the earliest scholarly writings on the inmate code and prison culture can be dated to 1940 when Donald Clemmer wrote "*The Prison Community*". This important piece was further developed in 1962 when sociologists John Irwin (a former inmate) and Donald Cressey described how inmates adapt to the prison environment using the skills and attitudes already possessed by those convicted of crimes. These classic writings shaped the academic study of the inmate code and prison culture; however, Garland and Wilson's study (2013) evidenced a problem in this line of research. As the authors mentioned, research about inmates' belief system and adaptations to prison life is in dire need of updating. The inmate code and prison culture is currently under studied in the modern era. Much has changed in prisons and among offenders since the original inmate code and prison culture studies were published in the mid-twentieth century and it is not clear whether the classical literature applies to prisons and their inmates in contemporary times. According to Trammell (2009a: 748), the prison setting of today is substantially different than prisons of the past: "American prisons now hold ten times more inmates than they did in 1974 and this incarceration trend is unprecedented in the history of the United States." To frame the current review of literature on the inmate code and prison violence, we begin with a contextualization of the current demographics of inmates in the U.S. to examine the evolution of the prison setting and how it has changed in recent history.

Current Inmate Population

In this section we briefly compare the demographics of the federal inmate population managed by the Bureau of Prisons (BOP) and state inmate population for the years 2007 and 2014. The earlier time frame of 2007 was chosen because a large proportion of the studies of the twenty-first century about the inmate code were completed before 2007 and contemporary literature brought the field up to date in the 2010s. Filling this temporal absence in the literature by highlighting changes in the inmate population can contribute to a better understanding of the current studies on inmate code and prison violence and,

Table 32.1 Comparison of Sentenced Inmates, 2007 and 2014

	2007			*2014*		
Total	*Inmate Population*	*Federal Inmates*	*State Inmates*	*Inmate Population*	*Federal Inmates*	*State Inmates*
Total	1,532,851	179,204	1,353,647	1,508,636	191,374	1,317,262
Gender						
Male	1,483,896	186,280	1,297,616	1,402,404	178,814	1,223,590
Female	114,420	13,338	101,082	106,232	12,560	93,672
Race						
White	521,900			506,600		
Black	586,200			539,500		
Hispanic	318,800			326,500		
Other	105,900			136,100		
Offense		(%)	(%)		(%)	(%)
Violent		8.7	51.2		7.3	53.2*
Property		5.7	19.6		6.0	19.3*
Drug		53.2	20.2		50.1	15.7*
Public Order		31.4	7.6		35.9	11.0*

Source: Bureau of Justice Statistics data from West and Sabol, 2008 and Carson, 2015.
*Offense data were for 2013.

more importantly, frame the present review of the historical and more recent literature on the inmate code.

At the end of 2007, the BOP housed 199,618[1] inmates in federal facilities (West and Sabol 2008). By year-end of 2014, that number had increased to 210,567 (Carson 2015). Though the federal numbers pale in comparison to the total number of state inmates, there was a decrease in the state inmate population over this time frame. In 2007, there were 1,397,217 inmates housed in state prisons, and this number had reduced by over 46,000 to 1,350,958 by the end of 2014 (Carson 2015). Turning now to the changing characteristics of inmates in 2007 and 2014, we focus on those who have been sentenced.[2] Looking at the total number of sentenced inmates, the state prison population is decreasing, while the federal inmate population is on the rise (see Table 32.1). It should be noted that the reduction in sentenced state inmates may reflect the current budget crises facing many jurisdictions rather than a true decrease in crime. In recent years, states have been forced to adjust their correctional policies to address the overcrowding experienced in their facilities, with more courts and correctional agencies opting for alternatives to incarceration for less serious offenders. Many prisons are releasing their lower-risk offenders (or opting for non-incarcerative punishments at sentencing) and reserving prison for the most egregious offenders, including those convicted of violent crimes. This is evidenced in the slight increase of violent offenders and decrease in drug offenders among sentenced state inmates in 2014 compared to 2007 (Table 32.1). This modest rise in the number of inmates who were convicted of violent crimes is an interesting trend to consider. Despite a 10-year decrease in the violent crime rate throughout the U.S. (Federal Bureau of Investigation 2014), the percentage of inmates serving prison sentences for violent crimes is up slightly from 51.2 percent in 2007 to 53.2 percent in 2013. Again, this change is perhaps best explained by the recent policy shift toward decarceration for less serious offenders.

Another interesting development during this time period is the increase in the number of inmates whose ethnicity is reported as Hispanic. This demographic change may mirror the increase in Latino/Latina persons in the U.S. population in general (see Passel, Cohn, and Lopez 2011). However, the uptick in the number of Hispanic inmates should be closely monitored as the U.S. Census estimates that by 2060 persons with a Hispanic ethnicity will constitute the majority of the U.S. population with 1 in 3 residents identifying as Latino/Latina (U.S. Census Bureau 2012). This shift in the race and ethnicity of the U.S. population may become more prominently reflected in correctional facilities.

Given these changes to the demographic landscape of the U.S. population and residents of its carceral facilities between 2007 and 2014, we question whether the current understanding of the inmate code, which was developed primarily with data from White and Black inmates, is appropriate for the new dynamics in modern prisons. An increase in the number of inmates who are Hispanic and the move towards decarcerating less violent offenders while retaining violent offenders suggests that it is time for scholars to turn their attention to these demographic shifts and how such changes may affect the experiences of inmates. Let us be clear—the data do not suggest any link (direct or indirect) between the increases in Hispanic inmates and violent offenders serving prison sentences. These changes are perhaps better explained by the decrease in nonviolent offenders behind bars and the increase of Hispanics in the general population. However, the joint influx of Hispanic inmates and retention, or additional increase of violent offenders behind bars suggests that the synergy of prison life may be changing. As such, this brief overview of current inmate characteristics serves as context as we explore the historical evolution of the inmate code, and consider future directions for its refinement and further development. After reviewing in the following sections the major perspectives on the inmate code, inmate adherence to the code, and applicability of the code to women inmates, we return to this discussion on current inmate characteristics in the conclusion to consider how correctional management practices and institutional policy are inherently linked to the inmate code and should be updated to reflect the evolving attributes of inmates.

Inmate Code

While there is some debate about whether there is an actual "inmate code"—a set of inmate rules formed to forge against the official administration and govern inmate behavior—there is ample discussion about how it is formed. Scholars take various approaches to studying the inmate code; often referring to it by different labels. It has been discussed primarily as the inmate code, though it has also been viewed as adaptations of the code of the street, labeled convict code or convict identity, and more generically recognized as a means of informal social control in prisons. Because of this variation in monikers different definitions also abound, though it can be broadly conceptualized as "informal rules about acceptable behavior and the consequences for failing to act accordingly" (Copes, Brookman, and Brown 2013: 841). While this definition brings together different factors from various perspectives, these codes and rules are very subjective and can be interpreted in different manners—not only by scholars, but also by inmates themselves (Copes et al. 2013; Irwin and Cressey 1962; Mears, Stewart, Siennick, and Simons 2013; Palermo 2011; Steiner, Butler, and Ellison 2014; Trammell 2009a; Wellford 1967).

Given this subjectivity surrounding the inmate code, we highlight the dominant perspectives in this chapter. While the concept of the inmate code is vast, it is primarily examined using two lenses: generation of the inmate code and use of the inmate code. First, we consider how the inmate code is developed by exploring three main theoretical perspectives on its development—deprivation, importation, and inmate management—to determine whether it arises from inside prison or begins in the outside world and is then transported behind walls. Second, we examine how it is adopted, violated, and followed by inmates and correctional officers to assert and maintain control over the prison environment.

Development of the Inmate Code

There are three primary theoretical explanations of the development of the inmate code: deprivation theory, importation theory, and the management perspective (Steiner et al. 2014). Together, these perspectives provide a well-rounded explanation of how the inmate code can be conceptualized. The major tenets and key literature on each theory are explicated below.

Deprivation theory

Deprivation theory can be summarized as the methods inmates use to reduce the pains of imprisonment through the incorporation of a new social system (see Sykes 1958). Deprivation theory purports that an inmate subculture is formed in prisons in response to the many deprivations experienced during prison life. Sykes (1958) identified these as the pains of imprisonment, which include deprivations of liberty, goods and services, heterosexual relationships, autonomy, and security. This theoretical perspective first surfaced around the mid 1900s. For example, one of the first scholars who discussed how individuals behave in a prison environment was the sociologist Donald Clemmer (1940). He described how inmates go through a process call *prisonization*. This process, according to Clemmer, is "the taking on in greater or less degree of the folkways, mores, customs, and general culture of the penitentiary" (as cited in Wellford 1967: 197). Later in 1961, Wheeler introduced the idea that the inmate code was a response of incapacitated individuals to mitigate the pains of imprisonment, meaning that those who adopted the inmate code were less susceptible to the prisonization process.

Building on this new literature, in the late 1960s, criminologist Charles Wellford identified two characteristics that must be analyzed when the inmate code is being explored: first, the rules established by the institution and, second, the norms of the inmate population itself. However, according to Wellford (1967), adherence to the inmate code means that an individual must reject the administrative rules, suggesting that these two previous characteristics are mutually exclusive and do not overlap. As such, an inmate can only adopt the institution code or the inmate code. In his study, Wellford pointed out two different though very poignant conclusions about the inmate code circa the late 1960s. On one hand, Wellford found that an inmate's phase of their "institutional career" (whether the inmate is experiencing his or her first contact with the criminal justice system or whether they had been incarcerated before, as well as the number of prior prison terms) and the "criminal social type" (roles that inmates acquire, such as "antisocial-inmate" or "prosocial-inmate") were related to an individual's decision to adopt the inmate code. Alternatively, he suggested that the adoption of the inmate code is not uniform because it is primarily organized by roles or levels inside the inmate community (e.g., first level are the core leaders with strict adoption of the code, though inmates at the third level participate occasionally, but do not consider themselves members of the group and do not routinely abide by the inmate code as the core members would).

A more contemporary study analyzed how the inmate code is formed and functions within the modern prison environment. In Trammell's study of California inmates, she found that inmates perceive the prison environment as an organized life and view the inmate code as a "set of rules that help regulate inmate behavior" (2009a: 756). Trammell also described how following the inmate code can lead inmates to adapt a convict identity, "which means doing solid time and acting tough" (2009a: 757). She suggested that the inmate code is generated by gangs who establish rules for inmates that are then enforced by the group members. The author pointed out that gangs and leaders are responsible for creating an inmate hierarchy. This order of power provides inmates with basic rules on how to behave and proffers an understanding that their actions may not be understood individually, and will be interpreted primarily as part of a group or a gang affiliation. Therefore, the behavior that an inmate displays inside prison reflects the group or gang to which he or she belongs. In addition, Trammell highlighted the connection between the inmate code and the illegal drug business—a more prevalent issue in the twenty-first century than when the inmate code was first uncovered by scholars. In this sense, Trammell's study provides insight into how the existing inmate code is further developed and shaped after incarceration begins, and how it is regulated by inmates within the prison hierarchy; with the similar goal of validating a positive convict identity in the social system of imprisonment.

Importation Theory

Importation theory is another perspective on the development of the inmate code. Contrary to the deprivation model, importation theory suggests that inmate subcultures are brought into prison from the outside and that this culture is shaped by factors independent from the prison environment. Steiner and colleagues (2014) remind us that prison is not a closed system and its inter-workings are influenced by pre-institutional characteristics, norms, and beliefs; suggesting that these factors are brought into prison by inmates. Sociologists John Irwin and Donald Cressey (1962) used importation theory as an explanation of the inmate code by acknowledging that norms inside prisons are not necessarily born behind bars. They argued that the manifestation of prison norms or the inmate code is not homogenous, suggesting that some inmates had values congruent with the inmate code before they were incapacitated and thus brought those predilections with them into the prison environment. Irwin and Cressey (1962) contended that criminal subcultures determine some belief and conduct codes, while they also explained that these subcultures are not causally linked to the act of being imprisoned or the incarceration experience. Contrary to the deprivation theory, they propose that the inmate code and subculture is not developed during periods of imprisonment, rather it is a manifestation of inmates' behavior, norms, and beliefs that they held prior to prison.

The idea that the inmate code is generated in the streets rather than in prison was elucidated by Elijah Anderson's (1999) ethnographic work published in his book *Code of the Street*. Using a structural and subcultural explanation of violence in inner-cities, Anderson suggested that youth use violence as a way of gaining prestige and respect, and the street code is invoked as a means to enforce informal social controls over situations. If youth experience any violation directed against their sense of respect, the disparaged individual must respond with force to ensure the recovery of their respect. More recently, Mears et al. (2013) studied how this code of the street is the main determinant in whether individuals adopt the inmate code. They examined how the street code continues during periods of imprisonment, suggesting that the street code is "an informal sets of beliefs that are learned during childhood and govern how some individuals . . . act" (Mears et al. 2013: 699). Analogously, the inmate code also governs behaviors and Mears and colleagues propose that this code is born outside the prison environment and can directly influence inmate behavior inside it. Like the inmate code, the street code includes the incorporation of a tough identity and securing the respect of others. Therefore, Mears et al. suggested that individuals who enter the prison setting and have a high adherence to the street code will adopt the inmate code easily, thereby also increasing violence during incarceration. This adherence to the code is likely fluid, and inmate identities can fluctuate to fit the situation (see Trammell 2012).

Management Perspective

The final theoretical explanation of the inmate code takes a different viewpoint and is related to prison management and administrative actions. According to the management perspective, inmates' behavior in institutions depends on how the prison is controlled and governed (Steiner et al. 2014). A classic example of how prison management and administrative actions influence the behavior of inmates is sociologist Mark Colvin's (1992) study of the prison riot in the Penitentiary in New Mexico. Colvin suggested that imprisonment creates specific psychological and environmental conditions in which a balance is established between the staff at the institution and the inmates. When the prison environment is stable, inmates form their own society to self-regulate their behavior and assist correctional officers with inmate management. However, when security lapses, overcrowding occurs, and there are changes in expectations and implementation of correctional officer control practices, a crisis, such as a riot, may ensue. The inmate code is not necessarily the opposite of the administrative norms, but instead lives parallel to it and functions to maintain equilibrium between the needs of inmates and the control sought by correctional officers. Therefore, if this balance and sense of wellbeing is broken by the institution, the inmate code will also suffer negative consequences; as evidenced in the New Mexico prison riot.

Similarly, Worley (2011) explored the role of informants in the inmate–guard relationship. He suggested that correctional officers may actively cultivate in the inmates the idea of becoming informants by reporting any misbehavior in the institution and especially those related to correctional employees' behavior. Worley proposed that an inmate who is assigned an "informant status" can lead to a hazardous situation because it can lead to mistrust, as well as disruption and chaos between inmates and guards. Worley's (2011) findings exemplify how the balance promoted by the management perspective is important in the prison setting. By allowing inmates to maintain some control over their social interactions, they assist correctional officers in keeping a safe and peaceful environment. A disruption in this management style can result in negative imbalance between any of the two parties while also threatening the placidity and balance that the inmate rules serve to establish.

In summary, these three theories provide varied explanations about the development and execution of the inmate code. Equally important, it cannot be denied that some scholars propose that the inmate code cannot be so neatly parsed into a taxonomic categorization. For example, Copes and colleagues (2013) suggested that the code can be explained as an "after-the-fact rationalization" of behavior; or in simpler words, the code is a concept that inmates use to justify their actions inside prison. Similarly, Victor Hassine (2007), an inmate turned prison reform advocate and author, refuted the idea that there is one specific inmate code, suggesting there are likely multiple codes reflecting varied inmate cultures, beliefs, and behaviors exhibited prior to incarceration. Other scholars support the idea that the inmate code is a compilation of deprivation and importation and that the inmate code may be best categorized using an integration model (Pollock 1997; Winfree, Newbold, and Tubb 2002). Therefore, the three main perspectives described here cannot explain the inmate code in its entirety, nor are they the only approaches to this topic.

Assuming, Breaking, or Denying the Inmate Code

We now move away from the theoretical underpinnings of the inmate code and turn to how the inmate code is adopted, violated, and overlooked by inmates and correctional officers as a means for asserting and maintaining control in correctional facilities. Even though the inmate code can be interpreted in multiple ways (Copes et al. 2013; Irwin and Cressey 1962; Palermo 2011; Mears et al. 2013; Steiner et al. 2014; Trammell 2009a; Wellford 1967), there are some clear patterns in how the inmate code is adopted, broken, or denied. In practice, two pillars of the inmate code are respect and refusal to report the wrongdoings ("snitch") of other inmates.

Overall, there seems to be substantial evidence that the inmate code is primarily adopted out of concern for *respect*. When someone inside the prison (inmate or staff) disrespects someone else, it is viewed by the inmate population as "breaking the rules" or breaking the inmate code. Respect coexists with the idea of social reputation inside prison (Copes et al. 2013; Mears et al. 2013). Retaliations resulting from disrespect can vary depending on the hierarchy of the people involved; though the most common way to balance an injustice is a physical fight between inmates. Inmate groups and hierarchy within those groups play a role in many of the situations regarding respect. For example, lower-status inmates may first ask group leaders or a higher-status inmate for guidance or permission before they retaliate against somebody who has aggrieved them (Trammell 2009a). These dynamics are important to understand because even if disrespect occurs, which is technically a violation of the inmate code, it does not mean that inmates will always react negatively to it or seek to right the wrong through violence. Inmates who follow the code are often careful to avoid creating a larger problem between individuals or groups, which would be more likely to occur if they responded to every disrespectful event. In the same way, inmates can also decide individually not to retaliate because they do not want to make their own legal situation worse or create more painful situations to their families (Copes et al. 2013; Trammell 2009a).

The inmate code also dictates that inmates do not "snitch" on each other. *No-snitching* means that inmates should not get into another inmate's "business" and should not divulge another inmate's wrongdoings to others, particularly the correctional officers. According to the code, inmates should mind their own business (e.g., do your own time), and not get involved with others' lives or affairs. To follow the inmate code, inmates generally want to stay away from prison staff and most often refuse to talk to them about any concerns related to inmate relations. However, some inmates may talk to the staff about hazardous issues and they will justify their actions and not follow the code in those situations. As Copes et al. (2013) suggest, inmates must consider whether a situation is hazardous to another inmate or themselves. If someone's life is in danger, the no-snitching requirement of the inmate code can be overlooked; suggesting that, in certain situations, human life is more important than the code.

This suggests that like many other doctrines, interpretation and responses to the code are subjective, and do not follow a hard-and-fast rule structure. Breaking the code can be justified depending on the circumstances. Likewise, this lack of general adherence to the code illuminates the existence of another group of inmates: those who do not adhere to the inmate code and whose behavior is not controlled by the rules (Copes et al. 2013; Steiner et al. 2014). This group of inmates purposefully defy the code because they do not feel that the code has any power over them, and therefore, they do not consciously act according to the inmate code. While the inmate code is prevalent, some inmates prefer to follow their own beliefs, those of their family, or would rather adopt a religious perspective to govern behavior (Copes et al. 2013). There is little published data on this group of inmates and how they manage the day-to-day prison life independent from the inmate code.

The Inmate Code, Offender Management, and Prison Culture

How the inmate code manifests within a particular correctional facility is determined primarily by the dyadic relationship between inmates and staff, as well as the degree of legitimacy afforded to management by both groups. It may be a vehicle to solidarity of inmates in an organizational culture characterized by conflict with staff and/or management, or it could serve as a means for acculturating new inmates into a positive prison culture (Goodstein, MacKenzie, and Shotland 1984). For example, a number of studies have shown that poor prison management is a significant predictor of inmate-on-inmate assaults, inmate-on-staff assaults, and generalized disorder (Byrne and Hummer 2007; Day, Brauer, and Butler 2015; McCorkle, Miethe, and Drass 1995; Ricciardelli and Sit 2016) or as an informal manual on everyday rules as part of the general population of inmates (Copes et al. 2013).

For many decades, the inmate code has been viewed as an essential governing mechanism in U.S. prisons, given the need to maintain institutional control in overcrowded facilities. Pervasive staffing issues, ranging from inadequate numbers of line employees to disproportionate numbers of inexperienced correctional officers coupled with the nature of the "total institution" have also necessitated a cooperative approach to institutional management, even if not formally acknowledged. Mass incarceration led high-security level facilities to rely more heavily on coercive methods of control. While more coercive management strategies are not necessarily anathema to coexistence with inmate self-regulation, such tactics are often present in facilities with greater violence and disorder problems, as inmates perceive these administrative attempts to maintain social order as heightening levels of stress and tension emerge within the population (Ricciardelli and Sit 2016). The twin concepts of "legitimacy" and "fairness" are critical components of a positive prison culture (Liebling 2011; Sparks and Bottoms 2008). When present, application of the inmate code develops in a layered manner, with inmates thoroughly engaged in self-regulation of their ranks within the institution, but with an overriding knowledge that administrative rules and regulations take precedence. If management is not seen as fair, and does not hold legitimacy with inmates (or line staff), the inmate code comes to be viewed as the final word on institutional life, and its existence vis-à-vis formal administrative rules becomes more confrontational and antagonistic.

Considering the aforementioned issues, the key question is whether the inmate code, within a context-specific form of shared institutional management, can be beneficial to prison administration. The answer to that question is neither simple, static, nor generalizable. What the literature makes clear is that the inmate code adapts to the management strategies in place at specific facilities, and in facilities that are more likely to employ remunerative control mechanisms, the inmate code serves to diminish violence and other undesirable behaviors (Ricciardelli and Sit 2016). Ultimately, the tone the inmate code adopts is dependent upon the perceived legitimacy of prison administration and management, and draconian efforts to suppress the impact of the inmate code on daily institutional life tend to be counter-productive.

Women's Code and Culture

Most studies about the inmate code and prison culture have focused on male inmates and/or correctional officers. Males are a practical focal point in the literature considering that the male population of inmates is significantly more substantial than female inmates. Because the literature on the inmate code is male-centric, there is a paucity of literature on female inmates' adaptation and reactions, despite studies suggesting that men and women interpret the code differently (see Trammell, Raby, Anderson, Hampton, and Stickney 2014). Contrary to females, male inmates are more focused on maintaining a balance between prisoners using their power as leaders and gang members to preserve inmate control, while also ensuring that adherence to the code reflects their toughness. Allegiance to the inmate code for male prisoners is also more corporeal and visceral. When retaliation has to be executed, males will use physical violence to keep the balance (Copes et al. 2013; Mears et al. 2013; Steiner et al. 2014).

Conversely, female inmates adapt and adhere to the inmate code without physical violence as a main objective (Trammell et al. 2014). Unlike their male counterparts, female inmates create pseudo-families in prison. Where male gangs have hierarchy levels, female families display figures and roles congruent with the traditional nuclear family (mother, father, and siblings) regardless of the fact that all the inmates are of the same gender. These families have the goal of serving as a replacement to biological families from whom inmates were separated when they were incarcerated. These family relationships are quite strong and serve a larger role than aiding in protection from guards and other inmates or the formation of friendships. Usually prison families are created between inmates who belong to the same neighborhood or cities. Members of these family groups will discuss post-release plans and those who have parental roles will serve as the disciplinarian and leadership figurehead. However, one important difference between males and females and their adaption of the inmate code is how they exact retaliation against other inmates. While male inmates generally engage in physical violence to redress disrespect from another inmate, women use *relational violence* to establish reputation, power, and control in the interpersonal relationships they have formed in the prison setting. This type of psychological violence aims to "ruin relationships and sever social ties" (Trammell et al. 2014: 268) and it is never physical. Relational violence is evidenced through the use of gossip, spreading of rumors, and ostracism to damage another's self-esteem and family relationships. It also creates social isolation. Female inmates prefer to use such relational violence rather than physical violence in response to any kind of disrespectful or threatening situation because, according to Trammell (2009b), they perceive this violence as more damaging and longer lasting than physical violence.

Conclusions

In this chapter we highlighted the changing demographics in the prison population followed by a discussion of the historical development of the inmate code, how the inmate code fits into the overall prison institutional culture, and how it has been adapted by female inmates. Given the decrease in the number of females in federal and state prisons, the critical focus of inquiry becomes Hispanic offenders and violent inmates. The shift in inmate population characteristics suggests a need by scholars to revisit the inmate code with systematic research that is mindful of what may become the new typical inmate, how such changes may alter our thinking about the inmate code, as well as how it is applied by inmates and correctional management teams. It is clear that additional research is necessary to address these changing demographics and determine how the inmate code is being used and adapted to serve the evolving prison culture. The current review of the literature serves as a base for future studies and assists in our understanding of the role of the inmate code and how its purpose is not only multifunctional but also malleable. It would be interesting to assess how the code is presently being used in conjunction with the focus on the decarceration of non-violent offenders in efforts to reduce prison overcrowding, and how it will be adapted and evolve as the inmate profile continues to shift.

Notes

1. This number reflects both inmates who were sentenced to a prison term and those who were awaiting a sentencing disposition.
2. Sentenced inmates in prison are less transient than those awaiting sentencing and their numbers are greater. Unlike jails, most offenders in prisons are sentenced (about 97 percent; Carson 2015), and are not being held on pretrial detention pending a hearing or awaiting final sentencing.

References

Anderson, Elijah. 1999. *Code of the Street*. New York: WW Norton.

Byrne, James. M., and Don Hummer. 2007. "In Search of the 'Tossed Salad Man' (and Others Involved in Prison Violence): New Strategies for Predicting and Controlling Violence in Prison." *Aggression and Violent Behavior* 12(5): 531–541.

Carson, E. Ann. 2015. *Prisoners in 2014*. U.S. Department of Justice, Office of Justice Programs. *Bureau of Justice Statistics*.

Clemmer, Donald. 1940. *The Prison Community*. New York: Rinehart.

Colvin, Mark. 1992. *The Penitentiary in Crisis: From Accommodation to Riot in New Mexico*. SUNY Press.

Copes, Heith, Fiona Brookman, and Anastasia Brown. 2013. "Accounting for Violations of the Convict Code." *Deviant Behavior* 34(10): 841–858.

Day, Jacob C., Jonathan R. Brauer, and H. Daniel Butler. 2015. "Coercion and Social Support Behind bars: Testing an Integrated Theory of Misconduct and Resistance in U.S. Prisons." *Criminal Justice and Behavior* 42(2): 133–155.

Federal Bureau of Investigation. 2014. *Crime in the United States, 2013*. Washington, DC: Federal Bureau of Investigation.

Garland, Brett, and Gabrielle Wilson. 2013. "Prison Inmates' Views of Whether Reporting Rape is the Same as Snitching: An Exploratory Study and Research Agenda." *Journal of Interpersonal Violence* 28(6): 1201–1222.

Goffman, Erving. 1961. *Asylums: Essays on the Social Situation of Mental Patients and other Inmates*. Garden City, NY: Anchor Books.

Goodstein, Lynne, Doris Layton MacKenzie, and R. Lance Shotland. 1984. "Personal Control and Inmate Adjustment to Prison." *Criminology* 22(3): 343–369.

Hassine, Victor. (2007). *Life without Parole: Living in Prison Today*, edited by R. Johnson and A. Dobrzanska. Oxford, UK: Oxford University Press.

Irwin, John, and Donald R. Cressey. 1962. "Thieves, Convicts and the Inmate Culture." *Social Problems* 10(2): 142–155.

Liebling, Alison. 2011. "Moral Performance, Inhuman and Degrading Treatment and Prison Pain." *Punishment & Society* 13(5): 530–550.

McCorkle, Richard C., Terance D. Miethe, and Kriss A. Drass. 1995. "The Roots of Prison Violence: A Test of the Deprivation, Management, and 'Not-so-total' Institution Models." *Crime & Delinquency* 41(3): 317–331.

Mears, Daniel P., Eric A. Stewart, Sonja E. Siennick, and Ronald L. Simons. 2013. "The Code of the Street and Inmate Violence: Investigating the Salience of Imported Belief Systems." *Criminology* 51(3): 695–728.

Palermo, George B. 2011. "Prisoner Misbehavior." *International Journal of Offender Therapy and Comparative Criminology* 55(8): 1183–1185.

Passel, Jeffrey S., D.V. Cohn, and Mark Hugo Lopez. 2011. *Hispanics Account for More than Half of Nation's Growth in Past Decade*. Washington, DC: Pew Hispanic Center, March. Retrieved May 8, 2017 from www.pewhispanic.org/2011/03/24/hispanics-account-for-more-than-half-of-nations-growth-in-past-decade/

Pollock, Joycelyn M. 1997. *Prisons: Today and Tomorrow*. Boston, MA: Jones & Bartlett Learning.

Ricciardelli, Rosemary, and Victoria Sit. (2016). "Producing Social (Dis) Order in Prison: The Effects of Administrative Controls on Prisoner-on-prisoner Violence." *The Prison Journal* 96(2): 210–231.

Sparks, Richard, and Anthony Bottoms. (2008). "Legitimacy and Imprisonment Revisited: Some Notes on the Problem of Order Ten Years After." Pp. 91–104 in *The Culture of Prison Violence*, edited by J.M. Byrne, D. Hummer, and F.S. Taxman. Boston, MA: Pearson, Allyn, & Bacon.

Steiner, Benjamin, H. Daniel Butler and Jared M. Ellison. 2014. "Causes and Correlates of Prison Inmate Misconduct: A Systematic Review of the Evidence." *Journal of Criminal Justice* 42(6): 462–470.

Sykes, Gresham M. 1958. *The Society of Captives: A Study of a Maximum Security Prison*. Princeton, NJ: Princeton University Press.

Trammell, Rebecca. 2009a. "Values, Rules, and Keeping the Peace: How Men Describe Order and the Inmate Code in California Prisons." *Deviant Behavior* 30(8): 746–771.

Trammell, Rebecca. 2009b. "Relational Violence in Women's Prison: How Women Describe Interpersonal Violence and Gender." *Women & Criminal Justice* 19(4): 267–285.

Trammell, Rebecca. 2012. *Enforcing the Convict code: Violence and Prison Culture*. Boulder, CO: Lynne Rienner.

Trammell, Rebecca, Jennifer Raby, Alexandra Anderson, Shannon Hampton, and Travis Stickney. 2014. "Maintaining Order and Following the Rules: Gender Differences in Punishing Inmate Misconduct." *Deviant Behavior* 35(10): 804–821.

U.S. Census Bureau. 2012. *U.S. Census Bureau Projections Show a Slower Growing, Older, More Diverse Nation a Half Century from Now*. Washington, DC: U.S. Census Bureau.

Wellford, Charles. 1967. "Factors Associated with Adoption of the Inmate Code: A Study of Normative Socialization." *The Journal of Criminal Law, Criminology, and Police Science* 58(2): 197–203.

West, Heather C., and William J. Sabol. 2008. *Prisoners in 2007*. Washington, DC: Department of Justice, Office of Justice Programs, Bureau of Justice Statistics.

Wheeler, Stanton. 1961. "Socialization in Correctional Communities." *American Sociological Review* 26(5): 697–712.

Winfree, L. Thomas, Greg Newbold, and S. Houston Tubb. 2002. "Prisoner Perspectives on Inmate Culture in New Mexico and New Zealand: A Descriptive Case Study." *The Prison Journal* 82(2): 213–233.

Worley, Robert M. 2011. "To Snitch or Not to Snitch, That is the Question: Exploring the Role of Inmate Informants in Detecting Inappropriate Relationships between the Keeper and the Kept." *International Review of Law, Computers & Technology* 25(1–2): 79–82.

33 When Women are Captive

Women's Prisons and Culture Within

L. Susan Williams and Edward L. W. Green

Introduction

Images of women held behind bars date from the 1956 film *Girls in Prison* to the *Caged Heat* genre of the 1970s, and most recently, the wildly popular Netflix series, *Orange Is the New Black* (OITNB), based on the autobiographical account of Piper Kerman's (2011) stint in a federal prison. The films are categorized as "sexploitation" dramas, at once characterizing women as sex objects ("what happens to women without men?") and slayers of men ("the shocking story of one man against 1000 women"). Contemporary news and reality-based programs follow suit, sensationalizing sex and violence (Cecil 2007). OITNB was "destined to be a classic" (Abramsky 2010) for bravely drawing overdue attention to the humanizing, little-known minutiae of life for women inmates; and simultaneously criticized for irresponsibly portraying women as too violent (Irwin 2015), too white (*Feminist Griote* 2013), or too Black (Samuels 2013). Similarly, critics claim the series is either too dark or too upbeat (Paskin 2015), while others critique it as two-dimensional and supportive of racist and classist portrayals of women (Nair 2014). Inexplicably, the series—designed to simultaneously showcase lives of incarcerated women while addressing a stark void in women's screen roles—also has been critiqued as rendering men marginalized and invisible (Berlatsky 2014). Though recent pop culture depictions such as OITNB may heighten awareness of incarcerated women's issues, they remain primarily an uncritical commodity.

As inaccurate and troubling as these pop-culture portrayals may be, a dearth of deep-seated prison scholarship, especially a paucity of work that focuses on women in prison, has failed to replace those hyper-sexualized images with reliable alternatives (recent exceptions include Haney 2013; Rockell 2012; Sexton 2012). Such voids create a despatialized dimension, one in which a new visibility (Thompson 2005) is shaped by distinctive properties of communication media (Cheliotis 2010). As a result, such single-lensed and conflicting simulacra tend to create barren connections to the group (in this case, women in prison) and shallow caricatures of the human experience, resulting in a "cultural remove" (Bouclin 2012) that insulates realities of punishment and pain from public consciousness (Brown 2009).

Ironically, female incarceration, representing the fastest growing population of prisoners, remains the least understood, due to androcentric bias (Bosworth and Kaufman 2012; Burgess-Proctor 2006; Chesney-Lind 2006) and scant primary research. The cultural milieu inside prison walls, and especially experiences of women prisoners, remains an area bereft of systematic study. As Kruttschitt concludes in her 2015 presidential address to the American Society of Criminology, women inmates represent the "group of offenders least acknowledged in our research—but the group most likely to have been saddled with common undifferentiated assumptions" (2016: 9).

Perhaps the omission is not surprising, given the historical silencing of women's voices more generally (dating back 3,000 years to Homer's *The Odyssey*, see Cameron 2014).

However, feminist scholars are gathering a body of work to address the propensity of male bias in research—a hefty part of what Dorothy Smith (1987) refers to as relations of ruling that arise from an expansive ruling apparatus (DeVault 2007) that dominates knowledge production. Such biases can only be corrected, according to Smith, by turning to the "standpoint" of those most intimately involved, in this case women, a point extended by Collins (2000) specifically to encompass women of color.

This chapter compiles various threads of scholarship in an attempt to address the void in prison culture studies. While Brown and Chesney-Lind (in this volume) provide a rich account of the historical, demographic, and political landscape of women's incarceration in the U.S., this review turns a lens inward, focusing on the context of carceral regimes for women captives. First, the chapter summarizes literature on prison culture in general. Second, we review research on women's prisons, both foundational and contemporary cultural configurations, highlighting intersectional junctures including race/ethnicity, class, and sexuality. Third, we offer a compilation of studies depicting institutional linkages between women's prison culture and universal structures of patriarchal power. Finally, a brief overview of identity transition research stretches the parameters of how we conceptualize gendered culture within the correctional facility. Here, we identify areas in which gender becomes more or less salient, and cultural "tryings," which may offer more malleable bearings on prison life. Concluding, we offer brief remarks concerning research, policy, and programming regarding women in prison. To frame the review, we are guided by a critical feminist criminology approach that considers culture as embedded in fluid gender dynamics (and vice versa) and underscores the dialectic between everyday interactions and structural power.

Culture, Subculture, and Interlocking Groups

The task of focusing on culture in women's prisons is not as straightforward as it may seem. General cultural studies have been informed by the Birmingham School tradition, relating cultural practices to broader systems of power (e.g., Peterson and Anand 2004; Wuthnow and Witten 1988); and the Chicago School, focusing on subgroups and "outsiders" (Becker 1963; Cohen 1955). Both have been critiqued as limited in explaining heterogeneous milieux and multiple, overlapping configurations (Patterson 2014). Three concepts respond to these limitations. First, Fine and Kleinman (1979) propose that various networks meet, merge, and diverge in "interlocking group networks;" Pachucki's (2010) concept of cultural holes refers to structural contingencies; and Patterson (2014: 1) advances the idea of cultural configurations where "people shift between multiple, overlapping configurations." These concepts may mark ways to explore multiple and diverse pockets of culture within women's prisons. Further, cultural criminology, developed by Ferrell and Sanders (1995), focuses on mediated frameworks, criminalization of particular groups and representations, and links between cultural processes and crime control, all of which holds promise in examining intersections of culture and inequalities apparent in incarcerated women's experiences. However, most work on women's prisons has emanated from studies employing a feminist approach, and much of this review targets this body of literature.

In overarching themes, several scholars punctuate the importance of situating prison culture within larger social forces. For example, Silberman (1995) analyzes violence in contemporary prisons as a product of social control including the symbolic role of the penitentiary and the state's coercive authority over inmates. Wacquant (2001: 95) draws attention to the prison's "historical sequence of peculiar institutions" that plays a critical role in maintaining and even deepening the oppression of certain groups, especially African Americans. Finally, Schept (2013) characterizes the rise in mass incarceration as a result of a "supportive culture of punishment . . . subject to diverse and context-specific formulations," constituting a pervasive "carceral habitus" in the U.S. that supports the largest era of mass incarceration in the world's history. Each of these perspectives helps to map a fairly divergent set of studies into a cohesive literature addressing culture in women's prisons.

Codes and Prison Culture

Following threads of subculture, early studies of prison culture in the U.S. focused narrowly on the assimilation of prisoners into an informal inmate normative system, generally known as "the convict code." Clemmer's *The Prison Community* (1940) and Sykes' *The Society of Captives* (1958) represent the first major texts on prison culture, based on studies of male inmates in Illinois and New Jersey state prisons, respectively. These pioneering studies identified a set of values and guidelines that harbored animosity toward prison staff and the correctional institution overall, including codes such as "Don't snitch"; "Don't interfere with inmate interests"; "Play it cool and do your own time"; "Don't break your word"; "Don't steal from the cons"; "Don't welsh on debts"; "Don't weaken"; and "Be sharp."

Following these early studies, a significant literature amassed, documenting "the code" as oppositional, pervasive, and durable. Research at Illinois (Jacobs 1977; Rasmussen 1940; Weinberg 1942), Kansas (Reimer 1937), Washington (Hayner and Ash 1940), California (Irwin 1970), and Rhode Island (Carroll 1988), extended the scope of a penal code that controls not only inmate behavior but also inmate–staff relationships (Sykes and Messinger 1960). Work surrounding "the code" continues in contemporary research (Hensley 2000; Sorensen, Wrinkle, and Gutierrez 1998; Wooldridge 1997), including international studies in the UK (Morris and Morris 1962), Australia (Boyle 1977), New Zealand (Newbold 1982), Korea (Reisig and Lee 2000); and multi-country comparisons (Akers, Hayner, and Grunninger 1977). Widely, the consensus is that Clemmer's ideas remain relevant today, concluding that "differences in correctional philosophy and prison populations notwithstanding, the culture of the incarcerated remains relatively unaltered" (Winfree, Newbold, and Tubb 2013: 230).

Two general theories guide this body of work. The first is deprivation theory as first articulated by Clemmer (1940) in describing prisoners' adaptation to pains of imprisonment or "deprivations" such as loss of liberty, material goods and services, heterosexual relationships, and personal security. Support for the deprivation thesis is related to length of confinement (Schwartz, 1971; Wheeler 1961), incarceration career phase (Garabedian 1963); alienation (Thomas and Zingraff, 1976); and interaction with inmates and staff (Schwartz 1971). The second theory, referred to as importation or diffusion, posits that pre-prison experiences and personal characteristics affect degree of assimilation into inmate subculture (Irwin 1970; Irwin and Cressey 1964). Supporters of importation contend that roles adopted in the convict code are not adjustments to deprivations of confinement, but are "composites of various criminal and conventional street identities" (Wright 1993: 162) produced outside the prison (Carroll 1977; Jacobs 1977). Examples of support include prior commitments and arrests (Schwartz 1971), social class (Thomas 1973), and pre-prison employment (Thomas and Peterson 1977), as well as race and gender. Most penologists agree that an integrated model provides the strongest explanatory model for assimilation (Schwartz 1971; Thomas and Foster 1972; Thomas and Peterson 1977; Tittle 1972; Wheeler 1961), but the debate over respective roles of prison's deprivations and imported values has never been fully resolved (Akers et al. 1977; Thomas 1973; Tittle 1972; Winfree et al. 2013).

The code also fostered a unification of prisoners into a community of sorts, a process that Clemmer termed "prisonization," creating a penal culture that helped to provide resistance and psychological survival for prisoners under extremely repressive systems of control.

At the same time, the prisoner is inculcated into a lifestyle that diminishes his chances at survival on the outside. All of these studies focused on men and male facilities.

Inside Women's Prisons: Infrastructure and Groundwork

A modest body of work addresses the convict code in women's prisons, much of which illustrates precisely what is referred to as the "add-women-and-stir" perspective (St. Pierre 1999)—one in which the androcentric tendencies of mainstream social science research proves to be intransigent (Rafter and Stank 1982; Stacey and Thorne 1985; Williams 2006) and almost never accounts for the ubiquitous reach of patriarchy in everyday life and institutional organization (Bosworth and Kaufman 2011; Burgess-Proctor 2006; Chesney-Lind 2006). General agreement remains that prisonization is found everywhere, but several significant differences emerge between men's and women's prison environments.

In the midst of the women's movement in the U.S., a trifecta of now-classic studies on women's prisons emerged. The first is Ward and Kassebaum's (1965) study of women at the high-security California Institution for Women, Frontera. A rich ethnographic-like study, these authors also used survey data to test the well-cited convict-code assimilation literature. They found no evidence of the mid-incarceration career spike in convict code adoption (known as the u-curve effect) documented in virtually all studies of men's prisons. They also found no support for time served, prior commitments, or offense type. They concluded that code adoption was not as salient for female as male prisoners, and that adoption was often dependent on their identity *as women* (1965: 87–88). In particular, they found no strong support for the "snitching" taboo, prevalent in male environments.

Giallombardo (1966) conducted a second major work at the women's federal mixed-security facility in West Virginia. Giallombardo found that certain outside roles, imported into the prison, at least partially determined assimilation into the prison culture. In particular, identity within the prison was based on familiar "feminine" roles in larger culture such as wife, mother, or daughter. Within the all-female environment, some women adopted "the stud" persona, taking on masculine characteristics, which moved them to higher status.

The third among the three pioneers in women's prison research is Heffernan's (1972) study at Virginia Women's Reformatory, Occoquan; she discovered "the square" (the non-criminal type) "the cool" (the professional criminal), and "the life" (the habitual criminal) role identities, noting that code adaptation varied widely among the three groups with "the square" least susceptible to assimilating into the prison code. Like Ward and Kassebaum, Heffernan found no direct support for the widely cited link between incarceration career phase and conformity to the convict code. Much of the support found in these early landmark studies remained relatively stable, with family structures and pre-prison roles more consistent than deprivation factors.

Beyond these landmark studies, a handful of studies addressed inmate code commitment for women. Jensen and Jones (1975) studied a minimum-security women's prison in North Carolina, identifying code components slightly different from men's and replicating the familiar u-curve in institutional careers (with highest scores in mid-career); Hartnagel and Gillan (1980) surveyed female inmates in two mixed-security correctional institutions in Canada, replicating many of the male inmate code indicators, but did not find the u-curve. Regarding background characteristics, younger inmates, married, and those with a criminal past and/or urban background scored higher on the inmate code and were more hostile towards the institution and staff. The authors concluded that both situational and background variables affect inmate perspectives, with background variables explaining relatively more variance; the strongest coefficient was age, with older offenders more likely to respect staff, agree with rules, and enjoy prison activities.

Four comparative studies add insight to the single-lens studies. Tittle (1969) compared male and female inmates committed to a federal hospital for narcotic addicts; women scored somewhat lower on the inmate code than men and were more involved in "pseudo-familial" relationships. Zingraff (1980) studied a female facility, which was centrally located and emphasized interaction, comparing it with a remotely located secure male institution. Zingraff concluded that females do assimilate into the subculture, although they differ from men in degree and were more influenced by importation variables. Third, Gartner and Krutschnitt (2004) compared experiences of incarcerated women at California Institution for Women during two eras—in the 1960s (the rehabilitative era) and mid 1990s (height of the "get tough" model). They found that despite changes in national politics, policy, and local regimes, consistency ruled; women rarely engaged in violence, racial conflict, or gang activity, and they tended to "do their time" in much the same way—by negotiating relationships, sometimes distancing themselves, participating in mundane forms of resistance, and wanting but doubting the hope of rehabilitation. Gendered assumptions of women prisoners also remained consistent among staff and officials, "not, on the whole, dangerous or predatory, but disabled and deficient" (299).

The fourth is Wilson's (1986) research in a Canadian minimum security co-ed living-unit type setting. The study found no difference between male and female commitment in three of four components related to convict code. Notably, Wilson compared these results with an all-male setting and found significant differences between the two settings on the same three components. The one significant difference was that males displayed greater distrust of staff than females, and women were more compliant; this held in comparisons between the two settings. As a set, these studies find differences between males and females, some due to certain pre-prison conditioning factors, but raise questions that gender differences may be due more to setting or environment than to inherent sex differences.

Inside Women's Prisons: Contemporary Configurations

Though few in number, a handful of weighty scholarly productions enriches the knowledge base of women's prison culture. In diverse fashion, these constructions contour the field with foundational feminist thought, fresh methodological approaches that reveal "women's way of knowing," and blueprints for action and activism. Four book reviews document this trend (Kerman 2011; Lempert 2016; Owen 1998; Talvi 2007). Second, this section briefly overviews selected studies that suggest additional ways to think about prison culture for women—sometimes in a whisper, other times flashy, loud, and high-pitched—representing contemporary cultural configurations that affect women's lives, inside and outside prison walls.

Rafter's (1985) comprehensive historical account of women's prisons in the U.S. provides a splendid backdrop to prepare the reader for Owen's (1998) ethnographic work in the largest women's prison in the U.S., the Central California Women's Facility. As mentioned, the classic trifecta of early women's prison work (Ward and Kassebaum 1965; Giallambardo 1966; Heffernan 1972) offered up a tapestry-like description of life in women's prisons about mid-twentieth century. However, amidst a general paucity of qualitative research in prison scholarship (Wacquant 2002) there remained an even more stark silence about culture in women's prisons beyond the 1970s. This is not entirely unexpected, given the male bias in criminology overall (Chesney-Lind 2006). As Belknap (1999) points out:

> almost everything bad about males' incarceration is worse for females. For example . . . the rate of incarceration is increasing at an even faster rate for females than the breakneck rate for males, the war on drugs has been more of a war on women than

men, the rate of incarcerating people of color is even more disproportionate in women's than men's prisons.

(1999:1)

Thus, the significance of Owen's three-year ethnographic work within a women's prison was noteworthy and remains significant today.

Within one chapter alone, Owen guides us through the "culture of imprisoned women," observing how inmates negotiate daily life, including safety, security, and reputation; their various "styles of doing time," which involve a much more nuanced sense of inmate code; and engagement in trouble (or not), as women encounter hustles, underground activities, and sheer boredom of prison life. Owen details these in-group dynamics, discovering how some women accrue "juice" (status) while others prefer (or are forced to deal with) isolation and loneliness. The book documents an inmate code, parts of which are similar to that described in earlier research (e.g., "do your own time"), but with important distinctions. First, the code is not as monolithic as earlier described; women tend to express loyalties in smaller cohorts, not as one large group. Second, divisions are not based on gangs or race as readily as in men's prisons, but do carry significant distinction by age; "old-timers" mostly disapprove of the younger generation of inmates, claiming the young ones (who are, in fact, increasing) are "crude, rude, and loud," with no respect for existing culture. Third, and as hinted in earlier studies, there is a much greater tolerance, even expectation, about "telling" in women's prisons, due, in part, to the lower degree of large-group cohesion. Perhaps most important, Owen eloquently demonstrates that culture inside women's prisons is not isolated from culture on the outside; it merely amplifies its "badness," as Belknap underscores. Owen concludes:

> Women in prison represent a very specific failure of conventional society—and public policy—to recognize the damage done to women through the oppression of patriarchy, economic marginalization, and the wider-reaching effects of such short-sighted and detrimental policies as the war on drugs and the over reliance on incarceration as social control.
>
> (1998:192)

Owen creates an "us" that does not separate incarcerated women from you and me.

A few notable journalistic accounts of women in prison add depth and detail to an otherwise sparse landscape. The most comprehensive is *Women Behind Bars* (2007) by Silja Talvi. Talvi blends history, facts, and figures with narratives of women prisoners, utilizing roughly 100 interviews and 300 letters. Several strengths lie in this accounting. First, Talvi visits nine U.S. prisons and jails, including some of the largest in California and Florida, as well as a private prison in New Mexico and a juvenile detention center in Seattle. She spent time in other settings such as transitional housing programs and policy-related hearings. Finally, she visited women's prisons in England, Finland, and British Columbia. The book is packed with detailed narratives, poetry, and other personal contributions from women prisoners, providing breadth and authenticity to the text. It addresses issues less well-known to prison literature, such as faith-based programming, medical neglect, and the criminalization of motherhood. In an extremely rare glimpse into a women's segregation unit, the reader peeks at a culture completely beyond reach of conventional measurement as the author tours through single cells filled with rage, despair, and suicide attempts. Talvi quotes Ellen Barry, founder of Legal Services for Prisoners in San Francisco:

> Women do their time differently from men . . . For men, the isolation is horrendous and people literally go nuts being so isolated. For women, I would argue that it takes

> on an even more significant dimension because . . . women turn to each other for support and basic survival in ways that men don't do as often. So the isolation issue takes on an even deeper [meaning] for women.
>
> (Talvi 2007: 126)

Kerman's (2011) autobiographical account of her year in a federal prison has drawn both acclaim and sharp criticism, primarily because of its link to the popular Netflix series. Nevertheless, it provides an insider perspective, albeit from her white middle-class position, about an all-woman society with a handful of men governing them. Descriptions range from poignant and emotional to humorous or starkly mundane. She intersperses a significant amount of facts and commentary, especially about policies that ill consider the unique needs of women inmates. As one small example, Kerman uses both intellectual and insider observations to offer rich descriptions of life in a women's prison:

> Psyche ward. That was my overwhelming impression. Dueling televisions blared at opposite sides of the small room. A cacophony of voices vibrated in the close crowded space. Women, disheveled and stooped blinked at us like moles. Although there was nothing playful about the place, it had an infantilized, nursery school vibe.
>
> (2011: 275)

Kerman has brought a face to the issues of women in prison through public appearances and Congressional testimonies; she has spoken passionately about the prison system as disproportionately affecting women of color.

In a recent publication long overdue, Lempert (2016) examines prison experiences of women serving life sentences. In a richly gendered analysis of 72 life-serving women (of approximately 5,000 in the U.S.), she interviews women with a collective 1,088 years of imprisonment. A doubly invisible population, they are widely stereotyped as ruthless, cold-blooded "monsters" who are seen as "less than human and often as betrayers of their sex" (Lempert 2016: 45). Lifers (who, as Irwin (1970) points out, "accumulate") become a repository of knowledge—a "village elder"—who often mentor others and may act as a stabilizing agent within prison culture. For example, they may mediate between inmates and officers, and both interpret and shape the culture around them. Typically rule-conforming, "staying busy" is their mainstay strategy but after a while they tend to settle into doing time alone "in the presence of over a thousand other women" (4121). Women lifers are usually distinct from other inmates in several ways. For those imprisoned on first- or second-degree homicide, this was the first and only criminal offense, and most often someone else (usually a male) was the "do-er." They all report regret; many interpret time as a "scaffolding for the constructions of their life changes" (4930). Still, as Lempert concludes, their prison experience is most often corrosive, an "institution of trauma" among those already disadvantaged by abusive pasts, inadequate education, limited employment opportunities, and delinquent peers.

Several contemporary studies approach slivers of prison life for women in ways that reflect how the culture external to prison becomes reinterpreted inside prison. For example, Smoyer (2014) examines feeding relationships developed in prison; foodways became a central part of social networks, as well as both symbolic and material connections to the outside world. Women inmates hoarded, smuggled, shared, and bartered with food, as well as produced a holiday communal "fatty cake," made entirely from commissary snacks (Smoyer 2016). Food also marks sacrifice, as some inmates forego help from home to bolster their children's support; an empty locker thus became a site of resistance. Similarly, Labotka (2014) identified "moments of discipline" through the topic of "hair" in women's prisons.

She observed the use of shackles, the "walk of shame," and administrative segregation as punishment for violations of personal appearance (such as hair coverings or untucked shirts). Unfortunately, the project seemed unaware of Weitz's (2004) groundbreaking work on women's hair, certainly an area primed for exploring the complex role body plays within women's prison culture. Finally, Fleetwood (2015) explored the poignant emotional work in the making, producing, viewing, and exhibiting of inmate photos taken inside makeshift corners and prison visiting rooms, though the subjects were all male; women prisoners' standpoint remains unrecorded (but see Han 2012).

Systems of Power: Institutional Ethnography

Institutional ethnography, first developed by Dorothy Smith, is known foremost as a research strategy inquiring into everyday interactions that are guided by, and become a part of, structural forces that shape human behavior over space and time. The purpose is to discover "'how things work,' [and] 'how they are actually put together'" (1987: 148). This means exploring the standpoint of those most intimately involved—marginalized women—while also uncovering the relationship of everyday interactions to the ruling apparatus, which is actually upheld by "those whose work has been both necessary to and unrecognized by it" (1987: 153). Far from viewing practices as simply local and individual, Smith claims that such problematizing of the everyday allows a revealing of power mechanisms. Microcosms of prison culture, by the very nature of its distillation and particulars, afford a lens with which to map power relations in the social world, elucidating the most vulnerable.

This review compiles interrelated areas of research that illustrate intersections between prison culture and larger patterns of behaviors, those that are mediated by ideologies governing social life and upholding existing power structures. This example centers on family ties and especially mothering—domains dominated by ideals of womanhood and femininity.

The gendered division of labor in which women are disproportionately responsible for sustaining relationships (especially with children) is amplified within the criminal justice system (Celinska 2013; Comfort 2008; Manby, Monchuk, and Sharratt 2013). More than 200,000 women are incarcerated, over 60 percent of whom were caring for minor children prior to their incarceration (Sentencing Project 2015), thus forcing them to rear children from afar and through intermediaries (Bosworth 1999). "Unlike male inmates, 86% of whom rely on their children's mothers for care while in prison, female inmates more often turn to female kin and friends for support" (Haney 2013: 110). The majority of incarcerated women were single-parent heads of households, and between 1991 and 2007 the number of children with an imprisoned mother increased by 131 percent (Lempert 2016). These dynamics are exacerbated for women of color; Black women are incarcerated at three times the rate of white women, and the differential for Latina women is 1.6 (Coutts and Greenberg 2015); these populations are already under the "triple threat" of drug and alcohol abuse, childhood and adulthood sexual and physical victimization, and mental health problems (Celinska 2013; Schuck, Lersch, and Verrill 2004). Added challenges unique to women inmates and their families include long distances to the (relatively) few women's facilities, limited transportation, child-unfriendly areas, and concerns of outside caretakers about exposing children to harsh conditions of imprisonment. Male inmates do not bear the same family responsibilities and yet have far more visitors while incarcerated (General Accounting Office 1999, as cited by Brown and Chesney-Lind in Chapter 12 of this volume).

Within systems of oppression, contradictions abound; control over women's minds and bodies is historically embedded in our culture, consistently remaking itself. Recent studies exemplify problematic and blurred boundaries of the body in several ways. Some studies turn attention to transgender issues within prisons (Jenness and Fenstermaker 2014, 2016;

Pemberton 2013; Sumner and Sexton 2014), illustrating the misfit between a (constructed) gender binary and real lives. Others document a multitude of social facts, illustrating the unrelenting effects of patriarchy within the criminal justice system. Women, previously punished for adultery or drinking, are now incarcerated primarily for drug-related offenses. Women, once convicted for bearing an illegitimate child, now give birth while in shackles. Women inmates live under heightened expectations of motherhood, yet multiple provisions within prisons doom them to fail. Motherhood is undermined, subsumed, and punished by prison staff (Haney 2013), "leaving mothering all the more bound up with power and punishment" (124); while non-mothering also bears a harsh burden (Jewkes and Letherby 2002). Incarcerated women absorb this stress (Flavin 2009) and nevertheless struggle to keep families afloat (Comfort 2008; Owen 1998). Yet, at least one-third lose parental rights, dramatically escalating the many problems that children of incarceration encounter. All of these incongruities exist within recurring and pervasive effects of race and class (Craig 2009) and pit women's needs against those of their children. Structurally, this trend deepens a child welfare crisis (Craig 2009) and mimics "a culture that idealizes the mothering of some women while thoroughly devaluing the parenting of others" (Haney 2013: 108).

Increasingly, scholars call for studies that examine tensions between reforms and the reformed (Craig 2009; Haney 1996), exemplified through cases in which women are convicted of murder for drug use during pregnancy (Talvi 2007; also see Coutts and Greenberg (2015) for report on abuses of incarcerated women). As Haney (2013) argues, the system "holds mothers accountable for what were largely societal failings" (120). This trend produces patterns that become inter-institutional and intergenerational, mirroring the feminization, racialization, and juvenilization of poverty (Foster and Hagan 2015; Schnyder 2010; Wakefield and Uggen 2010), and reproducing a culture harmful to women and their children, both behind and beyond prison walls.

Identity, Interstitial Moments, and Sites of Resistance

Throughout roughly five decades of research on women and crime, tensions remain between equality and "equality with a vengeance" (the latter ignoring gender sensitivity); questions of women's increasing participation in crime versus a "widening of the net" (to explain women's ballooning incarceration rate); and "push" factors such as punitive policies versus "pull" factors that disproportionately affect economically marginalized women. Undergirding these dialectics lies the question of instituting gender-specific treatment without sliding toward essentialism (Connell 2009). In this brief review, we do not suggest solutions to these questions, but do propose a niche that has been largely unexplored—interstitial moments that reveal mechanisms of gendering, instances when gender "doings" fade or become more pronounced, and "cultural holes" where resistance becomes most viable. We offer a brief snippet of our own work in identity transition from citizen to felon, considering gendered culture (both inside and outside prison walls) as more tentative than typically portrayed.

Green (2016) has depicted entry into the prison system as a new rite of passage, one which represents a threshold in contemporary U.S. culture for the more than two million incarcerated citizens; as we have seen, women represent the most dramatic increase despite declining crime rates. Because gender is most visible at boundaries and points of change, we argue that nowhere is gendering and identity transitions more apparent than at the moment of sentencing, that point where, as one of our participants exclaimed, "I was reborn a prisoner." Herein lies an opportunity to examine a critical life transition through a deeply gendered cultural lens. Is there, indeed, a "rebirth" of self? If so, what does the new "self" look like and how (and when) is it transformed? Does it vary by outside social trappings?

by the host milieu? Carceral geographies confine more than just the physical and material; they also define the social and emotional—the self, sense of belonging, purpose, and hope itself. Warehousing humans at historic proportions can best be exposed through amplifying voices of those living through society's binge on punitivity.

While we are limited in this brief section in answering these profound questions, we offer three laconic observations. First, our research demonstrates subtle differences between male and female inmates, especially in terms of pre-prison identity; women are more likely to describe themselves prior to prison as low in self-worth and life potential, while for men this reflection comes much later in their incarceration career. As a result, women are more likely to reflect on shorter periods of prison time as productive; men tend to produce what Irwin (2009) calls "redemptive narratives" after about ten years (among lifers), to demonstrate their prison transformation. Second, gender is more provisional than portrayed in the literature; women "try on gender," selectively experimenting with what works in the strange new world of women's prisons. Some of these "tryings" resemble accommodation (usually for survival), while certain subtle everyday practices (such as a sarcastic remark or gathering pieces of soap) constitute resistance. A reconfiguring of the "appropriate" woman is situational. Third, we found innumerable instances of self-empowerment, in ways large and small. Emphasized femininity, while enacted individually, constitutes a dogged persistence in woman-identified practices, and these seem to hold across race and ethnicity. But to do so wholesale, in the presence of others, demands a group consciousness among women *as women*, which ultimately reaches back to the original purpose of feminist projects and promise for real social change.

We suggest that "trying on gender" (Williams 2002) represents a useful concept for thinking about change and resistance in women's prisons. If this is true, we also should observe "cultural tryings" that help identify structural holes to challenge the masculine hegemony (Connell 1987) of life among those marginalized in women's prisons.

Conclusion and Implications

Leading feminist scholars conclude that researchers must continue to out-turn critical work, revealing power dynamics that allow vulnerable and voiceless women prisoners to remain largely invisible and the brunt of punitive policies. The women's penal culture literature reviewed here, with sparse numbers of studies largely upheld by a few researchers, speaks not only to prison environments, but also to larger social patterns, and to our own field of corrections research. The feminist movement in the U.S. has taught us that exclusion of marginalized groups leaves the entire field bereft of insight necessary for true advancement. Yet "women and crime" remains mostly the province of those who identify as feminist scholars, partitioned from mainstream scholarship, publications, and classrooms. Uncovering and understanding the pains of punishment for both women and men is critical to reversing the current punishment trend, a project best approached by inclusivity.

Similarly, Ferrell (1997) has argued that through reflexive developments in feminist literature, immersive approaches to research methods have not only expanded the scope of cultural criminology but also enhanced ethnographic techniques. Thus, an extension of critical feminism and broader cultural attunement in inquiry would further bolster gathering evidence against harshly punitive and supposedly "neutral" trends in U.S. corrections today. Reconsidering gender both as resistance and as fluid "tryings" opens up a theoretical space between rigid expectations of historical patriarchy and contemporary gendered identities; as well, it offers multiple paths toward exploring various cultural and contextual contingencies, supplying nuance into understanding human consequences of mass incarceration.

Integrating feminism and activism with critical sense-making of law, crime, justice, and state control will continue to forge a way toward reduction in incarceration. History teaches us, however, that we must guard against neoliberal strategies and unintended consequences (Hannah-Moffat 2000). The parity movement in justice for women was accompanied by increased arrests for women, despite differences in power and circumstance; concerns about mixed-sex prisons brought a proliferation of women's correctional facilities; and, as Jackson (2013) argues, the National Prison Rape Elimination Act has "reinforced fantasies of sexually violent black and brown bodies" (197) and expanded state-sanctioned control of women's bodies. Likewise, while decarceration remains a goal, Haney (2013) warns against a "starve the beast" approach, suggesting that "we may end up decarcerating in the way we deinstitutionalized mental hospitals in the 1970s: carelessly and irresponsibly" (108). Turning a gendered lens on cultural constructions of women prisoners, divulging consequences of incarcerating women, and voicing incarcerated women could work toward responsible reduction of captive women today.

References

Abramsky, Sasha. 2010. "American Justices: Two Distinct Takes on the Folly of Our Prison Policies." *Columbia Journalism Review*. Retrieved May 25, 2016 from www.cjr.org/review/american_justice.php

Akers, Ron L., Norman S. Hayner, and Werner Gruninger. 1977. "Prisonization in Five Countries." *Criminology* 14: 527–554.

Becker, Howard S. 1963. *Outsiders*. New York: Free Press.

Belknap, Joanne. 1999. "'In the Mix': Struggle and Survival in a Women's Prison" Book Review. *Western Criminology Review*. Retrieved May 30, 2016 from www.westerncriminology.org/documents/WCR/v01n2/Belknap/Belknap.html

Berlatsky, Noah. 2014. "Orange Is the New Black's Irresponsible Portrayal of Men." *The Atlantic*. June 30, 2014. Retrieved May 25, 2016 from www.theatlantic.com/entertainment/archive/2014/06/why-it-is-a-bad-thing-that-orange-is-the-new-black-leaves-men-out/373682/

Bosworth, Mary. 1999. *Engendering Resistance: Agency and Power in Women's Prisons*. Aldershot, UK: Ashgate.

Bosworth, Mary, and Emma Kaufman. 2012. "Gender and Punishment." Pp. 186–204 in *Handbook of Punishment and Society*, edited by Jonathan Simon and Richard Sparks. London: Sage.

Bouclin, Suzanne. 2012. "Book Review: The Culture of Punishment: Prison, Society, and Spectacle." *Crime Media Culture* 8: 233.

Boyle, Jimmy. 1977. *A Sense of Freedom*. London: Pan.

Brown, Michelle. 2009. *The Culture of Punishment: Prison, Society, and Spectacle*. New York: New York University Press.

Burgess-Proctor, Amanda. 2006. "Intersections of Race, Class, Gender, and Crime: Future Directions for Feminist Criminology." *Feminist Criminology* 1: 27–47.

Cameron, Janet. 2014. "Mary Beard on the Silencing of Women's Voices." *Decoded*. Retrieved May 25, 2016 from http://decodedpast.com/mary-beard-silencing-womens-voices/7393

Carroll, Leo. 1977. "Humanitarian Reform and Biracial Sexual Assault in a Maximum Security Prison." *Urban Life* 5(4): 417–437.

Carroll, Leo. 1988. "Race, Ethnicity, and the Social Order of the Prison." Pp. 181–203 in *The Pains of Imprisonment*, edited by Robert Johnson and Hans Toch. Prospect Heights, IL: Waveland.

Cecil, Dawn K. 2007. "Looking Beyond Caged Heat: Media Images of Women in Prison." *Feminist Criminology* 2: 304–326.

Celinska, Katarzyna. 2013. "The Role of Family in the Lives of Incarcerated Women." *Prison Service Journal* 207: 23–26.

Cheliotis, Leonidas K. 2010. "The Ambivalent Consequences of Visibility: Crime and Prisons in the Mass Media." *Crime Media Culture* 6: 169–184.

Chesney-Lind, Meda. 2006. "Patriarchy, Crime, and Justice: Feminist Criminology in an Era of Backlash." *Feminist Criminology* 1: 6–26.

Clemmer, Donald. 1940. *The Prison Community*. New York: Rinehart.

Cohen, Albert K. 1955. *Delinquent Boys: The Culture of the Gang*. New York: Free Press.

Collins, Patrica Hill. 2000. *Black Feminist Thought: Knowledge, Consciousness, and the Politics of Empowerment*. New York: Routledge.
Comfort, Megan. 2008. *Doing Time Together: Love and Family in the Shadow of the Prison*. Chicago, IL: University of Chicago Press.
Connell, Raewyn. 1987. *Gender and Power: Society, the Person, and Sexual Politics*. Stanford, CA: Stanford University Press.
Connell, Raewyn. 2009. "Accountable Conduct: 'Going Gender' in Transsexual and Political Retrospect." *Gender & Society* 23: 104–111.
Coutts, Sharona, and Zoe Greenberg. 2015. "Women, Incarcerated." *Prison Legal News* 26(6). Retrieved June 1, 2016 from www.prisonlegalnews.org/media/issues/06pln15.final-web.pdf
Craig, Susan C. 2009. "A Historical Review of Mother and Child Programs for Incarcerated Women." *Prison Journal* 89: 35S–52S.
DeVault, Marjorie L. 2007. "Ruling Relations." Pp. 3960–3961 in *Blackwell Encyclopedia of Sociology*, edited by George Ritzer. Malden, MA: Blackwell.
Feminist Griote. 2013. "Orange Is NOT the New Black." *The Feminist Griote*. August 19, 2013. Retrieved May 25, 2016 from http://thefeministgriote.com/orange-is-not-the-new-black/
Ferrell, Jeff. 1997. "Criminological Verstehen: Inside the Immediacy of Crime." *Justice Quarterly* 14: 3–23.
Ferrell, Jeff, and Clint R. Sanders. 1995. *Cultural Criminology*. Boston, MA: Northeastern University Press.
Fine, Gary Alan, and Sherryl Kleinman. 1979. "Rethinking Subculture: An Interactionist Analysis. *American Journal of Sociology* 85: 1–20.
Flavin. Jeanne. 2009. *Our Bodies, Our Crimes: The Policing of Women's Reproduction in America*. New York: New York University Press.
Fleetwood, Nicole R. 2015. "Posing in Prison: Family Photographs, Emotional Labor, and Carceral Intimacy." *Public Culture* 27: 487–511.
Foster, Holly, and John Hagan. 2015. "Punishment Regimes and the Multilevel Effects of Parental Incarceration: Intergenerational, Intersectional, and Interinstitutional Models of Social Inequality and Systemic Exclusion." *Annual Review of Sociology* 41: 135–158.
Garabedian, Peter G. 1963. "Social Roles and Processes of Socialization in the Prison Community." *Social Problems* 11: 140–152.
Gartner, Rosemary, and Candace Krutschnitt. 2004. "A Brief History of Doing Time: The California Institution for Women in the 1960s and the 1990s." *Law & Society Review* 38: 267–304.
Giallombardo, Rose. 1966. *Society of Women: A Study of a Women's Prison*. New York: Wiley.
Green, Edward L.W. 2016. "The Weight of the Gavel: Prison as a Rite of Passage." Ph.D. Dissertation, Department of Sociology, Anthropology, and Social Work, Kansas State University, Manhattan, KS.
Han, Sora Y. 2012. "The Purloined Prisoner." *Theoretical Criminology* 16: 157–174.
Haney, Lynne. 1996. "Homeboys, Babies, Men in Suits: The State and the Reproduction of Male Dominance." *American Sociological Review* 61: 759–778.
Haney, Lynne. 2013. "Motherhood as Punishment: The Case of Parenting in Prison." *Signs* 39: 105–130.
Hannah-Moffat, Kelly. 2000. "Prisons That Empower: Neo-liberal Governance in Canadian Women's Prisons." *British Journal of Criminology* 40: 510–531.
Hartnagel, Timothy F., and Mary Ellen Gillan. 1980. "Female Prisoners and the Inmate Code." *The Pacific Sociological Review* 23: 85–104.
Hayner, Norman S., and Ellis Ash. 1940. "The Prison as a Community." *American Sociological Review* 5: 577–582.
Heffernan, Esther. 1972. *Making It in Prison*. New York: Wiley.
Hensley, Christopher. 2000. "Attitudes Toward Homosexuality in a Male and Female Prison: An Exploratory Study." *The Prison Journal* 80: 434–441.
Irwin, Amos. 2015. "How 'Orange Is the New Black' Misrepresents Women's Federal Prison (and Why It Matters.)" *Everyday Feminism*. Retrieved May 25, 2016 from http://everydayfeminism.com/2015/07/oitnb-womens-federal-prison/

Irwin, John. 1970. *The Felon*. Los Angeles, CA: University of California Press.
Irwin, John. 2009. *Lifers: Seeking Redemption in Prison*. New York: Routledge.
Irwin, John, and Donald R. Cressey. 1964. "Thieves, Convicts and Inmate Culture." Pp. 225–245 in *The Other Side*, edited by Howard. S. Becker. New York: Macmillan.
Jackson, Jessi Lee. 2013. "Sexual Necropolitics and Prison Rape Elimination." *Signs* 39: 197–220.
Jacobs, James B. 1977. *Stateville: The Penitentiary in Mass Society*. Chicago, IL: The University of Chicago Press.
Jenness, Valerie, and Sarah Fenstermaker. 2014. "Agnes Goes to Prison: Gender Authenticity, Transgender Inmates in Prisons for Men, and Pursuit of 'The Real Deal.'" *Gender & Society* 28: 5–31.
Jenness, Valerie, and Sarah Fenstermaker. 2016. "Forty Years after Brownmiller: Prisons for Men, Transgender Inmates, and the Rape of the Feminine." *Gender & Society* 30: 14–29.
Jensen, Gary F., and Dorothy Jones. 1975. "Perspectives on Inmate Culture: A Study of Women in Prison." *Social Forces* 54(3): 589–603.
Jewkes, Yvonne and Gayle Letherby. 2002. "Women in Prison: Mothering and Non-Mothering Identities." *Prison Service Journal* 139: 26–28.
Kerman, Piper. 2011. *Orange Is the New Black: My Year in a Women's Prison*. New York: Random House/Spiegel & Grau.
Krutschnitt, Candace. 2016. "2015 Presidential Address to the American Society of Criminology: The Politics, and Place, of Gender in Research on Crime." *Criminology* 54: 8–29.
Labotka, Lori. 2014. "Healthy, Beautiful Hair: Cultivating the Self in a Women's Prison." Ph.D. Dissertation, School of Anthropology, The University of Arizona, Tucson, AZ.
Lempert, Lora Bex. 2016. *Women Doing Life: Gender, Punishment and the Struggle for Identity*. New York: New York University Press.
Manby, Martin, Leanne Monchuk, and Kathryn Sharratt. 2013. "The Importance of Maintaining Family Ties During Imprisonment—Perspectives of Those Involved in HMP New Hall's Family Support Project." *The Prison Journal* 209: 18–23.
Morris, Terrence, and Pauline Morris. 1962. *Pentonville: A Sociological Study of an English Prison*. London: Routledge & Kegan Paul.
Nair, Yasmin. 2014. "The Reign of Whitey Is Never Over." *In These Times*. Retrieved June 13, 2016 from http://inthesetimes.com/article/16819/the_reign_of_whitey_is_never_over
Newbold, Greg. 1982. *The Big Huey*. Auckland, NZ: Collins.
Owen, Barbara. 1998. *"In the Mix": Struggle and Survival in a Women's Prison*. Albany NY: State University of New York Press.
Pachucki, Mark A. 2010. "Cultural Holes: Beyond Relationality in Social Networks and Culture." *Annual Review of Sociology* 36: 205–224.
Paskin, Willa. 2015. "Prison as Playground." *Slate*. Retrieved May 25, 2016 from orange_is_the_new_black_season_3_review_why_did_the_show_lose_all_its_darkness.html
Patterson, Orlando. 2014. "Making Sense of Culture." *Annual Review of Sociology* 40: 1–30.
Pemberton, Sarah. 2013. "Enforcing Gender: The Constitution of Sex and Gender in Prison Regimes." *Signs* 39: 151–175.
Peterson, Richard A., and N. Anand. 2004. "The Production of Culture Perspective." *Annual Review of Sociology* 30: 311–334.
Rafter, Nicole Hahn. 1985. *Partial Justice: Women in State Prisons, 1800–1935*. Boston, MA: Northeastern University Press.
Rafter, Nicole Hahn, and E.A. Stank. 1982. *Judge, Lawyer, Victim, Thief*. Boston, MA: Northeastern University Press.
Rasmussen, Donald. 1940. "Prisoner Opinion About Parole." *American Sociological Review* 5: 584–595.
Reimer, Hans. 1937. "Socialization in the Prison Community." Pp. 151–155 in *Proceedings of the 67th Annual Conference of the American Prison Association*.
Reisig, Michael D., and Yoon Ho Lee. 2000. "Prisonization in the Republic of Korea." *Journal of Criminal Justice* 28: 23–31.
Rockell, Barbara. 2012. "Women and Jail: Life in the Gendered Cage." *Prison Service Journal* 201: 12–17.

Samuels, Allison. 2013. "Why I Don't Watch 'Orange Is the New Black.'" *The Daily Beast*. August 19, 2013. Retrieved May 25, 2016 from www.thedailybeast.com/articles/2013/08/19/why-i-don-t-watch-orange-is-the-new-black-or-any-shows-with-black-people-in-prison.html

Schept, Judah. 2013. "'A Lockdown Facility . . . with the Feel of a Small, Private College': Liberal Politics, Jail Expansion, and the Carceral Habitus." *Theoretical Criminology* 17: 71–88.

Schnyder, Damien. 2010. "Enclosures Abound: Black Cultural Autonomy, Prison Regime and Public Education." *Race Ethnicity and Education* 13: 349–365.

Schuck, Amie M., Kim Michelle Lersch, and Steven W. Verrill. 2004. "The 'Invisible' Hispanic? The Representative of Hispanics in Criminal Justice Research: What Do We Know and Where Should We Go?" *Journal of Ethnicity in Criminal Justice* 2: 5–22.

Schwartz, Barry. 1971. "Pre-institutional vs. Situational Influence in a Correctional Community." *Journal of Criminal Law, Criminology and Police Science* 62: 532–542.

Sentencing Project. 2015. "Incarcerated Women and Girls." The Sentencing Project. Retrieved June 20, 2016 from www.sentencingproject.org/wp-content/uploads/2016/02/Incarcerated-Women-and-Girls.pdf

Sexton, Lori. 2012. "Under the Penal Gaze: An Empirical examination of Penal Consciousness Among Prison Inmates." Ph.D. dissertation, Criminology, Law and Society, University of California, Irvine, Irvine, CA.

Silberman, Matthew. 1995. *A World of Violence: Corrections in America*. Belmont, CA: Wadsworth.

Smith, Dorothy E. 1987. *The Everyday World as Problematic: A Feminist* Sociology. Boston, MA: Northeastern University Press.

Smoyer, Amy B. 2014. "Feeding Relationships: Foodways and Social Networks in a Women's Prison." *Affilia: Journal of Women and Social Work* 30(1): 26–39.

Smoyer, Amy B. 2016. "Making Fatty Girl Cakes: Food and Resistance in a Women's Prison." *The Prison Journal* 96: 191–209.

Sorensen, J., R. Wrinkle, and A. Gutierrez. 1998. "Patterns of Rule-violating Behaviors and Adjustment to Incarceration Among Murderers." *The Prison Journal* 78: 222–231.

St. Pierre, Elizabeth A. 1999. "A Historical Perspective on Gender." *The English Journal* 88: 29–34.

Stacey, Judith, and Barrie Thorne. 1985. "The Missing Feminist Revolution in Sociology." *Social Problems* 32: 301–316.

Sumner, Jennifer, and Lori Sexton. 2014. "Lost in Translation: Looking for Transgender Identity in Women's Prisons and Locating Aggressors in Prison Culture." *Critical Criminology* 23: 1–20.

Sykes, Gresham. 1958. *The Society of Captives: A Study in a Maximum Security Prison*. Princeton, NJ: Princeton University Press.

Sykes, Gresham M., and Sheldon L Messinger. 1960. "The Inmate Social System." Pp. 5–19 in *Theoretical Studies in Social Organization of the Prison*, edited by Richard A. Cloward, Donald R. Cressey, George H. Grosser, Richard McCleery, Lloyd E. Ohlin, Gresham M. Sykes, and Sheldon L. Messinger. New York: Social Science Research Council.

Talvi, Silja J.A. 2007. *Women Behind Bars: The Crisis of Women in the U.S. Prison System*. Emeryville, CA: Seal Press.

Thomas, Charles W. 1973. "Prisonization or Resocialization? A Study of External Factors Associated with the Impact of Imprisonment." *Journal of Research on Crime & Delinquency* 10: 13–21.

Thomas, Charles W., and Samuel C. Foster. 1972. "Prisonization in the Inmate Contraculture." *Social Problems* 20: 229–239.

Thomas, Charles W., and David M. Peterson. 1977. *Prison Organization and Inmate Subcultures*. Indianapolis, IN: Bobbs-Merrill.

Thomas, Charles W., and Matthew T. Zingraff. 1976. "Organizational Structure as a Determinant of Prisonization." *Pacific Sociological Review* 19: 98–116.

Thompson, John B. 2005. "The New Visibility." *Theory, Culture & Society* 22: 31–51.

Tittle, Charles R. 1969. "Inmate Organization: Sex Differentiation and the Influence of Criminal Subcultures." *American Sociological Review* 34: 492–504.

Tittle, Charles R. 1972. "Institutional Living and Self-esteem." *Social Problems* 20: 65–77.

Wacquant, Loic. 2001. "Deadly Symbiosis: When Ghetto and Prison Meet and Mesh." *Punishment & Society* 3: 95–134.

Wacquant, Loic. 2002. "The Curious Eclipse of Prison Ethnography in the Age of Mass Incarceration." *Ethnography* 3: 371–397.

Wakefield, Sara, and Christopher Uggen. 2010. "Incarceration and Stratification." *Annual Review of Sociology* 36: 387–406.

Ward, David A., and Gene G. Kassebaum. 1965. *Women's Prison: Sex and Social Structure.* New Brunswick, NJ: Aldine Transaction.

Weinberg, S. Kirson 1942. "Aspects of the Prison's Social Structure." *American Journal of Sociology* 47: 717–726.

Weitz, Rose. 2004. *Rapunzel's Daughters: What Women's Hair Tells Us About Women's Lives.* New York: Farrar, Straus & Giroux.

Wheeler, Stanton. 1961. "Socialization in Correctional Communities." *American Sociological Review* 26: 697–712.

Williams, Christine L. 2006. "Still Missing?: Comments on the Twentieth Anniversary of 'The Missing Feminist Revolution in Sociology.'" *Social Problems* 53: 454–458.

Williams, L. Susan. 2002. "Trying on Gender: Gender Regimes, and the Process of Becoming Women." *Gender & Society* 16: 29–54.

Wilson, T.W. 1986. "Gender Differences in the Inmate Code." *Canadian Journal of Criminology* 28: 397–405.

Winfree, L. Thomas Jr., Greg Newbold, and S. Houston Tubb III. 2013. "Prisoner Perspectives on Inmate Culture in New Mexico and New Zealand: A Descriptive Case Study." *The Prison Journal* 82: 213–233.

Wooldredge, John D. 1997. "Explaining Variation in Perceptions of Inmate Crowding." *The Prison Journal* 77: 27–40.

Wright, Richard A. 1993. *In Defense of Prisons.* Westport, CT: Greenwood Press.

Wuthnow, Robert, and Marsha Witten. 1988. "New Directions in the Study of Culture." *Annual Review of Sociology* 14: 49–67.

Zingraff, Matthew T. 1980. "Inmate Assimilation: A Comparison of Male and Female Delinquents." *Criminal Justice and Behaviour* 7: 275–299.

34 Correctional Healthcare

Roberto Hugh Potter

The Problem of Health in U.S. Correctional Populations

Physical Health

Analysis of a social issue usually begins by framing the nature of the problem. Table 34.1 provides the most recently available medical information on nationally representative samples of jail inmates and prisoners (state and federal). The inmate and prisoner data are contrasted with a similar snapshot of self-reported health conditions taken in the early 2000s. And, for the first time, the 2011–12 data are contrasted with a nationally representative sample of citizens in the general U.S. population. Unfortunately, the data on prisoners between state and federal prisoners have been combined, losing some ability to see differences based on the types of crimes generally housed in each system. As one might suspect, the differences between a range of chronic and infectious diseases is substantial, and for the most part statistically significant.

On every disease comparison, jail inmates self-reported higher levels of disease burden than the community sample. This is especially important for the control of disease transmission in infectious diseases, as well as for planning for health care utilization. Jail inmates are likely to return to the community in a relatively brief period of time (24 hours to 28 days). For many, the only health care screenings and/or treatments they are likely to receive are in jail or the emergency room. Neither is cheap for the residents of communities.

When we compare the disease burden in the community sample to those in state and/or federal prison, we again see a significant difference towards higher health burden among the prisoners. Because fewer than 10 percent of those booked into jail will progress to prison in any given year, it is interesting to note that there are several disease categories that decline in proportion between jail inmates and prisoners. Self-reported asthma, heart, and kidney (renal) disease are less often self-reported among prisoners than inmates. Self-reported burden of arthritis, hypertension (high blood pressure), diabetes, general hepatitis (A, B, and C), and tuberculosis (TB) are higher among the prisoner population than the inmates. Among the prisoner population nearly one in 10 (9.8 percent) reported being positive for Hepatitis C (HCV). No similar data were available for the jail inmates or general population.

Some of these differences across groups are possibly due to the age structure of prisoners tending to be older than jail inmates. That is, for some diseases that require longer periods to develop, age provides a longer time of exposure for development. Overall, for any chronic disease, we see slightly higher rates in inmates than prisoners. Indeed, Maruschak, Berzofsky, and Unangst (2015) note that in the 2011–12 sample prisoners over the age of 50 reported chronic disease burden 2.4 times, and jail inmates two (2) times more often than those in the 18–24 age group. Self-reported cancers, bacterial sexually transmitted diseases, and liver problems are almost identical in the two groups, with rates of HIV identical in the groups.

Table 34.1 Medical Problems Reported by Jail Inmates and Prisoners Compared to the General Population

Medical Problem	*Jail Inmates*[1]		*Prisoners*[1,2]			
			State	*Federal*	*Combined*	*General Pop.*
	2002	*2011–12*	*2004*	*2004*	*2011–12*	*2011–12*
Chronic diseases						
Arthritis	12.9%	12.9%	15.3%	12.4%	15.0%	—%
Hypertension	11.2	26.3*	13.8	13.2	30.2*	18.1
Asthma	9.9	20.1*	9.1	7.2	14.9*	10.2
Heart problems	5.9	10.4*	6.1	6.0	9.8*	2.9
Renal (kidney) problems	3.7	6.7	3.2	3.1	6.1	—
Cancer	0.7	3.6	0.9	0.6	3.5	—
Diabetes	2.7	7.2*	4.0	5.1	9.0*	6.5
Hepatitis (unspecified)	2.6	6.5*	5.3	4.2	10.9*	1.1
Paralysis	1.3	—	1.4	1.6	—	—
Liver problems	0.9	1.7*	1.1	1.1	1.8*	0.2
Any chronic		44.7*			43.9*	31.0
Infectious diseases						
Tuberculosis (lifetime)	4.3	2.5*	9.4	7.1	6.0*	0.5
HIV	1.3	1.3*	1.6	1.0	1.3*	0.4
Other sexually transmitted diseases (STDs)	0.9	6.1*	0.8	0.4	6.0*	3.4

*p<.05
[1] Maruschak (2006, 2008)
[2] Maruschak, L.M., Berzofsky, M., and Unangst, J. (2015)

For infectious disease history, the older inmates reported three (3) times greater incidence than did the younger group.

The data collected in the 2011–12 surveys (Maruschak et al. 2015) also included some risk factor data for the first time. Obesity is one of those risk factors for chronic diseases measured. Nearly three-quarters (74 percent) of prisoners and two-thirds (62 percent) of inmates fell into the overweight (46 percent and 39 percent, respectively), obese (26 percent and 39 percent, respectively), or morbidly obese (2 percent and 2 percent, respectively) categories based on a body mass index (BMI) measure. It appears that the endomorphs are more likely to be among incarcerated adult populations these days than are the ecto- and mesomorphs! Incarcerated females were more likely to fall into the obese and morbidly obese categories than being just overweight compared to the males. Likewise, incarcerated females were more likely to report ever having a chronic condition than were males. Age is again related to obesity levels, as levels of overweight and obesity increase from younger through middle-aged and then drop back slightly in the older (50+) age group. Ethnicity also appears to play some role, with 44 percent of Hispanics being overweight.

Mental Health

The reader is no doubt aware that jails and prisons in the United States process and house more mentally ill individuals than do mental health hospitals. The second area of health concern, and the largest contributor to health burden in the criminal justice system, falls on local jails and prisons. Table 34.2 provides a comparison of self-report mental health burden at two points in time. The summary in Table 34.2 is intended only to illustrate the burden of mental health disorders encountered in correctional settings across the United States. The reader is cautioned that the data on various specific disorders were asked in different ways in the 2002–04 samples and the 2011–12 sample. This is also true of the "any mental health" versus "no mental health" problem questions in the first row. Thus, only the self-report data were asked in a consistent manner across the surveys and allow us to make direct comparisons.

The question about ever having been told by a professional that one has a mental health problem shows the greatest change over the course of a decade. Between the 2002–04 surveys and the 2011–12 survey, there was a four-fold increase in the number of jail inmates and prisoners, respectively, who reported this sort of conversation. It is unclear what explains this rapid increase. Reported hospitalizations for mental health conditions were also up sharply over the decade, as was reported mental health therapy. Use of medication for mental health purposes did not seem to have increased substantially over the decade between the surveys.

Reported mental health problems among jail inmates are higher than those reported among prisoners, as observed in the data on physical health problems. That is, the rates are higher in the community than among those who are sequestered in prison facilities. This suggests that something happens in criminal justice processing to reduce the level of mental health burden among longer-term inhabitants of correctional facilities. Exactly what that might be remains a matter for empirical study.

Substance Use/Abuse

Unfortunately, the most recent national-level study of mental health problems among inmates and prisoners did not include a measure of substance use and abuse—at least not as yet printed. Looking back a decade, however, we can see that just over half (53 percent) of jail inmates and state prisoners reported a substance use problem, and just under half (46 percent) of federal prisoners reported such.

The Treatment Episodes Data System (TEDS) operated by the Substance Abuse and Mental Health Services Agency (HRSA) does allow us a glimpse at the contribution to the substance abuse treatment population made by correctional populations. In 2011, 588,000

Table 34.2 Mental Health Problems Reported by Jail Inmates and Prisoners (Percentages), 2004 and 2011–12

	Jail Inmates[1] *2002*	*State Prisoners*[1] *2004*	*Federal Prisoners*[1] *2004*	*% Jail Inmates*[2] *2011–12*	*Prisoners (combined)*[2] *2011–12*
Any mental health problem	64	56	45	49	33
Recent history of mental health problem	21	24	14	Not asked	Not asked
Told had disorder by mental health professional	11	9	5	44	37
Had overnight hospital stay	5	5	2	13	9
Used prescribed medications	14	15	10	20	15
Had professional mental health therapy	10	8	15	39	36
Symptoms of mental health disorders	61	49	40	—	—
Major depressive disorder	29	24	16	22	18
Mania disorder	54	43	35	26	15
Psychotic disorder	24	15	10	—	—
Drug dependence or abuse	53	53	46	—	—

[1]James, D.J. & Glaze, L.E. (2006)
[2]Beck, A.J., Berzofsky, M., Kaspar, R. & Krebbs, C. (2013).

individuals, or 35 percent of all discharges from substance abuse treatment programs had entered from the criminal justice system (Smith and Strashny 2013). It is clear that criminal justice-involved persons are likely to be affected by substance abuse and misuse to a level that requires professional assistance. Often this involves other physical and mental health co-morbidities.

Disability

A first-of-its-kind report on disability status among those in jails and prisons during 2011–12 (Bronson, Maruschak and Berzofsky 2015) revealed that about 40 percent of jail inmates and 30 percent of prisoners (state and federal) reported at least one disability. These figures are nearly four times (among inmates) and three times (among prisoners) higher than observed in the general public. The *National Inmate Survey* measured "disability types include hearing, vision, cognitive, ambulatory, self-care, and independent living, which refers to the ability to navigate daily life schedules, activities, and events without assistance." Women tended to report higher levels of disability (49 percent in jails and 40 percent in prisons) than did men (39 percent and 31 percent, respectively). Non-Hispanic white and multi-racial/ethnic prisoners were more likely to report disability than African American (black) and Latino prisoners, but no significant differences among racial/ethnic groupings were noted at the jail level. As well, 53 percent of jail inmates and 54 percent of prisoners with a disability were more likely to report a chronic physical disease status than those without a disability (21 percent and 18 percent, respectively). Chronic conditions range from obesity to cancers, but no measure of mental health burden was included.

Complicating matters for correctional health purposes, older (aged 50 or greater) inmates in jails (60 percent) and prisons (44 percent) reported disabilities at a higher rate than younger incarcerated populations. According to Bronson et al. (2015: 5), older incarcerated individuals were "6 times more likely to report having a hearing disability, 4 to 5 times more likely to report a vision disability, and more than twice as likely to report an independent living disability." Cognitive disabilities, affecting the ability to perform a variety of mental tasks (but not including a mental health disorder), burdened approximately 30 percent of the jail population and 20 percent of the prison population. This compares to a rate of about 5 percent in the general population.

Summary of Disease and Disability Burden

The Pew Charitable Trusts (2014) found that 44 states spent 6.5 billion dollars on correctional health care in 2008, or nearly 18 percent of the total correctional budgets in those states. Pew reported a 28 percent median growth in correctional health care costs in those states between 2001 and 2008. These numbers do not include correctional health costs for jails. In the end, states and county governments are spending a great deal of their revenues on episodic health care required to meet a Constitutional mandate unlike that imposed on any other public institution (discussed hereafter).

The author will note two principle items of interest from the data presented, and the reader may note more. First, regardless of the stage of incarceration, physical and mental morbidity, as well as disability, are higher among criminal justice populations than among the general public (from which the incarcerated population is drawn). Second, as we move from jail (community-level) to prison (state- or national-level), those differences narrow, if only slightly. Other than the possible effect of an older average age among prisoners, it appears that the highest level of physical and mental health burden is observed closest to the community. The same relationship is noted in regards to disability.

One might ask where the observed difference goes between jail and prison, since less than 10 percent of those booked into jails proceed on to prisons in an average year. The author would suggest that the largest proportion of those under criminal justice supervision provides the answer—probationers. Probationers reflect the rates of disease and disability observed in jail inmate populations, yet they remain in the community. Yet, we have no monitoring/surveillance system for assessing the health of this community-based population. Nor do we have any systematic data on their access to or utilization of health services in the community. And, at least in non-Medicaid extension states (discussed below), we have no provision for health care for probationers or parolees such as exists inside correctional institutions. Until 2016 federal parolees and half-way house residents were not covered by medical insurance after release from prison; probationers are still not covered.

Thus, the data collected in these nationally representative samples of inmates and prisoners provide us with a description of the disease and disability burdens of those entering or remaining in correctional institutions. They do not provide us with an understanding of how that picture relates to those who are released into the community to serve out their remaining sentence period. That group represents approximately two-thirds of the annual population of individuals under some form of correctional supervision and/or control. This suggests a gap of major proportion in our knowledge of how health and disability status affect performance of sentenced individuals.

Knowledge of disability status becomes increasingly important in the design and operation of correctional facilities. This is not only to maintain compliance with federal laws and regulations such as the Americans with Disabilities Act (ADA). Disabilities also affect facilities operations to protect inmates and prisoners from unwanted sexual victimization and assaults of other kinds from fellow incarcerated individuals and staff. This knowledge should help also inform the development of legislation, regulation, and policy toward who is appropriate for incarceration and who might be best managed in alternative settings such as nursing homes. This may require a shift in thinking among the public and legislators about the function(s) of jails and prisons with regards to the health and safety of the incarcerated as well as the community.

To say that the burden of disease and disability among those who are processed through correctional facilities in a given year is bad, especially compared to the general population, would seem to be an understatement. The image of a young, healthy, mesomorphic criminal seems to be at odds with what these data suggest. Our correctional facilities at all levels are dealing with unprecedented levels of health burden, yet they are rarely staffed or funded to deal effectively with that charge. As we move through the remainder of this entry, we will examine the requirements for "adequate, reactive" health care provision and the reality of the burden of our populations. We will also examine the issue of "flow" or "churn" in the early stages of the process and how it affects the ability of corrections to address the burden of disease and disability that comes through the door.

A Brief History of Correctional Health Care in the U.S.

The start of modern correctional health care is generally traced to the 1976 *Estelle v. Gamble* decision. Prior to that, healthcare and corrections were rarely mentioned in the same sentence. Subsequent Supreme Court decisions, the HIV/AIDS, drug resistant tuberculosis (TB), and hepatitis C (HCV) epidemics, and the expansion of health care professional opportunities in correctional settings have raised the profile of and concern with health care in jails, detention centers, and prisons. Among corrections practitioners, health care is now recognized as an important and costly issue. Among correctional administrators and legislative bodies, correctional health care is viewed as an extremely costly, controversial, public good. Yet, in corrections and criminal justice educational programs, one is likely to note relatively little attention paid to this increasingly important aspect of corrections management and operations.

Both in teaching about correctional health care and in conversations with others not directly involved in correctional issues, the question of why inmates get "free" health care is raised. Generally speaking, prisoners' constitutional right to adequate health care centers around the concept of "deliberate indifference" (Kay and Branham 1991). Since inmates are almost completely at the mercy of the correctional facility (and by extension, the administration and officers), and are unable to obtain medical services when, where, and by whom they wish, the correctional institution must provide for their health care. In the 1976 *Estelle v. Gamble* ruling, it was the allegation that correctional officials ignored the inmate's medical condition and allowed the condition to worsen that caught the attention of the Supreme Court of the United States (SCOTUS). They reasoned that deliberate indifference to an inmate's medical condition was a form of "cruel and unusual punishment," and violated the Eighth Amendment prohibition against such punishment. Deliberate indifference generally requires that an inmate demonstrate either "an intentional delay in care, a denial of care, or callous indifference to obvious medical needs" (Kay and Branham 1991: 5)

The constitutional rights of persons detained in jails prior to conviction are based in Fourteenth Amendment protections of "due process." This was decided in the *Bell v. Wolfish* (1980) ruling by the SCOTUS. Even though one has not been convicted, if an individual is in the custody of the jail, one cannot freely obtain medical services. If jailers are aware of a medical need and do not respond (deliberate indifference), then the due process rights of the accused are violated. The SCOTUS determined that deliberate indifference to the medical needs of preconviction detainees amounted to punishment, which is illegal prior to conviction (Kay and Branham 1991: 6–7). Whether the Eighth or Fourteenth Amendment is the basis of health care provision to inmates, the key test becomes the "state of mind" of the correctional officer and official. If correctional personnel are aware of an inmate's serious medical need and do not respond appropriately, the deliberate indifference standard may be invoked.

Anno (2002: 36–37) stated that case law has led to three basic rights of inmate health care. First is access to care. She summarized: "Access to medical care must be provided for any condition, be it medical, dental or psychological, if the denial of care might result in pain, suffering, deterioration or degeneration." Second is the right to "care that is ordered" by medical personnel. Finally, there is the right to "professional medical judgment," medical professionals making decisions rather than correctional officials, officers, or inmates (as often happened pre-*Estelle*). Kay and Branham (1991: 14) note that the correctional system "must provide some assurance that needed medical treatment can be obtained." Whether such treatment will be the best or minimally adequate will depend on the resources available to the institution, as well as who is evaluating the quality of the care provided.

The legal environment surrounding correctional health care is fairly well established 40 years after *Estelle*. How it gets delivered is another matter. The next section will canvass some of the issues associated with correctional health care and explore issues of continuity of care outside of correctional facilities.

The Organization of Correctional Health Care in the U.S.

Governance of Correctional Health Care

The United States correctional system is the most complex formal system in the world. While there are criminal statutes at the Federal level, the primary responsibility for the development of criminal law is left to the 50 states and territories. Within those states and territories, the provision of correctional services is left to the states and 3,068 counties. The 3,245 jail facilities across those counties are operated mostly by Sheriff's Offices, but some are operated on a regional basis with multiple counties involved, and some are operated by county commissions. For most counties this means a directly elected Sheriff has operational responsibility for the jail. Budgets for the provision of health care come from County funds, appropriated by the County Commission or equivalent governmental body. While the locus of direct control over a jail might vary across the nation, the funds to support the jail are almost exclusively going to come from county tax payers, perhaps with some contractual funds coming in to house state or federal detainees and prisoners.

To summarize this section, the provision of health care (physical and mental) is a mandate from the Constitutional foundation of the United States. In an environment of non-universal health care it is, for the state and local governments, a generally unfunded health care mandate. Governance responsibility may rest at the county level, but mandates for health care requirements are generally developed at the federal level. This leaves the vast burden for the health care of detainees, inmates, and prisoners on county and state taxpayers.

Because our governance system in the United States is so locally focused with regard to correctional systems, we do not have a health care provision system similar to that found in many other developed nations. In Australia or England and Wales, for example, the care delivered in remand centers and prisons is often provided by the same organization that provides such care in the community. In the United States, however, it is rare to find a community-based hospital providing the health care inside a jail. Several states have utilized university medical schools to provide health care in state prisons, but that is a trend that appears to be fading. Some private prison (and jail) management companies incorporate a health care section or subsidiary in their contracts. In other settings, the health care provider may be distinct from other service providers in the jail or prison. And, it is likely that most of the jails in the United States, those in the "medium" jail category, are likely to hire their own staff to provide health care services.

The role of "voluntary compliance" standards in the governance of correctional health care should be addressed, if only briefly (see Anno 2002: 23–24). As a result of the *Estelle* and other decisions, the first association focusing on correctional health care exclusively was formed as a task force of the American Bar Association and the American Medical Association. This became the National Commission on Correctional Health Care (NCCHC). Other organizations, such as the American Public Health Association, have also promulgated correctional health standards, though they are rarely utilized for anything other than reference material. For at least two decades, the NCCHC provided the complimentary correctional health standards to the broader standards of the American Correctional Association (ACA). In the late 1990s and early 2000s, the relationship between the two organizations frayed and the ACA began to develop its own health care standards. This has resulted in two accrediting agencies for correctional health care (NCCHC and ACA). While many of the same individuals are involved in the development of the standards for both organizations, and conduct many of the accreditation visits, the two organizations have approached standards development in different ways at times. Thus, when we discuss the governance of correctional health care, we must include an analysis of whose standards are in use by a particular jail or prison system.

Perhaps foreshadowing the final section, the truth is that we know relatively little about how health care is provided across the nation for jail populations. Some state systems make this information available on their websites; others do not. In monitoring/surveillance terms, perhaps a first step in determining how correctional health care is structured would be to conduct a thorough survey of health care provision and providers. This brings us to the final section of the entry.

The Future of Correctional Healthcare in the U.S.

In the autumn of 2010 a new law was enacted that has the potential to change the provision of health care for inmates and prisoners from a local responsibility to a nationally shared system similar to those found in other developed democracies—the Affordable Care Act (The Patient Protection and Affordable Care Act, PL111–148). Generally speaking, the Act does not change previous legislation forbidding use of federal funds for in-facility health care (except for juveniles).

The use of Medicaid funding for prisoner health care had been a topic of discussion for many years. Because some proportion of those who spend time in jails and state prisons are Medicaid eligible, continuing to bill Medicaid for services received in jail or prison would seem to make sense. As a sweetener to states to expand Medicaid coverage as part of the passage of the Affordable Care Act, those states that expanded services are now allowed to use Medicaid funds (assuming the inmate/prisoner is covered by Medicaid) for inmate/prisoner treatment provided outside the institution. Those states that have resisted Medicaid expansion are still unable to access such Medicaid funds.

Several states and local jurisdictions in expansion states have begun to implement a process by which Medicaid-eligible inmates/prisoners are identified and the qualification and enrollment process begun during incarceration. If the individual is held long enough, s/he may walk out of the facility with a Medicaid card; if not, a referral to an agency that will continue to pursue the eligibility will be made. This example may well foreshadow the future of health insurance enrollment for eligible criminal justice-involved individuals until the advent of universal health care. Access, as Potter and Rosky (2012) noted, is a different issue.

What is the Role of Social Science Criminology/Criminal Justice in Correctional Health?

When the author worked at the Centers for Disease Control and Prevention as a member of the Corrections and Substance Abuse Team, fellow employees were often dismayed that I could not tell them how health care was delivered at any particular facility in the nation. After all, the Federal Bureau of Prisons utilized the services of the Public Health Services Corps (PHS) to deliver care to federal prisoners. What did the others do? As noted in the previous section, we don't really know.

Colleagues in the public health academic and federal government arenas have devoted a great deal of attention to the "epidemiology of" a variety of diseases among correctional populations. They have published a range of articles on how corrections and the criminal justice system contribute to health problems as a form of collateral damage from mass incarceration. We summarized many of these themes in *Epidemiological Criminology: A Public Health Approach to Crime and Violence* (Akers, Potter, and Hill 2012). As we noted, many to most of these articles are devoid of understanding of the criminal justice process or the laws associated with a variety of crimes that bring individuals to the attention of criminal justice agencies. They also tend to overlook the lack of a public health delivery system in the United States (see Potter and Rosky 2012).

Compared to the scant attention paid to issues of correctional health in academic criminology and criminal justice journals and texts, public health occupies the foreground in this area. An agenda for students (and faculty) to bring our academic enterprise into the leadership role might look something like this:

- Development of an empirically informed explanation of the relationship between poor health and criminal behavior; alternatively, the relationship between good health and conforming behavior. Looking at the data presented earlier, it appears that poor health is associated with finding oneself in jail and prison. Why? Are only those who are bad at avoiding detection due to poor health being caught?

- Development of a scientifically sound image of correctional health care provision across the United States. This agenda should pay particular attention to the issues of governance of correctional health care provision, privatization versus in-house, and continuity-of-care (COC) upon release to the community. They key question here is whether a particular form of health care delivery and COC produces better outcomes and under what conditions.
- A longitudinal study of the impact of correctional health care interventions on the immediate and longer-term health of criminal justice-involved individuals. This is the area where the situation of probationers with and without access to adequate health services in a community should reside. Basically, this is the question of whether correctional health care improves or diminishes the impact of community health care, and vice versa, and what factors facilitate/hinder the utilization of community care services among previously incarcerated and criminal justice-involved individuals.
- Finally, in this suggestion list, the impact of working in correctional settings on the health of staff of all types. Our emphasis has been to date almost exclusively on the plight of those caught in the mass incarceration boom since the late 1980s. Administering punishment may well have a direct impact in terms of work-related injuries and infections. It may also have a longer-term impact on the health and wellbeing of those charged with performing one of society's least desired functions.

Conclusion

In this Handbook entry I have tried to cover standard information covered in more detail elsewhere and bring in new data and developments in correctional health and health care. It has been suggested by others who research the area of correctional health issues that criminology and criminal justice academics have little interest in the topic. This is evidenced, they say, by the rejections of articles by journal reviewers as not being relevant to the discipline. At the same time, health journals are likely to reject the same articles because they are not focused enough on health. This situation reminds me of claims made by "critical theorists" about their marginalization by mainstream criminology and criminal justice. The only path forward for academic criminology and criminal justice professionals seems to lie in defining the actual relationship among health, criminality, and criminal justice, or the first agenda point. Until then, the "moveable feast" of that relationship being both protective and risk-producing, explaining everything and nothing simultaneously, will doom the topic to the margins. It remains for rigorous theorizing and researching scientists to address the topic or leave it to public health and think-tank researchers. Hopefully this entry will spur some of that rigorous thinking and research.

References

Akers, Timothy A., Roberto H. Potter, and Carl V. Hill. 2013. *Epidemiological Criminology: A Public Health Approach to Crime and Violence*. San Francisco, CA: Jossey-Bass.

Anno, B. Jaye. 2002. *Prison Health Care: Guidelines for the Management of an Adequate Delivery System*, Second Edition. Chicago, IL: National Commission on Correctional Health Care.

Beck, Allen J., Marcus Berzofsky, Rachel Caspar, and Christopher Krebs. 2013. *Sexual victimization in prisons and jails reported by inmates, 2011–12*. Washington, DC: U.S. Bureau of Justice Statistics.

Bronson, Jennifer, Laura M. Maruschak, and Marcsu Berzofsky. 2015. *Disabilities among Prison and Jail Inmates, 2011–2012*. Washington, DC: U.S. Department of Justice.

James, Doris J., and Lauren E. Glaze. 2006. "Highlights mental health problems of prison and jail inmates." Retrieved on June 23, 2017 from http://citeseerx.ist.psu.edu/viewdoc/summary?doi=10.1.1.694.3355

Kay, Susan L., and Lynn Branham. 1991. *The Constitutional Dimensions of an Inmate's Right to Health Care*. Chicago, IL: National Commission on Correctional Health Care.

Maruschak, Laura. 2006. *Medical Problems of Jail Inmates*. Washington, DC: U.S. Department of Justice.

Maruschak, Laura. 2008. *Medical Problems of Prisoners*. Washington, DC: U.S. Department of Justice.

Maruschak, Laura M., Marcus Berzofsky, and Jennifer Unangst. 2015. *Medical Problems of State and Federal Prisoners and Jail Inmates, 2011–12*. Washington, DC: U.S. Department of Justice.

Pew Charitable Trusts. 2014. Managing Prison Health Care Spending. Retrieved May 10, 2017 from www.pewtrusts.org/en/research-and-analysis/reports/2014/05/15/managing-prison-health-care-spending

Potter, Roberto Hugh, and Jeffrey W. Rosky. 2012. "The Iron Fist in the Latex Glove: The Intersection of Public Health and Criminal Justice." *American Journal of Criminal Justice* 38(2): 276–288.

Smith, Kelley, and Alexander Strashny. 2013. *Characteristics of Criminal Justice System Referrals Discharged from Substance Abuse Treatment and Facilities with Specially Designed Criminal Justice Programs*. The CBHSQ Report: April 26, 2016. Rockville, MD: Center for Behavioral Health Statistics and Quality, Substance Abuse and Mental Health Services Administration.

35 Solitary Confinement and Supermax Custody

Keramet Reiter

Solitary confinement has existed in Europe since the first prisons were built there in the early 1700s (Cajani 1996; O'Donnell 2014: 6) and in the United States since within a few decades of when the first prisons were built there, as early as the 1790s (O'Donnell 2014: 7; Wines 1895). The physical and administrative structures governing the practice of solitary confinement, as well as the definitions of what actually constitutes solitary confinement, have changed drastically over the last three centuries. But some form of isolation has remained integral to modern incarceration in jails, penitentiaries, and prisons. Disputes over whether solitary confinement "works" to deter, reform, or control, or alternatively, "works" to destroy, have plagued the practice continuously since its first inception. These disputes persist—remaining divisive and unresolved in the twenty-first century. This entry provides a brief overview of this history of solitary confinement, from the 1700s through the 2010s, touching on the purposes, physical and administrative structures, and critiques of the various forms of solitary confinement that have been deployed in prisons over the last three centuries. The focus is on the United States, but the entry touches on European and international practices, as well.

Simply for organizational purposes, the eras of solitary confinement are divided into four periods of interest: prototypes, 1700–1890; short-term containment, 1890–1971; long-term institutionalization, 1971–1986; supermaxes 1986–present. The demarcation of years in each period suggests a few moments of discontinuities in the practice of solitary confinement that are especially relevant to the overall history. These periods are hardly the only possible ways to organize the history of solitary confinement, however. In her periodization of solitary confinement, for instance, Sharon Shalev focused not on the administrative structure of solitary confinement, but rather on the changing goals of the practice: moral reform until the late nineteenth century, behavioral modification in the early part of the twentieth century, and risk-management in the late twentieth century (2009: 13–22). The subsequent sections touch on these themes as well, in describing and analyzing how the practice of solitary confinement has developed over time.

Prototypes, 1700–1890

The first western prisons—in Europe in the early 1700s, and in the United States in the late 1700s—sought to create monastic-like spaces, mingling isolation and silence in a range of different prison models. One of the earliest known prisons was the *Casa di Correzione* of San Michele, built in Rome, Italy in 1703. There, juvenile prisoners slept alone at night, and spent their days chained to desks in silence (O'Donnell 2014: 6). Visitors were impressed with the religious discipline imposed on the young wards (Cajani 1996: 301). In the United States, later in the eighteenth century, prison designs quickly bifurcated along two models: those that prioritized isolation, and those that prioritized silence (Rubin 2015: 373). Eastern

State Penitentiary, opened in Philadelphia in 1829 and completed in 1836, became the icon of the "Pennsylvania System": prisoners lived in isolation in single cells, equipped with bathrooms with modern plumbing and small outdoor spaces, so there was little need to leave. Pennsylvania system prisoners did piecework labor in their cells during the day and had limited contact with prison personnel. Auburn State Penitentiary, opened in upstate New York in 1821, became the icon of the "Auburn System": at first Auburn prisoners were in total isolation in single cells, with nothing but a bible; however, this regime was quickly replaced with a system of congregate but silent factory labor during the day, and solitude at night (O'Donnell 2014: 8–13; Rubin 2015: 378).

Both the Auburn System and the Pennsylvania system at first received interest, attention, and acclaim, but later, both faced sharp criticisms, too. Charles Dickens and Alexis De Tocqueville, for instance, both toured the United States and visited the new penitentiaries; both condemned the extremes of silence and solitude that had been imposed in the early days of Auburn and Eastern State (Beaumont and de Tocqueville 1833; Dickens 1842). Nonetheless, both models were widely replicated. The Pennsylvania model was especially popular in Europe (O'Donnell 2014: 17; Smith 2004), while the Auburn model became most popular in the United States. According to Rubin's study of the diffusion of the two prison models across the United States in the nineteenth century: "By 1860, almost all the country's 32 modern prisons followed the Auburn System" (2015: 373). Rubin explained the triumph of the silent, congregate Auburn system as the result of multiple contingencies, including the organized and vocal supporters of the Auburn model, its apparently greater potential for profit, and the "failed experiment with solitary confinement" documented in Auburn's early days and alleged throughout Eastern State's first decades of existence (Rubin 2015: 390). Death and insanity were documented at Auburn, in its first years of operation, before the silent labor program was introduced, and at Eastern State throughout its early years of operation. As the prevalence of the Auburn model over the Pennsylvania model in the United States suggests, most jurisdictions took steps to limit the use of solitary confinement, mitigate its harshness, and even to eliminate it entirely (Haney and Lynch 1997).

Some scholars have argued that stories of death and insanity were overblown and not representative of the vast majority of prisoners who survived their time in solitary. Moreover, the early penitentiaries quickly became overcrowded, compromising the operating principles of solitude (O'Donnell 2014: 19–26). Whether for philosophical or practical reasons, solitary confinement, especially in the long-term iterations first imagined for both the Auburn and Pennsylvania systems in the United States, fell out of favor by the end of the nineteenth century.

A U.S. Supreme Court decision in 1890 seemingly marked the end of this era of experimentation with long-term solitary confinement. *In Re Medley* concerned the death sentence of James Medley, who had been convicted of first-degree murder in Colorado in 1889. Between the time of Medley's crime and the time he was sentenced to death, Colorado passed a law requiring that death-sentenced prisoners be held in solitary confinement (instead of sharing cells with prisoners in the local jail). Medley challenged his death sentence on this basis, and the Supreme Court held that the conditions in solitary confinement amounted to such an extreme increase in the degree of punishment to which Medley was subjected that they violated the *ex post facto* prohibition on changing the punishment for a crime after the crime took place. The Court found the violation to be so egregious that it simply ordered Medley to be set free; his solitary confinement, the decision implied, had been punishment enough.

A brief excerpt of the opinion reveals just how decisive the Court's condemnation of solitary confinement was:

> A considerable number of the prisoners fell, after even a short confinement, into a semi-fatuous condition . . . and others became violently insane; others, still, committed suicide; while those who stood the ordeal better were not generally reformed, and in most cases did not recover sufficient mental activity to be of any subsequent service to the community.
>
> (*In Re Medley* 1890: at 168)

The 1890 *Medley* decision, in tone and effect, seemed like a conclusive end to the Pennsylvania System model of long-term solitary confinement in U.S. prisons.

Short-Term Containment, 1890–1971

Though *In Re Medley* dismissed solitary confinement as a barbaric practice of the past, the fact that the practice, already heavily criticized throughout the late nineteenth century, crept up in a Colorado case in 1890 is indicative of its persistence in prisons across the United States, albeit in more limited forms than the long-term isolation countenanced by the Pennsylvania System. For one, solitary confinement continued to be a condition of confinement often imposed on death row prisoners, into the present era. Though no longer idealized or normalized, solitary confinement also continued to be used as a short-term tool of control in prisons across the United States. Prison records, memoirs, and litigation from throughout the early twentieth century reveal frequent uses of short-term solitary confinement.

As early as 1891, just one year after its decision in the *Medley* case, the U.S. Supreme Court upheld the constitutionality of solitary confinement in a death-row prototype facility, where prisoners awaited execution in New York State (*McElvaine v. Brush* 1891). In the subsequent 50 years, the U.S. Supreme Court only mentioned solitary confinement a few more times—describing it as a severe, but constitutional form of punishment (*United States v. Moreland*, 258 U.S. 433, 449 (1922) (Brandeis, J., dissenting); *Chambers v. Florida*, 309 U.S. 227, 237–38 (1940); Haney and Lynch 1997: 540). Prison records from the early twentieth century provide further evidence of short-term uses of solitary confinement in prisons across the United States. For instance, records from Alcatraz, a high-security U.S. federal prison, which operated from 1932 to 1964, reveal that the warden would occasionally throw troublesome prisoners into the "Spanish dungeons" for a few days at a time (Odier 1982: 117).

In the 1960s, a new series of court cases across the United States again revealed the pervasiveness of solitary confinement—as a tool of control imposed on misbehaving prisoners. As with the Spanish dungeons at Alcatraz, this mid-century form of solitary confinement usually lasted anywhere from a few days to a few weeks but no longer. In *Sostre v. McGinnis*, for instance, Martin Sostre, a New York state prisoner, challenged his placement in segregation as punishment for his politics and in-prison organizing. The New York district court that heard the case found that segregation for more than 15 days could easily jeopardize a prisoner's sanity and, thereby, violated the Eighth Amendment prohibition against cruel and unusual punishment (*Sostre v. McGinnis* 1971; Gordon 2010: 96–132). *Sostre* was representative of the attitude of courts across the United States hearing challenges to the conditions of confinement in prisons and considering, especially, conditions in solitary confinement: the durations of such conditions of confinement were presumptively limited to a few weeks, 15–30 days at most (Reiter 2012a: 81). In what would become an even more expansive case, three prisoners in Arkansas legally challenged the abusive conditions of confinement in the Arkansas state penitentiary: electric shocks, punitive rape, forced labor, and long durations in punitive isolation. The case quickly expanded into the first class action case on behalf of an entire population of prisoners within a single prison (Reiter 2012a: 87).

Among other remedies, the Arkansas district court imposed—and the U.S. Supreme Court ultimately upheld—a 30-day limit on punitive isolation in Arkansas (*Holt v. Sarver* 1970; *Hutto v. Finney* 1978).

By the early 1970s, courts across the United States were considering challenges to the conditions of confinement and operational policies of more than 30 different state prison facilities (Feeley and Rubin 1998). The majority of these cases addressed conditions and durations of isolation (Reiter 2012a)—a clear indication that, in spite of the 1890 decision in *In Re Medley*, isolation continued to be used in prisons across the United States throughout the twentieth century. However, the facts detailed in these court cases reveal that most uses of isolation and solitary confinement in U.S. prisons were relatively short term, measured in days, weeks, and sometimes months, but not years. This started to change in 1971.

While prisoners litigated the conditions of their confinement, especially in isolation, they organized to resist the abuses they suffered in prison in other ways as well. Much of the 1960s and 1970s prisoners' rights litigation across the United States involved concerted, non-violent organizing. But this organizing and advocacy was not always non-violent. In fact, in many of the biggest state prison systems, violence, in the form of both prisoner and officer homicides, was growing. And in 1971, in the midst of all the litigation previously mentioned, the violence reached unprecedented levels. In August 1971, George Jackson allegedly attempted to escape from the isolation unit where he was being housed in San Quentin's Adjustment Center. Competing stories about exactly what Jackson intended to do and who killed whom on that fateful afternoon remain unresolved. But the death toll was clear: Jackson was shot dead on the prison yard, and two other prisoners and three guards were found stabbed to death on the "Adjustment Center" cell block (Reiter 2016: 34–58). Nineteen days later, prisoners at Attica State Prison in New York revolted. Prisoners took over the institution and negotiated with state officials for better conditions of confinement; when negotiations broke down, the National Guard entered the prison, and 40 people died. The violence was not confined to the coasts. Prisoners and guards fought, with fatal consequences, in Louisiana State Penitentiary, Iowa State Penitentiary, Norfolk Prison in Massachusetts, and the United States Penitentiary in Marion, Illinois, to name just a few examples (Reiter 2016: 57). To sum up, prisoners were fighting for their rights in court, but they were also fighting for their lives on cellblocks across the country. Prison officials felt under siege on multiple fronts, and they began to develop new tools of control.

Long-Term Institutionalization, 1971–1986

Following Jackson's death at San Quentin, the revolt at Attica, and the violence in places such as Louisiana, Iowa, and Massachusetts, a few prisoners at a time, and then entire blocks of prisons, were "locked down." Prison guards locked prisoners, who were believed to be or accused of being responsible for violence, into their cells and cancelled work programs, education programs, treatment programs, and group activities from recreation to eating in congregate dining halls. The lockdowns lasted first for months, and then years at a time (Bissonette 2008; Cummins 1994: 232; *Toussaint v. McCarthy* 1984: 1397, 1410; Ward and Breed 1984).

For example, Johnny Spain and Hugo Pinell, who were accused of plotting with George Jackson to escape from San Quentin prison, were locked into their cells following Jackson's death and not released again for any kind of group activity for the durations of their prison sentences. Spain challenged his conviction and was finally released from prison 17 years after Jackson's death, in 1988 (Reiter 2016: 127). Pinell died in prison in 2015, having spent more than 40 years in continuous solitary confinement (Reiter 2016: 1). In the year after Jackson died, the lockdowns expanded to include any prisoner believed to have been associated with Jackson, or the in-prison organization with which he was associated, the Black Guerrilla Family (Reiter 2016: 53).

Other states followed similar patterns. For instance, three (black) prisoners accused of killing a (white) guard at Louisiana's Angola State Penitentiary were locked down in 1972; each would spend between 29 and 42 years in total solitary confinement. After two guards were murdered in two separate incidents on the same day in October 1983 at the United States Penitentiary, Marion (a federal prison facility), all 435 cells at the facility were locked down. A few of the prisoners involved in that incident remain in solitary confinement, more than three decades later.

These extended lockdowns produced further litigation. In California, for instance, Johnny Spain and Hugo Pinell, along with the four other prisoners accused of conspiring with George Jackson to escape from San Quentin (known colloquially as the "San Quentin Six"), filed *Spain v. Procunier* in December 1973, in which they complained about both the lack of due process underlying their assignment to isolation in the San Quentin Adjustment Center and the harsh conditions of confinement there. Prisoners in Illinois and Louisiana, Massachusetts, and New York raised challenges not just to the conditions of their confinement, but to the long durations they were increasingly spending in solitary confinement. In spite of these legal challenges, states began building new facilities to maintain prisoners in even more restrictive conditions of indefinitely long-term solitary confinement.

Supermaxes, 1986–present

In 1986, the Arizona Department of Corrections opened the Special Management Unit (SMU) in Florence, Arizona. It had 786 total isolation beds. Officers in central control booths looked out over six pods at a time, each with six windowless cells. Prisoners would leave their rooms for an hour a day at most, when an officer pressed a series of buttons, opening one door at a time, in order to allow one prisoner at a time out into a solitary exercise yard, or for a shower. The facility was a technological marvel, from the centrally, computer-controlled, perforated steel cell doors to the smooth, poured concrete cells each with two concrete ledges for a bed and a desk. This was the first supermax: a hygienic, modern institution designed for long-term, total solitary confinement (Lynch 2010; Reiter 2016).

When California prison officials toured the country in 1986, looking for prototypes for a new high-security prison they planned to build, they stopped in Arizona last. They visited the SMU, and they were delighted by the carefully thought-out design details in the SMU. That was the prison they would build in California. Three years later, Pelican Bay State Prison opened in in Crescent City, California, on the state's northernmost border with Oregon. The prison's Security Housing Unit, or SHU, had 1,056 total isolation beds. Instead of grouping the pods into blocks of six, California prison officials had grouped them into blocks of eight. Otherwise, the similarities were striking—down to the perforated steel doors (Reiter 2016).

This was the beginning of the supermax phenomenon. Over the next ten years, most states followed the lead of Arizona and California and opened at least one supermax facility (National Institute of Corrections 1997). The federal bureau of prisons even opened its own supermax, the Administrative Maximum (or ADX) in Florence, Colorado, in 1994. The Vera Institute of Justice noted that between 1995 and 2000, the rate of solitary confinement use across the United States had increased far faster than the rate of incarceration (40 percent growth rate in solitary confinement versus a 28 percent growth rate in prison use) (Gibbons and Katzenbach 2006: 52–3). By 2000, the Bureau of Justice Statistics reported that there were 80,000 people in solitary confinement in U.S. prisons (2004). But scholars and justice department officials disagree over the exact numbers of people in solitary confinement in U.S. prisons today.

As it turns out, tracking the number of people in solitary confinement is hard to do for a number of reasons. First, every state prison system is different, which means they have different rules and definitions surrounding solitary confinement, including what the practice is called (e.g. the SHU in California and the SMU in Arizona), why prisoners get sent to solitary, and how long they spend there. Second, in all prison systems, the decision to send prisoners to solitary confinement, in supermax-like conditions, is an administrative one. Prison officials assess whether a prisoner (1) is too dangerous to be in the general prison population and must be confined indefinitely in solitary confinement (administrative segregation), (2) has broken a prison rule and must be placed in solitary confinement for a fixed period of time as punishment (disciplinary segregation), or (3) is too endangered in the general prison population and must be placed in solitary confinement for his or her own safety (protective custody). No judge or jury oversees this decision, so there is often no record of how the decision was made. Third, many state officials deny that the conditions in isolation units actually constitute solitary confinement, arguing that prisoners have access to lawyers and doctors when needed, televisions when available, and can shout at other prisoners through cell walls and drain pipes (Reiter 2016). In sum, many states likely underreport their use of solitary confinement, for a variety of definitional and labeling reasons.

In 2015, however, several major studies sought to reassess rates of solitary confinement use in the United States. A new Bureau of Justice Statistics report suggested that, in 2015, at least one in five prisoners had spent time in some form of solitary confinement in the prior year; given the U.S. prison population of just over 2 million, as many as 400,000 prisoners might be experiencing some form of isolation each year (Beck). A report co-produced by a Yale research institute and the Association of State Correctional Administrators estimated that between 80,000 and 100,000 prisoners were in some form of restricted housing (administrative, disciplinary, or protective) in 2015 (Baumgartel et al. 2015). The average lengths of stay in isolation can be as long as two to three years (Baumgartel et al. 2015: 27; Reiter 2012b: 548).

Recently, solitary confinement, especially its use in supermax facilities such as the Pelican Bay SHU and the Arizona SMU has come under sustained attack. Critics have argued that solitary confinement has been known to cause mental health problems since it was first used in the early nineteenth century, or at least as early as the Supreme Court's dismissal of the policy in 1890 in the *In Re Medley* decision (e.g., Haney and Lynch 1997). Some prisoners have been released directly from solitary confinement, after years in isolation, and have had trouble reintegrating into society, or worse, have committed horrific new crimes upon release (Reiter 2016: 166–193). Others have simply documented the serious psychological toll imposed by years on end of isolation (e.g., Casella, Ridgeway, and Shourd 2016; Reiter 2016). Between 2011 and 2013, prisoners in California's Pelican Bay SHU coordinated a series of massive hunger strikes, in which more than 30,000 prisoners participated, protesting the conditions of solitary confinement and the long durations of confinement in the SHU—more than 500 prisoners had been there more than ten years. During these hunger strikes, the U.N. Special Rapporteur on Torture declared that more than 15 days in solitary confinement potentially violated international human rights treaties (United Nations 2011). This touched off a new reform conversation across the United States about whether and when solitary confinement is an acceptable condition of confinement.

As U.S. prisons face a new era of critique and reform, one central question remains: will solitary confinement be abolished, will its use merely decline, or will its labels and forms change, while the practice, fundamentally, persists? The history of solitary confinement suggests that, in spite of fairly persistent critiques—from intellectuals, courts, prisoners, and human rights advocates—it has become more restrictive, more entrenched, and more widespread over the past two centuries.

References

Baumgartel, Sarah, Corey Guilmette, Johanna Kalb, Diana Li, Josh Nuni, Devon E. Porter, and Judith Resnik. 2015. "Time-In-Cell: The ASCA-Liman 2014 National Survey of Administrative Segregation in Prison." Retrieved May 13, 2017 from https://papers.ssrn.com/sol3/papers.cfm?abstract_id=2655627

Beaumont, Gustave de, and Alexis de Tocqueville. 1833. *On the Penitentiary System in the United States and Its Application to France*. Francis Lieber, trans. Philadelphia, PA: Casey, Lea & Blanchard. Retrieved May 10, 2017 from www.archive.org/details/onpenitentiarysy00beauuoft.

Beck, Allen J. 2015. *Use of restrictive housing in US prisons and jails, 2011–12*. Washington, DC: US Bureau of Justice Statistics.

Bissonette, Jamie. 2008. *When the Prisoners Ran Walpole: A True Story in the Movement for Prison Abolition*. With Ralph Hamm, Robert Dellelo, and Edward Rodman. Cambridge, MA: South End.

Bureau of Justice Statistics. 2004. *Census of State and Federal Adult Correctional Facilities*, 2000. Data available at National Archive of Criminal Justice Data. Retrieved May 10, 2017 from www.icpsr.umich.edu/NACJD.

Cajani, L. 1996. 'Surveillance and Redemption: The Casa di Correzione of San Michele in Ripa in Rome.' Pp. 301–324 in *Institutions of Confinement: Hospitals, Asylums and Prisons in Western Europe and North America, 1500–1950*, edited by N. Finzsch and R. Jutte. Cambridge: Cambridge University Press.

Casella, Jean, James Ridgeway, and Sarah Shourd. 2016. *Hell is a Very Small Place: Voices from Solitary Confinement*. New York: The New Press.

Chambers v. Florida, 309 U.S. 227, (1940).

Cummins, Eric. 1994. *The Rise and Fall of California's Radical Prison Movement*. Stanford, CA: Stanford University Press.

Dickens, Charles. 1842/1985. "Philadelphia and Its Solitary Prison." *American Notes for General Circulation*. London: Penguin. Available from the Literature Network, retrieved May 10, 2017 from www.online-literature.com/dickens/americannotes/8.

Feeley, Malcolm M., and Edward L. Rubin. 1998. *Judicial Policy Making and the Modern State: How the Courts Reformed America's Prisons*. New York: Cambridge University Press.

Gibbons, John J., and Nicholas J. Katzenbach (Commission Co-Chairs). 2006. *Confronting Confinement: A Report on the Commission on Safety and Abuse in America's Prisons*. New York: Vera Institute of Justice.

Gordon, Sarah Barringer. 2010. *The Spirit of the Law: Religious Voices and the Constitution in Modern America*. Cambridge, MA: Harvard University Press.

Haney, Craig and Mona Lynch. 1997. "Regulating Prisons of the Future: A Psychological Analysis of Supermax and Solitary Confinement." *New York University Review of Law and Social Change* 23(4): 477–570.

Holt v. Sarver, 309 F. Supp. 362 (E.D. Ark. 1970).

Hutto v. Finney, 437 U.S. 678 (1978).

In Re Medley, 134 U.S. 160 (1890).

Lynch, Mona. 2010. *Sunbelt Justice: Arizona and the Transformation of American Punishment*. Stanford, CA: Stanford University Press.

McElvaine v. Brush, 142 U.S. 155 (1891).

National Institute of Corrections, U.S. Department of Justice. 1997. *Supermax Housing: A Survey of Current Practice Special Issues in Corrections* (March). Retrieved May 10, 2017 from www.nicic.org/pubs/1997/013722.pdf

Odier, P. 1982. *The Rock: A History of the Fort/the prison*. Eagle Rock, CA: L'Image Odier.

O'Donnell, Ian. 2014. *Prisoners, Solitude and Time*. Oxford, UK: Oxford University Press.

Reiter, Keramet. 2012a. "The Most Restrictive Alternative: A Litigation History of Solitary Confinement in U.S. Prisons, 1960–2006." *Studies in Law, Politics, and Society* 57: 71–124.

Reiter, Keramet. 2012b. "Parole, Snitch, or Die: California's Supermax Prisons and Prisoners, 1987–2007," *Punishment and Society* 14(5): 530–563.

Reiter, Keramet. 2016. *23/7: Pelican Bay Prison and the Rise of Long-Term Solitary Confinement*. New Haven, CT: Yale University Press.

Rubin, Ashley. 2015. "A Neo-Institutional Account of Prison Diffusion." *Law & Society Review* 49(2): 365–399.

Shalev, Sharon. 2009. *Supermax: Controlling Risk through Solitary Confinement*. Devon, UK: Willan Publishing.

Smith, Peter Scharff. 2004. "Isolation and Mental Illness in Vridsløselille 1859–1873." *Scandinavian Journal of History* 29: 1–25.

Sostre v. McGinnis, 442 F.2d 178 (2d Cir. 1971), *en banc, rev'd in part sub nom Davidson v. Scully*, 694 F.2d 50 (2d Cir. 1982).

Spain v. Procunier, 600 F.2d 189, (9th Cir. 1979).

Toussaint v. McCarthy, 597 F. Supp. 1388 (N.D. Cal. 1984), *aff'd in part, rev'd in part,* 801 F.2d 1080 (9th Cir. 1986), *cert. denied,* 481 U.S. 1069 (1987).

United Nations. 2011. "Solitary Confinement Should Be Banned in Most Cases, UN Expert Says." U.N. News Centre, October 18. Retrieved May 10, 2017 from www.un.org/apps/news/story.asp?NewsID=40097

United States v. Moreland, 258 U.S. 433, (1922) (Brandeis, J., dissenting).

Ward, David A., and Alan F. Breed. 1984. *The United States Penitentiary, Marion, Illinois: A Report to the Judiciary Committee, United States House of Representatives*. Washington, DC: U.S. Government Printing Office, October.

Wines, F.H. 1895. *Punishment and Reformation: A Historical Sketch of the Rise of the Penitentiary System*. London: Swann Sonneschein.

36 The Importance of Prison Visitation in the Era of Mass Incarceration

Melinda Tasca

Despite evidence of slight declines in prison populations in some correctional systems, the United States continues to incarcerate its citizens at alarmingly high rates (Carson 2015). This get-tough approach to crime has resulted in significant segments of American society—notably poor, people of color—to experience incarceration directly or indirectly (Alexander 2012; Clear 2007; Lynch 2012; Pratt 2009). Nurse (2002) maintains that current crime control policies have been crafted to produce "deep breaks" among vulnerable family systems as a means to toughen community responses to crime. There is increasing evidence that incarceration can pose adverse short- and long-term effects on inmates, children, families, and communities (Braman 2004; Comfort 2009; Foster and Hagan 2007; Tasca, Rodriguez, and Zatz 2011; Turanovic, Rodriguez, and Pratt 2012; Wakefield and Wildeman 2014).

One way to mitigate potential harms of imprisonment, however, is through prison visitation (Tasca, Mulvey, and Rodriguez 2016). Prison visits offer an opportunity for inmates and their loved ones to maintain, build, and heal fragile and disrupted relationships (Maruna and Toch 2005). Garnering support and strengthening interpersonal ties during confinement are critical for improving inmate behavior, mental health, and post-release success. Visitation can also play a role in child wellbeing and overall family functioning (Arditti 2003, 2005' 2012). Research shows how institutional factors, family support capacities, interpersonal relationship dynamics, and inmate characteristics are contributors to both the likelihood and effects of prison visitation (Christian 2005; Cochran and Mears 2013). In short, there is a multifaceted linkage between prison visits and inmate, child, and family outcomes.

I organize this chapter along four dimensions. First, I discuss the purpose, goals, and typical policies associated with prison visitation. Second, I synthesize research on predictors of prison visitation. That is, who is visited and under what circumstances? Third, I take stock of the literature on the effects of such contact on inmates, children, and families. And finally, I highlight gaps in knowledge and conclude with ways to move this body of work forward.

Prison Visitation

For inmates and their families, visitation bridges prison and home (Arditti 2005; Beckmeyer and Arditti 2014). While other forms of contact are important, the ability to interact face-to-face is uniquely meaningful (Christian and Kennedy 2011; Maruna and Toch 2005). Visitation has the potential to benefit institutions, inmates, and visitors alike. To be sure, visitation is considered a useful tool for managing correctional populations by incentivizing good behavior (Cochran 2012). Although visits can be stressful experiences, they also provide a resource for inmates to cope with the pains of imprisonment and offer a chance to reset and strengthen interpersonal relationships. These encounters can signify a new beginning for inmates and visitors as the past can be confronted and plans for the future laid out as inmates are sober, attentive, and available often for the first time in a long time (Tasca et al. 2016). More broadly, visitation can improve reentry outcomes and the wellbeing of vulnerable families affected by mass incarceration (Bahr, Harris, Fisher, and Armstrong 2010; Brunton-Smith and McCarthy 2017).

Despite the widely held view that prison contact is advantageous in many ways, visitation has become less accessible to inmates and visitors over the past several decades in light of the get-tough approach to crime and justice (Tasca 2014). In particular, visitation restrictions were instituted in federal, state, and local correctional facilities across the country through a series of court rulings and administrative orders citing safety and fiscal concerns (Tewksbury and DeMichele 2005). Prior to the 1960s, the courts did not interfere in matters pertaining to prison contact, and instead left decisions and oversight to prison administrators. The rationale for this stance was grounded in the belief that judges lacked expertise in correctional management. As such, interference by the court might have a detrimental impact on prison order (see *Coffin v. Reichard* 1945; *Price v. Johnston* 1948; *Golub v. Krimsky* 1960). This position began to shift in the mid-to-late 1960s, however, as courts recognized that some inmate deprivations were a result of "capricious and arbitrary decisions" on behalf of prison officials. The courts subsequently determined that inmates were deserving of protection under the Civil Rights Act and encouraged courts to hear claims regarding constitutional rights violations (see *Cooper v. Pate* 1964; *Jackson v. Godwin* 1968). Prison visitation could not be restricted as an extended form of punishment during the 1970s, because visits were deemed to be a right afforded to all inmates (see *Agron v. Montanye* 1975; *Cooper v. Morin* 1979). These early rulings signaled the importance placed on protecting inmates' rights by the courts, which included prison visitation. As crime policies became increasingly punitive, this stance would later change.

Over the next several decades, philosophies of punishment began to shift away from rehabilitation towards incapacitation (Pratt 2009). Within the context of this swing in ideology, inmates' access to visitation was dramatically reduced. In *Overton v. Bazzetta* (2003), the U.S. Supreme Court decided that correctional administrators were best suited to define and determine appropriate means of achieving prison safety and security. This included allowing officials the ability to institute policies that limited inmates' access to visitation. In a 9–0 decision, the high court determined that although inmates retain some basic rights to contact, face-to-face visits are not constitutionally protected. Justice Kennedy wrote that "visitation alternatives need not be ideal, only available" in reference to non-contact visitation.

There have been significant ramifications resulting from the redefinition of prison visitation as a privilege as opposed to a right. For instance, prison officials started to restrict contact visitation as a disciplinary tool and severely limited visitation among inmates labeled "high institutional risk" (e.g., maximum security inmates; gang members) (Toch 2001, 2007). There have been additional restrictions placed on who is permitted to visit an inmate as well. Individuals frequently banned from visiting include those with criminal histories (even including arrests and misdemeanors in some correctional systems), undocumented immigrants, individuals applying to visit more than one inmate (which may result in a visitor having to choose between maintaining ties to a spouse or a family member, for example), some minors (e.g., non-relatives), and any individuals deemed to pose security or other risks to institutional order (e.g., correctional staff, known gang affiliates, victims) (Tasca 2014). Approved visitors commonly undergo searches of their person and property by dogs and/or staff, must adhere to strict dress codes and personal items allowances, and are limited in their ability to show affection to inmates (i.e. hugging, kissing, holding hands) (Comfort 2009). Some correctional facilities have been criticized for not offering child-friendly activities such as age-appropriate books or games that can help to encourage and enrich family interaction (Poehlmann, Dallaire, Loper, and Shear 2010).

Many institutions have also recently attached fees to visitation. Common practices include charging visitors' application and background fees or charging per-minute rates for virtual visitation (which is the only visiting option available in some correctional systems). Supporters of these for-profit strategies maintain that the collection of fees reduces the financial responsibility of taxpayers by lessening institutional operation costs. Opponents contend that these practices place undue burdens on visitors, many of whom are economically disadvantaged and have not been convicted of a crime (Tasca 2016). On the whole, visitation is generally viewed favorably by correctional administrators, inmates, families, and even the general public (Christian and Kennedy 2011). At the same time, institutional policies are not necessarily in line with promoting visitation access in practice.

Who Is Visited?

Prison visitation is an important source of social support for inmates during confinement. Such support can help to alleviate the pressures of prison life and contribute to the maintenance of relationships, which are important for reentry planning and to the reintegration process (Christian, Mellow, and Thomas 2006; Pierce 2015). Yet, a large number of inmates are never visited and far fewer are visited on a regular basis (Cochran, Mears, and Bales 2017). The literature points to a number of factors associated with the likelihood of prison contact, which I discuss hereafter.

Institutional barriers and family support capacities are important determinants of prison visitation (Connor and Tewksbury 2015; Lahm 2016). Access to reliable transportation is necessary; travel time and related costs are often high. For instance, visiting an inmate may require time off from work, the availability of sufficient funds not only for gas, but for food, and even lodging costs in some instances. Given the remote location of many prisons, nearby roads may be poorly maintained, making commutes stressful and even dangerous under adverse weather conditions. What is more, the farther an inmate is incarcerated from his or her family, the more challenging visitation becomes (Cochran, Mears, Bales, and Stewart 2016; Lindsey, Mears, Cochran, Bales, and Stults 2015). For some visitors, the barriers are simply too great. In a recent study, Cochran et al. (2016) found a negative relationship between distance and prison visitation. They explain how distance, as an obstacle to visitation, is intensified by community disadvantage. Separate research shows that inmates from economically marginalized areas and areas with high levels of social altruism actually receive a higher number of visits (Cochran et al. 2017). The authors suggest that communities most impacted by mass imprisonment may include large numbers of residents who work together to overcome visitation barriers. In other words, the most disadvantaged of families may need to rely on external social support in order to visit.

Relationship dynamics play a critical role in prison visitation patterns as well (Poehlmann et al. 2010). The motivation to keep the family together can be a primary driver of prison visitation, particularly when children are involved. Studies have documented caregivers' commitment to sustaining and repairing bonds with incarcerated parents for the sake of the children (Arditti 2012). In addition, research suggests that some romantic partners and relatives hold an idealized picture of inmates during incarceration, which may influence both the likelihood and frequency of visitation (Roy and Dyson 2005). Alternatively, other relationships may be too strained, resulting in family members distancing themselves or cutting off contact altogether with the inmate. This pattern might be most common among inmates who are high risk and high need (e.g., history of incarceration, mentally ill, substance abusers). Thus, prison contact can be dependent upon the status and strength of inmates' dynamic and complex relationship ties (Cochran and Mears 2013; Tasca 2016).

Prior work further demonstrates how visitation varies greatly by demographic characteristics. The majority of evidence indicates that women are more likely to be visited than men (Bales and Mears 2008; Clone and DeHart 2014). A primary explanation for this finding is that women are perceived as having stronger family ties, given most women inmates are mothers (Glaze and Maruschak 2010). The practical hurdles of visiting women may be even greater than visiting men, however. Since there are a higher number of male correctional facilities, men are typically housed closer to their families than are women. Other inmate characteristics such as race/ethnicity, age, marital status, material hardship, and educational attainment have also been linked to whether inmates are visited; although research is fairly mixed on the strength and direction of these relationships (Cochran et al., 2017).

Additionally, prior criminal history and offense-specific factors are commonly associated with the probability of visitation. Generally, inmates who have been previously incarcerated are less likely to be visited (Tewksbury and DeMichele 2005). Connor and Tewksbury (2015) found that an inmate's number of previous incarceration terms was among the strongest predictors of how many times he or she was visited. This relationship held across multiple visitor types including parents, children, siblings, and other extended relatives. The type of crime committed also emerged as a significant predictor of visitation in this study. Specifically, results revealed that inmates who were incarcerated for drug offenses were less often visited by children and siblings than inmates incarcerated for other types of crimes. A similar effect appeared for violent crime in which inmates incarcerated for violent offenses had lower odds of receiving visits from children relative to inmates in prison for other crimes. These findings are consistent with other work that shows the toll addiction takes on family relationships and how the incarceration of an individual prone to violence can be a reprieve for family members (Turanovic et al. 2012). Regarding sentence length, it is commonly suggested that the longer the term of confinement, the less likely an inmate is to be visited; though there are recent exceptions to this pattern in the literature. Cochran et al. (2017) found no association between sentence length and visitation among a population of Florida inmates while a separate study that specifically examined predictors of parent–child prison contact revealed a positive relationship between sentence length and maternal visits (Tasca 2016). Together, these results suggest that family members do not weigh the decision regarding if and when to visit in a vacuum, but rather consider their decision in the context of broader life circumstances and priorities.

Effects of Prison Visitation

A sizeable body of scholarship has been devoted to the consequences of prison visitation. Most of this work has centered on inmate-specific outcomes; however, a growing number of studies have begun to focus on the children and families of inmates as well (DeClaire and Dixon 2017; Poehlmann et al. 2010). Prison visitation has been shown to be linked to a wide array of outcomes including institutional misconduct, recidivism, and mental health (Duwe and Clark 2013; Mears, Cochran, Siennick, and Bales 2012; Mitchell, Spooner, Jia, and Zhang 2016). Visitation can play an important role in reentry planning and affect access to social capital, family relations, and child wellbeing (LaVigne, Naser, Brooks, and Castro 2005; Liu, Pickett, and Baker 2016).

While there is a consistent relationship demonstrated in the literature between prison visits and inmate misconduct, the direction of that relationship is mixed (Lindsey et al., 2015; Siennick, Mears, and Bales 2013). As part of a "carrots and stick" approach to correctional management, visitation is considered a useful incentive for promoting good behavior and overall prison order. This assumption has been supported in numerous studies that show visited-inmates commit fewer infractions than non-visited inmates (Cochran 2012; DeClaire and Dixon 2017). This is particularly evident in studies focused on incarcerated parents and contact with their children (Benning and Lahm 2014). By contrast, some studies show that visited inmates are at heightened risk of misconduct relative to their non-visited counterparts (Siennick et al. 2013). Scholars explain this seemingly contradictory effect by pointing out that visitation can be stressful and often stirs up intense emotions. In turn, such negative feelings and experiences can lead to increases in misconduct. Other work suggests that the visitation–misconduct relationship is mediated by distance between the prison and an inmate's home, age, and social ties (Lindsey et al. 2015).

Prison visitation has also been linked to decreases in recidivism (Barrick, Lattimore, and Visher 2014; Duwe and Clark 2013). Studies show that inmates who are visited more frequently (Mears et al. 2012), more consistently (Cochran 2014), and over an extended period of time (Bales and Mears, 2008) experience lower risks of recidivism. Previous research has identified positive effects of visitation with romantic partners, relatives, and friends on recidivism—with spousal visits producing the most favorable outcomes (Cochran and Mears 2013). Alternatively, visitation from children has been linked to increased recidivism (Bales and Mears 2008). In a recently published meta-analysis, Mitchell and colleagues (2016) found that visitation is associated with a 26 percent reduction in recidivism. Results indicated that this relationship varied along several key factors including gender, nature of the visit, length of time at risk, and the type of recidivism measure used. Relatedly, Duwe and Johnson (2016) found that visitation significantly reduced the likelihood of multiple reoffending measures but had no effect on technical violation revocations.

In addition, prison visits have been shown to contribute to improved mental health outcomes and increase the likelihood of post-release family reunification. Specifically, in-prison contact can reduce symptoms of depression—particularly among women and younger inmates (DeClaire and Dixon 2017). Given prior histories of relationship conflicts, disrupted parenthood, and other life stressors commonly experienced by the incarcerated population, inmates are often consumed with worry and guilt during confinement (Mancini, Baker, Sainju, Golden, Bedard, and Gertz 2016). Visitation offers an opportunity to ease such concerns, shift inmates' outlook on the future, and increase access to social capital available to them upon release (Liu et al. 2016). While a recent study by Wallace et al. (2016) did not find a significant relationship between social support received during incarceration—captured by in-prison contact—and inmates' mental health, findings revealed that family support received after release does improve this outcome. Importantly, prison visitation can serve as a springboard for receipt of social support following release.

Considering that most inmates are parents, studies examining the consequences of prison visitation have begun to extend empirical inquiry beyond individual inmates to children (Glaze and Marushak 2010; Tasca 2014). Research is mixed on whether visitation is positive or negative for children, however (Poehlmann et al. 2010). In other words, contact has been shown to be both good *and* bad for inmates' children. On one hand, research indicates that parental prison visitation can reduce children's anxiety surrounding their parent's incarceration. Similarly, there is evidence to suggest that children who visit an incarcerated mother or father exhibit fewer problem behaviors relative to children who don't visit, given their ability to maintain close ties to their parent (Nesmith and Ruhland 2008). On the other hand, children's exposure to various stressors in order to maintain contact with an incarcerated parent—such as commuting long distances and having to come to terms with leaving their parent behind once the visit has ended—can result in negative internalizing and externalizing behaviors (Dallaire and Wilson 2010; McDermott and King 1992; Schubert, Duininck, and Shlafer 2016).

One of the limitations of this line of research is that most studies are unable to control for institutional barriers and preincarceration factors related to living situation, relationship dynamics, and stressors that can shape children's responses to parental visitation. A recent study that was able to account for such factors found that more than half of children were reported by caregivers to react negatively to prison visitation with an incarcerated mother or father (Tasca 2014). Both institutional context and quality of parent–child attachment were the primary influences in children's responses to their visitation experiences.

In sum, while the majority of research suggests that visitation is positive for inmates, some research indicates that under certain circumstances visitation can have adverse effects (Bales and Mears 2008; Cochran and Mears 2013). Other research has examined the role of visitation on a broader set of outcomes that has linked visitation to family relationship quality, social capital, and offender attitudes. And, a small number of studies have explored the effects of visitation on inmates' children. Findings vary considerably in light of key differences in methodological approaches across studies. Far more work is needed to more clearly understand the consequences of visitation for children, families, and communities.

Current Gaps in Knowledge and Directions for Future Research

There is general consensus among scholars and professionals that visitation can be useful in mitigating the many harms of imprisonment. Although greater attention has been paid to prison visitation in the literature in recent years, important gaps in knowledge remain (Tasca, Wright, Turanovic, White, and Rodriguez 2016). Additional research is needed in three broad areas. These include achieving a better understanding of the correlates of contact, why visitation matters for behavioral and other inmate outcomes, and the influence of prison contact on children and family life.

First, we still know relatively little about who is visited, and the conditions under which visitation is most likely to occur (Cochran et al. 2017). A key area of focus for future studies should be to gain deeper insight into how relationship dynamics and family support capacities shape contact decisions. Second, research has consistently demonstrated that visitation is important, but it is not fully clear why. Research centered on the nature and quality of visitation experiences could be particularly helpful in uncovering the mechanisms underlying visitation effects. And third, there is a need for more work focused on the consequences of visitation for a broad array of child and family outcomes that account for preincarceration circumstances, using large samples and sophisticated methodological designs.

Without question, significant work has been done in the area of prison visitation. Research has shown how visits can serve as a protective factor for many individuals from a host of adversities. In a time when crime and punishment is once again front and center in the public policy dialogue, there is a real opportunity for research to inform and even shape correctional policy and practice. Thus, it is important to continue to build on existing work on the correlates and consequences of prison visitation in an effort to better the lives of those who have been affected by mass imprisonment in this country.

References

Alexander, Michelle. 2012. *The New Jim Crow: Mass Incarceration in the Age of Colorblindness*. New York: The New Press.

Arditti, Joyce A. 2003. "Locked Doors and Glass Walls: Family Visiting at a Local Jail." *Journal of Loss & Trauma* 8(2): 115–138.

Arditti, Joyce A. 2005. "Families and Incarceration: An Ecological Approach." *Families in Society: The Journal of Contemporary Social Services* 86(2): 251–260.

Arditti, Joyce A. 2012. *Parental Incarceration and the Family: Psychological and Social Effects of Imprisonment on Children, Parents, and Caregivers*. New York: New York University Press.

Bahr, Stephen J., Lish Harris, James K. Fisher, and Anita Harker Armstrong. 2010. "Successful Reentry: What Differentiates Successful and Unsuccessful Parolees?" *International Journal of Offender Therapy and Comparative Criminology* 54(5): 667–692.

Bales, William D., and Daniel P. Mears. 2008. "Inmate Social Ties and the Transition to Society: Does Visitation Reduce Recidivism?" *Journal of Research in Crime and Delinquency* 45(3): 287–321.

Barrick, Kelle, Pamela K. Lattimore, and Christy A. Visher. 2014. "Reentering Women: The Impact of Social Ties on Long-Term Recidivism." *The Prison Journal* 94(3): 279–304.

Beckmeyer, Jonathon J., and Joyce A. Arditti. 2014. "Implications of In-Person Visits for Incarcerated Parents' Family Relationships and Parenting Experience." *Journal of Offender Rehabilitation* 53(2): 129–151.

Benning, Carin L., and Karen F. Lahm. 2014. "Effects of Parent–Child Relationships on Inmate Behavior a Comparison of Male and Female Inmates." *International Journal of Offender Therapy and Comparative Criminology* 60(2): 189–207.

Braman, Donald. 2004. *Doing Time on the Outside: Incarceration and Family Life in Urban America*. Ann Arbor, MI: University of Michigan Press.

Brunton-Smith, Ian, and Daniel J. McCarthy. 2017. "The Effects of Prisoner Attachment to Family on Re-entry Outcomes: A Longitudinal Assessment." *British Journal of Criminology* 57(2): 463–482.

Carson, Ann E. 2015. "Prisoners in 2014." *Bureau of Justice Statistics Bulletin*. Washington, DC: U.S. Department of Justice, NCJ 248955.

Christian, Johnna. 2005. "Riding the Bus: Barriers to Prison Visitation and Family Management Strategies." *Journal of Contemporary Criminal Justice* 21(1): 31–48.

Christian, Johnna, and Leslie W. Kennedy. 2011. "Secondary Narratives in the Aftermath of Crime: Defining Family Members' Relationships with Prisoners." *Punishment & Society* 13(4): 379–402.

Christian, Johnna, Jeff Mellow, and Shenique Thomas. 2006. "Social and Economic Implications of Family Connections to Prisoners." *Journal of Criminal Justice* 34(4): 443–452.

Clear, Todd R. 2007. *Imprisoning Communities: How Mass Incarceration Makes Disadvantaged Neighborhoods Worse*. New York: Oxford University Press.

Clone, Stephanie, and Dana DeHart. 2014. "Social Support Networks of Incarcerated Women: Types of Support, Sources of Support, and Implications for Reentry." *Journal of Offender Rehabilitation* 53(7): 503–521.

Cochran, Joshua C. 2012. "The Ties That Bind or the Ties That Break: Examining the Relationship between Visitation and Prisoner Misconduct." *Journal of Criminal Justice* 40(5): 433–440.

Cochran, Joshua C. 2014. "Breaches in the Wall: Imprisonment, Social Support, and Recidivism." *Journal of Research in Crime and Delinquency* 51(2): 200–229.

Cochran, Joshua C., and Daniel P. Mears. 2013. "Social Isolation and Inmate Behavior: A Conceptual Framework for Theorizing Prison Visitation and Guiding and Assessing Research." *Journal of Criminal Justice* 41(4): 252–261.

Cochran, Joshua C., Daniel P. Mears, and William D. Bales. 2017. "Who Gets Visited in Prison? Individual-and Community-Level Disparities in Inmate Visitation Experiences."*Crime & Delinquency* 63(5): 545–568.

Cochran, Joshua C., Daniel P. Mears, William D. Bales, and Eric A. Stewart. 2016. "Spatial Distance, Community Disadvantage, and Racial and Ethnic Variation in Prison Inmate Access to Social Ties." *Journal of Research in Crime and Delinquency* 53(2): 220–254.

Comfort, Megan. 2009. *Doing Time Together: Love and Family in the Shadow of Prison*. Chicago, IL: University of Chicago Press.

Connor, David Patrick, and Richard Tewksbury. 2015. "Prison Inmates and Their Visitors: An Examination of Inmate Characteristics and Visitor Types." *The Prison Journal* 95(2): 159–177.

Dallaire, Danielle H., and Laura C. Wilson. 2010. "The Relation of Exposure to Parental Criminal Activity, Arrest, and Sentencing to Children's Maladjustment." *Journal of Child and Family Studies* 19(4): 404–418.

DeClaire, Karen, and Louise Dixon. 2017. "The Effects of Prison Visits from Family Members on Prisoners' Well-being, Prison Rule Breaking, and Recidivism: A Review of Research since 1991." *Trauma, Violence, & Abuse* 57(2): 463–482.

Duwe, Grant, and Valerie Clark. 2013. "Blessed Be the Social Tie That Binds: The Effects of Prison Visitation on Offender Recidivism." *Criminal Justice Policy Review* 24(3): 271–296.

Duwe, Grant, and Byron R. Johnson. 2016. "The Effects of Prison Visits from Community Volunteers on Offender Recidivism." *The Prison Journal* 96(2): 279–303.

Foster, Holly, and John Hagan. 2007. "Incarceration and Intergenerational Social Exclusion." *Social Problems* 54(4): 399–433.

Glaze, Lauren E., and Laura M. Maruschak. 2010. "Parents in Prison and Their Minor Children." *Bureau of Justice Statistics Special Report*. Washington, DC: U.S. Department of Justice, NCJ 222984.

Lahm, Karen F. 2016. "Factors Affecting Contact between Inmate Parents and Their Children: An Examination of Mothers and Fathers behind Bars." *Corrections* 1(1): 61–79.

LaVigne, Nancy G., Rebecca L. Naser, Lisa E. Brooks, and Jennifer L. Castro. 2005. "Examining the Effect of Incarceration and In-Prison Family Contact on Prisoners' Family Relationships." *The Prison Journal* 21(4): 314–335.

Lindsey, Andrea M., Daniel P. Mears, Joshua C. Cochran, William D. Bales, and Brian J. Stults. 2015. "In Prison and Far from Home: Spatial Distance Effects on Inmate Misconduct." *Crime & Delinquency*. Advance online publication, doi:10.1177/0011128715614017.

Liu, Siyu, Justin T. Pickett, and Thomas Baker. 2016. "Inside the Black Box: Prison Visitation, the Costs of Offending, and Inmate Social Capital." *Criminal Justice Policy Review* 27(8): 766–790.

Lynch, Mona. 2012. "Theorizing the Role of the 'War on Drugs' in US Punishment." *Theoretical Criminology* 16(2): 175–199.

Mancini, Christina, Thomas Baker, Karla Dhungana Sainju, Kristin Golden, Laura E. Bedard, and Marc Gertz. 2016. "Examining External Support Received in Prison and Concerns about Reentry among Incarcerated Women." *Feminist Criminology* 11(2): 163–190.

Maruna, Shadd, and Hans Toch. 2005. *The Impact of Imprisonment on the Desistance Process. Prisoner Reentry and Crime in America*. New York: Cambridge Press.

McDermott, Kathleen, and Roy D. King. 1992. "'Prison Rule 102: Stand by Your Man,' The Impact of Penal Policy on the Families of Prisoners." Pp. 50–73 in *Prisoners' Children: What are the Issues* edited by Roger Shaw. London: Routledge.

Mears, Daniel P., Joshua C. Cochran, Sonja E. Siennick, and William D. Bales. 2012. "Prison Visitation and Recidivism." *Justice Quarterly* 29(6): 888–918.

Mitchell, Meghan M., Kallee Spooner, Di Jia, and Yan Zhang. 2016. "The Effect of Prison Visitation on Reentry Success: A Meta-Analysis." *Journal of Criminal Justice* 47: 74–83.

Nesmith, Ande, and Ebony Ruhland. 2008. "Children of Incarcerated Parents: Challenges and Resiliency, in Their Own Words." *Children and Youth Services Review* 30(10): 1119–1130.

Nurse, Anne. 2002. *Fatherhood Arrested: Parenting from within the Juvenile Justice System*. Nashville, TN: Vanderbilt University Press.

Pierce, Mari B. 2015. "Male Inmate Perceptions of the Visitation Experience: Suggestions on How Prisons Can Promote Inmate–Family Relationships." *The Prison Journal* 95(3): 370–396.

Poehlmann, Julie, Danielle Dallaire, Ann Booker Loper, and Leslie D. Shear. 2010. "Children's Contact with Their Incarcerated Parents: Research Findings and Recommendations." *American Psychologist* 65(6): 575–598.

Pratt, Travis C. 2009. *Addicted to Incarceration: Corrections Policy and the Politics of Misinformation in the United States*. Thousand Oaks, CA: Sage.

Roy, Kevin M., and Omari L. Dyson. 2005. "Gatekeeping in Context: Babymama Drama and the Involvement of Incarcerated Fathers." *Fathering* 3(3): 289–310.

Schubert, Erin C., Megan Duininck, and Rebecca J. Shlafer. 2016. "Visiting Mom: A Pilot Evaluation of a Prison-Based Visiting Program Serving Incarcerated Mothers and Their Minor Children." *Journal of Offender Rehabilitation* 55(4): 213–234.

Siennick, Sonja E., Daniel P. Mears, and William D. Bales. 2013. "Here and Gone: Anticipation and Separation Effects of Prison Visits on Inmate Infractions." *Journal of Research in Crime and Delinquency* 50(3): 417–444.

Tasca, Melinda. 2014. "'It's Not All Cupcakes and Lollipops': An Investigation of the Predictors and Effects of Prison Visitation for Children during Maternal and Paternal Incarceration." PhD dissertation, Arizona State University.

Tasca, Melinda. 2016. "The Gatekeepers of Contact: Child–Caregiver Dyads and Parental Prison Visitation." *Criminal Justice and Behavior* 43(6): 739–758.
Tasca, Melinda, Philip Mulvey, and Nancy Rodriguez. 2016. "Families Coming Together in Prison: An Examination of Visitation Encounters." *Punishment & Society* 18(4): 459–478.
Tasca, Melinda, Nancy Rodriguez, and Marjorie S. Zatz. 2011. "Family and Residential Instability in the Context of Paternal and Maternal Incarceration." *Criminal Justice and Behavior* 38(3): 231–247.
Tasca, Melinda, Kevin A. Wright, Jillian J. Turanovic, Clair White, and Nancy Rodriguez. 2016. "Moving Visitation Research Forward: The Arizona Prison Visitation Project." *Criminology, Criminal Justice, Law and Society* 17(1): 55–67.
Tewksbury, Richard, and Matthew DeMichele. 2005. "Going to Prison: A Prison Visitation Program." *The Prison Journal* 85(3): 292–310.
Toch, Hans. 2001. "The Future of Supermax Confinement." *The Prison Journal* 81(3): 376–388.
Toch, Hans. 2007. "Sequestering Gang Members, Burning Witches, and Subverting Due Process." *Criminal Justice and Behavior* 34(2): 274–288.
Turanovic, Jillian J., Nancy Rodriguez, and Travis C. Pratt. 2012. "The Collateral Consequences of Incarceration Revisited: A Qualitative Analysis of the Effects on Caregivers of Children of Incarcerated Parents." *Criminology* 50(4): 913–959.
Wakefield, Sara, and Christopher James Wildeman. 2014. *Children of the Prison Boom: Mass Incarceration and the Future of American Inequality*. New York: Oxford University Press.
Wallace, Danielle, Chantal Fahmy, Lindsy Cotton, Charis Jimmons, Rachel McKay, Sidney Stoffer, and Sarah Syed. 2016. "Examining the Role of Familial Support during Prison and after Release on Post-Incarceration Mental Health." *International Journal of Offender Therapy and Comparative Criminology* 60(1): 3–20.

Cases Cited

Agron v. Montanye, 1975. 392 F.Supp. 454.
Coffin v. Reichard, 1945. 148 F. 2d 278.
Cooper v. Morin, 1979. 49 NY 2d 69.
Cooper v. Pate, 1960. 378 U.S. 546.
Golub v. Krimsky, 1960. 184 F.Supp. 783.
Jackson v. Godwin, 1968. 400 F.2d 529.
Overton v. Bazzetta, 2003. 539 U.S. 126.
Price v. Johnston, 1948. 334 U.S. 266.

37 Prison Gangs

David Skarbek and Danilo Freire

Introduction

Prison gangs have radically changed the dynamics of the United States penal system. These are inmate organizations that exist into perpetuity, and whose membership is restrictive, mutually exclusive, and often requires a lifetime commitment. Prior to the 1950s, prison gangs did not exist in the country, but by the late 1970s, inmate organizations were already a dominant force in American correctional facilities (e.g. Fleisher and Decker, 2001; Howell 2015; Wells, Minor, Angel, Carter, and Cox 2002). The strength of these groups can be inferred from their membership numbers. In 1985, there were about 113 gangs with 13,000 active members in American prisons (Camp and Camp 1985). By 2002, in contrast, about 308,000 prisoners were affiliated with inmate groups (Winterdyk and Ruddell 2010). The corrections director of California has attested that in 2006 there were up to 60,000 gang members in that state alone (Petersilia 2006). As these numbers do not include people who are indirectly involved with prison activities—such as visitors who smuggle narcotics into prisons for felons to trade (Crewe 2006)—the real influence of inmate gangs is probably more extensive than official figures suggest.

The emergence of prison gangs was far from peaceful. Gangs have been responsible for most cases of serious misconduct in jails, such as inmate assault (Cunningham and Sorensen 2007; Ralph and Marquart 1991; Reisig 2002), staff intimidation (Gaes, Wallace, Gilman, Klein-Saffran, and Suppa 2002), sexual misbehavior (Ralph and Marquart 1991; Wyatt 2005), and drug trafficking (Shelden 1991). Moreover, in recent years, prison groups have expanded their reach and made inroads into street-level drug markets, repeatedly resorting to force (e.g. Skarbek 2011; Valdez 2005). For all these reasons, it is unsurprising that inmate organizations are now regarded as the most serious threat to the American prison administration by staff and academics alike (Carlson 2001; DeLisi, Berg, and Hochstetler 2004; Fleisher and Decker 2001).

But despite their history of violence, prison gangs are not disorganized collectives. In fact, many gangs are highly structured organizations, often with strict hierarchies, elaborate internal rules, and comprehensive sets of norms (Leeson and Skarbek 2010; Skarbek 2012). Most importantly, gangs provide what the prison setting sometimes lacks: *social order*. The economics literature tells us that the private supply of public goods (with regulation of social order as a prime example) is not only theoretically possible (Olson 1965; Ostrom, Walker, and Gardner 1992), but in fact is commonly provided by a variety of social groups. Prison gangs are no exception.

Often, self-governing groups (such as mafias) play a prominent role in defining and securing property rights (Gambetta 1996; Skaperdas 2001; Varese 2011). Since inmates are constantly subject to extortion and violence, there is high demand for security from the incarcerated population. Convicts cannot always rely on prison staff for protection—

correctional officers may have limited resources, limited information, or both—therefore prisoners often turn to extralegal institutions for help. Evidence shows that gangs have been successful at protecting property and, perhaps surprisingly, their rise to power has coincided with a dramatic fall in victimization in prisons; the number of inmate riots, assaults, homicides, and suicides have all decreased over recent decades (Useem and Piehl 2006). Paradoxically, violent gangs are making prisons safer.

Prison gangs also help inmates to enjoy the benefits of trade. Although the state actively discourages illegal commerce among criminals, trade is widespread in the penal system (Davidson 1974; Kalinich 1986; Lankenau 2001; Williams and Fish 1974). The contraband marketplace is so important to inmate social life that some authors call it "the basis of legitimate power" within prisons (Kalinich and Stojkovic 1985). Nevertheless, market transactions are costly in jails. By the nature of their own business, criminals generally distrust one another (Gambetta 2009). Prison groups solve this social dilemma by enforcing contracts (through violence if required), monitoring transactions, providing general understanding of trade rules, and contacting potential suppliers of goods from street gangs (Blatchford 2008).

Academic works on street gangs greatly outnumber books and articles on prison gangs, and with few exceptions (e.g. Freire 2014; Skarbek 2010b, 2011, 2012, 2014), inmate institutions have been virtually ignored by political scientists and economists. Yet these two disciplines can offer valuable insights into the inner workings of criminal groups. Rational choice theory, widely employed by economists, appears particularly suited to this task. Rational choice is a variant of methodological individualism, and one of its basic premises is that macrobehavior can be explained by the purposive actions of self-interested individuals. The theory does not require agents to have complete information or perform perfect calculations of their pay-offs (Simon 1955), nor does it describe cognitive function or actual decision making.

Criminals are particularly inclined to behave rationally, as their environment forces them to do so. Mistakes are severely punished in jails. Errors in judgment may lead to death. Hence we see rational choice as a useful framework to analyze social preferences and collective outcomes in prisons. Furthermore, rational choice does not disregard the role social norms play in the formation of individual preferences (Crawford and Ostrom 1995; Elster 1989; Ostrom 2000). As we argue hereafter, shared perceptions have framed prison gangs since the earliest days of the phenomenon. However, if the inmate community grows larger and more diverse, norms have to be supplemented by other arrangements such as an organization. The rational choice framework can integrate these various mechanisms into a single, cohesive theory of gang behavior.

How Gangs Operate

What drives gang formation? The media generally portray prison gangs as racist, violent, and pathological. The idea does not seem far-fetched: many American gangs, such as the Aryan Brotherhood, the Black Family, or the Mexican Mafia, are indeed organized along racial lines (Fong 1990; Hunt, Riegel, Morales, and Waldorf 1993; Pelz, Marquart, and Pelz 1991). But while race does play a role in gang recruitment, ethnic competition is not the key factor behind the growth in gangs. Rather, we argue that prison gangs are created essentially to support contraband markets through the promotion of cooperation and trust between inmates (Fleisher and Decker 2001; Roth and Skarbek 2014).

This view is consistent with a vast literature on self-enforcing exchange. Several authors claim that it is possible for decentralized communities to engage in trade even without the presence of strong government institutions (e.g. Ostrom et al. 1992; Powell and Stringham

2009). Most people in the world still live under governments that are ineffective, weak or corrupt, and many firms run their businesses in areas where the state has only imperfect, if any, control. But how can we have governance without governments?

A common criticism of privately produced governance is based upon the assumption that if state regulations were absent, long-term exchange could not persist because every interaction would be characterized as a prisoner's dilemma. That is, even if both parties could gain from cooperation, they would still have an incentive to cheat due to the lack of external enforcement of property rights. However, in reality, many self-organizing groups devise private mechanisms to prevent predatory behavior. Historical examples abound. Leeson (2009) describes how late seventeenth- and early eighteenth-century pirates used reputation strategies to maximize profits. Stringham (2015) argues that stock exchange traders employed club membership as a signal of trustworthiness. De Soto (1990), in turn, analyzes the informal system of property rights in modern Peru and shows how a thriving illegal economy can subsist without, and sometimes in confrontation with, state institutions.

These cases demonstrate that seemingly erratic behavior may simply be rational responses to unusual economic incentives (Leeson 2009: 6). Prison gangs can also be understood through such a lens. Social coordination in gangs is often achieved with a community responsibility system (CRS). This institutional device was first employed by merchants in the late medieval period in Europe, and it comprises a system where the whole community is responsible for the actions and debts of their individual members (Greif 2006). A simple example may clarify how CRS induces trustworthiness:

> Consider a situation where a member of Group A borrows money from a member of Group B. If Member A defaults on the debt, then all members of Group A are responsible for repaying it. If Group A does not suitably compensate Member B, then Group B boycotts Group A. If there are substantial benefits available from future interactions with Group B, then the threat of boycott induces payment by Group A. . . . Moreover, the corporate nature of the group creates a repeated play scenario among groups even though particular members may never trade again. When groups have reputations for taking responsibility for its members' actions, then two members of different groups who do not know each other can still benefit from trade.
>
> (Roth and Skarbek 2014: 226)

Qualitative evidence indicates that gangs indeed operate within this type of system. There are two conditions for CRS to work in prisons. First, individuals should be able to signal their group affiliation, so that the other prisoners know with which group a person affiliates. This type of screening is not difficult in jail, as inmates routinely use costly signals to convey information (Gambetta 2009). One's race is a signal that is impossible to fake. Finally, inmates are eager to display voluntary signals of gang affiliation through slang, hand gestures, and other cultural displays (Kaminski 2010; Valentine 2000).

Second, the community must be able and willing to punish misbehaving members. This condition is also met in the penal system. Gangs routinely use force (or the threat thereof) to maintain social order and punish defectors (Skarbek 2011, 2012, 2014). A Californian inmate interviewed by Trammell (2009: 763) illustrates this point: "if one of my guys is messing up then we either offer him up to the other guys or we take him down ourselves."

What is remarkable about CRS is that it facilitates trade even if individuals are not of a cooperative type. Members of the same group have better information about one another and can more easily exert influence over each other than non-group members. This creates incentives for prisoners—even those who might be rivals in other contexts—to work together. Prison gangs may be divided by race, but inmates apparently do not let this factor interrupt exchange flows. As noted by a convict in California, "the races don't officially mix. That's true but you can buy drugs from whoever and the leaders control that stuff. . . . It's not as cut and dry as you think" (Trammell, 2009: 756). Racial tensions could easily escalate in prisons, but because gang wars are costly, groups have an incentive to be peaceful. Order is good for business.

This system becomes established because trade structures inmate relations. Goods that are easily accessible to the general population are notably scarce in prisons. Access to them therefore lends status and prestige to prisoners. Paul, a black British inmate in his early thirties, describes the role illegal trade plays in prisoner hierarchy:

> When I was [dealing] I could say: "I'm a top dog. I've got drugs, I've got this, I've got that, yeah, no-one can't fuck with me." . . . Drugs is power in here, yeah, so is tobacco, and without drugs, tobacco and phonecards [prisons] don't really work.
>
> (Crewe 2006: 360–361)

Prison gangs are key players in the contraband markets. As a prison official notes, "almost without exception . . . the gangs are responsible for the majority of drug trafficking in their institutions" (Camp and Camp 1985: 52). Crewe (2006: 361–362) quotes a dialogue with one interviewee where the inmate reflects on the link between money from illegal trading and group protection:

> "*If you have the drugs but you have no violence, does that mean the drugs just get taken off you?*"
>
> "You need backing. You yourself don't need violence. You've got bounty hunters in prison. . . . People who, for a price, will protect you. . . . Any smart person would get linked up with the right group."
>
> "*So you're saying that people then gang together because it's a form of protection?*"
>
> "Yes, it's a form of protection and it's power. If I've got half an ounce of heroin I can turn that into probably three or four grams, that's a lot of money in prison, and if you're keeping two or three guys sweet with you, they don't want that breaking up. They're thinking, 'fucking hell, we're living alright, we've got it easy in here, nobody is fucking up our little crew, we're sticking together'."

The story can be generalized to larger groups. Trammell (2009: 755) writes how Jack, an inmate in a California jail, explains the role of prison groups:

> "The boys inside, they follow the rules and that means you work with your own boys and do what they say. Look, there is a lot of problems caused by the gangs, no doubt. The thing is, they solve problems too. You want a structure and you want someone to organize the businesses so the gangs have their rules. You don't run up a drug debt, you don't start a fight in the yard and stuff. Gangs are a problem but we took care of business."

In summary, the fundamental role of prison gangs is to promote cooperation and stability between inmates who have strong reasons to distrust each other and who live in an environment that is potentially chaotic and violent. This is done to achieve an important goal: trade. As prisoners live in a resource-scarce world, trading acquires a significant importance, not only in terms of the gains it may bring to dealers, but also through the social relationship it forges. The community responsibility system ensures that commercial exchanges will not be interrupted by predatory individuals.

The Decline of the Convict Code

Before prison gangs and the community responsibility system, the main source of inmate governance in California was a set of informal norms known as "the convict code" (Irwin and Cressey 1962; Irwin 1970; Jacobs 1977; Sykes and Messinger 1960). The code relied on strong images of masculinity (Freeman 1999; Hua-Fu 2005) and emphasized the importance of being tough, and sometimes hostile, toward fellow prisoners and staff (Cole, Smith, and DeJong 2013: 369). Although the code does not include a fixed list of rules—its application varies significantly from case to case (e.g. Akers, Hayner, and Gruninger 1977; Copes, Brookman, and Brown 2013; Trammell 2012)—Sykes and Messinger (1960: 5–9) affirm that its chief tenets may be classified into five groups. First, there are norms that suggest caution to felons, and are usually condensed in the maxims, "Do not interfere with inmate interests" or "Do not rat on an inmate." These suggest that inmates should serve their time as freely as possible, with the minimum amount of interference from other prisoners. Second, there are rules that assert that prisoners should avoid engaging in conflict, such as "Do not fight with other inmates." Third, "Do not exploit other inmates." This dictates that deceiving and fraud should be not tolerated against other upstanding convicts. Fourth, the inmate code asks felons not to weaken under any circumstances: "Be strong." Fifth, there are many maxims that forbid convicts from cooperating with guards and authorities in the correction system in general, such as "Do not trust the staff" (Sutherland, Hardin, Cressey, and Luckenbill 1992: 525).

Those who lived by these rules were seen as "good cons" and generally enjoyed better reputations than prisoners who failed to comply with the code (Copes et al. 2013). In a setting where physical threats are frequent, enacting the code gave convicts an advantage. There is also evidence that similar prescriptions are followed in other parts of the world, such as the United Kingdom, New Zealand, Mexico, Spain, and Thailand (Akers et al. 1977; Sirisutthidacha and Tititampruk 2014; Winfree, Newbold, and Tubb 2002). While not uniformly enforced in these countries, the inmate code apparently serves as a guide to felons abroad (Copes et al. 2013: 843).

Scholars have proposed two theories to explain inmate culture and the origins of the convict code. The first is called the deprivation model. This theory suggests that inmate behavior is largely a product of prison life itself (Clemmer 1940; Irwin 1980; McCorkle and Korn 1954). According to this view, the convict code expresses a collective "situational response" (Akers et al. 1977) to the problems of "prisonization" (Clemmer 1940), that is, the deprivation of freedom, security, heterosexual relations, goods and services, and personal autonomy felons routinely endure (Sykes 1958). The model also stresses that this feeling of deprivation is pervasive in jails, and to a varying extent all inmates are familiar with it. This shared experience is what binds prisoners together and it is the main reason why felons adopt the convict code.

Conversely, other authors contend that the convict code is merely an institutionalized version of the thieves' code. This theory is called the importation model and, as the name suggests, it states that criminals bring their former beliefs and behavior to jails (Irwin and Cressey 1962; Irwin 1970, 1980). A number of inmates come from neighborhoods with high levels of violence or notable presence of gangs; hence, it is not surprising that there are strong links between street subculture and the convict code (Sirisutthidacha and Tititampruk 2014: 96). Irwin (1980: 12) points out the many similarities:

> The central rule to the thieves' code was "thou shalt not snitch." In prison, thieves converted that to the dual form of "do not rat on another prisoner" and "do your own time." Thieves were also obliged by their code to be cool and tough, that is to maintain respect and dignity; not to show weakness; to help other thieves; and to leave most prisoners alone.

Nonetheless, these two hypotheses are not fundamentally incompatible, and scholars now agree that both factors help explain the emergence of the inmate culture (Schwartz 1971; Trammell 2009). On the one hand, prisoners do not enter jails like a *tabula rasa* as the deprivation model seems to predict. On the other hand, inmate behavior is also mediated by prison conditions. Whereas the exact causal mechanisms are yet to be specified (DeLisi et al. 2004), the convict code is likely a result of both social deprivation and previous criminal behavior.

Regardless of its origins, over the past decades the inmate code has clearly declined in importance (Irwin 1970; Jacobs 1975; Skarbek 2014). This does not mean that the code's prescriptions are outdated: inmates continue to refer to them and often punish those who systematically violate the code's core tenets (Copes et al. 2013; Trammell 2012). However, the growth of the American incarcerated population has significantly weakened the influence of old norms and the most efficient institutions for enforcing them.

The code's effectiveness declined because of dramatic shifts in inmate demographics. California provides a relevant example. Between 1945 and 1970, the inmate population grew from 6,600 to about 25,000, and from 1950 to 2012 the number of prisons increased from five to 33 (Bass 1975; Skarbek 2014). This inflow of new prisoners indicates that spreading and enforcing the convict code became more costly than in the past. Consequently, young inmates are less likely to know and internalize such informal rules (Hunt et al. 1993).

The expansion of the prison population has also diminished the influence of the inmate code through other channels. Norms are very effective at promoting coordination in small groups, but as the number of interactions increases, the opportunities for an individual to defect multiply (Bowles and Gintis 1998). In groups with loose social ties, people have only imperfect information about one another, so reputation effects are not a strong deterrent to uncooperative behavior. Furthermore, in a large community, individuals have additional incentives to free ride and let others bear the costs of punishing norm violators (Olson 1965). Thus, a norm-based system such as the convict code tends to break down as the number of felons increases.

The demand for protection in prisons has not declined with a growing inmate population. Rather, the opposite has occurred. However, inmates responded to this unprecedented situation by devising a new type of organization to provide order in jails. This is how prison gangs turned into powerful institutions. Prison gangs are well equipped to enforce rules in a large and heterogeneous penal system. As we noted in the previous section, gangs can monitor their members through the community responsibility system. Moreover, these groups provide valuable information to felons. Inmate organizations usually have rigid admission criteria, and they often publicize their acceptable standards of behavior in written documents (Skarbek 2010a, 2012). This enhances cooperation as inmates know that prisoners who are affiliated with gangs are likely to be trustworthy. The affiliation process itself is already a costly and credible signal. Finally, prison gangs can mobilize a significant amount of money, violence, and merchandise through their networks. The scale of their operations allows them to offer protection and material benefits to hundreds or even thousands of members (Blatchford 2008; Camp and Camp 1985). In an overcrowded penal system, these are all desirable qualities.

Prison gangs are interpreted as an unintentional consequence of the massive demographic shift that has taken place in American prisons in the last years. This shift has made the previous system of norms, the convict code, insufficient to meet prisoners' demands for social order. Gangs provide security and facilitate trade in a diverse penal system by using effective enforcement mechanisms and transmitting reliable information to inmates. Prison gangs are therefore not a cause, but a solution to many of the inmates' problems.

Conclusion

In this chapter, we have offered a brief overview of the current literature on prison gangs. We have discussed how inmate gangs are a rational response to several challenges of prison life, and how they promote illegal trade and provide security to inmates. We have also argued that prison gangs sustain internal order through a community responsibility system, and discussed how this system fosters trust between inmate communities. Moreover, in the third section we presented the main rules of the convict code and explained why the code has decreased in importance over the past few years. These are the conditions that allowed gangs to increase their dominance behind bars and later to expand their protection services to street criminals.

However, there are many under-researched topics in the prison gang literature. Although there are several relevant academic works on gang formation, comparative studies are still uncommon in the field. There is too little work on global variation in prison gang activity. Testing causal mechanisms in a range of prison gangs could help scholars isolate the necessary and sufficient conditions for gang formation and development. Likewise, past studies have relied on comparative case studies (Skarbek 2016), but complementary work with quantitative methods would yield valuable insights. This would require collecting and standardizing large sample data, an effort that is yet to be done but that would be fruitful for scholarship on prison gangs (Fleisher and Decker 2001).

Illicit markets in prisons are also not well understood. Thus far, there are only a small number of studies about how prisoners engage in trade, mostly focused on the inmates' demand for drugs and other goods behind bars. Little is known about how drug dealers establish their networks, and how hard drugs determine other aspects of prison life such as internal hierarchies or inmate financing and credit tools (Crewe 2006: 348).

Another topic that deserves further attention is how inmate groups decide their "repertoire of violence," that is, which type of violence prison gangs use against their own members or non-affiliated convicts. Whereas some gangs employ physical threats only as a last resort (Crewe 2006; Trammell 2012), others make extensive use of violence as a means to enforce rules. In prisons, violence also has a clearly communicative purpose (Gambetta 2009), so comparing and analyzing violence strategies would enable us to gain a better grasp of gangs' relative positions in the inmate community and to analyze how these groups manage (or fail) to influence others' decisions.

Finally, the relationship between the state and prison gangs can be further explored by scholars. It is important to know under what conditions the state chooses to confront, appease, or collude with an inmate group. It is important to identify which mechanisms lead the state to adopt different approaches when dealing with extralegal groups. As mass incarceration has become one of the most pressing issues not only in the United States but also abroad, a call for evidence-based policies seems timely. Taken together, these efforts will allow researchers and policymakers to formulate better, more efficient approaches for managing prison gangs.

References

Akers, Ronald L., Norman S. Hayner, and Werner Gruninger. 1977. "Prisonization in Five Countries: Type of Prison and Inmate Characteristics." *Criminology* 14(4): 527–554.

Bass, Richard A. 1975. *An Analysis of the California Department of Corrections Work Furlough Program in Fiscal Year 1969–1970.* Number 57. Sacramento, CA: California Department of Corrections.

Blatchford, Chris. 2008. *The Black Hand: The Bloody Rise and Redemption of "Boxer" Enriquez, a Mexican Mob Killer.* New York: Harper Collins.

Bowles, Samuel, and Herbert Gintis. 1998. "The Moral Economy of Communities: Structured Populations and the Evolution of Pro-Social Norms." *Evolution and Human Behavior* 19(1): 3–25.

Camp, George M., and Camille Graham Camp. 1985. *Prison Gangs: Their Extent, Nature, and Impact on Prisons*. Washington, DC: U.S. Department of Justice, Office of Legal Policy, Federal Justice Research Program.

Carlson, Peter M. 2001. "Prison Interventions: Evolving Strategies to Control Security Threat Groups." *Corrections Management Quarterly* 5(4): 10–22.

Clemmer, Donald. 1940. *The Prison Community*. New York: Holt, Rinehart & Winston.

Cole, George F., Christopher E. Smith, and Christina DeJong. 2013. *Criminal Justice in America*. Boston, MA: Cengage Learning.

Copes, Heith, Fiona Brookman, and Anastasia Brown. 2013. "Accounting for Violations of the Convict Code." *Deviant Behavior* 34(10): 841–858.

Crawford, Sue, and Elinor Ostrom. 1995. "A Grammar of Institutions." *American Political Science Review* 89(3): 582–600.

Crewe, Ben. 2006. "Prison Drug Dealing and the Ethnographic Lens." *The Howard Journal of Criminal Justice* 45(4): 347–368.

Cunningham, Mark D. and Jon R. Sorensen. 2007. "Predictive Factors for Violent Misconduct in Close Custody." *The Prison Journal* 87(2): 241–253.

Davidson, R. Theodore. 1974. *Chicano Prisoners: The Key to San Quentin*. Prospect Heights, IL: Waveland Press.

DeLisi, Matt, Mark T. Berg, and Andy Hochstetler. 2004. "Gang Members, Career Criminals and Prison Violence: Further Specification of the Importation Model of Inmate Behavior." *Criminal Justice Studies* 17(4): 369–383.

De Soto, Hernando. 1990. *The Other Path: The Invisible Revolution in the Third World*. London: I.B. Tauris.

Elster, Jon. 1989. "Social Norms and Economic Theory." *The Journal of Economic Perspectives* 3(4): 99–117.

Fleisher, Mark S., and Scott H. Decker. 2001. "An Overview of the Challenge of Prison Gangs." *Corrections Management Quarterly* 5(1): 1–9.

Fong, Robert S. 1990. "The Organizational Structure of Prison Gangs: A Texas Case Study." *Federal Probation* 54(1): 36–43.

Freeman, Robert M. 1999. *Correctional Organization and Management: Public Policy Challenges, Behavior, and Structure*. Boston, MA: Butterworth Heinemann.

Freire, Danilo. 2014. "Entering the Underworld: Prison Gang Recruitment in São Paulo's Primeiro Comando da Capital." Master's thesis, The Graduate Institute of International and Development Studies, Geneva, Switzerland.

Gaes, Gerald G., Susan Wallace, Evan Gilman, Jody Klein-Saffran, and Sharon Suppa. 2002. "The Influence of Prison Gang Affiliation on Violence and Other Prison Misconduct." *The Prison Journal* 82(3): 359–385.

Gambetta, Diego. 1996. *The Sicilian Mafia: The Business of Private Protection*. Cambridge, MA: Harvard University Press.

Gambetta, Diego. 2009. *Codes of the Underworld: How Criminals Communicate*. Princeton, NJ: Princeton University Press.

Greif, Avner. 2006. *Institutions and the Path to the Modern Economy: Lessons from Medieval Trade*. Cambridge: Cambridge University Press.

Howell, James C. 2015. *The History of Street Gangs in the United States: Their Origins and Transformations*. Lanham, MD: Lexington Books.

Hua-Fu, Hsu. 2005. "The Patterns of Masculinity in Prison." *Critical Criminology* 13(1): 1–16.

Hunt, Geoffrey, Stephanie Riegel, Tomas Morales, and Dan Waldorf. 1993. "Change in Prison Culture: Prison Gangs and the Case of the Pepsi Generation." *Social Problems* 40(3): 398–409.

Irwin, John. 1970. *The Felon*. Englewood Cliffs, NJ: Prentice Hall.

Irwin, John. 1980. *Prisons in Turmoil*. Boston, MA: Little, Brown.

Irwin, John, and Donald R. Cressey. 1962. "Thieves, Convicts and the Inmate Culture." *Social Problems* 10(2): 142–155.

Jacobs, James B. 1975. "Stratification and Conflict Among Prison Inmates." *The Journal of Criminal Law and Criminology* 66(1): 476–482.

Jacobs, James B. 1977. *Stateville: The Penitentiary in Mass Society*. Chicago, IL: University of Chicago Press.

Kalinich, David B. 1986. *Power, Stability, and Contraband: The Inmate Economy*. Prospect Heights, IL: Waveland Press.

Kalinich, David B., and Stan Stojkovic. 1985. "Contraband: The Basis for Legitimate Power in a Prison Social System." *Criminal Justice and Behavior* 12(4): 435–451.

Kaminski, Marek M. 2010. *Games Prisoners Play: The Tragicomic Worlds of Polish Prison*. Princeton, NJ: Princeton University Press.

Lankenau, Stephen E. 2001. "Smoke'em if You Got'em: Cigarette Black Markets in US Prisons and Jails." *The Prison Journal* 81(2): 142–161.

Leeson, Peter T. 2009. *The Invisible Hook: The Hidden Economics of Pirates*. Princeton, NJ: Princeton University Press.

Leeson, Peter, and David Skarbek. 2010. "Criminal Constitutions." *Global Crime* 11(3): 279–297.

McCorkle, Lloyd W., and Richard Korn. 1954. "Resocialization Within Walls." *The Annals of the American Academy of Political and Social Science* 293: 88–98.

Olson, Mancur. 1965. *The Logic of Collective Action: Public Goods and the Theory of Groups*. Cambridge, MA: Harvard University Press.

Ostrom, Elinor. 2000. "Collective Action and the Evolution of Social Norms." *Journal of Economic Perspectives* 14(3): 137–158.

Ostrom, Elinor, James Walker, and Roy Gardner. 1992. "Covenants With and Without a Sword: Self-governance Is Possible." *American Political Science Review* 86(2): 404–417.

Pelz, Mary E., James W. Marquart, and C. Terry Pelz. 1991. "Right-Wing Extremism in the Texas Prisons: The Rise and Fall of the Aryan Brotherhood of Texas." *The Prison Journal* 71(2): 23–37.

Petersilia, Joan. 2006. *Understanding California Corrections*. Berkeley, CA: California Policy Research Center.

Powell, Benjamin, and Edward P. Stringham. 2009. "Public Choice and the Economic Analysis of Anarchy: A Survey." *Public Choice* 140: 503–538.

Ralph, Paige H., and James W. Marquart. 1991. "Gang Violence in Texas Prisons." *The Prison Journal* 71(2): 38–49.

Reisig, Michael D. 2002. "Administrative Control and Inmate Homicide." *Homicide Studies* 6(1): 84–103.

Roth, M. Garrett, and David Skarbek. 2014. "Prison Gangs and the Community Responsibility System." *Review of Behavioral Economics* 1(3): 223–243.

Schwartz, Barry. 1971. "Pre-Institutional vs. Situational Influence in a Correctional Community." *Journal of Criminal Law, Criminology and Police Science* 62(4): 532–542.

Shelden, Randall G. 1991. "A Comparison of Gang Members and Non-Gang Members in a Prison Setting." *The Prison Journal* 71(2): 50–60.

Simon, Herbert A. 1955. "A Behavioral Model of Rational Choice." *The Quarterly Journal of Economics* 69(1): 99–118.

Sirisutthidacha, Warissara, and Dittita Tititampruk. 2014. "Patterns of Inmate Subculture: A Qualitative Study of Thai Inmates." *International Journal of Criminal Justice Sciences* 9(1): 94–109.

Skaperdas, Stergios. 2001. "The Political Economy of Organized Crime: Providing Protection when the State Does Not." *Economics of Governance* 2(3): 173–202.

Skarbek, David. 2010a. "Putting the 'Con' into Constitutions: The Economics of Prison Gangs." *Journal of Law, Economics, and Organization* 26(2): 183–211.

Skarbek, David. 2010b. "Self-Governance in San Pedro Prison." *The Independent Review* 14(4): 569–585.

Skarbek, David. 2011. "Governance and Prison Gangs." *American Political Science Review* 105(4): 702–716.

Skarbek, David. 2012. "Prison Gangs, Norms, and Organizations." *Journal of Economic Behavior & Organization* 82(1): 96–109.

Skarbek, David. 2014. *The Social Order of the Underworld: How Prison Gangs Govern the American Penal System*. Oxford, UK: Oxford University Press.

Skarbek, David. 2016. "Covenants without the Sword? Comparing Prison Self-Governance Globally." *American Political Science Review* 110(4): 845–862.

Stringham, Edward Peter. 2015. *Private Governance: Creating Order in Economic and Social Life*. Oxford, UK: Oxford University Press.

Sutherland, Edwin Hardin, Donald Ray Cressey, and David F. Luckenbill. 1992. *Principles of Criminology*. Lanham, MD: Rowman & Littlefield.

Sykes, Gresham M. 1958. *The Society of Captives: A Study of a Maximum Security Prison*. Princeton, NJ: Princeton University Press.

Sykes, Gresham M., and Sheldon L. Messinger. 1960. "The Inmate Social System." Pp. 5–19 in *Theoretical Studies in Social Organization of the Prison*, edited by Richard A. Cloward. New York: Social Science Research Council.

Trammell, Rebecca. 2009. "Values, Rules, and Keeping the Peace: How Men Describe Order and the Inmate Code in California Prisons." *Deviant Behavior* 30(8): 746–771.

Trammell, Rebecca. 2012. *Enforcing the Convict Code: Violence and Prison Culture*. Boulder, CO: Lynne Rienner Publishers.

Useem, Bert, and Anne M. Piehl. 2006. "Prison Buildup and Disorder." *Punishment & Society* 8(1): 87–115.

Valdez, Avelardo. 2005. "Mexican American Youth and Adult Prison Gangs in a Changing Heroin Market." *Journal of Drug Issues* 35(4): 843–867.

Valentine, Bill. 2000. *Gangs and Their Tattoos: Identifying Gangbangers on the Street and in Prison*. Boulder, CO: Paladin Press.

Varese, Federico. 2011. *Mafias on the Move: How Organized Crime Conquers New Territories*. Princeton, NJ: Princeton University Press.

Wells, James B., Kevin I. Minor, Earl Angel, Lisa Carter, and M. Cox. 2002. *A Study of Gangs and Security Threat Groups in America's Adult Prisons and Jails*. Indianapolis, IN: National Major Gang Task Force.

Williams, Vergil L., and Mary Fish. 1974. *Convicts, Codes, and Contraband: The Prison Life of Men and Women*. Cambridge, MA: Ballinger.

Winfree, L. Thomas, Greg Newbold, and S. Houston Tubb. 2002. "Prisoner Perspectives on Inmate Culture in New Mexico and New Zealand: A Descriptive Case Study." *The Prison Journal* 82(2): 213–233.

Winterdyk, John, and Rick Ruddell. 2010. "Managing Prison Gangs: Results From a Survey of US Prison Systems." *Journal of Criminal Justice* 38(4): 730–736.

Wyatt, Rachel. 2005. "Male Rape in US Prisons: Are Conjugal Visits the Answer?" *Case Western Reserve Journal of International Law* 37(2): 579–614.

38 Prison Inmate Economy

Kyle A. Burgason

What Is the Prison Economy

The words "prison" and "inmate" invoke images of steel bars or electrified fences strung on top with razor wire. The words may remind us of hulking, tattooed, and ominous images of "career criminals" perpetuated and distorted by the media. In reality, some prisons in the United States serve as little more than warehouses for offenders (Irwin 2005) that must deal with a variety of problems including but not limited to physical and sexual violence, staff misconduct including excessive use of force, isolation from family and friends, and a host of life-altering deprivations that all inmates experience.

First identified by Sykes (1971), prison subculture and inmates' adjustment to incarceration are closely aligned to the conditions of imprisonment, and these circumstances represent all of the kinds of deprivations that inmates face. Inmates are deprived of both material possessions as well as psychological stability. They are deprived of clothes they want to wear and the food they want to eat. They are denied access to heterosexual relationships, as well as family and friends. Lastly, they are deprived of freedom and of any expectations of privacy. These deprivations help shape an inmate's adjustment to prison. Therefore, a conceivable solution consistent with the value placed on materialism in the general community would be that of manipulating the prison environment (Guenther 1975). Sykes suggested the systematic deprivation that inmates suffer provides them with the motivation to develop an identifiable social system, which in turn provides mechanisms that help lessen the pains of incarceration. The prison environment is organized in a way to deprive individuals, not only from achieving high goals, but also from satisfying basic needs, the safe environment they long to live in, and making decisions they choose to make. However, by depriving individuals of their material possessions, personhood, autonomy, and freedom, the state is able to deny people opportunities to satisfy their needs. However, simply because these needs cannot be satisfied does not repudiate their existence, because these needs are internal characteristics of individuals and cannot be detached from the persons. Therefore, as long as these desires remain unsatisfied, individuals will search for both legitimate and illegitimate avenues to satisfy their needs (Karpova 2013).

The prison economy takes the form of two almost independent and exhaustive systems. The first model is a formal economic system that is comprised of legitimate exchanges of goods and services (Karpova 2013). Within the formal economic system there are generally three avenues for lawfully acquiring goods and services in the prison. (1) The prison store sells goods for scrip, which range from toiletries to television sets. (2) Purchases inside and outside the institution may be made with a check written against an inmate's account with some restrictions; for example, cigarettes, drugs, alcohol, and other contraband may not be purchased. (3) Many goods, such as clothing, may be sent inside as gifts (Gleason 1978). The formal prison economy provides, at best, the essentials, while at worst, even less. "It is true that the prisoner's basic material needs are met—in the sense that he does not go hungry, cold or wet" (Sykes 1971: 65). Furthermore, prisoners seek not only necessities, but also amenities such as different goods and services, the number of which is very limited. Finally, the formal system provides very little opportunity to earn income, and if it does, there is no fairness in the distribution of income (Lankenau 2001), as prison has deliberately been made an island of poverty (Williams and Fish 1974).

The second model is an informal economic system comprised of both legitimate and illegitimate exchanges of goods and services. Prior research has suggested that informal economic systems or the sub-rosa economy circulate throughout the inmate population within all penal institutions (Casella 2000). The reason for this is simple: the prison's formal economic system provides only the essentials if not less. As a means of fulfilling basic needs in an environment inundated with rules and regulations, inmates have developed this underground/informal economic system. This system provides inmates the benefit of greater quality of life (e.g., additional phone time, freshly ironed clothing, special meals, a clean cell, hair care), access to contraband (e.g., drugs, alcohol, pornography, tobacco, cell phones, cash), and/or forbidden services (e.g., sex, tattooing, physical protection, gambling) (Copes, Higgins, Tewksbury, and Dabney, 2010). This economy allows inmates to locate and secure the restricted goods they desire (Irwin 1970; Kalinich 1980; Kalanich and Stojkoviv 1985). The range of the prison economy generally extends into restricted services or enhancements. For example, according to Irwin and Cressey (1962), an inmate can work in a kitchen storeroom and steal and sell food to acquire status. While there are few opportunities for worthwhile work within the formal system, there are a number of informal opportunities to make money. The jobs differ from transporting contraband to doing laundry, or from drawing tattoos to gambling and taking bets. Each job is paid, so it is highly desirable. The authors found that a steady income of cigarettes, which was the medium of exchange in prison, could promote prisoners to a level of influence that will allow them to purchase symbols of status to separate them from the others. As such, inmates exchange capital (such as the aforementioned cigarettes) for desired enhancements (e.g., candy, haircare, and cell cleaning) and forbidden services (e.g., tattooing, drugs, and sex).

In yet other cases, unauthorized payment or trade agreements are attached to legitimate services such as legal assistance or tutoring (Copes et al. 2010); thus, when goods and services are heavily regulated, they can often become forms of capital. These forms of capital are discussed and traded readily within the institutional setting. The presence of rules and the absence of currency mean nothing in a location where supply and demand can be innovatively defined and managed (Copes et al. 2010). Those who participate in the underground prison economy are granted advantages beyond access to scarce goods (Kalinich and Stojkovic 1985). Among the most valuable material goods there are cell phones, coffee, candies, chocolate bars, sandwiches, alcohol, cigarettes, and of course, drugs. Whereas in the outside world a candy bar is merely a candy bar, inside the prison it is a sought-after commodity and in some cases currency. Each of these goods can be sold, traded, and gambled because each item is essentially money. So the underground/informal economy indeed exists in prison. Inmates generally identify this economy as a hustle. It exists despite walls, fences or deprivation of freedom. It exists because of necessity. It brings money, and with that the ability to bring comfort when incarcerated (Karpova 2013). The inmate economy penetrates all facets of prison life. Inmate economic relations have a potential to maintain stable market relationships between prisoners when rules are clear, resources are accessible, and regulation of social relations are certain and straightforward (Karpova 2013).

A major aspect of the informal system is the contraband market; which, as highlighted earlier, provides (a) material goods and services to inmates that they otherwise would not have access to, and (b) a sense of psychological satisfaction, both from seeing the formal system "beat" and from feeling they have at least some control over their lives (Kalinich and Stojovic 1985). Contraband goods and services can be produced within an institution or smuggled in from the outside world. Drugs and real money, for example, must be smuggled in, while weapons and alcohol can be produced using resources found within the institution. Contraband can be smuggled into a prison in a myriad of ways; it is smuggled in by inmate trustees who can leave and enter with some freedom. Inmates often obtain contraband during visitation. It is also planted on vehicles making otherwise legitimate deliveries (Kalinich and Stojkovic 1987). As a result, the contraband system is instrumental to the development of informal rules and regulations among prisoners and serves as one of the most important ways that inmates ease the pains of imprisonment (Roth and Skarbek 2014). In effect, the sub-rosa market provides, in part, not only a forum for exchange but also a foundation for inmate behavior.

Contraband items can generally be divided into two large classes: "nuisance" and "serious" contraband. *Nuisance* contraband derives its lure primarily from the outlawing against or regulating of free-world goods and services. The various types of prohibited materials within this class pertain to needs for recreation, expression, making a profit, supplementing the official diet, and engaging in sexual fantasy or expression (Guenther 1975). Thus, gambling paraphernalia, pornographic novels, and devices for heating stolen food are commonly found in prison. Correctional staff believe that these items are contraband because they involve theft or because their rental, e.g., of pornography, creates debts that may not be collectable. Failure to pay on a debt has a potential for violence since the delinquent debtor commonly suffers an assault. Conversely, *serious* contraband is viewed as a threat to security or is expected to affect inmates in objectionable ways. From the inmate's perspective, serious contraband serves three basic functions: to defend against or to perpetrate assaults, to escape from confinement, or to induce intoxication through drugs (Guenther 1975).

Kalinich (1980) identified several major categories of goods and services available including: drugs, alcoholic beverages, gambling, appliances (TV sets, hot plates, radios, and so on), clothing, buying of institutional privileges and reports, weapons, food and snack services, and prostitution. A common and approved contraband service was the "inmate store." Each cell block had a couple of inmates, two of whom kept a large stock of snacks, pop, instant coffee, and so on, that they purchased at the inmate commissary and resold to inmates in the evenings after the commissary was closed. This form of "convenience store," while unauthorized, added to the smooth running of the cell block (Kalinich 1980).

In the same way that participation in the stock market can bring positive and negative outcomes for free members of society, so too can participation in the prison economy (Copes et al. 2010). Having these services and amenities at one's disposal or being a supplier of said items can increase one's status among fellow inmates. However, acquiring goods or status can also make an inmate a target for victimization by those who seek to acquire their capital and status by force (Copes et al. 2010). Thus it is clear that the contraband marketplace is an important focal point for inmates, around which they focus a great deal of their activities, as well as structure their behaviors and interactions with each other and the correctional staff (Kalinich and Stojkovic 1985).

The Hustle

Inmate hustling exists in prison regardless of place and time. As some may recall from Morgan Freeman's performance as the hustler Ellis Redding in *The Shawshank Redemption*, hustling is a concept authorities in the field are aware of and continue to fight. Already residing in a deprived setting, it gets even harder for inmates to retain their identities. As such, a prisoner's natural response to authorities is to adapt to prison culture through rebellion, which can mean engaging in illegal activities and hustling (Karpova 2013).

Hustling requires some imagination to see the opportunities available, as well as initiative to pursue the opportunities, access to goods and services or working capital, and a willingness to take the necessary risks (Gleason 1978). A hustler must have access to goods and services sought by other inmates and/or access to working capital. Generally, the more profitable the hustle, the more highly the job is valued; consequently, there is competition among inmates for such positions.

Gleason identified six factors that influence inmates' choice of a hustle. (1) The more time inmates have spent incarcerated, the more knowledgeable they become about the available hustles and how to establish themselves within their chosen hustle. (2) The skills that inmates bring in from outside or acquire while inside will limit their opportunities. (3) The rules governing gifts can impact the potential breadth of the hustles. (4) The influence of increasing inmates' legitimate income by raising pay scales as an increased legitimate income would decrease the need for certain hustles but might also provide more working capital. (5) The amount, quality, and variety of rival goods in the prison store can impact the earning power of certain hustles. (6) Lastly, the hustlers' preference for risk determines whether they choose a relatively safe hustle or the more risky hustles. Gleason defined the degree of risk as a function of the probability of receiving punishment and the expected punishment (Gleason 1978).

Gleason (1978) contended the probability of receiving the aforementioned punishments is contingent upon four factors: (1) The frequency of a given hustle, or (2) the quantity of goods and services hustled, as the greater the amount of goods and services hustled the more likely it is to be observed. There are limits to how much hustling can occur. Some hustling is tolerated by correctional staff; however, if hustling becomes excessive and leads to increased threats to security or institutional cost, the rules against such activities will become more severe. (3) The vigilance of correctional staff varies and thus impacts the chances of being caught. Recall that some small hustles can be tolerated if not encouraged on the part of correctional staff as they can aid in running a stable cellblock. (4) Lastly, the time inmates have spent incarcerated provides them with opportunities to observe and learn methods to protect their hustle from discovery.

The demand for hustled goods and services is a function of taste, income availability, the going price of the commodity, and the prices of similar goods available in the store, from other hustlers, and those receivable as gifts. Gleason noted that the price inmates are willing to pay for a given commodity can be influenced by buyers' concern for the trustworthiness and reliability of the hustlers and the quality of their products. Gleason highlights three reasons for such concerns: (1) The buyer may be implicated in the transaction and is then subject to punishment or at least confiscation of the contraband. (2) If hustlers do not satisfy their part of the deal the buyer has no recourse but strong-arming or other forms of force. (3) In some instances, such as the purchase of a used watch, the buyer is concerned that hustlers provide a good-quality watch in working condition and guarantee their product for some period of time (Gleason 1978).

Gangs

So who are the hustlers that facilitate the informal economic system and where do they come from? A surprising answer to this question can be found in the formation of prison gangs. Most of us are only aware of the portrayal of prison gangs we see in movies, pop culture, and the media, that of chaotic bands of violent, racist thugs. However, recent research has shown that one reason for the formation of prison gangs is to provide extralegal governance in social and economic interactions (Roth and Skarbek 2014; Skarbek 2014). In short, inmates join gangs to promote cooperation and trust, which facilitates illegal contraband markets. Therefore, prison gangs play a central role in contraband activity (Blatchford 2008; Camp and Camp 1985; Irwin 1980).

Roth and Skarbek's argument is based on the premise that members in prison gangs watch out for the good of their members and have a since of togetherness among their members much the same way the members of a community would on the outside. In particular, they advocate for a community responsibility system (CRS) which has often played an important role in governing social interactions (Fearon and Laitin 1996; Greif 2006). In such a system, all members of the group are responsible for the actions and debts of any other member. The authors argued prison gangs are the "communities" that inmates join. For instance, they cannot rely on correctional staff to enforce agreements made in drug deals, punish inmates who do not pay their drug debts, or knowingly protect a drug stash. For these illicit markets to operate, inmates must create extralegal governance institutions (Roth and Skarbek 2014).

McCleery (1962) reported similar findings in his study, describing active and prosperous contraband market systems that were controlled by powerful inmate groups and leaders. Irwin (1970) described links between inmates' street behaviors and their behaviors in the informal economic system in prison and the tenuous connection contraband provides among prison gangs. The more extensively inmates wish to engage in the underground economy, the more important it is they affiliate with a gang. When conflicts arise, inmates can appeal to these powerful leaders to meet. If inmates are not affiliated with a group, then there is no community that can put pressure on them to make restitution or to do so themselves (Roth and Skarbek 2014).

Consequently, Roth and Skarbek (2014) opine that active participation in the informal economy often requires membership in the community responsibility system, and all gang members are responsible for any member's actions. For example, if a member of Gang A purchases drugs on credit from someone in Gang B, then Gang A is responsible for his payment of that debt. If the inmate does not pay, then the drug dealer can appeal to the leaders of Gang A for relief. The leader will either pay the debt, force his member to pay the debt, or work for them, assault the inmate to appease the drug dealer, or hand him over to Gang B to be assaulted (Roth and Skarbek 2014).

Guards

Guards, just like inmates, are adapting to a particular prison culture generally dominated by mindless, confident, and brutal custodians (Johnson 1997). As previously stated, to an extent guards are dependent on inmates for the satisfactory performance of their duties, and like many figures of authority, guards are evaluated in terms of the inmates they control; a troublesome, loud, unkempt cellblock reflects on the guard's ability to "handle prisoners," and this can be an important component used as the basis for pay raises and promotions (Guenther 1975). The institution cannot totally control its inmate body for a variety of reasons: low officer-to-inmate ratio, lack of normative commitment to the organizational rules by inmates, and the inability to implement an efficient reward/punishment system to gain compliance among inmates (Kalinich and Stojkovic 1985). As such, guards cannot rely on the direct application of force to attain compliance, for they are few against hundreds, and if guards continually call for additional help they can become a serious problem and safety concern for the shorthanded prison administration.

Guards, then, are under pressure to achieve a smoothly running cellblock by persuasion of rewards rather than by the threat of punishment. One of the best strategies guards can implement is ignoring minor offenses or making sure that they do not find themselves in a position to discover minor infractions of the rules. Guards attempt to establish a working relationship with inmates by using their discretion in enforcing rules, which becomes the basis for cooperation with the inmates, as well as providing the guards with a reputation among inmates as being fair (Lombardo 1981). However, guards must be aware they are walking a "slippery slope" by allowing some transgressions while looking the other way with others. They can easily find themselves at odds with a particular group of inmates or even as key members in the prison economy. Guards can often escalate the problem. Poorly paid and often lacking ethics, the officers may take advantage of deprived inmates and the miserable condition of the prison (Karpova 2013). Therefore, those motivated by profit may become smugglers of contraband going both in and out of the prison (Kalinich 1980). As Davidson (1977) reported, a correctional officer at San Quentin Prison earned $60,000 in one year bringing heroin into the prison. By smuggling or helping the smuggling of illegal goods into a facility, correctional officers directly fuel the prison economy (Karpova 2013). In short, the management of inmates requires that officers determine the consequences of minor rule violation, while simultaneously avoiding blackmail (Guenther 1975) and the slippery slope that can lead to becoming a member in the prison economy.

Contraband

Traditionally, cigarettes have been used by inmates as a standard form of currency in informal prison economies. Radford's (1945) description of a Nazi Germany prisoner of war (POW) camp was the first to discuss the economic and social importance of cigarettes in an inmate economy. He indicated that although active trading of other goods and services existed, only cigarettes were transformed from a commodity to a form of currency due to their durability, portability, supply, and demand. Likewise, Williams and Fish (1974) reported that cigarettes functioned as an ideal currency in prison because they were often smoked and replaced by new packs before the old packs became mangled and worn out. Similarly, Irwin and Cressey (1962) found with a steady income of cigarettes, inmates possessed a great deal of influence and purchased those things that were symbols of status among inmates. Even if there is no well-developed medium of exchange, inmates could trade goods acquired for equally desirable goods possessed by other inmates; including, but not limited to, information, specially laundered clothing, fancy belts, belt buckles, billfolds, shoes, or any other type of dress that would set them apart and indicate that they have both the influence to get and keep the goods despite prison rules that outlaw doing so (Irwin and Cressey 1962).

Smoking has historically been a normative part of prison culture (Butler, Richmond, Belcher, Wilhelm, and Wodak 2007). In fact, most people entering U.S. prisons are smokers, and this group has relatively high rates of smoking related health problems (National Commission on Correctional Health Care 2006). This, coupled with changes in public perceptions of smoking, increased concern over these adverse health effects, and fear of lawsuits by incarcerated people involuntarily exposed to cigarette smoke has driven correctional institutions to implement smoking bans (Marrett and Sullivan 2005; Thibodeau, Seal, Jorenby, Corcoran, and Sosman 2012). Since the mid 1980s, cigarette-smoking policies have become increasingly restrictive in correctional facilities across the United States (Lankenau 2001). According to a survey of 49 state correctional departments and the Federal Bureau of Prisons, 60 percent of prison systems report having total smoking bans, and 87 percent do not allow smoking indoors (Kauffman, Ferketich, and Wewers 2008).

Officer attitudes toward the smoking bans influenced the development of cigarette black markets in two ways. Officers who overlooked smoking violations, indirectly stimulated demand for cigarettes by allowing inmates to develop or maintain a smoking habit. More serious, officers who smuggled cigarettes or aided smugglers fueled both a supply and a demand for cigarettes among inmates (Lankenau 2001). Lankenau also found that tobacco smuggling is far more common in minimum security facilities, due to more inmate movement off site (to jobs, etc.) compared to higher security prisons. The new tobacco ban policy also had ramifications for inmates. The majority of inmates were compelled to pay considerably higher prices to continue their cigarette habits. Consequently, the high cost of cigarettes prompted many inmates to undertake various hustles or to become low-level dealers because paying for only a few cigarettes could cost a third of an inmate's monthly institutional pay (Lankenau 2001). Another problem identified by Lankenau was the purity of the product. Just as the criminalization of cocaine and heroin gave way to increased impure drugs, cigarettes sold on the black market are often more harmful than those sold legally and may be combined with less healthy smoking practices. For instance, some inmates rolled cigarettes with toilet paper wrappers or pages from a Bible. Both contain ink or dyes that are harmful when burned.

The smoking prevalence is estimated at 60–80 percent in US criminal justice populations (Kauffman et al. 2008), about four times higher than in the general population. County jails in Illinois, Tennessee, Alabama, Nebraska, and Kentucky, for example, have begun to sell e-cigarettes to prisoners through commissaries (Curry, Lee, and Rogers 2014). With the introduction of this alternative into a correctional setting came with it unique risks as jailers discovered that inmates were using the hard metal casings of standard e-cigarettes to create weapons so one company researched and redesigned an e-cigarette with a "soft plastic" rather than metal casing, which limits its utility as a weapon (Curry et al. 2014). Recently several companies, *Crossbar*, *Lock-ups*, and *Precision Vapor*, are marketing directly to the correctional population (Williams 2014). According to these companies, these new e-cigarettes not only increase revenue from commissary sales, but also decrease the presence of contraband, since "inmates no longer needed to try to sneak in tobacco."

Correctional facilities ban cigarettes for a variety of reasons, including tobacco control laws and ordinances that legislate bans throughout state and county buildings, the aforementioned inmate lawsuits and grievances that sue for smoke-free environments, overcrowding that increases the amount of cigarette smoke within facilities, and new institutional architecture and technology that are harmed by tobacco smoke (Lankenau, Falkin, and Strauss 1999). However, in spite of these bans in a majority of U.S. correctional institutions, just as in life on the outside, e-cigarettes may be quickly becoming an acceptable alternative on the inside.

Cell Phones

At one time, drugs, cigarettes, and special clothing served as contrabands of choice by inmates; however, within the last few years, wireless phones are quickly becoming popular and are being used not just for communication purposes, but may allow inmates to continue operating their criminal enterprise from behind bars. Cell phones represent the latest concern in the battle against contraband in American correctional settings. A recent report concluded that "a significant number of inmates use prison telephones to commit serious crimes" (Burke and Owen 2010: 10). While inmates no doubt use their cell phones for harmless communicative purposes, the devices also provide inmates with an avenue for conducting criminal activity. For example, during a massive search in a Texas institution, authorities recovered approximately 300 wireless phones, including 18 from death row inmates (Burke and Owen 2010). More recently, the California Department of Corrections and Rehabilitation confiscated some 15,000 phones from inmates in 2011 alone. During a two-week period at one institution, correctional staff used a special device to detect more than 25,000 unauthorized calls, texts, and internet requests (California Council on Science and Technology 2012).

With the numbers previously highlighted this is more than just a common hustle, inmates are being aided substantially from visitors and correctional staff who smuggle wireless phones and related paraphernalia into prisons. In some cases, staff members have accepted bribes from inmates to sneak cell phones into facilities. For example, one correctional officer reported earning more than $100,000 by charging prisoners $100 to $400 per device. Smuggled wireless phones also provide a source of additional income to inmates who charge other prisoners up to $50 for each call placed (Burke and Owen 2010). Burke and Owen highlighted one case in which officials discovered wireless devices outside a perimeter fence and determined that a makeshift catapult had been constructed to launch phones over the prison wall.

The original contrabands of choice of cigarettes and drugs may very well be outdated as wireless phones are becoming popular. Inmates, civilians, and correctional staff alike have smuggled cell phones into institutions, allowing them to be utilized by inmates for numerous purposes, some illegal and even dangerous. Inmates argue that wireless phones are less expensive than pay phones for maintaining contact with family as well as offering inmates a means of private communication with minimal oversight by correctional staff. Thus, it appears that cell phones as a means of contraband in correctional facilities are here to stay.

Sex

Sex can be an important part of the informal economy in prison, as sex is both a highly valued item and a relatively cheap commodity. For many prisoners, the only commodity they have to trade is themselves. In some institutions, there is a menu of sexual practices that are bartered for common items such as cigarettes, food, toiletries, or a phone call (Smith 2006). Imprisonment can arouse the fear of losing control over one's personhood. As discussed earlier, upon imprisonment, inmates may feel deprived of functions that are core to survival such as eating, drinking, sleep, communication, and self-care. All of these functions are either controlled or limited by external authority. Often, concern for physical safety and wellbeing is a main motivator for sex between inmates and between inmates and correctional staff. Smith states the concept of "protective pairing" signifies inmates have sex or become involved with someone to protect themselves from a greater harm from other inmates or staff. Legal and other narratives are inundated with stories of prisoners having sex with other prisoners or with correctional staff to ensure their safety (Smith 2006).

However, research has also posited that many sexual relationships are based predominantly on manipulation rather than on a homosexual alliance (Greer 2000). That is, inmates participate in sexual relationships to advance economic standing as access to money or material goods was found to be a major motivation for engaging in homosexual activity (Greer 2000; Ward and Kassebaum 1965) while others utilized sex to settle a debt. For instance, Robertson (2003) contends when the "mark," usually an inexperienced, drug addicted inmate, cannot make good on his debt, he will be given the option of "servicing" the debt through copulation or face continual beatings.

Interestingly, sex between inmates and correctional staff is often considered consensual, particularly in women's institutions. The rationality is that women seek particular favors from male officers in exchange for sexual attentions (Karpova 2013) in much the same way that inmates do for protection, and are therefore willing participants. As such, prior research on sexual relationships between female inmates and correctional staff has considered such relationships to be more consensual than forced (Bothworth 1999; Girshick 1999; Owen 1998; Rierden 1997). Sex in prison has been shown to be more than just an expression of power or love, but can be legitimately used as a commodity to be bartered and traded within the informal prison economy.

Conclusion

The environment of incarceration is notorious for the deprivation and limitation of freedom and other liberties, so neither material possessions nor outside status can be fully brought to the facility. Wealth and status are the major concepts in the facility. Prison life is inherently mantled with many temptations, such as choosing the path of gambling, hustling, and other illegal activities. Those inmates who receive money from family and friends may be able to afford to buy certain things while confined. However, those without money are often forced to get involved in illegal activities. It is important to note that these experiences and adaptations of prisoners are not constant over time (Diaz-Cotto 1996; Greer 2000; Rierden 1997); that is the prison subculture and economy is being influenced by broader political, cultural, economic, and social forces (Clemmer 1940; Jacobs 1977; Sykes 1971). In fact, Gartner and Kruttschnitt (2004) found evidence that broader social and economic changes had shaped prison economic relationships. Comparing prison economic relationships in the 1960s with those in the 1990s, they found that by 1990 there was a reduction in the personal property exchange among prisoners because of the potential for conflict (Karpova 2013).

It needs to be stated that the informal economic system itself can present additional problems beyond security concerns. Identified by Kalinich and Stojkovic (1987), the sub-rosa economic system is a class structure within the prison environment. The old adage that "the rich get richer while the poor get poorer" is particularly relevant in this context. The informal economic system makes this a definite reality in prison. Additionally, for those inmates who thrive on the sub-rosa economy, the system rationalizes and reinforces their existing criminal patterns of behavior. This can have an adverse effect on any program of rehabilitation, since these illegal activities encourage greater criminal tendencies as opposed to inmates adopting a pro-rules stance and becoming more accepting of society's laws and norms. There is little doubt that the informal economic system runs counter to any optimism of personal rehabilitation on the part of inmates (Kalinich and Stojkovic 1987).

Lastly and most importantly, the illegal system of goods and services definitely produces a situation where the corruption of authority among correctional staff is inevitable. Since officers are evaluated on how well they control their respective areas and the inmate leaders' power is founded in the ability to facilitate the flow of illegal goods and services, there is a necessary linkage between the two to encourage prison stability. Thus, the prison organization is forced to trade off some corruption for order (Kalinich 1980).

Therefore, just as in the real world, in prison, those inmates who are willing to betray solidarity and collaboration, victimize fellow inmates, get involved in speculative activities, and are willing to take risks, are the inmates who have a chance to escape from material deprivation and prosper (Karpova 2013).

References

Blatchford, Chris. 2008. *The Black Hand: The Bloody Rise and Redemption of "Boxer" Enriquez*. New York: William Morrow Paperbacks.

Bothworth, Mary. 1999. "Resistance and Compliance in Women's Prisons: Towards a Critique of Legitimacy." *Critical Criminology* 7: 5–19.

Burke, Tod W., and Stephen S. Owen. 2010. "Cell Phones as Prison Contraband." *FBI Law Enforcement Bulletin* 79(7): 10–15.

Butler, Tony, R. Richmond, J. Belcher, K. Wilhelm, and A. Wodak. 2007. "Should Smoking be Banned in Prisons?" *Tobacco Control* 16(5): 291–293.

California Council on Science and Technology, and United States of America. 2012. *The Efficacy of Managed Access Systems to Intercept Calls from Contraband Cell Phones in California Prisons*. Sacramento, CA. Retrieved from https://assets.documentcloud.org/documents/355647/2012cell.pdf

Camp, George, and Camille Camp. 1985. *Prison Gangs: Their Extent, Nature, and Impact on Prisons*. Washington DC: U.S. Department of Justice, Federal Justice Research Program.
Casella, Eleanor. 2000. "Doing Trade': A Sexual Economy of Nineteenth-Century Australian Female Convict Prisons." *World Archaeology* 32(2): 209–221.
Clemmer, Donald. 1940. *The Prison Community*. New York: Holt, Rinehart Winston.
Copes, Heith, George E. Higgins, Richard Tewksbury, and Dean A. Dabney. 2010. "Participation in the Prison Economy and Likelihood of Physical Victimization." *Victims and Offenders* 6(1): 1–18.
Curry, Laurel, Youn Ok Lee, and Todd Rogers. 2014. "E-cigarettes Made Especially for Inmates." *Tobacco Control* 23(e2): e87–e88.
Davidson, R. Theodore. 1977. "The Prisoner Economy." Pp. 204–219 in *Correctional Institutions*, 2nd ed., edited by Robert Melvin Carter, Daniel Glaser, and Leslie T. Wilkins. Philadelphia, PA: J.B. Lippincott.
Diaz-Cotto, Juanita. 1996. *Gender, Ethnicity, and the State: Latina and Latino Prison Politics*. Albany, NY: SUNY Press.
Fearon, James, and David Laitin. 1996. "Explaining Interethnic Cooperation." *American Political Science Review* 90(4): 715–735.
Gartner, Rosemary, and Candace Kruttschnitt. 2004. "A Brief History of Doing Time: The California Institution for Women in the 1960s and 1990s." *Law & Society Review*, 38(2): 267–304.
Girshick, Lori. 1999. *No Safe Haven: Stories of Women in Prison*. Boston, MA: Northeastern University Press.
Gleason, Sandra E. 1978. "Hustling: The Inside Economy of a Prison." *Federal Probation* 42: 32–40.
Greer, Kimberly. 2000. "The Changing Nature of Interpersonal Relationships in a Women's Prison." *The Prison Journal* 80(4): 442–468.
Greif, Avner. 2006. "The Birth of Impersonal Exchange: The Community Responsibility System and Impartial Justice." *Journal of Economic Perspectives* 20(2): 221–236.
Guenther, Anthony L. 1975. "Compensations in a Total Institution: The Forms and Functions of Contraband." *Crime & Delinquency* 21(3): 243–254.
Irwin, John. 1970. *The Felon*. Los Angeles, CA: University of California Press.
Irwin, John. 1980. *Prisons in Turmoil*. Boston, MA: Little, Brown.
Irwin, John. 2005. *The Warehouse Prison: Disposal of the New Dangerous Class*. Los Angeles, CA: Roxbury Pub.
Irwin, John, and Donald R. Cressey.1962. "Thieves, Convicts and the Inmate Culture." *Social Problems* 10(2): 142–155.
Jacobs, James. 1977. *Stateville: The Penitentiary in Mass Society*. Chicago, IL: University of Chicago Press.
Johnson, Robert. 1997. *Hard Time: Understanding and Reforming the Prison*, 2nd ed. Belmont, CA: Wadsworth Publishing.
Kalinich, David B. 1980. *The Inmate Economy*. Lexington, MA: Lexington Books.
Kalinich, David B., and Stan Stojkovic. 1985. "Contraband: The Basis for Legitimate Power in a Prison Social System." *Criminal Justice and Behavior* 12(4): 435–451.
Kalinich, David B., and Stan Stojkovic. 1987. "Prison Contraband Systems: Implications for Prison Management." *Journal of Crime and Justice* 10(1): 1–21.
Karpova, Polina A. 2013. "Predicting Inmate Economic Conflict in Female Housing Units: Individual Factors versus Social Climate Factors." MS thesis, College of Justice and Safety, Eastern Kentucky University.
Kauffman Ross, Amy K. Ferketich, and Mary E. Wewers. 2008. "Tobacco Policy in American Prisons, 2007." *Tobacco Control* 17(5): 357–360.
Lankenau, Stephen E. 2001. "Smoke 'em if you Got'em: Cigarette Black Markets in US Prisons and Jails." *The Prison Journal* 81(2): 142–161.
Lankenau, Stephen, Greg Falkin, and Strauss, S. 1999. "Social Forces Shaping and Resisting the Trend toward Banning Cigarettes in U.S. Jails and Prisons." National Development and Research Institutes, New York: Unpublished manuscript.
Lombardo, Lucien. 1981. *Guards Imprisoned: Correctional Officers at Work*. New York: Elsevier.
Marrett, A., and D. Sullivan. 2005. "Stubbing out Smoking in Prisons." Paper presented at the 3rd Australian Tobacco Control Conference, Sydney, New South Wales, Australia.

McCleery, Richard. 1962. *Communication Patterns as Bases of Systems of Authority and Power.* Indianapolis, IN: Bobbs-Merril.

National Commission on Correctional Health Care. 2006. *The Health Status of Soon to Be Released Inmates: A Report to Congress.* Chicago, IL. Retrieved from https://www.ncjrs.gov/pdffiles1/nij/grants/189735.pdf

Owen, Barbara. 1998. *In the Mix: Struggle and Survival in a Women's Prison.* Albany, NY: State University of New York Press.

Radford, Robert. 1945. "The Economic Organization of a POW Camp." *Economica* 12(48): 189–201.

Rierden, Andi. 1997. *The Farm: Life inside a Women's Prison.* Amherst, MA: University of Massachusetts Press.

Robertson, James E. 2003. "Rape among Incarcerated Men: Sex, Coercion and STDs." *AIDS Patient Care and STDs* 17(8): 423–430.

Roth, M. Garrett, and David Skarbek. 2014. "Prison Gangs and the Community Responsibility System." *Review of Behavioral Economics* 1(3): 223–243.

Skarbek, David. 2014. *The Social Order of the Underworld: How Prison Gangs Govern the American Penal System.* Oxford, UK: Oxford University Press.

Smith, Brenda V. 2006. "Rethinking Prison Sex: Self-expression and Safety." *Columbia Journal Gender & Law* 15: 185–234.

Sykes, Gresham. 1971. *The Society of Captives: The Study of a Maximum Security Prison.* Princeton, NJ: Princeton University Press.

Thibodeau, Laura, David W. Seal, Douglas E. Jorenby, Kerri Corcoran, and James M. Sosman. 2012. "Perceptions and Influences of a State Prison Smoking Ban." *Journal of Correctional Health Care* 18(4): 293–301.

Ward, David, and Gene Kassebaum. 1965. *Women's Prison: Sex and Social Structure.* Chicago, IL: Aldine Press.

Williams, Timothy. 2014. "In Rural Jails, E-cigarettes are a Calming Vapor." *The New York Times,* January 23, p. A1.

Williams, Vergil L., and Mary Fish. 1974. *Convicts, Codes, and Contraband: The Prison Life of Men and Women.* Cambridge, MA: Ballinger.

39 Sexuality in Correctional Facilities

Richard Tewksbury and John C. Navarro

Same-sex relationships among the incarcerated are regarded to be an intensely neglected field of inquiry for scholars (Hensley and Tewksbury 2002). Yet, pervasive misconceptions have raised alarms among the public about tales of rampant inmate-on-inmate sexual victimization, and male and female inmates being forced into same-sex relations. These myths about the sexual behaviors of the incarcerated have further perpetuated folklores to be acquired by the public.

Emerging research has uncovered the true reality about inmates' expressions of sexuality during their incarcerations. Coerced sexual behaviors do occur between both the male and female incarcerated populations, but so do consensual and bartered sexual acts between inmates, staff, and visitors (Hensley and Tewksbury 2002; Warren, Jackson, Loper, and Burnette 2010). In whole, there exist three forms of sexual interactions in correctional facilities: bartered sex, coerced sex, and consensual sex. Thus, the inmate subculture is not solely defined by coerced sexual encounters, but rather there are alternative forms of sexuality that inmates can express when incarcerated. Of note, due to the sensitive nature of the topic at hand, we decided to differentiate legal and personal consent. Hereafter, the term consensual will reflect legal consent, which is also a term frequently used by scholars and we will continue to honor their terminology use, whereas the use of the term willing will reflect personal consent.

Sexual identity is one such expression that is rather fluid in the inmate subculture. Inmates may vacillate between identifying as heterosexual, homosexual, or bisexual (Hensley, Tewksbury, and Koscheski 2002; Hensley, Tewksbury, and Wright 2001). Longer incarceration periods result in a greater likelihood to report same-sex sexual relations and/or self-identification as a homosexual (Hensley et al. 2002). Regardless of an inmate's sexual orientation, same-sex encounters can generate into meaningful relationships among inmates. Nevertheless, inmates still have a continued risk of being a victim of rape and/or sexual assault (Tewksbury and Connor 2014), most notably by persons that hold the institutional power of the correctional facility (Warren et al. 2010). However, contrary to popular belief, incidents of unwanted sexual encounters are rather rare occurrences in correctional facilities (Beck, Berzofsky, Caspar, and Krebs 2013).

In response to public concerns, government bodies become involved in the study of sexual victimization reported by inmates. The passage of the Prison Rape Elimination Act (PREA) in 2003 was a catalyst in the evolution of prison rape research that examined and dissected sexual expressions exhibited by inmates. Consequently, scholarly works have offered a grander perspective of the sexual lifestyle of male and female inmates that have operated inside the inmate subculture, and inmates' persistent issues with sexual victimization, especially from staff members.

This chapter is separated into five sections. The historical aspects of prison sexuality are detailed in the first section. The second section entails a discussion of how scholars promoted legislative responses and encouraged the development of enhanced methodological research to gauge sexual violence and sexual behaviors in correctional facilities. With the background of prison sexuality established, the third section is the heart of the chapter, which covers the sexual behaviors of male and female inmates, as well as prevalence, types, and motivations for same-sex relations. In the fourth section, the prevalence of inmate-to-staff sexual relationships and its dynamics will be discussed. The fifth and final section includes a segment regarding the health consequences faced by inmates who engaged in sexual relations inside closed environments such as correctional facilities.

History of Prison Sexuality

Joseph Fishman paved the road for future prison sexuality and sexual violence scholars with his classic work published in 1934 about American prisons, entitled *Sex in Prison*. Fishman's contributions included a theoretical basis that postulated as to why same-sex relations occurred inside correctional facilities, which was termed the deprivation theory. Sykes (1958) reworked this theoretical argument some decades later into the five cardinal deprivations faced on a daily basis by the incarcerated, which included the prohibition of heterosexual relationships. However, emerging scholarship has argued against the deprivation theory and re-oriented the discussion that indicated sexual relations inside correctional facilities are more strongly related to hypersexuality (Warren et al. 2010).

Other contributions by Fishman (1934) also include the exposure of terminology used within correctional facilities. Such prison slang terms—otherwise known as prison argot—are designed to define the inmate's position in the social-sexual hierarchy found in correctional institutions, a hierarchy that has dominated male institutions. For instance, known homosexual males were termed as "fairies," "pansies," or "fish" (Fishman 1934; Hensley, Wright, Tewksbury, and Castle 2003). Male inmates who failed to express stereotypical masculine characteristics are identified as "fags" or "punks." In contrast to the roles of effeminate inmates, "Wolves" are heterosexual males who exhibit masculine qualities and pursue (or, "hunt") sexual relations with others because of a supposed sexual deprivation (Hensley et al. 2003).

Like male inmates, but not as apparent, the female inmate subculture also operated within the architecture of a social-sexual hierarchy in the form of two sexual roles (Alarid 2000). Black women and/or females that identified themselves as lesbians typically occupied the "stud" role, which encompassed masculine characteristics. In contrast, "femmes" included effeminate women of all races and ethnicities, and were generally "turned out" heterosexual females. In fact, "studs" faced several bouts of sexual coercion by the sexually aggressive "femmes"; taken into consideration that "femmes" maintained the advantage due to outnumbering "studs," and that staff persons find it hard to believe that the feminine female inmates can sexually coerce the masculine female characters in a female correctional institution. These terms reinforced the inmate subculture and further encouraged the acceptance of same-sex relations in an institutional environment.

Prison sexuality research began to capture the social dynamics of same-sex relations between the 1930s and early 1960s, but its prevalence inside these facilities was largely unknown. In 1968, the first valid and reliable rate of prison rape originated from nearly 3,300 interviews with inmates from the Philadelphia jail system (Davis 1968). Rates of prison rape from this study indicated that the issue of sexual activities in correctional facilities was much more problematic than originally believed, considering that an estimated 2,000 (of 60,000) male inmates experienced a sexual assault. Davis (1968) excluded consensual same-sex sexual relationships from his study because of the difficulty in disentangling the true decision-making process of a same-sex relationship in male correctional facilities. Nevertheless, the remarkable efforts set by Davis (1968) would later promote future scholars to pursue sexual violence studies in order to bring greater attention to the issues faced by inmates. Ultimately, government officials became involved with the creation of a federal mandate that enacted procedures to gauge the prevalence of sexual victimization in various correctional facilities across the U.S.

Legislative Responses

The federal passage of the PREA in 2003 brought national attention to rape inside correctional institutions. Not only did PREA assist researchers to further the scholarship in prison rape and promote attention to this issue based on reliable information, but PREA also standardized various definitions of prison rape as to not confound estimates of sexual victimization in correctional institutions. Rape, as defined by PREA, is "the carnal knowledge, oral sodomy, sexual assault with an object, or sexual fondling of a person, forcibly or against that person's will" (PREA 2003: 988). Different from rape, PREA defined prison rape as "the rape of an inmate in the actual or constructive control of prison officials." PREA also acknowledged the presence of inmate-to-staff sexual interactions and labeled them as staff sexual misconduct. In addition to establishing clear definitions that distinguished prison rape from other forms of rape, this multi-purpose Act eventually led to the development of standards for the prevention and intervention of sexual victimization among inmates and opened up greater treatment options and grander resources to be accessible for inmates. In efforts to reinforce PREA's agenda, legislators placed responsibility onto the Bureau of Justice Statistics (BJS) for the production of annual reports of sexual victimization experienced by inmates.

The BJS, via the National Inmate Survey (NIS), began to compile inmate reports and rates of sexual violence beginning in 2007 (Beck 2015; PREA 2003). Various responsibilities to address sexual violence in correctional institutions were given to other governmental bodies, which included the National Institute of Corrections (NIC) and the National Prison Rape Elimination Commission (NPREC). These two institutions should be viewed as checks and balances for PREA as they ensured that the federal Act fulfilled its responsibilities. The NIC's cardinal duty was to encourage prison rape prevention through education and training of correctional administrators, whereas the NPREC maintained broader responsibilities where they oversaw the grander impact of prison rape. Prison-related issues that the NPREC assessed included the prevalence of STDs and HIV/AIDS and the characteristics of victims prone to sexual victimization (PREA 2003). Altogether, these governmental bodies pushed forth toward a monumental task in standardizing methodological standards for sexual violence research and allowed inmates a voice to report their sexual victimization to institutional bodies whose agenda is to fulfill the overall goals set by PREA.

Unlike previous scholarly research, PREA set rigorous methodological standards when conducting sexual victimization research inside U.S. based correctional facilities. In doing so, PREA established a national standard of research methods for future researchers to adopt and offered the ability for comparisons to a national baseline of inmate sexual victimization. Due to such standards, organizations affiliated with PREA have produced empirical results that are widely considered reliable. Further, PREA amassed a great number of correctional facilities to be involved in data collection (Beck 2015), thereby a broader reach of several types of facilities and a larger number will result in a much more reliable estimate of sexual victimization. Specifically, BJS calculated that less than 4 percent of both prison and jail inmates reported sexual victimization when incarcerated (Beck et al. 2013). This represents a notable decrease in sexual victimization rates among prison inmates compared to previous BJS reports, but the rate has remained unchanged among jail inmates.

However, some inmates are substantially more susceptible to sexual victimization. Non-heterosexual inmates reported the highest rates of sexual victimization (Beck et al. 2013; Beck 2014). About 10 percent of prison (12.2 percent) and jail inmates (8.5 percent) that identified as gay, lesbian, bisexual, or another form of non-heterosexuality reported sexual victimization by other inmates. Within the non-heterosexual category, transgender inmates reported the greatest rates of sexual victimization. About one-quarter of transgender prison (21.4 percent) and jail inmates (22.8 percent) reported a sexual victimization by an inmate within the past 12 months of their incarceration (Beck 2014). A majority of transgender inmates reported that the sexual experience was in conjunction with a threat of force or force by other inmates (72.2 percent). Given these points, non-heterosexual inmates are highly vulnerable to sexual victimization, which may be attributed to their perceived absence of masculine features.

Inmate Sexuality Subculture

Inmate subculture has held the notion of sex to be substantially different from how it is viewed in general society. Unlike the outside world, sex has become a normalized commodity used for the benefits of protection and other matters (Zaitzow 2014). One school of thought is that prohibition of sexual activities in correctional facilities has promoted unwanted sexual encounters, and thus, increased violence. In effect, a social-sexual hierarchy is created based on the characteristics of inmates and functions as a form of social control exercised by the inmates. On the other end, a restriction of sexual activities placed upon the inmate population can be seen as a form of institutional control (Potter and Rosky 2014).

Types of Sexuality

Sexual encounters occur among inmates, as well as visitors and institutional staff persons, despite being universally prohibited by institutional policies. For some inmates, sex inside is an extension and continuation of their sexual ways prior to incarceration. Other inmates experience a reshaping and redefinition of sexuality and yet other inmates seemingly discontinue sexual activities while incarcerated. As with sexuality in any setting, there are a number of ways that individuals experience and enact sexuality in prison.

Inmates who have entered the confines of correctional facilities must acclimate to their newfound surroundings, which do not socially operate with norms found in the free world. In an attempt to acclimate and survive in a turbulent, violent environment, some inmates adopt a new (social and sexual) role (Blackburn, Fowler, and Mullings 2014). While some inmates report no sexual contacts or encounters during their period of incarceration (Warren et al. 2010), other inmates—including heterosexuals—do report same-sex arrangements (Hensley et al. 2002).

One important adjustment to the incarcerated lifestyle is sexual orientation, which has been documented to be rather fluid among inmates (Hensley, Tewksbury, and Wright 2001; Hensley et al. 2002). To demonstrate, some inmates have identified as heterosexuals prior to their incarceration, but the more time they serve, the more likely they are to identify as a homosexual as well as report a greater rate of same-sex encounters (Hensley, Tewksbury, and Wright 2001; Levan 2014). Notably, an even greater portion of male inmates later self-identified as bisexual following their incarceration (Hensley, Tewksbury, and Wright 2001). Taken together, inmates who have engaged in same-sex relationships in correctional facilities can be labeled as situational homosexuals—those who engage in same-sex sexual activities so as to relieve sexual desires—or dispositional homosexuals—those with an inclination to be homosexual or bisexual (Levan 2014). As such, persons deprived of heterosexual relations while incarcerated (Sykes 1958) may alter their sexuality to maintain a sexual life.

Sexual relationships in correctional facilities can be seen as, and actually be, consensual interactions (Hensley, Tewksbury, and Wright 2001; Warren et al. 2010). Being involved in same-sex sexual relations, however, may also increase the likelihood of an inmate's risk of economic or sexual exploitation (Pardue, Arrigo, and Murphy 2011). Regardless of these risks, inmates report a constellation of feelings that motivate their behavior to become sexually involved with other persons when incarcerated (Warren et al. 2010).

Male Inmates

Homosexuality

Few scholars have pursued the topic of male inmate same-sex sexual relations (Hensley and Tewksbury 2002). Ranges of one-in-five to one-in-three male inmates have engaged in same-sex sexual encounters during their imprisonment (Hensley, Tewksbury, and Wright 2001; Tewksbury 1989). The most compelling evidence is that male inmates who have engaged in same-sex relations are 52 times more likely to transform their sexual orientation identity during incarceration. This transformative process may be because of the exposure to variant sexual behaviors during their incarceration (Gibson and Hensley 2013).

Male inmates that identified as homosexual or bisexual prior to the incarceration stated that they sexually sought out other inmates for various reasons that included a desire for intimacy and/or a new outlook on life, boredom, and provocation (Barth 2012). Of interest, only non-heterosexual male inmates noted that they had an intention of intimacy during their pursuit of same-sex sexual relationships. Even so, male inmates are not as accepting of prison homosexuality when compared to female inmates (Blackburn, Fowler, Mullings, and Marquart 2011).

Types of Inmate Sexual Behavior

Male inmates tend to face a number of sexual behaviors consecutively, which graduate from one to the other, whereas female inmates generally experience only either coerced or consensual sexual encounters (Warren et al. 2010). Ordered by the level of violence, these forms of sexual behavior included consensual sex, bartered sex, victimization, and predation. Like consensual sex, male inmates reported greater rates of bartered sex to occur with visitors and the correctional staff rather than other inmates. In fact, male inmates reported the greatest rate of consensual sexual acts with visitors, followed by staff, and other inmates. Male inmates were more likely to self-describe their pursuit for sexual encounters as predatory in nature when compared to female inmates. Comparable to consensual and bartered sexual pursuits, male inmates aimed their sexual predatory behavior toward staff persons or visitors. The element of sex was a constant topic in the lifestyle of male inmates, which was directed not at inmates but outsiders.

Self-sexual pleasure is perhaps the most common form of sexual activity in correctional facilities. However, it has received very little attention from scholars (Hensley, Tewksbury, and Wright 2001). Unfortunately, institutions have frowned upon this alternative sexual behavior, even though it may reduce coerced sexual encounters in correctional institutions. Regardless of the prohibition of masturbation, nearly all inmates have reported acts of masturbation while incarcerated.

However, international inquiries have suggested that masturbation is not a frequent occurrence for French male inmates (Merotte 2012). However, the rate of their masturbation slightly increased when compared to their masturbatory behaviors when not incarcerated. In support, German male inmates reported a decreased libido when incarcerated (Barth 2012). Of note, Barth's German inmates failed to support Sykes' (1958) deprivation theory, in which heterosexual German male inmates did not cite sexual deprivation as a reason for same-sex relations (Barth 2012). However, Barth's (2012) inmates were older, and in light of Blackburn et al.'s (2011) findings, older male inmates generally found homosexual sexual activities distasteful.

Motivations

Not until the 1980s did empirical work begin to emerge that discussed consensual/willing same-sex sexual activities among male incarcerated populations. Anywhere from 25 percent to 40 percent of incarcerated males reported consensual sex during their imprisonment (Tewksbury 1989). This theme of consensual/willing same-sex relations among male inmates persisted into the millennium. In fact, most same-sex sexual relationships in correctional facilities are consensual/willing (Hensley, Tewksbury, and Wright 2001; Levan 2014).

Recent research revealed that religion and race predicted the likelihood of consensual same-sex male inmate relations (Hensley, Tewksbury, and Wright 2001). Specifically, non-Protestants and Whites were more likely to engage in same-sex sexual behaviors at greater rates. Typical predictors of same-sex relationships among incarcerated males that failed to predict such sexual activities included age, amount of time served, and education.

Although on the surface male same-sex relations generally appear to be consensual/willing, there are underlying processes that are not being advertised (Hensley and Tewksbury 2002). A power differential exists between male inmates who exhibit effeminate qualities and those with stereotypical masculine characteristics (Levan 2014). The environment socially pressures many male inmates to engage in same-sex acts in exchange for protection and financial support, among other favors (Blackburn et al. 2014; Hensley and Tewksbury 2002). Even though actual sexual assaults are low in male correctional facilities, the concern of sexual victimization is so great that inmates are relegated to same-sex relations to mitigate potential victimization (Hensley and Tewksbury 2002). In support, male inmates tended to cite a desire to please and comfort their partner at greater rates (Warren et al. 2010). Further, once male inmates are released back into society they typically revert to their preincarceration sexual identities and practices. Such a transformation in sexual identity lends credences that perhaps being a product of a social environment such as a correctional facility encouraged inmates to engage in same-sex relations.

Female Inmates

In spite of the wealth of male inmate research, scholars began their empirical exploration of female inmate–inmate sexuality in 1913—prior to the research on sexuality among male inmates (Hensley and Tewksbury 2002). However, the lack of statistical analyses in early research about the relationship between female inmates and sexuality contributed much skepticism to the findings. Robust research methods found their way into regular practice by the early 1960s. Beginning in the 1990s, ample amounts of scholarly work focused on female inmates and understandings of their sexual victimization experiences gradually emerged (Struckman-Johnson, Struckman-Johnson, Rucker, Bumby, and Donaldson 1996). Nevertheless, female inmates have not received the same attention by scholars as male inmates when it comes to sexual victimization experiences (Tewksbury and West 2000).

Prevalence

First estimates reported 1-in-14 female inmates were sexually victimized (Struckman-Johnson et al. 1996). Since then, and due largely to PREA, more attention has been devoted to the topic and it has supported the 1-in-14 estimate being valid (Beck et al. 2013). Other research found that nearly one in five female inmates experienced a form of sexual victimization while incarcerated (Blackburn, Mullings, and Marquart 2008). Initially, these numbers do not appear to be shocking, but female inmates only comprise about 1-in-20 of the total U.S. inmate population. Compared to male inmates, female inmates tended to report greater rates of inmate-on-inmate sexual victimization (Marcum 2014).

Sexual relations tend to escalate much more quickly among female than male inmates (Warren et al. 2010). A majority of female inmates (75 percent to 80 percent) have reported being involved in same-sex sexual relationships during their incarceration (Alarid 2000); this rate has essentially stayed unchanged over a decade (Einat and Chen 2012). In reality, sexual assault is not as common when compared to the level of sexual pressuring and harassment experienced by incarcerated females (Alarid 2000).

But, female inmates' attempts to sexually pressure and harass other female inmates generally subside over time (Alarid 2000). Unique among female inmates is that their choice to resist same-sex relationships is generally respected (Alarid et al. 2000; Blackburn et al. 2014). This option is not readily available for male inmates. Female inmates can willingly volunteer to participate in same-sex acts (Hensley and Tewksbury 2002). Due to this level of respect shared among female inmates, consensual relationships are much more common in female correctional institutions than in male facilities (Blackburn et al. 2014).

Types of Sexual Behavior

Female inmates are likely to experience one of two distinct types of sexual behaviors, sexual contact or coerced sex. These two categories of sexual behaviors are mutually exclusive (Warren et al. 2010), with the occurrences of coerced sexual acts being rather rare among the female inmate population (Hensley and Tewksbury 2002). Moreover, female inmates with greater periods of incarceration report greater instances of consensual same-sex relationships (Hensley et al. 2002). However, such themes do not hold true for all populations of female inmates. For instance, homosexual or bisexual female inmates report greater rates of sexual abuse (Blackburn et al. 2008).

Scholars have developed a five-part typology to describe the continuum of female inmate sexuality (Pardue et al. 2011). In order of escalating aggression, this typology includes suppressed sexuality; autoeroticism; consensual, true homosexuality; consensual situational homosexuality; and sexual violence. In detail, the absence of any sexual activity, but the formation of pseudofamilies and/or kinships is termed as suppressed sexuality. More information about pseudofamilies can be found in the later section of this chapter. The following stage in the typology labeled as autoerotic sexual behavior involved self-pleasure/masturbation. Notably, masturbation is a form of sexual behavior that is practiced twice as much among incarcerated females than women in a free society (Hensley, Tewksbury, and Koscheski 2001). The third stage—consensual, true homosexuality—involved female inmates self-identified as homosexuals and engaged in consensual sexual acts, with the potential risk of various types of exploitation. Similar to true homosexuality, the fourth stage—consensual, situational homosexuality— maintained the same risk of exploitation, but the individual likely engaged in same-sex sexual behaviors to adapt to a unisex environment. The final stage, or sexual violence, is a form of sexual behavior that involved severe aggression, which included aspects such as manipulation, compliance, and coercion.

Motivation

Although female inmates mentioned a number of motivating factors for same-sex sexual relations when incarcerated, most were related to strong feelings of love and affection (Warren et al. 2010). Like male inmates, a large portion of female inmates admitted that they engaged in same-sex relations for sexual favors (Alarid 2000). Over time, these same-sex relationships among female inmates graduated into truly intimate sexual relationships (Marcum 2014). In support, female inmates reported the greatest rate of consensual sexual acts with other inmates (26.2 percent) versus visitors (3.8 percent) and staff persons (2.7 percent).

Two primary factors that predicted a female's likelihood to engage in same-sex relations when incarcerated include race and age. Black female inmates reported greater rates of same-sexual relationships when incarcerated. Although this may be due to Black female inmates being more forthright about their same-sex relations during their incarceration compared to White female inmates (Hensley et al. 2002). Comparatively, younger female inmates were more likely to report instances of same-sex relationships. Several reasons can contribute to this finding. It may be that the scholars have captured evolving beliefs found among females in a contemporary society regarding homosexuality. Suggested by the scholars, female inmates may have experimented with same-sex relationships prior to their incarceration due to the reduced stigma associated with homosexuality. In support, younger, female inmates, especially those that identified as non-heterosexual are more accepting of homosexuality compared to other inmates (Blackburn et al. 2011). Liberal attitudes aside, young female inmates may be in pursuit of an emotional relationship to adapt to their current situation (Hensley et al. 2002).

Pseudofamilies

Unlike male inmates, female inmates often engage in same-sex relationships to re-create a family support system within a correctional facility, otherwise known as pseudo-families (Hensley and Tewksbury 2002; Marcum 2014; Merotte 2012; Owen 1998). Empirical evidence of pseudo-families first appeared in the 1930s from research in female juvenile institutions. Desires for sexual relations may be the initial reason for these relationships within pseudo-families, but such sexual desires evolve into the need for emotional support (Marcum 2014). Female inmates willingly pursued same-sex relationships largely for emotional purposes; as such, arrangements are a coping mechanism to incarceration (Blackburn et al. 2014). Support for this is seen in the fact that homosexual or bisexual female inmates reported sexual encounters with self-identified heterosexual female inmates (Warren et al. 2010).

Sexual Victimization by Staff

Staff persons are common perpetrators of inmate sexual victimization (Beck et al. 2013). In fact, staff persons in both prisons and jails are identified as offenders of sexual violence more frequently than inmates. Among staff persons, it is correctional officers that are the most frequently reported to have sexually engaged with inmates, with female correctional officers being the most common offender (McDonald and Miller 2014; Warren et al. 2010). Female staff persons were identified as the offender in over half of the substantiated cases of sexual misconduct, and around a quarter of the substantiated cases involved sexual harassment (Beck 2015). Because staff persons are the most common offenders coupled with the fact that they are the superiors in correctional facilities, reporting sexual victimization is much more difficult (Barth 2012; McDonald and Miller 2014; Zaitzow 2014).

One explanation for the high rate of staff–inmate sexual relations is that such relationships may be consensual, if not romantic (Warren et al. 2010). However, from 2007 to 2012, rates of willing sexual relations with staff persons have decreased in prisons and jails (Beck et al. 2013). Although this may be true, nearly one in four male inmates reported consensual sex with correctional staff persons (Warren et al. 2010), representing a much higher rate when compared to the one in seven male inmates that reported consensual sex with inmates. In contrast, female inmates reported the highest rate of consensual acts with inmates when compared to staff persons.

However, not all inmate-to-staff sexual encounters may be romantic in nature. Male inmates reported exhibiting frequent behaviors of predatory sexual encounters toward prison staff persons (Warren et al., 2010). At the same time, male inmates reported nearly equal rates of sexual misconduct by staff persons as is also reported by female inmates (Beck et al. 2013). Interestingly enough, female inmates reported greater rates of inmate-on-inmate sexual victimization than staff sexual misconduct. Paradoxically, although inmates displayed predatory sexual encounters toward staff members, especially male inmates, inmates themselves as a whole also reported a high rate of staff sexual misconduct.

Other inmates vulnerable to staff sexual misconduct are inmates that do not identify as heterosexual. Non-heterosexuals were twice as likely to report a sexual misconduct by staff persons when compared to heterosexuals. Specifically, about one in 20 prison (5.4 percent) and jail inmates (4.3 percent) reported a staff person as a perpetrator (Beck et al. 2013). Transgender prison inmates are also highly susceptible to staff sexual misconduct (16.7 percent), with an even greater rate of transgender jail inmates that have reported sexual misconduct by staff persons (22.9 percent) (Beck 2014).

A power differential exists between staff persons and inmates that is unique to the incarcerated population. For that reason, there is no ambiguity in whether the sexual act was consensual between these two roles inside a correctional facility; it simply cannot be consensual in legal terms considering the authoritarian role of a staff person (McDonald and Miller 2014). However, criminal prosecutions are rare. Inmates who choose to speak out about their sexual victimization risk potential threatening situations by experiencing negative responses by staff persons (Barth 2012; Zaitzow 2014), such as staff retaliation (Zaitzow 2014). When actions are taken, female correctional officers typically face different types of punishment than their male counterparts (Warren et al. 2010). Termination is the most common outcome for female correctional officers, whereas male correctional officers were likely to be prosecuted. In the long run, prevention of staff sexual misconduct must begin with effective training, especially among females considering their increased likelihood to engage in sexual relations with the inmates (Warren et al. 2010).

In spite of the aforementioned evidence, recent estimates indicated that staff persons and inmates were more or less just as likely to perpetuate a sexual act against an inmate (Beck 2015). Additionally, in contrast to the BJS findings, inmates interviewed by Warren and her colleagues (2010) found inmates were the most common perpetrators of sexual victimization rather than staff persons. Among male inmates, the rate of sexual misconduct from staff and inmates was twice as great (5.9 percent vs. 2.4 percent), whereas, female inmates reported nearly a threefold difference in sexual victimization committed by inmates and staff persons (6.6 percent vs. 2.7 percent). This pattern of inmates committing a greater rate of offenses than staff persons was sustained even when non-contact sexual acts were assessed.

Health Consequences

Implementation of harm-reduction strategies in order to promote pro-social behaviors inside correctional facilities is frequently met with much trepidation by policymakers. Although highly criticized, conjugal visits are one such harm-reduction technique that has been practiced. Now, few U.S. states maintain conjugal visits, in spite of the evidence that has indicated that conjugal visits effectively decreased sexual violence in correctional facilities (Castle 2014; Potter and Rosky 2014). One of the primary criticisms is that conjugal visits promote the transmission of infectious diseases such as HIV/AIDS among visitors, which have the potential to be passed on to persons in general society (Castle 2014). The feasibility to treat and prevent these infectious diseases among the inmate population is hindered by issues unique to correctional facilities, such as the lack of financial resources, lack of access to medical treatment, high traffic of persons, etc. (Potter and Rosky 2014). For these reasons, conjugal visits have waned in their existence since the early 1970s due to the qualms held by administrators (Castle 2014).

Administrators are also weary of the supposed benefits delivered by the introduction of condoms in their institutions, in which they have cited safety issues as well as doubt in their effectiveness for reducing sexual violence (Potter and Rosky 2014). Empirically, the introduction of condoms in certain Australian prisons has reduced consensual and/or nonconsensual sexual relations among the incarcerated populations. However, if condoms were introduced and accessible among the incarcerated, it may be viewed as an admittance that sexual relations have and are occurring inside these facilities. Additionally, inmates have committed criminal acts that in effect have made it difficult for practitioners, administrators, and other policymakers to become amenable to the promotion of "enjoyable" activities in their facilities (Castle 2014; Potter and Rosky 2014).

Conclusion

Modern inmate sexuality research has revealed findings that combat the misconception of systemic sexual victimization. The majority of same-sex relationships in correctional institutions are consensual/willing rather than coercive. In a similar vein, sexual orientation has operated on a spectrum among inmates as they may initially identify as heterosexual, but over the period of their incarceration their likelihood to identify as homosexual or bisexual increases (Hensley et al. 2001; Hensley et al. 2002). However, caution should be noted here regarding an inmate's transformative process with their sexual orientation. Perhaps an inmate's environment influenced their sexual orientation or it was the exposure to variant sexual behaviors (Gibson and Hensley 2013), especially when inmates reported reverting to a heterosexual identity once released (Warren et al. 2010). Nonetheless, the association between incarceration and the fluctuation of sexual orientation is quite strong. Altogether, sexual violence may not be a result from the deprivation of sexual encounters but perhaps is related to homosexual inclinations, which may ultimately develop into grander personal sexual relationships between inmates.

Policymakers should encourage safe sex practices with the introduction of harm reduction techniques given that same-sex sexual relations occur in correctional facilities. This is especially true considering that international research found that harm reduction techniques are effective in the reduction of sexual violence (Potter and Rosky 2014). However, it may be that the dynamic of the inmate subculture is unique in the U.S. Cross-cultural studies should be conducted in light of the research overseas that indicated a seemingly divergent inmate subculture as compared to the U.S. One reason may be that the U.S. imposed excessively harsh punitive sanctions onto inmates that consequently resulted in longer sentences, thus a further immersion into inmate subculture. Given their contextual and social position, inmates are socially invisible persons in society who have committed criminal infractions (McDonald and Miller 2014). Thus, an inmate's claim of sexual victimization is not as valid due to their criminal history.

In the end, prison sexuality is diverse, dynamic, and gender-based, and includes the full range of types of sexual expression found in free society. Sexual behavior does occur in prison and jail, and although not legally permitted, is relatively common and not necessarily based on violence, intimidation, or coercion.

References

Alarid, Leanne F. 2000. "Sexual Assault and Coercion among Incarcerated Women Prisoners: Excerpts from Prison Letters." *The Prison Journal* 80(4): 391–406.

Barth, Thomas. 2012. "Relations and Sexuality of Imprisoned Men in the German Penal System—A Survey of Inmates in a Berlin Prison." *International Journal of Law and Psychiatry* 35(3): 153–158.

Beck, Allen J. 2014. *Sexual Victimization in Prisons and Jails Reported by Inmates, 2011–12: Supplement Tables: Prevalence of Sexual Victimization Among Transgender Adult Inmates* (NCJ 241399). Bureau of Justice Statistics, Office of Justice Programs. Washington, D.C: U.S. Department of Justice.

Beck, Allen J. 2015. *PREA Data Collection Activities, 2015* (NCJ 248824). Bureau of Justice Statistics, Office of Justice Programs. Washington, DC: U.S. Department of Justice.

Beck, Allen J., Marcus Berzofsky, Rachel Caspar, and Christopher Krebs. 2013. *Sexual victimization in prisons and jails reported by inmates, 2011–12—National inmate survey 2011–12* (NCJ 241399). Bureau of Justice Statistics, Office of Justice Programs. Washington, DC: U.S. Department of Justice.

Blackburn, Ashley, G., Shannon K. Fowler, Janet L. Mullings, and James W. Marquart. 2011. "Too Close for Comfort: Exploring Gender Differences in Inmate Attitudes toward Heterosexual in Prison." *American Journal of Criminal Justice* 36(1): 58–72.

Blackburn Ashley, G., Shannon L. Fowler, and Janet L. Mullings. 2014. "Gay, Lesbian, Bisexual, and Transgender Inmates." Pp. 87–112 in *Sex in Prison: Myths and Realities*, edited by Catherine D. Marcum and Tammy L. Castle. Boulder, CO: Lynne Rienner Publishers.

Blackburn, Ashley, G., Janet L. Mullings, and James W. Marquart. 2008. "Sexual Assault in Prison and Beyond: Toward an Understanding of Lifetime Sexual Assault among Incarcerated Women." *The Prison Journal* 88(3): 351–377.

Castle, Tammy L. 2014. "Conjugal Visitation." Pp. 77–86 in *Sex in Prison: Myths and Realities*, edited by Catherine D. Marcum and Tammy L. Castle. Boulder, CO: Lynne Rienner Publishers.

Davis, Alan J. 1968. "Sexual Assaults in the Philadelphia Prison System and Sheriff's Vans." *Transaction* 6(2): 8–17.

Einat, Tomer, and Gila Chen. 2012. "What's Love Got to Do with It? Sex in a Female Maximum-security Prison." *The Prison Journal* 92(4): 484–505.

Fishman, Joseph. F. 1934. *Sex in Prison: Revealing Sex Conditions in American Prisons*. New York: National Library.

Gibson, Lauren E., and Christopher Hensley. 2013. "The Social Construction of Sexuality in Prison." *The Prison Journal* 93(3): 355–370.

Hensley, Christopher, and Richard Tewksbury. 2002. "Inmate-to-Inmate Prison Sexuality: A Review of Empirical Studies." *Trauma, Violence, & Abuse* 3(3): 226–243.

Hensley, Christopher, Richard Tewksbury, and Mary Koscheski. 2001. "Masturbation Uncovered: Autoeroticism in a Female Prison." *The Prison Journal* 81(4): 491–501.

Hensley, Christopher, Richard Tewksbury, and Mary Koscheski. 2002. "The Characteristics and Motivations Behind Female Prison Sex." *Women and Criminal Justice*, 13(2–3): 125–139.

Hensley, Christopher, Richard Tewksbury, and Jeremy Wright. 2001. "Exploring the Dynamics of Masturbation and Consensual Same-Sex Activity Within a Male Maximum Security Prison." *Journal of Men's Studies* 10(1): 59–71.

Hensley, Christopher, Jeremy Wright, Richard Tewksbury, and Tammy Castle. 2003. "The Evolving Nature of Prison Argot and Sexual Hierarchies." *The Prison Journal* 83(3): 289–300.

Levan, Kristine. 2014. "Consensual Sex." Pp. 13–24 in *Sex in Prison: Myths and Realities*, edited by Catherine D. Marcum and Tammy L. Castle. Boulder, CO: Lynne Rienner Publishers.

Marcum, Catherine D. 2014. "Examining Prison Sex Culture." Pp. 1–12 in *Sex in Prison: Myths and Realities*, edited by Catherine D. Marcum and Tammy L. Castle. Boulder, CO: Lynne Rienner Publishers.

McDonald, Danielle, and Alexis Miller. 2014. "Local Perspectives." Pp. 139–152 in *Sex in Prison: Myths and Realities*, edited by Catherine D. Marcum and Tammy L. Castle. Boulder, CO: Lynne Rienner Publishers.

Merotte, L. 2012. "Sexuality in Prison: Three Investigation Methods Analysis." *Sexologies* 21(3): 122–125.

Owen, Barbara. 1998. *In the Mix: Struggle and Survival in a Women's Prison*. New York: State University of New York Press.

Pardue, Angela, Bruce A. Arrigo, and Daniel S. Murphy. 2011. "Sex and Sexuality in Women's Prisons: A Preliminary Typological Investigation." *The Prison Journal* 91(3): 279–304.

Potter, Roberto H., and Rosky, Jeffrey. 2014. "Health Issues." Pp. 113–128 in *Sex in Prison: Myths and Realities*, edited by Catherine D. Marcum and Tammy L. Castle. Boulder, CO: Lynne Rienner Publishers.

Prison Rape Elimination Act of 2003, 42 USC §§15601–15609.

Struckman-Johnson, Cindy, David Struckman-Johnson, Lila Rucker, Kurt Bumby, and Stephen Donaldson. 1996. "Sexual Coercion Reported by Men and Women in Prison." *The Journal of Sex Research* 33(1): 67–76.

Sykes, Gresham. M. 1958. *The Society of Captives*. Princeton, NJ: Princeton University Press.

Tewksbury, Richard. 1989. "Measures of Sexual Behavior in an Ohio Prison." *Sociology and Social Research* 74(1): 34–39.

Tewksbury, Richard, and David Patrick Connor. 2014. "Who Is Having Sex Inside Prison?." *Deviant Behavior* 35(12): 993–1005.

Tewksbury, Richard, and Angela West. 2000. "Research on Sex in Prison During the Late 1980s and Early 1990s." *The Prison Journal* 80(4): 368–378.

Warren, Janet I., Shelly L. Jackson, Ann B. Loper, and Mandi L. Burnette. 2010. *Risk Markers for Sexual Predation and Victimization in Prison* (NIJ 2004-RP-0004). NCJRS. Washington, DC: U.S. Department of Justice. Retrieved January 30, 2016 from www.ncjrs.gov/pdffiles1/nij/grants/230522.pdf

Zaitzow, Barbara. 2014. "Responding to Sexual Assault." Pp. 53–76 in *Sex in Prison: Myths and Realities*, edited by Catherine D. Marcum and Tammy L. Castle. Boulder, CO: Lynne Rienner Publishers.

40 Examining the World of Correctional Officers

Robert M. Worley and Vidisha Barua Worley

Even though the United States has only 5 percent of the world's population, it has 25 percent of the world's prisoners, giving it the dubious distinction of having the highest incarceration rate of any other country (Garland 2010). Correctional officers are the primary agents of social control who are entrusted with maintaining the security of prison and jail facilities and ensuring that the incarcerated persons within these institutions are safe. In the United States, there are approximately 427,790 correctional officers responsible for the safety and security of more than 2.4 million inmates (mostly males) in state and federal correctional institutions, county and city jails, juvenile detention facilities, and private facilities (Bureau of Labor Statistics 2016; Guerino, Harrison, and Sabol 2011). According to the Bureau of Labor Statistics (2016), prison and jail officers nationwide have a mean salary of $43,500, which is fairly low compared to police officers, who enjoy a mean salary of $57,800. As a result of this pay disparity, most individuals interested in pursuing careers in law enforcement, especially those with two-and four-year college degrees, often seek employment in police organizations rather than correctional agencies. Though the educational requirements for correctional officers tend to be quite modest, with most jails and prisons requiring applicants to have only a high school degree or GED (Worley and Cheeseman 2006), many correctional agencies require prospective employees to successfully pass oral interviews, physical fitness tests, written exams, and drug screenings (American Correctional Association 2013).

One of the most important responsibilities of correctional officers is to protect offenders from threats of violence, and sexual violence, in particular. As mandated by the Prison Rape Elimination Act of 2003 (PREA), the Bureau of Justice Statistics (BJS) collects data on sexual assaults involving inmates as one way to assess whether or not correctional officers are keeping inmates safe (Worley, Worley, and Mullings 2010). In one fairly recent study, researchers estimated that roughly 2 percent of the total incarcerated population were victims of either a nonconsensual or abusive sex act (Beck and Harrison 2007). This is consistent with Gaes and Goldberg (2004) who found a 1.91 percent incidence of national prison rape.

Most inmates perceive that correctional officers work hard to keep them safe, and some offenders make it a point to get to know officers as a form of protection (Fleisher and Krienert 2009). Officers who are vigilant, well-trained, and consistently enforce the rules tend to be the most effective at deterring inmate-on-inmate sexual assaults (Beck, Rantala, and Rexroat 2014). As Fleisher and Krienert (2009: 3) suggest, "an inmate pressed for sex in prison is probably safer than a coed pressed for sex at a drunken fraternity party."

Besides protecting prisoners from one another, correctional officers must also occasionally protect inmates from themselves. Prisons and jails have become the de facto mental health system, with the number of mentally ill persons in correctional facilities ranging somewhere between 16 percent and 50 percent (James and Glaze 2006). In fact, the three largest providers of psychiatric services within the United States are the Los Angeles Jail (CA), the Rikers

Island Jail (NY), and the Cook County Jail (IL) (Johnson 2011). Today's correctional officers must be willing to work with prisoners who may "rub feces on themselves, stick pencils in their penises, bite chunks of flesh from their bodies [or] slash themselves" (Human Rights Watch 2003: 30). In fact, nearly one-third of inmates engage in self-injurious behavior during some point in their incarceration, and most correctional institutions deal with these types of incidents on a routine basis (Appelbaum, Savageau, Trestman, Metzner, and Baillargeon 2011).

Correctional officers must often work in noisy, tense, and stressful environments that are all too often characterized by long hours with very little pay. Worley (2016), in an autoethnographic study, reflects upon his seven years as a "guard-researcher" and provides real-life examples of how correctional organizations often produce feelings of low morale, anxiety, and professional inadequacy among the guards who work within these institutions. He writes about one instance where a correctional officer was ostracized by her fellow officers:

> I remember one occasion when several officers, both male and female, secretly worked in cahoots to make sure that a female guard who had designed a homemade bracelet and given it to a male offender was reprimanded and punished by the unit warden. Although this may seem harsh to outsiders, the social norms of the prison organization permeated the belief that if a staff member gave an inmate minor, nuisance contraband, it would only be a matter of time before he or she was smuggling dangerous contraband such as drugs, money, cell phones, or weapons into the facility, which could put everyone at risk.
>
> (Worley 2016: 7)

Worley's (2016) passage illustrates that not all correctional officers are immediately embraced by the guard subculture. On the contrary, some officers may be viewed as "outsiders," and much to their chagrin, find they have to work hard to become accepted by veteran officers and supervisors. There is also evidence that female correctional officers may be especially likely to experience burnout and high levels of stress and feelings of exclusion from the guard subculture (Carlson, Anson, and Thomas 2003; Dial, Downey, and Goodlin 2010; Paoline, Lambert, and Hogan 2015). In a recent study, inmates in a Midwestern state prison facility told researchers that male guards may even objectify and sexualize their female co-workers by calling them names such as "bitches" and "sluts" (Trammel and Rundle, 2015). Some male correctional officers may deliberately ignore, undermine, and taunt female officers. For example, one correctional officer explained to researchers how some of his male co-workers failed to show female guards the proper amount of respect:

> They harass the women and make them look dumb in front of the inmates. It's not all of them but it's enough to make me mad. It's going to cause problems because the inmates already say sexual stuff to women here all the time and this makes it worse. If they think the women are incompetent, they won't listen to them about the rules. They won't follow orders.
>
> (Trammell, Raby, Anderson, Hampton, and Stickney 2014: 815)

It is likely that gender dynamics may influence how an officer responds to inmate misconduct. For example, researchers have discovered that female officers are more likely than male officers to work closely with offenders to provide meaningful, transformative rehabilitation opportunities (Carlson et al. 2003; Gordon 2006; Hemmens and Stohr 2000).

Even though the addition of females to the guard workforce has had a positive impact on the overall quality of prison life (Cheeseman and Worley 2006), some male guards are nevertheless leery of their female co-workers who tend to prefer verbal intervention strategies rather than brute force to control inmates. Within the confines of a male-dominated correctional institution, the heteronormative response often casts a cloud of suspicion on female employees, and sadly, female officers who use their interpersonal skills to manage male prisoners may be perceived as instigating romantic relationships with inmates—even when they are not (Trammell et al. 2014; Worley 2011). A similar observation was made by Worley, Tewksbury, and Frantzen (2010) as part of a larger project that assessed, among other things, the institutional culture within the Texas Department of Criminal Justice. As one inmate told the lead author:

> It's not fair that most all women guards at one time or another are suspected of having a boyfriend. If a woman has even a conversation with an inmate, she's made to feel like she's doing wrong. A boss man can be talking to an inmate all day and no one thinks anything of it. I ain't down with that.
>
> (Worley, Tewksbury, and Frantzen 2010: 350)

Interestingly, there is literature that has suggested that lesbian correctional officers may actually have an advantage over *straight* female officers, in that much like male guards, they can work closely with the male inmates without having their motives called into question (Trammell et al. 2014). However, in the hypermasculine environment of male prisons, it is likely that *all* female correctional officers (regardless of their sexual orientation) could find themselves to be victims of "inmate public autoerotism," an aggressive form of behavior where prisoners expose themselves to female staff and violently masturbate in their presence (*Beckford v. Department of Corrections* 2010; Dial and Worley 2008). In a study by Worley and Worley (2013b), the lead author interviewed 15 inmates who admitted to masturbating in the presence of female prison staff. When one respondent was asked why he engaged in this behavior, the inmate justified this as a way to seek revenge on a female officer who he believed had wronged him.

> I had this one boss lady who used to chew me out all the time for no good reason. I didn't forget about this. I waited until she was working my cellblock. Then when she was doing her last count, I pulled out my junk and went to town [masturbated]. She was so shook up. The best part is I didn't even catch a case. I had to stand in the hallway in my boxers for a while, but that was it. It was worth it.
>
> (Worley and Worley 2013b: 861)

Even though casual observers might perceive inmate-on-officer masturbation to be exceedingly rare or uncommon, correctional officers who work behind the prison walls know better. In some correctional facilities, it occurs on an almost daily basis and invariably creates a hostile work environment. Worley and Worley (2013b) argue that it is essential for male correctional employees to lead the efforts in condemning acts of inmate public autoerotism, as prisoners might look to these individuals for subtle cues as to what type of behavior will be tolerated, regardless of the official rules. Female correctional officers must also do their part and promptly write a disciplinary case for any inmate who uses masturbation as a weapon to antagonize his captors (Worley and Worley 2013b). It is especially important for this behavior to be reported, for if it goes unchecked, the inmate may perceive (incorrectly) that the employee-victim is amenable to engaging in boundary violations, or even worse, having an inappropriate relationship with an offender.

While most correctional agencies have policies that prohibit correctional officers from fraternizing with offenders, some officers cross the line by engaging in boundary violations with the very inmates they supervise. Boundary violations are behaviors that "blur, minimize, or disrupt, the professional distance" between those who work in correctional facilities and those who reside in them (Marquart, Barnhill, and Balshaw-Biddle 2001: 878). These behaviors can range from being fairly benign (e.g., giving or receiving a bag of chips or soft drink to an inmate) to outright illegal (e.g., aiding and abetting an escape). Despite the fact that the norms of the guard subculture strongly discourage correctional officers from becoming overly familiar with inmates, factors such as poor supervision, dreary work conditions, a lack of family support, abysmal pay, and perhaps even boredom, have the potential to entice some officers to establish "inappropriate relationships" with inmates, a severe type of boundary violation, which is often sexual or economic in nature and poses a significant threat to the security of a correctional facility (Worley, Marquart, and Mullings 2003; Worley and Worley 2013a).

Even though the layperson might perceive that inappropriate relationships between guards and inmates are rare, they actually occur with surprising regularity in day-to-day prison operations (Ross 2013; Worley et al. 2010; Worley and Worley 2016). In many cases, when these infractions occur, wayward officers are quietly dismissed or resign in lieu of termination. This may be due to the fact that correctional officers work in what Goffman (1961) famously referred to as "total institutions," facilities where administrators are often able to limit access to outsiders and restrict the flow of any information that might tarnish the image of the prison regime.

Typically, administrators prefer to keep cases of inappropriate relationships out of the public eye; however, there have been occasions where this phenomenon has received national attention in the wake of public scandals. For example, in 2015, Joyce Mitchell, a 51-year old grandmother and correctional employee, assisted two convicted murderers at the Clinton Correctional Facility in New York in an elaborate *Shawshank Redemption*-style escape. Mitchell, who was married to a correctional officer at the same facility, also admitted to having a consensual sexual relationship with one of the men on multiple occasions (Hill 2015).

In another well-publicized incident, it was revealed in 2013 that prison gang members from the Black Guerrilla Family essentially took control of the Baltimore City Detention Center. One notorious gang leader, Tavon "Bulldog" White, impregnated four female guards and oversaw a sophisticated drug smuggling operation. This manipulative inmate would later tell investigators that he earned at least $16,000 a month from corrupting correctional officers (Marimow and Wagner 2013). In yet another egregious example of guard misconduct, in 2006, a rogue guard at an all-female facility used a personal handgun he smuggled into the Federal Correctional Institution in Tallahassee to shoot and kill an agent with the Office of Inspector General who was serving arrest warrants on six male correctional officers accused of providing female inmates with contraband in exchange for sex. Certainly, this incident is highly atypical, yet it illustrates that when correctional officers cross the line with inmates, this can have deadly consequences.

As Gresham Sykes (1958) observed in his classic book, *The Society of Captives*, the operational realities of correctional institutions often encourage officers to ignore inmates who commit small rule violations in return for securing cooperation in major areas. If officers depend too much on inmates in order to perform their job, this erodes professional distance between the keeper and the kept and can lead a guard down a slippery slope of boundary violations (Allen and Bosta 1981; Elliot and Verdeyen 2003). More recently, Worley and Worley (2016) proposed the burgeoning "economics of crossing over," thesis, which purports that poor pay, a turbulent family life, feeble supervisor support, and poor public image, *the economics*, lead some guards to feel relatively deprived (compared to other professionals), and entice them to behave inappropriately with inmates.

It is possible, at least in theory, that given enough time and the right opportunity, virtually any correctional officer could find himself or herself behaving in an unprofessional or overly familiar manner with an inmate. Nevertheless, there is literature that indicates some guards are more susceptible than others to crossing professional boundaries with offenders. For example, Worley and Cheeseman (2006) suggest that correctional officers who have inappropriate relationships with offenders may possess certain types of "non-shareable problems," including relationship failures, as originally described by Cressey (1973) in his study of embezzlers. For example, as one inmate reported to Worley:

> I hooked up with this one new officer who went through a rough divorce and was left with two kids. We got to be close and in a couple of weeks we started fooling around. I told her I was HIV positive, but she didn't care. We still had sex without a condom because she was alone and wanted to be with me so bad. She would have brought me in a weapon if I had wanted one.
>
> (Worley and Worley 2006: 214)

This statement made by a manipulative inmate at a medium security state prison facility is consistent with a study conducted by Marquart and colleagues (2001: 902) who concluded that deviant guards who engage in boundary violations may often have "sexual frustration, marital strife, or discord, boredom, ruptured dreams, or separation from their spouses." In addition to this finding, there is also indication that supervisory practices (or lack thereof) can have an impact on whether or not a correctional officer crosses the line and behaves inappropriately with an inmate. Worley and Worley (2013a) examined 501 self-report questionnaires administered to Texas correctional officers and found that, compared to their coworkers, guards who perceived supervisors to be unsupportive were significantly more likely to report favorable attitudes towards employee misconduct, including being overly familiar with inmates. Also, in this same study, it was discovered that if a correctional officer perceived his or her job to be less dangerous than other respondents, he or she was at a higher risk of committing a boundary violation with an inmate. Intuitively, this makes sense; simply put, guards who fail to appreciate that correctional institutions can often be dangerous, perhaps even deadly places to work, may begin to "view their work environments as *nightclubs* or places to converse with members of the opposite sex, rather than as institutions that warehouse dangerous criminals" (Worley and Worley 2013a: 128).

While inappropriate relationships between guards and inmates are prevalent and occur daily at prison and jail institutions all across the United States (and elsewhere), it should be noted that most correctional officers do not engage in these behaviors. In fact, throughout the history of incarceration, there has been a well-established folkway that frowns upon officers who violate the "no-friendship with inmates" norm (Marquart et al. 2001; Worley and Worley 2016). Correctional administrators and supervisors also encourage officers to maintain a professional distance from inmates, and this sense of space is reinforced through socially constructed barriers. For example, guards wear uniforms and typically require inmates to use formal modes of address when addressing them (Sir, Mrs., Ms., Mr., Officer, Boss) (Marquart et al. 2001). From the moment an individual is hired by a correctional agency, he or she is indoctrinated into the guard subculture, which legitimizes and enforces boundaries between inmates and correctional employees (Marquart et al. 2001; Worley et al. 2010).

The infamous Stanford Prison Experiment reminds us that correctional officers wield "a great deal of power over a population that is essentially powerless" (Baker, Gordon, and

Taxman 2015: 1038; Haney, Banks, and Zimbardo 1973; Zimbardo 2007). Correctional officers often work in regimented, quasi-military environments that have the potential to crush individuality and independent thinking (Stojkovic and Farkas 2003; Worley 2016). COs are also subject to a myriad of rules, policies, and regulations, and must often answer to multiple supervisors (e.g. sergeant, lieutenant, captain), many of whom lack leadership and interpersonal skills (Worley and Worley 2011). On top of this, correctional officers have one of the highest rates of workplace injuries of any occupation in the United States (U.S. Department of Labor, Bureau of Justice Statistics, 2010).

Given the stressful and dangerous nature of working in prisons and jails, it is no wonder that correctional officers are more likely than those in other occupations to be victims of heart attacks, ulcers, and high blood pressure (Whiteacre 2006). Prisons and jails are also notoriously understaffed which can heighten stress levels as well as generate anxieties among officers about having to work mandatory overtime (Mahfood, Wolfe, Pollock, and Longmire 2013; Minor, Wells, Earl, and Matz 2011). As Higgins, Tewksbury, and Denney (2012: 342) assert:

> Shortages of correctional officers has also resulted in correctional facilities using creative and unique shift work structures in order to cover necessary posts essential to the operation of the prison . . . There have been a number of issues documented as a result of shift work being that of cognitive impairment, fatigue, lack of vigilance, and decreases in motor skills due to the disruption of the biological clock from the lack of the body being on a normal schedule.

As a result of spending virtually their entire careers contending with irate inmates, meager paychecks, unsupportive supervisors, and dreary work conditions, correctional officers often die at a significantly younger age compared to the national average (Lambert and Paoline 2008). In order to remedy this problem and also elevate the public image of corrections as a profession, policymakers must improve the pay of all prison and jail officers. Doing this will have a substantial impact on the self-esteem of correctional officers and also instill a sense of pride in their profession (Worley and Worley 2016).

References

Allen, Bud, and Diana Bosta. 1981. *Games Criminals Play*. Susanville, CA: Rae John Publishers.

American Correctional Association. 2013. Correctional Officer Education and Training: Survey Summary. *Corrections Compendium* 37: 13–25.

Appelbaum, Kenneth L., Judith A. Savageau, Robert L. Trestman, Jeffrey L. Metzner, and Jacques Baillargeon. 2011. "A National Survey of Self-Injurious Behavior in American Prisons." *Psychiatric Services* 62: 285–290.

Baker, Thomas, Jill A. Gordon, and Faye S. Taxman. 2015. "A Hierarchical Analysis of Correctional Officers' Procedural Justice Judgments of Correctional Institutions: Examining the Influence of Transformational Leadership." *Justice Quarterly* 32: 1037–1063

Beck, Allen J., and Paige M. Harrison. 2007. *Sexual Victimization in State and Federal Prisons Reported by Inmates, 2007* (Special Report No. NCJ 219414). Washington, DC: Bureau of Justice Statistics.

Beck, Allen J., Ramona R. Rantala, and Jessica Rexroat, J. 2014. *Sexual Victimization Reported by Adult Correctional Authorities, 2009–11* (NCJ 243904). Washington, DC: U.S. Department of Justice.

Beckford v. Department of Corrections. 2010. 605 F.3d 951

Bureau of Labor Statistics. 2016. "Occupational Employment and Wages, May 2015: Correctional Officers and Jailers." Retrieved May 12, 2017 from www.bls.gov/oes/current/oes333012.htm

Carlson, Joseph, Richard Anson, and George Thomas. 2003. "Correctional Officer Burnout and Stress: Does Gender Matter?" *The Prison Journal* 83: 277–288.

Cheeseman, Kelly Ann, and Robert M. Worley. 2006. "Women on the Wing: Inmate Perceptions about Female Correctional Officer Job Competency in a Southern Prison System." *Southwestern Journal of Criminal Justice* 3: 86–102.

Cressey, Donald. R. 1973. *Other People's Money*. Montclair, NJ: Patterson Smith.

Dial, Kelly C., Ragan A. Downey, and Wendi E. Goodlin. 2010. "The Job in the Joint: The Impact of Generation and Gender on Work Stress in Prison." *Journal of Criminal Justice* 38: 609–615.

Dial, Kelly C., and Robert M. Worley. 2008. "Crossing the Line: A Quantitative Analysis of Inmate Boundary Violators in a Southern Prison System." *American Journal of Criminal Justice* 33: 69–84.

Elliot, Bill, and Vicki Verdeyen. 2003. *Game Over: Strategies for Redirecting Inmate Deception*. Lanham, MD: American Correctional Association.

Fleisher, Mark S., and Jessie L. Krienert. 2009. *The Myth of Prison Rape: Sexual Culture in American Prisons*. Lanham, MD: Rowman & Littlefield.

Gaes, Gerald G., and Andrew L. Goldberg. 2004. *Prison Rape: A Critical Review of the Literature* (Executive Summary No. NCJ 213365). Washington, DC: National Institute of Justice.

Garland, David. 2010. *A Peculiar Institution: America's Death Penalty in an Age of Abolition*. Cambridge, MA: Belknap Press of Harvard University.

Goffman, Erving. 1961. *Asylums: Essays on the Social Situation of Mental Patients and Other Inmates*. Garden City, NY: Anchor Books.

Gordon, Michael. 2006. "Correctional Officer Control Ideology: Implications for Understanding a System." *Criminal Justice Studies* 19: 225–239.

Guerino, Paul, Paige M. Harrison, and William J. Sabol. 2011. *Prisoners in 2010*. (NCJ 236096). Washington, DC: U.S. Department of Justice.

Haney, Craig, Curtis Banks, and Philip Zimbardo. 1973. "Interpersonal Dynamics in a Simulated Prison." *International Journal of Criminology and Penology* 1: 69–97.

Hemmens, Craig, and Mary Stohr. 2000. "The Two Faces of the Correctional Role: An Exploration of the Value of the Correctional Role Instrument." *International Journal of Offender Therapy and Comparative Criminology* 44: 326–349.

Higgins, George, Richard Tewksbury, and Andrew S. Denney. 2012. "Validating a Measure of Work Stress for Correctional Staff: A Structural Equation Modeling Approach." *Criminal Justice Policy Review* 24: 338–352.

Human Rights Watch. 2003. *Ill Equipped: U.S. Prisons and Offenders with Mental Illness*. New York: Author.

Hill, Michael. 2015. "New York Prison Worker Pleads Guilty in Escape of 2 Killers." *Associated Press State Wire*, July 29: NEWS.

James, Doris J., and Lauren D. Glaze. 2006. *Mental Health Problems of Prison and Jail Inmates* (NCJ 213600). Washington, DC: U.S. Department of Justice, Bureau of Justice Statistics. Retrieved May 12, 2017 from http://bjs.ojp.usdoj.gov/content/pub/pdf/mhppji.pdf.

Johnson, William W. 2011. "Rethinking the Interface between Mental Illness, Criminal Justice, and Academia." *Justice Quarterly* 28: 15–22.

Lambert, Eric G., and Paoline, Eugene A. 2008. "The Influence of Individual, Job, and Organizational Characteristics on Correctional Staff Job Stress, Job Satisfaction, and Organizational Commitment." *Criminal Justice Review* 33: 160–184.

Mahfood, V. Wolfe, Wendi Pollock, and Dennis Longmire. 2013. "Leave it at the Gate: Job Stress and Satisfaction in Correctional Staff." *Criminal Justice Studies* 26: 308–325.

Marimow, Anne E., and John Wagner. 2013. "Md. Guards Accused of Aiding Prison Gang." *The Washington Post*, April, 254: AO1.

Marquart, James W., Maldine B. Barnhill, and Kathy Balshaw-Biddle. 2001. "Fatal Attraction: An Analysis of Employee Boundary Violations in a Southern Prison System, 1995–1998." *Justice Quarterly* 18: 878–910.

Minor, Kevin I., James B. Wells, Angel Earl, and Adam K. Matz, 2011. "Predictors of Early Job Turnover among Juvenile Correctional Facility Staff." *Criminal Justice Review* 36: 58–75.

Paoline, Eugene A., Lambert, Eric G., and Nancy L. Hogan. 2015. Job Stress and Job Satisfaction Among Jail Staff: Exploring Gendered Effects." *Women and Criminal Justice* 25: 339–359.

Ross, Jeffrey Ian. 2013. "Deconstructing Correctional Officer Deviance: Toward Typologies of Actions and Controls." *Criminal Justice Review* 38: 110–126.

Stojkovic, Stan, and Mary Ann Farkas. 2003. *Correctional Leadership: A Cultural Perspective*. Belmont, CA: Wadsworth.

Sykes, G.M. 1958. *The Society of Captives: A Study of a Maximum Security Prison*. Princeton, NJ: Princeton University Press.

Trammell, Rebecca, Jennifer Raby, Alexandra Anderson, Shannon Hampton, and Travis Stickney. 2014. "Maintaining Order and Following the Rules: Gender Differences in Punishing Inmate Misconduct." *Deviant Behavior* 34: 805–821.

Trammel, Rebecca, and Mackenzie Rundle. 2015. "The Inmate as the Nonperson: Examining Staff Conflict from the Inmate's Perspective." *Prison Journal* 95: 472–492.

U.S. Department of Labor, Bureau of Labor Statistics. 2010. *Correctional officers (Occupational Outlook Handbook)*. Retrieved May 12, 2017 from www.bls.gov/oco/ocos156.htm

Whiteacre, Kevin W. 2006. "Measuring Job Satisfaction and Stress at a Community Corrections Center: An Evidenced-Based Study." *Corrections Today* 68: 70–73.

Worley, Robert M. 2011. "To Snitch or not to Snitch, That is the Question: Exploring the Role of Inmate Informants in Detecting Inappropriate Relationships Between the Keeper and the Kept." *International Review of Law, Computers, and Technology* 25: 79–82.

Worley, Robert M. 2016. "Memoirs of a Guard-Researcher: Deconstructing the Games Inmates Play behind the Prison Walls." *Deviant Behavior* 37(11): 1215–1226.

Worley, Robert M., and Kelly Ann Cheeseman. 2006. "Guards as Embezzlers: The Consequences of Non-Shareable Problems in Prison Settings." *Deviant Behavior* 27: 203–222.

Worley, Robert M., James W. Marquart, and Janet L. Mullings. 2003. "Prison Guard Predators: An Analysis of Inmates Who Established Inappropriate Relationships with Prison Staff, 1995–1998." *Deviant Behavior* 24: 175–198.

Worley, Robert M., Richard Tewksbury, and Durant Frantzen, D. 2010. "Preventing Fatal Attractions: Lessons Learned from Inmate Boundary Violators in a Southern Penitentiary System." *Criminal Justice Studies* 23: 347–360.

Worley, Robert M., and Vidisha B. Worley. 2011. "Guards Gone Wild: A Self-Report Study of Correctional Officer Misconduct and the Effect of Institutional Deviance on Care within the Texas Prison System." *Deviant Behavior* 32: 293–319.

Worley, Robert M., and Vidisha B. Worley. 2013a. "Games Guards Play: A Self-report Study of Institutional Deviance in the Texas Department of Criminal Justice. *Criminal Justice Studies* 26: 115–132.

Worley, Robert M., and Vidisha B. Worley. 2013b. "Inmate Public Autoerotism Uncovered: Exploring the Dynamics of Masturbatory Behavior within Correctional Facilities." *Deviant Behavior* 34: 11–24.

Worley, Robert M., and Vidisha B. Worley. 2016. "The Economics of Crossing Over: Examining the Link between Correctional Officer Pay and Guard-Inmate Boundary Violations." *Deviant Behavior* 37, 16–29.

Worley, Vidisha B., Robert M. Worley, and Janet L. Mullings. 2010. "Rape Lore in Correctional Settings: Assessing Inmates' Awareness of Sexual Correction in Prisons." *Southwest Journal of Criminal Justice*, 7: 65–86.

Zimbardo, Philip. 2007. *The Lucifer Effect: Understanding How Good People Turn Evil*. New York: Random House.

Section 6

Effects of Corrections and Post-Sanction Issues

41 The Effects of Corrections on Communities and Families

Bridget Brew, Alyssa Goldman, and Christopher Wildeman

The notion of a criminal offender who is solely responsible for his punishment in the era of mass incarceration is a "useful fiction" (Braman 2004: 63), because it ignores the profound impact of individual sentences on offenders' families and community networks. The majority of prisoners are parents to children under the age of 18 (Glaze and Maruschak 2008), suggesting that the ramifications of mass incarceration have the potential to extend beyond the confined to the next generation. Indeed, a burgeoning literature has begun to document the collateral consequences of mass incarceration on the families and communities that share in its burdens.

Any discussion of these consequences is incomplete without acknowledging that mass incarceration is distributed unequally across the population. Its heavy concentration among black men (Bonczar 2003; Bonczar and Beck 1997) with low levels of educational attainment (Pettit and Western 2004) means that the majority of incarceration's spillover affects families and communities who are already socially and economically disadvantaged. This focus on families and communities is essential in order to appreciate the magnitude of the disproportionate impact that mass incarceration has on some segments of American society.

Effects of Incarceration on the Family

Family Dynamics

Incarceration can have profound and lasting effects on family functioning and relationship stability. Married men who experience incarceration are at a significant risk for separation and divorce (Lopoo and Western 2005), and relationship dissolution is especially likely among couples with children (Turney 2015). Fathers with a history of incarceration are also less likely than other fathers to live with their children (Geller, Garfinkel, and Western 2011). Unmarried black men who experience imprisonment have lower chances of ever marrying, suggesting that mass incarceration has potentially significant implications for declines in marriage and the rise in single-parent households (Western and Wildeman 2009).

The link between incarceration and compromised family functioning can be attributed to a host of strains that emanate from a prisoner's absence and return. Imprisoned partners are unable to contribute to caregiving and other household responsibilities, and their incarceration often demands considerable time, money, and attention from family members trying to maintain contact from outside (Braman 2004). Although the majority of inmates are granted some degree of visitation privileges, these opportunities are often far from conducive to maintaining family cohesion. Families may be required to travel long distances to visit inmates, undergo invasive searches, conduct visits in crowded and heavily supervised visitation rooms, and be restricted to certain visitation time limits, all of which can ultimately damage the quality and stability of family ties over the course of one or more sentences (Comfort 2009).

Those left behind may also face significant stigma as a result of having a family member incarcerated. This stigma can undermine family cohesion by leading wives, girlfriends, parents, and children to conceal information about a family member's incarceration from neighbors and extended family, leading to withdrawal from potential support networks (e.g., Braman 2004). Even following release, concerns about the lasting stigma and tarnished reputation of a formerly incarcerated partner can further compromise relationship quality (Edin 2000). Likewise, ongoing police evasion after or between periods of incarceration can result in avoiding family gatherings out of fear of arrest, as well as implicating partners and parents in hiding their whereabouts (Goffman 2009).

A family member's incarceration also leaves a number of household responsibilities unfulfilled in their absence, including childcare and housework. Older siblings may have to assume more family obligations, which can negatively impact their educational trajectories (Foster and Hagan 2007). Mothers of the incarcerated often experience psychological distress in response to responsibilities for grandchildren assumed in their child's absence (Green, Ensminger, Robertson, and Juon 2006). Among the most detrimental of consequences is the finding that, especially in the case of maternal incarceration, children are at increased risk of being placed in foster care (Andersen and Wildeman 2014).

Despite these adverse consequences, it is important to acknowledge that incarceration is not universally detrimental to family dynamics. In some cases, incarceration is a means of removing physically violent or otherwise abusive men from their households, and can provide family members with a reprieve from caring for an addict (Braman 2004) or mentally ill family member (Comfort 2007). However, even in cases where incarceration may temporarily improve family functioning, family members typically experience mixed emotions, including guilt, betrayal, and anger as a result of a family member's incarceration (Comfort 2007).

Economic Consequences

Poverty and interaction with the criminal justice system are linked (Watts and Nightingale 1996), as economic hardship is both a cause and a consequence of incarceration (Braman 2004; Harris, Evans, and Beckett 2010). Ethnographic (Braman 2004; Comfort 2009), interview-based (Arditti, Lambert-Shute, and Joest 2003), and quantitative research (Geller, Garfinkel, Cooper, and Mincy 2009; Phillips, Erkanli, Keeler, Costello, and Angold 2006) all consistently find that the incarceration of a parent (generally a father) is associated with decreased economic stability for the family. There is evidence of a causal relationship between paternal incarceration and material hardship (Schwartz-Soicher, Geller, and Garfinkel 2011) and reduced financial contributions to children's wellbeing (Geller et al. 2011).

Most inmates are working-age males (Watts and Nightingale 1996), the majority of whom are employed just prior to their incarceration (Braman 2004), so their absence means lost income for the family. Whether the income was derived from legitimate or illegal work (Clear 2007), the loss is consequential for family finances (Geller et al. 2011; Schwartz-Soicher et al. 2011). Although most prisoners were not high-income earners prior to incarceration, the loss of their income can be especially consequential for poor families (Comfort 2007; Wakefield and Uggen 2010). Nevertheless, the aggregate impact on inequality is likely insignificant given that the majority of these families were already economically disadvantaged prior to the family member's incarceration.

Partners of the incarcerated (generally women) often assume the majority of domestic burdens during prisoners' absence, which can be detrimental to their ability to earn a formal income. In their sample of 56 caregivers of children visiting a jail, Arditti and colleagues find that a significant portion of women had to leave paid positions following their partner's incarceration due to the overwhelming demands of family responsibilities (Arditti et al. 2003: 201). There is also an increase in food stamp and Medicaid receipt following a paternal incarceration (Sugie 2012).

In addition to lost income and family support, staying in contact with a prisoner is costly. Family members, especially female partners, use resources to provide letters, packages, calls, and visits to incarcerated loved ones (Comfort 2009). The exorbitant costs of these efforts can significantly exacerbate financial burdens, especially for low-income families. Grinstead and colleagues' (2001) study is unique in its attempt to capture the exact cost of maintaining contact with an inmate. Analyzed by income level, they find that women are likely to spend between 7 and 36 percent of their incomes on this undertaking.

Maintaining contact is a financial burden, as is incarceration itself. Fees, fines, and restitution orders that stem from a criminal charge are common and this debt is significant when compared to the expected earnings of the convicted (Harris et al. 2010). Though these legal financial obligations are officially the prisoner's responsibility, Comfort (2009) finds that part of the money that women send to their partner's account for food and toiletries gets deducted to help pay his legal debts, thus extending these financial burdens to families.

While prisoners' lost income can strain family finances, serious economic impediments often continue after their release. Research strongly emphasizes the challenges that former inmates face in finding employment upon release (Geller et al. 2011; Pager 2003), possibly due to stigma (Wakefield and Uggen 2010; Pager 2003), making their return a continued financial burden on their household (Braman 2004; Comfort 2007). Of course, returning partners and fathers can contribute in non-financial ways, such as assisting with childcare (Schwartz-Soicher et al. 2011), but fathers who have been incarcerated tend to live apart from their children following release (Geller et al. 2011). This separation may undermine opportunities to assist with childcare and other household responsibilities.

Health

Incarceration carries both physical and mental health implications for family members left behind. The stress that results from increased caregiving and financial responsibilities assumed in the absence of an incarcerated partner can be particularly consequential for family wellbeing. Among women, an incarcerated family member is associated with higher odds of obesity, heart attack, stroke and fair or poor self-rated health. These findings may be due in part to the compromised attention women in such positions are able to devote to preventative self-care (Lee, Wildeman, Wang, Matusko, and Jackson 2014).

Women with incarcerated male partners are also at significantly higher risk of contracting HIV. Not only are HIV and other infectious diseases more prevalent among prisoners than in the general population, but the spread of HIV is also facilitated by risky, unprotected sexual behavior among inmates. Likewise, partners left behind may develop new sexual relationships during spells of their partner's incarceration, and sexual concurrency may continue following a prisoner's release, further contributing to exposure risk among both inmates and their non-incarcerated partners (Johnson and Raphael 2009; Kahn et al. 2009). Other infectious diseases such as tuberculosis and hepatitis are also more common among prisoners than the general population, and therefore more likely to spread to family members upon a prisoner's release and return to their household (Fazel and Baillargeon 2011).

Children of the incarcerated are especially vulnerable to negative health consequences. Experiencing parental incarceration is associated with higher levels of attention deficit disorder, attention deficit hyperactivity disorder, aggressive behaviors, various learning and communication disorders, and even infant mortality (Turney 2014; Wakefield and Wildeman

2013). Following release, mortality rates are higher among former prisoners, suggesting that parents, partners, and children are at greater risk of experiencing the death of a family member immediately following incarceration (Binswanger, Stern, Deyo, and Heagerty 2007). This permanent loss on the heels of the temporary loss compounds family trauma and hardship.

A significant way that family members are impacted by an incarceration is psychosocial. Female partners experience depression (Wildeman, Schnittker, and Turney 2012). Mothers of the incarcerated also experience high levels of distress, especially near the start of their son's incarceration (Green et al. 2006). Children experience the loss of a parent (Comfort 2007) and possible trauma of witnessing an arrest (Braman 2004). In ethnographic work and studies using only one or a few respondents (small-n), researchers report that parental incarceration leads to emotional problems for kids, such as acting out or the desire to isolate, which negatively impacts their performance in school (Arditti et al. 2003; Braman 2004). These children have more depressive symptoms (Wilbur et al. 2007) and more self-reported antisocial behaviors (Haskins 2015).

As with adults, stigma is important for children. Foster and Hagan (2007) propose stigma as one mechanism to explain their finding that children who have experienced a paternal incarceration have a 15 percent chance of being socially excluded in their transition to adulthood. There is evidence that children's feelings of stigma are well founded, as teachers perceive children of the incarcerated to be less academically proficient than their peers (Turney and Haskins 2014).

Education and Delinquency

The psychosocial consequences for children are frequently measured by their performance in school, including their behavior and educational attainment. As the majority of children with incarcerated parents are elementary aged (Haskins 2015), scholars have leveraged data from the Fragile Families and Childhood Wellbeing Study to consider how experiencing paternal incarceration shapes educational outcomes. Paternal incarceration is associated with lower non-cognitive school readiness, which impacts chances of later special education placement (Haskins 2014). Young students are also more likely to experience early grade retention (Turney and Haskins 2014) and show both internalizing and externalizing behaviors (Geller at al. 2012; Haskins 2015; Wakefield and Wildeman 2011; Wilbur et al. 2007). Young boys seem especially vulnerable to paternal incarceration in the form of lower school readiness (Haskins 2014) and more behavior problems (Geller et al. 2009), including physical aggression (Wildeman 2010).

Even among older children, parental incarceration is causally associated with lower educational attainment (Foster and Hagan 2009). Researchers posit that this educational detainment may be an intervening mechanism between parental incarceration and a child's social exclusion during the transition to adulthood (Foster and Hagan 2007: 406). In a review of the literature including data from the United Kingdom, Murray and Farrington (2008) conclude that parental incarceration is a risk factor for school failure. There is even evidence that students in schools where a high percentage of children have incarcerated parents receive lower grades and complete college at inferior rates than their counterparts in schools without a high concentration of paternal incarceration (Hagan and Foster 2012).

In addition to negative educational impacts, children of the incarcerated are also at risk of later involvement with the criminal justice system (Hagan and Dinovitzer 1999; Huebner and Gustafson 2007). Parental incarceration impacts delinquent behaviors beyond what is predicted by other kinds of parental absence (Murray and Farrington 2005). There are multiple mechanisms to explain why parental incarceration and youth delinquency may be linked (Murray, Loeber, and Pardini 2012), but the strongest connection seems to be between fathers and their sons (Farrington, Jolliffe, Loeber, Stouthamer-Loeber, and Kalb 2001). As with other negative consequences, it is not clear whether this intergenerational involvement with the criminal justice system is due to the parental incarceration itself or to other preexisting family factors (Roettger and Swisher 2011).

Maternal incarceration has not been established to be so definitively adverse for children. While there are studies demonstrating negative outcomes (Huebner and Gustafson 2007; Trice and Brewster 2004), others have shown null (Cho 2009; Wildeman and Turney 2014) or mixed effects (Turney and Wildeman 2015). Though the rate of increase for women's incarceration is high (Glaze and Maruschak 2008) and 70 percent of incarcerated women are mothers (Cho 2009), maternal incarceration is still much less common than paternal incarceration (Wildeman 2009). More mothers than fathers are co-resident with their children prior to incarceration (Glaze and Maruschak 2008), but the most at-risk mothers may not live with their children, which helps explain these mixed findings.

It is important to emphasize that families are negatively impacted by incarceration even after accounting for the fact that they are already socially disadvantaged, and are therefore at greater risk of poor economic, health, and educational outcomes anyway. Additionally, families that have experienced one incarceration are likely to experience multiple family member incarcerations (Wildeman and Wakefield 2014), so some of these negative impacts may be multiplied over various incarcerations. Though negative consequences are not always differentiated by race (Roettger and Swisher 2011), incarceration has significant effects on racial disparities given that poor, black families disproportionately experience a family member's imprisonment.

Effects of Incarceration on Communities

Just as mass incarceration disproportionately impacts poor men of color and their families, its effects are also concentrated in disadvantaged communities (Sampson and Loeffler 2010). These neighborhoods, sometimes called "million dollar blocks" because of the money spent on imprisoning residents (Gonnerman 2004), are also the places where former prisoners return after their release (Clear, Rose, and Ryder 2001; Petersilia 2001). Spatially concentrated mass incarceration and its mirror issue of mass reentry (Travis 2005) lead to population churning that undermines community cohesion, further destabilizing already fragile neighborhoods (Petersilia 2001).

Safety and Crime

Testing for community-level effects of incarceration is extremely challenging, so much of this work is preliminary and theoretical. Still, scholars tend to agree that the incarceration of the most serious, violent offenders promotes community safety, while the drastic rise in imprisonment of low-level, non-violent offenders is unlikely to benefit societal safety in any substantial way (Western 2006). According to some estimates, after accounting for the costs of incarceration and its consequences, the benefit–cost ratio on the margin is likely to be substantially less than 1 and has diminished with rising incarceration (Johnson and Raphael 2012).

Some theoretical perspectives (e.g., the coercive mobility thesis) propose that the social and emotional strain of prison cycling on social ties attenuates the degree of community social capital, collective efficacy, and capacity for informal social control (Rose and Clear 1998). By weakening norms of coordination and in some cases facilitating social isolation of family members left behind, mass incarceration may actually contribute to, rather than lessen, community crime rates (Clear 2008).

The idea that harsh punishment may have a "counterdeterrent" (Fagan and Meares 2008) effect on crime can be attributed to a number of factors that impact children in these high incarceration neighborhoods. Children who are socialized in these communities may believe that their future involvement with the criminal justice system is a normal, unavoidable part of the life course (Fagan, West, and Holland 2003). Prison churning further contributes to family disruption, weakening youth supervision, which can influence their tendency to commit crimes (Drakulich, Crutchfield, Matsueda, and Rose 2012).

Economic Impacts

During spells of incarceration, human capital is wasted, in addition to wasting away. Inmates are not formally employed, leaving families to endure the lost income (Clear et al. 2001; Watts and Nightingale 1996). Upon release, former inmates are barred from obtaining certain jobs (Clear 2007; Petersilia 2001) and generally struggle to secure employment (Pager 2008; Rose and Clear 1998; Western and Pettit 2010), ultimately contributing to higher rates of unemployment in neighborhoods with concentrated incarceration (Sampson and Loeffler 2010). Eroded local labor market conditions increase the likelihood that residents will turn to crime as a means of income (Clear 2007). These circumstances, combined with a larger number of community members cycling in and out of prison, weaken the capacity of neighborhood social networks to help with job searches (Fagan et al. 2003).

Just as stigma is often cited as a powerful mechanism explaining the collateral consequences of incarceration for families, it also negatively impacts communities. Businesses may be reluctant to open in communities with high incarceration rates because of the stigma associated with that neighborhood (Clear et al. 2001; Fagan et al. 2003; Western, Kling, and Weiman 2001). Whereas ex-felons often face labor market discrimination on the basis of reporting their conviction history when required (Pager 2003), neighborhood stigma may also transfer to individual residents (Besbris, Faber, Rich, and Sharkey 2015), making potential employers less likely to hire someone based on beliefs about their neighborhood's incarceration rate, regardless of whether he or she actually has a criminal history (Fagan et al. 2003; Wakefield and Uggen 2010).

Mass incarceration also drains communities of economic resources. Though prisoners are overwhelmingly sent from urban neighborhoods (Clear et al. 2001; Drakulich et al. 2012; Fagan et al. 2003; Sampson and Loeffler 2010), prisons are generally located in more rural areas (Braman 2004; Gonnerman 2004). Therefore, any local economic boon that results from an increase in prison populations bypasses the residents of high incarceration communities (Rose and Clear 1998; Watts and Nightingale 1996). Additionally, because census counts enumerate the incarcerated, political and economic resources are shifted away from poor inner cities to the communities where prisons are located (Gonnerman 2004; Manza and Uggen 2006; Travis 2005).

Community and Public Health

In some instances, the community-level effects of incarceration can be traced to the aggregation of individual-level consequences, given the spatial concentration of families affected by incarceration. The high rates of HIV and other communicable disease transmission among inmates also elevate the risk of infection in the communities to which they return following release (Johnson and Raphael 2009). Mass incarceration plays such a central role in the spread of infectious disease, in fact, that the population-level incidence of tuberculosis increases with prison rate growth (Stuckler, Basu, McKee, and King 2008). There is even evidence that concentrated incarceration impacts mental health as residents of these neighborhoods are at a significant risk of experiencing depression or anxiety, regardless of their own incarceration history (Hatzenbuehler, Keyes, Hamilton, Uddin, and Galea 2015).

These risks are exacerbated by the fact that disadvantaged communities tend to be ill equipped to treat and manage physical and mental health conditions. For many inmates suffering health issues, including substance abuse, incarceration is an opportunity for diagnosis and treatment, which ends abruptly upon their release. The formerly incarcerated also face difficulties in re-establishing social bonds and securing employment and housing, which may increase their likelihood of engaging in drug and alcohol use and risky sex behaviors as a means of coping (Fazel and Baillargeon 2011). Community-based treatment of communicable diseases is important to prevent their spread. Likewise, the timely treatment of former inmate mental health conditions (including addiction) can be a critical step in preventing recidivism (Fazel and Baillargeon 2011).

The concentration of incarceration among men of certain races and age ranges in narrow geographic areas negatively impacts local marriage markets (Charles and Luoh 2010). Not only can the stigma of a prison record be unappealing to potential partners, but high male incarceration and mortality rates also result in a decreasing number of marriageable men in disadvantaged communities (Braman 2004; Western and Wildeman 2009). Mass incarceration may therefore contribute to the number of female-headed households in poor urban areas. Additionally, by altering the community sex ratio and leaving women with fewer choices in partnering, women may be less likely to negotiate contraception and other forms of protection, further contributing to the number of unintended pregnancies and transmission of sexually transmitted diseases (Johnson and Raphael 2009).

Political Consequences

Neighborhoods with high incarceration rates have diminished political power. In most states, those who have been convicted of a felony are legally barred from voting during their sentence, supervision, and sometimes longer (Manza and Uggen 2006). The spatial concentration of felon disenfranchisement undermines that community's ability to influence local policies. At a higher level, felon disenfranchisement may have swayed multiple senate races and a presidential election that could have favored a candidate with pro social welfare leanings if convicted felons had been able to vote (Uggen and Manza 2002).

Spatially concentrated incarceration impacts beliefs about the government. Neighborhoods with high rates of incarceration have elevated levels of policing and surveillance (Fagan et al. 2003; Goffman 2009; Justice and Meares 2014), causing some to argue that criminal justice institutions are a primary source of civic socialization in these areas (Lee, Porter, and Comfort 2014; Weaver and Lerman 2010). Frequent interactions with police in these neighborhoods can erode residents' willingness to cooperate with legal authorities (Tyler, Fagan, and Geller 2014). Those who have been arrested and/or incarcerated have compromised trust in the government (Manza and Uggen 2006), as do their families (Lee et al. 2014). As incarceration rates have risen, so too have beliefs about the harshness and racial bias of the criminal justice system among those directly or proximally affected (Muller and Schrage 2014).

Living in a high incarceration neighborhood seems to shape political behaviors such as voting, joining an organization, volunteering, and serving on a jury. Though there is some disagreement about the direction (e.g., Walker 2014), most scholars show that political participation among partners and neighbors of the incarcerated are dampened (Lee et al. 2014; Sugie 2015; Weaver and Lerman 2010), especially in predominately black neighborhoods (Bowers and Preuhs 2009). Lee and colleagues (2014) propose two mechanisms for the transmission of these beliefs and behaviors: indirectly through hearing about their loved one's experience and directly through their own interactions with criminal justice institutions. Indeed, there is evidence of a causal relationship between the amount of interaction with the criminal justice system and negative beliefs about the government and civic behavior (Weaver and Lerman 2010).

As with incarceration rates, community consequences of incarceration are racialized (Bowers and Preuhs 2009; Manza and Uggen 2006; Ochs 2006; Roberts 2004). Regardless of their own incarceration history, the disadvantaged population in these communities experience the "hidden curriculum" of civic institutions that tell them they are not full citizens, rather members of a class that need to be excluded and monitored (Justice and Meares 2014). The disengagement of neighborhood residents who have not been disenfranchised is particularly significant when considering that these individuals may otherwise be political advocates of criminal justice reform (Sugie 2015).

Limitations and Conclusion

While researchers have made considerable progress in understanding the effects of mass incarceration on families and communities, a number of areas warrant further investigation. A primary challenge that scholars face is disentangling which of these effects, if any, is truly caused by incarceration. Indeed, selection into prison is nonrandom, with most inmates coming from already disadvantaged familial and community backgrounds. To this end, it is difficult to discern whether the adverse consequences experienced by families and communities would have taken place even in the absence of mass incarceration, as those who are incarcerated may be demographically, genetically, environmentally, and/or behaviorally distinct from the never-incarcerated (Hagan and Dinovitzer 1999). Longitudinal datasets and analytic approaches designed to attenuate selection effects will likely remain important tools for this field.

Much of the scholarship to date has established a connection between incarceration and family and community outcomes; future research should also explore the mechanisms that explain how these consequences occur. As the phenomenon of mass incarceration ages, researchers should also focus on its long-term impacts on social, economic, political, and health inequalities. The imprint of this criminal justice experiment will likely depend in part on future changes, if any, in the policies that have upheld the drastic rise in incarceration in recent decades.

References

Andersen, Signe Hald, and Christopher Wildeman. 2014. "The Effect of Paternal Incarceration on Children's Risk of Foster Care Placement." *Social Forces* 93(1): 269–298.

Arditti, Joyce A., Jennifer Lambert-Shute, and Karen Joest. 2003. "Saturday Morning at the Jail: Implications of Incarceration for Families and Children." *Family Relations* 52(3): 195–204.

Besbris, Max, Jacob William Faber, Peter Rich, and Patrick Sharkey. 2015. "Effect of Neighborhood Stigma on Economic Transactions." *Proceedings of the National Academy of Sciences* 112(16): 4994–4998.

Binswanger, Ingrid A., Marc F. Stern, Richard A. Deyo, and Patrick J. Heagerty. 2007. "Release from Prison—A High Risk of Death for Former Inmates." *The New England Journal of Medicine* 356(2): 157–165.

Bonczar, Thomas P. 2003. "Prevalence of Imprisonment in the US Population, 1974–2001." *Bureau of Justice Statistics Special Report*. Washington, DC: U.S. Department of Justice, NCJ 197976.

Bonczar, Thomas P., and Allen J. Beck. 1997. "Lifetime Likelihood of Going to State or Federal Prison." *Bureau of Justice Statistics Bulletin*. Washington DC: U.S. Department of Justice, NCJ 160092.

Bowers, Melanie, and Robert R. Preuhs. 2009. "Collateral Consequences of a Collateral Penalty: The Negative Effect of Felon Disenfranchisement Laws on the Political Participation of Nonfelons." *Social Science Quarterly* 90(3): 722–743.

Braman, Donald. 2004. *Doing Time on the Outside: Incarceration and Family Life in Urban America*. Ann Arbor, MI: University of Michigan Press.

Charles, Kerwin Kofi, and Ming Ching Luoh. 2010. "Male Incarceration, The Marriage Market, And Female Outcomes." *The Review of Economics and Statistics* 92(3): 614–627.

Cho, Rosa Minhyo. 2009. "Impact of Maternal Imprisonment on Children's Probability of Grade Retention." *Journal of Urban Economics* 65(1): 11–23.

Clear, Todd R. 2007. *Imprisoning Communities: How Mass Incarceration Makes Disadvantaged Neighborhoods Worse*. New York: Oxford University Press.

Clear, Todd R. 2008. "The Effects of High Imprisonment Rates on Communities." *Crime and Justice* 37(1): 97–132.

Clear, Todd R., Dina R. Rose, and Judith A. Ryder. 2001. "Incarceration and the Community: The Problem of Removing and Returning Offenders." *Crime & Delinquency* 47(3): 335–351.

Comfort, Megan. 2007. "Punishment beyond the Legal Offender." *Annual Review of Law and Social Science* 3: 271–296.

Comfort, Megan. 2009. *Doing Time Together: Love and Family in the Shadow of the Prison*. Chicago, IL: University of Chicago Press.

Drakulich, Kevin M., Robert D. Crutchfield, Ross L. Matsueda, and Kristin Rose. 2012. "Instability, Informal Control, and Criminogenic Situations: Community Effects of Returning Prisoners." *Crime, Law and Social Change* 57(5): 493–519.

Edin, Kathryn. 2000. "Few Good Men." *The American Prospect* 11(4): 26–31.

Fagan, Jeffrey, and Tracey L. Meares. 2008. "Punishment, Deterrence and Social Control: The Paradox of Punishment in Minority Communities." *Ohio State Journal of Criminal Law* 6: 173–229.

Fagan, Jeffrey, Valerie West, and Jan Holland. 2003. "Reciprocal Effects of Crime and Incarceration in New York City Neighborhoods." *Fordham Urban Law Journal* 30: 1551–1602.

Farrington, David P., Darrick Jolliffe, Rolf Loeber, Magda Stouthamer-Loeber, and Larry M. Kalb. 2001. "The Concentration of Offenders in Families, and Family Criminality in the Prediction of Boys' Delinquency." *Journal of Adolescence* 24(5): 579–596.

Fazel, Seena, and Jacques Baillargeon. 2011. "The Health of Prisoners." *The Lancet* 377(9769): 956–965.

Foster, Holly, and John Hagan. 2007. "Incarceration and Intergenerational Social Exclusion." *Social Problems* 54(4): 399–433.

Foster, Holly and John Hagan. 2009. "The Mass Incarceration of Parents in America: Issues of Race/ethnicity, Collateral Damage to Children, and Prisoner Reentry." *The Annals of the American Academy of Political and Social Science* 623(1): 179–194.

Geller, Amanda, Carey E. Cooper, Irwin Garfinkel, Ofira Schwartz-Soicher, and Ronald B. Mincy. 2012. "Beyond Absenteeism: Father Incarceration and Child Development." *Demography* 49(1): 49–76.

Geller, Amanda, Irwin Garfinkel, Carey E. Cooper, and Ronald B. Mincy. 2009. "Parental Incarceration and Child Well-Being: Implications for Urban Families." *Social Science Quarterly* 90(5): 1186–1202.

Geller, Amanda, Irwin Garfinkel, and Bruce Western. 2011. "Paternal Incarceration and Support for Children in Fragile Families." *Demography* 48(1): 25–47.

Glaze, Lauren E., and Laura M. Maruschak. 2008. *Parents in Prison and Their Minor Children*. Washington, DC: U.S. Department of Justice, Office of Justice Programs.

Goffman, Alice. 2009. "On the Run: Wanted Men in a Philadelphia Ghetto." *American Sociological Review* 74(3): 339–357.

Gonnerman, Jennifer. 2004. "Million-Dollar Blocks: The Neighborhood Costs of America's Prison Boom." *Village Voice* 9.

Green, Kerry M., Margaret E. Ensminger, Judith A. Robertson, and Hee-Soon Juon. 2006. "Impact of Adult Sons' Incarceration on African American Mothers' Psychological Distress." *Journal of Marriage and Family* 68(2): 430–441.

Grinstead, Olga, Bonnie Faigeles, Carrie Bancroft, and Barry Zack. 2001. "The Financial Cost of Maintaining Relationships with Incarcerated African American Men: A Survey of Women Prison Visitors." *Journal of African American Men* 6(1): 59–69.

Hagan, John, and Ronit Dinovitzer. 1999. "Collateral Consequences of Imprisonment for Children, Communities, and Prisoners." *Crime and Justice* 26: 121–162.

Hagan, John, and Holly Foster. 2012. "Intergenerational Educational Effects of Mass Imprisonment in America." *Sociology of Education* 85(3): 259–286.

Harris, Alexes, Heather Evans, and Katherine Beckett. 2010. "Drawing Blood from Stones: Legal Debt and Social Inequality in the Contemporary United States." *American Journal of Sociology* 115(6): 1753–1799.

Haskins, Anna R. 2014. "Unintended Consequences: Effects of Paternal Incarceration on Child School Readiness and Later Special Education Placement." *Sociological Science* 1(1): 141–158.

Haskins, Anna R. 2015. "Paternal Incarceration and Child-Reported Behavioral Functioning at Age 9." *Social Science Research* 52: 18–33.

Hatzenbuehler, Mark L., Katherine Keyes, Ava Hamilton, Monica Uddin, and Sandro Galea. 2015. "The Collateral Damage of Mass Incarceration: Risk of Psychiatric Morbidity Among Nonincarcerated Residents of High-Incarceration Neighborhoods." *American Journal of Public Health* 105(1): 138–143.

Huebner, B. M. and R. Gustafson. 2007. "The Effect of Maternal Incarceration on Adult Offspring Involvement in the Criminal Justice System." *Journal of Criminal Justice* 35(3): 283–296.

Johnson, Rucker C., and Steven Raphael. 2009. "The Effects of Male Incarceration Dynamics on Acquired Immune Deficiency Syndrome Infection Rates among African American Women and Men." *The Journal of Law & Economics* 52(2): 251–293.

Johnson, Rucker, and Steven Raphael. 2012. "How Much Crime Reduction Does the Marginal Prisoner Buy?" *The Journal of Law & Economics* 55(2): 275–310.

Justice, Benjamin, and Tracey L. Meares. 2014. "How the Criminal Justice System Educates Citizens." *The Annals of the American Academy of Political and Social Science* 651(1): 159–177.

Khan, Maria R., Irene A. Doherty, Victor J. Schoenbach, Eboni M. Taylor, Matthew W. Epperson, and Adaora A. Adimora. 2009. "Incarceration and High-Risk Sex Partnerships among Men in the United States." *Journal of Urban Health* 86(4): 584–601.

Lee, Hedwig, Lauren C. Porter, and Megan Comfort. 2014. "Consequences of Family Member Incarceration Impacts on Civic Participation and Perceptions of the Legitimacy and Fairness of Government." *The Annals of the American Academy of Political and Social Science* 651(1): 44–73.

Lee, Hedwig, Christopher Wildeman, Emily A. Wang, Niki Matusko, and James S. Jackson. 2014. "A Heavy Burden: The Cardiovascular Health Consequences of Having a Family Member Incarcerated." *American Journal of Public Health* 104(3): 421–427.

Lopoo, Leonard M., and Bruce Western. 2005. "Incarceration and the Formation and Stability of Marital Unions." *Journal of Marriage and Family* 67(3): 721–734.

Manza, Jeff, and Christopher Uggen. 2006. *Locked Out: Felon Disenfranchisement and American Democracy*. New York: Oxford University Press.

Muller, Christopher, and Daniel Schrage. 2014. "Mass Imprisonment and Trust in the Law." *The Annals of the American Academy of Political and Social Science* 651(1): 139–158.

Murray, Joseph, and David P. Farrington. 2005. "Parental Imprisonment: Effects on Boys' Antisocial Behaviour and Delinquency through the Life-Course." *Journal of Child Psychology and Psychiatry* 46(12): 1269–1278.

Murray, Joseph, and David P. Farrington. 2008. "The Effects of Parental Imprisonment on Children." *Crime and Justice* 37(1): 133–206.

Murray, Joseph, Rolf Loeber, and Dustin Pardini. 2012. "Parental Involvement in the Criminal Justice System and the Development of Youth Theft, Marijuana Use, Depression, and Poor Academic Performance." *Criminology* 50(1): 255–302.

Ochs, Holona Leanne. 2006. "'Colorblind' Policy in Black and White: Racial Consequences of Disenfranchisement Policy." *Policy Studies Journal* 34(1): 81–93.

Pager, Devah. 2003. "The Mark of a Criminal Record." *American Journal of Sociology* 108(5): 937–975.

Pager, Devah. 2008. *Marked: Race, Crime, and Finding Work in an Era of Mass Incarceration*. Chicago, IL: University of Chicago Press.

Petersilia, Joan. 2001. "When Prisoners Return to the Community: Political, Economic, and Social Consequences." *Corrections Management Quarterly* 5(3): 1–11.

Pettit, Becky, and Bruce Western. 2004. "Mass Imprisonment and the Life Course: Race and Class Inequality in U.S. Incarceration." *American Sociological Review* 69(2): 151–169.

Phillips, Susan D., Alaattin Erkanli, Gordon P. Keeler, E. Costello, and Adrian Angold. 2006. "Disentangling the Risks: Parent Criminal Justice Involvement and Children's Exposure to Family Risks." *Criminology & Public Policy* 5(4): 677–702.

Roberts, Dorothy E. 2004. "The Social and Moral Cost of Mass Incarceration in African American Communities." *Stanford Law Review* 56(5): 1271–1305.

Roettger, Michael E., and Raymond R. Swisher. 2011. "Associations of Fathers' History of Incarceration with Sons' Delinquency and Arrest Among Black, White, and Hispanic Males in the United States." *Criminology* 49(4): 1109–1147.

Rose, Dina R., and Todd R. Clear. 1998. "Incarceration, Social Capital, and Crime: Implications for Social Disorganization Theory." *Criminology* 36(3): 441–480.

Sampson, Robert J., and Charles Loeffler. 2010. "Punishment's Place: The Local Concentration of Mass Incarceration." *Daedalus* 139(3): 20–31.

Schwartz-Soicher, Ofira, Amanda Geller, and Irwin Garfinkel. 2011. "The Effect of Paternal Incarceration on Material Hardship." *The Social Service Review* 85(3): 447–473.

Stuckler, David, Sanjay Basu, Martin McKee, and Lawrence King. 2008. "Mass Incarceration Can Explain Population Increases in TB and Multidrug-Resistant TB in European and Central Asian Countries." *Proceedings of the National Academy of Sciences of the United States of America* 105(36): 13280–13285.

Sugie, Naomi F. 2012. "Punishment and Welfare: Paternal Incarceration and Families' Receipt of Public Assistance." *Social Forces* 90(4): 1403–1427.

Sugie, Naomi F. 2015. "Chilling Effects: Diminished Political Participation among Partners of Formerly Incarcerated Men." *Social Problems* 62(4): 550–571.

Travis, Jeremy. 2005. *But They All Come Back: Facing the Challenges of Prisoner Reentry*. Washington, DC: The Urban Institute.

Trice, Ashton D., and JoAnne Brewster. 2004. "The Effects of Maternal Incarceration on Adolescent Children." *Journal of Police and Criminal Psychology* 19(1): 27–35.

Turney, Kristin. 2014. "Stress Proliferation across Generations? Examining the Relationship between Parental Incarceration and Childhood Health." *Journal of Health and Social Behavior* 55(3): 302–319.

Turney, Kristin. 2015. "Liminal Men: Incarceration and Relationship Dissolution." *Social Problems* 62(4): 499–528.

Turney, Kristin, and Anna R. Haskins. 2014. "Falling Behind? Children's Early Grade Retention after Paternal Incarceration." *Sociology of Education* 87(4): 241–258.

Turney, Kristin, and Christopher Wildeman. 2015. "Detrimental for Some? Heterogeneous Effects of Maternal Incarceration on Child Wellbeing." *Criminology & Public Policy* 14(1): 125–156.

Tyler, Tom R., Jeffrey Fagan, and Amanda Geller. 2014. "Street Stops and Police Legitimacy: Teachable Moments in Young Urban Men's Legal Socialization." *Journal of Empirical Legal Studies* 11(4): 751–785.

Uggen, Christopher, and Jeff Manza. 2002. "Democratic Contraction? Political Consequences of Felon Disenfranchisement in the United States." *American Sociological Review* 67(6): 777–803.

Wakefield, Sara, and Christopher Uggen. 2010. "Incarceration and Stratification." *Annual Review of Sociology* 36: 387–406.

Wakefield, Sara, and Christopher Wildeman. 2011. "Mass Imprisonment and Racial Disparities in Childhood Behavioral Problems." *Criminology & Public Policy* 10(3): 793–817.

Wakefield, Sara, and Christopher Wildeman. 2013. *Children of the Prison Boom: Mass Incarceration and the Future of American Inequality*. New York: Oxford University Press.

Walker, Hannah L. 2014. "Extending the Effects of the Carceral State: Proximal Contact, Political Participation, and Race." *Political Research Quarterly* 67(4): 809–822.

Watts, Harold, and Demetra Smith Nightingale. 1996. "Adding It up: The Economic Impact of Incarceration on Individuals, Families, and Communities." Pp. 91–104 in *The Unintended*

Consequences of Incarceration. Paper presented at the Vera Institute of Justice Conference: The Unintended Consequences of Incarceration.

Weaver, Vesla M., and Amy E. Lerman. 2010. "Political Consequences of the Carceral State." *The American Political Science Review* 104(4): 817–833.

Western, Bruce. 2006. *Punishment and Inequality in America*. New York: Russell Sage Foundation.

Western, Bruce, Jeffrey R. Kling, and David F. Weiman. 2001. "The Labor Market Consequences of Incarceration." *Crime & Delinquency* 47(3): 410–427.

Western, Bruce, and Becky Pettit. 2010. "Incarceration & Social Inequality." *Daedalus* 139(3): 8–19.

Western, Bruce, and Christopher Wildeman. 2009. "The Black Family and Mass Incarceration." *The Annals of the American Academy of Political and Social Science* 621: 221–242.

Wilbur, MaryAnn B., Jodi E. Marani, Danielle Appugliese, Ryan Woods, Jane A. Siegel, Howard J. Cabral, and Deborah A. Frank. 2007. "Socioemotional Effects of Fathers' Incarceration on Low-Income, Urban, School-Aged Children." *Pediatrics* 120(3): e678–e685.

Wildeman, Christopher. 2009. "Parental Imprisonment, the Prison Boom, and the Concentration of Childhood Disadvantage." *Demography* 46(2): 265–280.

Wildeman, Christopher. 2010. "Paternal Incarceration and Children's Physically Aggressive Behaviors: Evidence from the Fragile Families and Child Wellbeing Study." *Social Forces* 89(1): 285–309.

Wildeman, Christopher, Jason Schnittker, and Kristin Turney. 2012. "Despair by Association? The Mental Health of Mothers with Children by Recently Incarcerated Fathers." *American Sociological Review* 77(2): 216–243.

Wildeman, C., and K. Turney. 2014. "Positive, Negative, or Null? The Effects of Maternal Incarceration on Children's Behavioral Problems." *Demography* 51(3): 1041–1068.

Wildeman, Christopher, and Sara Wakefield. 2014. "The Long Arm of the Law: The Concentration of Incarceration in Families in the Era of Mass Incarceration." *Journal of Gender, Race and Justice* 17: 367–389.

42 Sex Offender Civil Commitment

Georgia M. Winters and Elizabeth L. Jeglic

Overview

Twenty states and the federal government have established Sexually Violent Predator (SVP) laws (Association for the Treatment of Sexual Abusers 2010). These laws allow for the civil commitment of a select group of sexual offenders who are deemed by a court to be highly likely to recidivate following the completion of their prison sentence. The basis of sex offender commitment stems from the general mental health civil commitment model, in which an individual who is at high risk for harming themselves or others is legally committed to a secure psychiatric facility where they receive treatment to diminish this risk. Thus, SVP laws are designed to target a small group (e.g., 1 percent of sex offenders in Washington State and 5 percent of sex offenders in Minnesota; Janus and Meehl 1997) of the "most dangerous" sexual predators (Kirwin 1995), with the ultimate goal of SVP legislation being to keep communities safe by incapacitating high risk offenders and utilizing risk management strategies to prevent future sexual reoffending (Fabian 2005; La Fond 2005).

SVP laws have proven to be both controversial and costly. Opponents of SVP legislation have argued that they violate an offenders' civil liberties (Calkins, Jeglic, Beattey, Zeidman, and Perillo 2014). Further, there have been debates over the criteria used to civilly commit SVPs and the legitimacy of committing these offenders when there is questionable access to effective treatment. While constitutional challenges to these laws have thus far been upheld (Calkins et al., 2014), there has also been debate about whether the high cost of this legislation outweighs the benefits (Perillo and Jeglic 2013). The costs of civilly committing a SVP can range from $47,555 in Florida to upwards of $138,000 in North Dakota (La Fond 2005). On average, the cost per person for one year under SVP laws is around $100,000 (La Fond 2005; Washington State Institute for Public Policy 2007). Further, the proceedings involved in committing a sex offender incurs court expenses, such as hiring forensic evaluators, which is estimated to be as high as $450,000 per offender (Willmsen 2012).

There are also concerns about the ultimate purpose of civil commitment given that the large majority of sex offenders who have been civilly committed as SVPs have not been released (Janus 2000). A total of 4,534 individuals had been committed under SVP Laws as of 2006, though only 494 had been discharged or released (Washington State Institute for Public Policy 2007). As significantly fewer sex offenders are released than detained, these numbers will only continue to rise. Thus, this chapter will provide an overview of sex offender civil commitment, including the history, criteria, legal processes, treatment, and reform.

History of SVP Legislation

In 1987, a sex offender named Earl Shriner completed a ten-year prison term in Washington State for abducting and sexually assaulting two young girls (Lieb 1996). Despite warnings by correctional staff based on drawings Shriner had made while incarcerated depicting the torture and murders of children, he was released from the prison at the termination of his sentence. Two years later, Shriner brutally raped and physically assaulted a young boy, nearly resulting in the loss of the victim's life. The public was outraged that a dangerous sexual offender was released into the community knowing that he remained a risk. Subsequently, the Washington State legislature created a Task Force to address the issue of what to do with high risk sex offenders upon expiration of their sentence. This resulted in the development of a law known as the Sexually Violent Predator (SVP) statute that permitted the civil commitment of sex offenders following incarceration. Numerous states soon followed suit by passing similar SVP laws. The implementation of the SVP law was also followed by several constitutional challenges delineated hereafter.

In 1994, the Kansas State legislature enacted an SVP law that allowed for the civil commitment of sexually violent predators who posed a "likelihood of engaging in repeat acts of predatory sexual violence" (*Kansas v. Hendricks* 1997). The law, referred to as the SVP Act, mirrored the legislation imposed in Washington State. The first utilization of the law was for the petition of commitment of convicted sex offender, Leroy Hendricks, who had several sexual assaults against children over the past 40 years. Hendricks was set to be released to a halfway house after serving 10 years of his 5–20-year sentence. During the trial, Hendricks reported that he has pedophilic interests and was unable to control his urge to sexually assault children when under stress (*In re Hendricks* 1996). Hendricks also reported that while he did not want to commit another sexual crime, the only way this would be ensured was "to die." The jury determined that Hendricks qualified as an SVP given his identified sexual interest toward children and self-reported inability to control his behavior when under stress (Mercado, Schopp, and Bornstein 2005).

Hendricks' case was brought to the Supreme Court in *Kansas v. Hendricks* (1997), where the SVP law was challenged on the basis of two constitutional issues. The first issue was that the SVP laws were punitive in nature, which would violate *ex post facto* laws and the double jeopardy clause. Second, it was argued that the SVP laws violate substantive due process by unconstitutionally expanding civil commitment beyond domains for which it was established. In a 5–4 decision, the U.S. Supreme Court upheld the SVP law that allowed for the indefinite civil commitment of sexual offenders following the completion of their prison sentence. The Court argued that the laws are not punitive in nature, but rather aim to incapacitate as is done in traditional civil commitment and that the civil commitment facilities would provide treatment to the committed offenders. Further, the court held that those sex offenders eligible for this civil commitment must be found to have a "mental abnormality" or "personality disorder"; and as such SVP civil commitment does not expand beyond the traditional civil commitment laws given it does not serve a punitive purpose. The court further stressed that the established mental abnormality must place the offender at a high risk for future "predatory acts of sexual violence" (1997: 350). The Court's decision alluded to the fact that SVP commitment should only be limited to those offenders who have an inability to their control behavior, also referred to as "volitional impairment."

Another landmark case in SVP legislation arose in 2002 in the decision of *Kansas v. Crane*. This decision addressed the ambiguity of the volitional impairment criteria established in *Kansas v. Hendricks*. Michael Crane was a convicted sex offender who had repeated sexual offenses and was diagnosed with both pedophilia and antisocial personality disorder (*Kansas v. Crane* 2002). The psychiatrist in the case testified that Crane's behaviors were both "willful and uncontrollable" (*In re Crane* 2000, 7 P.3d at 290). The Court held that it must be demonstrated the offender finds it "particularly difficult to control their behavior." Therefore, under this new decision, the law required something less than a complete loss of control, in contrast to the previously held *Kansas* finding of complete loss of control.

The third constitutional challenge to SVP laws came following the passage of the Adam Walsh Child Protection and Safety Act in 2006, which allowed for the federal government to civilly commit a sexual offender following the completion of a federal sentence (Adam Walsh Child Protection and Safety Act 2006). In 2010, this issue was brought to the U.S. Supreme court following a petition to commit an offender nearing release, Graydon Early Comstock. Comstock served 37 months in prison for child pornography charges and the government sought to commit him under the Adam Walsh Child Protection and Safety Act. The petitioners argued federal SVP commitment violated the clauses of double jeopardy and *ex post facto*, as well as the individual's Sixth and Eighth Amendment rights. The Supreme Court held in *United States v. Comstock* (2010) that the federal government is authorized to commit dangerous sexual offenders who served federal sentences.

Criteria for SVP Commitment

The Evaluation Process

While some variability exists across states, determination of SVP status for civil commitment typically involves four elements (Jackson and Hess, 2007; Jackson, Rogers, and Shuman 2004; Janus 2000): 1) conviction history of at least one sexual offense; 2) a mental abnormality or personality disorder; 3) determination to be high risk to commit another sexual offense; and 4) the diagnosed mental abnormality results in an individual being at increased likelihood to engage in future sexually violent acts.

In order to establish whether an offender qualifies as an SVP, clinical evaluations are conducted using a variety of techniques, such as interviews with the offender, record review, collateral information, psychological testing, physiological testing, and risk assessment tools (Witt and Conroy 2009). These evaluations are typically conducted by state-appointed evaluators and, oftentimes, an expert for the defense. The clinical interview with the offender is an integral part of the evaluation process, this is the opportunity for the evaluator to speak with the offender in order to obtain the offender's perspective on his background, criminal and psychological history, and thoughts about the likelihood he would commit another crime. Additionally, the clinical interview also serves as a means for the evaluator to observe the offender's behavior and mental processes. The clinical interview forms but one piece of the final SVP evaluation. Important information is also gleaned from record review wherein the evaluator looks for records pertaining to criminal history, psychological/psychiatric history, medical history, police reports of the crimes, victim impact statements, institutional behavior, and treatment records. These records provide information to complete risk assessment tools as well as form the basis of determining whether a sex crime was committed by the offender and the degree to which he can control his behavior. Collateral contacts can include speaking to arresting officers, correctional staff, parole and probation officers, treatment providers, family members, and friends. This provides additional observation of the offender's past and present behaviors as well as insight into any psychological or behavioral problems that may not be noted in the records. Psychological testing such as IQ tests, personality, diagnostic interviews, or symptom checklists can also be administered, but should only be those that add to the diagnostic clarity or the determination of volitional impairment. In certain instances, assessments of deviant sexual interest such as the penile plethysmograph (PPG) may also be employed where such tests are available and are needed for diagnostic clarity. Finally, actuarial risk assessments are conducted based upon interview and file review.

History of Conviction of a Sexual Offense. The first prong of the SVP criteria is the presence of a sexual offense history. The offender must have been convicted of, and completed a prison sentence for a sexually violent crime. At a minimum, the offender must have been convicted of at least one statutorily defined sexual offense, against either a child or adult victim (Jumper, Babula, and Casbon 2011; Lieb and Matson 1998).

Mental Abnormality or Personality Disorder. As expressed by the Court in *Kansas v. Hendricks* (1997) an SVP offender must have a "mental abnormality" or "personality disorder", which was often defined as a "congenital or acquired condition affecting the emotional or volitional capacity which predisposes the person to the commission of criminal sexual acts" (Jackson and Roesch 2015). An assessment of psychopathology must be conducted to evaluate for the presence or absence of a mental abnormality or personality disorder. In addition, the Court specified that the diagnosis must make the offender more likely to reoffend sexually. Although the term mental abnormality is a legal term and vaguely defined (Miller, Amenta, and Conroy 2005), evaluators tend rely on the use of the *American Psychiatric Associations Diagnostic and Statistical Manual of Mental Disorders Fifth Edition* (*DSM-5*; APA 2013). In addition to a thorough clinical interview, self-report measures of personality such as Minnesota Multiphasic Personality Inventory-2 (MMPI-2; Butcher, Dahlstrom, Graham, Tellegen, and Kaemmer 1989), Millon Clinical Multiaxial Inventory-III (MCMI-III; Millon and Davis 1997), and the Personality Assessment Inventory (PAI; Morey 2007) have also been utilized to establish a diagnosis as they are thought to be less face valid than some other diagnostic measures and have validity indices to assess for malingering.

The most commonly used diagnoses in SVP hearings include: pedophilia (48 percent), substance use disorder (31 percent), paraphilia not otherwise specified (NOS) (31 percent), and antisocial personality disorder (28 percent; Perillo, Spada, Calkins, and Jeglic 2014). Research has shown that SVPs have higher rates of paraphilia diagnoses, personality disorders, and psychopathy, and lower rates of serious mental illness when compared to non-committed sexual offenders and general inpatient civilly committed patients (e.g., Becker, Stinson, Tromp, and Messer 2003; Elwood, Doren, and Thornton 2010; Jackson and Richards 2007; Janus and Walbek 2000; Levenson, 2004b). Paraphilias (i.e., abnormal sexual desires or acts) are most the most common diagnoses in SVP cases given their association with sexual behaviors (Becker et al. 2003; Janus and Walbek 2000; Levenson 2004a; Levenson and Morin 2006; McLawsen, Scalora, and Darrow 2012; Perillo et al. 2014), especially pedophilia and paraphilia NOS (Doren and Elwood 2009; Jumper et al. 2011; Levenson and Morin 2006). Other paraphilia diagnoses are typically diagnosed at lower frequencies, including sexual sadism, voyeurism, exhibitionism, frotteurism, and fetishism (Jumper et al. 2011).

Overall, there is no evidence to confirm the valid use of *DSM* diagnoses as evidence of the legal term of mental abnormality (Wollert 2007). The *DSM* notes that the intended use of the diagnoses is not to answer psycho-legal questions, including civil commitment, without further information (APA 2013). While the *DSM* provides common criteria to assess mental abnormality across various clinicians, there may be variations in what the criteria mean and who meets criteria for the diagnosis (Doren and Ellwood 2009). Despite these potential pitfalls, the *DSM* remains the most widely used method to establish the presence or absence of a mental abnormality in SVP evaluations. Even with the use of standardized diagnostic criteria established in the *DSM*, there is evidence to suggest the reliability and validity of diagnosing offenders under SVP statues is questionable (Levenson 2004a). The interrater reliability of *DSM-IV* diagnoses in SVP cases has been examined, with results suggesting only "fair" agreement, although improvement was shown with semi-structured interviews (Meyer 2002; Packard and Levenson 2006; Perillo et al. 2014). Thus, the use of DSM diagnoses in SVP cases remains of high concern.

As with DSM diagnoses in general, questions have been raised about the use of paraphilia diagnoses in SVP cases (Miller, Amenta, and Conroy 2005; O'Donohue, Regev, and Hagstrom 2000; Schopp, Pearce, and Scalora 1998; Schopp, Scalora, and Pearce 1999).

It has been suggested that paraphilias may be applied too broadly or are being misapplied (First and Halon 2008; Levenson 2004b). Evaluators must be careful to examine the underlying mental state of a sex offender, rather than applying a paraphilia diagnosis solely due to the fact that a deviant sexual act occurred (Perillo et al. 2014). For example, convictions for child sexual abuse or rape are not sufficient to establish that the offender has a long-standing pattern of deviant sexual interests (First and Halon 2008). It has also been argued that some of the terminology used in the diagnostic criteria for paraphilias is subjective in nature (e.g., "recurrent," "intense," "distress," "impairment"; Perillo et al. 2014).

One of the most highly controversial areas in SVP diagnoses involves the use of paraphilia NOS, which is the second most commonly used diagnosis following pedophilia (Perillo et al. 2014). While most of the research has focused on the *DSM-IV*'s paraphilia NOS, it should be noted this diagnosis has been bifurcated in the *DSM-5* into paraphilia other specified paraphilic disorder (OSPD) and paraphilia unspecified paraphilic disorder (UPD). Two subtypes of paraphilia OSPD/UPD nonconsent (i.e., interest in sexual activities involving nonconsenting individuals) and hebephilia (i.e., sexual interest in adolescent children), have been subject to intense criticism. The *DSM-IV* or *DSM-5* does not contain specific criteria for diagnosing the subtypes of nonconsent or hebephilia, though these diagnoses are being used by experts in the field (Doren 2002; Perillo et al. 2014; Prentky, Coward, and Gabriel 2008). During the development of the *DSM-5*, there was a Paraphilia Subwork Group comprised of experts in the field and it was concluded that these subtypes of nonconsent or hebephilia would not be included as formal diagnoses and further it was decided that there was insufficient evidence to list them in the areas for future research. It has argued that paraphilia OSPD/UPD nonconsent is used by evaluators as a catch-all category for individuals who committed the act of rape, despite questions regarding the reliability of the diagnosis (Spitzer 1986). The paraphilia OSPD/UPD hebephilia diagnosis has been criticized for questionable reliability and subjective nature in diagnosing the disorder given the lack of established criteria (Franklin 2009; Perillo et al. 2014). In sum, despite an absence of diagnostic criteria, paraphilia OSPD/UPD diagnoses, especially nonconsent and hebephilia, are being used in SVP evaluations.

To ensure most ethical and valid use of paraphilia diagnoses, First and Halon (2008) proposed steps for evaluating these disorders in SVP cases. First, the clinician should provide reasonable evidence in establishing the presence of the paraphilia, through assessing the offender's arousal fantasies and urges. Second, should a paraphilia be established, the evaluator should examine whether the prior sexual misconducts were a direct result of the paraphilia. Third, evidence on the paraphilia's direct effect on volitional impartments should be provided, rather than assuming the diagnosis impairs ability to control behavior.

Volitional Impairment. In *Kansas v. Hendricks* (1997), the Supreme Court stressed there must be a link between the mental abnormality and an offender's inability to control their behavior. Then in *Kansas v. Crane* (2002), it was further stressed that this demonstrated lack of control, or "volitional impairment" distinguished offenders under the SVP laws and a typical criminal recidivist. While there have been several attempts through case law, legal theory, and psychological theory to clarify what this means, there has yet to be an established definition or way of measuring volitional impairment (Mercado et al. 2005).

Within the legal context, various court decisions have implied that volitional impairment may be related to repeated engagement of deviant acts regardless of the negative consequences (Held 1999) or poor insight into one's own behaviors (*In re Irwin* 1995). Others have suggested lack of control refers to situations when it is unreasonable to expect that an offender can refrain from engaging in certain behaviors under given circumstances (Schopp 1991). Still, some contend that the court in *Crane* and *Hendricks* alluded that volition refers to an individual's choice to not reoffend, a decision that may be impacted by a personality disorder or paraphilia, such as pedophilia (Elwood 2009). In their stance on the volitional impairment criteria, the Association for the Treatment of Sexual Abusers (ATSA 2010) stressed that volitional impairment is "untenable," "meaningless," and "unworkable" (p. 2) and has not been accepted by the legal and medical fields. Overall, it is argued that there is no standardized way of measuring this construct given the lack of a definition and criteria for assessing volitional impairment (Mercado et al 2005).

Deviant Sexual Interest. An offender's deviant sexual interests are important to consider within SVP diagnoses as they relate to both diagnosis and recidivism risk. Assessment procedures designed to assess deviant sexual interests most commonly include phallometric testing. Phallometric testing, such as the penile plethysmograph, measures erectile circumference or volume changes in response to deviant and nondeviant images, video, and/or audio. A meta-analysis has shown phallometric responses to deviant sexual stimuli were the strongest predictor of sexual recidivism (Hanson and Bussiere 1998). Penile plethysmograph evaluations have been criticized for ethical and practical concerns (e.g., the invasive nature of the measures), as well as issues regarding the validity and reliability of the measure (e.g., the measure can be faked; 25 percent of individuals do not respond to the measure) (Council on Sex Offender Treatment, forthcoming; Marshall and Fernandez 2000; Wilson 1998; Witt and Conroy 2009).

High Risk of Sexual Recidivism. SVP law requires the person be found to be at high likelihood to engage in future acts of criminal sexual acts. In order to address this prong of the statutory criteria, clinicians use a variety of measures to assess risk for recidivism (Jackson and Hess 2007). Commonly, evaluators will utilize actuarial risk tools for assessing risk for sexual recidivism (Douglas, Cox, and Webster 1999; Levenson 2004b). Dynamic risk factors also are frequently considered and integrated into the findings of structured risk assessment tools (Levenson and Morin 2006).

Several actuarial instruments have been developed to examine risk for sexual recidivism. Tools designed to specifically assess for sexual recidivism include: the *Static-99* (Hanson and Thornton 2000), and its revision the *Static-99R* (Helmus, Thornton, Hanson, and Babchishin 2012), the *Sex Offender Risk Appraisal Guide* (*SORAG*; Quinsey, Harris, Rice, and Cormier 1998), and the *Minnesota Sex Offender Screening Tool-Revised* (*MnSOST-R*; Epperson, Kaul, Huot, Goldman, and Alexander 2003). The *Static-99* is a 10-item scale to assess risk of sexual recidivism. *Static-99* scores have been shown to correlate with violent and sexual recidivism (e.g., Blair, Marcus, and Boccaccini 2008; Hanson and Morton-Bourgon 2007; Harris et al. 2003) The *SORAG*, which was adapted from the *Violence Risk Appraisal Guide* (*VRAG*; Harris, Rice, and Quinsey, 1993), assesses both psychological variables and static factors. The measure has been found to be a good predictor of sexual recidivism, and may be a stronger predictor of violent and non-sexual reoffending compared to the Static-99 (Hanson and Thornton 2000). The *MnSOST-R* utilizes 16 items to address both static (non-changing) and dynamic (changing) factors related to reoffending. The measure has also been shown to be a strong predictor of sexual recidivism (Hanson and Morton-Bourgon 2007).

The *Psychopathy Checklist-Revised* (*PCL-R*; Hare 1991, 2003) is another measure that has been used in SVP evaluations. The *PCL-R* is a 20-item measure that utilizes clinical interview and record review to establish levels of psychopathy. Research has shown that psychopathy is a risk factor for general, violent, and sexual recidivism (Hemphill, Templeman, Wong, and Hare 1998; Salekin, Rogers, and Sewell 1996). A meta-analysis of 95 studies revealed a positive correlation between *PCL-R* scores and sexual recidivism (Hanson and Morton-Bourgon 2005).

Overall, research has shown that sex offenders who qualified for commitment had higher scores on actuarial measures, including the *Static-99* (Hanson and Thornton 1999) and MnSOST-R (Epperson et al. 2003). Importantly, however, some research has shown that there are high levels of variance between clinicians on risk instruments used to assess sexual offenders (Murrie et al. 2009). Several concerns have also been raised regarding the use of risk assessment tools (Miller et al. 2005). First, sex offenders are a heterogeneous group (e.g., rapists, child molesters, child pornographers) and classifying everyone into a group based on risk may provide a more narrow view than is needed to examine risk. Second, research tends to focus solely on static factors (i.e., those that cannot change) versus dynamic ones (i.e., can change). Evidence has shown that dynamic risk factors are related to risk for reoffending (e.g., Beech, Friendship, Erikson, and Hanson 2002; Dempster and Hart 2002; Hanson and Bussiere 1998; Hanson and Harris 2000; Thornton 2002), such as criminal attitudes, social factors, and levels of hostility. While some measures have been developed to address dynamic factors (e.g., *Sex Offender Need Assessment Rating*; *SONAR*; Hanson and Harris 2001), more empirical evidence is needed.

Legal Processes Involved in SVP Commitment

Although legal procedures may vary across jurisdictions, there are several stages involved in legal processes of SVP cases: screening, probable-cause hearing, trial, and release. First, state agencies screen sex offenders who are nearing their release from prison by examining their records in order to identify those sex offenders who may quality under SVP laws (La Fond 2005). This process typically occurs within three months of the offender's release from prison (Terry 2006). The names of the individuals who may meet criteria to be SVPs are then forwarded to the prosecutors who have the power to petition for commitment under SVP statutes. Subsequently, a probable-cause hearing is held where the judge determines whether there is enough evidence to suggest that the sex offender meets criteria to be an SVP.

If probable cause is established, the government arranges for the offender to be evaluated by licensed mental health professionals (MHP) who are either state-licensed psychiatrists or psychologists. Should the government MHP determine the offender meets criteria for SVP, an independent evaluation is arranged by the defense attorney or one is provided by the state if the offender is indigent. A trial is then held to make the final determination of whether the sex offender will be committed as an SVP. In most states, either the defense or the prosecution can request a jury trial; an option that is almost always requested by the prosecution. During the trial, which may last days or weeks, the prosecutor has one or more MHP testify, and may even have a past victim take the stand. Then, the defense has the opportunity to present an opposing MPH, though there may be instances where the case solely relies on state experts (Witt and Conroy 2009).

If committed, a sexual offender is sent to a secure facility for an indefinite period, according to most state statues. However, some states require renewal of commitment after a given time period (e.g., 2-year period in California; Lieb 2003). Nearly all states house civilly committed sex offenders in secure facilities (i.e., psychiatric hospitals, mental health facility in a correctional setting, free standing secure facilities) (Deming 2008). In Texas, however, sex offenders are mandated to outpatient treatment, where they undergo supervision in the community as opposed to an inpatient setting.

A sex offender committed under SVP laws can only be released if they are deemed to be safe to return to the community. This is typically determined by a judicial hearing, where a jury will decide if the offender should be released. For instances where the offender is deemed safe for release, they may be subject to either conditional or final release. Conditional release involves the release of an offender into the community while still under strict monitoring, whereas final release involves the complete discharge from state control.

As of 2006, a total of 4,534 individuals had been held under SVP Laws, while only 494 had been discharged or released (Washington State Institute for Public Policy 2007).

The low number of offenders being released may be due to a number of factors. First there is a lack of resources dedicated to treat the offenders in an outpatient setting; therefore, SVPs are contained in inpatient settings for long periods of time. Additionally, treatment within commitment facilities has been shown to be a slow process and it is unclear when treatment progress is significant enough to warrant release from an inpatient setting. It has also been suggested that the high political stakes of releasing a dangerous offender into the community has resulting in many prosecutors resisting conditional release. Notably, analyses on the estimated rate of recidivism showed about one in ten SVPs would be expected to reoffend within four years (Duwe 2014), which has been used to argue that the vast majority of SVPs could be managed safely in the community.

Treatment of SVPs

One of the aims of SVP commitments is to provide committed offenders the appropriate treatment needed to assist in reducing the risk for future sexual violence (Fabian 2005; La Fond 2005). Importantly, only 53 percent of the civilly committed or detained sex offenders received sex offender specific (SOS) treatment according to a survey in May 2006 (Deming 2008), although with increased litigation aimed at civil commitment facilities this may be changing. In an examination of treatment provision for SVPs, Jackson, Schneider, and Travia (2007) found that 15 of the 16 programs sampled reportedly provide a structured treatment to civilly committed sex offenders. Structured treatment involves specific stages or phases of treatment whose goals must be completed before progressing to subsequent phases. The survey also showed that 85 percent of the programs were providing relapse prevention and cognitive behavioral therapy. An additional 80 percent also reportedly provided group therapy targeting topics such as dynamic risk, management of sexual arousal, and offense cycle.

Cognitive-behavioral therapy (CBT) is the most commonly used treatment model for sex offender treatment both in the community and correctional settings (Marshall, Anderson, and Fernandez 1999) in which sex offenders are taught new behaviors and skills to prevent offending as well as challenge and modify cognitions that are supportive of offending behavior. The objectives of CBT for sex offenders include: recognizing problematic behaviors, understanding emotions that precede deviant behaviors, identifying and modifying cognitive distortions, accepting responsibility for the sexual offense, evaluating attitudes and beliefs, acquiring prosocial expression of sexuality, developing social skills, identifying high-risk situations, and gaining an understanding of the offense cycle in order to break the sequence in the future (Terry 2006). It should be noted that while the treatment may be more intensive in a civil commitment facility, the foundations of the treatment are the same as that provided to non-SVPs.

There are several obstacles to treating civilly committed sex offenders versus those of the general sexual offender population (Terry 2006). First, in many cases sex offenders may be receiving treatment for the first time following years in prison; therefore, it may be their psychiatric or behavioral problems have been exacerbated by then. Second, while CBT has been shown most effective for sex offenders in general, there is a dearth of evidence to show this is effective for sex offenders who have been shown to have a mental abnormality. Third, there may be a treatment paradox, which suggests that information an offender discloses during the course of treatment, a necessary component to making positive changes, could be later used to argue against their release and thus this may prevent sex offenders from being open and honest in the disclosures as it may be used against them at a later date (Terry 2006).

Reform of SVP Legislation

It has been suggested that the SVP laws are in need of reform or ultimate abolition. Arguments for the abolition of SVP laws are largely based upon the vague criteria for SVP commitment and that there is no clear pathway to release for those sex offenders who are committed under SVP statutes. Further, it has been argued that SVP laws are punitive in nature, rather than rehabilitative. In response to these critiques, several recommendations have been made to reform SVP statutes.

La Fond (2005) outlined eleven suggestions for reform of SVP laws:

1. The use of the medical model would limit SVP commitment for only individuals who have been diagnosed with a recognized mental illness. Thus, SVP evaluators would be provided with a scientific basis for establishing the presence of a "mental abnormality."
2. While most laws only require a single conviction in order to be committed, it has been suggested that having a requirement of more than one prior conviction would assist in narrowing the scope of offenders eligible for commitment.
3. Currently, filing SVP petitions is often the responsibility of prosecuting attorneys who may be motivated by political concerns. As an alternative, the state could have MHP involved in the filing decision for SVP cases given they possess more knowledge of sex offender evaluations and treatment and are not motivated by the same political pressures as prosecutors.
4. Following the probable-cause hearings for SVP cases, the offender is temporarily committed in a correctional setting for offenders awaiting trial. Therefore, MHP should conduct evaluations prior to the probable-cause hearing so that a judge can inquire about the presence of a mental abnormality that would impact volitional impairment. Should there be insufficient evidence, then the petitions for those offenders should be dismissed.
5. The prosecution and defense attorneys in SVP cases should ensure that SVP cases are tried within a reasonable amount of time. Time requirements should be established between the initial petition and probable-cause hearing, and the subsequent trial should probable-cause be established.
6. There are states that allow for prosecuting attorneys to choose a jury or bench trial in an SVP case. Prosecutors will be drawn to the jury option, given that citizens are likely to decide to commit rather than release a potentially dangerous sex offender. Instead of allowing prosecutors to have this discretion, the decision for a jury or bench trial should rest in the hands of the defendant.
7. SVP commitment is a civil case (as opposed to a criminal case) which means a prosecutor could retry a sex offender even after they were found not eligible at trial by a jury or judge. Therefore, if an offender is found not to meet criteria for SVP civil commitment following trial, the government should then release the offender and not allow for future trials for commitment of that offender unless new sex crimes are committed.
8. In applicable cases, use of outpatient treatment from the onset of commitment should be considered rather than solely utilizing inpatient facilities. Effective risk management strategies can be implemented in community-based treatment settings as a more economic method of reducing risk for reoffending. For example, Texas utilizes supervised outpatient treatment rather than containing SVPs in an inpatient setting (Deming 2008).
9. Provide limits for a term of commitment that can be renewed if needed. This would require treatment staff to provide effective and intensive treatment. This would also assist in lowering the number of SVP in state facilities, which would save money and resources.
10. Under some SVP laws, prosecutors are allowed to oppose treatment staff's decision to release a civilly committed sex offender; a decision that may be based on political factors.

Allowing staff to release offenders would assist in allowing committed individuals who have improved through treatment to return to the community.

11. There is often political pressure not to release SVPs given the possibility of the person committing a new sexual offense. Therefore, the SVP system in general should be protected from these political motivations from entering the decisions to commit or release offenders. For example, utilizing independent evaluators rather than government employees when conducting SVP evaluations.

References

Adam Walsh Child Protection and Safety Act of 2006, 42 U.S.C. § 16901 et seq. (2006).

American Psychiatric Association. 2013. *Diagnostic and Statistical Manual of Mental Disorders*, 5th ed. Washington, DC: Author.

Association for the Treatment of Sexual Abusers. 2010. *Civil Commitment Of Sexually Violent Predators*. Retrieved March 29, 2016 from www.atsa.com/civil-commitment-sexually-violent-predators.

Becker, Judith V., Jill Stinson, ShannonTromp, and Gene Messer. 2003. "Characteristics of Individuals Petitioned for Civil Commitment." *International Journal of Offender Therapy and Comparative Criminology* 47: 185–195.

Beech, Anthony, Caroline Friendship, Matt Erikson, and Karl R. Hanson. 2002. "The Relationship Between Static and Dynamic Risk Factors and Reconviction in a Sample of U.K. Child Abusers." *Sexual Abuse: A Journal of Research and Treatment* 14(2): 155–167.

Blair, Pamela, David K. Marcus, and Marcus T. Boccaccini. 2008. "Is There an Allegiance Effect for Assessment Instruments? Actuarial Risk Assessment as an Exemplar." *Clinical Psychology: Science and Practice* 15: 346–360.

Butcher, James N., William G. Dahlstrom, John R. Graham, Auke Tellegen, and Stefan B. Kaemmer. 1989. *The Minnesota Multiphasic Personality Inventory-2 (MMPI-2): Manual for Administration and Scoring*. Minneapolis, MN: University of Minnesota Press.

Calkins, Cynthia, Elizabeth Jeglic, Robert A. Beattey, Steven Zeidman, and Anthony D. Perillo. 2014. "Sexual Violence Legislation: A Review of Caselaw and Empirical Research." *Psychology, Public Policy, and Law* 20(4): 443–462.

Council on Sex Offender Treatment. Forthcoming. *Use of the Penile Plethysmograph (PPG) in the Assessment and Treatment of Sex Offenders*. Retrieved March 29, 2016 from file:///C:/Users/gwinters/Downloads/csot_pleth2.pdf.

Deming, Adam. 2008. "Sex Offender Civil Commitment Programs: Current Practices Characteristics, and Resident Demographics. *Journal of Psychiatry & Law* 36(3): 439–461.

Dempster, Rebecca J., and Stephen D. Hart. 2002. "The Relative Utility of Fixed and Variable Risk Factors in Discriminating Sexual Recidivists and Nonrecidivists." *Sexual Abuse: A Journal of Research and Treatment* 14(2): 121–138.

Doren, Dennis M. 2002. *Evaluating Sex Offenders: A Manual for Civil Commitment and Beyond*. Thousand Oaks, CA: Sage.

Doren, Dennis M., and Richard Elwood. 2009. "The Diagnostic Reliability of Sexual Sadism." *Sexual Abuse: A Journal of Research and Treatment* 21: 251–261.

Douglas, Kevin S., David N. Cox, and Christopher D. Webster. 1999. "Violence Risk Assessment: Science and Practice." *Legal and Criminological Psychology* 4: 149–184.

Duwe, Grant. 2014. "To What Extent Does Civil Commitment Reduce Sexual Recidivism? Estimating the Selective Incapacitation Effects in Minnesota." *Journal of Criminal Justice* 42(2): 193–202.

Elwood, Richard W. 2009. "Mental Disorder, Predisposition, Prediction, and Ability to Control: Evaluating Sex Offenders for Civil Commitment." *Sexual Abuse: Journal of Research and Treatment* 21(4): 395–411.

Elwood, Richard W., Dennis M. Doren, and David Thornton. 2010. "Diagnostic and Risk Profiles of Men Detained Under Wisconsin's Sexually Violent Person Law." *International Journal of Offender Therapy and Comparative Criminology* 54(2): 187–196.

Epperson, Douglas L., James D. Kaul, Stephen Huot, Robin Goldman, and Will Alexander. 2003. *Minnesota Sex Offender Screening Tool–Revised (MnSOST-R) Technical Paper: Development, Validation, and Recommended Risk Level Cut Scores*. Retrieved May 26, 2006 from www.psychology.iastate.edu/~dle/TechUpdatePaper12–03.pdf

Fabian, John. 2005. "The Risky Business of Conducting Risk Assessments for Those Already Civilly Committed as Sexually Violent Predators." *William Mitchell School of Law* 32(1): 81–159.

First, Michael B., and Robert L. Halon. 2008. "Use of DSM Paraphilia Diagnoses in Sexually Violent Predator Commitment Cases." *The Journal of the American Academy of Psychiatry and the Law* 36: 443–454.

Franklin, Karen. 2009. "The Public Policy Implication of 'hebephilia': A response to Blanchard et al." *Archives of Sexual Behavior* 38: 319–320.

Hanson, Karl R., and Monique T. Bussiere. 1998. "Predicting Relapse: A Meta-Analysis of Sexual Offender Recidivism Studies." *Journal of Consulting and Clinical Psychology* 66: 348–362.

Hanson, Karl R., and Andrew J.R. Harris. 2000. "Where Should We Intervene? Dynamic Predictors of Sex Offense Recidivism." *Criminal Justice and Behavior* 27: 6–35.

Hanson, Karl R., and Andrew J. R. Harris. 2001. "A Structured Approach to Evaluating Change Among Sexual Offenders." *Sexual Abuse: A Journal of Research and Treatment* 13(2): 105–122.

Hanson, Karl R., and Kelly E. Morton-Bourgon. 2005. "The Characteristics of Persistent Sexual Offenders: A Meta-Analysis of Recidivism Studies." *Journal of Consulting and Clinical Psychology* 73: 1154–1163.

Hanson, Karl R., and Kelly E. Morton-Bourgon. 2007. *The Accuracy of Recidivism Risk Assessments for Sexual Offenders: A Meta-Analysis*. Ottawa, ON: Department of the Solicitor General of Canada.

Hanson, Karl R. and David Thornton. 1999. *Static-99: Improving Actuarial Risk Assessments for Sex Offenders (User Report No. 99–02)*. Ottawa, ON: Department of the Solicitor General of Canada.

Hanson, Karl R., and David Thornton. 2000. "Improving Risk Assessments for Sex Offenders: A Comparison of Three Actuarial Scales." *Law and Human Behavior* 42(1): 119–136.

Hare, Robert D. 1991. *The Hare Psychopathy Checklist-Revised*. Toronto, ON: Multi-Health Systems.

Hare, Robert D. 2003. *Manual for the Revised Psychopathy Checklist*, 2nd ed. Toronto, ON: Multi-Health Systems.

Harris G, Rice M, and Quinsey V. 1993. "Violent Recidivism of Mentally Disordered Offenders: The Development of a Statistical Prediction Instrument." *Criminal Justice and Behavior* 20(4): 315–335.

Harris, Grant T., Marnie E. Rice, Vernon L. Quinsey, Martin L. Lalumiere, Douglas Boer, and Carol Lang. 2003. "A Multisite Comparison of Actuarial Risk Instruments for Sex Offenders." *Psychological Assessment* 15: 413–425.

Held, A. 1999. "The Civil Commitment of Sexual Predators: Experience under Minnesota's Law." Pp. 2-1–2-54 in *The Sexual Predator: Law, Policy, Evaluation, and Treatment*, Vol. 1 edited by A. Schlank and F. Cohen. New Jersey: Civic Research Institutes.

Helmus, Leslie, David Thornton, R. Karl Hanson, and Kelly M. Babchishin. 2012. "Improving the Predictive Accuracy of Static-99 and Static-2002 with Older Sex Offenders: Revised Age Weights." *Sexual Abuse: Journal of Research And Treatment* 24(1): 64–101.

Hemphill, James F., Ron Templeman, Stephen Wong, and Robert D. Hare. 1998. "Psychopathy and Crime: Recidivism and Criminal Careers." Pp. 375–398 in *Psychopathy: Theory, Research, and Implications for Society*, edited by D. Cooke and R.D. Hare. Dordrecht, The Netherlands: Kluwer Academic.

In re Crane, 269 Kan. 578, 7 P.3d 285 (Kan. 2000), Cert. granted, U.S., 121 S. Ct. 1483, 149 L. Ed. 2d 372 (2001).

In re Hendricks, 912 P.2d 129 (Kan. 1996).

In re Irwin, 529 N.W.2d 366 (Minn. Ct. App. 1995).

Jackson, Rebecca L., and Derek T. Hess. 2007. "Evaluation for Civil Commitment of Sex Offenders: A Survey of Experts." *Sexual Abuse: A Journal of Research and Treatment* 19: 425–448.

Jackson, Rebecca L., and Henry J. Richards. 2007. "Diagnostic and Risk Profiles Among Civilly Committed Sex Offenders in Washington State." *International Journal Of Offender Therapy and Comparative Criminology* 51(3): 313–323.

Jackson, Rebecca L., and Ronald Roesch. 2015. *Learning Forensic Assessment: Research and Practice*. New York: Routledge.

Jackson, Rebecca L., Richard Rogers, and Daniel W. Shuman. 2004. "The Adequacy and Accuracy of 474 Sexually Violent Predator Evaluations: Contextualized Risk Assessment in Clinical Practice." *International Journal of Forensic Mental Health* 3(2): 115–129.

Jackson, R., J. Schneider, and T. Travia, T. 2007, October. "Surveying Sex Offender Civil Commitment Programs: Program and Resident Characteristics." Paper presented at the Annual Meeting of the Association for the Treatment of Sexual Abusers (ATSA), San Diego, CA.

Janus, Eric S. 2000. "Sexual Predator Commitment Laws: Lessons for Law and the Behavioral Sciences." *Behavioral Sciences & The Law* 18(1): 5–21.

Janus, Eric S., and Paul E. Meehl. 1997. "Assessing the Legal Standard for Predictions of Dangerousness in Sex Offender Commitment Proceeding." *Psychology, Public Policy, and Law* 3: 33–64.

Janus, Eric S., and Nancy H. Walbek. 2000. "Sex Offender Commitments in Minnesota: A Descriptive Study of Second Generation Commitments." *Behavioral Sciences & the Law* 18: 343–374.

Jumper, Shan, Mark Babula, and Todd Casbon. 2011. "Diagnostic Profiles of Civilly Committed Sexual Offenders in Illinois and Other Reporting Jurisdictions: What We Know So Far." *International Journal of Offender Therapy and Comparative Criminology* 56: 838–855.

Kansas v. Crane, 2002 WL 75609.

Kansas v. Hendricks, 117 S.Ct. 2072 (1997).

Kirwin, John L. 1995. "Civil Commitment of Sexual Predators: Statutory and Case Law Developments." *The Hennepin Lawyer* 66(7): 22–26.

La Fond, John Q. 2005. *Preventing Sexual Violence: How Society Should Cope with Sex Offenders.* Washington, DC: American Psychological Association.

Levenson, Jill S. 2004a. "Reliability of Sexually Violent Predator Civil Commitment Criteria in Florida." *Law & Human Behavior* 28: 357–368.

Levenson, Jill S. 2004b. "Sexual Predator Civil Commitment: A Comparison of Selected and Released Offenders." *International Journal of Offender Therapy and Comparative Criminology* 48: 638–648.

Levenson, Jill S., and John W. Morin. 2006. "Factors Predicting Selection of Sexually Violent Predators for Civil Commitment." *International Journal of Offender Therapy and Comparative Criminology* 50: 609–629.

Lieb, Roxanne. 1996. "Washington's Sexually Violent Predator Law: Legislative History and Comparisons with Other States." Retrieved March 29, 2016 from www.wsipp.wa.gov/ReportFile/1244/Wsipp_Washingtons-Sexually-Violent-Predator-Law-Legislative-History-and-Comparisons-With-Other-States_Full-Report.pdf.

Lieb, Roxanne. 2003. "State Policy Perspectives on Sexual Predator laws." Pp. 41–59 in *Protecting Society from Sexually Dangerous Offenders: Law, Justice, and Therapy,* edited by Bruce J. Winick, and John Q. La Fond. Washington, DC: American Psychological Association.

Lieb, Roxanne, and Scott Matson. 1998. *Sexual Predator Commitment Laws in the United States [No. 38].* Olympia, WA: Washington State Institute for Public Policy.

Marshall, William L., Dana Anderson, and Yolanda Fernandez. 1999. *Cognitive Behavioral Treatment of Sexual Offenders.* Toronto, ON: Wiley.

Marshall, William L., and Yolanda M. Fernandez. 2000. "Phallometric Testing with Sexual Offenders: Limits to Its Value." *Clinical Psychology Review* 20(7): 807–822.

McLawsen, Julia E., Mario J. Scalora, and Charles Darrow. 2012. "Civilly Committed Sex Offenders: A Description and Interstate Comparison of Populations." *Psychology, Public Policy, and Law* 18: 453–476.

Mercado, Cynthia C., Ronert F. Schopp, and Brian H. Bornstein. 2005. "Evaluating Sex Offenders Under Sexually Violent Predator Laws: How Might Mental Health Professionals Conceptualize the Notion of Volitional Impairment?" *Aggression and Violent Behavior* 10(3): 289–309.

Meyer, Gregory L. 2002. "Implications of Information-Gathering Methods for a Refined Taxonomy of Psychopathology." Pp. 69–106 in *Rethinking the DSM: A Psychological Perspective,* edited by Larry E. Beutler, and Mary L. Malik. Washington, DC: American Psychological Association.

Miller, Holly A., Amy E. Amenta, and Mary A. Conroy. 2005. "Sexually Violent Predator Evaluations: Empirical Evidence, Strategies for Professionals, and Research Directions." *Law and Human Behavior* 29(1): 29–54. Retrieved March 29, 2016 from http://doi.org/10.1007/s10979–005–1398-y.

Millon, Theodore, and Roger R. Davis. 1997. "The MCMI-III: Present and Future Directions." *Journal of Personality Assessment* 68(1): 69–85.
Morey, Leslie C. 2007. *Personality Assessment Inventory Professional Manual*, 2nd Lutz, FL: Psychological Assessment Resources.
Murrie, Daniel C., Marcus T. Boccaccini, Darrel B. Turner, Meredith Meeks, Carol Woods, and Chriscelyn Tussey. 2009. "Rater (Dis)Agreement on Risk Assessment Measures in Sexually Violent Predator Proceedings: Evidence of Adversarial Allegiance in Forensic Evaluation?" *Psychology, Public Policy, and Law* 15: 19–53.
O'Donohue, William., Lisa G. Regev, and Anne Hagstrom. 2000. "Problems with the DSM–IV Diagnosis of Pedophilia." *Sexual Abuse: Journal of Research and Treatment* 12: 95–105.
Packard, Richard L., and Jill S. Levenson. 2006. "Revisiting the Reliability of Diagnostic Decisions in Sex Offender Civil Commitment. Sexual Offender Treatment." Retrieved March 29, 2016 from sexualoffender-treatment.org
Perillo, Anthony D. and Elizabeth L. Jeglic. 2013. "The Cost of Sex Offender Civil Commitment: How Much is Too Much?" *Sex Offender Law Report* 14(2): 21–23.
Perillo, Anthony D., Ashley H. Spada, Cynthia Calkins, and Elizabeth L. Jeglic. 2014. "Examining the Scope of Questionable Diagnostic Reliability in Sexually Violent Predator (SVP) Evaluations. *International Journal of Law and Psychiatry* 37(2): 90–197.
Prentky, Robert A., Anna I. Coward, and Adeena M. Gabriel. 2008. "Muddy Diagnostic Waters in the SVP Courtroom." *Journal of the American Academy of Psychiatry and the Law* 36: 455–458.
Quinsey, Vernon L., Grant T. Harris, Marnie E. Rice, and Catherine A. Cormier. 1998. *Violent Offenders: Appraising and Managing Risk*. Washington, DC: American Psychological Association.
Salekin, Randall T., Richard Rogers, and Kenneth W. Sewell. 1996. "A Review and Meta-Analysis of the Psychopathy Checklist and Psychopathy Checklist–Revised: Predictive Validity of Dangerousness." *Clinical Psychology: Science and Practice* 3: 203–215.
Schopp, Robert F. 1991. *Automatism, Insanity, and the Psychology of Criminal Responsibility: A Philosophical Inquiry*. New York: Cambridge University Press.
Schopp, Robert F., Marc Pearce, and Mario J. Scalora. 1998. "Expert Testimony and Sexual Predator Statutes After Hendricks." *Expert Evidence* 6: 1–21.
Schopp, Robert F., Mario, J. Scalora, and Marc Pearce. 1999. "Expert Testimony and Professional Judgment: Psychological Expertise and Commitment as a Sexual Predator After Hendricks." *Psychology, Public Policy, and Law* 5: 120–174.
Spitzer, Robert L. 1986. *Memo to Advisory Committee on Paraphilias*. Washington, DC: APA Library.
Terry, Karen J. 2006. *Sexual Offenses and Offenders: Theory, Practice, and Policy*. Belmont, CA: Thompson/Wadsworth.
Thornton, David. 2002. "Constructing and Testing a Framework for Dynamic Risk Assessment." *Sexual Abuse: A Journal of Research and Treatment* 14(2): 139–153.
U.S. v. Comstock, 130 S. Ct. 1949 (2010).
Washington State Institute for Public Policy. 2007. Comparison of State Laws Authorizing Involuntary Commitment of Sexually Violent Predators: 2006 Update, Revised. Retrieved March 29, 2016 from www.wsipp.wa.gov/ReportFile/989/Wsipp_Comparison-of-State-Laws-Authorizing-Involuntary-Commitment-of-Sexually-Violent-Predators-2006-Update-Revised_Full-Report.pdf.
Willmsen, Christine. 2012. "State Wastes Millions Helping Sex Predators Avoid Lockup." *Seattle Times*. Retrieved March 29, 2016 from http://SeattleTimes.com/html/ localnews/2017301107_civilcomm22. html
Wilson, Robin J. 1998. "Psychophysiological Signs of Faking in the Phallometric Test." *Sexual Abuse: A Journal of Research and Treatment* 10: 113–126.
Witt, Philip H., and Mary A. Conroy. 2009. *Evaluation of sexually violent predators*. New York: Oxford University Press.
Wollert, Richard. 2007. "Poor Diagnostic Reliability, the Null-Bayes Logic Model, and Their Implications for Sexually Violent Predator Evaluations." *Psychology, Public Policy, and Law* 13: 167–203.

43 Felon Disenfranchisement

C. Cory Lowe and Bryan Lee Miller

Introduction

The question of who should be included and excluded in the democratic process has been the source of internal tension in democracies since classical antiquity (Ewald 2002; Pettus 2013). Ancient Athens is touted as the "prototypical democracy" even though women were denied the right to vote and slavery was commonplace (Katz 1997: 4). In the past 200 years, however, the world has witnessed the proliferation of democracies and an expansion of the right to vote (Blais, Massicotte, and Yoshinaka 2001). Today, universal adult suffrage has been idealized as the *sine qua non* of liberal democracy in the Universal Declaration of Human Rights (United Nations 1948). Although universal suffrage is the ideal, most democracies restrict the right to vote on the basis of age, mental disability and illness, citizenship, residency, and criminal conviction (Blais et al. 2001). Felon disenfranchisement, or the loss of voting rights, is a collateral consequence of felony conviction. Such consequences are called "collateral" because they are "typically located outside the penal code, implemented by non-criminal justice institutions, and interpreted as civil regulations rather than criminal penalties" (Uggen and Stewart 2015: 1875).

During the past two decades, there has been a renewed and growing scholarly interest in felon disenfranchisement across several disciplines. Much of the renewed interest among American scholars can be attributed to the contested 2000 U.S. presidential election which, for reasons discussed later, highlighted the political consequences of felon disenfranchisement. However, there has been a growing global interest in expanding the franchise since the international resurgence of democracy after World War II (Hull 2009; Keyssar 2000; Whitman 2003), and democracies have generally been moving towards "re-enfranchising" prisoners (Ewald and Rottinghaus 2009; Ispahani 2006; Uggen and Inderbitzin 2010).

In recent years, some jurisdictions in the U.S. have also liberalized their policies on felon disenfranchisement (Eisenberg 2012; Ewald 2009; Porter 2010), and between 1960 and 2002 the "number of states that disenfranchise some or all ex-felons dropped from 36 to 14" (Yoshinaka and Grose 2005:50). However, the U.S. remains an outlier among liberal democracies in both the application and scope of disenfranchisement (Ewald and Rottinghaus 2009; Ziegler 2011). Uggen, Van Brakle, and McLaughlin (2009) surveyed 105 nations and found that 40 allowed prisoners to vote while incarcerated, while the other 65 nations disenfranchised citizens during incarceration. In the U.S., Maine and Vermont are the only states that allow incarcerated felons to vote (Uggen, Shannon, and Manza 2012). The policies of the remaining 48 states and the District of Columbia comprise what officials with the U.S. Department of Justice have referred to as "a national crazy-quilt of disqualifications and restoration procedures" (Love, Kuzma, and Waters 1996). This "crazy-quilt" consists of 48 jurisdictions that bar prisoners from voting, among which 22 also disenfranchise those under direct state supervision (i.e. parole and probation), and 12 disenfranchise some or all felons after the completion of their sentence (Chung 2016).

These policies have had significant consequences for the voting population. The U.S. disenfranchises more citizens post-incarceration than any other democratic country (Ispahani 2006), and an estimated 5.85 million American citizens are prohibited from voting because of a felony conviction (Uggen et al. 2012). Further, since minorities and the poor are disproportionately represented in the criminal justice system, disenfranchisement disproportionally affects the poor and people of color (Manza and Uggen 2006). Whether this effect is intentional has been the source of debate and legal challenge. U.S. federal courts have often examined the historical foundations of felon disenfranchisement policies to determine their constitutionality; therefore, to better understand these policies in relation to their consequences we must explore their historical, political, and philosophical foundations.

Historical Foundations of Felon Disenfranchisement

Political status can be summarized as an individual's power, privileges, and obligations relative to others' in a political community that decides who gets what, when, and how (Benoit-Smullyan 1944; Lasswell 1936). Political statuses delineate the boundaries of the body politic, thus serving to include and exclude individuals and groups (Ewald 2002). It should be no surprise then, that political statuses have been used since classical antiquity to control crime and punish criminals (Pettus 2013; Whitman 2003). The right to vote, or franchise, is an element of political status that holds both instrumental and symbolic significance. Over time, the U.S. has become more democratic and has come to guarantee the rights of broader segments of the population. However, this progress is being threatened by the dramatic increase in incarceration as well as the increasing number of collateral consequences that are attached to conviction (Gottschalk 2014). As Ewald (2013: 335) noted, in 1860, the incarceration rate was about 61 people per 100,000 residents, while in 2010 the figure was closer to 500 per 100,000. Because of this trend and the expansion of collateral sanctions, Gottschalk (2008: 245) argued that "gradations of citizenship are on their way to becoming a new norm in America," where entire categories of people receive differential treatment on the basis of criminal conviction. Although the United States is unique in its application and scope of these sanctions, collateral consequences have a long history in Western society. Pettus (2013) explored the genealogy of felon disenfranchisement, and traced its roots in Greek *atimia* (dishonor), Roman *infamia* (infamy), and later European practices of civil death and outlawry.

In classical antiquity, criminals who were proclaimed "infamous" were prohibited from various civic activities including voting, serving on juries, holding public office, and making public speeches (Ewald 2002; Holloway 2014). Others were outright banished from the community or executed, which are forms of the ultimate exclusion from the body politic. After the fall of the Roman Empire, Germanic tribes relied on outlawry to "punish those who committed particular crimes involving serious harm . . . and to compel wrongdoers to obey orders of the court" (Itzkowitz and Oldak 1973: 722). "Outlaws" were considered to be "outside the law," and could be killed on sight without penalty (Itzkowitz and Oldak 1973; Pettus 2013; Roth 2011). In England, the practice of attainder led to a person's "civil death," which meant they "could not perform any legal function" (Ewald 2002: 1059). Attainder not only put one "outside of the law," but also punished capital crimes with the forfeiture of property (to the king) and "corruption of blood," which removed all rights to inheritances or to transmit titles and property to heirs (Blackstone and Sprague 1915; Itzkowitz and Oldak 1973; Pettus 2013). The common law tradition of civil death is the thread that connects the American tradition of felon disenfranchisement directly to England's practice of civil death (Pettus 2013).

However, the American Revolution marked a break with England and a radical change in the structure of government, the understanding of rights, and the nature of relationships in society (Wood 1992). In the Declaration of Independence, Thomas Jefferson posited that:

> We hold these truths to be self-evident, that all men are created equal, that they are endowed by their Creator with certain inalienable Rights, that among these are Life, Liberty and the Pursuit of Happiness. That to secure these rights, Governments are instituted among Men, deriving their just powers from the consent of the governed.
>
> (United States of America 1776)

The U.S. founders sought to implement a government where the power to govern belonged to those who are governed. In 1789, David Ramsey, one of the first historians of the American Revolution, considered the change that had taken place and stated:

> A citizen of the United States [is] a member of this new nation. The principle of government [was] radically changed by the revolution, [and] the political character of the people was also changed from subjects to citizens. The difference is immense. Subject is derived from the Latin words, *sub* and *jacio*, and means one who is under the power of another; but a citizen is [a] unit of a mass of free people, who, collectively, possess sovereignty.
>
> (Ramsay 1789: 3)

These statements, taken together, summarize early American thinking on rights; rights were not mere privileges that were to be granted or denied without due process, they were essential in-born characteristics of citizens. This belief was established in Article 1, Section 9 of the U.S. Constitution, which prohibits bills of attainder. However, this did not end civil death, it just required that the judicial process precede the removal of rights.

Even though Ramsay and Jefferson both wrote loftily, it must be noted that they were both slave owners (Shaffer 1984), and that voting was restricted on the basis of race, gender, age, religion, and property ownership during their lives. This highlights an ever-present question in American history, which is, who should be included in the body politic and what rights should they have? After war, centuries of political battles, and massive social movements, Americans have answered this question with the prohibition of slavery and the universal suffrage of adult citizens, with the exception of the mentally ill and felons. The debate over felons' right to vote continues today.

Felon Disenfranchisement: The Debate

The U.S. founders and their enlightenment contemporaries argued that people are "endowed by their Creator with certain inalienable rights," therefore, arguments in support of felon disenfranchisement have approached the issue with the intent to limit the in-born right of self-government (Ewald 2002). In recent years, most scholarship has focused on the disproportionate effect that felon disenfranchisement laws have on racial minorities. However, most felon disenfranchisement laws were not directly created with the intent of disenfranchising racial minorities, which is why these laws have been so resilient in the face of legal challenges. Scholars have demonstrated that felon disenfranchisement policies were established for four general purposes: (1) responding to a breach of the social contract, (2) protecting society from the less virtuous, (3) deterring crime, and (4) politically incapacitating members of racial minorities (Dinan 2007; Ewald 2002; Uggen, Behrens, and Manza 2005). These roughly correspond to three of the four primary justifications for punishment:

(1) retribution, (2) incapacitation, and (3) deterrence. The fourth justification, rehabilitation, is typically associated with arguments for the restoration of voting rights (Miller and Spillane 2012a; Uggen et al. 2005).

Breach of social contract. Social contract theories generally posit that civil society is established through the mutual consent of the governed for the purposes of protecting certain rights (Boucher and Kelly 1994). Some proponents of felon disenfranchisement argued that criminals infringe on the rights of others, and in so doing, break the social contract, thus forfeiting their right to participate in self-government (Dinan 2007; Ewald 2002). This argument aligns most with retributive justifications for punishment. However, disenfranchisement is often applied to all felons, regardless of the nature of their crime, which is in direct conflict with the principle of proportionality. Early criminologists argued that punishments that were not proportional to the crime would be an unjust breach of the "contract between the state and its citizens" (Manza and Uggen 2006: 26). In some states, disenfranchisement is permanent, which means that the criminal will never be able to vote to change the laws that led to their punishment.

Protecting the ballot and maintaining civic virtue. Some have argued that felons should lose the franchise because they have proven that they lack the necessary virtue to participate in self-governance (Dinan 2007; Ewald 2002). This contrasts with social contract arguments in subtle but important ways. Throughout history, criminals have been incapacitated through mutilation, imprisonment, and/or death. Felon disenfranchisement politically incapacitates criminals by removing their ability to commit electoral crimes or shape the law according to their allegedly wicked intents (Dinan 2007; Ewald 2002); therefore, this is most closely aligned with an incapacitative justification for punishment. This argument was especially popular in the late nineteenth century, when the secret ballot and voter registration had not yet been widely adopted, and there was growing concern about voter fraud and vote buying (Keyssar 2000). It was also popular during the late nineteenth and early twentieth century because of the influx of immigrants who were widely seen as a threat to the political order (Bensel 2004; Ewald 2004).

This argument in support of felon disenfranchisement has been criticized on multiple grounds. First, there is no connection between many types of crime and election fraud. For example, Thompson (2002) noted that it does not follow that a person who breaks into an outhouse, or conspires to operate a motor vehicle without a license in Tennessee is likely to commit election fraud. Second, supporters of the civic-virtue arguments believe that if felons are allowed to vote that they will undermine the criminal law (Ewald 2004). Of course, it is easy to see how disenfranchising citizens based on fears of how they might vote is problematic. In fact, in *Carrington v. Rash*, the Supreme Court ruled that "[disenfranchising] a sector of the population because of the way they may vote is constitutionally impermissible" (1965: 94).

Deterrence. There is also the relatively straightforward argument of disenfranchising criminals for the purposes of deterring crime. These proponents argue that potential criminals will avoid committing crimes to avoid the penalty of disenfranchisement. Dinan (2007) found that this was a prominent argument in state constitutional convention debates throughout U.S. history. For example, a legislator in Maine argued that "young persons would be more cautious of committing crimes, and courts would be more careful of convictions, when they saw [disenfranchisement] as a result" (Maine 1894: 125). However, scholarship on deterrence has shown that this argument is tenuous. For punishments to have a deterrent effect, they must be swift, certain, and severe (Nagin 2013); felon disenfranchisement fails on at least two counts. First, felon disenfranchisement is a collateral civil sanction above and beyond the criminal penalty for offending. If imprisonment and other punishments contained in the criminal law do not deter a crime, then it is unlikely that civil penalties will have an effect sufficient to deter crime (Miller and Agnich 2015; Uggen et al. 2005). Second, felon disenfranchisement is an "invisible punishment" and is often not even considered by judges, prosecutors, and/or defense attorneys in the justice process, therefore it is unlikely that offenders fully understand the potential civil consequences of conviction (Travis 2005). If potential criminals do not recognize that disenfranchisement is a possible consequence, then it is unlikely there is any deterrent effect.

Racist political motivations. Finally, some legislators have supported felon disenfranchisement for the express purpose of disenfranchising black voters, and clearly these policies have had disproportionate effect on racial minorities. However, we have also seen that there are a number of "race-neutral" arguments in support of felon disenfranchisement. These "race-neutral" arguments complicate historical analysis of the role that racial animus has played in the development of felon disenfranchisement policies. Nevertheless, there is circumstantial and direct evidence that some felon disenfranchisement laws were passed with the intent of politically incapacitating members of minority groups. To better understand the role that racism played in the development and expansion of these policies, we must consider felon disenfranchisement in the context of a broader set of policies that sought to disenfranchise racial minorities.

In 1870, 90 percent of all blacks in the U.S. lived in the American South. Several Southern states had majority black populations, including South Carolina (58.9 percent), Mississippi (53.7 percent) and Louisiana (50.1 percent), while other states had black populations that exceeded 40 percent of the state population including Virginia (41.9 percent), Alabama (47.7 percent), Georgia (46.0 percent), and Florida (48.8 percent; Gibson and Jung 2002). After the Civil War and Reconstruction, many states, and particularly those in the South, began enacting policies with the express intent of limiting the black vote such as poll taxes, literacy tests, grandfather clauses, and understanding clauses (Keyssar 2000). At the same time, these states were adopting allegedly "race-neutral" criminal disenfranchisement policies. In fact, 9 of the 11 former Confederate States established their first felon disenfranchisement laws after the Civil War and Reconstruction (Manza and Uggen 2006). However, by this time felon disenfranchisement had been established in most states on the basis of civic-virtue and social contract arguments (Dinan 2007; Keyssar 2000).

There is direct evidence of racial animus in the formation and expansion of some criminal disenfranchisement laws. For example, the president of Alabama's 1901 State Constitutional Convention, John B. Knox, argued:

> So far as the exclusion of the negro race is concerned, any scheme which could be devised for the purpose of separating the competent from the incompetent would exclude more negroes tha[n] white men for the reason that the negro is so unfortunate as to be wanting in those qualities which go to make a good citizen. If you select the education test, . . . the test of ownership of property, . . . the test of patriotism, . . . the test of freedom from commission of crime—every such test, when properly applied, will exclude largely more of one race than another.
>
> (State of Alabama 1940: 2924–2925)

The author of Alabama's felon disenfranchisement amendment, John Fielding Burns, included the crimes of "vagrancy, living in adultery, and wife beating" in the amendment specifically because they "were thought to be more commonly committed by blacks" (*Hunter v. Underwood* 1985: 232). In 1985, Alabama's disenfranchisement provisions were declared unconstitutional in *Hunter v. Underwood* (1985). Justice Rehnquist cited Knox and Burns in the majority opinion which, declared that the 1901 provisions violated the Equal Protection Clause of the Fourteenth Amendment because they "had been expressly adopted and designed to target black voters" (Re and Re 2012). Other states also attempted to disenfranchise blacks by including minor crimes that blacks were allegedly prone to commit, notably in Virginia, South Carolina, Georgia and Mississippi (Kousser 1999; Shapiro 1993).

In a study of 114 Constitutional Conventions, Alabama's 1901 Convention was the only one where racist intentions were voiced during debate (Dinan 2007). However, this study only included state constitutional conventions with existing debate records, and did not examine debates over piecemeal amendments to constitutions or other legislation. Therefore, most of the Southern constitutional conventions were excluded because the records simply do not exist. The study found that the majority of the debates revolved around felon disenfranchisement for the purposes of preserving civic virtue, responding to breaches of the social contract, and deterring crime (Dinan 2007). The history of motivations for creating felon disenfranchisement creates a legal quandary in which a law is deemed constitutional despite its immense and disproportionate effect on racial minorities. The inequities that are produced by felon disenfranchisement seem to stand in opposition to the egalitarian spirit of the Fourteenth and Fifteenth Amendments, as well as the Voting Rights Act. However, the constitutionality of felon disenfranchisement rests largely on Section 2 of the Fourteenth Amendment.

Legal Challenges to Felon Disenfranchisement

There have been many challenges to felon disenfranchisement in U.S. Courts, and scholars have proposed a number of strategies for challenging felon disenfranchisement in the future. However, felon disenfranchisement has remained durable in the face of most legal challenges, which is largely due to Section 2 of the Fourteenth Amendment. Felon disenfranchisement has also been challenged on the basis of the Voting Rights Act, Eighth Amendment, Fifteenth Amendment, Twenty-fourth Amendment, and the Attainder Clause of Article 1, Section 8 of the U.S. Constitution. Here we present an overview of the relevant case law regarding felon disenfranchisement.

Fourteenth Amendment Challenges

In 1974, the felon disenfranchisement provisions of California's Constitution and statutes were challenged before the U.S. Supreme Court in *Richardson v. Ramirez* (1974). In *Richardson*, three plaintiffs had been prohibited from registering to vote on the basis of their prior criminal conviction, and argued that they had been denied the equal protection of the laws provided by Section 1 of the Fourteenth Amendment. However, the court ruled that California's provisions did not violate the Equal Protection Clause, because Section 2 contains an "affirmative sanction" for disenfranchisement of those convicted of "rebellion, or other crime" (1974: 55). *Richardson v. Ramirez* is generally recognized "as having closed the door on [equal protection challenges] to state statutory voting disqualifications for conviction of crime" (*Allen v. Ellisor* 1981: 395).

However, *Richardson v. Ramirez* did not foreclose all equal protection challenges. As discussed earlier, an equal protection challenge was brought before the Supreme Court in *Hunter v. Underwood* (1985). Here the plaintiffs challenged Alabama's felon disenfranchisement on the grounds that the State provisions had been designed to intentionally disenfranchise blacks. The Supreme Court reviewed the historical record and found that the provisions were the product of racist motivations. The Court ruled that the Fourteenth Amendment was "not designed to permit . . . purposeful racial discrimination," and struck down felon disenfranchisement in Alabama (*Hunter v. Underwood* 1985: 233). However, some felon disenfranchisement provisions have been upheld, despite their racist origins. For example,

Mississippi's felon disenfranchisement law was upheld in *Cotton v. Fordice* when the Fifth Circuit found that "a facially neutral provision . . . might overcome its odious origins" (1998: 391). This precedent was cited in *Johnson v. Bush* where the court found that, despite "any invidious discriminatory purpose that may have prompted" Florida's 1868 felon disenfranchisement policy, it's 1968 revision "cleansed" it of any such scheme (2002: 1339). Alternatively, in *Williams v. Taylor* (1982), the appellant had been convicted of a crime that carried the consequence of disenfranchisement in Mississippi. Despite this, the appellant was allowed to vote for many years after completing his sentence until the Marshall County Board of Election Commissioners revoked his right to vote. The appellant claimed that this revocation was racially and politically motivated, and therefore, had been selectively enforced. Because the district court had ruled on the case without considering this point, the Fifth Circuit remanded the case to the district court thus leaving open the possibility of future equal protection challenges where selective enforcement is at issue.

Voting Rights Act Challenges

Likewise, selective enforcement of disenfranchisement provisions could also be challenged under the Voting Rights Act (VRA) of 1965 and its 1982 revisions. The VRA was enacted to enforce the Fifteenth Amendment which prohibited the denial or abridgement of the right to vote based on race, color, or previous condition of servitude. In 1982, this was revised to establish a "results test" in which policies would be prohibited based on whether they have racially discriminatory results, rather than the intent to discriminate (Handelsman 2004; Shapiro 1993). However, there has not been a successful VRA challenge to date. In *Hayden v. Pataki* (2006), the plaintiffs challenged New York's felon disenfranchisement policies on the grounds that they violated the 1982 revisions to the VRA. Despite the racially discriminatory results, the Second Circuit upheld felon disenfranchisement in New York citing a number of reasons, including the "explicit approval given such laws in the Fourteenth Amendment," the history of such provisions throughout the U.S., and the statements made by judiciary committees of the House and Senate "explicitly excluding felon disenfranchisement laws from provisions of the statute" (*Hayden v. Pataki* 2006: 315). Most recently, a VRA challenge was heard before a three-judge panel of the Ninth Circuit in *Farrakhan v. Gregoire* (2010a), which declared Washington's felon disenfranchisement provisions as unconstitutional and temporarily created a circuit split. However, the case was reconsidered later that year *en banc* and felon disenfranchisement was upheld (*Farrakhan v. Gregoire* 2010b).

Other Challenges

Felon disenfranchisement has also been challenged on the grounds that it violates other provisions of the Constitution. For example, in *Green v. Board of Elections* (1967), the plaintiff argued that felon disenfranchisement amounted to a bill of attainder, which is prohibited by Article 1, Section 9. However, the court ruled that the Attainder Clause only applies to statutes imposing penalties, and that felon disenfranchise was a "nonpenal exercise of the power to regulate the franchise" (1967: 449), which invalidated the challenge. A similar logic has been applied to challenges based on the Eighth Amendment's Cruel and Unusual Punishment Clause, in that if felon disenfranchisement is a regulation of the franchise and not a punishment, then it cannot be cruel and unusual (Thompson 2002). Finally, some have challenged felon disenfranchisement with the provision of the 24th Amendment which prohibits poll taxes or any other taxes as a requirement for voting. In many states there is a process for the restoration of voting rights; of course, this process often includes paying any fines, fees, or restitution as part of the sentence prior to being eligible to restore voting rights (Miller and Spillane 2012b). Some have challenged that these fines and fees amount to taxes that must be paid prior to voting; however, this challenge has failed in *Howard v. Gilmore* (2000) and *Johnson v. Bush* (2002) where the courts ruled that the payment of such fees was not simply a condition for the right to vote, because that right had already been removed, rather they are a condition for the restoration of the plaintiffs' civil rights.

Consequences of Felon Disenfranchisement

Because felon disenfranchisement has been so resilient in the face of legal challenges, scholars have argued that if felon disenfranchisement policies are to be changed, then it will likely require legislation at the state and federal level (Ewald 2013; Liles 2006). In recent years, legislatures throughout the nation have changed their felon disenfranchisement provisions (Eisenberg 2012). However, changing the laws in some states has been a daunting task fraught with high costs and legislative hurdles. For example, in 2015 there was a proposed ballot initiative in Florida to change the felon disenfranchisement provisions (Riggs 2015). In order to get the initiative on the 2016 ballot, the sponsors needed to collect valid petitions from 10 percent of Floridians; however, the sponsors of the initiative were only able to collect 59,484 signatures of the required 683,149 (Florida Department of State 2016). Legislative proposals to change felon disenfranchisement provisions also face the obvious challenge of changing the law without the support of those who are most affected by the laws—disenfranchised felons. The political ramifications of felon disenfranchisement extend beyond simply changing disenfranchisement provisions; it also affects local, state, and federal elections throughout the United States.

Felon disenfranchisement has received increased scholarly attention ever since the contested 2000 U.S. presidential election, because it highlighted the political consequences of felon disenfranchisement. Manza and Uggen (2006) argue that both the 2000 and 2004 presidential elections, as well as numerous congressional and state elections would have had different outcomes if felons had been allowed to vote. They argue that felon disenfranchisement disproportionately affects minorities and the poor, which decreases the popular support that one party or another receives. In recent years, disenfranchisement has reduced the political base of the Democratic Party, whereas it reduced the popular support of Republicans from the Post-Civil War period until the mid-twentieth century (Manza and Uggen 2006). However, there are deeper consequences of felon disenfranchisement than the outcomes of elections, such as the effect that felon disenfranchisement has on political engagement within communities.

Effects of Felon Disenfranchisement on Political Engagement

There are ways that the political consequences of felon disenfranchisement can be addressed, especially in states where the right to vote is restored after the completion of sentences. Many ex-felons do not fully understand how conviction affects their rights (McCahon 2016), but some research has shown that by simply informing ex-felons that they are eligible to vote may increase political participation (Gerber, Huber, Meredith, Biggers, and Hendry 2015). However, Bowers and Preuhs (2009) found that, in addition to the immediate political consequences, felon disenfranchisement reduces political participation of *nonfelons* in black communities. They argue that disenfranchisement reduces "the probability that individuals will be exposed to families, social networks, or community norms that promote political participation" (Bowers and Preuhs 2009: 726). However, this is only one of many social consequences of felon disenfranchisement.

Social and Criminal Consequences of Felon Disenfranchisement

Approximately 600,000 prisoners are released from prison every year (Carson and Golinelli 2013) and they face a number of challenges to reentry and reintegration, including potential collateral consequences. Felon disenfranchisement is only one potential collateral consequence; others include losing eligibility for certain occupational licenses, public housing, student loans, and Temporary Assistance for Needy Families (TANF) benefits (Travis 2005). The cumulative effect creates a phenomenon that Uggen and Stewart (2015) have called "piling on." They borrowed this term from American football, and it is apt because it refers to "when one or more players jumps on top of a downed player after a tackle has been made." They go on to explain that "it is illegal because it is unnecessary, slows the progress of the game, and often results in serious injury" (Uggen and Stewart 2015: 1872).

Adam Winkler has argued that voting is a "meaningful participatory act through which individuals create and affirm their membership in the community and thereby transform their identities both as individuals and as part of a greater collectivity" (1993: 331). Maruna (2001: 7) has argued that successful reintegration relies on the development of "a coherent prosocial identity for themselves" of which civic engagement is part and parcel. Disenfranchisement removes the opportunity for an individual to affirm their identity as a member of their community by voting. While disenfranchisement may not be the most important concern for many ex-felons (Petersilia 2003), voting is still a very important aspect of one's place in society. The relative importance of voting in reintegration was voiced by a participant in a study on felon disenfranchisement and reintegration, who noted that the most important things were obtaining food, clothes, and shelter, but that "civil rights are the finishing touches on coming back to civilization and community, you know coming back to being a citizen" (Miller and Spillane 2012a: 418). Another participant explained his perceptions of how disenfranchisement affected his relationship to his community, stating:

> People look at me differently, because I'm a convicted felon, you know, so I don't feel like I'm part of the community, so, a lot of people who don't feel like they're a part of the community do other things: they either go back to selling drugs, smoking drugs, or doing crime.
>
> (Miller and Spillane 2012a: 415)

Manza and Uggen noted the difficulties of establishing a causal relationship between felon disenfranchisement and recidivism, stating that this "would require a large-scale longitudinal survey that tracked released felons in their communities and closely monitored changes in their criminal and political behavior" and lamented that "no such data exists" (2006: 129). However, using data from the Youth Development Survey, they found that among arrestees, 27 percent of nonvoters in their sample were rearrested, while only 12 percent of voters were rearrested (Manza and Uggen 2006: 131–133). Unfortunately, researchers currently lack the ability to establish a direct causal link between voting and recidivism.

Conclusion

In the past 30 years, scholars have made great strides in understanding the effects of felon disenfranchisement in contemporary society. Historians have explored the ideological foundations of disenfranchisement, legal scholars have challenged the constitutionality of the practice, and social scientists have sought to explain its consequences. Despite this growing body of scholarship, there are still many potential avenues for research. First, more research can be done on the relationship of disenfranchisement, reintegration, and recidivism.

If scholars find that there is a causal relationship between voting and recidivism, then it will also be important to examine strategies for increasing political engagement among ex-felons and at-risk populations.

Another opportunity for research is to examine whether felon disenfranchisement actually achieves the purposes of its advocates. In other words, we should answer whether felon disenfranchisement actually deters crime, preserves civic virtue, or whether it is an appropriate and effective form of retributive punishment. Twenty-three leading criminologists filed an amicus brief for *Farrakhan v. Gregoire* (2010a), and argued that felon disenfranchisement did not serve any of these purposes. The authors provided rational legal and theoretical arguments; however, they did not cite any studies that empirically tested whether felon disenfranchisement served its proposed legitimate purposes. Currently, the strongest empirical evidence available relating to felon disenfranchisement supports that these policies disproportionately impact the vote of racial minorities and the poor.

References

Allen v. Ellisor, 664 F.2d 391 (1981).

Benoit-Smullyan, Emile. 1944. "Status, Status Types, and Status Interrelations." *American Sociological Review* 9(2): 151–161.

Bensel, Richard Franklin. 2004. *The American Ballot Box in the Mid-Nineteenth Century*. New York: Cambridge University Press.

Blackstone, William, and William C. Sprague. 1915. *Blackstone's Commentaries, Abridged*. Chicago. IL: Callaghan.

Blais, André, Louis Massicotte, and Antoine Yoshinaka. 2001. "Deciding Who Has the Right to Vote: A Comparative Analysis of Election Laws." *Electoral Studies* 20(1): 41–62.

Boucher, David, and P.J. Kelly. 1994. *The Social Contract from Hobbes to Rawls*. London; New York: Routledge.

Bowers, Melanie, and Robert R. Preuhs. 2009. "Collateral Consequences of a Collateral Penalty: The Negative Effect of Felon Disenfranchisement Laws on the Political Participation of Nonfelons." *Social Science Quarterly* 90(3): 722–743.

Carrington v. Rash, 85 S. Ct. 775 (1965).

Carson, E. Ann and Daniela Golinelli. 2013. *Prisoners in 2012: Trends in Admissions and Releases, 1991–2012*. NCJ 243920. Washington, DC: Bureau of Justice Statistics.

Chung, Jean. 2016. "Felony Disenfranchisement: A Primer." *The Sentencing Project*. Retrieved May 26, 2016 from www.sentencingproject.org/publications/felony-disenfranchisement-a-primer/

Cotton v. Fordice, 157 F.3d 388 (1998).

Dinan, John. 2007. "The Adoption of Criminal Disenfranchisement Provisions in the United States: Lessons from the State Constitutional Convention Debates." *Journal of Policy History* 19(3): 282–312.

Eisenberg, Lynn. 2012. "States as Laboratories for Federal Reform: Case Studies in Felon Disenfranchisement Law." *NYU Journal of Legislation and Public Policy* 15: 539–583.

Ewald, Alec C. 2002. "'Civil Death': The Ideological Paradox of Criminal Disenfranchisement Law in the United States." *Wisconsin Law Review* 2002: 1045–1137.

Ewald, Alec C. 2004. "An 'Agenda for Demolition': The Fallacy and the Danger of the 'Subversive Voting' Argument for Felony Disenfranchisement." *Columbia Human Rights Law Review* 36(1): 109–144.

Ewald, Alec C. 2009. "Criminal Disenfranchisement and the Challenge of American Federalism." *Publius: The Journal of Federalism* 39(3): 527–556.

Ewald, Alec C. 2013. "Escape from the 'Devonian Amber': A Reply to Voting and Vice." *Yale Law Journal Online* 122: 319–837.

Ewald, Alec C., and Brandon Rottinghaus. 2009. *Criminal Disenfranchisement in an International Perspective*. Cambridge, UK: Cambridge University Press.

Farrakhan v. Gregoire, 590 F.3d 989 (2010a).

Farrakhan v. Gregoire, 623 F.3d 990 (2010b).

Florida Department of State. 2016. "Voter Restoration Amendment 14–01." *Florida Department of State, Division of Elections*. Retrieved June 13, 2016 from http://dos.elections.myflorida.com/initiatives/initdetail.asp?account=64388&seqnum=1

Gerber, Alan S., Gregory A. Huber, Marc Meredith, Daniel R. Biggers, and David J. Hendry. 2015. "Can Incarcerated Felons Be (Re) Integrated into the Political System? Results from a Field Experiment." *American Journal of Political Science* 59(4): 912–926.

Gibson, Campbell, and Kay Jung. 2002. *Historical Census Statistics on Population Totals by Race, 1790 to 1990, and by Hispanic Origin, 1790 to 1990, for the United States, Regions, Divisions, and States*. Washington, DC: Bureau of the Census.

Gottschalk, Marie. 2008. "Hiding in Plain Sight: American Politics and the Carceral State." *Annual Review of Political Science* 11(1): 235–260.

Gottschalk, Marie. 2014. "Democracy and the Carceral State in America." *The Annals of the American Academy of Political and Social Science* 651(1): 288–295.

Green v. Board of Elections of the City of New York, 380 F. 2d 445 (1967).

Handelsman, Lauren. 2004. "Giving the Barking Dog a Bite: Challenging Felon Disenfranchisement under the Voting Rights Act of 1965." *Fordham Law Review* 73: 1875–1940.

Hayden v. Pataki, 449 F.3d 305 (2006).

Holloway, Pippa. 2014. *Living in Infamy: Felon Disfranchisement and the History of American Citizenship*. New York: Oxford University Press.

Howard v. Gilmore, 205 F.3d 1333 (2000).

Hull, Elizabeth A. 2009. "Our 'Crooked Timber': Why Is American Punishment So Harsh." Pp. 79–108 in *Criminal Disenfranchisement in an International Perspective*, edited by A.C. Ewald and B. Rottinghaus. New York: Cambridge University Press.

Hunter v. Underwood, 105 S. Ct. 1916 (1985).

Ispahani, Laleh. 2006. *Out of Step with the World: An Analysis of Felony Disfranchisement in the US and Other Democracies*. New York: American Civil Liberties Union.

Itzkowitz, Howard, and Lauren Oldak. 1973. "Restoring the Ex-Offender's Right to Vote: Background and Developments." *American Criminal Law Review* 11(3): 721–770.

Johnson v. Bush, 214 F. Supp. 2d 1333 (2002).

Katz, Richard S. 1997. *Democracy and Elections*. New York: Oxford University Press.

Keyssar, Alexander. 2000. *The Right to Vote: The Contested History of Democracy in the United States*. New York: Basic Books.

Kousser, J. Morgan. 1999. *Colorblind Injustice: Minority Voting Rights and the Undoing of the Second Reconstruction*. Chapel Hill, NC: The University of North Carolina Press.

Lasswell, Harold D. 1936. *Politics: Who Gets What, When, and How*. London: Whittlesey House.

Liles, William Walton. 2006. "Challenges to Felony Disenfranchisement Laws: Past, Present, and Future." *Alabama Law Review* 58: 615–629.

Love, Margaret C., Susan M. Kuzma, and Keith Waters. 1996. *Civil Disabilities of Convicted Felons: A State-by-State Survey*. Washington, DC: U.S. Department of Justice, Office of the Pardon Attorney.

Maine. 1894. *The Debates and Journal of the Constitutional Convention of the State of Maine 1819–1820: and Amendments subsequently made to the Constitution*. Augusta, ME: Maine Farmers' Almanac Press.

Manza, Jeff, and Christopher Uggen. 2006. *Locked out: Felon Disenfranchisement and American Democracy*. New York: Oxford University Press.

Maruna, Shadd. 2001. *Making Good: How Ex-Convicts Reform and Rebuild Their Lives*. Washington, DC: American Psychological Association.

McCahon, David S. 2016. "Combating Misinformation in the Ex-Felon Population: The Role Probation and Parole Agencies Can Play to Facilitate Civic Reintegration in the United States." *Probation Journal* 63(1): 9–22.

Miller, Bryan Lee, and Laura E. Agnich. 2015. "Unpaid Debt to Society: Exploring How Ex-Felons View Restrictions on Voting Rights after the Completion of Their Sentence." *Contemporary Justice Review* 1–17.

Miller, Bryan Lee, and Joseph F. Spillane. 2012a. "Civil Death: An Examination of Ex-Felon Disenfranchisement and Reintegration." *Punishment & Society* 14(4): 402–428.

Miller, Bryan Lee and Joseph F. Spillane. 2012b. "Governing the Restoration of Civil Rights for Ex-Felons: An Evaluation of the Executive Clemency Board in Florida." *Contemporary Justice Review* 15(4): 413–434.

Nagin, Daniel S. 2013. "Deterrence in the Twenty-First Century." *Crime and Justice* 42(1): 199–263.

Petersilia, Joan. 2003. *When Prisoners Come Home: Parole and Prisoner Reentry*. New York: Oxford University Press.

Pettus, Katherine Irene. 2013. *Felony Disenfranchisement in America: Historical Origins, Institutional Racism, and Modern Consequences*. New York: LFB Scholarly Publishing.

Porter, Nicole D. 2010. *Expanding the Vote State Felony Disenfranchisement Reform, 1997–2010*. Washington, DC: Sentencing Project.

Ramsay, David. 1789. *A Dissertation on the Manner of Acquiring the Character and Privileges of a Citizen in the United States*. Charleston, S.C. Retrieved May 29, 2016 from http://quod.lib.umich.edu/e/evans/N17114.0001.001?rgn=main;view=fulltext

Re, Richard M., and Christopher M. Re. 2012. "Voting and Vice: Criminal Disenfranchisement and the Reconstruction Amendments." *Yale Law Journal* 121(7): 1584–1670.

Richardson v. Ramirez, 94 S. Ct. 2655 (1974).

Riggs, Allison J. 2015. "Felony Disenfranchisement in Florida: Past, Present and Future." *Journal of Civil Rights and Economic Development* 28(1): 107–123.

Roth, Mitchel P. 2011. *Crime and Punishment: A History of the Criminal Justice System*, 2nd ed. Belmont, CA: Wadsworth/Cengage Learning.

Shaffer, Arthur H. 1984. "Between Two Worlds: David Ramsay and the Politics of Slavery." *The Journal of Southern History* 50(2): 175–196.

Shapiro, Andrew L. 1993. "Challenging Criminal Disenfranchisement under the Voting Rights Act: A New Strategy." *The Yale Law Journal* 103(2): 537–566.

State of Alabama. 1940. *Official Proceedings of the Constitutional Convention of the State of Alabama, May 21st, 1901, to September 3rd, 1901*. Wetumpka: Wetumpka Printing Co. Retrieved May 28, 2016 from www.legislature.state.al.us/aliswww/history/constitutions/1901/proceedings/1901_proceedings_vol1/day55.html

Thompson, Mark E. 2002. "Don't Do the Crime If You Ever Want to Vote Again: Challenging the Disenfranchisement of Ex-Felons as Cruel and Unusual Punishment." *Seton Hall Law Review* 33: 167–205.

Travis, Jeremy. 2005. *But They All Come Back: Facing the Challenges of Prisoner Reentry*. Washington, DC: Urban Institute Press.

Uggen, Christopher, Angela Behrens, and Jeff Manza. 2005. "Criminal Disenfranchisement." *Annual Review of Law and Social Science* 1(1): 307–322.

Uggen, Christopher, and Michelle Inderbitzin. 2010. "The Price and the Promise of Citizenship: Extending the Vote to Non-Incarcerated Felons." in *Contemporary Issues in Criminal Justice Policy: Policy Proposals from the American Society of Criminology Conference*, edited by N. Frost, J.D. Freilich, and T.R. Clear. Belmont, CA: Wadsworth, Cengage Learning.

Uggen, Christopher, Sarah Shannon, and Jeff Manza. 2012. *State-Level Estimates of Felon Disenfranchisement in the United States, 2010*. Washington, DC: Sentencing Project.

Uggen, Christopher, and Robert Stewart. 2015. "Piling On: Collateral Consequences and Community Supervision." *Minnesota Law Review* 99(5): 1871–1912.

Uggen, Christopher, Mischelle Van Brakle, and Heather McLaughlin. 2009. "Punishment and Social Exclusion: National Differences in Prisoner Disenfranchisement." Pp. 59–78 in *Criminal Disenfranchisement in an International Perspective*, edited by A. Ewald and B. Rottinghaus. Cambridge, UK: Cambridge University Press.

United Nations. 1948. "The Universal Declaration of Human Rights." Retrieved May 28, 2016 from www.un.org/en/universal-declaration-human-rights/

United States of America. 1776. "The Declaration of Independence."

Whitman, James Q. 2003. *Harsh Justice: Criminal Punishment and the Widening Divide between America and Europe*. New York: Oxford University Press.

Williams v. Taylor, 677 F.2d 510 (1982).

Winkler, Adam. 1993. "Expressive Voting." *New York University Law Review* 68: 330–388.

Wood, Gordon S. 1992. *The Radicalism of the American Revolution*. New York: A.A. Knopf.

Yoshinaka, Antoine and Christian R. Grose. 2005. "Partisan Politics and Electoral Design: The Enfranchisement of Felons and Ex-Felons in the United States, 1960–99." *State and Local Government Review* 37(1): 49–60.

Ziegler, Reuven. 2011. "Legal Outlier, Again? U.S. Felon Suffrage: Comparative and International Human Rights Perspectives." *Boston University International Law Journal* 29: 197–266.

44 Reentry in the United States

A Review

Holly Ventura Miller

Introduction

The incarceration boom of the last three decades has resulted in a range of latent consequences for the criminal justice system including overcrowded prisons, strained correctional resources, and a sharp rise in the number of children with an incarcerated parent. One of the most significant challenges is the reintegration of offenders into society following a period of incarceration—commonly referred to as *reentry*. Reentry is not monolithic but rather encompasses a range of programmatic elements and approaches that aim to improve offender outcomes following release. Reentry programs most often focus on offender behavioral modification through cognitive behavioral interventions that may include additional components such as educational/vocational training and assistance, substance abuse treatment, or life skills development. Some reentry programs are situated entirely in community settings, while others begin during incarceration and continue following release. Ideally, reentry programs are intended to address the offender's multifaceted needs in areas such as housing, education, employment, mental health treatment, and addiction recovery. Overall, prior research has produced inconsistent findings regarding the effectiveness of reentry programs, as not all programs are equipped to address the full range of offenders' needs nor are programs necessarily individualized (Lattimore and Visher 2009; Petersilia 2004; Roman, Brooks, Lagerson, Chalfin, and Tereshchenko 2007; Seiter and Kadela 2003; Wilson and Davis 2006; Wright, Zhang, Farabee, and Braatz 2014).

Reentry presents a significant challenge for the criminal justice system and allied services such as health care and mental health agencies. There are currently more than two million Americans incarcerated in the nation's prisons and jails (1 in every 136 citizens) and an additional five million under some form of community supervision (i.e., probation or parole; 1 in every 32 citizens) (U.S. Bureau of Justice Statistics (BJS) 2016). More than 600,000 inmates are released from correctional facilities each year in the U.S., or about 2,000 individuals per day. Since more than 9 in 10 inmates are eventually released back to the community (BJS 2016), attention to offender needs has emerged as a leading policy shift in the system toward the rehabilitative ideal as a way to decrease recidivism and increase public safety (Petersilia 2004; Solomon, Osborne, LoBuglio, Mellow, and Mukamel 2008; Travis, 2005; Travis and Waul 2004).

The reentry movement received a boost from the passage of the Second Chance Act (SCA) in 2008, which appropriated millions of dollars for reentry funding. This legislation had several goals including expunging criminal records, providing services to high-risk offenders most in need, enhancing public safety, reducing correctional costs through recidivism reduction, and offering opportunities for studying the effectiveness of reentry and rehabilitation approaches (Council of State Governments 2013). The SCA Grant Program funds eight separate projects: demonstration projects for the planning and implementation of reentry initiatives for juveniles or adults; mentoring programs for juveniles or adults; family-based substance abuse treatment programs for incarcerated parents; reentry courts; programs for co-occurring offenders; state departments of correction; probation-specific programming; and training programs for technological careers. Juvenile programs are administered through the Office of Juvenile Justice and Delinquency Prevention (OJJDP), while adult programs are administered through the Bureau of Justice Assistance (BJA). Prior to the SCA, the federal government appropriated more than $100 million to fund the Serious and Violent Offender Reentry Initiative (SVORI) providing monies to all 50 states to implement initiatives designed to reduce recidivism among high-risk offenders (Lattimore and Visher 2009). These federal efforts, combined with what has been largely bipartisan and public support for prisoner reentry, have resulted in the implementation and evaluation of a significant number of initiatives.

Prison Reentry

The prisoner reentry literature suffers from a number of methodological shortcomings including a lack of experimental research that has produced largely inconsistent findings (MacKenzie 2012; Seiter and Kadela 2003; Visher, Lattimore, Barrick, and Tueller 2017; Vito and Tewksbury 1999; Wright et al. 2014). Prior research on reentry varies considerably in focus, ranging from rehabilitative approaches rooted in cognitive-behavioral therapy to work and vocational programs designed to increase job readiness. Many published evaluations have focused on the effectiveness of drug treatment while overlooking other program elements (Butzin, Scarpetti, Nielsen, Martin, and Inciardi 1999; Hiller, Knight, and Simpson 1999; Knight, Simpson, Chatham, and Camacho 1997; Knight, Simpson, and Hiller 1999; Miller and Miller 2011; Rhodes, Pelisser, Gaes, Saylor, Camp, and Wallace 2001; Wexler, Falkin, and Lipton 1990). During the 1990s and early 2000s, many programs focused on addiction treatment were rooted in the federal Residential Substance Abuse Treatment (RSAT) grant program, which provided monies to state prison systems to provide substance abuse treatment for inmates. Though these programs were not necessarily conceived or described as "reentry" programs at the time, they nonetheless represent the federal government's earlier efforts to reduce recidivism and relapse among returning drug offenders. Collectively, prior evidence produces modest support for the effectiveness of substance abuse treatment in reducing recidivism among returning offenders.

The Serious and Violent Offender Reentry Initiative (SVORI), the precursor to the SCA, has produced a wealth of evaluation research across its 89 sites. Lattimore and Visher (2009) evaluated 12 original SVORI sites reporting mixed results. Participants experienced favorable outcomes relative to a comparison group on variables such as housing and employment, but failed to have the expected reductions in reincarceration. Participation in SVORI had no effect on self-reported offending and by 24 months, both male and female offenders had a higher rate of incarceration than the comparison group. Visher, Lattimore, and colleagues also examined the effectiveness of *type* of reentry services to determine the most salient program components (Visher et al. 2017). Findings revealed the varied nature of SVORI initiatives, which included elements such as case management, life skills training, employment programming, CBT, and mental health treatment. Case management, anger management, and educational programs were associated with a lower incidence of recidivism (i.e., arrests), while life skills assistance, reentry classes, and employment services were associated with a shorter time to arrest.

An evaluation of Kansas' SVORI program reported that program participants had a greater incidence of failed urinalysis, more returns to prison, and fewer days released to the community (Severson, Bruns, Veeh, and Lee 2011). The Boston SVORI produced significantly lower failure rates for the treatment group on recidivism (i.e., arrest and violent arrest) (Braga, Piehl, and Hureau 2009). Time to arrest was also significantly longer for participants for all crime and violent crimes, in particular. Collectively, the SVORI literature paints an inconsistent picture of the effectiveness of reentry programming but does reveal some important empirical points. First, reentry programming is varied, making it difficult to compare one program or initiative to another. Second, much of what is considered critical to effective reentry is often neglected, even among well-funded initiatives (i.e., individualized reentry plans, case managers, CBT, medicated assisted treatment). Third, many evaluations lack adequate implementation and process components, making it difficult to discern the contextual realties of these failures.

Other research has also identified negative or inconclusive effects of reentry programming. New York's Project Greenlight is a large-scale reentry initiative shown to exert negative effects on program participants such that those who received treatment fared worse than members of an untreated comparison group (Wilson and Davis 2006). Project Greenlight was a CBT-oriented intervention that included substance abuse, housing, family counseling, and life skills training. Despite inclusion of individualized reentry plans and attention to other best practices, the treatment group experienced higher recidivism rates than those of the controls. Another large-scale effort, the Maryland Reentry Partnership Initiative, similarly failed to reduce the likelihood of rearrest among participants, but did lead to significant cost-savings for the state, especially in public health costs (Mellow and Griefinger 2007; Roman et al. 2007).

Jail Reentry

Although much of the extant literature relates the experiences and outcomes of prison-based reentry programming, the scientific knowledge on jails has increased in the past decade (see, for example, Lurigio, Fallon, and Dincin 2000; H. Miller and Miller 2010, 2015; Miller and Miller 2016; H. Miller, Miller, and Barnes 2016; M. Miller, Miller, and Barnes 2016; Osher 2006, 2007; Osher, Steadman, and Barr 2002; Solomon et al. 2008; Ward and Merlo 2016). The increase in jail-based reentry is due in large part to three factors: (1) SCA reentry funding made available to local municipalities, (2) state legislation that has reclassified many lower level felonies as punishable by sentence to jails (instead of state prisons), and (3) the burgeoning heroin epidemic which has increased the number of drug-involved offenders in local corrections, especially in suburban and rural areas. Although jail sentences are shorter compared to prisons, the sheer number of offenders cycling through the nation's local correctional facilities provides a unique opportunity to intervene in the criminal trajectories of lower level offenders and increase the likelihood of successful reentry.

Similar to larger prison reentry literature, prior jail-based studies have reported inconsistent levels of effectiveness across program approaches. In an early study of jail reentry in NYC, Freudenberg and colleagues (1998) found that women who participated in pre- and post-release substance abuse treatment had lower rates of offending compared to non-participants. In a more recent study of reentry programming at Rikers Island, however, White and colleagues (2012) reported that participants had no better outcomes than the comparison group. The results did show that those who completed at least 90 days of post-release services (i.e., aftercare) had significantly fewer returns to jail and a greater number of days in the community following release. Most recently, additional research in the NYC jail system reported that CBT for inmates suffering from co-occurring mental disorders was able to significantly reduce recidivism compared to a matched comparison group (Glowa-Kollisch, Lim, Summers, Cohen, Selling, and Venters 2014).

Miller and colleagues have examined the effectiveness of a number of recently funded SCA jail-based reentry initiatives (Auglaize County, OH ACT Program; Delaware County, OH DCT Program and Substance Abuse Treatment Program; Middle Tennessee Rural Reentry Initiative). Each of these programs was designed in accordance with reentry best practices and implemented with varying degrees of program fidelity. Outcome evaluations revealed inconsistent levels of program success, though generally positive. For example, the ACT program, which is featured on crimesolutions.gov as a "promising" rural reentry program, was found to be effective in reducing the likelihood of rearrest for the first cohort (Miller and Miller 2010) but not for the second (H. Miller and Miller 2015). The DCT program, modeled after the nearby ACT, also produced somewhat inconsistent findings. Participants in the DCT program had significantly lower rates of recidivism relative to the comparison group (70.15 percent of comparison group recidivated versus 32.35 percent of treatment group) and also had significantly lower odds of probation revocation. No significant differences were found, however, between the two groups on new charge recidivism. The number of days to recidivism was also significantly longer for the treatment group (Miller, Miller, and Barnes 2014; H. Miller, Miller, and Barnes 2016). Finally, this author group studied the effectiveness of a family-based reentry program housed in the same jail facility (Delaware County Jail) designed for male offenders with histories of addiction and familial dysfunction. Results from a quasi-experimental design revealed significant differences in the rate of recidivism between program participants (27.7 percent) and a comparison group (75 percent), while participation significantly lowered the odds of both new-charge recidivism and any recidivism. No significant differences were found between the treatment and comparison groups for probation revocations, and similar to the DCT program, the number of days to recidivism was longer for the treatment group (M. Miller, Miller, and Barnes 2016).

Prior research in jails has also focused on mental health and drug-using behavior in addition to recidivism related outcomes (e.g., rearrest, reincarceration, probation violation) as a means of evaluating program impact. Gordon, Barnes, and VanBenschoten (2006) evaluated a jail diversion program for mentally ill offenders and reported that participants showed signs of mental health improvement along with reductions in substance use and serious offending. Lamberti and colleagues (2001) assessed a program for justice-involved mentally ill patients and found the program to be effective in reducing recidivism and improving community adjustment among participants. In a mainly descriptive study, Spjeldnes, Jung, Maguire, and Yamatni (2012) reported that post-release factors such as family support were associated with lower levels of self-reported substance use among offenders, although this study did not use a rigorous causal design (i.e., experimental or quasi-experimental design). With respect to treatment outcomes, prior research also indicated that jail-based programs can significantly improve the likelihood of entering treatment, maintaining treatment after release, and avoiding relapse (Scott and Dennis 2012).

Though much of the reentry literature is purely quantitative in nature, other research has employed mixed-methodological designs to identify additional aspects of program effectiveness or benefits not accurately measured through outcome designs. For example, Bahr and his colleagues (2012) interviewed a sample of Utah jail inmates and reported that treatment group participants experienced elevated recognition of the consequences of their behavior and altered their perspective regarding drug use. Research also has indicated that participation in programming is associated with a range of positive outcomes including fewer inmate altercations, improved facility climate, and improved race relations (Miller 2014). Given the shortcomings of purely quantitative outcome analyses, reentry research can benefit from mixed methods designs spanning implementation and process phases (in addition to outcome) by identifying the elements of programming perceived as most effective by participants, contextualizing quantitative findings, determining offender engagement, and, perhaps most importantly, establishing program fidelity (Miller 2014; M. Miller and Miller 2015, 2016; Miller, Tillyer, and Miller 2012).

Best Practices in Reentry

A number of studies have attempted to review, categorize, or meta-analyze reentry research in an effort to determine "what works". In a review of reentry programs spanning more than two decades, Seiter and Kadela (2003) categorized evaluations according to the Maryland Scientific Ratings Scale to determine the strength of the evidence for various reentry approaches. Their review identified vocational and work assistance initiatives that attempt to develop particular marketable skills or trades as one of the most promising reentry strategies capable of exerting a modest effect on recidivism and relapse rates. Prior work has indicated these programs reduce recidivism (or time to recidivism), improve job readiness, and decrease incidence of inmate misconduct (Duwe 2015; Finn 1999; Saylor and Gaes 1992, 1997; Turner and Petersilia 1996), although some recent research has produced less positive evidence (Visher et al. 2017). Seiter and Kadela's review (2003) also showed that halfway houses (Dowell, Klein, and Krichmar 1985; Seiter 1975) and cognitive-behavioral therapies for violent and sex offenders (Barberee, Seto, and Maric 1996; Robinson 1996) hold promise for reducing recidivism.

In a narrative review of prisoner reentry research between 2000 and 2010, Wright and his colleagues (2014) found that the most common components in reentry programs were life skills and substance abuse treatment while those that provided aftercare and housing assistance were most likely to produce favorable results. Surprisingly, programs that included CBT produced the least favorable outcomes (Wright et al. 2014: 51). Jonson and Cullen (2015) assessed the reentry literature within the context of the RNR (risks, needs, responsibility) model (Andrews, Bonta, and Hoge 1990) and concluded that reentry programming is most effective when it provides a continuity of care, is implemented with fidelity, targets high-risk offenders, and employs therapeutic communities.

In an effort to make sense of the divergent literature on reentry (among other topics), the National Institute of Justice (NIJ) created crimesolutions.gov, a publicly available website designed to rate criminal justice policies and practices as "effective," "promising," or "no effects." NIJ surveys the extant literature for experimental and quasi-experimental research that informs best practices in reentry and then summarizes the relevant information for general public consumption. Crimesolutions.gov offers a centralized location to disseminate accessible information about the scientific knowledge base related to a variety of programs and practices.

Table 44.1 presents a summary of the reentry programs and practices currently rated as "effective" or "promising" by crimesolutions.gov. Programs that are not reentry per se but rather single approach rehabilitative initiatives are not included. For Table 44.1, reentry program or practice is conceived as a system of continuous care that begins in custody and continues following release. Under these criteria, there are significantly fewer programs and practices than are listed under a general "reentry" search on crimesolutions.gov.

Second Chance Act grant funding has adopted its own definitions and criteria of what is considered "best practices" in reentry and outlines these each year in their annual requests for proposals. The most recent criteria identified by the Bureau of Justice Assistance (BJA) in their 2016 Second Chance Act Reentry Program for Adults with Co-occurring Substance Abuse and Mental Health Disorders include 16 interrelated components that all applicants must incorporate into program design and implementation in order to be considered for funding. These elements include: (1) use of an actuarial risk screening instrument, (2) target

Table 44.1 Reentry Programs Rated Effective or Promising on Crimesolutions.gov

Program	*Rating*	*Description*[1]	*No. of Studies*
Amity In-Prison Therapeutic Community	Promising	Provides intensive treatment to male inmates with substance abuse problems during the last 9 to 12 months of their prison term. The volunteer participants must reside in a dedicated program housing unit during treatment. The program is rated Promising. Overall, participants had lower levels of reincarceration rates compared to the control groups.	3
Auglaize County (OH) Transition Program (ACT)	Promising	The program works to reduce recidivism of jail inmates once they reenter the community, in part by linking inmates to various resources. The program is rated Promising. The program was successful in reducing recidivism rates among participants.	2
Boston Reentry Initiative	Promising	An interagency public safety initiative to help incarcerated violent adult offenders transition back to their neighborhoods following release from jail through mentoring, social service assistance, and vocational development. The program is rated Promising. The study found participants, relative to the control group, had significantly lower failure rates, arrests for violent crime, or arrests for any crime. The differences between the two groups narrowed somewhat over time.	1
Community Based Residential Programs (OH)	Promising	The programs include halfway houses and community-based correctional facilities in Ohio. The goal of the community-based correctional programs is to reduce recidivism by offering a wide range of programming related to chemical dependency, education, employment, and family relationships. The program is rated Promising. Offenders in community-based residential programs were less likely to recidivate (measured by new arrests and re-incarcerations) than those not in the programs.	1
Delaware KEY/Crest	Promising	A prison-based therapeutic community for offenders with a history of substance abuse and a residential work release center that allows offenders to continue their treatment as they transition to the community. The program is rated Promising. Program completers and aftercare recipients were less likely to be arrested or use drugs. Also, the treatment group did better at follow-up in remaining arrest- and drug-free.	3
Forever Free	Promising	The first comprehensive, in-prison, residential substance abuse treatment program designed for incarcerated women. The program is rated Promising. The intervention group reported fewer arrests during parole, less drug use and were employed more at follow-up than the comparison group.	1

Table 44.1 continued

Program	*Rating*	*Description*[1]	*No. of Studies*
Mental Health Services Continuum Program	Promising	The program targets parolees with mental health problems and provides services to enhance their level of individual functioning in the community. The overall goal is to reduce recidivism of mentally ill parolees and improve public safety. The program is rated Promising. Parolees who participated in the program and received a pre-release assessment or who had one or more contacts with the Parole Outpatient Clinic showed a significant reduction in the odds of being returned to custody.	1
Modified Therapeutic Community for Offenders with Mental Illness and Chemical Abuse (MICA) Disorders	Promising	An adaptation of the therapeutic community models for use with offenders who have both drug abuse problems and mental health disorders. This modified version uses a more flexible, more personalized, and less intense program that targets reductions in substance use and recidivism. The program is rated Promising. Participants in the treatment group were less likely to abuse substances; and if they did start, it was later than the control group.	1
Offender Reentry Community Safety Program	Promising	Formerly called the Dangerous Mentally Ill Offender Program, this is a reentry-planning and service program aimed at reducing recidivism for dangerously mentally ill offenders in Washington State. The program is rated Promising. Program participants had significantly lower violent felony and overall felony recidivism rates compared with the matched control group 4 years following release from prison.	1
Prison Initiated Methadone Treatment (practice)	Promising	This program offers methadone maintenance to heroin-addicted prisoners and provides referrals to community-based treatment programs to encourage continued treatment during reentry. The program is rated Promising. The counseling + methadone group were significantly more likely to spend more days in treatment compared to the other groups. There were fewer positive urine drug tests for opioids and cocaine for the counseling + methadone group compared to those who received counseling only in prison.	2
Opiate Maintenance Therapy (practice)	Effective	A medication-assisted treatment for opioid dependence, including methadone, buprenorphine, and Levo-Alpha-Acetymethadol (LAAM). The overall goals are to help opioid-addicted patients alleviate withdrawal symptoms, reduce or suppress opiate cravings, and reduce the illicit use of opioids (such as heroin). The practice is rated Effective for achieving higher sustained heroin abstinence for dual heroin–cocaine abusers, but No Effects for cocaine abstinence for dual abusers.	1

[1] Descriptions are from crimesolutions.gov; search term = reentry

high-risk offenders, (3) establish baseline recidivism and collect/report recidivism data, (4) enhance intrinsic motivation, (5) target criminogenic needs, (6) determine dosage and intensity of services, (7) provide evidence-based substance use and mental disorder treatment services, (8) provide integrated treatment for co-occurring disorders, (9) provide evidence-based pharmacological treatment, (10) cognitive-behavioral interventions, (11) transition planning procedures, (12) comprehensive range of recovery support services, (13) provide sustained aftercare and case planning/management in the community, (14) evidence-based community supervision following release, (15) data collection, management, and evaluation, and (16) strategies for increasing access to health care.

The criteria identified by BJA are comprehensive and intended to touch on many aspects of offender reentry. It is important to note that a number of these components are often overlooked or outright neglected in many reentry programs, including those that have received SCA funding. For example, medicated assisted treatment (MAT) for treatment of heroin, opioid, and alcohol addiction has been a staple of the public health response to substance abuse for more than four decades, although this has not translated into criminal justice policy (O'Brien and Cornish 2006). This is unfortunate because the rate of addiction among those involved in the criminal justice system is significantly higher than that of the general population, addiction is highly interrelated with criminality, and the system is actually one of the largest providers of drug treatment in the U.S. (Mumola and Karberg 2006; SAMHSA 2014). One of the most effective MAT strategies involves the use of extended-release naltrexone (XR-NTX) for opioid, opiate, and/or alcohol addiction disorders.

Naltrexone was first developed by the National Institute on Drug Abuse in the 1970s and approved by the FDA for the treatment of heroin addiction in 1984 and alcohol addiction in 1995 (O'Brien, Greenstein, Mintz, and Woody 1975; Greenstein, Arndt, McLellan, O'Brien, and Evans 1984; Volpicelli, Alterman, Hayashida, and O'Brien 1992). Earlier versions of naltrexone were administered orally, typically once or twice weekly, while the new sustained-release version is administered through injection that can last up to one month. Few studies have examined the use of naltrexone among system-involved individuals (Cornish et al. 1997; Coviello et al. 2012; Crits-Cristoph, Lundy, Stringer, Gallop, and Gastfriend 2015) and only one has addressed effectiveness of the newer extended release naltrexone—signaling the need for additional assessment. Recent research on parolees and probationers in Missouri who received either naltrexone, other MAT, or psychosocial counseling found those receiving extended-release naltrexone (XR-NTX) had longer duration of care and were more likely to become abstinent (Crits-Cristoph et al. 2015). Overall, prior evidence indicates that the use of naltrexone is associated with successful outcomes for those under community supervision and may be an important strategy for the larger reentry movement.

Discussion and Conclusions

The reentry movement has shifted the focus of correctional systems back to the rehabilitative ideal and spawned the rapid growth of many new programs and initiatives. Unlike rehabilitative efforts of the past, reentry ideally encompasses a broad, comprehensive, and holistic attempt to assist offenders in a successful return to the community. Reentry acknowledges that offenders tend to suffer from clusters of problems such as co-occurring psychiatric disorders, housing insecurity, unemployment, and poor physical health, and that the best way to ameliorate these issues is to target them in an integrated manner. Unfortunately, prior research has produced inconsistent findings regarding the effectiveness of reentry programs, as not all initiatives are equipped to address the full range of offenders' needs nor are programs necessarily individualized.

Despite the shortcomings of the extant literature, there have nonetheless been attempts to identify the most effective reentry practices. Generally, programs that feature a continuum of care that begins during incarceration and continues following release are best suited to assist the offender in a successful transition to the community. Optimal interventions begin with accurate screening and assessment using validated actuarial screening instruments and continue with individualized approaches that target criminogenic needs in programs that are implemented with high levels of fidelity. Successful reentry programs also provide critical aftercare and case management components that allow offenders to continue to receive services in the community and maintain connectivity to the treatment milieu that begins during incarceration.

Fundamentally, an increase in the number and quality of researcher–practitioner partnerships is necessary if reentry programs are to become institutionalized in corrections and operate at maximum effectiveness. A better effort is needed to disseminate academic knowledge to practitioner audiences, since many of the problems plaguing both reentry program operation and assessment are attributable to this gap. Reentry in the real world can suffer from poor program fidelity and disparate researcher–practitioner expectations, both of which can be reduced or avoided through careful planning and collaboration. Partnering with practitioners prior to the conception or at least implementation of a program is a necessity to ensure that the intervention is designed in accordance with best practices. Well-developed partnerships also allow for rigorous implementation and process evaluations that are critical to describing and documenting program components and operations as well as providing critical real time feedback to practitioners to increase adherence to fidelity. Successful researcher–practitioner partnerships also increase the chances of obtaining quality data for outcome analyses and may enable agreement for randomized designs.

The research designs employed by program evaluators also require improvement. There are far too few randomized control trials within the reentry literature and even fewer that feature mixed methodological implementation, process, and outcome phases. A mixed methods approach featuring both qualitative (interviews, observations) and quantitative (experimental/quasi-experimental design) techniques can better enable determinations of program fidelity than a single-method design. As noted by Miller and Miller (2016: 10):

> Establishing program fidelity in evaluation research is critical for several reasons. First, process evaluations can generate immediate feedback to practitioners for program improvement and document program accountability in terms of whether service providers are compliant with grant conditions and treatment delivery expectations. Process evaluation also enables collection of data directly from key program stakeholders including administrators, staff, and participants, as well as observation of program activities and content to ensure consistency with intervention design. Perhaps most importantly, program fidelity research can elucidate the "black box" of evaluation, through insight into how and why a program is or is not effective.

There are similar deficiencies with respect to outcome analyses. The vast majority of reentry evaluations have relied on quasi-experimental designs and often these are fairly weak, featuring unmatched comparison groups or, even worse, within-group single sample designs. The obvious solution is the use of randomized experiments within evaluation research but even this apparently simple solution is simple only to those unfamiliar with the criminal justice system as it operates day to day. Many judges are loath to randomly assign offenders to any kind of treatment program; conservatives often don't believe they deserve treatment and liberals often believe everyone deserves treatment. Unfortunately, researchers must work around these political realities when designing and conducting program evaluations.

The good news is that strong researcher–practitioner partnerships can make it more likely that randomization is achieved when explained fully to stakeholders and planned prior to program implementation. In lieu of true experiments, researchers should aim to utilize the most rigorous quasi-experimental approaches such as propensity score matching and regression discontinuity designs. Additional weak designs do little to add to the extant evidence and are a disservice to work done by reentry program staff. A best practices model of reentry cannot be realized until the body of research rests on strong experimental evidence.

References

Andrews, Don A., James Bonta, and Robert D. Hoge. 1990. "Classification for Effective Rehabilitation: Rediscovering Psychology." *Criminal Justice and Behavior* 17: 19–52.

Bahr, Stephen J., Paul E. Harris, Janalee Hobson Strobell, and Bryan M. Taylor. 2012. "An Evaluation of a Short-term Drug Treatment for Jail Inmates." *International Journal of Offender Therapy and Comparative Criminology* 57(10): 1275–1296.

Barbaree, H.E., M.T. Seto, and A. Maric. 1996. "Effective Sex Offender Treatment: The Warkworth Sexual Behavior Clinic." *Forum on Corrections Research* 8(3): 13–15.

Braga, Anthony A., Anne M. Piehl, and David Hureau. 2009. "Controlling Violent Offenders Released to the Community: An Evaluation of the Boston Reentry Initiative." *Journal of Research in Crime and Delinquency* 46(4): 411–436.

Butzin, Clifford A., Frank R. Scarpetti, A.L. Nielsen, Steven S. Martin, and J.A. Inciardi. 1999. "Measuring the Impact of Drug treatment: Beyond Relapse and Recidivism." *Corrections Management Quarterly* 3(4): 1–7.

Cornish, James W., David Metzger, George E. Woody, David Wilson, Thomas A. McLellan, Barry Vandergrift, and Charles P. O'Brien. 1997. "Naltrexone Pharmacotherapy for Opioid Dependent Federal Probationers." *Journal of Substance Abuse Treatment* 14(6): 529–534.

Coviello, Donna M., James W. Cornish, Kevin G. Lynch, Tamara Y. Boney, Cynthia A. Clark, Joshua D. Lee, Peter D. Friedmann, Edward V. Nunes, Timothy W. Knlock, Michael S. Gordon, Robert P. Schwartz, Elie S. Nuwayser and Charles P. O'Brien. 2012. "A Multisite Pilot Study of Extended-release Injectable Naltrexone Treatment for Previously Opioid-dependent Parolees and Probationers." *Substance Abuse* 33(1): 48–59.

Crits-Christoph, Paul, Christie Lundy, Mark Stringer, Robert Gallop, and David R. Gastfriend. 2015. "Extended-Release Naltrexone for Alcohol and Opioid Problems in Missouri Parolees and Probationers." *Journal of Substance Abuse Treatment* 56: 54–60.

Council of State Governments. 2013. *Second Chance Act*. Washington, DC: Author. Retrieved May 13, 2017 from http://csgjusticecenter.org/nrrc/projects/second-chance-act/

Dowell, David A., Cecelia Klein, and Cheryl Krichmar. 1985. "Evaluation of a Halfway House." *Journal of Criminal Justice* 13: 217–226.

Duwe, Grant. 2015. "The Benefits of Keeping Idle Hands Busy: An Outcome Evaluation of a Prisoner Reentry Employment Program." *Crime & Delinquency* 61(4): 559–586.

Finn, Peter. 1999. "Job Placement for Offenders: A Promising Approach to Reducing Recidivism and Correctional Costs." *National Institute of Justice Journal* 240: 2–11.

Freudenberg, Nicholas, Ilene Wilets, Michael B. Greene, and Beth E. Richie. 1998. "Linking Women in Jail to Community Services: Factors Associated with Rearrest and Retention of Drug-using Women Following Release from Jail." *Journal of the American Medical Women's Association* 53: 89–93.

Glowa-Kollisch, Sarah, Sungwoo Lim, Cynthia Summers, Louise Cohen, Daniel Selling, and Homer Venters. 2014. "Beyond the Bridge: Evaluating a Novel Mental Health Program in the New York City Jail System." *American Journal of Public Health* 104(11): 2212–2218.

Gordon, Jill A., Christina M. Barnes, and Scott W. VanBenschoten. 2006. "The Dual Treatment Track Program: A Descriptive Assessment of a Mew "In-House" Jail Diversion Program." *Federal Probation* 27(2): 9–18.

Greenstein, Robert A., C. Arndt, A.T. McLellan, C.P. O'Brien, and B. Evans. 1984. "Naltrexone: A Clinical Perspective." *Journal of Clinical Psychiatry* 45: 25–28.
Hiller, Mathew L., Kevin Knight, and D. Dwayne Simpson. 1999. "Prison-based Substance Abuse Treatment, Residential Aftercare and Recidivism." *Addiction*, 49(6): 833–842.
Jonson, Cheryl Lero and Francis T. Cullen. 2015. "Prisoner Reentry Programs." *Crime and Justice* 44: 517–557.
Knight, Kevin, D. Dwayne Simpson, Lois R. Chatham, and L. Mabel Camacho. 1997. "An Assessment of Prison-based Drug treatment: Texas' In-prison Therapeutic Community Program." *Journal of Offender Rehabilitation* 24(3/4): 75–100.
Knight, Kevin, D. Dwayne Simpson, and Matthew L. Hiller. 1999. "Three-year Reincarceration Outcomes for in Prison Therapeutic Community Treatment in Texas." *The Prison Journal* 79(3): 337–351.
Lamberti, J. Steven, Robert L. Weisman, Steven B. Schwarzkopf, Nancy Price, Rudo Mundondo Ashton, and John Trompeter. 2001. "The Mentally Ill in Jails and Prisons: Towards an Integrated Model of Prevention." *Psychiatric Quarterly* 72(1): 63–77.
Lattimore, Pamela K., and Christy Ann Visher. 2009. *The Multi-site Evaluation of SVORI: Summary and Synthesis*. Washington DC: Urban Institute.
Lurigio, Arthur J., John R. Fallon, and Jerry Dincin. 2000. "Helping the Mentally Ill in Jails Adjust to Community Life: A Description of a Post-release ACT Program and its Clients." *International Journal of Offender Therapy and Comparative Criminology* 44: 532–548.
MacKenzie, Doris L. 2012. "The Effectiveness of Corrections-based Work and Academic and Vocational Education Programs." Pp. 492–520 in *The Oxford Handbook of Sentencing and Corrections*, edited by J. Petersilia and K.R. Reitz. New York: Oxford University Press.
Mellow, Jeff, and Robert B. Greifinger. 2007. "Successful Reentry: The Perspective of Private Correctional Health Care Providers." *Journal of Urban Health* 84(1): 85–98.
Miller, Holly Ventura, and J. Mitchell Miller. 2010. "Community In-reach through Jail Reentry: Findings from a Quasi-experimental Design." *Justice Quarterly* 27(6): 893–910.
Miller, Holly Ventura, and J. Mitchell Miller. 2015. "A Promising Jail Reentry Program Revisited: Results from a Quasi-experimental Design." *Criminal Justice Studies* 28(2): 211–225.
Miller, Holly Ventura, J. Mitchell Miller, and J.C. Barnes. 2016. "Reentry Programming for Opioid and Opiate Involved Female Offenders: Findings from a Mixed Methods Evaluation." *Journal of Criminal Justice* 46: 129–136.
Miller, Holly Ventura, Rob Tyller, and J. Mitchell Miller. 2012. "Recognizing the Need for Prisoner Input in Correctional Research: Observations from the Texas In-Prison DWI Reduction Program." *The Prison Journal* 92(2): 274–289.
Miller, J. Mitchell. 2014. "Identifying Collateral Effects of Offender Reentry Programming through Evaluative Fieldwork." *American Journal of Criminal Justice* 39(1): 41–58.
Miller, J. Mitchell, and Holly Ventura Miller. 2011. "Considering the Effectiveness of Drug Treatment behind Bars: Findings from the South Carolina RSAT Evaluation." *Justice Quarterly* 28(1): 70–86.
Miller, J, Mitchell, and Holly Ventura Miller. 2015. "Rethinking Program Fidelity for Criminal Justice." *Criminology and Public Policy* 14(2): 339–349.
Miller, J. Mitchell, and Holly Ventura Miller. 2016. "Validating Program Fidelity: Lessons from the Delaware County Second Chance Initiatives." *American Journal of Criminal Justice* 41(1): 112–123.
Miller, J. Mitchell, Holly Ventura Miller, and J.C. Barnes. 2014. *Process and Outcome Evaluation of the Delaware County, OH Second Chance Act Offender Treatment and Reentry Initiatives*. Final Report submitted to U.S. Bureau of Justice Assistance.
Miller, J. Mitchell, Holly Ventura Miller, and J.C. Barnes. 2016. "Outcome Evaluation of a Family-based Jail Reentry Program for Substance Abusing Offenders." *The Prison Journal* 96(1): 53–78.
Mumola, Christopher J., and Jennifer C. Karberg. 2006. *Drug Use and Dependence, State and Federal Prisoners, 2004*. Washington, DC: U.S. Department of Justice, Office of Justice Programs, Bureau of Justice Statistics.
O'Brien, Charles, and James W. Cornish. 2006. "Naltrexone for Probationers and Parolees." *Journal of Substance Abuse Treatment* 31(2): 107–111.

O'Brien, Charles P., Robert A. Greenstein, Jim Mintz, and George W. Woody. 1975. "Clinical Experience with Naltrexone." *The American Journal of Drug and Alcohol Abuse* 2(3–4): 365–377.

Osher, Fred C. 2006. *Integrating Mental Health and Substance Abuse Services for Justice-involved Persons with Co-occurring Disorders*. Baltimore, MD: National GAINS Center.

Osher, Fred C. 2007. "Short-term Strategies to Improve Reentry of Jail Populations." *American Jails* January/February: 9–18.

Osher, Fred C., Henry J. Steadman, and Heather Barr. 2002. *A Best Practice Approach to Community Reentry from Jails for Inmates with Co-occurring Disorders: The APIC Model*. Delmar, NY: The National GAINS Center.

Petersilia, Joan R. 2004. "What Works in Prisoner Reentry? Reviewing and Questioning the Evidence." *Federal Probation* 68: 4–8.

Rhodes, William, Bernadette Pelisser, Gerald Gaes, William Saylor, Scott Camp, and Susan Wallace. 2001. "Alternative Solutions to the Problem of Selection Bias in an Analysis of Federal Residential Drug Treatment Programs." *Evaluation Review* 25: 19–45.

Robinson, David. 1996. "Factors Influencing the Effectiveness of Cognitive Skills Training." *Forum on Corrections Research* 8(3): 6–9.

Roman, John, Lisa Brooks, Erica Lagerson, Aaron Chalfin, and Bogdan Tereshchenko. 2007. *Impact and Cost-benefit Analysis of the Maryland Reentry Partnership Initiative*. Washington, DC: Urban Institute.

Saylor, William G., and Gerald G. Gaes. 1992. "The Post-release Employment Project: Prison Work has Measurable Effects on Post-release Success." *Federal Prisons Journal* 2(4): 33–36.

Saylor, William G., and Gerald G. Gaes. 1997. "Training Inmates through Industrial Work Participation and Vocational Apprenticeship Instruction." *Corrections Management Quarterly* 1(2): 32–43.

Scott, Christy K., and Michael L. Dennis. 2012. "The First 90 Days following Release from Jail: Findings from the Recovery Management Checkups for Women Offenders (RMCWO) Experiment." *Drug and Alcohol Dependence* 125(1): 110–118.

Seiter, Richard P. 1975. *Evaluation Research as a Feedback Mechanism for Criminal Justice Policy Making: A Critical Analysis*. PhD dissertation, School of Public Administration, Ohio State University.

Seiter, Richard P., and Karen R. Kadela. 2003. "Prisoner Reentry: What Works, What Does Not, and What is Promising." *Crime & Delinquency* 49: 360–388.

Severson, Margaret E., Kimberly Bruns, Christopher Veeh, and Jaehoon Lee. 2011. "Prisoner Reentry Programming: Who Recidivates and When?" *Journal of Offender Rehabilitation* 50: 327–348.

Solomon, Amy L., Jenny W. Osborne, Stefan F. LoBuglio, Jeff Mellow, and Debbie Mukamal. 2008. *Life after Lockup: Improving Reentry from Jail to the Community*. Washington, DC: Urban Institute.

Spjeldnes, Solveig, Hyunzee Jung, Lambert Maguire, and Hide Yamatani. 2012. "Positive Family Social Support: Counteracting Negative Effects of Mental Illness and Substance Abuse to Reduce Jail Ex-inmate Recidivism Rates." *Journal of Human Behavior in the Social Environment* 22(2): 130–147.

Substance Abuse and Mental Health Services Administration (SAMHSA). 2014. *Results from the 2013 National Survey on Drug Use and Health: Summary of National Findings*. Rockville, MD: SAMHSA.

Travis, Jeremy. 2005. *But They All Come Back: Facing the Challenges of Prisoner Reentry*. Washington, DC: Urban Institute.

Travis, Jeremy, and Michelle Waul. 2004. *Prisoners once Removed: The Impact of Incarceration and Reentry on Children, Families, and Communities*. Washington, DC: Urban Institute.

Turner, Susan, and Joan Petersilia. 1996. "Work Release in Washington: Effects on Recidivism and Corrections Costs." *The Prison Journal* 76(2): 138–164.

U.S. Bureau of Justice Statistics. 2016. *Correctional Populations in the U.S. 2014*. Washington, DC: Author. Retrieved May 13, 2017 from www.bjs.gov/content/pub/pdf/cpus14.pdf

Visher, Christy A., Pamela K. Lattimore, Kelle Barrick, and Stephen Tueller. 2017. "Evaluating the Long-term Effects of Prisoner Reentry Services on Recidivism: What Types of Services Matter?" *Justice Quarterly* 34(1): 136–165.

Vito, Gennaro F., and Richard Tewksbury. 1999. "Improving the Educational Skills of Inmates: The Results of an Impact Evaluation." *Corrections Compendium* 24(10): 46–51.

Volpicelli, Joseph R., Arthur I. Alterman, Motoi Hayashida, and Charles P. O'Brien. 1992. "Naltrexone in the Treatment of Alcohol Dependence." *Archives of General Psychiatry* 49(11): 876–880.

Ward, Kyle C., and Alida V. Merlo. 2016. "Rural Jail Reentry and Mental Health: Identifying Challenges for Offenders and Professionals." *The Prison Journal* 96(1): 27–52.

Wexler, Henry K., Gregory P. Falkin, and Douglas S. Lipton. 1990. "Outcome Evaluation of a Prison Therapeutic Community for Substance Abuse Treatment." *Criminal Justice and Behavior* 17: 71–92.

White, Michael D., Jessica Saunders, Christopher Fisher, and Jeff Mellow. 2012. "Exploring Inmate Reentry in a Local Jail Setting: Implications for Outreach, Service Use, and Recidivism." *Crime & Delinquency* 58(1): 124–146.

Wilson, James A., and Robert C. Davis. 2006. "Good Intentions Meet Hard Realities: An Evaluation of the Project Greenlight Reentry Program." *Criminology and Public Policy* 5: 303–338.

Wright, Benjamin J., Sheldon X. Zhang, David Farabee, and Rick Braatz. 2014. "Prisoner Reentry Research from 2000 to 2010 Results of a Narrative Review." *Criminal Justice Review* 39(1): 37–57.

45 Offender Recidivism

Kevin A. Wright and Natasha Khade

The "what works" evidence-based movement in corrections is largely driven by the need to reduce offender recidivism. To be sure, when it was concluded that "nothing works" based in part on Robert Martinson's (1974) article in the *Public Interest*, the conclusion was more appropriately "nothing works to reduce recidivism." Whether through the fear of future punishment, the modification of antisocial attitudes, or some other black-boxed mechanism, it is expected that involvement with the criminal justice system will curtail further criminal behavior. And given that correctional budgets have often been tightened in times of economic uncertainty (Turner et al., 2015), it is essential that programs provide the best bang for the buck when it comes to preventing future crime and increasing public safety (Maxwell 2005). Thus, understanding recidivism—its definition, its measurement, and its implications—is of critical importance toward understanding the effectiveness of the criminal justice system.

Defining and Measuring Recidivism

At the most basic level, recidivism can be defined as "the reversion of an individual to criminal behavior after he or she has been convicted of a prior offense, sentenced, and (presumably) corrected" (Maltz 1984: 1). It is very much a criminal justice concept. Whereas the study of criminology might be more concerned with explaining the onset, persistence, and cessation of criminal behavior, the study of criminal justice is more concerned with the relationship between the justice system and the individual. As such, recidivism requires that some sort of involvement (and perhaps intervention) has taken place within the justice system, and then the individual must again come into contact with the system after additional transgressions. Recidivism is therefore officially detected, repeat unlawful behavior.

Of course, multiple measures of officially detected behavior exist. Rearrest could be considered the least restrictive form that recidivism could take and is likely to produce the highest rates of offender recidivism. This measure casts the widest net and includes individuals who may later have charges dropped or are found to be innocent of the alleged crime committed. Reconviction is another form that recidivism could take and this moves the measure one step further along in the adjudication process. Finally, reimprisonment is one of the more stringent measures of offender recidivism and likely of greatest concern for determining whether a particular correctional approach reduces a reliance on imprisonment. As discussed later, the indicator of recidivism is likely to impact the extent of recidivism, and producers and consumers of recidivism statistics should be clear in what the indicator is actually measuring.

The official measurement of reoffending does have at least one critical difference with official measurements of offending: those who previously came into contact with the system may be placed on community supervision and thus be subject to a host of conditions that can result in them being more likely to be "caught" recidivating. These supervision conditions can be rather common and general, such as the need to notify an officer if leaving the county or state, or can be specific to the individual, such as the need to submit to random drug testing. Violations of these conditions—often referred to as technical violations—can result in a recidivism event, and probation and parole officers often have the discretion to decide whether or not to report their client's violation. Including technical violations within the measurement of recidivism has a significant impact on overall rates, and states often vary widely in making the decision to return someone to prison. For example, within three years, 40 percent of those released in California in 2004 were returned to prison for technical violations whereas 3 percent of those released in neighboring Oregon were returned for technical violations during the same time period. California's overall recidivism rate during this time was 58 percent; Oregon's was 23 percent (Pew Center on the States 2011). The intensity of supervision is also likely to affect recidivism rates—an issue discussed in more detail later (see Petersilia and Turner 1993).

Another critical factor in measuring recidivism is in determining how long a follow-up period to allow for the detection of unlawful behavior. Most recidivism assessments use a follow-up of at least six months, which is considered to be a critical period for those returning from prison in particular (Petersilia 2003). Longer follow-up periods are likely to produce higher rates of recidivism. It is often argued that at least a three-year follow up is necessary to truly assess recidivism (King and Elderbroom 2014). Scholars who study desistance liken crime to an addiction in which no one truly becomes a "nonrecidivist" until death (see the discussion in Maruna 2001), and still others have argued that after the passage of a certain amount of time, a person with a criminal record is of no greater risk to offend than someone of the same age without a record (Blumstein and Nakamura 2009). Finally, the actual amount of time until someone recidivates may be of interest—with quicker times to "failure" perhaps indicating difficulty with the moment of reentry, and longer times to "failure" perhaps indicating difficulty finding and maintaining stable housing or employment.

The unique time characteristics associated with recidivism require analyses that take into account the time at risk for individual offenders. Cox proportional hazard models are often estimated in recidivism analyses. These models begin with all subjects "surviving" in the community upon release and then estimate the effect of various risk and protective covariates of failure as risk ratios proportional to a common baseline hazard ratio. In so doing, it allows for speculations to be made about differences in recidivism among subjects, and also allows for the handling of censored data where failure has not yet occurred. An additional statistical technique often used in recidivism analyses is that of propensity score matching, which allows for researchers to more closely approximate a random assignment of individuals to programs or interventions (Frost and Clear 2012). Specifically, certain characteristics may lead an individual to "select in" to a particular program or policy that may bias outcomes of that program (e.g., a low-risk offender with a willingness to change his or her behavior). When an organization or program proudly touts that "only 5% of our graduates have recidivated" it is worth questioning whether its graduates were atypical—perhaps individuals who were unlikely to recidivate in the first place. A more rigorous approach would be to "match" these individuals to counterparts who did not complete the program. This allows for a better isolation of the true program effect on recidivism, given that all other critical risk and protective factors are presumed to be equal between the individuals.

Wright and Rosky (2011) used both propensity score matching and Cox proportional hazard modelling in their analysis of an early release cohort in Montana. The authors were interested in whether a group who were released early from prison (n = 434; released early to overcome a budget deficit) were more likely to recidivate (and to do so sooner) as compared to a group released from prison through a traditional parole release (n = 1,422).

First, propensity score matching was used to make the two groups more similar. Specifically, those chosen for early release were more likely to be female, younger, and with shorter sentences served in prison. The matching process balanced these to reduce the likelihood of selection bias and to more closely isolate the effect of being released from prison. Second, a Cox proportional hazard model determined that the early release cohort was more likely to recidivate, and to do so more quickly, than those traditionally released from prison. The authors speculated that the early release group may have not been adequately prepared to "seize the moment of release," given that they recidivated more quickly (Travis 2005; see Bird and Grattet 2016 for additional discussion on early release and recidivism).

Taken altogether—different definitions, the combination of unlawful behavior with technical violations, varying levels of supervision, different follow-up periods, and more—recidivism becomes "a complex measure of criminal behavior combined with formal and informal policy and procedure mechanisms" (Wilson 2005: 494).

Extent of Recidivism

With these complexities in mind, what is the extent of recidivism in America? A number of national assessments have documented high recidivism rates, regardless of the chosen indicator of reoffending. The Bureau of Justice Statistics (BJS) produced one of the most often cited recidivism studies tracking 272,111 formerly incarcerated individuals for a period of three years from 1994–1997 (Langan and Levin 2002). These individuals represented two-thirds of all releases that year and they were discharged from prisons in 15 states. Recidivism rates were found to be as high as 68 percent when rearrest for a new offense was the indicator of recidivism. However, when reconviction or reincarceration for a new offense was measured, 47 percent and 25 percent, respectively, were found to have recidivated. And, when including technical violations, 52 percent had been returned to prison within the three years. Thus, depending on the chosen measure of recidivism, recidivism rates varied from 25 percent to 68 percent, and even return-to-prison could be reported as low as 25 percent or as high as 52 percent.

BJS produced an updated report on 404,638 formerly incarcerated individuals from 30 states that were followed for a period of five years from 2005–2010 (Durose, Cooper, and Snyder 2014). Similar to the earlier report, 68 percent of individuals were rearrested within three years. When the follow-up period was extended to five years, however, the rearrest rate increased to 77 percent. Within five years, over half (55 percent) of the released individuals had a parole or probation violation or a new offense that resulted in reimprisonment.

The United States Sentencing Commission (2016) produced a report on 25,431 federal offenders released in 2005 and followed for a period of eight years. Nearly half were rearrested, nearly one-third were reconvicted, and nearly one-quarter were reimprisoned during that period. A critical difference between this study and the BJS studies is that it included individuals who were previously sentenced to only probation. These individuals had a rearrest rate of 35 percent whereas individuals sentenced to prison had a rearrest rate of 53 percent.

Finally, the Pew Center on the States (2011) published a report titled "State of Recidivism: The Revolving Door of America's Prisons" that provided aggregate recidivism rates between 2004 and 2007 for 33 states. The overall three-year recidivism rate, measured as return-to-prison, was 43 percent. This rate masked wide variation among states, with six states reporting recidivism rates above 50 percent (led by Minnesota's 61 percent) and five states reporting recidivism rates under 30 percent (led by Oregon's 23 percent). Again, technical violations often contributed to this wide variation, with states such as Missouri

(45 percent) having a high percentage of individuals reincarcerated for violating conditions of their supervision. The report concluded by suggesting a number of promising avenues to reduce recidivism, including defining success as recidivism reduction and incentivizing individuals on supervision to succeed.

Understanding Recidivism

A number of national recidivism studies have shown that when it comes to recidivism, the United States correctional system—particularly the prison system—is simply not working (see also Nagin, Cullen, and Jonson 2009). A better understanding of offender recidivism may be able to suggest ways to reduce recidivism. Along these lines, Wright and Cesar (2013: 389) provided a framework for understanding recidivism that considers the individual-, community-, and system-levels of reoffending, and they argued that "any assessment of recidivism or the efficacy of offender reentry programs will be incomplete unless all of these dimensions are taken into account" (see also Visher and Travis 2003). Each of these levels is related to specific approaches or disciplines that study recidivism, which often leads to them being presented independently.

The individual characteristics that may contribute to recidivism have received a significant amount of attention in the correctional literature. Scholars have been focused on identifying and targeting risk factors that might increase the likelihood of recidivism. These individual-level risks are classified into two categories: static and dynamic (Andrews and Bonta 2003). *Static risk* factors are features of the offender that cannot be changed such as age, race, or criminal record. Research has consistently found that those released at a young age, males, minorities, and those with past criminal history have a higher risk for recidivism (Benedict, Huff-Corzine, and Corzine 1998; Gainey, Payne, and O'Toole 2000; Gendreau, Little, and Goggin 1996; Hepburn and Albonetti 1994; Listwan, Sundt, Holsinger, and Latessa 2003). *Dynamic risk* factors, on the other hand, are characteristics that are malleable and therefore make appropriate targets for treatment. Some dynamic risk factors include antisocial values, beliefs, and behaviors and are sometimes referred to as criminogenic needs (Andrews et al. 1990).

The correctional rehabilitation literature has appropriately focused on dynamic risks to reoffending that can possibly be targeted and altered through programming. Specifically, the Risk-Needs-Responsivity (RNR) approach provides a blueprint for how to attend to the individual-level correlates of recidivism (Andrews et al. 1990; Taxman, Thanner, and Weisburd 2006). In general, the RNR approach follows three principles. First, delivering services to high-risk offenders (risk); second, addressing criminogenic needs while avoiding factors that are inconsequential and unrelated to crime (need); third, using treatment styles and modes that are consistent with the ability and learning style of offenders (responsivity) (Andrews et al. 1990). This method of risk/need assessment has a natural appeal in today's correctional environment, where agencies need to determine how best to allocate scarce resources. Focusing on high-risk cases in particular diverts these resources to those most in need and also avoids the possibility of actually increasing the probability of recidivism by low-risk individuals (Lowenkamp and Latessa 2005). Further, focusing on risks and needs related to criminal behavior, such as antisocial attitudes, while avoiding those that are not, such as self-esteem, ensures that programs target the appropriate offender characteristics for change.

Research is beginning to document that changes in these important individual characteristics may lead to reductions in recidivism. For example, Cohen and colleagues (2016) examined how changes in risk levels among 64,716 federal offenders placed on supervision affected their likelihood of rearrest within one year of risk assessment. Using scores on the Post Conviction Risk Assessment (PCRA), which includes important dynamic risk factors such as substance abuse and cognitions, offenders were placed into high-, moderate-, and low/moderate-risk categories. The PCRA was administered within the community at two different time points that were, on average, nine months apart. Offenders who experienced decreases in risk classifications over that time period were less likely to recidivate as compared to those who experienced no change or increased in risk classification. It is clear, then, that understanding and changing individual criminogenic characteristics is a critical component of recidivism reduction (see also Labrecque, Smith, Lovins, and Latessa 2014; Latessa 2016; Vose, Smith, and Cullen 2013).

An emerging literature has begun to look beyond the individual to better understand how community characteristics may also impact recidivism. The communities into which formerly incarcerated individuals reenter vary greatly on a number of dimensions, possibly influencing the likelihood of reoffending. For example, some individuals may return to communities characterized by high poverty and unemployment rates, high residential turnover, and high crime with little to no resources whereas others return to communities characterized by low crime, low poverty, greater opportunities for employment and better quality housing. Further, community characteristics influence a variety of other individual-level outcomes including victimization (Miethe and McDowall 1993; Rountree, Land, and Miethe 1994; Velez 2001), adolescent development (Elliott et al. 1996), delinquency (Simcha-Fagan and Schwartz 1986; Wikstrom and Loeber 2000), and violence (Sampson, Raudenbush, and Earls 1997; Silver 2000). These findings suggest that neighborhood context could play a crucial role in offender recidivism (Wright, Byungbae, Chassin, Losoya, and Piquero 2014).

Kubrin and Stewart (2006) examined this possibility in their study of 4,630 formerly incarcerated individuals living in 156 neighborhoods (i.e., census tracts) within Multnomah County, Oregon. Controlling for key individual-level characteristics such as age, race, and prior arrests, they documented that living in disadvantage (i.e., a construct representing economic indicators such as poverty and employment) increased the likelihood of rearrest within one year. Additionally, they found that living in neighborhoods with high concentrations of affluent families (as compared to poor families) decreased the likelihood of rearrest, and they suggested that this may be due to the presence of available resources in those neighborhoods. This line of research suggests that changing the individual may not be enough to reduce recidivism, and changing the environments to which they return could lead to more sizeable reductions in reoffending (see also Reisig, Bales, Hay, and Wang 2007; Wright, Pratt, Lowenkamp, and Latessa 2012; 2013).

The system-level of offender recidivism is probably the least researched of the three—at least in the criminological literature. Rooted primarily in organizational theory, the system-level of recidivism implicates organizational pressures, formal and informal practices, and widespread discretion on the part of community corrections officers (CCOs) as being influential for recidivism rates. As noted previously, the study of recidivism is different than the study of initial criminal behavior due to the fact that ex-offenders are often under some form of supervision and have to abide by conditions set by a CCO. These CCOs operate within a larger bureaucratic framework with a number of rules and regulations, constraints, and expectations that are often adapted to by using discretion at the street level (Lipsky 1980). This, in turn, can affect recidivism rates—particularly when it comes to decisions to violate individuals for technical violations.

Grattet and colleagues (2011) examined official reactions to parolee deviance as part of a "supervision regime" that shaped the detection and reporting of deviant behavior on the part of 254,468 parolees in California in 2003 and 2004. The authors found that supervision intensity and tolerance were both related to the likelihood of violation. Supervision intensity referred to the type and intensity of supervision, with categories for minimum (no drug testing; monthly reporting via mail), medium, high (one drug test per month; biweekly face-to-face meeting), and higher intensity increased the risk of violations, controlling for key individual characteristics such as age and offense history. Supervision tolerance referred to characteristics of the parole officer shown to be related to whether an officer uses formal sanctions to manage parolee deviance. Specifically, parolees with Black CCOs and CCOs with more than three years of experience had lower risk of violation. Additionally, the likelihood of violation varied by region, with Los Angeles County being more tolerant of violations. Finally, the authors found that certain individual characteristics were less important with the inclusion of the supervision regime measures, suggesting that some of the increased risk of serious, violent offenders to violation is partially attributable to the increased supervision that they face (for additional works see Gray, Fields, and Maxwell 2001; Lin, Grattet, and Petersilia 2010; Wright and Gifford 2017).

Moving Recidivism Research Forward

Offender recidivism is complex. Whenever statements are made such as "over three-fourths of individuals recidivated"—more questions should follow. The way that recidivism is defined and measured has a great impact on the extent of recidivism. Further, offender recidivism is not simply about the offender; the social, economic, and system-level contexts within which offenders live and work is likely to impact reoffending. Nevertheless, recidivism will remain a critical indicator of policy and program success. Reducing recidivism will therefore always be a prominent concern for criminologists, practitioners, policymakers, and the general public.

Despite the challenges and complexities with measuring and understanding recidivism, a wealth of information exists as to "what works" in reducing recidivism. This information can be organized under the umbrella concept of social support (Cullen 1994; see also Wright and Cesar 2013). Delivering and maintaining social support—both formally and informally—to formerly incarcerated individuals, their families, and their communities may serve to strengthen prosocial associations while weakening antisocial associations. A socially supportive correctional system may not require a major overhaul of existing practice. For example, an existing feature of prison life could be reimagined in a more supportive way. Prison visitation has received increased attention, particularly with regard to whether it may reduce recidivism (Bales and Mears 2008; Cochran 2014; Mears, Cochran, Siennick, and Bales 2012). Thus far, however, existing studies have primarily examined whether being visited, how many times visited, or how frequently visited is related to recidivism. Untouched are the specific qualities or conditions of certain visits that may be more indicative of social support than others, and moving toward an evidence-based visitation might produce even larger reductions in recidivism (Tasca, Wright, Turanovic, White, and Rodriguez 2016).

Reimagining the study of recidivism in general may provide the best step forward towards also reducing recidivism. The study of recidivism is currently a study of failure—with risk assessments and survival analyses focusing on the "bad things" that will inevitably lead to a return to prison. The study of desistance, however, often focuses on the resilient characteristics and conditions that promote a law-abiding lifestyle. Integrating recidivism and desistance research may lead to a better understanding of reoffending in general (Nakamura and Bucklen 2014), and the focus may shift from what the two-thirds who did recidivate did wrong to what the one-third who did not recidivate did right. Then, a whole host of new conceptual and measurement challenges can be tackled when the focus shifts from risk-based recidivism to resiliency-based nonrecidivism.

References

Andrews, Don A., and James Bonta. 2003. *The Psychology of Criminal Conduct*. Cincinnati, OH: Anderson.

Andrews, Don A., Ivan Zinger, Robert D. Hoge, James Bonta, Paul Gendreau, and Francis T. Cullen. 1990. "Does Correctional Treatment Work? A Clinically Relevant and Psychologically Informed Meta-Analysis." *Criminology* 28: 369–404.

Bales, William D., and Daniel P. Mears. 2008. "Inmate Social Ties and the Transition to Society: Does Visitation Reduce Recidivism?" *Journal of Research in Crime and Delinquency* 45: 287–321.

Benedict, W. Reed, Lin Huff-Corzine, and Jay Corzine. 1998. "Clean Up and Go Straight: Effects of Drug Treatment on Recidivism among Felony Probationers." *American Journal of Criminal Justice* 22: 169–187.

Bird, Mia, and Ryken Grattet. 2016. "Recidivism and Realignment." *The ANNALS of the American Academy of Political and Social Science* 664: 176–195.

Blumstein, Alfred, and Kiminori Nakamura. 2009. "Redemption in the Presence of Widespread Criminal Background Checks." *Criminology* 47: 327–359.

Cochran, Joshua C. 2014. "Breaches in the Wall: Imprisonment, Social Support, and Recidivism." *Journal of Research in Crime and Delinquency* 51: 200–229.

Cohen, Thomas H., Christopher T. Lowenkamp, and Scott W. VanBenschoten. 2016. "Does Change in Risk Matter? Examining Whether Changes in Offender Risk Characteristics Influence Recidivism Outcomes." *Criminology & Public Policy* 15: 263–296.

Cullen, Francis T. 1994. "Social Support as an Organizing Concept for Criminology: Presidential Address to the Academy of Criminal Justice Sciences." *Justice Quarterly* 11: 527–560.

Durose, Matthew R., Alexia D. Cooper, and Howard N. Snyder. 2014. *Recidivism of Prisoners Released in 30 States in 2005: Patterns from 2005 to 2010*. Washington, DC: Bureau of Justice Statistics.

Elliott, Delbert S., William J. Wilson, David Huizinga, Robert J. Sampson, Amanda Elliott, and Bruce Rankin. 1996. "The Effects of Neighborhood Disadvantage on Adolescent Development." *Journal of Research in Crime and Delinquency* 33: 389–426.

Frost, Natasha A., and Todd R. Clear. 2012. "New Directions in Correctional Research." *Justice Quarterly* 29: 619–649.

Gainey, Randy R., Brian K. Payne, and Mike O'Toole. 2000. "The Relationships Between Time in Jail, Time on Electronic Monitoring, and Recidivism: An Event History Analysis of a Jail-Based Program." *Justice Quarterly* 17: 733–752.

Gendreau, Paul, Tracy Little, and Claire Goggin. 1996. "A Meta-Analysis of the Predictors of Adult Offender Recidivism: What Works!" *Criminology* 34: 575–607.

Grattet, Ryken, Jeffrey Lin, and Joan Petersilia. 2011. "Supervision Regimes, Risk, and Official Reactions to Parolee Deviance." *Criminology* 49: 371–399.

Gray, M. Kevin, Monique Fields, and Sheila R. Maxwell. 2001. "Examining Probation Violations: Who, What, When." *Crime & Delinquency* 47: 537–557.

Hepburn, John R., and Celesta A. Albonetti. 1994. "Recidivism Among Drug Offenders: A Survival Analysis of the Effects of Offender Characteristics, Type of Offense, and Two Types of Intervention." *Journal of Quantitative Criminology* 10: 159–179.

King, Ryan, and Brian Elderbroom. 2014. *Improving Recidivism as a Performance Measure*. Washington, DC: Urban Institute.

Kubrin, Charis E., and Stewart, Eric. 2006. "Predicting who Reoffends: The Neglected Role of Neighborhood Context in Recidivism Studies." *Criminology*, 44, 171–204.

Langan, Patrick A., and David J. Levin. 2002. "Recidivism of Prisoners Released in 1994." *Federal Sentencing Reporter* 15: 58–65.

Labrecque, Ryan, Paula Smith, Brian Lovins, and Edward J. Latessa. 2014. "The Importance of Reassessment: How Changes in the LSI-R Risk Score Can Improve the Prediction of Recidivism." *Journal of Offender Rehabilitation* 53: 116–126.

Latessa, Edward J. 2016. "Does Change in Risk Matter? Yes, It Does, and We Can Measure It." *Criminology & Public Policy* 15: 297–300.

Lin, Jeffrey, Ryken Grattet, and Joan Petersilia. 2010. "'Back-End Sentencing' and Reimprisonment: Individual, Organizational, and Community Predictors of Parole Sanctioning Decisions." *Criminology* 48: 759–795.

Lipsky, Michael. 1980. *Street-Level Bureaucracy*. New York: Russell Sage Foundation.

Listwan, Shelley J., Jody L. Sundt, Alexander M. Holsinger, and Edward J. Latessa. 2003. "The Effect of Drug Court Programming on Recidivism: The Cincinnati Experience." *Crime & Delinquency* 49: 389– 411.

Lowenkamp, Christopher T., and Edward J. Latessa. 2005. "Increasing the Effectiveness of Correctional Programming Through the Risk Principle: Identifying Offenders for Residential Placement." *Criminology & Public Policy* 4: 263–290.

Maltz, Michael D. 1984. *Recidivism*. Orlando, FL: Academic Press.

Martinson, Robert. 1974. "What Works? Questions and Answers about Prison Reform." *The Public Interest* 35: 22–54.

Maruna, Shadd. 2001. *Making Good: How Ex-Convicts Reform and Rebuild their Lives*. Washington, DC: American Psychological Association.

Maxwell, Sheila R. 2005. "Rethinking the Broad Sweep of Recidivism: A Task for Evaluators." *Criminology & Public Policy* 4: 519–526.

Mears, Daniel P., Joshua C. Cochran, Sonja E. Siennick, and William D. Bales. 2012. "Prison Visitation and Recidivism." *Justice Quarterly* 29: 888–918.

Miethe, Terance D., and David McDowall, David. 1993. "Contextual Effects in Models of Criminal Victimization." *Social Forces* 71: 741–759.

Nagin, Daniel S., Francis T. Cullen, and Cheryl L. Jonson. 2009. "Imprisonment and Reoffending." Pp. 115–200 in *Crime and Justice: An Annual Review of Research*, edited by M. Tonry. Chicago, IL: University of Chicago Press.

Nakamura, Kiminori, and Kristofer B. Bucklen. 2014. "Recidivism, Redemption, and Desistance: Understanding Continuity and Change in Criminal Offending and Implications for Interventions." *Sociology Compass* 8: 384–397.

Petersilia, Joan. 2003. *When Prisoners Come Home: Parole and Prisoner Reentry*. New York: Oxford University Press.

Petersilia, Joan, and Susan Turner. 1993. "Intensive Probation and Parole." Pp. 281–335 in *Crime and Justice: An Annual Review of Research*, edited by M. Tonry. Chicago, IL: University of Chicago Press.

Pew Center on the States. 2011. *State of Recidivism: The Revolving Door of America's Prisons*. Washington, DC: The Pew Charitable Trusts.

Reisig, Michael D., William D. Bales, Carter Hay, and Xia Wang. 2007. "The Effect of Racial Inequality on Black Male Recidivism." *Justice Quarterly* 24: 408–434.

Rountree, Pamela, Kenneth C. Land, and Terance D. Miethe. 1994. "Macro-Micro Integration in the Study of Victimization: A Hierarchical Logistic Model Analysis Across Seattle Neighborhoods." *Criminology* 32: 387–414.

Sampson, Robert J., Stephen W. Raudenbush, and Felton Earls. 1997. "Neighborhoods and Violent Crime: A Multilevel Study of Collective Efficacy." *Science* 277: 918–924.

Silver, Eric. 2000. "Extending Social Disorganization Theory: A Multilevel Approach to the Study of Violence Among Persons with Mental Illnesses. *Criminology* 38: 1043–1073.

Simcha-Fagan, Ora, and Joseph E. Schwartz. 1986. "Neighborhood and Delinquency: An Assessment of Contextual Effects." *Criminology* 24: 667–699.

Tasca, Melinda, Kevin A. Wright, Jillian J. Turanovic, Clair White, and Nancy Rodriguez. 2016. "Moving Visitation Research Forward: The Arizona Prison Visitation Project." *Criminology, Criminal Justice, Law & Society* 17: 55–67.

Taxman, Faye S., Meridith Thanner, and David Weisburd. 2006. "Risk, Need, And Responsivity (RNR): It All Depends." *Crime and Delinquency* 52: 28–51.

Travis, Jeremy. 2005. *But They All Come Back: Facing the Challenges of Prisoner Reentry*. Washington, DC: Urban Institute Press.

Turner, Susan F., Lois M. Davis, Terry Fain, Helen Braithwaite, Theresa Lavery, Wayne Choinski, and George Camp. 2015. "A National Picture of Prison Downsizing Strategies." *Victims & Offenders* 10(4): 401–419.

United States Sentencing Commission. 2016. *Recidivism Among Federal Offenders: A Comprehensive Overview*. Retrieved May 15, 2017 from www.ussc.gov/sites/default/files/pdf/research-and-publications/research-publications/2016/recidivism_overview.pdf

Velez, Maria. 2001. "The Role of Public Social Control in Urban Neighborhoods." *Criminology* 39: 837–863.

Visher, Christy A., and Jeremy Travis. 2003. "Transitions from Prison to Community: Understanding Individual Pathways." *Annual Review of Sociology* 29: 89–113.

Vose, Brenda, Paul Smith, and Francis T. Cullen. 2013. "Predictive Validity and the Impact of Change in Total LSI-R Score on Recidivism." *Criminal Justice and Behavior* 40: 1383–1396.

Wikstrom, Per-Olof H., and Rolf Loeber. 2000. "Do Disadvantaged Neighborhoods Cause Well-Adjusted Children to Become Adolescent Delinquents? A Study of Male Juvenile Serious Offending, Individual Risk and Protective Factors, and Neighborhood Context." *Criminology* 38: 1109–1142.

Wilson, James A. 2005. "Bad Behavior or Bad Policy? An Examination of Tennessee Release Cohorts, 1993–2001." *Criminology & Public Policy* 4: 485–518.

Wright, Kevin A., Kim Byungbae, Laurie Chassin, Sandra H. Losoya, and Alex R. Piquero. 2014. "Ecological Context, Concentrated Disadvantage, and Youth Reoffending: Identifying the Social Mechanisms in a Sample of Serious Adolescent Offenders." *Journal of Youth and Adolescence* 43: 1781–1799.

Wright, Kevin A., and Gabriel T. Cesar. 2013. "Toward a More Complete Model of Offender Reintegration: Linking the Individual-, Community-, and System-Level Components of Recidivism." *Victims and Offenders* 8: 373–398.

Wright, Kevin A., and Faith Gifford. 2017. "Legal Cynicism, Antisocial Attitudes, and Recidivism: Implications for a Procedurally-Just Community Corrections." *Victims and Offenders* 12(4): 624–642.

Wright, Kevin A., Travis C. Pratt, Christopher T. Lowenkamp, and Edward J. Latessa. 2012. "The Importance of Ecological Context for Correctional Rehabilitation Programs: Understanding the Micro- and Macro-Level Dimensions of Successful Offender Treatment." *Justice Quarterly* 29: 775–798.

Wright, Kevin A., Travis C. Pratt, Christopher T. Lowenkamp, and Edward J. Latessa. 2013. "The Systemic Model of Crime and Institutional Efficacy: An Analysis of the Social Context of Offender Reintegration." *International Journal of Offender Therapy and Comparative Criminology* 57: 92–111.

Wright, Kevin. A., and Jeffrey W. Rosky. 2011. "Too Early is Too Soon." *Criminology & Public Policy* 10: 881–908.

Index